Financial Institutions, Valuations, Mergers, and Acquisitions

Subscription Notice

This Wiley product is updated on a periodic basis with supplements to reflect important changes in the subject matter. If you purchased this product directly from John Wiley & Sons, Inc., we have already recorded your subscription for this update service.

If, however, you purchased this product from a bookstore and wish to receive (1) the current update at no additional charge, and (2) future updates and revised or related volumes billed separately with a 30-day examination review, please send your name, company name (if applicable), address, and the title of the product to:

Supplement Department
John Wiley & Sons, Inc.
One Wiley Drive
Somerset, NJ 08875
1-800-225-5945

For customers outside the United States, please contact the Wiley office nearest you:

Professional & Reference Division	John Wiley & Sons, Ltd.
John Wiley & Sons Canada, Ltd,	Baffins Lane
22 Worcester Road	Chichester
Rexdale, Ontario M9W 1L1	West Sussex PO19 1UD
(416) 675-3580	United Kingdom
1-800-567-4797	(44)(243)779777
FAX (416) 675-6599	

Financial Institutions, Valuations, Mergers, and Acquisitions:
The Fair Value Approach

Second Edition

Zabihollah Rezaee

John Wiley & Sons, Inc.

New York • Chichester • Weinheim • Brisbane • Singapore • Toronto

Library of Congress Cataloging-in-Publication Data:
Rezaee, Zabihollah, 1953-
    Financial institutions, valuations, mergers, and acquisitions: the fair value approach /
Zabihollah Rezaee.—2nd ed.
        p. cm.
    ISBN 0-471-39449-1 (cloth: alk. paper)
    1. Banks and banking—Valuation—United States. 2. Bank mergers—United States. 3.
    Sale of banks—United States. 4. Financial institutions—Valuation—United States. 5.
    Financial institutions—Mergers—United States. 6. Financial institutions—Purchasing—United States. 7. Consolidation and merger of corporations—Law and legislation—United States. I. Title.
    HG1707.7 .R49 2001
    332.1′6—dc21
                                                                00-046264

Formerly titled *Commercial Bank Valuation* by William D. Miller

10 9 8 7 6 5 4 3 2 1

About the Author

Zabihollah Rezaee is a professor of accounting at Middle Tennessee State University. He received his B.A. degree from Iranian Institute of Advanced Accounting, his M.B.A. from Tarleton State University in Texas, and his Ph.D. from the University of Mississippi. Professor Rezaee holds several certifications including certified public accountant (CPA), certified management accountant (CMA), certified internal auditor (CIA), certified government financial manager (CGFM), and certified fraud examiner (CFE).

Professor Rezaee has published over 130 articles in a variety of accounting, finance, banking, and economic journals including *Journal of Accounting and Economics; Journal of Business, Finance and Accounting; Journal of Accounting, Auditing and Finance; Advances in Public Interest Accounting; Journal of Accountancy, Internal Auditors Management Accounting, Strategy Finance; and Bankers' Economic and Investment Alert.*

Active within the accounting profession and the academic and financial communities, Dr. Rezaee has made over 120 presentations at conferences and workshops throughout the world. He teaches financial, management, and international accounting and auditing and has been involved in financial and management consulting with national and international organizations including the United Nations. Dr. Rezaee has received numerous research grants from various sources. He received the 1998 distinguished research award at Middle Tennessee State University and the Lybrand Bronze Medal for the outstanding article in 1999 selected by the Institute of Management Accountants.

This book is dedicated to
the loving memory of my mother,
Fatemeh Rezaee

Contents

Acknowledgments   xviii

Preface   xix

Part I   The Foundation: Financial Institutions, Valuations, Mergers, Acquisitions, Regulatory and Accounting Environment   1

Chapter 1   Introduction to Financial Institutions   3
   1.1   Introduction   3
   1.2   Structural Changes in the Financial Services Industry   5
        1.2.1   Consolidation   5
        1.2.2   Convergence   7
        1.2.3   Competition   15
   1.3   Historical Perspective of American Banking   16
   1.4   Current Trends in the Banking Industry   17
        1.4.1   Changes in Regulations   19
        1.4.2   Information Technology   25
        1.4.3   Global Marketplace   28
        1.4.4   Capital Standards   29
        1.4.5   Supervisory Activities   30
        1.4.6   Continuous Quality Improvement   32
        1.4.7   Valuation Process   34
   1.5   Conclusion   35

Chapter 2   Overview of the Valuation Process   38
   2.1   Introduction   38
   2.2   Valuation Services   39
   2.3   Valuation Profession   41

2.4 Attracting Valuation Clients 44
2.5 Accepting a Client 51
2.6 Pricing Valuation Services 58
2.7 Importance of the Engagement Letter 59
2.8 Planning an Appraisal Engagement 59
    2.8.1 Conference with Client Personnel 59
    2.8.2 Knowledge of the Business 61
    2.8.3 Legal Structure 62
    2.8.4 Policies 62
    2.8.5 Industry and Economic Conditions 62
2.9 General Planning 64
    2.9.1 General Planning Decisions to be Made 64
    2.9.2 Evidence and Knowledge Obtained to Prepare
           Preliminary Appraisal Plan 64
    2.9.3 Procedures in Preparing the Preliminary Appraisal Plan 66
2.10 Appraiser's Traits 67
    2.10.1 Able to Function Well Under Intense Pressure 68
    2.10.2 Communicate Well Both Orally and in Writing 68
    2.10.3 Utilize Both Qualitative and Quantitative Data 68
    2.10.4 Be Unfazed by Ambiguity and Uncertainty 68
    2.10.5 Continuous Improvement of Valuation Expertise and
           Skills through Ongoing Professional Education 68
    2.10.6 Continuous Marketing Strategies 69
2.11 Appraiser's Due Diligence Process 69
2.12 Conclusion 69

Chapter 3 Overview of Mergers and Acquisitions 73
3.1 Introduction 73
3.2 Historical Perspective of M & A 74
3.3 Recent Trends in M & A 74
3.4 Regulations of Bank Mergers 77
    3.4.1 Antitrust Regulations 78
3.5 Trends Toward Business Combinations in the Financial Services
    Industry 82
3.6 Motives for Business Combinations 84
3.7 Determinants of Mergers and Acquisitions 84
3.8 Perceived Shortcomings of M & A 85
    3.8.1 Diminished Services 85
    3.8.2 High Financial Services Fees 88
    3.8.3 Credit Availability 89
    3.8.4 Undesirable Impacts on Competition 89
3.9 Studies on Mergers and Acquisitions 90

3.10   Mergers and Acquisitions Process   93
    3.10.1   Strategy Development   95
    3.10.2   Target Identification and Selection   95
    3.10.3   Identifying Key Issues and Contacting Targets   99
    3.10.4   Structuring the Acquisition Transaction   99
    3.10.5   Due Diligence Process   99
    3.10.6   Risk Assessment   100
    3.10.7   Negotiation   102
    3.10.8   Financial Structure   103
    3.10.9   Closing the Deal   103
    3.10.10 Integration   104
3.11   Conclusion   105

Chapter 4   Regulatory Environment and Financial Reporting
               Process of Financial Institutions   111

4.1   Introduction   111
4.2   Consolidation   111
    4.2.1   Technological Innovations   113
    4.2.2   Geographical and Activity Diversification   114
    4.2.3   National and Global Competition   114
4.3   Regulatory Environment   116
4.4   Bank Supervision   118
    4.4.1   Market Discipline   118
    4.4.2   Supervision   119
    4.4.3   Minimum Capital Regulation   123
    4.4.4   Safety and Soundness   126
4.5   Financial Modernization: The Gramm-Leach-Bliley Act   127
4.6   Financial Reporting Process of Financial Institutions   130
4.7   Statement of Financial Accounting Standards (SFAS) No. 115   133
4.8   Auditing Proper Classifications of Marketable Securities   135
4.9   Tax Consideration of Fair Value   136
4.10   Recent Development of Fair Value Accounting   137
4.11   Financial Reporting Requirements of Financial Institutions   143
    4.11.1   Reports Required Under Regulation H and the SEC
            Act of 1934   144
    4.11.2   Reporting Requirement for International Activities   145
4.12   Corporate Governance of Financial Institutions   147
    4.12.1   Financial Reporting   150
    4.12.2   Internal Control Structure   150
    4.12.3   Independent Audit Committee   154
    4.12.4   Functions of Audit Committees   155
4.13   Conclusion   157

Part II   Fundamentals of Valuations: Concepts, Standards, and
          Techniques   163

Chapter 5   Value and Valuation: A Conceptual Foundation   165

  5.1   The Nature of Value   165
  5.2   Twelve Concepts of Value   166
  5.3   Types of Property That Can Be Valued   172
  5.4   Relationship Among Different Types of Value   173
  5.5   Principles of Valuation Theory   174
          5.5.1   Principle of Alternatives   174
          5.5.2   Principle of Replacement   174
          5.5.3   Principle of Substitution   174
          5.5.4   Principle of Future Benefits   175
  5.6   Pricing Value Versus Reporting Value   175
  5.7   Limitations of the Valuation Process   176

Chapter 6   Approaches to Measuring Value   177

  6.1   Overview of the Valuation Process   177
  6.2   The Cost Approach to Valuation   178
  6.3   The Market Approach to Valuation   180
          6.3.1   Identifying Comparables   180
          6.3.2   Adjusting for Lack of Comparability   181
  6.4   The Income Approach to Valuation   182
          6.4.1   The Stabilized Income Method   183
          6.4.2   The Discounted Future Income Method   184
          6.4.3   Discounted Cash Earnings   185
          6.4.4   Selecting the Type of Income to Use   186
          6.4.5   Estimating the Stabilized Level of Income   187
          6.4.6   Projecting Future Income Levels   189
          6.4.7   Selecting the Capitalization and Discount Rates   189
          6.4.8   Dividend Capitalization Model   197
          6.4.9   The Effects of Inflation   198
  6.5   Special Topics—Approaches to Intangible Asset Valuation   199
          6.5.1   Cost of Replacement of Intangible Asset   199
          6.5.2   Income from Intangible Asset   199
          6.5.3   Cost Savings from Intangible Asset   200
          6.5.4   Excess Earnings Method   201
  6.6   Special Topics—Business Valuation   202
          6.6.1   Market-to-Book Value Method   202
          6.6.2   Total Enterprise Value Versus Value of Equity   202
          6.6.3   Existence of Preferred Stock   203
          6.6.4   Adjusted Book Value to Compute Market Value of Equity   206
          6.6.5   Liquidation of Business   206

6.7   Valuation and Business Concentrations   207
6.8   Special Topics—Closely Held Stock   207
        6.8.1   Revenue Ruling 59-60   208
        6.8.2   Discounts for Minority Position/Premium for
                  Control   209
        6.8.3   Discount for Lack of Marketability   211
6.9   Special Topics—Valuing Widely Traded Companies   211

Chapter 7   Valuations for Tax and Accounting Purposes   213
7.1   Tax Aspects of Mergers and Acquisitions   213
        7.1.1   Nontaxable Transactions   213
        7.1.2   Taxable Transactions   214
7.2   Typical Tax-Oriented Valuations   215
7.3   Accounting Aspects of Mergers and Acquisitions   217
        7.3.1   Pooling Versus Purchase Accounting   217
        7.3.2   Requirements for Use of Pooling Accounting   217
        7.3.3   Advantages and Disadvantages of Purchase and Pooling
                  Accounting   220
7.4   Typical Accounting-Oriented Valuations   220

Chapter 8   Intangible Asset Valuation   223
8.1   Nature and Types of Intangible Assets   223
        8.1.1   Criteria for Defining Intangible Assets   223
        8.1.2   Core Deposit Base   224
        8.1.3   Loan Servicing Contracts   224
        8.1.4   Safe Deposit Box Contracts   224
        8.1.5   Proprietary Computer Software   224
        8.1.6   Trust Accounts   224
        8.1.7   Leasehold Interests   225
        8.1.8   Assembled Work Force   225
        8.1.9   Goodwill   225
8.2   Amortizable Versus Nonamortizable Intangible Assets   225
        8.2.1   Benefits of Amortization   225
        8.2.2   Requirements for Amortization   226
8.3   Measuring the Useful Life of an Intangible Asset   227
        8.3.1   Unique Experience   227
        8.3.2   Individual Component Analysis   228
8.4   Establishing Value of Intangible Assets   229
        8.4.1   The Cost Approach   229
        8.4.2   The Market Approach   229
        8.4.3   The Income Approach   230
8.5   Amortization Methods   230
8.6   Supporting Intangible Asset Valuation and Amortization   231

Part III   Assessment of Financial Institutions   233

Chapter 9   Financial Analysis of Banks and Bank Holding
            Companies   235
    9.1   Types and Sources of Financial Data   235
           9.1.1   The Uniform Bank Performance Report   235
           9.1.2   The Bank Holding Company Performance Report   236
           9.1.3   Other Public Sources   236
           9.1.4   Private Sources   237
           9.1.5   Internal Data Sources   237
    9.2   Overview of Financial Statements   238
           9.2.1   Income Generation and Income Statement   238
           9.2.2   Balance Sheet   240
    9.3   Composition of Bank Assets   241
           9.3.1   Cash and Due Froms   242
           9.3.2   Investment Securities   242
           9.3.3   Fed Funds Sold and Reverse Repos   242
           9.3.4   Loans and Lease Financing Receivables   243
           9.3.5   Assets Held in Trading Accounts   244
           9.3.6   Premises and Fixed Assets   244
           9.3.7   Other Real Estate Owned   244
           9.3.8   Investments in Unconsolidated Subsidiaries and
                    Associated Companies   244
           9.3.9   Customer Liabilities to Bank on Acceptances
                    Outstanding   244
           9.3.10   Intangible Assets   245
           9.3.11   Other Assets   245
    9.4   Composition of Bank Liabilities   245
           9.4.1   Deposits   245
           9.4.2   Fed Funds Purchased and Repos   246
           9.4.3   Demand Notes Issued to U. S. Treasury   246
           9.4.4   Other Borrowed Money   246
           9.4.5   Mortgage Indebtedness/Capitalized Leases   247
           9.4.6   Bank's Liability on Acceptances Executed and
                    Outstanding   247
           9.4.7   Subordinated Notes and Debentures   247
           9.4.8   Other Liabilities   247
    9.5   Off-Balance Sheet Items   247
    9.6   Composition of Bank Capital   248
           9.6.1   Par Value of Stock   248
           9.6.2   Surplus   248
           9.6.3   Undivided Profits   249
           9.6.4   Capital Reserves   249

9.7   Regulatory Capital Components   249
        9.7.1   Capital Components—Banks   249
        9.7.2   Capital Components—Bank Holding Companies   251
9.8   Risk-Based Capital   252
9.9   Value-at-Risk (VAR) Models   255
9.10   Composition of Bank Income   256
        9.10.1   Interest Income   256
        9.10.2   Noninterest Income   257
        9.10.3   Extraordinary Gains (Losses)   258
9.11   Composition of Bank Expenses   258
        9.11.1   Interest Expense   258
        9.11.2   Noninterest Expense   259
        9.11.3   Provision for Loan and Lease Losses and Allocated
                  Transfer Risk   260
        9.11.4   Income Taxes   260
9.12   Balance Sheet Analysis Illustration   261
        9.12.1   Asset Growth Rates   266
        9.12.2   Asset Composition   266
        9.12.3   Asset Composition—Peer Group Comparison   266
        9.12.4   Liability Growth Rates   267
        9.12.5   Liability Composition   267
        9.12.6   Liability Composition—Peer Group Comparison   267
        9.12.7   Capital Levels and Trends   267
9.13   Income Statement and Profitability Analysis Illustration   267
        9.13.1   Overall Income and Expenses   272
        9.13.2   Sources of Profitability   272
9.14   Loan Risk Analysis Illustration   273
        9.14.1   The Magnified Impact of Loan Losses   273
        9.14.2   Delinquent and Classified Loan Analysis   274
        9.14.3   Historical Loan Risk Analysis   277
9.15   Liquidity and Investment Portfolio Analysis Illustration   277
9.16   Portfolio Equities Analysis (Realm Model)   278
9.17   Special Bank Holding Company Considerations   278

Chapter 10   Internal Characteristics Assessment   280
10.1   Objectives and Benefits of an Internal Characteristics
        Assessment   281
10.2   The "Ten P Factor" Framework   281
        10.2.1   Profits   282
        10.2.2   People   283
        10.2.3   Personality   285
        10.2.4   Physical Distribution   286
        10.2.5   Portfolio   287

10.2.6   Products   287
10.2.7   Processes   288
10.2.8   Property   288
10.2.9   Planning   289
10.2.10   Potential   290
10.3 Shareholder Value Creation   291
10.3.1   Risk Assessment   291
10.3.2   Economic Value Added   291
10.3.3   Balanced Scorecard (BSC)   292

Chapter 11   External Environment Assessment   294
11.1 Impact of External Environment on Value   294
11.2 Sources of Data   294
11.3 Market-Wide Versus Small Area Analysis   295
11.4 Demographic Analysis   296
11.5 Economic Analysis   297
11.6 Competitive Analysis   298

Part IV   Valuation of Mergers and Acquisitions   301

Chapter 12   The Bank Merger and Acquisition Process   303
12.1 Strategy Phase   303
12.1.1   Overall Strategic Plan   304
12.1.2   Merger and Acquisition Team   305
12.1.3   Merger and Acquisition Plan   306
12.1.4   Candidate Criteria   306
12.1.5   Candidate Identification   307
12.1.6   Candidate Analysis   307
12.1.7   Preliminary Valuation and Financial Feasibility   307
12.2 Negotiation and Investigation Phase   308
12.2.1   Negotiation Strategy   308
12.2.2   Candidate Contact and Preliminary Negotiations   308
12.2.3   Letter of Intent   309
12.2.4   Due Diligence   309
12.3 Finalization and Integration Phase   310
12.3.1   Final Agreement   311
12.3.2   Regulator and Shareholder Approval   311
12.3.3   Final Review   312
12.3.4   Transaction Finalization   313
12.3.5   Integration   313

Chapter 13   Accounting Standards on Mergers and Acquisitions   315
13.1 Accounting for Business Combinations   316
13.2 Alternative Proposals to ED   317

13.3 Potential Impacts of New Accounting Standards on M & A
Deals 319
    13.3.1 Effect on M & A Deals 320
    13.3.2 Cash Flow 320
    13.3.3 More Efficient M & A Deals 321
    13.3.4 Impact on Earnings 322
13.4 Empirical Research on the Effects of Accounting Methods for
Business Combinations 322
13.5 Implementation of New Accounting Standards on M & A 323
    13.5.1 Develop Bank Merger Strategy 323
    13.5.2 Examine the Risks Inherent in Mergers 326
    13.5.3 Determine How the Proposed Accounting Standards Will
        Affect Bank Mergers, Before and After their
        Adoption 326
    13.5.4 Consider the Appropriate Accounting Treatment of the
        Business Combination Transaction 327
    13.5.5 Consider the Cash Flow Implications of the Proposed
        Accounting Standards 327
    13.5.6 Recalculate the Tax Implications of Mergers Under the
        New Proposed Accounting Standards 329
    13.5.7 Review all of the Above with Independent Bank
        Accounting Firms and Tax Advisors 329
    13.5.8 Provide Full Disclosure of Merger and Acquisition
        Transactions 330
    13.5.9 Inform Financial Statement Users about Bank Business
        Combinations 330
13.6 Conclusion 330

Chapter 14 Valuing a Bank as a Business Enterprise 333
14.1 Business Enterprise Versus a Collection of Assets 333
14.2 The Concept of the Banking Franchise 334
14.3 Difference Between Strategic and Tactical Valuations 335
14.4 Why the Cost Approach Is Not Used For Strategic Bank
Valuations 336
14.5 Application of the Market Approach to Valuing a Bank 336
    14.5.1 Identification of Comparable Transactions 336
    14.5.2 Basis of Comparability 337
    14.5.3 Publicly Traded Companies as Comparables 337
    14.5.4 Value Estimation by Market Approach—
        An Example 339
    14.5.5 Advantages and Disadvantages of Market Approach 339
14.6 Application of the Income Approach to Valuing a Bank 340
    14.6.1 Measuring Available Cash Flow 340
    14.6.2 Overview of Income Approach Model 341

14.6.3   Projection of Key Balance Sheet Items   341
14.6.4   Projection of Income, Expenses, and Available Cash
          Flow   342
14.6.5   Value Estimation by Income Approach—An Example   345
14.7   Sensitivity of Value Estimate to Assumption Changes   348
14.8   Value Creation Opportunities and the Acquisition Price   348
14.9   Valuation Methods for Mergers and Acquisitions   351
       14.9.1   Income Approach   352
       14.9.2   Balance Sheet Approach   354
       14.9.3   Market Approach   356
14.10 Sophisticated Valuation Techniques for Mergers and Acquisitions   357
       14.10.1   The Capital Asset Pricing Model (CAPM)   358
       14.10.2   Accounting-Based Valuation Approach
                 (Ohlson Model)   359
14.11 Relation Between Price and Value and Effect on Stockholders   360

Chapter 15   Valuation of Tangible Bank Assets   363
15.1   Tangible Physical Assets   364
15.2   Tangible Financial Assets   364
       15.2.1   Investment Securities Valuation   365
       15.2.2   Loan Portfolio Valuation   366
       15.2.3   Commercial Loans   367
       15.2.4   Consumer Loans   368
       15.2.5   Mortgage Loans   368
       15.2.6   Lease Financing   369
       15.2.7   Nonperforming Loans   369
15.3   Tangible Assets in Bank Mergers and Acquisitions   369

Chapter 16   Core Deposits as a Special Type of Intangible Asset
             Valuation   370
16.1   The Concept of Core Deposit Base as an Intangible Asset   370
16.2   Internal Revenue Service Position on Core Deposits   370
16.3   Important Core Deposit Tax Court Cases   371
       16.3.1   The Midlantic Case   371
       16.3.2   The Banc One Case   371
       16.3.3   The AmSouth Case   372
       16.3.4   The Citizens & Southern Case   374
       16.3.5   The Newark Morning Ledger Case   376
16.4   Deposits to be Included in Valuation   377
16.5   Alternative Approaches to Valuing a Core Deposit Base   377
       16.5.1   Historical Development Cost Approach   377
       16.5.2   Cost Savings Approach   378
       16.5.3   Future Income Approach   378

16.6   Core Deposit Base Life Estimation   379
        16.6.1   Historical Retention   379
        16.6.2   Projecting Lifing of Acquired Core Deposit Accounts   382
16.7   Application of the Cost Savings Approach   382
16.8   Application of the Future Income Approach   385
        16.8.1   Earnings Per Account Calculation   385
        16.8.2   Projection of Earnings from Acquired Deposit Base   387
        16.8.3   Computation of Deposit Base Value   387

Chapter 17   Derivative Financial Instruments   388
17.1   Authoritative Guidelines on Derivatives   389
17.2   Derivative Markets   390
17.3   Derivatives Risk Management   391
17.4   Derivatives Risk Management Policy   393
        17.4.1   The Extent of Derivatives' Use   393
        17.4.2   Identification and Analysis of All Types of Derivatives   393
        17.4.3   Identification and Assessment of Derivative Risk   393
17.5   Accounting of Derivatives   397
        17.5.1   Financial and Managerial Impacts of SFAS No. 133   401
        17.5.2   How Does This SFAS No. 133 Work?   403
        17.5.3   Financial Requirements   403
        17.5.4   Disclosure Requirements   404
17.6   Tax Considerations of Derivatives   405
17.7   Audit of Derivative Transactions   406
17.8   Sources of Information on Derivatives   407
17.9   Derivatives Valuation Models   408
        17.9.1   Binomial Model   408
        17.9.2   Binomial Model—An Illustrative Example   409
        17.9.3   The Black-Scholes Call Option Valuation Model   409
        17.9.4   An Illustrative Example of the Black-Scholes Valuation
                 Formula   410
        17.9.5   Digital Contracts for Valuation of Derivatives   411
17.10 Conclusion   411

Chapter 18   Real World Bank Valuation Complications   414
18.1   Banks Experiencing Recent Losses   414
18.2   Banks with Low Equity Capital   418
18.3   Banks with Uncertain Future Loan Loss Exposure   419
18.4   Preferred and Common Stock   420
18.5   Highly Leveraged Banks   420
18.6   Branch Acquisitions   421
18.7   European Banking Model   422
18.8   Initial Public Offering (IPO)   424

Acknowledgments

I acknowledge the American Institute of Certified Public Accountants, American Society of Appraisers (ASA), Appraisal Foundation (AF), Institute of Business Appraisers (IBA), National Association of Certified Valuation Analysts (NACVA), SNL Securities, Federal Reserve Board (FRB), Federal Deposit Insurance Corporation (FDIC), and American Bankers Association (ABA) for permission to quote and reference valuation standards, codes of professional conduct, and other publications. The willingness of these organizations to permit the use of their materials is a significant contribution to the book.

The encouragement and support of my family and colleagues are also acknowledged. I thank the members of the John Wiley and Sons, Inc., team for their hard work and dedication, including Louise Jacob for managing the book through the production process, Colleen Scollans for marketing efforts, and Judy Howard and John De Remigis for their editorial guidance.

Special thanks go to Professor E. James Burton, Dean of the College of Business at MTSU, for his valuable inputs, encouragement, and continuous support. A special acknowledgement is due to William D. Miller, the main author of the first edition of this book. His efforts were needed to develop the second edition and improve it from the first edition. Saving the best to the end, words cannot express the extent of support freely given by my wife, Soheila, and my son, Nick, in writing this book. Without their love, enthusiasm, and support, this book would not have come to fruition when it did.

Zabihollah Rezaee

Preface

The past decade has witnessed significant changes in the structure, characteristics, and types of products and services offered by financial services providers. The most significant changes were in three areas: consolidation, convergence, and competition. Financial institutions are also facing numerous new challenges caused by the rapid changes occurring in information technology, deregulation, geographic and product expansion, globalization of business, statutory laws, accounting standards, the marketplace, and trends toward business combinations. The modern financial services being offered by banks, insurance companies, and mutual funds, coupled with a new trend toward combinations between banks and financial services organizations, make the subject matter of valuations and mergers and acquisitions timely and relevant.

Traditionally financial services provided by banks, insurance companies, and mutual funds and their roles have been somewhat separate. Today, the differences between functions of these financial services providers are becoming less noticeable, especially since the Gramm-Leach-Bliley Financial Modernization Act (GLB) of 1999 permits combinations between banks, insurance companies, and mutual funds. The implementation of the GLB Act will create numerous challenges for financial services providers, including restructuring their business operations and entering the areas of investment management, insurance, and a variety of other financial services.

In recent years, the field of business valuation has truly undergone a revolution. Mergers and acquisitions also continue to play an important role in business valuation and strategy. Every day a significant number of business executives, business owners, accountants, attorneys, investment bankers, tax and regulatory authorities, and judges are involved in various stages of business valuation and the merger and acquisition process. Knowledgeable and experienced valuation specialists can play a vital role in this exciting, dynamic, and rewarding process.

This book is intended to assist valuation, merger, and acquisition practitioners in applying their knowledge and expertise in providing their services. No prior knowledge of financial institutions, valuations, mergers, and acquisitions is assumed in the second edition. The author has attempted to present current developments in the areas of valuations, mergers, and acquisitions, which have progressed significantly since the first edition of the book in 1995.

The second edition is designed primarily for audiences (business executives, banks, financial services organizations, attorneys, accountants, appraisers) interested in the valuation, mergers, and acquisitions areas of the financial services industry. Throughout the book, every effort is made to integrate on-line, fair value valuation techniques into the due diligence process and practices for internal and external assessment purposes as well as merger and acquisitions deals. Our goals in preparing this edition are to (1) make refinements in the style and clarity of presentations to maximize the effectiveness of the book as an authoritative guide and learning resource for users; (2) make further refinements in the content and organization of the book to enhance its relevance and flexibility in accommodating new on-line valuation techniques for the financial services industry; and (3) provide comprehensive and integrated coverage of the latest developments in the environment, accounting standards, laws, regulations, and methodologies pertaining to the valuation process, as well as the due diligence practices for merger and acquisition deals.

The second edition is designed to provide a useful reference for anyone wishing to obtain understanding and knowledge of financial institutions and their valuation, as well as the wave of mergers and acquisitions in the financial services industry. The substantial changes in the second edition reflect the intent of the book.

HIGHLIGHTS OF CHANGES FROM THE FIRST EDITION

The following changes are made in the second edition to achieve the book's aforementioned goals.

1. The first four new chapters (1–4) constitute the foundation of the book.

2. Chapter 1 presents the major topics of the book, including consolidation, convergence, and competition in the financial services industry.

3. Chapter 2 provides background information regarding the market and demand for valuation services, valuation services providers (appraisers) and the various appraisal organizations and their standards, codes of ethical conduct, and certifications. The valuation process, including preparation of engagement letters, documents requests, internal and external sources of information gathered by the appraisers, and valuation reports, is also discussed in this chapter.

4. Chapter 3 discusses mergers and acquisitions in general and consolidation and convergence in the financial services industry in particular. Merger and acquisition decisions involve proper analysis and assessment of strategic, financial, and integration factors discussed in this chapter.

5. Chapter 4 presents the regulatory environment, corporate governance, and financial reporting process of financial institutions.

6. A brief historical perspective on valuation and mergers and acquisitions in the financial services industry is added to Chapter 1.

7. All chapters containing material on valuations are updated to integrate on-line valuation techniques and incorporate authoritative accounting standards.

8. The passage and implementation of the Gramm-Leach-Bliley Financial Modernization Act of 1999 for the financial services industry and its impact on future business combinations among banks, insurance companies, stock brokerages, and mutual funds are thoroughly discussed in Chapters 1 and 3.

9. A new Chapter 13 on provisions of the new proposal accounting standards for business combinations and valuations of intangible assets is added. This chapter also presents in-depth discussion of fair value accounting and regulatory capital requirements for banks.

10. Increased attention is given to the global banking services and relevance of international accounting standards for the U.S. financial services industry and globalization of the financial services industry.

11. Citation of relevant accounting standards, related literature, and applicable laws and regulations pertaining to valuations, mergers, and acquisitions is provided in chapter end notes.

12. Specific illustrations on financial statement presentations of fair value of financial items for the financial services industry are incorporated in all related chapters throughout the book.

13. End-of-chapter citations are included to support materials added in each chapter and to provide references to new accounting standards, applicable statutory changes, and trends in valuations and business combinations.

14. A new Chapter 17 is added to discuss the concept of theoretical fair value of derivatives. Accounting standards set forth for the proper measurement, recognition, and reporting of fair value of derivatives are provided in this chapter.

15. Changes in accounting and trends of mergers and acquisitions that are taking place in the coming years are thoroughly examined throughout the book.

16. Updated materials pertaining to on-line (Internet) sources of comparative financial and valuation data are added to provide numerous data sources for international, regional, and local economic data, banking industry information, and bank financial statement data.

ORGANIZATION OF THE BOOK

The organization of the second edition continues to provide maximum flexibility in choosing the amount and order of materials on valuations, mergers, and acquisitions for financial institutions. The entire valuation process is examined from a mergers and acquisitions perspective. Thus, in addition to valuation theory, concepts, methodology, and techniques, the merger and acquisition process, target bank analysis, applicable laws and regulations, and related accounting standards are thoroughly examined.

The second edition is organized into four parts as follows:

Part	Subject	Chapters
I	Financial Institutions and Their Valuation	1–4
II	Fundamentals of Valuation	5–8
III	Financial Analysis of Banks and Bank Holding Companies	9–11
IV	Applying Valuation to the Acquisition Process	12–18

The 18 chapters of this book are organized into four parts. The first part contains four chapters that constitute the foundation of the book. Chapter 1 discusses the major topics of the book, and Chapter 2 describes its focus valuation. The third chapter discusses mergers and acquisitions in general and convergence in the financial services industry in particular. Part I concludes with Chapter 4, which examines the regulatory environment, corporate governance, and the financial reporting process of financial institutions.

Part II, containing Chapters 5 through 8, addresses the fundamental issues related to valuation, including different types of value, approaches to measuring value, and the differences between tangible and intangible assets. The four chapters in Part II provide a thorough background on the basic principles needed to understand the calculation of value of a bank.

Part III (Chapters 9, 10, and 11) addresses the various types of research that will likely be undertaken as part of a proper valuation. A major portion of the discussion relates to the financial analysis of the banking company, but with an ample discussion on the nonfinancial aspects of the bank's operations and organizations as well as the external market environment in which it operates. Taken together, the discussions in Parts II and III provide a solid foundation for applying the principles of valuation to the calculation of a banking company's value.

Part IV contains Chapters 12 through 18, which focus on specific issues related to calculation of value for purposes of merger or acquisition. A description of the bank merger and acquisition process is provided as a background to put into context the role that valuation can play at various points in that process. Also covered are topics that are unique to banking, such as core deposits, branch acquisitions, unknown loan losses, derivatives, and accounting standards on merger and acquisitions.

The analyses in this book are described so as to be useful to both buyers and sellers. As a buyer, a banker must be able to assess the value of a target bank and gauge the underlying business, which has "created" that value. As a seller, a banker should understand how the value of the institution will be assessed, whether a buy offer is fair, and possible strategies to enhance value. Where possible, examples are given from both the buyer's and seller's perspective. However, whether the reader is a buyer or seller (or a professional assisting either), the concepts, principles, and techniques described can assist in making the merger and acquisitions process more successful.

In one book, it is not possible to address the valuation of every type of subsidiary business a bank holding company may operate. Consequently, the focus is on what is commonly thought of as a "commercial bank," often referring to the bank holding company legal structure that is common in U.S. banking. While the discussions that unfold generally focus on commercial banks and on those bank holding companies where the principal subsidiaries are commercial banks, the same valuation principles and techniques apply to nonbanking entities.

Most terms are defined where appropriate throughout the book; however, some should be clarified at this point. The use of the term "financial institution" refers to banks, bank holding companies, mutual saving banks, saving banks, stock-owned thrift institutions, credit unions, and savings and loan associations. Although the title of the book is *Financial Institutions: Valuations, Mergers, and Acquisitions* and therefore the focus is on financial institutions, the issues of valuations, mergers, and acquisitions are relevant to all organizations in all industries. The first part of the book examines these issues in generic terms as they relate to all organizations. The other parts of the book discuss these issues as they pertain to financial institutions: Technical distinctions exist between mergers and acquisitions. Mergers often occur when two separate entities combine and both parties to the merger wind up with common stock in a single combined entity. In contrast, in an acquisition deal, the acquirer (bidding entity) buys the common stock or assets of the seller (target entity). However, in this book mergers and acquisitions are used interchangeably to describe the method in which separate institutions are combined under the control of one entity. The vast majority of all business combinations are acquisitions rather than mergers.

The Foundation: Financial Institutions, Valuations, Mergers, Acquisitions, Regulatory and Accounting Environment

CHAPTER 1

Introduction to Financial Institutions

1.1 INTRODUCTION

The past decade has witnessed significant changes in the structure, characteristics, and types of products and services provided by the financial services industry. The most significant changes were in three areas: consolidation, convergence, and competition. These changes, which are expected to continue to occur at a higher speed in the future, have been motivated and caused by a number of factors and forces, including deregulation, globalization of business, geographic expansion, highly valued stock prices, product line expansion, technological advances, relatively low interest rates, and considerable economic stability and growth. Consolidation, convergence, and competition have transformed the financial services industry from traditional organizations such as banks, brokers, insurance companies, mutual funds, and securities providers to asset management companies such as bank holding companies and financial holding companies.

The structure and characteristics of banks and banking organizations are changing from traditional brick-and-mortar branches to universal banking, PC-banking, and Internet banking. Until recently, customers could not do one-stop shopping for all of their financial services, and very little shopping at all for financial services. The range of options often was limited by geographic restrictions, product limitations, and even inefficiencies, cost, and time-consuming searches for the best option. The majority of households and businesses used local banks within 20 miles for their financial service needs because of availability, convenience, and personalized banking relationships.

Today, financial holding companies are developed to provide the opportunity for one-stop shopping for all financial services and products, including checking and saving accounts, loans, asset management, insurance, and investment services, as well as unlimited efficiency in finding the best financial services at the lowest cost nationwide or even across international borders. For example, customers now can easily find information about loans or mortgages on-line by visiting eloan.com or loanweb.com sites. This information efficiency offered to customers through e-commerce and Internet banking, coupled with the creation of financial holding companies, would accelerate the financial services movement toward commoditization. The new information technology not only

Exhibit 1.1   Composition of the Financial Services Industry

		Number			
SIC/NAICS	Organization	1985	1990	1995	1999
6021/52211	Commercial Banks	14,430	12,347	9,910	8,580
6035/52212	Savings and Loan Associations	3,640	2,358	2,030	1,640
6311/52411	Life Insurance Companies	2,261	2,195	2,079	1,512
6282/52392	Mutual Funds:				
	Number of Funds	1,530	3,081	5,790	7,791
	Fund Complexes	220	361	370	433
6211/52311-5231	Investment Banking and				
	Brokerage firms	6,300	5,800	5,400	5,100

Sources: Federal Deposit Insurance Corp. (FDIC)
            Federal Home Loan Bank Board (FHLB)
            Federal Finance Board (FFB)
            Investment Company Institute (ICI)
            American Council of Life Insurance (ACLI)
            Securities Industry Association (SIA)

empowers customers to shop for their financial services easily and effectively but also provides opportunities for competitors to identify, match, and duplicate any innovative financial services.

Financial institutions are also facing numerous challenges caused by the rapid changes occurring in information technology, trends toward business combinations, statutory laws, marketplace, global competition, and accounting standards. Traditionally, financial services provided by banks, insurance companies, and mutual funds and their roles have been somewhat separated. Today, the differences between functions of these financial services provided by entities in the financial services industry are becoming less noticeable. Entities in the financial services industry are classified in this book as: (1) banks and thrifts; (2) finance companies; (3) securities and investments companies; and (4) insurance companies. Exhibit 1.1 shows the composition of the financial services industry's previously used standard industrial classification (SIC) code along with the new classification coding system, called the North American Industry Classification System (NAICS) for entities in the financial services industry.

Many of the traditional barriers including both geographic (e.g., interstate banking) and products (e.g., a variety of financial services) that once had separated banks from insurance companies, mutual firms, or investment funds are now diminishing in the financial services industry. Thus, the ever-changing nature, structure, and competition in the financial services industry have currently received great attention primarily because of the recent elimination of geographic barriers and product barriers especially those that related to cross-industry mergers and affiliations. The passage of the Gramm-Leach-Bliley Act of 1999 (hereafter, GLB) will significantly increase the number and size of mergers within the financial services industry. The importance of the current environment of the financial services industry is underscored by the fact that the main theme of the 36th Annual Bank Structure Conference, held in Chicago in May 2000, was "The Changing Financial Industry Structure, Regulation, and Competition." Among the key issues discussed at the 36th conference were:

- Opportunities and challenges that the current changes (e.g., regulations, technologies) present for financial services providers.
- Motivational factors and forces behind the merger trend in the financial services industry.
- The implications of the current merger wave for antitrust methodologies and for industry competition.
- The role of universal banking or one-stop shopping.
- The impact of Internet banking on industry structure, competition, and related regulatory issues.
- The effects of these changes on small banks.

These issues will be addressed throughout the book, especially in Chapters 1, 3, and 4.

1.2   STRUCTURAL CHANGES IN THE FINANCIAL SERVICES INDUSTRY

The financial services industry is undergoing unprecedented changes driven by consolidation, convergence, and competition. Until recently financial service organizations (e.g., banks, insurance companies, mutual funds, brokerage firms) in the financial services industry were structurally and functionally distinct. Consolidation, convergence, and competition have brought these organizations together. The distinctions between banks, insurance companies, securities, and brokerage firms are melting away as the financial services industry transforms into a more consolidated, converged, competitive industry.

1.2.1   Consolidation

Consolidation, in this book, refers to the integration and consolidation of financial institutions' resources into larger and fewer institutions by means of mergers and acquisitions (hereafter, M & A). The driving forces behind current growing consolidation, especially among financial institutions, are (1) deregulation of geographical and product restrictions; (2) technological advances; (3) global competition; (4) healthy financial positions and profitable financial conditions; and (5) growing stock prices. These factors are not listed in any order of importance, and they will be discussed thoroughly in this chapter and Chapter 3. However, deregulation and technological advances are viewed as the most important factors shaping up future consolidation. The elimination of geographic restrictions under the Riegle-Neal Interstate Banking and Branching Efficiency Act of 1994, which allowed virtually nationwide branching as of June 1, 1997, was the biggest impetus for the consolidation of banks and banking organizations. Technological progress has made consolidation more feasible.

Recent changes in technology, global competition, deregulation, interest rates, and merger trends have profoundly affected the financial services industry. Internet banking has changed the "low-touch" customized financial services provided to local customers. The use of derivative financial instruments is becoming more common as a means of managing risk. Foreign banks are now competing more freely and frequently in the United States and the global market. The wave of megamergers has substantially reduced the number of financial institutions as the industry consolidated. The Glass-Steagall Act (also called the Banking Act of 1933); (1) separates commercial banking (e.g., receiving deposits and making loans) from investment banking (e.g., underwriting, market maker of securities); (2) prohibits banks from paying interest on deposits; (3) restricts the types of assets banks could own; and (4) prohibits bank distribution of mutual funds.

The banking problems of the early 1990s encouraged the issuance of the 1991 Federal Deposit Insurance Corporation (FDIC) Act amendments, which sharply raised bank deposit insurance premiums. The reduction of short-term interest rates by the Federal Reserve in the early 1990s encouraged banks to borrow short and lend long, which helped banks to get back to better financial health and generate excess capital for new acquisitions. In 1994, Congress passed the Riegle-Neal Interstate Banking Act, which allowed combinations across state lines. This Act made interstate banking much easier by putting a cap on the amount of domestic deposits that a bank could hold at 10 percent of the national aggregate. The economic growth of the mid-1990s coupled with the low interest rates and diversity in financial institutions' operations gave large banks higher valuation and the currency of higher stock prices with which to pursue future mergers and acquisitions (M & A) deals. Small banks, on the other hand, became more profitable which made them a good target for acquisition at prices attractive to their shareholders.

Traditionally, banks have expanded by adding more branches staffed by many salaried employees to provide retail transactions and costly commercial services to their customers. Banks have faced regulatory restrictions that kept them from moving out of the commercial business into investments and insurance services. The recent wave of mergers in the financial services industry is driven by the emerging technologies to make the industry more competitive and efficient. There is no compelling evidence that the new mergers are motivated by a desire to monopolize markets and increase fees for financial services. Indeed, the financial services industry, especially the banking industry, remains far less concentrated than many other competitive industries such as automobiles and communication. However, it is vital that the Fed continues to exercise its oversight responsibility to ensure that M & A deals and resulting changes in the structure of financial institutions are consistent with and in compliance with applicable laws and regulations and in the best interest of the public.

Banks are, by law, protected by a so-called "federal financial safety net" (e.g., deposit insurance, access to the Fed's discount window and payment services) designed to protect banks' customers and to serve the public. This provision of the banking industry, when it is not properly monitored, may create adverse incentives of "moral hazard" in the sense that depositors may think that their deposits are always safeguarded regardless of the banks' severe financial difficulties. Banks, on the other hand, may be motivated to take more than prudent business risk of undertaking risky loans and investments expecting that higher returns will ease their financial difficulties. In the absence of proper balance between banks' risk and return assessment and in the light of financial difficulties, the insurance fund and ultimately taxpayers are left to absorb the losses (e.g., the savings and loan debacle of the 1980s). The existence of "moral hazard" can be very detrimental to the success of megamergers in the financial services industry because the failure of a large combined financial institution could be very costly to resolve. Thus, the current merger wave may necessitate a reform in the financial services industry at least in the areas of safety net and deposit insurance coverage.

1.2.2 Convergence

Webster's third new international dictionary (1986) defines "convergence" as the "tendency or movement toward union or uniformity." Convergence in the financial services industry is defined in this book as the integration of banking organizations and other financial services providers (e.g., insurance companies, mutual funds, and securities firms) through the combination and expansion of the scope or breadth of their financial products and services. Convergence may occur through (1) M & A between financial institutions and other financial services organizations now permitted under the GLB Act of 1999; (2) the creation of bank holding companies under the Bank Holding Company Act of 1956; and (3) the establishment of financial holding companies under the GLB Act of 1999.

Traditionally, the functional services of banks, insurance companies, mutual funds, and brokerage firms were distinguishable, and their roles were separated. Banks were engaged in offering traditional services such as deposits, loans, and transaction activities. Insurance companies provided auto, property, and life insurance products. However, the financial services industry has experienced the evolutionary disappearance of the distinctions in their offered financial services. Today, the differences between functions of these financial services providers are becoming less noticeable. For example, pension funds have grown far more rapidly than traditional life insurance, requiring more investment services expertise and competence that can best be provided by banks. Thus, commercial banks took an interest in mutual funds and insurance services at their branches. Indeed, Exhibit 1.2 shows

Exhibit 1.2

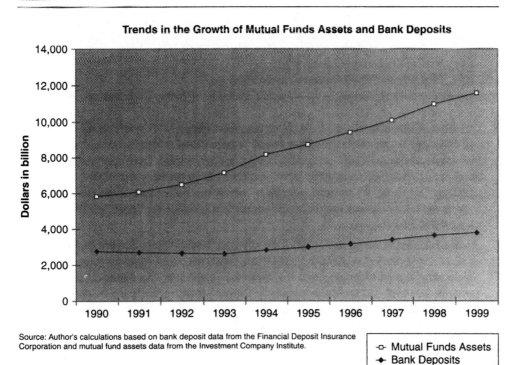

Trends in the Growth of Mutual Funds Assets and Bank Deposits

Source: Author's calculations based on bank deposit data from the Financial Deposit Insurance Corporation and mutual fund assets data from the Investment Company Institute.

-□- Mutual Funds Assets
-◆- Bank Deposits

that during the past decade the total assets of mutual funds have exceeded total bank deposits. Insurance companies, on the other hand, started getting into banks' traditional credit markets and business loans by providing financial services such as securitized instruments, mortgages, derivatives, and loan syndications.

The logic of a universal financial service (e.g., one-stop shopping for all financial services and products) offering a variety of financial products and services is compelling. Furthermore, technological advances facilitate one-stop shopping for all financial products and services. Indeed, universal banking has been practiced in Germany, Canada, and other countries, yet, until recently, it has not been permitted in the United States. The trend toward convergence in financial services organizations can be viewed as desirable and socially beneficial in the sense that it would lead to offerings of more financial products and services at a single location and more competition for customer dollars.

The Gramm-Leach-Bliley (hereafter, GLB) Act of 1999 (better known as the Financial Modernization Act), which officially went into effect in March 2000, repeals the Glass-Steagall Act of 1933, which prohibits the line of business expansion for banks. The GLB Act permits banks, securities firms, insurance companies, mutual funds, brokerage firms, and asset managers to freely enter each others' business or consolidate. It also allows creation of financial holding companies that may conduct a broad range of financial services including insurance and securities underwriting, commercial banking, investment banking, asset management and distribution, and real estate development and investment, typically under separate subsidiaries. The passage of the GLB Act has raised some concerns that its implementation may: (1) create concentration of economic power in the financial services industry; and (2) cause lack of ability of regulators and government to properly oversee the industry's activities and to manage risk. Proponents of the GLB Act believe that its implementation would: (1) provide long-sought financial services supermarkets and one-stop shopping for all financial services; and (2) improve the ability of U.S. financial services providers to compete effectively in the global financial services market.

1.2.2(a)   Provisions of the Gramm-Leach-Bliley Act
Provisions of the GLB Act can be summarized into the following eight categories:

1. Creation of the new types of regulated entities—namely, "financial holding companies"—that are authorized to offer a broad range of financial products and services. A financial holding company is a bank holding company whose depository institutions are well-capitalized, well-managed, and Community Reinvestment Act (CRA)-rated "satisfactory" or better. A financial subsidiary, which can offer most of the newly-authorized activities, is a direct subsidiary of a bank that satisfies the same conditions as the financial holding company.

2. Authorization of a wide variety of the newly-permissible financial activities for financial holding companies including securities, insurance, merchant, banking/equity investment, financial in nature, and complementary activities. Provisions of the GLB Act permit banking organizations to engage in virtually every type of activity currently recognized as financial as well as new activities that will be authorized by the Federal Reserve and Treasury Department as "incidental" or "complementary" to a financial activity. The "merchant banking" provisions of the GLB Act permit a financial holding company to make a controlling investment virtually in any kind of company, financial or commercial.

3. Restrictions for commercial companies to acquire thrifts through unitary thrift holding companies. However, the existing commercial unitary thrift holding companies are grandfathered as of May 4, 1994, but such companies may not sell their thrifts to any other commercial company.

4. Substantial changes to laws governing the Federal Home Loan Bank System. The GLB Act created a new type of Federal Home Loan Bank member called a Community Financial Institution (CFI) which is a community bank or thrift with less than $500 million in assets. A CFI may pledge small business and agricultural advances.

5. Requirements for protecting the privacy of customers' information. The GLB Act established four privacy requirements pertaining to the sharing of customer information with others, which apply equally to all financial institutions. The GLB Act requires each financial institution to: (1) establish and annually disclose a privacy policy; (2) provide customers the right to opt-out of having their information shared with non-affiliated third parties; (3) not share customer account numbers with non-affiliated third parties; and (4) abide by regulatory standards to protect the security and integrity of customer information.

6. Community Reinvestment Act (CRA) Provisions. The GLB Act addressed the three controversial CRA provisions that nearly prevented the legislation from passing. These provisions are related to requirements for: (1) establishing "satisfactory" CRA ratings as a condition for engaging in the Act's new activities; (2) disclosing of CRA agreements between financial institutions and third parties; and (3) establishing a lengthened CRA exam cycle for community banks and thrifts.

7. Other Regulatory Provisions. Other important regulatory provisions of the GLB Act affecting banks and financial institutions are: (1) the Federal Reserve's "umbrella" supervisory authority over financial holding companies; (2) those affecting foreign banks; (3) limitations on the state's ability to establish regulations that discriminate against banking organizations; (4) revisions to federal antitrust authority affecting financial holding companies; (5) ATM disclosure provisions; and (6) elimination of the "special reserve" of the Savings Association Insurance Fund. The GLB Act states that bank holding companies cannot become financial holding companies or engaged in the newly-authorized financial activities unless all of their subsidiaries and affiliates have CRA ratings of satisfactory or better.

8. Effective dates of key provisions of the Act. These include the 120-day delayed effective date for the financial holding company and financial subsidiary sections of the Act (e.g., through mid-March 2000).

1.2.2(b)   Implementation of the Gramm-Leach-Bliley Act

Exhibits 1.3 through 1.6 show banks' and thrifts' activities and affiliates before and after the implementation of the GLB Act. The proper implementation of the landmark GLB Act will create both opportunities and challenges for the financial services industry including the following:

• The act will likely increase certain trends already underway in the financial services industry causing further consolidation of the industry.

• New authorized financial activities can be conducted only by a subset of bank holding companies (BHCs) to be called financial holding companies (FHCs.) To be an FHC, each

Exhibit 1.3

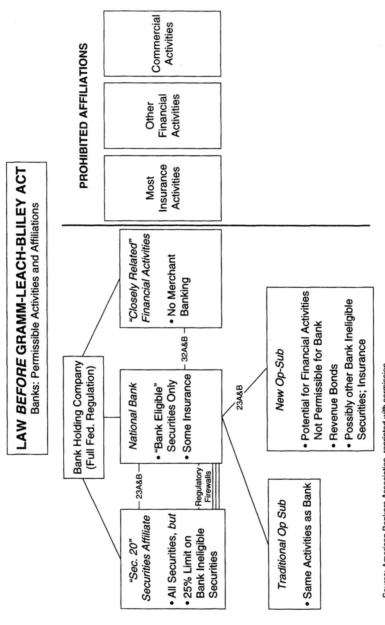

LAW *BEFORE* GRAMM-LEACH-BLILEY ACT
Banks: Permissible Activities and Affiliations

Bank Holding Company
(Full Fed. Regulation)

"Sec. 20" Securities Affiliate
- All Securities, *but*
- 25% Limit on Bank Ineligible Securities

National Bank
- "Bank Eligible" Securities Only
- Some Insurance

"Closely Related" Financial Activities
- No Merchant Banking

23A&B

32A&B

23A&B

Regulatory Firewalls

Traditional Op Sub
- Same Activities as Bank

New Op-Sub
- Potential for Financial Activities Not Permissible for Bank
- Revenue Bonds
- Possibly other Bank Ineligible Securities; Insurance

PROHIBITED AFFILIATIONS

Most Insurance Activities

Other Financial Activities

Commercial Activities

Source: American Bankers Association, reprinted with permission.

Exhibit 1.4

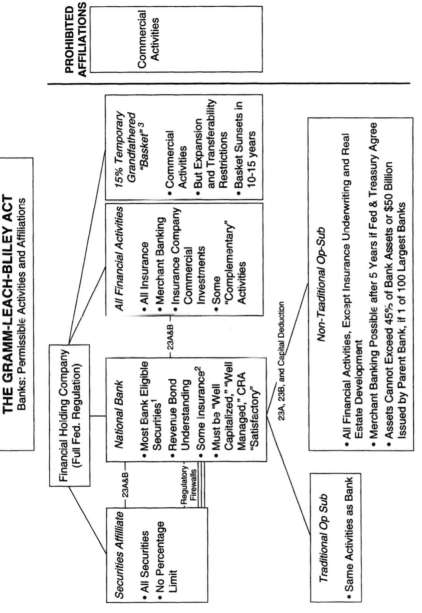

THE GRAMM-LEACH-BLILEY ACT
Banks: Permissible Activities and Affiliations

PROHIBITED AFFILIATIONS

Commercial Activities

Financial Holding Company
(Full Fed. Regulation)

Securities Affiliate — 23A&B
- All Securities
- No Percentage Limit

— Regulatory Firewalls

National Bank
- Most Bank Eligible Securities[1]
- Revenue Bond Understanding
- Some Insurance[2]
- Must be "Well Capitalized," "Well Managed," CRA "Satisfactory"

— 23A&B

All Financial Activities
- All Insurance
- Merchant Banking
- Insurance Company Commercial Investments
- Some "Complementary" Activities

15% Temporary Grandfathered "Basket"[3]
- Commercial Activities
- But Expansion and Transferability Restrictions
- Basket Sunsets in 10-15 years

23A, 23B, and Capital Deduction

Traditional Op Sub
- Same Activities as Bank

Non-Traditional Op-Sub
- All Financial Activities, Except Insurance Underwriting and Real Estate Development
- Merchant Banking Possible after 5 Years if Fed & Treasury Agree
- Assets Cannot Exceed 45% of Bank Assets or $50 Billion Issued by Parent Bank, if 1 of 100 Largest Banks

[1]Some bank eligible Securities activities and some banking products would be "pushed out" (or exposed to push-out) from bank.
[2]Insurance underwriting is generally prohibited.
[3]Applies to newly-formed FHCs Annual gross revenues from FHCs commercial activities may not exceed 15% of FHC's gross revenues (excluding depository institution revenue).

Source: American Bankers Association, reprinted with permission.

Exhibit 1.5

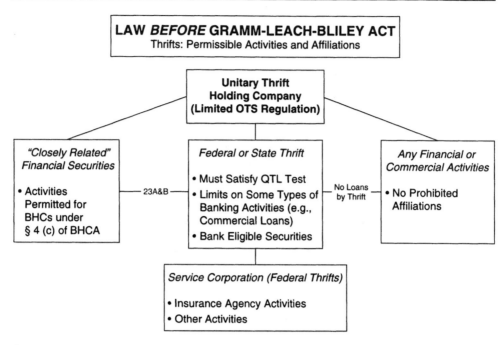

LAW *BEFORE* GRAMM-LEACH-BLILEY ACT
Thrifts: Permissible Activities and Affiliations

Unitary Thrift Holding Company (Limited OTS Regulation)

"Closely Related" Financial Securities
- Activities Permitted for BHCs under § 4 (c) of BHCA

23A&B

Federal or State Thrift
- Must Satisfy QTL Test
- Limits on Some Types of Banking Activities (e.g., Commercial Loans)
- Bank Eligible Securities

No Loans by Thrift

Any Financial or Commercial Activities
- No Prohibited Affiliations

Service Corporation (Federal Thrifts)
- Insurance Agency Activities
- Other Activities

Source: American Bankers Association, reprinted with permission.

subsidiary bank must be well-capitalized, well-managed, and have a Consumer Reinvestment Act (CRA) rating of satisfactory or better.

- The "sunshine" language of the Act requires public disclosure of all written agreements made in fulfillment of the CRA involving payments by banking organizations in excess of $10,000 or loans in excess of $50,000.

- Financial services organizations affected by the Act should establish disclosure requirements and consumer "opt-out" procedures that protect consumer privacy without significantly burdening financial institutions or consumers. The purpose of the privacy provision of the Act is to restrict the ability of financial institutions to disclose to unrelated third parties nonpublic personal information pertaining to individuals who obtain financial products and/or services from the financial institution.

- Prior to the passage of the Act, a BHC could own no more than five percent of the voting equity and 25 percent of total equity of a company. The Act allows "merchant banking," which means that any FHC with a securities affiliate may engage in merchant banking by obtaining ownership of securities of a company.

- FHCs are authorized to engage in a broad range of financial activities including insurance underwriting and sales, securities underwriting and dealing, merchant banking, lending, investment advisory, financial data processing services, travel agency, and certain management consulting services.

- There will be a new challenge for bank supervisors to implement the new blend of umbrella and functional supervision established in the Act. The extent of the challenge depends on

Exhibit 1.6

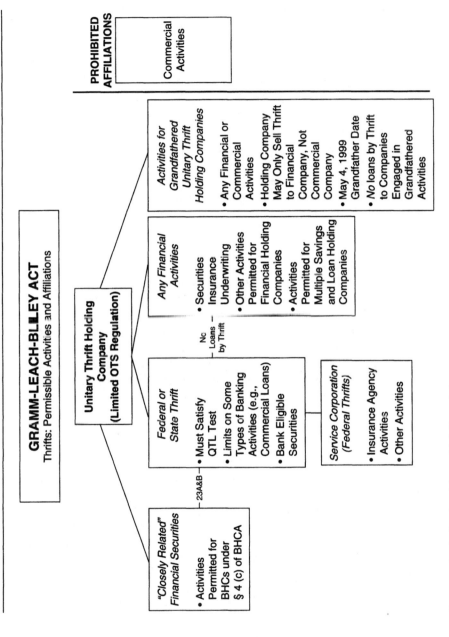

GRAMM-LEACH-BLILEY ACT
Thrifts: Permissible Activities and Affiliations

PROHIBITED AFFILIATIONS

Commercial Activities

Unitary Thrift Holding Company (Limited OTS Regulation)

"Closely Related" Financial Securities
- Activities Permitted for BHCs under § 4 (c) of BHCA

— 23A&B —

Federal or State Thrift
- Must Satisfy QTL Test
- Limits on Some Types of Banking Activities (e.g., Commercial Loans)
- Bank Eligible Securities

Service Corporation (Federal Thrifts)
- Insurance Agency Activities
- Other Activities

— No Loans by Thrift —

Any Financial Activities
- Securities Insurance Underwriting
- Other Activities Permitted for Financial Holding Companies
- Activities Permitted for Multiple Savings and Loan Holding Companies

Activities for Grandfathered Unitary Thrift Holding Companies
- Any Financial or Commercial Activities
- Holding Company May Only Sell Thrift to Financial Company, Not Commercial Company
- May 4, 1999 Grandfather Date
- No loans by Thrift to Companies Engaged in Grandfathered Activities

Source: American Bankers Association, reprinted with permission.

the degree of integration of financial activities within financial holding companies and the relative size of the bank and nonbank activities within such organizations.

- The Act requires communication, cooperation, and coordination among multiple banking regulators to share information among the umbrella, financial, and bank supervisors in a manner that is satisfactory to all regulatory agencies. However, the Act states that the first level supervisory authority lies with the functional regulators (e.g., state, SEC.)

- The Act limits extensions of the safety net by eliminating the need to impose bank-like regulation on nonbank subsidiaries and affiliates of organizations that contain a bank.

- The privacy provisions of the Act prohibit financial institutions from disclosing information to third parties unless customers first are given the opportunity to opt-out of information sharing. Furthermore, all financial institutions including banks, brokerage firms, and insurance companies must establish a privacy policy which should be presented to all current and future customers. The privacy policy must: (1) list all types of personal information the institution collects (e.g., accounting activity, credit reports); (2) inform the customer of precisely where this information will be shared; and (3) disclose the security measures undertaken to safeguard the confidentiality of the information.

The 1994 Riegle-Neal Act, which went into effect in 1997, practically removed all geographic barriers to M & A activities within the banking industry. The 1999 GLB Financial Modernization Act, which went into effect in March 2000, removed the remaining products and services restrictions for convergence within the financial services industry. These two acts substantially deregulated the financial services industry by removing geographic and product barriers and have set the stage for unprecedented consolidation and convergence in the financial services industry. The 1997 removal of all geographic barriers to M & A made it theoretically possible, subject to antitrust policy restrictions, for the top 50 U.S. banks to merge into just six megabanks and the next 50 banks to combine into seven banks of almost equal size.[1] The 2000 removal of products and services barriers allowed the potential six megabanks to become full-line financial service providers under the universal banking system.

The passage of the GLB Act of 1999 brought the financial services industry one step closer to the effective convergence of financial services and utilization of universal banking common in other countries. However, the full convergence necessitates resolution of obstacles and issuance of standard and universally applicable regulatory and supervisory laws and rules in the financial services industry. For example, the global banking community, with the issuance of the Basel Accord, is virtually establishing standards and globally acceptable risk-based capital requirements for banks. The National Association of Insurance Commissioners (NAIC) has also established risk-based capital guidelines for insurance companies to prevent insurance company failures. While there are some similarities in these two sets of requirements, they are not currently applicable to both banks and insurance companies. Schott (1996) argued the most severe obstacles to complete implications of financial-services convergence are the differences in corporate culture associated with financial services providers.[2] Schott (1996) provided several examples of these differences, including the contrast between insurance agents and stock market brokers. Insurance agents seek high-margin, modest-volume operations, while stock market brokers are often low-margin, high-volume oriented.

1.2.3   Competition

Consolidation and convergence resulting from deregulation, technological advances, and favorable economic and business prospects have to be profitable, productive, and cost effective to survive. Productive and profitable consolidation and convergence cause cost efficiency, which in turn creates higher competitive intensity and tighter pricing. It is expected that consolidation and convergence in the financial services industry will create more competitive prices for commoditized offered financial products and services. Future pricing of financial services is likely to follow examples of other consolidated, deregulated industries, such as long distance telecommunications companies, electricity providers, and airlines. In these industries, prices declined about 20 percent in the first five years following deregulation-consolidation and then another 20 percent in the subsequent five years.[3] Higher competitive intensity resulting from consolidation and convergence causes high cost. High-price providers are either acquired and restructured or driven out of the industry entirely.

Increased competition nationally and worldwide in the financial services industry is viewed as an important factor shaping the industry. Global competition in providing financial services can be achieved by striving to be the low-cost provider of financial products and services or by developing a niche product of differentiating offered financial services and products. Being low-cost providers requires banks to be large enough to generate economies of scale. Differentiation is difficult to achieve in the banking industry because of relatively homogenous financial services and products (e.g., checking, saving, loans), which is why many financial services organizations are currently engaged in a variety of activities such as asset management, insurance, and mutual funds. Furthermore, differentiation often requires substantial investment in technology that is not readily available to small banks. Thus, for banks to become either low-cost providers or offer niche financial products and services, they ought to grow through mergers and acquisitions.

The profound effects of consolidation and convergence are increases in local market concentration, the move toward universal banking, and the commoditization of financial services and products. Banks and banking organizations are moving toward offering retail banking, insurance, and asset management services. The financial services market will become relatively homogenous. Global competition and easy accessibility of financial services through the Internet will force financial institutions to provide a variety of financial services and products at relatively competitive and similar rates through extensive branch networks. Financial products and services will be viewed mostly as commodities available to everyone through the Internet.

Commoditization of financial products and services for small business includes checking, savings, lines of credit, mortgages, transactions, cash management, and credit-related services. Transaction services consist of the processing of credit card receipts, wire transfers, the provision of currency and coin, and the collection of night deposits. Cash management services include lockbox services, zero-balance accounts, and the provision of sweep accounts. Credit-related services consist of letters of credit, factoring, and bankers' acceptances. The 1995 Survey of Consumer Finances revealed that 98 percent of households use a local depository institution, while the 1993 National Survey of Small Business Finances indicated that 92 percent of small businesses use a local depository institution.[4]

Many banks have adopted a new management philosophy of being driven more by markets than by regulations to be able to compete successfully in the highly competitive global market. In the highly competitive global market of the 1990s, banks that were strong and well capitalized acquired other banks and got stronger, and weak banks got weaker. The strong banks and banking organizations with effective and efficient performance and high capital ratios are often viewed and treated favorably by both financial markets and regulators. Banks also found that competitive edge and market value are the ultimate performance measures.

Financial institutions are in the midst of a transformation with advances in technology, financial engineering, financial innovation, and deregulation. Consolidation, convergence, and competition have caused profound changes in the role of financial institutions. Traditionally, financial institutions have issued claims to back their holdings of primarily private illiquid assets. Today, financial institutions assist their customers in holding and managing highly diversified portfolios of marketable securities (e.g., pension funds; mutual funds) at low cost. Financial institutions are different from most other businesses. To demonstrate and better understand these differences, it is helpful to discuss the historical perspective of American banking.

1.3   HISTORICAL PERSPECTIVE OF AMERICAN BANKING

During the early life of the banking industry in the United States (the post-World War II) period), banks operated locally with strict branch restrictions and negative perceptions toward large and centralized financial institutions. This is evident by the opposition and refusal of renewal of charters of the First and Second Banks of the United States in the early nineteenth century.[5] There was a deep-seated distrust that large federal financial institutions would seek financial power and attempt to maximize their owners' profit at the expense of the broader public.

During the early years of American banking, branching was not common and possible primarily because of lack of sufficient technology to support inexpensive long-distance communication. Another impediment to branching by national banks was the general belief that the National Banking Act passed during the Civil War prohibited it. To promote more banking activities, an act was passed in 1900 that lowered the minimum capital requirements to establish a new national bank in a small town. As a result, during the early years of the twentieth century, there were over 13,000 banks in the United States with only 119 branches. The significant number of bank failures, especially of small banks during the 1920s and in the early years of the Great Depression, proves that large banks with branches were more resistant to failure. Thus, policymakers started considering liberalization of the banking system by allowing branching as a means of diversifying individual bank portfolios and failure risk and by strengthening the banking system.

High interest rates and inflation in the late 1970s and early 1990s, coupled with inadequate and inappropriate policy and regulatory response, forced deposits out of banks and thrifts into money-market funds and open-market instruments. This move was the major cause of the S&L crises of the 1980s and banks' problems of the late 1980s and early 1990s. However, this crisis underscores the importance of market discipline and market-oriented forces over the regulatory requirements, which in turn encourage deregulation in the financial services industry.

The passage of national deposit insurance in 1933, which guaranteed the stability of the banking system, encouraged many states to liberalize their branching laws. During the past

three decades, several factors have encouraged substantial increases in the number of mergers and acquisitions in the banking industry. First, in the early 1990s more than 36 states
authorized statewide branching. Second, states passed laws allowing bank holding companies from other states to buy banks within their borders with the restriction of operating
these interstate acquisitions as separate banks. Third, the passage of the Riegle-Neal Interstate Banking Act of 1994 eliminated interstate banking restrictions which provided opportunities for banks to have branches nationwide and, accordingly, set the stage for the significant acceleration for mergers and acquisitions of financial institutions.

1.4 CURRENT TRENDS IN THE BANKING INDUSTRY

During the late 1980s and the early 1990s, conditions in the banking industry were horri-
bly signified by record losses, record failure, and record-low valuations. However, the number of bank and thrift failures during the past five years has been very low as shown in Exhibit 1.7 (e.g., eight in 1995, six in 1996, one in 1997, three in 1998, and eight in 1999.)
Exhibit 1.7 reveals numbers of bank and thrift failures and their related total assets and deposits from 1994 through 1998. When the banking environment was troubled in the late
1980s and early 1990s, hundreds of banks failed because of the problems in real estate

Exhibit 1.7

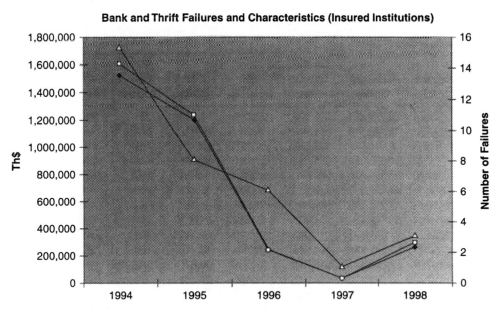

Source: Author's calculations based on data from the Federal Deposit Insurance Corporation.

markets, economic recessions, and lax lending standards. For example, in 1991 the number of commercial banks on the FDIC's problem bank list exceeded 1,000 institutions with over half a trillion dollars in assets. As the real estate market, the economy, and banking conditions improved during the 1990s, for eight consecutive years banks and thrifts have reported earnings and the number of failures and problems have substantially decreased. Exhibit 1.8 presents selected statistics for the FDIC-insured commercial banks (CB) including number of banks, their assets, income, branches, offices, charters, mergers, and failures from 1984 to the third quarter of 1999.

Today's ever-changing business environment has created substantial challenges for all businesses, especially those in the financial services industry. These changes require management to establish a proper business strategy to effectively compete in the global market. Management should focus on value-added activities that contribute to the improvement of the cash flow-based value of the business and its potential market value by identifying the key drivers of value. In the late 1990s, the banking industry showed record profits, improvement, and diversity in operations, which are reflected in their valuations. In addition, reasonable stable interest rates and favorable regulatory changes are helping banks to improve their values. Exhibits 1.9 and 1.10 present a state banking performance summary for FDIC-insured institutions including national commercial banks and national savings institutions for the years 1997–1999, respectively. The return on assets ratios of commercial banks, on average, for all three years are above one (1.23, 1.19, and 1.31 for 1997, 1998, and 1999, respectively). Commercial banks' return on equity ratios for all institutions reported as 14.69, 13.93, and 15.34 for 1997, 1998, and 1999, respectively. Percentage of unprofitable national commercial banks for all three years is less than 10 percent. Commercial banks

Exhibit 1.8 Selected Statistics for the FDIC-Insured Commercial Banks (CB)

Year	Number of CB	CB Assets (millions)	CB Net Income (millions)	CB Branches	CB Offices	CB Charters	CB Mergers	CB Failures
1999	8,580	$5,734,843	$71,703	62,544	71,142	231	417	7
1998	8,775	$5,440,944	$61,921	61,085	69,879	194	564	3
1997	9,143	$5,014,946	$59,161	59,525	66,734	188	601	1
1996	9,528	$4,578,314	$52,351	57,181	65,828	145	554	5
1995	9,940	$4,312,676	$48,745	55,856	65,052	102	609	6
1994	10,451	$4,010,517	$44,622	54,563	63,611	50	548	11
1993	10,958	$3,706,165	$43,035	52,612	63,267	61	481	42
1992	11,462	$3,505,663	$31,987	51,766	63,832	72	428	100
1991	11,921	$3,430,682	$17,935	51,876	63,832	106	447	108
1990	12,343	$3,389,490	$15,991	50,333	62,710	165	393	159
1989	12,709	$3,299,362	$15,575	47,936	60,678	192	411	206
1988	13,123	$3,130,796	$24,812	46,327	59,451	229	598	221
1987	13,703	$2,999,949	$2,803	45,307	59,010	219	543	201
1986	14,199	$2,940,699	$17,418	44,316	58,515	257	341	144
1985	14,407	$2,730,672	$17,977	43,250	57,657	331	336	118
1984	14,496	$2,508,749	$15,500	41,850	56,332	391	330	78

Source: FDIC (Graph Book and Historical Statistics on Banking)
http://www.fdic.gov/bank/analytical/index.html
Reprinted with permission

with total assets greater than $100 million, on average, reported higher return on assets ratios and return on equity ratios for 1997, 1998, and 1999 than those commercial banks with assets of less than $100 million. Core capital (leverage) ratios for all commercial banks during 1997, 1998, and 1999 are above seven with larger commercial banks reporting higher core capital ratios (10.66, 10.79, and 10.68 for 1997, 1998, and 1999, respectively).

Exhibit 1.10 reveals a national savings institutions performance summary for 1997 through 1999 as follows: (1) number of savings institutions decreased by about eight percent (from 1,780 savings institutions in 1997 to 1,640 in 1999); (2) return on assets ratios have been about one; (3) return on equity ratios of around 11; (4) core capital (leverage) ratios of approximately eight and; (5) larger savings institutions with total assets of greater than $100 million reported higher performance ratios and condition ratios than those with total assets of less than $100 million. Exhibits 1.11 and 1.12 show selected characteristics of banking organizations, including total assets, loans, and revenue as well as ratios of total loans/total assets, return on equity, and return on assets from 1980–1999. These statistics indicate profitable and financially healthy, safe, and sound banking organizations since 1991.

Consolidation, convergence, and competition may increase systematic risk and expand the safety net of financial institutions by changing the risk profiles of individual institutions. Especially as financial institutions are becoming larger through M & A, their activities and systematic risk would affect many other financial services organizations. This universal impact may give a wrong impression of "too-big-to-fail" and discourage the market and policymakers, including bank regulators, from responding to banks' problems in a timely manner. One may argue that larger banks are in a better position to manage their risk through diversification rather than incurring additional risks. However, the reality is that combined financial institutions are more interested in maximizing shareholders' return by reallocating their portfolios to higher-risk, higher-return investments. Current forces and trends in the financial services industry that have encouraged consolidation, convergence, and competition in the industry are (1) changes in regulations; (2) information technology; (3) global marketplace; (4) capital standards; (5) supervisory activities; (6) continuous quality improvement; and (7) valuation process.

1.4.1 Changes in Regulations

Financial regulation has a number of objectives, including safety and soundness, fair disclosure, avoidance of abuses, competitiveness, resource allocation, and fair treatment. These objectives are not mutually exclusive and independent and often conflict. For example, the requirements of the Community Reinvestment Act (CRA) may conflict with permission to branch and combination within the financial services industry. Another example is the capital adequacy requirement and the permission to expand by consolidation and convergence. Aspinwall (1997) argued that any new proposals for possible changes in regulatory agencies should address these apparent conflicts and suggested that these areas of regulatory process need more attention and delineation: (1) safety and soundness, including capital adequacy requirement; (2) the financial reporting process, including accounting and disclosure standards; (3) chartering and powers responsibilities; (4) oversight for allocative preferences; and (5) conflicts and abuses.[6]

Consolidation and convergence resulting from deregulation and technological advances require proper attention to safety and soundness in the financial services industry. Vigilant, prudential supervision is essential to prevent excessive risk-taking by financial institutions

Exhibit 1.9 State Banking Performance Summary (FDIC-Insured Institutions)

(dollar figures in millions)	Commercial Banks National 31-Mar-00		
	All Institutions	Assets less than $100 million	Assets greater than $100 million
Number of institutions reporting	8,518	5,093	3,425
Total employees (full-time equivalent)	1,648,952	105,986	1,542,966
AGGREGATE CONDITION AND INCOME DATA			
Net income (year-to-date)	19,549	682	18,866
Total assets	5,847,134	238,723	5,608,411
Earning assets	5,046,782	219,686	4,827,096
Total loans & leases	3,568,368	143,831	3,424,537
Other real estate owned	2,763	266	2,497
Total deposits	3,878,291	202,773	3,675,518
Equity capital	491,784	25,783	466,002
PERFORMANCE RATIOS (YTD, %)			
Yield on earning assets	8.02	8.17	8.02
Cost of funding earning assets	4.02	3.64	4.04
Net interest margin	4	4.53	3.98
Noninterest income to avg. earning assets	3.07	1.23	3.15
Noninterest expense to avg. earning assets	4.15	3.88	4.17
Net charge-offs to loans & leases	0.57	0.16	0.59
Credit-loss provision to net charge-offs	114.69	209.91	113.58
Net operating income to average assets	1.38	1.13	1.39
Retained earnings to average equity	6.56	3.85	6.71
Return on assets	1.35	1.15	1.36
Return on equity	16.08	10.66	16.38
Percent of unprofitable institutions	6.4	9.64	1.6
Percent of institutions with earning gains	68.63	66.87	71.24
CONDITION RATIOS (%)			
Net loans and leases to assets	60	59.39	60.03
Loss allowance to:			
Loans and leases	1.68	1.42	1.69
Noncurrent loans and leases	173.12	148.95	174.12
Noncurrent loans & leases to			
total loans & leases	0.97	0.96	0.97
Nonperforming assets to assets	0.65	0.69	0.64
Core deposits to total liabilities	51.14	81.81	49.86
Equity capital to total assets	8.41	10.8	8.31
Core capital (leverage) ratio	7.8	11.04	7.66
Total capital to risk-weighted assets	12.25	17.81	12.05
Gross 1–4 family mortgages to gross assets	14.6	16.72	14.51
Gross real estate assets to gross assets	34.28	39.32	34.06

Source: Call Report and Thrift Financial Report:
Prepared by the FDIC-Division of Research and Statistics

Research@fdic.gov
Reprinted with permission

Last Updated 08/02/1999

	Commercial Banks National 31-Mar-99			Commercial Banks National 31-Mar-98		
	All Institutions	Assets less than $100 million	Assets greater than $100 million	All Institutions	Assets less than $100 million	Assets greater than $100 million
	8,722	5,375	3,347	9,023	5,742	3,281
	1,619,878	115,739	1,504,139	1,557,251	124,952	1,432,299
	17,966	683	17,284	15,918	780	15,138
	5,411,797	250,512	5,161,285	5,109,111	263,839	4,845,272
	4,674,403	231,060	4,443,343	4,413,492	242,884	4,170,608
	3,251,097	144,498	3,106,598	3,023,466	154,184	2,869,283
	3,138	277	2,861	3,734	338	3,396
	3,637,338	214,195	3,423,143	3,467,394	226,719	3,240,675
	469,603	27,724	441,879	429,788	28,716	401,073
	7.72	7.82	7.71	8.12	8.29	8.11
	3.67	3.5	3.67	4.05	3.72	4.07
	4.05	4.32	4.04	4.06	4.58	4.03
	2.97	1.45	3.05	2.66	1.39	2.74
	4.25	3.95	4.26	4.19	3.95	4.21
	0.62	0.18	0.64	0.62	0.17	0.65
	108.39	196.03	107.26	103.25	208.38	101.78
	1.3	1.09	1.31	1.17	1.18	1.17
	7.51	3.54	7.76	6.49	3.48	6.7
	1.32	1.09	1.33	1.26	1.19	1.26
	15.4	9.88	15.75	15.02	10.92	15.32
	6.07	8.93	1.49	4.56	6.37	1.4
	52.67	46.41	62.71	63.57	58.84	71.83
	59	56.83	59.11	58.1	57.57	58.13
	1.78	1.48	1.79	1.83	1.48	1.84
	179.66	133.71	182.06	187.09	139.55	189.88
	0.99	1.11	0.99	0.98	1.06	0.97
	0.67	0.75	0.67	0.67	0.75	0.67
	53.41	83.3	52	54.15	84.06	52.57
	8.68	11.07	8.56	8.41	10.88	8.28
	7.68	10.84	7.53	7.56	10.72	7.38
	12.42	18.19	12.19	12.37	18.07	12.12
	13.68	16	13.56	14.25	16.82	14.11
	32.99	37.9	32.76	32.51	37.92	32.21

Exhibit 1.10   State Banking Performance Summary (FDIC-Insured Institutions)

(dollar figures in millions)	Savings Institutions* National 31-Mar-00		
	All Institutions	Assets less than $100 million	Assets greater than $100 million
Number of institutions reporting	1,633	651	982
Total employees (full-time equivalent)	244,711	12,551	232,160
AGGREGATE CONDITION AND INCOME DATA			
Net income (year-to-date)	2,943	46	2,897
Total assets	1,156,195	32,572	1,123,623
Earning assets	1,073,936	30,620	1,043,616
Total loans & leases	772,933	21,907	751,026
Other real estate owned	1,152	35	1,117
Total deposits	711,960	25,755	686,205
Equity capital	94,770	4,090	90,680
PERFORMANCE RATIOS (YTD, %)			
Yield on earning assets	7.55	7.47	7.56
Cost of funding earning assets	4.51	4.01	4.53
Net interest margin	3.04	3.46	3.03
Noninterest income to avg. earning assets	1	1.43	0.99
Noninterest expense to avg. earning assets	2.32	3.9	2.27
Net charge-offs to loans & leases	0.18	0.07	0.18
Credit-loss provision to net charge-offs	122.67	183.77	122.03
Net operating income to average assets	0.99	0.55	1
Retained earnings to average equity	6.36	1.45	6.59
Return on assets	1.03	0.56	1.05
Return on equity	12.53	4.49	12.9
Percent of unprofitable institutions	8.26	15.2	3.66
Percent of institutions with earning gains	57.5	55.29	58.96
CONDITION RATIOS (%)			
Net loans and leases to assets	66.26	66.77	66.24
Loss allowance to:			
Loans and leases	0.89	0.72	0.89
Noncurrent loans and leases	126.63	92.13	127.76
Noncurrent loans & leases to			
total loans & leases	0.7	0.78	0.7
Nonperforming assets to assets	0.57	0.64	0.57
Core deposits to total liabilities	54.92	76.93	54.32
Equity capital to total assets	8.2	12.56	8.07
Core capital (leverage) ratio	7.79	12.38	7.66
Total capital to risk-weighted assets	14.26	23.93	14
Gross 1–4 family mortgages to gross assets	46.37	49.83	46.27
Gross real estate assets to gross assets	77.32	69.38	77.55

Source: Call Report and Thrift Financial Report:
Prepared by the FDIC-Division of Research and Statistics

*Data do not include institutions in Resolution Trust Corporation Conservatorship.

Last Updated 08/02/1999

Research@fdic.gov

Reprinted with permission

	Savings Institutions* National 31-Mar-99			Savings Institutions* National 31-Mar-98		
All Institutions	Assets less than $100 million	Assets greater than $100 million	All Institutions	Assets less than $100 million	Assets greater than $100 million
1,668	690	978	1,756	743	1,013
240,336	13,296	227,040	243,508	14,672	228,836
2,684	58	2,625	2,584	76	2,508
1,109,761	35,705	1,074,056	1,040,292	38,986	1,001,306
1,035,630	33,659	1,001,970	971,708	36,791	934,918
726,400	23,385	703,015	704,916	26,186	678,730
1,529	40	1,490	1,992	60	1,932
699,203	29,054	670,149	707,997	31,976	676,020
95,696	4,331	91,365	91,463	4,682	86,781
7.24	7.34	7.23	7.68	7.78	7.68
4.16	4.01	4.17	4.5	4.23	4.51
3.08	3.33	3.07	3.18	3.55	3.16
0.91	1.22	0.9	0.81	1.09	0.8
2.4	3.52	2.36	2.42	3.34	2.38
0.16	0.08	0.16	0.21	0.11	0.21
135.98	161.69	135.58	116.7	146.46	116.12
0.84	0.55	0.84	0.83	0.69	0.84
6.8	2.04	7.03	5.29	2.89	5.42
0.98	0.66	0.99	1.01	0.79	1.02
11.36	5.4	11.64	11.55	6.6	11.82
5.99	11.01	2.45	4.78	7.67	2.66
44.9	35.5	51.53	58.14	48.99	64.85
64.83	64.98	64.82	67.09	66.65	67.11
0.96	0.79	0.97	0.99	0.77	1
115.42	78.44	116.92	96.57	75.12	97.39
0.83	1.01	0.83	1.02	1.02	1.02
0.68	0.77	0.68	0.89	0.84	0.89
57.73	79.75	57.03	63.94	81.25	63.29
8.62	12.13	8.51	8.79	12.01	8.67
7.87	11.79	7.73	8.02	11.64	7.87
14.98	23.51	14.72	15.24	23.04	14.96
46.44	48.59	46.37	38.99	50.75	48.92
78	67.54	78.35	78.5	69.85	78.84

Exhibit 1.11

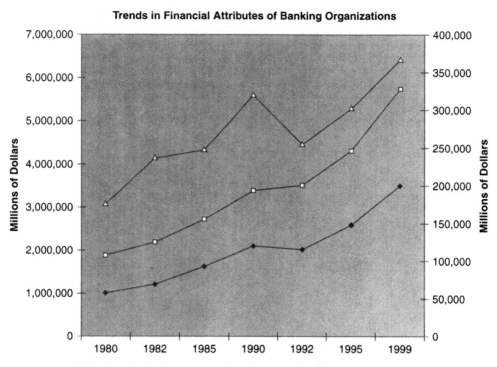

Trends in Financial Attributes of Banking Organizations

Source: Author's calculations based on data from the Federal Deposit Insurance Corporation.

-□- Total Assets (Left Scale)
-◆- Total Loans (Left Scale)
-△- Total Revenues (Right Scale)

under the newly established financial structure. Consolidation and convergence create large financial services organizations that present special challenges for regulatory authorities and supervisors because the failure of a large financial organization can have a severe effect on the financial system. Thus, bank supervisors in many countries have a "too-big-to-fail policy," which protects all depositors at a big bank (whether insured or uninsured) if the bank fails. The problem with this policy is that it may increase big banks' moral hazard incentives to take on excessive risk and therefore reduce market discipline.

Banks are regulated organizations operating under specific regulations issued by states and national agencies. One of these regulations is the requirement of the safety net by lowering the cost of banking, which (1) places banks in competitive advantages over other financial institutions; (2) reduces substantially the concern about banks' financial risk, going concern, and creditworthiness; (3) encourages banks' management to take more risk, which may impair the realistic balance between risk and reward (moral hazard) and create risk incentive distortions, permit banks to obtain funds more cheaply by protecting customers who deal with banks through governmental subsidy; and (4) taxpayers who will eventually bear this cost of troubled bail-out banks must protect themselves through the supervision and

Exhibit 1.12

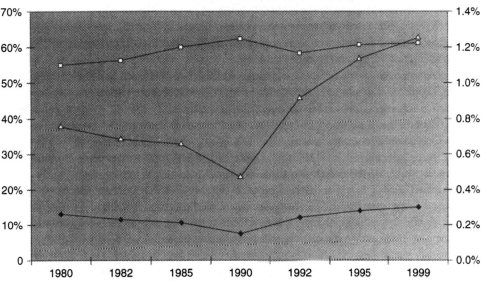

Source: Author's calculations based on data from the Federal Deposit Insurance Corporation.

-ʊ- Total Loans/Total Assets (Left Scale)
◆ Return on Equity (Left Scale)
-△- Return on Assets (Right Scale)

regulations of banks' activities. Governor Lawrence H. Meyer in his speech on *"Financial Modernization: The Issues,"* on March 12, 1999 at the Washington University School of Law, pointed out "that the safety net creates a whole category of problems for financial modernization . . . banks have a competitive advantage through the subsidy implicit in the safety net."[7] The regulatory environment of the banking industry will be further discussed in Chapter 4.

1.4.2 Information Technology

The rapid progress in information technology has had a profound effect on the economy in general and the financial services industry in particular. Mishkin and Strahan (2000) argued that the progress in information technology has reduced both transaction costs and asymmetric information problems.[8] They found evidence that technological advances have caused three profound changes in financial markets: (1) debt markets now substantially consist of tradable debt instruments, which are becoming larger and less dominated by financial institutions; (2) derivatives markets have significantly grown as risk management and speculation tools, which allow financial institutions to act as dealers in these markets at low cost; and (3) payment systems are virtually moving toward an electronic system, which reduces the need for households to invest their wealth in the form of bank deposits.

Technological advances have increased economies of scale and scope in the financial services industry. The increases in economies of scale and scope have encouraged more consolidation, convergence, and competition in the financial services industry. Technological advances have changed the traditional delivery of retail financial services toward electronic delivery modes that do not rely on a branch network. Indeed, many banks have replaced their full-service branches with supermarket branches that offer a variety of financial services including ATMs and Internet banking.

The new technology, including e-commerce, business-to-business, and Internet banking, provides both financial services organizations and their customers with a greater degree of information efficiency. This information efficiency created by the use of new technology can also significantly speed up the movement of financial institutions' financial services and products toward commoditization. Global access to the Internet and especially Internet banking make customization of financial products and services less possible because they can be easily replicated by competitors. As customers gain access to more and readily available information, they can shop more competitively for financial products and services and can easily change providers. This suggests that future markets for financial services and products will be very competitive, and only those large institutions with opportunities for economics of scale and scope that offer the best quality financial services and products and lowest costs will survive. Technological advances may have increased economies of scale and scope in producing financial services by creating opportunities to improve efficiency and increase value through consolidation.

Electronic banking is a generic term that covers a broad range of financial services provided by banks. These services are: (1) the traditional electronic services such as telephone banking, credit cards, ATMs, and direct deposits; (2) maturing electronic services such as debit cards and electronic bill payment (e.g., Financial Electronic Data Interchange); and (3) developing electronic services such as stored-value cards, Internet banking, and on-line investing. One of the current challenges in the financial services industry, especially banking, is the proper development of electronic commerce including the issues of customer identification and account verification for on-line purchases. The Internet is also changing the way financial institutions operate because customers now have unlimited choice of both financial services and pricing on-line, and it is often cheaper to complete transactions electronically than use paper or telephone. For example, banks now can conduct the majority of their financing and cash management services to automobile dealers across the nation over the Internet. The use of the web in the financial services industry can achieve the three goals of marketing information, delivering financial services, and improving customer relationships.

Electronic banking is growing rapidly as a result of continued development and advances in processing, analyzing, and transmitting vast quantities of data electronically. The key factors that are encouraging and facilitating the rapid growth of the use of electronic commerce and banking, as pointed out by Vice Chairman Ferguson, are convenience, confidence, and complexity.[9] **Convenience** reflects the availability of both human and physical resources required to optimize the use of electronic commerce in conducting and processing business transactions. **Confidence** refers to the assurance provided by electronic commerce in security, privacy, and the authentication of transactions and parties as well as safeguarding resources and data and reducing the risk. **Complexity** refers to the extent that the key features of electronic transactions can be easily standardized, automated, understood, and used by the parties to the transactions.

Electronic banking has created convenience and an efficient financial services environment within which banks and their customers are able to transact a variety of financial services at virtually any time. Financial institutions' recent statistics reveal that: (1) approximately 40 percent of U.S. banks now have Web sites through which they communicate with their customers; (2) about 15 percent provide Web sites that can be used to conduct financial services transactions; and (3) over 50 percent of large banks (over $500 million in assets) provide Web sites for their customers' convenience to conduct banking transactions.[10] Through the use of Internet and Web sites, banks are now able to standardize and automate many of their financial services such as loan services. In the past several years, business-to-business (B2B) has evolved from being a facilitator of traditional business to a transformer of business in its entirety. While B2B has revolutionized the global marketplace, it has not been fully utilized in the financial services industry. A survey conducted by Arthur Andersen attempted to gather expert opinions regarding the attitudes and perceptions toward the transition of e-business from potential to reality in the financial services industry. The survey sought to find answers to the following questions.

1. If e-business is the future, what is really stopping institutions from seizing the opportunity?
2. Is there a future outside the Internet? Will "chips-and-clicks" fully replace "bricks-and-mortar?"
3. Will today's cannibals become tomorrow's conquerors? In the new economy, does fortune favor the early entrant or the cautious late-comer?
4. How will tax and regulation shape the e-business landscape?
5. In a world without boundaries, where do today's players see tomorrow's successes?[11]

The survey results indicate that (1) e-business remains a passive or background factor, rather than a positive strategic initiative; (2) e-business is a reality, but for many financial service companies, e-business remains locked within old models; (3) retail e-business growth is expected to be over 90 percent in the next two years; (4) 18 percent of respondents viewed e-business as more important than consolidating, cost reduction, and streamlining; (5) 33 percent of respondents viewed global financial institutions as the e-business winners five years from now; (6) the perceived drivers and potential advantages in using e-business are customer acceptance, reduced costs of Internet access, increased security, and cross-border deregulation; and (7) barriers that hinder the use of e-business were transaction security issues, the cost of making wrong decisions, the ability of their organizations to support eStrategy, the difficulty of projecting return on e-business, and the lack of Internet infrastructure accessible to customers.

Businesses of all sizes can benefit from Internet banking. Small businesses where cash flow is king, benefit from Internet banking just as much as large corporations where continuous improvement in efficiency and effectiveness is the main goal of top executives. Internet banking can provide an on-line, real-time cash management tool by: (1) offering on-line banking of up-to-the-minute cash balances on checking and money market accounts; (2) making free domestic wire transfers; (3) viewing checks that have cleared; (4) transferring funds; (5) authorizing automatic payments; and (6) downloading data to computer applications.

Internet banking can also be beneficial to large corporations in: (1) promoting business-to-business transaction processing; (2) establishing direct deposits for employee paychecks; and (3) authorizing payment of funds electronically that are immediately deposited into a vendor's account. Internet banking has not yet been universally accepted and used by businesses because breaking away from the traditional brick-and-mortar banks and moving into on-line banking takes time. Internet banking is now considered a handy (but still optional) way of doing banking transactions, but soon it will evolve into a high-priority requirement for conducting effective financial services activities.

Innovations in payment systems (e.g., ATMs, debit cards) have provided more convenient ways of conducting banking transactions. In July 1999, the Federal Reserve Board established the Payments System Development Committee, to address public policy issues pertaining to the development of the retail payment system to: (1) ensure the safety and soundness of the payment and financial system; (2) promote competitive markets; (3) provide adequate levels of consumer protection; (4) work with the public to identify barriers to the future development of the payment system; and (5) recommend solutions to the Board and other authorities.

Technological innovations have made financial products and services more standardized and commoditized, and these products and services are offered through electronic media (phone, e-mail, Internet, PC), which is much cheaper than offering them through traditional brick-and-mortar buildings. The 1999 Special Report: Technology in Financial Services prepared by the CPA firm Ernst and Young predicts the following changes in the financial services industry: "(1) most transactions (financial services) have already become a commodity, with virtual players offering low-priced loans, trades, and mortgages in an online auction format, while niche players offer specialized transactions such as complex risk-management derivatives; (2) unless regulators decide to intervene, we believe that auction markets will predominate in many areas of financial services; and (3) financial services firms will have little choice here: informal customers will demand 'best-of-breed' products, and few companies that fail to offer 'best-of-breed' will survive."[12]

In summary, technological advances including the Internet are significantly changing the ways in which banks conduct their business in offering financial products and services. The Internet provides banks new opportunities and challenges of reevaluating their existing delivery channels and business activities, developing new online financial products and services, taking advantage of cost efficiencies, satisfying existing customers' demands, reaching new customers, and securing customers' privacy. Bank regulators including the Office of the Comptroller of the Currency (OCC) have revised their regulations to reflect the use of new technologies by banks. For example, in 1996, the OCC revised its data-processing regulation to reflect the use of electronic activities by banks (61 FR 4849, February 9, 1996). The OCC, in 1999, issued a comprehensive handbook that: (1) addresses the risks presented by Internet banking activities; (2) provides guidelines to banks engaging in Internet banking activities; (3) describes electronic banking issues including technology risk management, retail personal computer banking, certification authority systems, Web privacy statements, consumer compliance, computer-related crime reporting, and cyber-terrorism; and (4) discusses procedures for examining Internet banking activities. This Internet Banking Handbook and other OCC-related technology handbook series are available on the OCC Web site (http://www.occ.treas.gov).

1.4.3   Global Marketplace

Global financial considerations are important issues that should be thoroughly examined to determine whether the financial sector is functioning effectively toward its goal of facilitating capital accumulation and enhancing real economic growth. The social cost of the global financial crises can be significant due to high unemployment rates following the crises. A sound macroeconomic policy of anticipating the potential financial crises in the financial services industry and taking proactive actions to prevent them can be an effective way of dealing with the national financial crises. However, even good macroeconomic policies would not be effective in dealing with global financial crises. More reliance on global market forces can be the most effective and efficient way of preventing global financial crises.

Market-driven forces would be the result of: (1) the global competition in the financial services industry through the use of Internet banking and (2) demand by global customers for more convenient and broader financial services provided by technology. There have been profound and fundamental changes in the way customers handle their financial services mostly driven by the Internet. In the near future, providing financial services through national branching may become a less relevant way of conducting the banking business. Local banking and even national branching may become obsolete under the new electronic delivery of financial services. Thus, the requirement for reform, particularly in the area of electronic delivery of financial services, becomes critical in order to keep up with all the changes that are affecting the financial services industry.

To compete successfully in the global marketplace, financial institutions are adopting a new management philosophy of becoming more aggressive, leaner, more adaptable, more performance-oriented, and more responsive to market value. Frieder and Hedges (1994) suggested seven key areas in which banks should position themselves to elevate both their performance and value. Banks are encouraged to pay more attention to market value as the ultimate performance measure in the following key areas: (1) mergers and acquisitions; (2) portfolio mix; (3) cost management; (4) retail distribution; (5) relationship banking; (6) credit risk; and (7) management leadership and culture.[13] Banks are also realizing that to compete successfully in a global market, they have to move away from traditional commercial services into investment and asset-management businesses.

1.4.4 Capital Standards

Recent vibrant economic conditions and strong financial conditions of financial institutions signify healthy financial environments in the financial services industry, especially banks. However, infrequent bank failures resulting from inadequate capital or the existence of fraudulent activities can cause substantial losses to the insurance fund. During the 1980s and early 1990s, hundreds of banks failed because of lax lending standards, economic recessions, high interest rates, and troubled real estate markets. (See Exhibit 1.8.) These failures almost deprived the Bank Insurance fund. As the economic conditions improved and banks began to become more profitable during the 1990s, the number of bank failures substantially decreased. The number of state member banks as of year-end 1999 were 1,010 with combined assets of $1.3 trillion of which only six state member banks have failed since the beginning of 1993.[14]

Banks and banking organizations have established internal risk-management processes in evaluating risks for capital adequacy. These processes consist of four elements: (1) identifying and measuring all material risks; (2) relating capital to the level of risk; (3) stating explicit capital adequacy goals with respect to risk; and (4) assessing conformity to the institution's stated objectives. In 1988 the Basel Accord established the Basel Committee on

Banking Supervision in an attempt to (1) create a level playing field for international banks to effectively compete in the global market; (2) provide a common international definition of bank capital; and (3) establish risk-based capital standards for banking organizations worldwide.

The Basel Committee assesses capital adequacy based on a set of three so-called pillars of minimum capital standards, supervisory oversight, and market discipline.[15] Pillar one requires sound minimum capital standards that effectively and accurately distinguish degrees of credit risk based on (1) a standardized approach that ties capital requirements to external credit assessments (e.g., credit ratings), and (2) banks' own internal ratings according to their estimates of default probabilities and unique risk profiles.

The second pillar of the Basel Committee requires vigilant supervisory oversight and review of capital adequacy by focusing on the following principles that supervisors:

- have the authority to require banks to operate above the minimum regulatory capital ratios;
- should require banks to assess and maintain overall capital adequacy in relation to underlying risks;
- should review and evaluate the internal capital adequacy assessments and strategies of banks, as well as their compliance with regulatory capital ratios; and
- should intervene at an early stage to prevent capital from falling below prudent levels and should require remedial action quickly if capital becomes inadequate.

The third pillar of the new Basel capital framework relates to market discipline, which gives banks more incentive to manage their risks and maintain adequate capital. The effectiveness of market discipline and supervision depends on whether or not banks disclose timely, accurate, and reliable information regarding their capital structure and risk exposures. Based on the relevant and objective information disseminated to the market, market participants can assess and decide about their own risks in dealing with such institutions. The effectiveness of market discipline in controlling the risk-taking of banks depends on the adequacy of disclosure provided to the market and the reliability and quality of disclosure practices in banks.

Financial institutions should continuously measure and assess their capital adequacy. The 1988 Basel Capital Accord may not be relevant to and adequate for megamerged, large, and complex financial institutions. The current technological advancements have made financial institutions more effective and efficient in managing their risks. The use of the current standard frequently provides a poor assessment of capital adequacy and, accordingly, there is a need for a more vigorous, effective, and efficient capital standard. Currently, the Basel Committee on Bank Supervision is expecting to propose a new capital standard more sensitive to economic, market, and credit risk than the existent standard which would more accurately measure the capital strength of financial institutions.[16] Capital standards for banks will be further described in Chapter 4.

1.4.5 Supervisory Activities

Consolidation, convergence, and competition in the financial services industry have created a new set of challenges for policymakers, regulatory authorities, and supervisors in (1) defining geographic and product markets for antitrust policy implications; (2) establishing more vigilant methods based on new market parameters to preserve the safety and soundness of the financial systems; and (3) establishing a more relevant disclosure system to provide information on the current values of assets and liabilities. The new technological innovations should be used to create secure and reliable disclosure systems based on a real-time, on-line basis. Since the financial services industry is experiencing an unprecedented merger movement, which is changing the structure of the industry, the role of the Federal Reserve in effective implementation of its merger policy in encouraging competition in the industry is becoming vital.

The current changes in the financial services industry (e.g., 3Cs) driven by the technological innovations, deregulations, and healthy economic and financial environment have raised several important policy issues.[17] The first and most important policy issue is the potential effect of the rapid pace of consolidation and convergence on the combined financial services organizations' concentration and market power. Thus, the traditional antitrust policies monitoring market power should be reconsidered in this ever-changing environment. The second issue is the reassessment of policies pertaining to safety and soundness of operations of the emerging financial services organizations. The third policy issue relates to proper regulatory and supervisory provisions.

Deregulations in the financial services industry (e.g., GLB Act of 1999), coupled with technological innovations, have two profound effects on the implications and proper implementation of the existing antitrust policies. First, deregulations and technological advances have substantially reduced geographical and product restrictions and barriers to entry and expanded the size of markets. The market for financial services providers is now far more competitive and open. This universal competitive financial market necessitates modification of the existing antitrust policies in properly defining the relevant geographic and product market. Second, consolidation, convergence, and competition driven by deregulation and technological innovations have created greater opportunities for financial services organizations to expand their market share. This increased market share, power, and concentration can be a source of concern for policymakers and regulatory authorities. With the implementation of both the Riegle-Neal Interstate Banking and Branching Efficiency Act of 1994 (IBBEA) and the Gramm-Leach-Bliley Financial Modernization Act of 1999 (GLB), more concentration of financial services organizations will occur at the national level. Currently, level of concentration for geographic markets is defined locally in terms of a metropolitan statistical area (MSA) or a non-MSA county. For research and policy purposes, the level of concentration is measured as the deposit share of the top three banks in a specified local market. It is expected that in light of the rapid pace of consolidation and convergence in the financial services industry, the national measures of concentration will become the important and relevant indicator of market power in the future.

Empirical findings on the effects of concentration and market openness for standardized financial products and services are inconsistent and controversial. A number of studies[18, 19, 20] found that (1) consolidations resulting from deregulation caused improvement of the efficiency of the banking industry through reduction in non-interest costs and loan losses; (2) costs of financial services and products fell because the more efficient banks gained market share at the expense of less efficient banks; (3) deregulation of the banking industry has led to higher bank profits because a more active takeover market provided more incentives for managers to maximize bank value; and (4) profits grew as local banking markets became more concentrated only in states that restricted branching. Other empirical studies[21, 22,23] on the other hand, found that banks in more concentrated markets (1) pay lower rates on retail deposits; (2) have less deposit-rate sensitivity to changes in market interest rates; (3) charge higher rates on small business loans; and (4) pay lower interest rates on interest-bearing checking and saving accounts. Furthermore, Keeley (1990) found that the value of bank franchises decreased subsequent to deregulation of barriers to expand possibly due to less access to more profitable markets following deregulation.[24]

Financial institutions' financial reporting should properly disclose the distribution of their internal ratings, asset quality, risk measurement, and management practices. Large banks should also attempt to strengthen their supervisory information systems. The Federal Reserve is in the process of designing a brand-based system called the Banking Organization National Desktop (BOND) to strengthen banks' supervisory information systems. The supervisor's role in identifying and assessing weakness in financial institutions in the midst of strong economic conditions is crucial primarily because bank supervisors are assuming an important public trust with a great responsibility of: (1) minimizing fraud incidents and excesses in the banking system; (2) reducing losses to insurance funds; and (3) maintaining a stable and productive banking system. The proposed H.R. 3374, the "Federal Deposit Insurance Corporation Examination Enhancement and Insurance Fund Protection Act," would allow the Chairperson of FDIC to authorize a special examination of any insured depository institution. It would also require the FDIC to make all reasonable efforts to coordinate any special examination with the primary federal banking supervisor.

1.4.6 Continuous Quality Improvement

An important asset of financial services organizations is their reputation and customer satisfaction and confidence which is not measurable and unrecognized in their financial statements. Financial institutions whose reputation is sound can more effectively compete in the global market and prevent regulators from following up on them. On the other hand, an institution whose reputation is impaired would have a harder time regaining the confidence of customers, employees, creditors, shareholders, and regulators.

Recent trends of increased complexity of doing business, globalization of the economy, worldwide competition, deregulation, consolidation, and convergence have encouraged financial institutions to apply strategies of continuous improvement in the quality of their services. To remain competitive, financial institutions have begun to place a high premium on improving the quality of their services, meeting customers' expectations, and assuring financial integrity. In 1992, the American Quality Foundation and Ernst & Young conducted the International Quality Study (IQS) to examine the quality management practices of retail banks in the United States, Canada, Germany, and Japan.[25] The IQS concluded that quality, as defined by customer satisfaction, is the single most important element of a bank's reputation. The IQS also found that reliability, performance, convenience, responsiveness, and adaptability, are the most important components of quality.

The Malcolm Baldrige National Quality Award (MBNQA) Improvement Act was signed into law in 1987 and established an annual national MBNQA to promote quality awareness and make quality an integral part of product development and service delivery in the United States.[26] The award is given to the U.S. firms that have achieved total quality management to the highest extent possible. Although there is no direct financial reward, chosen entities will receive national recognition for attaining excellent quality that indirectly will translate into more satisfied customers wanting to acquire goods or services from a topnotch quality entity. Each year up to two awards are given in each of the three categories of manufacturing, small business, and service entities.

Financial institutions can achieve continuous improvements in the quality of their financial products and services by:

1. Identifying the nature of their financial products and services, categories of customers, markets, competitors, regulatory environment, and the key quality attributes. For example, direct competitors would be other banks, credit unions, savings and loan associations, and finance companies. Indirect competitors would include brokerage firms, insurance companies, and other financial service providers. However, the direct competition among banks, insurance companies, and securities and brokerage firms increases as financial services providers continue to take advantage of convergence opportunities provided by the GLB Act of 1999.

2. Financial institutions should state their quality mission and goals, as they are perceived by customers, and establish appropriate methods of execution to attain these goals. This typically involves establishment of the mission of attaining high levels of customer satisfaction with a goal of attracting and retaining customers. The method of execution entails eliminating a customer's "expectation gap" by understanding customers' expectations and meeting them. To eliminate the expectation gap, the bank should consider the quality expectations of different segments of customers served including individual depositors, small businesses, commercial customers, institutional customers, and services provided to other financial institutions.

3. Obtaining top-level management commitment to continuous quality improvements. Top-level executives should set a "tone at top" that customer satisfaction is the important mission of their financial institution because lack of leadership can cause any quality initiative to fail. The role of senior management should include the communication of an understandable mission statement of quality to all employees. Top executives must assume an active role in dealing with customers' complaints, quality problems, and customer service.

4. Empowering employees to use their judgment in dealing with customers. Internet banking, global competition, consolidation, and convergence caused by technological advances, and deregulation create a need for better-trained, highly motivated, more productive, and more empowered employees. Development of quality programs for employees consists of: monthly quality meetings, assignment of senior executives to quality programs, discussion of quality issues in general management meetings, quality recognition programs, and quality videos.

5. Gathering and analyzing relevant information related to customers' needs, products, and services as well as internal operations, suppliers, and competitors. The information gathered should be analyzed to develop actionable responses in both short- and long-run planning. These actionable responses include criteria for targeting problem areas, proving appropriate information, and implementing responses. Surveys of customers chosen at random, or chosen as members of special groups (e.g., closing out accounts, opening new accounts, special services) can provide valuable quality information. These surveys can evaluate adherence to appropriate procedures as well as determine

why customers are leaving or opening new accounts. Furthermore, surveys can be used to answer various regulatory compliance questions including affirmative action requirements and the provisions of the Community Reinvestment Act (CRA). The 1997 CRA requires that banks that take deposits in a community must also make a certain level of loans available to that community including low- and moderate-income areas. Under the CRA, banks are reviewed on their lending, investment, and community development activities (e.g., support of schools, cultural events, charitable organizations) in particular areas and can earn one of four ratings: outstanding, satisfactory, needs to improve, and substantial noncompliance. The Financial Modernization Act of 1999 (Gramm-Leach-Bliley Act) requires that a bank holding company (BHC) can qualify as a financial holding company (FHC) and, therefore, expand to other financial services (e.g., insurance, mutual funds) only if it has received at minimum a satisfactory rating on its last CRA examination.

6. Ensuring compliance with four privacy requirements of the GLB Act as well as other privacy legislation to protect and safeguard the privacy of customers' personal information. The GLB Act requires each financial institution to (1) establish and annually disclose a privacy policy; (2) provide customers the right to opt out of having their personal identifiable information shared with non-affiliated third parties; (3) not share customer account numbers with non-affiliated third parties; and (4) abide by regulatory standards to protect the security and integrity of customer information. The passage of the GLB Act and the public outcry over privacy issues has encouraged almost all states to introduce privacy bills primarily directed toward financial institutions to give consumers choice and control over the information collected about them.

    • Providing training for all personnel including executives, managers, and employees to get involved in quality-related activities to make continuous improvement in quality and productivity. This training process must constantly communicate the message of total quality to the various levels of employees and empower them to make appropriate decisions to support this goal. Training programs should teach employees what quality means to customers and how this quality can be provided through each employee's function. Continuous employee training in focusing on customer retention, personal interaction, and customer feedback is necessary to assure day-to-day quality.
    • Recognizing and awarding employees for their commitment to quality. Satisfied and rewarded employees would be more dedicated to improve the quality of their performance. Periodic surveys of employees and information on percentages and causes of turnover can provide valuable input regarding employee satisfaction.

1.4.7 Valuation Process

The current changes in the financial services industry raise two fundamental questions: (1) how much these financial services organizations are actually worth, and (2) how their value should be measured. It is the primary goal of this book to assist readers in understanding current changes in the industry and their possible impact on the valuation of financial services organizations, specifically financial institutions. During the past decades, bank earnings grew and many stock prices continuously increased, thereby encouraging more consolidation and convergence in the financial services industry. This continuous rapid pace of business combination in the financial services industry has been criticized on the grounds that consolidation and convergence are happening at high costs and acquirer banks are paying too much for the target banks. The three primary issues being addressed in this book are: (1) how much banks are actually worth; (2) how to value the target bank; and (3) how much premium over the book value of the target bank the acquirer should pay.

Traditionally, financial institutions have been defined by geographical markets. Thus, when Bank A sought to buy Bank B, it knew what it was buying (e.g., a number of branches, deposits, loans, market share). Today, financial institutions may enter and exit distant markets more freely, they may provide a variety of financial services (e.g., loans, insurance, credit cards, investment, financing) and their customers may also buy financial services from a dozen institutions. It is becoming more difficult to properly value an institution because branch networks, bricks, and mortar do not count for as much as they used to. Thus, factors that should be considered in the valuation of financial institutions are: (1) reasonably well-run institutions and management operating style; (2) simple earnings streams with stable, straight-forward, basic earnings components not too sensitive to macro events such as interest rate changes and regulatory changes; and (3) the lowest P/E ratios. The current wave of consolidation and convergence is going to continue, which in turn may result in reduction in numbers of financial institutions that provide full financial services and their valuation process.

1.5 CONCLUSION

In this chapter we examined the current changes such as consolidation, convergence, and competition that have significantly affected the structure and characteristics of financial institutions. The potential impact of these changes on the value of financial institutions will be discussed throughout this book. However, the traditional valuation methods of focusing on branches, deposits, and market share may not be appropriate for the valuation of currently formed financial holding companies. Core deposits, branch networks, and bricks and mortar are worth less than they once were. Technology and deregulation have been considered two major factors driving the wave of consolidation and convergence in the financial services industry. Technological advances such as image-processing, networking, and Internet banking enable larger banks to achieve additional cost savings and synergies, which might have resulted in the booming consolidation and convergence activities in the industry.

Deregulation (e.g., Riegle-Neal Act of 1994; Gramm-Leach-Bliley Act of 1999) virtually eliminated both geographic and product barriers in the U.S. financial services industry, which has been through significant structural changes in the past decade. Product and geographic deregulation, especially in the banking industry, coupled with increased global competition and technological innovations, has produced evidence of potential and likely acceleration of consolidation and convergence in the industry. Financial services organizations have responded to these changes by attempting to strategically position themselves for future challenges and opportunities. Invariably, the consideration of consolidation, convergence, and competition is a significant part of management strategic planning to succeed in this ever-changing economic and business environment. Thus, the valuation and financing aspects of M & A activities in the financial services industry will continue to be of significant interest to the business community in general and financial institutions in particular.

The passage of the GLB Act in 1999 publicly and officially permits cross-industry financial conglomerates in the United States, although the cross-industry consolidation has been practiced often in the United States and abroad. For example, the convergence of Citicorp, Travelers, and Salomon Smith Barney in the United States in 1998 created Citigroup, Inc., which provides a variety of financial services to its customers and is one of the largest financial services organizations in the world. A universal bancassurance corporation, which originated in Europe, provides its customers with the potential of low cost and convenience, one-stop shopping for a variety of financial services including banking, insurance, investment, financial, and accounting services. These examples of cross-industry and even cross-border business combinations may reflect upon the future financial holding companies under the GLB Act of 1999. Financial holding companies can provide a broad range of financial services including investment and commercial banking, asset management and distribution services, insurance and securities underwriting services, and even real estate development and investment services. These future financial holding companies, by consolidating their human and physical resources, will be able to gain economies of scale and scope. This perceived benefit of economies of scale and scope will increase mergers and acquisitions (M & A) in the financial services industry.

The convergence in the financial services industry has raised many concerns including potential excessive market concentration and monopoly power in the industry and creation of too much systematic risk in the economy resulting from fewer but larger financial services organizations. Furthermore, the bull market in stocks has caused high valuation multiples paid by the acquirer to buy the target especially when the target is a public rather than private company. The study of M & A activities requires consideration and assessment of numerous issues, including strategic planning, valuation, legal and regulatory, accounting, tax, negotiating, and integration strategies. These issues are discussed throughout this book, with the primary focus on the relevance of these issues for financial institutions.

ENDNOTES

1. Mendonca, Lenny, and Greg Wilson. 1998. "Financial Services Consolidation and Convergence: Advancing to the Endgame." *Business Economics* (October): 7–13.

2. Schott, Francis H. 1996. "Consolidation and Convergence of Financial Institutions." *Business Economics* (October 1996): 31–36.

3. Crandall, Robert, and Jerry Ellig. 1997. "Economic Deregulation and Customer Choice: Lessons for the Electric Industry." Center for Market Processes.

4. Kwast, Myron L. 1999. "Bank Mergers: What Should Policymakers Do?" *Journal of Banking and Finance* 23: 629–636.

5. Sec. J. Alfred Broaddus, Jr., "The Bank Merger Wave: Causes and Consequences," *Economic Quarterly* (Summer), V84, i3 (1998): 1.

6. Aspinwall, Richard. 1997. "Conflicting Objectives of Financial Regulation." In Robert Guttmann, ed., *Reforming Money and Finance: Toward a New Monetary Regime.* M. E. Sharpe.

7. Governor Lawrence H. Meyer, "Financial Modernization: The Issues," 1999 Hodge O'Neal Corporate and Securities Law Symposium, Washington University School of Law, St. Louis, Missouri, March 12, 1999. The Federal Reserve Board.

8. Mishkin, Frederic S., and Philip E. Strahan. 2000. "What Will Technology Do to Financial Structure?" *Brooking-Wharton Papers on Financial Services* 1: 249–287.

9. The Federal Reserve Board. Remarks by Vice Chairman Roger W. Ferguson, Jr., at the 36th Annual Conference on Bank Structure and Competition, Chicago, Illinois, May 4, 2000.

10. Ibid.

11. Arthur Andersen, 2000. "Thriving in the New Economy: Perception vs. Reality." *Financial Services Research Papers* (Survey): 3–4.

12. Ernst and Young. 1999. "Special Report: Technology in Financial Services." *E-Commerce.*

13. Frieder, Larry A., and Robert B. Hedges. 1994. "Market Value: The Ultimate Performance Measure." *Bank Management* (September/October) Vol. 7 No. 5: 60–66.

14. The Federal Reserve Board. Testimony of Governor Lawrence H. Meyer, 1999 Banking Failure before the Committee on Banking and Financial Services, U. S. House of Representatives, February 8, 2000.

15. The Federal Reserve Board. 2000. Remarks by Vice-Chairman Roger W. Ferguson, Jr., at the Institute of International Bankers, Washington, D.C. (March 6).

16. Richard Spillenkothen, 1999. Bank Supervision and Regulation in the Next Millennium, Federal Reserve Board. Speech at the New York State Banking Department, New York, October 25, 1999.

17. loct. Mishkin and Strahan (2000) addressed these policy issues as affected by technological progress.

18. Jayaratne, Jith, and Philip E. Strahan. 1998. "Entry Restrictions, Industry Evolution, and Dynamic Efficiency: Evidence from Commercial Banking." *Journal of Law and Economics* 41 (April): 239–273.

19. Schranz, Mary S. 1993. "Takeovers Improve Firm Performance: Evidence from the Banking Industry." *Journal of Political Economy* 101 (April): 299–326.

20. Evanoff, Douglas D., and Diana L. Fortier. 1988. "Reevaluation of the Structure-Conduct-Performance Paradigm in Banking." *Journal of Financial Service Research* 1 (June): 277–294.

21. Berger, Allen N., and Timothy H. Hannan. 1989. "The Price-Concentration Relationship in Banking." *Review of Economics and Statistics* 71 (May): 291–299.

22. Jackson, William E. III. 1997. "Market Structure and the Speed of Price Adjustment: Evidence of Non-Monotonicity." *Review of Industrial Organization* 12 (February): 37–57.

23. Radecki, Lawrence J. 1998. "The Expanding Geographic Reach of Retail Banking Markets." Federal Reserve Bank of New York *Economic Review* 4 (June): 15–34.

24. Keeley, Michael C. 1990. "Deposit Insurance, Risk, and Market Power in Banking." *American Economic Review* 80 (December): 1183–1200.

25. American Quality Foundation and Ernest and Young. 1992. "The International Quality Study: Best Practices Report." American Quality Foundation, N.Y.

26. U.S. Department of Commerce, 1993. "Award Criteria: Malcolm Baldrige National Quality Award." (Milwaukee: American Society for Quality Control, 1993.)

CHAPTER 2

Overview of the Valuation Process

2.1 INTRODUCTION

Business valuation is a specialized field with a variety of valuation standards, statutory guidelines, case laws, and techniques offering valuation services for a variety of purposes. Traditionally, a business value (e.g., selling price) has been determined based on bargaining power of negotiation between the buyer and the seller. Today's business climate is made up of executives, investors, suppliers, customers, government, and employees who are looking for customized valuation services. Businesses have built infrastructures that not only deliver timely, relevant, reliable, and useful information but also consist of networks of specialists who can provide critical assistance and advice to constantly changing situations. The appraisers can play an important role and be a key member of this team.

The business valuation market has grown at a steady pace and will continue to grow as long as the demand for business valuation services increases due to factors such as (1) ever-increasing M & A activities in all industries especially financial services; (2) high-volume establishment of employee stock ownership plans; (3) enhanced financing opportunities for individuals and businesses; and (4) litigation involving shareholder disputes, small businesses, taxation issues, business damages, and divorce. A number of professionals and individuals including academics, accountants, attorneys, bankers, business brokers, economists, financial analysts, and real estate appraisers can engage in performing a variety of valuation services for their clients. An appraiser is defined in this book as a person or firm who has expertise in providing valuation services based on relevant and reliable information, standards, methodology, knowledge, integrity, and objectivity.

Appraisers provide value-added advice, assistance, or services to their clients. Appraisers are those experts with adequate educational training, experience, proficiency, and knowledge about valuation concepts, standards, and techniques, as well as reporting and documentation requirements. Appraisers should have both educational and technical understanding and knowledge of tax, accounting, financial, theory, and valuation methods. Appraisers should possess both appraisal and industry qualifications to provide a credible valuation opinion. Appraisers are typically members of one or more valuation professional organizations such as the American Society of Appraisers (ASA), Institute of Business Appraisers (IBA), American Institute of Certified Public Accountants (AICPA), National Association of Certified Valuation Analysts (NACVA), or other appraisal organizations that are required to observe and comply with the Business Valuation Standards, the Principles of Appraisal Practice, and Code of Ethics of the American Society of Appraisers.

Appraisers often possess professional valuation certification and designation and prepare their valuations report in accordance with the requirements of their professional affiliations such as Uniform Standards of Professional Appraisal Practice issued by the Appraisal Foundation. The current demand for and interest in business valuation services have encouraged professional organizations such as AICPA to offer a vast product line of BV tools and methodologies to their members. Valuation professionals including AICPA, NACVA, ASA, and IBA offer certification, conferences, publications, continuing professional education self-study, and software programs to their members in order to provide a framework, foundation, and continuing education in business valuation.

2.2 VALUATION SERVICES

Valuation services are becoming interesting, profitable, and exciting market niches for appraisers. The types of valuation services, their purposes, and related valuation standards are summarized in Exhibit 2.1. The four basic standards of value commonly used in the valuation process are fair market value, fair value, investment value, and intrinsic value. These and other valuation standards are thoroughly described in Chapter 5. Fair market value is the most commonly used standard of value, especially for estate, gift, or marital disputes valuation purposes. Fair market value is defined in Revenue Ruling 59-60 as what a willing buyer would pay a willing seller at a specific date based on the best educated judgment using all the knowledge available on that date. Fair value is defined statutorily, applies to certain specific transactions such as shareholders' disputes, and is an estimate of the price that would have been realized by selling an asset under normal business considerations. More specifically, fair value is the amount at which an asset could be bought or sold or a liability could be incurred or settled in the normal course of business between willing parties. Investment value is the strategic value to the specific group of investors and is the specific value assigned to goods or services by this group of investors based on investment requirements. Intrinsic value is the fundamental or theoretical value often determined based on the discounted value of future operating cash flows.

Valuation services as they pertain to financial institutions (banks and thrifts) are typically performed for the following reasons:

- At any time during the life of a business to determine the value of the institution.
- Merger and acquisition transactions or takeover deals.
- Changes in ownership.
- Selling part or the entire stock.
- Giving all or a portion of the institution's stock as gifts.
- Exercising stock option or warrant.
- Establishing employee stock ownership plan.
- Initial public offerings.
- Damages litigation.

Exhibit 2.1 Valuation Services, Purposes, and Standards

Number	Valuation Services	Purposes	Standards
1.	Ad Valorem Taxes	To establish the value of property used in a trade or business for tax purposes	Fair market value
2.	Allocation of Purchase Price	To support uniform allocation of the total purchase price to the component parts for tax purposes based on an appraisal of the underlying assets	Fair market value
3.	Buy-Sell Agreements	To determine a value for a transaction between the partners or shareholders in the event of withdraws, death, disability, or retirement	Investment value (agreed-upon value)
4.	Charitable Contributions	To establish the value of the gift that exceeds $10,000 to charity	Fair market value
5.	Employee Stock Ownership Plans (ESOP)	To determine the price per share to support ESOP transactions with participants, plan contributions, and allocations within the ESOP	Intrinsic value (public price quotations) if available
6.	Damages Litigation	To estimate the amount of damage resulting from the disputed issues such as breach of contract, lost business opportunities, and discrimination	Fair value
7.	Eminent Domain Actions	To establish the value of the property seized by government	Fair value
8.	Estate and Gift Taxes	To determine the value of a business interest for the purpose of the unified estate and gift tax credit	Fair market value
9.	Financing	To establish the value for the business to obtain additional funds	Fair value
10.	Incentive Stock Option Considerations (ISOC)	To determine the price of the exercised stock option mostly for income tax purposes	Fair market value
11.	Initial Public Offerings	To establish the price of the stock for the initial public offering purposes	Intrinsic value (proforma estimate of earnings, market price of comparable stock)
12.	Liquidation or Reorganization of a Business	To determine the value of distributed assets in the case of split-up or spin-off for financial reporting or tax purposes	Fair value
13.	Marital Dissolution	To establish value for asset and liability interests of a couple involved in a divorce case	Fair value
14.	Mergers and Acquisitions	To determine the value of both the target and acquirer entities involved in the business combination	Investment value/ Intrinsic value
15.	Stockholder Disputes	To establish the value for shares of dissenting shareholders	Fair value
16.	S-to-C Corporation Conversions	To determine the value of business interest in the case of S-to-C Corporation conversions	Fair value/Investment value
17.	Casualty Loss	To estimate the value of assets lost due to casualty	Fair value
18.	Allocation of Lump-Sum Assets	To allocate the cost of assets in a bulk purchase between depreciable and non-depreciable assets such as land and goodwill	Fair value

- Valuation of assets donated to charitable organizations.
- Valuation of assets lost due to casualty.
- Allocation of the cost of assets in a bulk purchase between depreciable and non-depreciable assets such as land and goodwill.
- Financing.

A number of factors, valuation standards, and a variety of valuation methodologies can be utilized in valuing a financial institution. Financial institutions may be valued differently for different purposes. Practically, the appraisal value depends on the purpose for which the institution is being assessed, not what the institution is worth in an appraisal. For example, in merger and acquisition deals, the value depends on what a potential acquirer is willing and able to pay for the target institution. This willing and able price is known in accounting, finance, and business literature as fair market value or simply fair value. The general public may confuse fair market value with fairness. Fair market value is not about fairness; rather, it is determined as of a specific date based on the price that a willing buyer would pay a willing seller, using all available relevant knowledge. In addition, the net income of the target institution and the price to earnings ratio of the potential acquirer's stock can play an important role in the valuation process.

2.3 VALUATION PROFESSION

In contrast to the centuries-old preeminence of medicine, law, and engineering as professions, valuation services gained prominence as a profession only during the twentieth century. The evolution of the valuation profession is summarized by Trugman (1993)[1] as follows:

- Prior to the 1920s, a business's selling prices were primarily a matter of negotiation between the buyer and the seller based on their horse-trading sense.
- During the 1920s, business valuation began changing when breweries and distilleries incurred substantial losses in the intangible value of their business. Thus, the Internal Revenue Service (IRS) issued Appeals and Review Memorandum (ARM) 34 suggesting consideration of the value of intangibles and goodwill for estate and gift tax purposes. Business specialists then started applying ARM 34 by adding the value of intangibles including goodwill to the tangible assets in establishing the total value of a business.
- In 1959, the IRS issued Revenue Ruling 59-60, which established basic guidelines for business appraisers by identifying eight factors to be considered in the valuation of closely-held businesses for estate and gift tax purposes. Exhibit 2.2 discusses these eight factors, their description, and related court cases. The application of these factors for appraisers will be discussed later in this chapter. Revenue Ruling 65-192 extended the applicability of Revenue Ruling 59-60 to other business valuations.
- The IRS issued Revenue Ruling 68-609 in 1968 suggesting the use of a formula in determining the fair market value of intangible assets.
- During the 1970s and 1980s, the demand for business valuation expanded greatly due to a downward slide in the real estate market and economic losses suffered by banks and

Exhibit 2.2 Revenue Ruling 59-60, Its Description, and Related Court Cases

Factor	Description	Court Cases
1. Nature of the business and history of the entity	Nature and history of an entity reveals its condition and past performance (e.g., stability, growth, diversification), which is very important in determining the degree of risk involved in the business.	Estate of Victor P. Clarke (35 TCM. 1482, 1976). Characteristics of the company, its products, markets, management, and position in industry, book value, dividend-paying capacity, and earnings considered to be important in determining value.
2. Economic outlook in general, and specific outlook for industry	Analysis of economic conditions and industry specifications and considerations (e.g., economic growth, interest rates, government regulations, market share) are very important in the valuation.	Tallichet v. Commissioner (33 TCM. 1133, 1974). Nature of competition considered as a factor in determining value.
3. Book value of stock and the financial condition of the entity	Financial statements analysis (comparative analysis of balance sheets, ratio analysis) can be helpful in assessing book value and financial condition.	McIntosh (26 TCM 1164, 1967); Turner (23 TCM 952, 1964). The book value by itself is not relevant in determining the fair market value of the stock. The book value, however, should serve as a basis if the result is to be anything more than a dignified guess.
4. Earnings capacity	Earnings capacity is a major factor in many valuations of closely held stock. Historical earnings records are often the most useful and reliable sources of assessing future earnings and recurring earnings components should be given special attention in the valuation. The capitalization rate for earnings and dividends is focal in determining the value.	Knowles (24 TEM 129, 1965); Harrison (17 TCM 776, 1958); Huntsman (66 TC 861, 1976); Tebb (27 TC 671); Clarke (35 TCM 1482, 1976). Significant considerations were given to recurring earnings capacity and prospects for future profits.

5. The dividend-paying capacity	Revenue ruling states that primary consideration should be given to dividend-paying capacity, not actual dividends paid in the valuation of closely held corporations. In a close corporation, dividends are often authorized based on the needs of executives and/or shareholders (e.g., avoiding double taxation, executive compensation), which may not be a good measure of dividend capacity.	C. D. Baker (172 F. Supp. 833, 1959). Dividend-paying capacity was given considerable weight in determining value. The three factors considered important in determining value were earnings (50 percent weight); book value (25 percent weight); and dividend-paying capacity (25 percent weight).
6. Goodwill and other intangibles	Goodwill (the excess of appraised value of the assets over the book value of the assets) and other intangibles (patents, trademarks, copyrights) should be considered in the business valuation.	Richard M. Boe and Marglois Boe v. C.T.R. (307 F.2d 339, 1962). Goodwill is an unidentifiable intangible asset that affects the earning entity.
7. Previous sales and the size of block of stock to be valued	Previous sales of stock in a closely held corporation should be considered carefully to ensure that the sales were made at arm's length, not distress sales, which may not reflect fair market value. The size of the lock of stock is also relevant because isolated sales in small amounts may not provide an accurate measure of value.	White (35 TCM 1726, 1976), Levenson (18 TCM 535, 1959); DuPont (19 TC 281, 1960); Brown (25 TCM 498, 1966); and Thalheimer (36 TCM 101, 1977). Prior sales that were based on "arm's length" were given much weight in these cases.
8. Market price of stocks or corporations engaged in a similar line of business	The value of unlisted stocks and securities is to be determined partly by the market price of stocks of corporations engaged in a similar line of business. For example, a business in an expanding market should not be compared with one in a declining market.	Tallichet v. Commissioner (33 TCM 1133, 1974). Factors such as capital structure, credit status, depth of management, personnel experience, nature of competition, and maturity of the business were used in determining comparability.

thrifts. This period was also considered as the period of the emergence and growth of professional appraisal organizations such as the American Society of Appraisers, the Institute of Business Appraisers, Inc., and the Appraisal Foundation.

- In 1984, the Financial Institutions Reform, Recovery, and Enforcement Act (FIRREA) was enacted, which mandates the licensing and certification of real estate appraisers. Although the FIRREA was intended to affect only real estate appraisers, several states have expanded its applicability to cover other business valuations. Business valuation as a profession has evolved from simple valuation of intangible assets for estate and gift tax purposes under ARM 34 in 1920 to a complex and sophisticated valuation of megamergers of the 1990s that promulgated standards and certifications. Exhibit 2.3 shows organizations that have influenced the development of business valuation as a profession with prospect and prosperity.

- The Appraisal Foundation (AF) is authorized by Congress as the source of appraisal standards and appraiser qualifications. The AF has formed the Appraisal Standard Board (ASB), which has promulgated a set of Uniform Standards of Professional Appraisal Practice (USPAP). All real estate appraisers must comply with USPAP in accordance with the Financial Institutions Reform, Recovery, and Enforcement Act of 1989 (FIRREA). Other organizations and agencies such as state appraiser certification and licensing boards, appraisal services, appraisal trade associations, and federal, state, and local agencies require compliance with USPAP. The ASB has issued a set of (1) USPAP, which provide guidelines for real property, mass, business, and personal property appraisal and consulting; (2) statements that clarify, interpret, explain, and elaborate on appraisal standards; (3) advisory opinions that offer advice and resolutions for appraisal issues; and (4) uniform commercial and industrial summary appraisal report (UCISAR) manuals, which guide appraisers in appraising existing income-producing and small, uncomplicated income-producing properties. Exhibit 2.4 summarizes the content of the 2000 USPAP. The 2000 USPAP, which is 191 pages and can be purchased from the AF for $25, is discussed in depth throughout the book.

2.4 ATTRACTING VALUATION CLIENTS

Appraisers are constantly seeking new valuation clients or looking for ways to expand valuation services to existing clients. Today's competitive valuation environment dictates that every appraiser consider how best to market their valuation services. Appraisers can market their valuation services through target advertising, surveys of client needs, and the identification of targeted industries and companies for unsolicited preliminary proposals. New clients can be obtained by the following means:

- Referrals from existing clients. Referrals and recommendations from existing clients are not only the best source of obtaining new clients but also attest to the quality of valuation services.

- References from other professionals, especially accountants, lawyers, bankers, and analysts. This is the best method of establishing a network of professional contacts. Appraisers often work closely with accountants, CPAs, lawyers, bankers, and analysts in providing comprehensive services to mutual clients. This coordination and cooperation can lead to valuable future references.

- On-line advertising. In today's era of information technology using the Internet or Web is the most effective and efficient method of marketing valuation services and obtaining new clients. Exhibit 2.5 shows the list of valuation services specialists searched by using the keyword of "valuation services" from the Internet.

- Professional and social contacts with key business executives. Becoming acquainted with key executives in the business community is a sure way of obtaining new clients. Business relationships fostered in community activities, at a country or golf club, in voluntary organizations, or membership at the Chamber of Commerce often expand the appraiser's potential client base.

- Mergers, acquisitions. The potential for mergers and acquisitions often leads to the expansion of valuation services for most appraisers. Appraisers can establish merger and acquisition valuation and consulting services to assist their clients in the merger and acquisition process.

- Advertising. Advertising is one method of creating images for your quality and commitment to valuation services. Appraisers can highlight their areas of valuation expertise, qualifications, certification, and associations. Advertising not only brings new clients to the business but also creates a positive image of, and positive recognition for, the appraisers.

- Requests for proposals. In this demanding environment for business valuation services, many organizations are shopping for valuation services or reassessing their current level of valuation services and related fees. Within a competitive environment, clients often shop for valuation services by testing the market to determine whether significant cost savings can be achieved by changing appraisers. Appraisers are often asked to submit proposals for potential new clients. The appraiser must be able to write an effective proposal that thoroughly explains the valuation services that can be provided and properly demonstrates understanding and knowledge of the client's business, industry, and potential problems. This written proposal should typically include an overview of the valuation services, particular areas of expertise, a description of the qualifications, designations of appraisers, types of valuation services, the service fee structure, and billing requirements for the engagement. Exhibit 2.6 shows a more detailed description of the contents of a proposed package.

- Direct proposals to a targeted industry or company. Many valuation appraisers or organizations establish strategies to target a specific industry or a company. For example, an appraiser wishing to become known as a merger and acquisition specialist might target all potential business combination companies as clients. This targeted approach includes building key contacts with the important decision makers in the organization, developing an understanding of the business and industry, and promoting a positive image.

- Referrals by other valuation appraisers or organizations. Referrals by other valuation appraisers or organizations, as surprising as this may sound, are the most effective method of obtaining new clients. For example, when an appraiser is providing valuation services to a growing client with business throughout the nation, the needs of the client may come to exceed the ability of the appraiser to serve the client effectively and efficiently and the client's local valuation services may be referred to a local valuation appraiser. Thus, it is

Exhibit 2.3 Organizations Influencing Business Valuation

Organization	Purpose	Certification, Publication, Standards

American Institute of Certified Public Accountants
1211 Avenue of the Americas
New York, NY 10036-8775
Phone: (212) 596-6200
Fax: (212) 596-6213
Web: www.aicpa.org/members/div/mcs/abv.htm
	1. The Management Consulting Services (MCS) Division of the AICPA issues Management Consulting Standards which are typically applicable to all consulting engagements including business valuations.
	2. The AICPA Consulting Services Team also assists CPAs to develop specific consulting non-technical core competencies to create specializations, certificates in educational achievement (CEA) programs including business valuation programs.
	3. In December 1999, the Accounting and Review Services Committee of the AICPA issued an exposure draft which would exempt financial statements included in written business valuations from the applicability of Statement on Standards for Accounting and Review Services (SSARS).
		1. AICPA MCS Division's Business Valuation and Appraisal Subcommittee has been working on standards relevant to business valuations.
		2. In 1997, the AICPA developed the Accredited in Business Valuation (ABV) accreditation program.
		3. To earn the ABV designation a candidate must:
		  a. Be a member in good standing of the AICPA and hold an unrevoked CPA certificate or license.
		  b. Provide evidence of ten (10) business valuation engagements.
		  c. Take and pass a written examination.
		  d. Meet CPE requirements of sixty (60) hours and involvement in five (5) business valuation engagements every three-year period.

American Society of Appraisers (ASA)
555 Herndon Parkway
Suite 125
Herndon, VA 20170
Phone: (703) 478-2228
Fax: (703) 742-8471
Web: www.appraisers.org
	1. The ASA offers education and professional accreditation in many appraisal disciplines including business valuation, real property, machinery and equipment, and personal property.
	2. The ASA through its Business Valuation Committee issued a set of business valuation standards. These standards provide guidance for implementation of business valuation approaches and methods and must be observed by members of ASA.
		1. The ASA sponsors Accredited Senior Appraiser (ASA) and Accredited Member (AM) professional designations.
		2. To obtain the ASA or AM designation, candidates must:
		  a. Have work experience in the discipline in which the designation is granted (two-five years of full-time equivalent experience.)
		  b. Pass the relevant examinations (both technical and ethics exams.

c. Submit two appraisal reports that meet the examining committee's standards. These two levels of accreditation are granted based on the experience of the applicant.

3. The ASA publishes a multidisciplinary appraisal Journal of Valuation and the Business Valuation Committee of the ASA publishes the quarterly Journal of Business Valuation Review.

The Appraisal Foundation (AF)
1029 Vermont Avenue, NW
Suite 900
Washington, DC 20005-3517
Phone: (202) 347-7722
Fax: (202) 347-7727
Web: www.appraisalfoundation.org

1. The AF is a foundation consisting of nine (9) appraisal organizations which was established in 1987. The Board of Trustees of the AF consists of representatives of the sponsoring organizations plus fourteen (14) trustees-at-large.

2. The Board of Trustees appoints two independent boards of the Appraisal Standards Board (ASB) and the Appraisal Qualifications Board (AQB).

1. The Appraisal Standards Board has promulgated the Uniform Standards of Professional Appraisal Practice (USPAP). The content of the USPAP is summarized in Exhibit 2.4.

2. The USPAP Standards and the Statements of Appraisal Standards are mandatory for members of professional appraisal organizations that have adopted USPAP. Advisory opinions are, however, illustrative and offer advice, and therefore, are not mandatory.

3. The Appraisal Qualifications Board issues appraiser qualifications for different disciplines such as real estate, personal property, and business appraisers.

Association for Investment
Management and Research (AIMR)
560 Ray C. Hunt Dr., P.O. Box 3668
Charlottesville, VA 22903-0668
Phone: (804) 951-5499,
         (800) 247-8132
Fax: (804) 951-5262
Web: www.aimr.org
E-mail: info@aimr.org

1. The AIMR is not an appraisal organization; however, it does provide educational materials, conduct seminars, and publish monographs on valuation services.

1. The AIMR sponsors a professional designation and Chartered Financial Analyst (CFA). The AIMR requires a minimum three-year program for passing examinations given annually for three consecutive years.

2. CFAs are well qualified to conduct the analysis of publicly-traded securities, the management of investment portfolios, and valuation of companies in the case of mergers, acquisitions, and spin-offs.

Exhibit 2.3 *(Continued)*

Organization	Purpose	Certification, Publication, Standards
Institute of Business Appraisers (IBA) P.O. Box 17410 Plantation, FL 33318 Phone: (954) 584-1144 Fax: (954) 584-1184 Web: www.instbusapp.org E-mail: ibohg@instbusapp.org	1. The IBA offers seminars on business appraisal topics. publishes a code of ethics, and issues a set of business appraisal standards. 2. IBA standards are very comprehensive and fully embrace USPAR and provides in-depth guidance for business appraisals.	1. The IBA grants the professional designation of Certified Business Appraiser (CBA). The CBA designation requires an examination and the approval of reports but no requirement for experience.
National Association of Certified Valuation Analysts (NACVA) 1245 E. Brickyard Road, Suite 110 Salt Lake City, UT 84106 Phone: (801) 486-0600 Fax: (801) 486-7500 Web: www.nacva.com E-mail: nacva@nacva.com	1. The NACVA is a professional association providing business valuation and litigation consulting education and training support programs. 2. The NACVA offers a range of support services including marketing tools, software, reference materials, and customized databases. 3. The NACVA assists its members to seize the opportunities providing valuation, litigation, and consulting services to the business community. 4. NACVA has issued a set of valuation standards.	1. NACVA currently offers three (3) designations in the field of business valuation, Certified Valuation Analyst (CVA), Government Valuation Analyst (GVA), and Accredited Valuation Analyst (AVA.) 2. To obtain a CVA designation, the practitioner should be a licensed CPA. To become a GVA, the candidate must be employed by a government agency and have a college degree. The AVA designation requires a business degree. All three designations require successful completion of a comprehensive exam.
Canadian Institute of Chartered Business Valuation (CICBV) 277 Wellington Street, W. 5th Floor Toronto Ontario, Canada M5V3H2 Phone: (416) 204-3396 Fax: (416) 977-8585 Web: www.businessvaluators.com E-mail: admin@cicbv.ca	1. The CICBV was founded in 1971 and provides educational meetings and publishes a code of ethics and practice standards.	1. The CICBV sponsors the professional designation of Chartered Business Valuator (CBV). 2. The CBV designation requires candidates to successfully complete an examination and provide either three years of full-time experience, five years of part-time experience, or two years of experience and a required course of study.

Employee Stock Ownership Plans (ESOP) Association
1726 M Street, NW, Suite 501
Washington, DC 20036
Phone: (202) 293-2971
Fax: (202) 293-7568
Web: www.the-esop-employer.org
E-mail: esop@esopassociation.org

1. The ESOP Association is an organization of companies that have ESOPs and those that provide professional advisory services to ESOP companies. The ESOP has created the Valuation Advisory Committee composed of 25 members that meet twice a year to discuss issues concerning the valuation of ESOP shares.

1. The ESOP Association does not sponsor any certification or designation nor does it endorse business appraisers or any other specialists. It has not yet issued any valuation standards.
2. The ESOP Association has published a book entitled, "Valuing ESOP Shares" providing guidance for the valuation of ESOP shares of most closely held companies.

Internal Revenue Service
1111 Constitution Avenue, NW
Washington, DC 20224
Phone: (202) 566-5000
Web: www.irs.gov

1. The IRS has issued a number of regulations and pronouncements (e.g., Revenue Rulings, Revenue Procedures, Letter Rulings, Technical Advice Memorandums, and General Counsel Memorandums) on various tax matters including the valuation of businesses, business interests, and related intangible assets. Although the IRS regulations and pronouncements are intended to provide valuation guidance for tax purposes, they often contain general valuation guidance that can be used for a variety of valuation purposes.

1. The most important IRS rulings pertaining to valuations discussed throughout this book are:

59-60   Provides guidance on minimum factors to consider for valuation of estate and gift taxes.

61-193 Modified Revenue Ruling 59–60 regarding separation of tangible and intangible assets.

66-49   Provides guidance for making appraisals of donated property for federal income tax purposes.

68-609 Suggests "formula approach" or excess earnings methods of appraisals for determining fair market value of intangible assets.

77-12   Suggests methods for allocating a lump-sum purchase price to inventories.

77-287 Covers marketability discounts related to restricted stock.

Exhibit 2.3 *(Continued)*

Organization	Purpose	Certification, Publication, Standards
Internal Revenue Service *(continued)*		81-253 Describes allowance of minority discounts.
		83-120 Discusses factors that should be considered in valuing the common and preferred stock.
		85-75 Describes the basis for determining depreciation deductions or income taxes on capital gains from a subsequent asset sale.
		93-12 Allows appropriate minority discounts to be applied when the minority interests of family members in a closely held corporation are valued.

important to develop cooperation and better relationships with peers throughout the nation and even internationally.

- Other professional contacts. Contact through other professional organizations such as CPA firms, banks, attorneys, and valuation and appraiser associations can be an effective way of getting referrals. Thus, membership in these professional organizations and associations would be very helpful in attracting more clients.

2.5 ACCEPTING A CLIENT

Within the valuation profession, there is considerable competition among appraisers. Although selling valuation services is important, appraisers do not want to accept all potential clients. Associations with the wrong valuation client can be detrimental to the appraiser's financial situation as well as reputation. The client with financial difficulties or lack of management integrity may not be able to pay the valuation fee or create additional risk for the appraiser. An appraiser is not obligated to perform valuation services for every client that requests it. Before accepting a new client, an appraiser should investigate the client to determine its acceptability. To the extent possible, the prospective client's standing in the business community, financial stability, and relations with its previous appraiser should be evaluated. Thus, a decision to accept new valuation clients or continue services to existing clients should not be taken lightly.

In summary, the appraiser should make preliminary assessment of the following factors and take them into consideration when making decisions to accept the new client or continuing with the existing client:

- Client's standing in the community.
- Client management's integrity and reputation.
- Any legal proceedings involving the client's organization.
- The overall financial position of the client's organization.
- The client's working relationships with the predecessor appraiser.

These factors, to some extent, are interrelated. There are several sources of information regarding management integrity, honesty, and trustworthiness available to the appraiser, including correspondence with other professionals and predecessor appraisers' information in regulatory findings and various news media and interviews with management. The appraiser should be prepared to pursue many of the sources of information shown in Exhibit 2.7 if there are any indications that management integrity issues may be important in accepting a potential client or continuing relationships with existing clients.

Many appraisers have developed a checklist to assist them in determining whether to accept or continue with a valuation client:

- Competency and capability to do the job. Almost all appraisal organizations and associations (e.g., USPAP, ASCPA, ASA) have competency standards for their members who perform valuation services.

Exhibit 2.4   2000 Uniform Standards of Professional Appraisal Practice

Introduction	Standards and Standards Rules	Statements on Appraisal Standards	Advisory Opinions
Preamble	Standard 1: Real Property Appraisal, Development	SMT-1: Standard Rule 3-1(g) (Appraisal Review)	AO-1: Sales History
Ethics Rule	Standard 2: Real Property Appraisal, Reporting	SMT-2: Discounted Cash Flow Analysis	AO-2: Inspection of Subject Property Real State
Competency Rule	Standard 3: Real Property and Personal Property Appraisal Review, Development and Reporting	SMT-3: Retrospective Value Opinions	AO-3: Update of an Appraisal
Departure Rule	Standard 4: Real Property/Real Estate Consulting, Development	SMT-4: Prospective Value Opinions	AO-4: Standards Rule 1-5(b)
Jurisdictional Exception Rule	Standard 5: Real Property/Real Estate Consulting, Reporting	SMT-5: Confidentiality Section of the Ethics Rule	AO-5: Assistance in the Preparation of an Appraisal
Supplemental Standard Rule	Standard 6: Mass Appraisal, Development and Reporting	SMT-6: Reasonable Exposure Time in Real Property and Personal Property Market Value Opinions	AO-6: The Appraisal Review Function
Definitions	Standard 7: Personal Property Appraisal, Development	SMT-7: Permitted Departure from Specific Requirements for Real Property and Personal Property Appraisal Assignments	AO-7: Marketing Time Opinions
	Standard 8: Personal Property Appraisal, Reporting	SMT-8: Electronic Transmission of Reports	AO-8: Market Value vs. Fair Value in Real Property Appraisals
	Standard 9: Business Appraisal, Development	SMT-9: Identification of the Client's Intended Use in Developing and reporting Appraisal, Appraisal Review, or Consulting Assignment Opinions and Conclusions	AO-9: Responsibility of Appraisers Concerning Toxic or Hazardous Substance Contamination

Standard 10: Business Appraisal, Reporting

AO-10: The Appraiser-Client Relationship

AO-11: Content of the Appraisal Report Options of Standards Rules 2-2 and 8-2

AO-12: Use of Appraisal Report Options of Standards Rules 2-2 and 8-2

AO-13: Performing Evaluations of Real Property Collateral to Conform with USPAP

AO-14: Appraisals for Subsidized Housing

AO-15: Using the DEPARTURE RULE in Developing a Limited Appraisal

AO-16: Fair Housing Laws and Appraisal Report Content

AO-17: Appraisal of Real Estate Property with Proposed Improvements

AO-18: Use of an Automated Valuation Model (AVM)

AO-19: Unacceptable Assignment Conditions in Real Property Appraisal Assignments

Source: Uniform Standards of Professional Appraisal Practice (USPAP) 2000 USPAP is available from the Appraisal Foundation, 1029 Vermont Avenue, NW, Suite 900, Washington, DC 20005, Phone (202) 347-7722.

Exhibit 2.5   Valuation Services Organizations

Organization	Specialization	Address, Telephone, Website
American Valuation Group Woodland Hills, CA	Provides business valuation, economic analysis, and expert witness services for taxation, litigation, mergers and acquisitions, and condemnation	21860 Burbank Blvd., Suite 110 Woodland Hills, CA 91367 Tel: 818-992-4917 Fax: 818-992-4925 *www.amvalgroup.com*
Backer-Meekins Company, Inc.— Lutherville, MD	Business valuation analysts, consultants, and advisors	1404 Front Avenue Lutherville, MD 21093 Tel: 410-823-2600 Fax: 410-823-8455 *www.bakermeekms.com*
Banister Financial, Inc.— Charlotte, NC	Valuations of closely held companies, professional practices and family limited partnerships	1914 Brunswick Ave., Suite 1-B Charlotte, NC 28207 Tel: 704-334-4932 Fax: 704-334-5770 *www.businessvalue.com*
Bear, Inc.—San Carlos, CA	Provides a snapshot valuation of companies or small businesses by submitting a web form	865 Laurel St., San Carlos, CA 94070 Tel: 650-592-6041 Fax: 650-508-4410 *www.bearval.com*
Business Valuation Services, Dallas, TX	Provides business and business asset valuations for merger and acquisition, taxation, litigation, and management consulting purposes	3030 LBJ Freeway, Suite 1650 Dallas, Texas 75234 Tel: 972-620-0400 Fax: 972-620-8650 *www.bvs-inc.com*
Business Valuation Services, Orlando, FL	Provides a coordinated approach to business damages, valuation and litigation issues for privately held corporations	529 North Ferncreek Ave., Suite A Orlando, FL 32803 Tel: 407-898-7099 Fax: 407-898-7095 *www.valuationanalysis.com*
Columbia Financial Advisors— Portland, OR	One of the top business valuation firms in the U.S. Also offering investment banking and research consulting services	650 Morgan Building, 720 S.W. Washington Street, Portland, Oregon 97205 Tel: 503-222-0562 Fax: 503-222-1380 *www.cfai.com*
Corporate Appraisal, Inc.—Eden Prairie, MN	Specializing in the valuation of closely-held businesses, partnerships, and proprietorships	10452 Fawns Way Eden Prairie, MN 55347 Tel: 612-829-5406 Fax: 612-829-7464 *www.corpappraisal.com*
D. L. Heisey & Co, Inc.— Parker, CO	Business valuation for purchases and sales, estates and gifts, litigation support, lost profits damages, and intellectual property matters	D.L. Heisey & Co, Inc. Parker, CO 80134 Tel: 303-840-2875 Fax: 303-840-2875 *www.dlheisey.com*

Exhibit 2.5 *(Continued)*

Organization	Specialization	Address, Telephone, Website
Edward G. Detwiler & Associates— Schaumburg, IL	Valuations of high technology businesses in medical and scientific fields	1515 East Woodfield Road, Suite 730 Schaumburg, IL 60173 Tel: 847-995-9885 Fax: 847-995-9887 *www.egdetlwiler.com*
Equipment Appraisal Group, Inc.	Provides machinery and equipment appraisals following USPAP guidelines	P.O. Box 90255 San Antonio, TX 78209 Tel: 210-822-7473 Fax: 210-822-7144 *www.eagi.com*
Financial Resources Management—Rolling Hills Estates, CA	Provides authoritative business valuations, forensic economic services and books, including appraisals, estate planning and economic analysis in commercial and personal litigation	904 Silver Spur Road Rolling Hills Estates, CA 90274-3802 Tel: 310-377-2270 Fax: 310-377-8227 *www.csz.com/frm*
Fowler Valuation Services, LC	Offers services for merger and acquisition, taxation, shareholder transactions, and provides litigation support	211 W. 7th Street, Suite 920 Austin, TX 78701 Tel: 512-476-8866 Fax: 512-476-4625 *www.fowlervalue.com*
Gordon Associates	Business valuation, damage analysis and corporate financial consulting	One State Street, Suite 750 Boston, MA 02109 Tel: 617-227-2707 Fax: 617-227-7625 *www.gordonassociates.com*
Halas & Associates— Charlotte, NC	Uses the HBVS appraisal system to determine the reasonable market value for any present or planned U.S. or offshore business	425 Rose Lawn Place Charlotte, NC 28211 Tel: 704-364-4440 Fax: 704-364-1494 *www.halas.com*
Institute of Business Appraisers—IBA	IBA is a professional society devoted to the appraisal of closely-held businesses, and a pioneer in business appraisal education and accreditation	P.O. Box 17410 Plantation, FL 33318 Tel: 954-584-1144 Fax: 954-584-1184 *www.instbusapp.org*
Judges and Lawyers Business Valuation Update	Monthly newsletter offering the expert valuation professional up-to-date analytical tools, regulations, and court case decisions	Business Valuation Resources, LLC 7412 SW Beaverton-Hillsdale Hwy #106 Portland, OR 97225 Tel: 503-291-7963 Fax: 503-291-7955 *www.bvulegal.com*
MB Valuations, Inc.— Dallas, TX	Offers business valuations for industries such as aviation, real estate, and machinery	1111 Empire Central Place Dallas, Texas 75247-4301 Tel: 214-631-4707 Fax: 214-638-2576 *www.mbval.com*

Exhibit 2.5 *(Continued)*

Organization	Specialization	Address, Telephone, Website
Mentor Group, Inc.	Investment banking firm specializing in valuations and appraisals	777 E. Tahquitz Canyon Way, Suite 200 Palm Springs, CA 92262 Tel: 760-325-6411 Fax: 760-325-7260 *www.mentorgroup.com*
Mercer Capital— Memphis, TN	Provides independent business valuation services for ESOPS, litigation support, estate and gift tax, mergers and acquisitions, fairness opinions, corporate transactions, and research services	5860 Ridgeway Center Parkway, Suite 410 Memphis, TN 38120 Tel: 901-685-2120 Fax: 901-685-2199 *www.bizval.com*
Shannon Pratt's Business Valuation Update	Monthly newsletter that keeps valuation professionals up-to-date with the latest data, analytical tools, regulations and court case decisions. Fully indexed searchable back issues	Business Valuation Resources, LLC 7412 SW Beaverton-Hillsdale Hwy #106 Portland, OR 97225 Tel: 503-291-7963 Fax: 503-291-7955 *www.bvupdate.com*
Strogen & Associates, Inc.	Specializes in the valuation and sale of medical practices	443 Lantern Lane Berwyn, PA 19312 Tel: 610-644-5890 Fax: 610-644-5080 *www.strogen.com*
Trugman Valuation Associates, Inc.	Business valuation and litigation firm performs appraisals of closely held businesses and economic damages	270 A Route 46 East Rockaway, NJ 07866 Tel: 973-983-9790 Fax: 973-983-6686 *www.trugmanvaluation.com*
Wharton Valuation Associates, Inc.— Livingston, NJ	Provides valuation studies for manufacturing, distribution, financial, and service	P.O. Box 2042 Livingston, NJ 07039 Tel: 973-992-4979 Fax: 973-992-1128 *www.whartonvaluation.com*

- The nature of the relationship between the appraiser and the client. Validity and reliability of the appraiser's opinion, to a great extent, determines the degree of independence from the client. Thus, the appraiser or the appraisal firm should assess the impact of any previous or existing business or personal relationships with the client and the ability to express valuation opinions unbiasedly and independently. Existence of such relationships, however, should be disclosed in the valuation report to enable potential readers or users of the report to make their own judgment about the independence of the appraiser and possible impact on reliability and objectivity of appraisal opinions. In accordance with ethical standards of most appraisal professional organizations (USPAP, AICPA, ASA) the relationship between the appraiser and the client is confidential in nature. This

Exhibit 2.6   Proposal Package for a New Client

Overview of the Appraiser Team

This section provides an overview of the appraiser team, their expertise, qualifications, designations, achievements, and affiliations.

Valuation Service Capabilities

This section normally emphasizes the appraiser team's ability to provide a variety of valuation services including mergers and acquisitions, estate and gift taxes, allocation of purchase price, and employee stock ownership plans. Included are descriptions of unique valuation capabilities of the team suitable for this particular client.

Valuation Approach

This section describes the appraiser team's overall valuation approach and standard of value that will be used (standards of value are defined and discussed in the next section). The team should also use this opportunity to extol its computerized on-line valuation capabilities.

Timing and Fees

This section contains a detailed description of the valuation service fees and the method of determining the fee. The basis of billing is generally outlined and fees allocated among various valuation services. The section also includes the preliminary valuation service schedule, including any plans and a target date for completion of the agreed-upon valuation services.

Qualifications and Resumes of the Valuation Engagement Team

This section contains a description of the qualifications of the members of the valuation engagement team, their education, experience, designations, certifications, and unique expertise in relation to valuation of the client's industry. This narrative description should be followed by a formal resume of all members of the valuation engagement team.

Client List and References

This section includes a list of all local office clients and selected individual references from the client list. Any industry references on a regional or national basis are also included to emphasize the firms' overall qualification for valuation services in that industry.

Publications and Periodicals

Any publications or periodicals, including manuals and membership rosters published by the appraiser organization either on-line or in hard copies, should be described here.

Web site

The Web site of the appraiser team or organization is a focal point and the most effective means of introducing, marketing, and advertising the appraiser valuation capabilities, services, expertise, knowledge, and qualifications.

---

confidential relationship requires that the appraiser disclose information about an appraisal assignment only to the client or to other parties with the client's permission unless demanded by court of law.

- Purposes of the valuation. The purpose of the valuation assignment should be to determine the standard of valuation being used, the valuation approach employed, the type of appraisal opinions furnished, and the intended use of the valuation report.

- Form and extent of the valuation report. The form and extent of the anticipated appraisal report plays an important role in the determination of the fees to be charged and the amount of time required to complete the assignment. Furthermore, the nature and amount of paperwork and documentation necessary to support the appraisal report helps the appraiser

Exhibit 2.7   Sources of Information Regarding Management Integrity

1. **Preliminary Interviews with Management.**

    Such interviews can be very helpful in better understanding your client's valuation needs as well as management operating style and frankness in dealing with important issues affecting the valuation.

2. **Communication with Predecessor Appraiser(s).**

    Information obtained directly through inquiries of the predecessor appraisers regarding integrity and operating style of client's management, any disputes with the client over valuation fee or method of determining the fee can be very helpful to the successor appraiser in making acceptance decisions.

3. **Communication with Other Professionals in the Business Community.**

    Inquiries of lawyers, accountants (CPAs), and bankers known to the appraiser with whom the client has working relationships is a good way of obtaining knowledge about the client and its management.

4. **News Media.**

    Information about the client's organization and its management may be available through on-line Internet, financial journals or magazines, or industry trade magazines.

5. **Public Databases.**

    On-line public databases such as Internet (Yahoo, America OnLine, Lycos, Oracle) can be searched to obtain sufficient information and knowledge about the client, its business, industry, and management. In addition, on-line databases such as the NAARS and LEXIS/NEXIS can be searched to obtain sufficient information about the financial situation as well as other information such as the existence of legal proceedings against the client's organization or its key members of management.

6. **Inquiries of Government Regulatory Agencies.**

    These inquiries should be done when the preliminary assessment of the potential client indicates any reasons or justifications to make inquiries of specific regulatory agencies regarding pending actions against the client's organization or its management.

7. **Hiring Private Investigation Firms.**

    While the use of this method of obtaining information about the potential client may be rare, it can be very helpful when there are serious issues regarding the creditworthiness or the integrity of management.

to assign personnel to the assignment, budget staff time, and meet the time budget. The appraiser should ensure that the assignment meets the minimum documentation standards for appraisal reports set forth in the Uniform Standards of Professional Appraisal Practice (USPAP) and the Business Appraisal Standards (BAS).

2.6   PRICING VALUATION SERVICES

Valuation appraisers should price their valuation services to support their continuous growth and to attract and retain competent personnel as well as to attract and retain valuation clients. Competition within the valuation profession demands that valuation services be reasonably priced. An appraiser can, on occasion, cut valuation prices to obtain a key client in an important industry, but services cannot routinely be priced at unprofitable levels.

2.7   IMPORTANCE OF THE ENGAGEMENT LETTER

A clear understanding of the terms of the valuation engagement should exist between the client and the appraiser. It is a good professional practice to confirm the terms of each engagement in an engagement letter as illustrated in Exhibit 2.8. The form and content of engagement letters may vary for different clients, but they should generally include the following:

- Clear identification of the client and their appraiser.
- Precise specification of the valuation subject including the business interests or the legal interest being valued.
- The objective or purpose of the valuation.
- Reference to the standard of value that will be used or any applicable valuation professional standards.
- An explanation of the nature and scope of the valuation and the appraiser's responsibility.
- Date(s) of the valuation.
- Form and type of the valuation report (e.g., written, oral).
- A statement regarding the intended use of the valuation report including any assumptions and limitations of the report.
- The responsibilities of the client to provide valid and timely records and documentation necessary to complete the appraisal report.
- The valuation fee or the method of determining the fee and any billing arrangement.
- A request for the client to confirm the terms and conditions of the engagement by signing and returning a copy of the letter to the appraiser.
- The date of the engagement letter.

2.8   PLANNING AN APPRAISAL ENGAGEMENT

The preliminary planning of an appraisal engagement consists of: (1) arranging a conference with client personnel; (2) obtaining knowledge of the client business; and (3) understanding the client's industry and economic conditions.

2.8.1   Conference with Client Personnel

Soon after acceptance of a valuation assignment, the appraiser should have conferences with key client personnel. The appraiser should meet with principal administrative, financial, operating officers, and executives to discuss matters expected to have a significant effect on the conduct of the valuation assignment and the appraiser's opinion.

   Client personnel assistance is often needed to obtain documents, records, evidence, and explanations of various matters. Thus, effective early conferences can establish a foundation for a good working relationship with all client personnel. Effective communication with top management is particularly important.

Exhibit 2.8   Sample Engagement Letter

Smith & Jones Associates
(Hereafter the Appraiser)
123 Courtside
Any City, NY 10011

Mr. John Clark
(Hereafter the Client)
500 West Main Street
Any City, NY 10011

Dear Mr. Clark:

Thank you for meeting with us to discuss the requirements and terms of our forthcoming engagement. This will confirm our understanding of the arrangements for appraisal of the fair market value of a 100 percent, nonmarketable, controlling interest in the outstanding common stock of XYZ Company, Inc., a New York Corporation, held by Mr. John Clark, as of May 30, 2000 for gift tax purposes. Fair market value standard used in this engagement is defined as "value at which a willing seller and willing buyer, both being informed of the relevant facts about the business, could reasonably conduct a transaction, neither party acting under any compulsion to do so."

Client warrants that this appraisal report will be relied on for the use and the date indicated in this engagement. The appraisal will be subject to, at least, the following contingent and limiting conditions.

1. The appraiser needs prompt and free access to all related documents, materials, records, facilities, and/or client's personnel to effectively and efficiently perform the agreed-upon valuation services in a timely and professional manner. Lack of proper cooperation in this regard may result in withdrawal from the assignment and/or a delay of the completion date of the assignment.
2. Information, estimates, opinions, and evidence contained in this report are gathered from reliable sources. However, no independent verification of such evidence is performed by the appraiser.
3. Client warrants that the information and evidence provided to the appraiser is reliable and accurate to the best of the client's knowledge.
4. Other contingent and limiting conditions may be required, and the client agrees that all conditions disclosed by the appraiser will be accepted and incorporated into the appraiser's report.

Our engagement will also include providing expert witness testimony as it may require. The client agrees that payment of all fees and expenses related to this service be paid prior to the performance of expert witness testimony. The client agrees to indemnify and hold the appraiser harmless against any and all liability, claim loss, cost, and expenses that the appraiser may incur as a result of providing expert witness testimony.

It is our intention to complete this assignment by agreed-upon date (e.g., 120 days from the receipt of signed agreement and all requested documents). Our billings for the services set forth in this engagement will be based upon our per diem rates for this type of work plus out-of-pocket expenses; billings will be rendered at the beginning of each month on an estimated basis and are payable upon receipt. This engagement includes only those valuation services specifically described in this letter, and appearance before judicial proceedings or government organizations such as the Internal Revenue Service, or other regulatory bodies, arising out of this engagement will be billed to you separately.

Exhibit 2.8   *(Continued)*

We look forward to providing the valuation services described in this letter as well as other valuation services agreed upon. The appraiser reserves the right to withdraw from this engagement at any time for reasonable cause. In the unlikely event that any differences concerning our services or fees should arise that are not resolved by mutual agreement, we reserve the right not to make a court appearance in this matter.

If you are in agreement with the terms of this letter, please sign one copy and return it for our files. We appreciate the opportunity to (continue to) work with you.

Sincerely,

Smith & Jones Associates
Robert E. Smith
Engagement Partner

The foregoing letter fully describes our understanding and is accepted by us.

May 30, 2000	Signature of John Clark
Date	John Clark

2.8.2   Knowledge of the Business

The appraiser's knowledge of the client's business and industry is very important in understanding the events, transactions, and practices that affect business valuation. The evidence-gathering part of the valuation assignment typically requires the appraiser to obtain knowledge of the client's business and the factors affecting its value. The knowledge of the client's business that the appraiser should obtain includes:

- Organization Structure. In any business the structure of the organization is important in specifying the tasks and responsibilities of the various components of the organization. The organization structure and operating style are based on the abilities of management, tax and legal issues, regulatory considerations, product diversification, and geographical location. In a large complex business, the organization structure takes the form of organization charts, charts of accounts, rules, office memos, manuals, contracts, and internal control structure including control environment, communication, monitoring, and control activities and risk assessment.

- Operations. The appraiser should obtain an understanding of the client's operating characteristics, its legal structure, applicable laws, rules, and regulations as well as managerial policies and procedures. Operating characteristics consist of types of products and services, locations, and methods of production, distribution, and compensation. The appraiser should prepare brief operating characteristics of the client and other significant factors that have a bearing on valuation. To properly and intellectually interpret the evidence gathered throughout the valuation, the appraiser must understand the client's business and many factors that will have an influence on the client's operations. A review of legal documents is important for rational interpretation of the evidence gathered throughout the valuation assignment. The appraiser should review the corporate charter and bylaws or partnership agreements, the corporate minute book, tax return, regulatory requirement, and filing systems, and consider their implications for the valuation process. For example, the corporate charter includes information on the corporate structure, the authorized capital, and the power and rights granted to, as well as responsibilities and restrictions placed on, the corporation by state law. A partnership agreement includes similar information about the organization and operating requirements of a business organized as a partnership.

2.8.3 Legal Structure

The legal status of the business (e.g., partnership, corporation) plays an important role in the valuation engagement and can have a significant impact on the valuation opinions. In the case of limited partnership or when earnings allocation among partners is different from allocation in the liquidation process, the value assigned to different groups or partners may not be the same. Thus, the appraiser should read the partnership agreement first to understand the partner's legal rights and privileges and then consider their implications for the valuation assignment.

2.8.4 Policies

Minutes of the meetings of the corporate board of directors contain an official record of important information, economic events, transactions, and agreements which can have a significant impact on the valuation conclusions. The declaration of dividends, capital expenditures, and authorization of stock-based compensation plans are examples of the important information contained in corporate minutes. Contracts and correspondence with customers, suppliers, employees, labor unions, and various government agencies contain information that will enable the appraiser to understand the business practices and problems of the clients as well as provide information for valuation reports.

2.8.5 Industry and Economic Conditions

The appraiser must understand the broad economic environment in which the client operates, including the effects of national economic polices (e.g., various government regulations), the geographic location and its economy (Northeastern states versus Southwestern states), and the developments in taxation and regulatory requirements. The appraiser should have a basic understanding of the global market and economy, national economic conditions, government regulations, changes in technology, and competitive conditions that affect the value of the client's business or business interest. Information about the industry in which the client operates may be obtained by searching for data from on-line sites, trade journals, and books of industry statistics and publications. To obtain knowledge about the client's business and business interest the appraiser may:

- Review the articles of incorporation and bylaws or partnership agreements.
- Read the minutes of the board of directors' and shareholders' meetings to gather information about dividend declarations, employee stock-based compensation plans, and approval of mergers and acquisitions.

Exhibit 2.9   Sources of Economic, Industry, and Business Information

General Economic Information
 1. Federal Reserve Bulletin
 2. Survey of Current Business (U.S. Department of Commerce)
 3. Statistical Abstract of the United States (U.S. Department of Commerce)
 4. Economic Report of the President (U.S. Council of Economic Advisers)
 5. Economic and Business Outlook (Bank of America)
 6. Economic Trends (Federal Reserve Bank of Cleveland)
 7. U.S. Financial Data (Federal Reserve Bank of St. Louis)
 8. Monthly Labor Review (U.S. Bureau of Labor Statistics)
 9. Congressional Information Service
10. Regional Economics and Markets
11. The Complete Economic and Demographic Data Source
12. Office of the Comptroller of the Currency

Industry Information
 1. Federal Deposit Insurance Corporation
 2. U.S. Industrial Outlook
 3. Standard & Poor's Industry Surveys
 4. Moody's Investor's Industry Review
 5. National Trade and Professional Association of the United States
 6. Statistical Abstracts of the United States
 7. Encyclopedia of Associations
 8. Moody's Manuals (various industries)

Business Information
 1. Dun & Bradstreet Principal International Business
 2. Standard & Poor's Register of Corporations, Directors, and Executives
 3. Value Line Investment Survey
 4. Standard & Poor's Corporation Records
 5. Dun & Bradstreet, Key Business Ratios
 6. Business Press (e.g., The Wall Street Journal, Forbes, Fortune, and Barron's)
 7. National Mortgage News
 8. United States Banker
 9. Federal Reserve Banks
10. SNL Securities
11. On-Line Data Sources (e.g., Yahoo, Lycos, America OnLine, and LEXIS/NEXIS)

- Review and analyze recent (e.g., past five years) annual financial statements, tax returns, and reports to regulatory agencies.

- Review the client's applicable governmental laws and regulations.

- Read important continuing contracts such as labor contracts, loan agreements, and bond indentures.

- Read trade and industry publications regarding current business and industry developments. Exhibit 2.9 shows some sources of business and industry information.

- Obtain nonfinancial information such as the form of organization and ownership of the client's business, products and services, through inquiries of client's management, key personnel, or a document request.

- Search available Web sites to gather general economic, industry, and business information. The on-line information search provides powerful flexibility, easy and fast accessibility, and relatively cheap availability and control for the appraiser. Exhibit 2.10 provides a list of Web sites that can be very helpful to the appraiser in gathering sufficient and competent information.

2.9 GENERAL PLANNING

The valuation process and appraisal plan consist of three interrelated and sequential aspects: (1) the decisions the appraiser needs to make; (2) the knowledge to be obtained and the evidence to be gathered in making these decisions; and (3) the valuation procedures that are typically applied to obtain that evidence and knowledge. To clearly distinguish these aspects, consider the following separate listings of valuation decisions, knowledge, and evidence as well as procedures. These aspects of the valuation process for financial institutions will be discussed in-depth in Chapters 5 through 18 of this book.

2.9.1 General Planning Decisions to Be Made

- The agreed-upon purpose(s) of the valuation.
- Detailed description of the valuation subject (e.g., business or business interest).
- The applicable standard of value that will be used (e.g., fair market value, fair value, investment value, intrinsic value).
- The type, nature, form, and extent of the report to be issued.
- Overall timing of the valuation assignment.
- Staffing requirements and the expected assistance for the client personnel in valuation evidence-gathering and data preparation.
- Any assumptions and limiting conditions that will be part of the valuation report.
- Other services such as providing expert witness or litigation testimony.

2.9.2 Evidence and Knowledge Obtained to Prepare Preliminary Appraisal Plan

- Business. Description of the business and its operations, types of products and services, capital structure, location, and methods of production, marketing, and distribution. The purpose is to obtain knowledge of how effectively and efficiently the client is carrying out its operations.
- Industry. Specification of the industry in which the client operates including economic conditions, government regulations, changes in technology, and competitive conditions can assist the appraiser in learning more about the client's business and industry. This knowledge can have a significant impact on valuation conclusions.
- Interview. Interviews with the client's key personnel can provide information regarding management integrity, operating style, and business operations to develop a realistic process of establishing an appropriate valuation conclusion.

Exhibit 2.10   On-Line Sites Economic, Industry, Business Information

Site	Feature
www.megafinancial.com	Provides links to other sites for financial services including commercial and investment banks, mutual funds, on-line stock trading, loans, and financial planning.
Icweb.loc.gov/rr/business/brs.html	Has a section called Business Reference Services for searching topics in business, technology, and economics.
www.bbbonline.org/business/code/ Index.htm	Offers the Better Business Bureau (BBB) full text on an exposure draft and Code of Online Business Practices.
Stats.bls.gov/blshome.htm	Provides a section on Economy at a Glance, which gives a statistical breakdown of the labor market in hours, earnings, and productivity.
www.bog.frb.fed.us/releases	Posts daily, weekly, monthly, quarterly, and annual statistics releases and historical data of commercial banks.
www.smallcapcenter.com	Provides information about earnings, investments, and trades.
www.businessjeeves.com	Provides a list of links to sites on a variety of business topics including banking services, bond brokers and markets, currency markets, general financial services, and international trade.
www.edgar-online.com www.tenkwizard.com www.sec.gov www.freedgar.com bamboo.tc.pw.com www.gsionline.com	All these sites provide information on publicly traded companies often needed in performing valuations on estate and gift taxes, ESOPs, and mergers and acquisitions. Especially, the SECs' EDGAR data base provides information on more than 15,000 publicly traded companies.
www.hoovers.com	Provides extensive information on more than 12,000 publicly traded companies in easy-to-use format.
www.justquotes.com	Offers a financial data search engine to find company name, stock symbol, quotes, financial data, and links to related Web sites.
www.marketguide.com	Offers comprehensive research on more than 10,000 publicly traded companies' stock information, earnings estimates, comparison ratios, and brokerage reports.
www.the-esop-emplowner.org/	Provides ESOP statistics on the number of ESOPs, the magnitude, and types of ESOP.
www.american-capital.com	Maintains the employee ownership index (EOI).
www.stockpicker.net	Finds the best stock selections.
www.nceo.org/nceo.journal.html	Publishes the employee ownership index (EOI) quarterly.
www.numeraive.com	Provides global value investing with stock valuation including detailed information about value investing, the process of stock screening, selection, and pricing.

- Audited Financial Statements. Audited financial statements (Statement of Financial Position, Income Statement, Statement of Cash Flows, Statement of Owner's Equity) can provide reliable and useful financial information regarding the client's financial position, results of operations, and cash flows as well as equity situations. Although audited financial statements prepared in conformity with generally accepted accounting principles (GAAP) are based on historical cost not the fair market value, they provide financial information that is relevant to the appraisal.

- Normalized Financial Statements. Appraisers often use audited historical financial statements to develop and present their appraisal report of a business's value. The primary purpose of using financial statements is to assist in developing and presenting the value of an entity. These financial statements, which are utilized in the preparation of the valuation report and often included in the written business valuations, frequently contain departures from generally accepted accounting principles (GAAP) or other comprehensive basis of accounting (OCBOA). The accounting and review services committee of the AICPA issued an Exposure Draft (ED) in December 1999 titled "Financial Statements Included in Written Business Valuations." The ED defines normalized financial statements as "financial statements that contain necessary and appropriate adjustments in order to make an entity's financial information more meaningful when presenting and comparing on a consistent basis the financial results of that entity to those of a comparable entity as part of a business valuation engagement." The ED exempts such financial statements from the provisions of Statements on Standards for Accounting and Review Services (SSARS) No. 1, Compilation and Review of Financial Statements, which requires compliance. The ED exempts from SSARS No. 1 historical financial statements and normalized financial statements included in a written business valuation.

- Other Financial Data. Financial information other than financial statements such as federal income tax returns, reports with regulatory agencies, management forecasts and projects, internal and managerial reports, and capital and operating budgets can provide relevant data for the valuation assignment.

- Operating Information. A history of the client's organization, its business, mission, and a brief chronology of major changes in the form and ownership of organization, background of key personnel, brochures, catalogs, price lists, organization charts, major customers and suppliers as well as information regarding long-term and continuous agreements and obligations (e.g., leases, loans, bonds) can assist the appraiser in completing the valuation assignment effectively and successfully.

2.9.3 Procedures in Preparing the Preliminary Appraisal Plan

Every appraisal engagement requires the choice of certain valuation procedures. Valuation procedures performed as part of the preliminary appraisal plan are an important component of the valuation process. These procedures include:

- Reviewing and analysis of economic data to (a) determine its impact on the future performance of the client's organization and (b) assess the economic risk that the client organization is exposed to.

- Reviewing various sources of industry information such as industry or trade publications and annual reports of companies in the industry.

- Reviewing and analyzing financial information including trend analysis, comparative analysis, ratio analysis, and common-size financial analysis assists the appraiser in assessing the client's future trends, performance, risk, and unusual items (abnormalities) that may have an impact on valuation conclusions.
- Considering the applicable valuation standards and methods issued by professional appraisal organizations (e.g., ASA, IBA, NACVA, AICPA).
- Inquiring of management about current business developments.
- Reading current year's interim financial statements.
- Discussing the type, scope, and the timing of the valuation assignment with the client.
- Touring the client's physical facilities, plants, and offices.
- Reading the corporate charter, bylaws, major contracts, and minutes of directors' and shareholders' meetings.
- Completing a generalized questionnaire, checklist, or narrative memorandum that organizes and summarizes the information needed to complete the valuation assignment.

The appraiser should choose valuation techniques that best combine reliable values with relevant information about the economic characteristics of the business or business interest under consideration. The usual approach to valuation is to determine the present value of the future cash flows. In other words, the projected cash flows are discounted at an appropriate discount rate and then the sum of the discounted cash flows is an indication of the value. Appraisers often try to be realistic by providing a clear caveat in their report stating that "the value developed in this report is calculated based on the premises that the firm will be able to continue its existence according to its business plan. If the plan is fulfilled in terms of projected revenues, expenses, and cash flows, then the value determined in this report can be relied on."

The second approach is the comparable method. The appraiser looks at revenue trends, earnings potential, and the firm's competitive position relative to other comparable firms in the same industry. The most commonly used valuation approaches are presented and described in depth in Chapter 6 of this book. The appraiser should consider the following questions in selecting the appropriate valuation approach(es).

- What future economic, industry, and business factors should be included in or excluded from the valuation process?
- To what extent should joint inputs, interaction, and grouping affect the valuation?
- How and to what extent should the assessed risk be factored into the valuation estimates?
- What valuation standard(s) should be used?
- What discount rate should be used?
- How should changes in value be reported?

2.10   APPRAISER'S TRAITS

Danziger (2000) discussed that CPAs who have been successful in offering business valuation services share the following traits.[2]

2.10.1 Able to Function Well under Intense Pressure

Business valuation clients often have a specified goal (e.g., marital dissolution, mergers and acquisitions, stockholder disputes, estate and gift taxes), and they also know whether a high or low valuation will benefit them most. In performing valuation services, the appraisers should maintain their objectivity and independence by refraining from the influence of being pressured by a client to reach a particular value. The appraiser should also be able to handle the pressures of meeting the deadline and being cross-examined by attorneys when serving as an expert witness or litigation consultant.

2.10.2 Communicate Well Both Orally and in Writing

Successful appraisers are typically effective communicators who can convey their findings (valuation opinions) succinctly to the interested parties (e.g., client, judge, jury, tax authorities, bank regulators). Good public relations with the business community, appraisal professionals, and other professionals (banks, accountants, attorneys) can assist in establishing appraisal services and secure future growth. Effective writing skills in preparing the appraisal report is essential in conveying valuation findings to interested parties.

2.10.3 Utilize Both Qualitative and Quantitative Data

Successful appraisers should have the training and experience of meshing the data by using both quantitative information (e.g., historical financial statements, market value, discount rate, cash flows) and qualitative information (e.g., economic conditions, market trends, judgment, goodwill, management reputations and skills) in reaching valuation conclusions. Appraisers should have adequate skills of gathering, analyzing, synthesizing, and interpreting data by employing appropriate valuation methodologies to generate reliable and relevant valuation information.

2.10.4 Be Unfazed by Ambiguity and Uncertainty

In performing valuation services, the appraisers often use their judgment and experience in estimating appraisal data (e.g., future cash flows, discounted rate, growth rate). Thus, appraisers should support their findings by applying several valuation methods, test these methods for their sensitivities to ambiguities and uncertainties, and be able to justify estimations used in forming valuation opinions.

2.10.5 Continuous Improvement of Valuation Expertise and Skills through Ongoing Professional Education

Being a successful appraiser requires proper training, education, work experience, and proficiency. To achieve these credentials and skills in the professional valuation community, appraisers must first earn a business valuation designation offered by a number of organizations (e.g., American Society of Appraisers, Institute of Business Appraisers, National Association of Certified Valuation Analysts, Association for Investment Management and Research, American Institute of Certified Public Accountants). Exhibit 2.11 presents appraisal certifications and their attributes. The knowledge base of understanding of business valuation theory, concepts, and methods is a prerequisite for getting into the business valuation profession but is not sufficient. After achieving the knowledge base and initial designation, the appraiser should obtain proper experience and continuous training and education to be successful.

2.10.6   Continuous Marketing Strategies

Obtaining valuation clients requires an effective marketing and contacting strategy. There are several ways that the appraiser can obtain clients: (1) targeting your marketing efforts and expertise to a particular profession or industry (e.g., valuing ESOPs, estate and gift taxes, mergers and acquisitions); (2) contacting other professionals for assisting them with valuation services (e.g., attorneys, accountants, bankers, security brokers); (3) personal direct contact of local businesses; (4) advertising in the local and national business and appraisal journals; (5) getting referrals from fellow appraisers; (6) attending conventions, conferences, and other meetings of professional associations (e.g., appraisal organizations, accountant's societies, attorneys, chamber of commerce, banks); and (7) creating a Web site to get local, national, and even global exposure.

2.11   APPRAISER'S DUE DILIGENCE PROCESS

Conducting effective business valuation services requires appraisers to develop proper valuation strategies and perform the due diligence valuation process of using different valuation methods, concepts, a number of sources of financial and strategic information, various state and federal valuation regulations, and professional valuation standards. Evans (2000) suggested the following tips for the appraiser in performing a business valuation due diligence.[3]

- Understand the valuation assignment.
- Comply with competency and independence standards.
- Watch the market.
- Know the difference between fair market and investment value.
- Know when to use the invested capital vs. equity model.
- Don't let rates of return distort value.
- Beware of earnings measures—cash is king.
- Verify all rates of return.
- Always challenge long-term growth rates.
- Challenge premiums or discounts.
- Have pride in your report.

2.12   CONCLUSION

This chapter has provided background information regarding the market and demand for valuation services, valuation service providers (appraisers), the various appraisal organizations,

Exhibit 2.11 Appraisal Certifications and Their Attributes

Certifications/ Attributes	Sponsoring Organization	Years of Establishment	Education
1. Accredited in Business Valuation (ABV)	American Institute of Certified Public Accountants (AICPA)	1997	Education requirements for CPA designation
2. Accredited Senior Appraiser (ASA)	American Society of Appraisers (ASA)	1952	College degree or equivalent
3. Accredited Senior Member (ASM)	ASA	1952	College degree or equivalent
4. Chartered Financial Analysts	Association for Investment Management and Research (AIMR)	1963	College degree
5. Certified Business Appraiser (CBA)	Institute of Business Appraisers (IBA)	1978	College degree or equivalent
6. Business Valuator Accredited for Litigation	IBA	1998	None
7. Accredited by IBA (AIBA)	IBA	1991	None
8. Certified Valuation Analyst (CVA)	National Association of Certified Valuation Analysts (NACVA)	1991	Education requirements of CPAs
8. Government Valuation Analyst (GVA)	NACVA	1996	College degree
9. Accredited Valuation Analyst (AVA)	NACVA	1999	Business degree
10. Chartered Business Valuator (CBV)	Canadian Institute of Chartered Business Valuation (CICBV)	1971	Business degree

Experience	Examination	Continuing Education	Others
Ten business valuation engagements	Written examination	60 hours and involvement in five business valuation engagements every three-year period	CPA in good standing
1. Five years of full-time equivalent 2. Two appraisal reports	1. Technical and ethics examination 2. Four courses and related technical exams	40 hours every five years	Two appraisal reports
None	Eight hours of technical exam and one hour of ethics exam before sitting for the exam	40 hours every five years	No continuing experience
Significant professional experience	A minimum three-year program for passing examination; three extensive annual examinations	Professional continuing education	Public company orientation Investment management
None	Four-hour written examination	None	Two full valuation reports
None	Four-hour written examination	None	None
None	Four-hour exam	None	None
Licensed CPAs	1. Two-day AICPA course with open-book take-home exam; or 2. Five-day other related course and take-home exam	Continuing education requirements of CPAs; 24 hours first two years; 36 hours every three years thereafter	Periodic report writing course and quality enhancement
Governmental employee	Five-day course with open-book take-home exam	24 hours first year and 36 hours every three years thereafter	Quality Enhancement
Holding ASA or CFE designation	Five-day course with open-book take-home exam	24 hours first year and 36 hours every three years thereafter	Quality Enhancement
1. Three years of full-time experience; 2. Five years of part-time; or 3. Two years of experience and a required course	Written exam	40 hours every five years	

and their standards and certifications. This chapter also discusses the appraisal process, including information about engagement letters, the initial document request, and internal and external sources of information gathered by the appraiser. Gathering and analyzing the foregoing information will provide a framework for the appraiser to conduct a variety of valuation service assignments including those pertaining to financial institutions (e.g., M & A, IPO, ESOP). An understanding of background materials presented in this chapter is crucial to the further development and application of valuation methodologies and techniques to financial institutions presented in Parts II, III, and IV of this book.

ENDNOTES

1. Trugman, Gary R., 1993. "Conducting a Valuation of a Closely Held Business." Management Consulting Services Division of ASCPA, p. 13/100–1.
2. Danziger, Elizabeth, 2000. "Is Business Appraising For You?" Journal of Accountancy (March): 28–33.
3. Evans, Frank C., 2000. "Tips for the Valuator." Journal of Accountancy (March): 35–41.

CHAPTER 3

Overview of Mergers and Acquisitions

3.1 INTRODUCTION

Mergers and acquisitions (hereafter M & A) are occurring at a record pace in almost every industry, especially in the financial services industry. Falling regulatory and geographic barriers (e.g., interstate and even global banking, the passage of the Financial Modernization Act, GLB Act) along with banks' unprecedented performance and levels of private equity, are contributing to this increased M & A activity. The objective of this chapter is to present a basic understanding of the M & A process from the standpoints of both the target and the acquirer. This chapter provides a generic discussion of M & A transactions that can be used by all entities wishing to grow through business combinations. More in-depth discussion of M & A transactions for financial institutions is presented in Chapters 12 and 13. M & A deals are typically viewed by both the acquirer and the target as an important means of achieving economies of scale especially in a multiple-product market such as the financial services industry.

The wave of M & A activities and the determinants of their behavior in the financial services industry have begun to gain importance and have surfaced as a core issue in the financial community. The terms *mergers* and *acquisitions* are often used interchangeably by laypeople. In a merger deal, two separate entities combine and both parties to the deal wind up with common stock in a single, combined entity. In contrast, in an acquisition transaction, the acquirer (bidding entity) buys the common stock or assets of the seller (target entity). The vast majority of all business combinations are acquisitions rather than mergers. M & A activities within the financial services industry have continued with varying levels of intensity since the end of World War II. Recent waves of M & A in financial institutions have been motivated by a favorable regulatory environment (e.g., elimination of intrastate and interstate branching restrictions), continuous increase in bank earnings and stock prices, opportunities for market expansions, favorable stock prices and strong stock market, substantial advances in communication and data processing technologies (e.g., e-commerce, Internet banking), greater efficiency following acquisition, and economies of scale. As M & A deals continue to grow, as shareholders lean toward liquidity, and as acquirers offer higher premiums for their targets, the use of the appropriate valuation process in considering the pros and cons of these deals and estimating their values become more apparent.

3.2 HISTORICAL PERSPECTIVE OF M & A

Prior to World War II, the primary motivations for mergers and acquisitions in corporate America were centered around the effectiveness and efficiency in operations expected to be generated from the incorporation of economies of scale. Prior to the 1980s, geographic restrictions, especially the prohibition against interstate banks and even intrastate branching, limited where and how banks could compete. The formation of bank holding companies (BHC) allowed banks to acquire banks and other non-banking companies in different geographic locations or markets, lower their inherent tax burden, and issue commercial paper. During the 1980s, banks began to acquire other financial services companies such as mutual funds, investment, and finance companies. Many banks focused on acquiring other banks and thrifts or commercial banks to have immediate access to the federal funds market.[1] In contrast to M & A during the 1980s that were primarily motivated to remove troubled banks and thrifts, the most recent M & A in the financial services industry focused on additional growth, increase in efficiency and effectiveness in operations, and diversification of financial services. Exhibit 3.1 shows large bank mergers in the United States during the 1990s for target banks with assets over $10 billion.

3.3 RECENT TRENDS IN M & A

M & A in the banking sector have increased substantially during the 1990s. The development of regional banking agreements and the relaxation of federal legislation have paved the way for a continued increase in M & A deals for financial institutions. The number of banks in the United States decreased about 30 percent between 1988 and 1997, while the share of total assets held by the largest 10 banks increased from one-fifth to one-third, and several hundred M & A occurred each year. This massive wave of M & A activities, especially in the financial services industry, will continue at least for the next several years, according to a nationwide survey of financial consultants. The survey of 230 financial consultants conducted by RHI Management Resources in 1999 reveals that more than two-thirds (68 percent) of the respondents believe that the current level of M & A activities will increase from 2000 through 2002.[2] These survey results mirror findings of a comparable survey of 1,400 chief financial officers (CFOs) conducted in 1997 in which 65 percent of responding CFOs expected increased M & A activity through the year 2000.

M & A transactions are either the in-market type, between banks with deposits in the same metropolitan area or rural country, or the market-extension variety between banks in different local markets. The distinction between in-market and market-extension business combinations is important for evaluating the causes and effects of M & A and the policy responses to M & A deals. Exhibit 3.2 presents frequency of M & A deals of banks and thrifts from 1990 to 1999. Exhibit 3.3 shows the value of M & A deals of banks and thrifts from 1990 to 1999. The megamergers of the 1990s are Citicorp and Travelers; Bank America and Nations Bank; Deutsche Bank and Bankers Trust; Union Bank of Switzerland and Swiss Bank Corp.; Wells Fargo and Norwest; Société Générale and Paribas; Bank One and First Chicago; and BankBoston Corp. and Fleet Financial Group, Inc.

In 1998, the value of M & A in the financial services industry reached the highest ever level of $674 billion.[3] The most publicized megamerger was Citicorp and Travelers with

Exhibit 3.1   Large Bank Mergers in 1990s

Year	Target Bank	Acquiring Bank	Total Assets of Target ($billions)
1991	Security Pacific Corporation	Bank America Corporation	88.0
1991	Manufacturers Hanover Corporation	Chemical Banking Corporation	61.5
1991	C&S Sovran Corporation	NCNB Corporation	51.4
1991	Manufacturers National Corporation	Comerica Inc.	12.1
1991	Ameritrust Corporation	Society Corporation	11.0
1992	MNC Financial Inc.	NationsBank Corporation	17.5
1993	Key Corp, Albany, NY	Society Corporation	25.5
1994	Continental Bank Corporation	Bank America Corporation	22.5
1995	Chase Manhattan Corporation	Chemical Banking Corporation	114.0
1995	First Chicago Corporation	NBD Bancorp	65.9
1995	First Interstate Bancorp	Wells Fargo & Company	55.8
1995	First Fidelity Bancorporation	First Union Corporation	36.2
1995	Shawmut National Corporation	Fleet Financial Group Inc.	31.3
1995	Meridian Bancorp Inc.	Corestate Financial Corporation	15.0
1995	Integra Financial Corporation	National City	13.7
1995	Midlantic Corporation	PNC Bank Corporation	13.3
1995	BayBanks	Bank of Boston Corporation	10.8
1995	Michigan National Corporation	National Australia Bank Ltd.	10.2
1996	Boatmen's Bancshares	NationsBank Corporation	33.7
1996	Standard Fed Bancorp	ABN-AMRO Holding NV	13.3
1997	Corestates Financial Corporation	First Union Corporation	45.6
1997	Barnett Banks	NationsBank Corporation	41.4
1997	US Bancorp	First Bank System	31.9
1997	First of American Bank	National City	22.1
1997	Signet Banking Corporation	First Union Corporation	11.7
1997	Central Fidelity Banks Inc.	Wachovia Corporation	10.6
1998	BankAmerica Corporation	NationsBank Corporation	260.0
1998	First Chicago NBD Corporation	Banc One Corporation	114.1
1998	Wells Fargo & Company	Norwest Corporation	97.5
1999	Fleet Financial Group Inc.	BankBoston Corp.	73.5
1999	Republic New York Corp.	HSBC USA Inc.	50.4
1999	Firstar Corp.	Mercantile Bancorp.	35.6
1999	Zions Bancorp.	First Security Corp.	22.0
1999	Amsouth Bankcorp.	First American Corp.	20.3

Source: Federal Deposit Insurance Corporation and American Banker, Inc. for target banks with assets over $10 billion.

the estimated combined assets of $669 billion[4] which provide a variety of financial services including traditional commercial banking, investment banking, asset management, securities brokerages, and property, casualty, and life insurance. M & A, consolidations, and convergence are all valid positioning tactics intended to assist combined companies to compete more effectively in the global marketplace by: (1) shoring up existing lines of business; (2) extending into new lines of business, and (3) eliminating former competitors. The currently overvalued stock has motivated shareholders of both the acquirer and target firms to

Exhibit 3.2   Business Combination

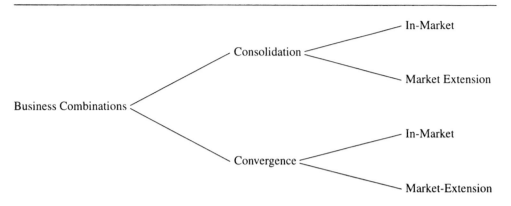

consummate megamergers. Acquirers can now afford to exchange overvalued stocks for shares of target banks and pay them high premiums without jeopardizing their operations and cash flows. Shareholders of target banks will also receive higher prices for their shares.

There are two types of business combinations in the financial services industry; namely consolidation and convergence. Consolidation entails combination of resources of similar financial institutions (e.g., banks) through M & A of, for example, banks and bank holding companies. Convergence means the expansion of the scope or breadth of financial institutions into a variety of financial services through M & A between banks and other financial

Exhibit 3.3

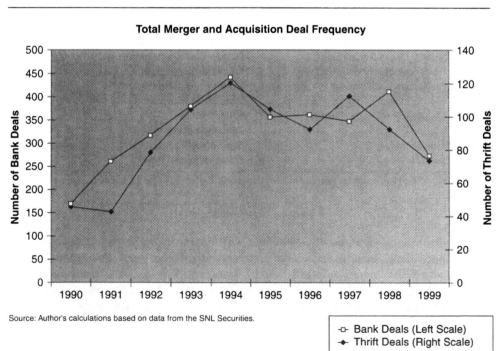

Source: Author's calculations based on data from the SNL Securities.

Exhibit 3.4

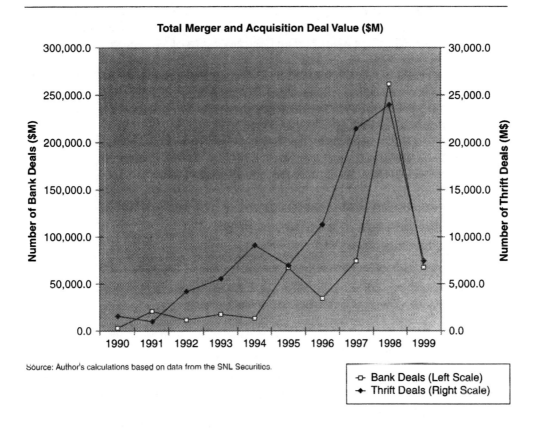

Total Merger and Acquisition Deal Value ($M)

Source: Author's calculations based on data from the SNL Securities.

-□- Bank Deals (Left Scale)
-◆- Thrift Deals (Right Scale)

services firms (e.g., insurance companies, securities underwriting, and mutual funds). Exhibit 3.4 shows classification of business combination in the financial services industry. Consolidation is very common in the financial services industry, while convergence of banks with other financial service providers has been rare. However, there have been significant acquisitions of investment banking institutions with holding companies since 1996, and it is expected that this trend will continue at a higher pace with the passage of the GLB Act of 1999. Although banks are now enjoying high profit margins, they will be facing increasing competition from insurance companies, brokerage houses, mutual funds, credit unions, and the like, which will be able to make consumer and business loans as well as offer other banking services (e.g., savings and checking accounts) under the GLB Act. This new wave of convergence will bring banks, mutual funds, insurance companies, and investment firms under one corporate roof.

3.4   REGULATIONS OF BANK MERGERS

Examination of M & A laws and regulations is important in understanding the continuous trend toward M & A deals in the financial services industry. A number of laws and regulations are applicable to M & A proposals in the financial services industry, and they influence their approvals. M & A proposals are being reviewed by both the financial institutions' regulatory agencies and the Department of Justice for compliance with applicable laws and regulations. The two major federal regulations pertaining to bank mergers are the Bank Merger Act (BM Act) of 1960 and the Bank Holding Company Act (BHC Act) of 1956 and its 1970 Amendment.

The BM Act requires that applications for M & A by banks be processed through bank regulators. The federal regulator responsible for bank M & A typically has regulatory authority over the final form of the bank emerging from the M & A deal regardless of the agency that regulated the bank prior to the merger.

The BHC Act requires approval by the Board of Governors of the Federal Reserve System of any M & A action making a bank part of a BHC affiliation. Chapter 3(c) of the BHC specifies the required forms that disclose the following information:

- The financial history and condition of the company or companies and the banks concerned.
- Prospects after the merger, if the merger is permitted.
- The Charter of Management.
- Effects of the proposed merger on the needs and welfare of the communities.
- Whether or not the proposed M & A would expand the size or extent of the bank involved beyond limits consistent with adequate and sound banking.

3.4.1 Antitrust Regulations

The Antitrust Department of the Department of Justice has advisory responsibility over bank merger activities primarily because the Sherman Act and the Clayton Act often apply to M & A deals in the banking industry. The antitrust policy, as related to M & A, is designed to prevent business combinations that would lead to a substantial increase in market power. Market power is not easily determinable and can be driven by a variety of forces (e.g., profitability, efficiency) unrelated to business combinations. Thus, regulators and antitrust authorities examine the structural characteristics of the affected markets measured by market concentration to determine the likely market power and competitive impact of a proposed business combination.

The two regulatory authorities assessing M & A transactions among commercial banks in the United States, the Federal Reserve Board and the Department of Justice (DOJ), have traditionally employed different approaches in enforcing antitrust policies. The Office of the Comptroller of the Currency (OCC) and the Federal Deposit Insurance Corporation (FDIC) also have regulatory jurisdiction for antitrust enforcement in the banking industry. The OCC and the FDIC have followed more lenient antitrust policies than the Federal Reserve Board and the DOJ in recent years. This is evidenced by the fact that neither the OCC nor the FDIC has denied a proposed M & A deal on competitive grounds in the past ten years while the Board and DOJ have challenged and caused modification of many proposed M & A transactions.

The four important antitrust issues relevant to all M & A in the banking industry are:

- Geographic market definition.
- Product market definition.

- Structural guidelines.
- Mitigating factors.

(a)   Geographic Market Definition

The first step in antitrust assessment is to determine the proper market definition, which can be defined as a product (or group of products) and a geographic area in which the product is sold.[5] Geographic markets are often defined locally, such as a metropolitan statistical area (MSA) or a non-MSA county. Since financial institutions provide a wide variety of financial services to a wide variety of customers throughout the nation and now, with the use of Internet banking, worldwide, it is difficult to define geographic banking markets. Global competition opportunities and technological advances have reduced barriers to entry and expanded the size of markets. Markets are becoming more open, which in turn makes it more difficult for antitrust policymakers to precisely define the relevant geographic and product market.

(b)   Product Market Definition

The Federal Reserve Board and DOJ have traditionally defined the relevant banking product market for antitrust assessment and purposes as the cluster of financial services offered by commercial banks. Financial institutions provide a cluster of financial services to their clients, including deposits, loans, transaction activities, and other asset management services. However, regulators have commonly used total deposits as measures of concentration. These agencies have traditionally used total deposits as a proxy for the ability of commercial banks to provide this cluster of financial services to both businesses and individuals in a given local geographic banking market. However, the use of Internet banking has expanded the geographic boundaries of banking markets and made it possible and easier for bank customers to split their various financial services among a number of providers. This may result in a substantial weakening of the clustering of bank services, which makes the antitrust policies in banking less predictable. Furthermore, the new wave of consolidation and convergence makes the use of total deposits less relevant as a proxy for the measure of concentration and market power.

(c)   Structural Guidelines

The impact of the proposed M & A deals on market structure is the next step in assessing the deal for antitrust policy purposes after clearly defining geographic and product markets. The primary purpose of U.S. antitrust policy is to prevent M & A activities that could lead to a substantial increase in market power, which may discourage healthy competition in the market. Determination of direct market power is not easily attainable because of the lack of specific, reliable, and relevant information for measuring market power. Thus, antitrust authorities generally investigate the structural characteristics of the affected market to determine the likely competitive effect of a proposed M & A deal. The competitive impact is measured in terms of the potential effect of the proposed M & A deal on market concentration.

The Justice Department and banking authorities use the Herfindahl-Hirschman Index (HHI) as a first-cut assessment of the likely impact of a proposed M & A on competition. The HHI is calibrated as the sum of the squares of the deposit market shares of all entities (e.g., banking organizations) in the market. The HHI is a static measure that determines market concentration at a single point in time. Mathematically, it can be depicted as:[6]

$$HHI = \sum_{i=1}^{n} (MS_i)^2$$

where

MS is the market share of the bank *i*, and
N is the number of banks in the market.

Market structure (e.g., number, size, distribution, market shares) affects the degree of competition in the banking industry, which is often measured by the HHI. The HHI is calculated by adding up the squares of the deposit shares of participants in a banking market and multiplying by 10,000. For example, if there are four banks in a given market and their deposit shares are 25 percent each, the HHI would be calculated as $[(.25)^2 + (.25)^2 + (.25)^2 + (.25)^2] \times 10,000 = 2500$. The HHI index of 10,000 is set for a monopoly market and decreases as the number of banks entering the market increases. Here is another example: if the number of banks increases to five, each having 20 percent of the market, the HHI would be 2000 $[(5)(.20)^2 (10,000)]$. This shows that an M & A deal may cause increases in the HHI because the number of banks in a given market decreases. Thus, antitrust regulators often use the HHI to screen bank M & A applications for potential monopoly or anticompetition. According to the 1982 DOJ guidelines, the HHI level of less than 1,000 is presumed to be unconcentrated and therefore not anticompetitive. The HHI level of 1,000 is considered moderately concentrated, and the HHI level of greater than 1,800 is viewed as highly concentrated and therefore anticompetitive.

The DOJ has issued merger guidelines based on the HHI for all industries, including the banking industry. The HHI is relevant in assessing the proposed bank M & A by considering every competitor in a market and by measuring the structural effect of the proposed merger in a particular market. The antitrust enforcement agencies have developed a numerical standard using the Herfindahl-Hirschman Index (HHI) to determine the degree of concentration resulting from a proposed M & A. If a proposed M & A would result in an HHI less than 1,800 (equivalent to having five or six equal-sized firms) or would increase the HHI by fewer than 200 points (market share of 10 percent), then the proposal would be very unlikely to raise antitrust concerns.[7] These numerical standards are not deciding rules, but rather are guidelines to assess the changes and level of concentration that may be caused by the M & A proposal. The Federal Reserve Board has also employed the acquiring firm's market share as an additional merger screen. For example, if an acquirer's proforma market share would exceed 35 percent, the acquisition proposal would be subject to a more stringent antitrust assessment.

(d)   Mitigating Factors

The primary purpose of antitrust analysis is to determine whether a merger is likely to result in the exercise of market power. The Federal Reserve Board or DOJ assess the effects of each merger or market concentration and the ability of the combined institution to influence the pricing of financial services both to individuals and businesses. Thus, in addition to other considerations, the mitigating factors in M & A transactions are important in assessing M & A proposals. The Federal Reserve Board, in 1997, performed a major review of its antitrust policies and procedures. This review confirmed existing policies in the areas of (1) use of the cluster of banking services as the standard product line for this assessment of the effects of M & A activities on competition, and (2) use of local geographic markets as the standard for defining a market or changes in market concentration. In assessing the effectiveness of current antitrust policies and procedures, Kwast (1999, p. 636) wrote "while antitrust constraints will occasionally affect the terms and conditions for consummation of a bank merger, the antitrust laws do not significantly constrain the vast majority of bank mergers and acquisitions."[8]

When a proposed M & A would violate the benchmark 1800/200/35 percent initial merger screen, the Board examines various factors that might mitigate any anti-competitive effects that might arise from the change in structure. Examples of mitigating factors considered in assessing a proposed banking M & A are: (1) the competitive effect of potential entrants into local banking markets; (2) long-term market decline, acquisition of a failing banking organization; and (3) improved efficiency and effectiveness of combined institution.[9]

Noncompliance with the established antitrust policies should prevent M & A deals. Nevertheless, the number of proposed M & A denials for financial institutions has been very low during the past several years. Indeed, the Board has denied only two merger applications in the past several years and both denials were of acquisitions of thrift institutions in rural banking markets.[10] However, simulations have indicated that the number of banking organizations in the United States could drop from its current level of 7.300 to 6 without ever violating the Board HHI M & A guidelines.[11]

A number of studies have investigated the relationship between measures of market concentration and combined companies' profitability or prices. These studies (Werden, Joskow, and Johnson, 1989; Brorenstein, 1990; Kim and Singal, 1993)[12, 13, 14] examine the effects on airfares of horizontal mergers in the airline industry and they concluded that: (1) these mergers led to increased fares and reduced services on the affected routes; (2) the fare increases tended to occur prior to merger consummation, and (3) the increased market power was associated with business combinations.

Two recent studies (Akhavein, Berges, and Humphrey, 1998; Prager and Hannan, 1998)[15, 16] examined the profit efficiency and pricing effects of mergers in the banking industry. These studies found: (1) no evidence of significant price effects (service fees) attributable to these business combinations; and (2) that merged banks, on average, exhibited greater reduction in deposit interest rates (a price paid to customers by banks) than non-merged banks.

The DOJ and bank authorities apply the HHI to all mergers in the banking industry to assess the effects of a proposed bank merger on competition and to determine the possible violation of antitrust laws. The DOJ has issued M & A guidelines based on the HHI for banking and other industries. The guidelines suggest that if a banking merger shows an increase in the HHI of over 200 points in a given market (50 points in other industries) to a level greater than 1,800, the bank should be further assessed for antitrust enforcement. It is obvious that the more lenient standard, as measured by the changes in the HHI, applies to the banking industry as compared to other industries. This more lenient standard is designed to account roughly for competition from nonbank financial services providers (e.g., credit unions and finance companies). Furthermore, the Federal Reserve Board takes into consideration the 50 percent of the deposits held by nonbank thrift institutions in a market in calculating the HHI. This HHI is typically used on a first-cut indicator of the effects of a proposed merger on competition and, thus, merging banks that violate these standards are often approved upon the presence of some mitigating factors demonstrating potential competition. Even the disapproved mergers may eventually get approved conditional on the merging bank selling some of its branches to other banks to reduce the noncompetitive structural impact of the merger.

Traditionally, banks were restricted by law to operate locally. Restrictions on interstate and intrastate banking made them unable to expand their geographical markets. These restrictions were somehow relaxed in the 1980s and especially with the passage of the Riegle-Neal Interstate Banking and Branching Efficiency Act of 1994. This act allows interstate branching into almost all states that promote M & A in the banking industry. The deregulation of geographical restraints on bank competition has improved banks' performance in increasing shareholder value by becoming more efficient or otherwise being acquired by more profitable banks. However, the Riegle-Neal Act, by restricting the total amount of deposits of the merged banks to 30 percent in a single state and 10 percent nationally, did not significantly liberalize consolidation and integration in the banking industry. The Glass-Steagall Act and related legislation significantly restricted convergence in the financial services industry by limiting banks' ability to underwrite securities. Liberalization of these restrictions began in the late 1980s with the Federal Reserve allowing: (1) bank holding companies to underwrite corporate debt and equity through "Section 20" affiliates and (2) revenue from underwriting corporate debt and equity to be as much as 25 percent of the affiliate's total revenue. This liberalization has been a powerful force behind several large M & A between bank holding companies and securities firms. Finally, the passage of the GLB financial modernization act of 1999 significantly liberalized M & A in the financial services industry by allowing business combinations between banks, insurance companies, investment firms, and mutual funds.

A study conducted by the Federal Deposit Insurance Corporation in 1999 concluded that merger mania during the 1990s has made the Bank Insurance Fund more likely to become insolvent in coming years.[17] The recent bank failures in 1999 (e.g., First National Bank of Keystone in West Virginia and Best Bank of Boulder, Colorado) have created some interest in the need for bank deposit insurance reform. Large banks are far less likely to fail than small banks because of economies of scale, less dependence on domestic deposits for funding, better risk diversification, and fewer insured deposits per asset dollar. However, given that large banks now control a great portion of all industry deposits, the failure of just one large megamerged bank could be very detrimental to the future solvency of the bank insurance deposit fund.

3.5 TRENDS TOWARD BUSINESS COMBINATIONS IN THE FINANCIAL SERVICES INDUSTRY

Traditionally, customers have had their checking and savings accounts at a bank, their mortgages at the saving and loan association (mortgage company), their insurance services with insurance firms, and their investment activities with investing companies, mutual funds, and brokerage firms. This traditional model of receiving and providing financial services is deemed to disappear upon the proper implementation of the GLB financial modernization act of 1999. The global financial markets are becoming more interconnected, and the financial services industry has moved toward expanding its financial services through more global competition driven by advances in technology, communication, and global financial innovations. Finally, the Congress has passed the GLB Act to recognize these realities by changing old laws and now permitting business combinations

Exhibit 3.5   M & A Policy Responses

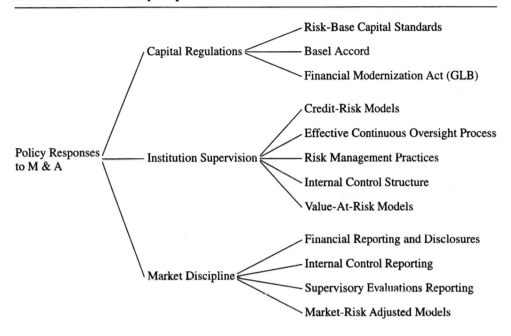

in the financial services industry. Market-driven responses and discipline are probably the best policy responses to changes in the combined institutions. Banking authorities, regulators, and supervisors should not get involved directly in micro-managing the merging institutions; however, they should assume oversight responsibility to prevent substantial negative externalities to the institutions, customers, financial services industry and system, and taxpayers who provide the ultimate funding behind the safety net. Policymakers and regulators should also prevent significant increases in market power from either in-market or market-extension M & A.

Policymakers should disregard this public and market misconception and moral hazard of "too-big-to-fail." Institutions of any size, especially merged institutions, are subject to failure, resulting from inefficiency and ineffectiveness. In the case of convergence, when banks combine with other financial services providers (e.g., insurance, mutual funds) it is possible that the safety net may extend beyond banking. While it is difficult to completely prevent the risks of non-banking activities spreading to the insured bank and giving some of the benefits of the safety net to the non-banking activity, banking authorities should take proper actions to ensure that no assistance or bail-out of non-banking affiliates is provided. Exhibit 3.5 shows suggested policy responses to the wave of M & A in the financial services industry.

The evolution of M & A in the financial services industry starts with consolidation of local banks to improve their efficiency and effectiveness, to mergers across the nation to expand geographical services and create synergies, and now convergence to consolidate all financial services. The ultimate liberalization in the financial services industry would be achieved by globalization of the industry through cross-border integration. The torrid role of M & A in the financial services industry is expected to continue in the twenty-first century. Future M & A deals will be motivated by a loosening in regulations, technological advancements, a desire by large financial institutions to offer a variety of financial services (e.g., insurance, loans, and investments), and the lure of new markets.

3.6 MOTIVES FOR BUSINESS COMBINATIONS

The primary goal and motive behind almost all M & A deals in the financial services industry is congruent with the main purpose for the existence of business entities—maximizing shareholder value. The increase in the shareholder's wealth of the acquiring entity either could be a result of value created by the M & A deal or could result from a wealth transfer from bondholders to shareholders with no change in the total market value of the combined entity. This can be achieved by: (1) improving the efficiency and effectiveness of the combined institutions through economies of scale and cost saving; (2) increasing their market power in selling prices and service fees, and (3) increasing their access to the safety net. When two entities combine, the merged entity is expected to make more money. Other factors that may be important in an M & A deal are synergies, economies of scale, market presence, culture, cost cutting, revenue improvement, and expanding operations and territory.

Several hypotheses have been advanced to explain the motives for business combinations, especially the current M & A wave. These hypotheses, their justifications and rationales, and empirical evidence substantiating the hypotheses are presented in Exhibit 3.6. These hypotheses attempt to explain the capital market reaction to target and acquirer firms. Some of these hypotheses assume a non-wealth creating behavior on the part of acquirers (e.g., hubris hypothesis) and predict that the share price of target firms will rise and those of acquirers will drop with no net aggregate wealth creation. Other hypotheses assume a wealth-creating behavior predicting that the share prices of target firms will rise with no impact on share prices of acquirers. The current megamergers in the financial services industry have created an offering of universal financial services. For example, the merger of Citicorp and the Travelers group as Citigroup has provided one-stop shopping for all financial services. Citicorp has been a leader in consumer and corporate banking, credit cards, and consumer loans. Travelers has been a major provider of insurance, securities, and investment banking services. The combined Citigroup now serves as a kind of supermarket for a variety of financial services.

3.7 DETERMINANTS OF MERGERS AND ACQUISITIONS

The wave of the current megamerger is part of a convergence trend in the financial services industry that began in the early 1980s to share risk and save costs. This is evident by a substantial decrease in the number of financial institutions in the past decade. For example, between 1981 and 1997, the number of banks and savings and loan associations decreased to about 40 percent (from more than 18,000 to less than 11,000).

M & A deals are becoming a common practice in the financial services industry; thus, related challenges should be properly addressed to ensure success of these deals. The challenges to execute an M & A deal include both the opportunities to achieve a profitable M & A deal (e.g., financial benefits to both shareholders of the acquirer and target institution) and obstacles during the combination process where both human and physical resources are eventually forced to join. Thus, both financial opportunities and the related obstacles (e.g., different corporate cultures) should be examined and assessed when contemplating an M & A deal.

Admitting that it is impossible to identify all causes and effects of the current merger wave in the financial services industry, the purpose is to explain and understand the most recent mergers. Nevertheless, the current rapid pace of M & A can be attributed to several factors. Exhibit 3.7 presents the summary of possible determinants of current M & A in financial institutions. First, the ever-increasing number of M & A would have been impossible without the elimination of the traditional interstate and branching restrictions. Second, the level of concentration gives more market power and purchasing power to acquire other banks. Although banking in the United States is relatively fragmented nationally compared to other industries (e.g., automobile, soft drink), the five largest banks have recently doubled their market share. Unlike other industries (automobile, manufacturing) banks have traditionally provided financial services to local customers, which discourages excessive concentration at the national level. Thus, most mergers occur across local markets rather than within them, which in turn makes measures of concentration virtually constant at the local level, despite the wave of the consolidation nationally.

Third, the substantial advances in information technology, communications, and data processing play an important role in facilitating and making M & A virtually possible in the banking industry. The use of automated teller machines (ATMs), electronic data interchange (EDI), financial EDI (FEDI), and Internet banking enables banks to manage information databases more effectively and efficiently. The benefits of the technological advances in offering financial services via Internet and computer networks and reducing the data processing costs can be more effectively realized by bigger banks. Thus, technology is considered as the fundamental force driving the merger wave. Fourth, the extraordinary abundance of financial capital (money) and stock prices resulting from high earnings available for investment has encouraged the ever-increasing merger wave. The excess capital has gone into stocks, which has pushed their values to a high level in the past decade and encouraged shareholders of both the acquirer and target to take advantages of M & A deals. The globally abundant financial capital resulted from globalization of economies and businesses, lower trade barriers, technological advances, and privatization, which are considered other important forces driving M & A transactions.

3.8 PERCEIVED SHORTCOMINGS OF M & A

Merger critics have argued several perceived shortcomings of an M & A deal: diminished services, higher service fees, decreased credit availability, and undesirable impacts on competition.[18]

3.8.1 Diminished Services

People are naturally resistant to change, and especially when a bank is taken over, they find it easier to complain about the quality of financial services they receive. The perception toward diminished services can be explained by three main reasons. First, the consolidation

Exhibit 3.6 Motivational Hypotheses for Mergers and Acquisitions

Motivational Hypothesis	Justifications and Reasonings	Empirical Evidence
1. Economies of Scale	1. Combination of two or more entities yields an increase in effectiveness and efficiency of the combined business (e.g., increases in productivity and outputs; decreases in long-term costs.) 2. Unit cost decreases as size increases.	Jensen and Ruback (1983) found evidence of economies of scale resulting from M & A deals.
2. Inefficient Management	1. The acquirer tends to buyout inefficient management of the target firms and make it efficient.	Hannan and Rhoades (1987) rejected the hypothesis that poorly-managed firms are more likely acquisition targets than other firms.
3. Re-Engineering	1. Cost savings resulting from the divestiture and internal restructuring decisions made prior to or subsequent to the business combination.	Cheng, Gup, and Wall (1989) found evidence in support of re-engineering as a motivation factor for bank acquisition.
4. Power	1. Optimizing size by eliminating duplication and lowering unit costs of financial services. 2. Increases in the size of the business resulting from M & A and the relationship between the size and the proposed management compensation and self interest.	Phillips and Pavel (1986) found acquiring firms use mergers as a vehicle to increase their market share and profits.
5. Geographic and Product Diversification	1. Enhanced profitability and risk moderation through geographic and product diversification.	Piper and Weiss (1971) argued M & A occurs to overcome geographical limits on bank expansion.
6. Revenue Enhancement	1. The impact of the business combination on the wealth of shareholders of the combined entity (e.g., shareholder wealth maximization.)	Hunter and Wall (1989) found that profitability measured by return on equity and core-deposit growth of acquired banks had consistently

7. Tax	1. A merger will create wealth to shareholders whenever the tax liability of the combination is smaller than the sum of the tax liability of the two individual firms.	Rose (1988) concluded that expected: (1) increases in profitability, market share, growth rate, market power, and stock price; and (2) decrease in tax liabilities were considered as the important motives to pursue merger activities.
8. New Business Opportunities	1. Creation of new business opportunities and market expansion through M & A.	Cheng, Gup, and Wall (1989) and Palia (1993) concluded that new business opportunities play an important role in bank's takeover.
9. Decrease Risk	1. Reduction in inherent business risk resulting from diversification.	Asquith and Kim (1982) did not find evidence in support of the diversification hypothesis.
10. Hubris	1. There is no gain to be realized from corporate takeovers primarily because financial markets, product markets, and labor markets are assumed to be totally efficient.	Roll (1986) concluded that any perceived monetary gains of mergers are offset by the true economic value of the combined firm.
11. Synergy	1. There is a potential reduction in production and/or administrative costs when two or more entities combine.	Mueller (1980) found that non-merging firms outperformed merging firms indicating that mergers lead to a reduction in profitability with no synergic effect.
12. Information	1. The shares of some firms are incorrectly valued by the market because relevant information about those firms are not available to the public.	Firth (1980) found a permanent rise in the price of target firms even in the case of unsuccessful tender offers.

Exhibit 3.7   Determinants of M & A

1. Regulations	1. Lowering the restrictions on branching.
	2. The passage of the Reigle-Neal Interstate Banking Act of 1994 eliminating interstate banking restrictions.
	3. The passage of the Financial Modernization Act of 1999 (GLB) allowing consolidation in the financial services industry.
2. Reporting and Accounting Standards	1. Generally Accepted Accounting Principles (GAAP) vs. Regulatory Accounting Principles (RAP).
	2. Fair value standards.
	3. Exposure Draft on eliminating pooling of interest methods.
3. Technological Advancements	1. Advances in communication and data processing technology.
	2. Internet banking.
	3. Use of Web sites.
4. Business Practices	1. Increases in the nationwide level of concentration in financial institutions.
	2. Increases in earning power and earning quality.
	3. Expanding financial services provided.
	4. Steady increases in bank stock prices.
	5. Increases in number of banks.
	6. Reduction in bank failures.
5. Economic Factors	1. Economic growth.
	2. Low interest rates.
	3. Abundance of money available for investment.
	4. Excess financial capital.

and convergence may cause changes in the mix and pricing of financial services, which may not be viewed favorably by customers preferring the traditional financial services mix. Second, the economies of scales that make the merger more cost effective may dictate the standardization of financial services offered by the combined financial institution, which can inconvenience customers who are accustomed to tailored services. Third, as banks merge into larger institutions, there is a possibility that the combined institution may lose its focus on providing high-touch financial services tailored to satisfy their customers' demands. The possibility of lower-touch banking may adversely affect the well-established banking relationships with many customers.

3.8.2   High Financial Services Fees

There is no empirical evidence that indicates that the merged financial institutions charge higher fees for similar services after the combination. However, service fees on deposits as a percentage of deposits have risen by 42 percent for all banks and by 67 percent for large banks during the past decade.[19] This steady increase in service charges, especially by bigger banks, may increase customers' perception that merged banks charge higher fees than smaller local community banks. Larger national banks often do charge higher fees for services such as checking accounts, overdrafts, and the use of automated teller machines than small local commercial banks.

3.8.3 Credit Availability

Small community banks, in most cases, by virtue of having high-touch banking relation-ships with their local customers can tailor their financial services to their customers' needs. These specialized customized financial services can positively affect the availability of credit to small businesses. The larger megamerged banks may not be able to maintain close lines of communication between their lending officers and customers. However, large banks can overcome this perceived negative effect of mergers by offering loan convenience such as loan applications being made over the phone or the Web.

3.8.4 Undesirable Impacts on Competition

The recent wave of mergers in the financial services industry has raised concern with their impact on competition. This concern has gotten the attention of policymakers and bank au-thorities to assess the social and private benefits of M & A and to ensure that consolidations in financial institutions are not detrimental to potentially vulnerable bank customers. Stra-ham and Weston[20] found that smaller banks tend to invest a greater proportion of their as-sets in smaller loans than do larger banks. Berger et al.[21] and Berger et al.[22] concluded that consolidations resulting from loosening of geographical restrictions led to a decline in the supply and quality of small business loans. Prager and Hannan[23] found evidence that indi-cates merging banks tend to significantly decrease deposit interest rates compared to non-merging banks during the twelve months prior to and subsequent to a merger suggesting that merging banks are not passing on efficiency gains to their customers.

There is a gap between what managers and investors expect from an M & A deal and what employees and customers desire from such a deal. Generally speaking, shareholders and managers are expecting a more efficient and effective combined institution resulting from an M & A deal. Employees and customers, on the other hand, may view business com-binations as reductions in jobs and services. One reason for these expectations is too much emphasis on management and financial issues and inadequate attention to other factors such as corporate culture, team-spirit chemistries, technological advances, banking systems, and human resources, general negative attitudes toward M & A deals, and hostile feelings as-sociated with convergence.

Employees typically view M & A deals as threats to their position by jeopardizing their job security through cost reduction, downsizing and resulted layoffs, or competition be-tween staff. Non-managerial employees might view an M & A deal as a threat and react with apathy due to the lack of proper participation and involvement during the initial plan-ning stages. Managerial employees, on the other hand, may view the M & A deal as an op-portunity to seize power and to advance, especially if they were involved during the tran-sition phase of the M & A deal. Thus, proper communication with affected employees and encouragement of their participation during the various stages of M & A could prevent many problems during the due diligence, execution, and implementation of the business combination.

Continuous communication with all affected management, employees, shareholders, and major customers of both the acquiring and target institution is an effective means of re-ducing and controlling rumors and wild predictions during the M & A process. Since there can be a long period of time between the announcement of a merger and the consummation of the M & A deal, negotiation teams should continuously communicate steps of the process to the affected employees by means of conferences, speeches, newsletters, direct mail, lobby displays, and videotapes. This allows people to feel that they are participating in the process and gives them an opportunity to understand the changes that will be taking place and the reasons for them. This communication should focus on the advantages of the consolidation and convergence, the growth potential and opportunities to improve services, the role of employees in the combined institution, and how the business combination can contribute to the achievement of their personal and professional goals.

3.9   STUDIES ON MERGERS AND ACQUISITIONS

Early empirical studies on M & A (e.g., Smith)[24] found that the profitability of acquired firms was not significantly greater than that of non-merging firms. Empirical results on capital market reactions to M & A announcements are controversial and inconsistent. For example, Piper and Weiss[25] found that acquisitions by bank holding companies between 1947 and 1967 yielded no increase in earnings per share. James and Wier[26] concluded that gains to acquirer firms are positively related to the number of alternative target firms and negatively associated with the number of other potential bidders in the market. More recent studies[27, 28] found that merger premiums were associated with the regulatory environments for both acquirer and target banks and their characteristics (e.g., inefficient management, synergy, and new business opportunities). Exhibit 3.8 summarizes the findings of a number of studies on M & A.

Rose[29] surveyed 591 national and state-chartered banking institutions to gather information on their motives for M & A deals. The survey results indicate that expected increases in profitability, market share, growth rate, market power, and stock price were considered as the important motives needed to pursue their merger activities.

Curry[30] examined a large sample (1,156 banks) to determine the pre-acquisition characteristics of the banks acquired by multi-bank holding companies (MBHCs) during the period of 1969 to 1972. Curry found significant associations between dependent variables such as risk, pricing behavior, operating efficiency, and profitability and independent variables of market growth, bank growth, the state branching code, and the size of banks. Curry concluded that MBHCs tend to acquire "typical" commercial banks instead of acquiring the target banks with unique operating attributes.

Hannan & Rhoades[31] analyzed 201 Texas banking organizations acquired between 1971 and 1982 according to the locations of their acquiring banks (e.g., outside or inside the target banking organizations' markets). They found that: (1) a poorly managed bank measured by several different ratios (e.g., return on equity, return on assets) did not have significant influence on the probability of being acquired; (2) bank capitalization ratio (e.g., capital assets) showed a significant negative relationship with the probability of being acquired; and (3) a higher market share of a target bank increased the probability of being acquired, especially when its acquirer comes from the outside market.

Beatty et al.[32] examined a number of factors that may determine a bank merger premium and found that higher merger premiums (purchase price to book ratio) were paid to target banks that had a higher proportion of risky assets in the asset portfolio, were well managed and profitable, and were located in a non-competitive banking environment.

Exhibit 3.8 Empirical Studies of M & A

Studies	Findings
Smith 1971	Found that the profitability of acquired banks was not significantly greater than that of non-merging banks.
Lev and Mandelker 1972	Focusing on the areas of risk, growth rate, and financial structure, they found that the monetary returns to shareholders of the acquiring firm were higher but not statistically different than those of shareholders of non-merging firms.
Dodd 1980	Shareholders of target firms earned large positive abnormal returns from the announcement of merger proposals.
Piper and Weiss 1971	Acquisitions by bank holding companies between 1947–1967 yielded no increase in earnings per share.
Hannan and Wolken 1989	Found evidence that indicates that target firms show positive returns on an average of 11.2 percent the day before merger announcement while acquiring firms accrue negative returns of four percent of the day prior to the day of merger announcements.
Asquith and Kim 1982	Using a paired comparison of bond returns, found no evidence in support of the diversification hypothesis.
James and Weir 1987	Found that gains to acquirer firms are positively related to the number of alternative target firms and negatively associated with the number of other potential bidders in the market.
DeAngelo, DeAngelo, and Rice 1984	The offers (bids) are made in cash when a bidding firm perceives its stock to be undervalued. The bid offers are typically made with stock when the bidding firm perceives its stock to be overvalued.
Varaiya 1986	Found that any premium paid over the market price in an M & A deal is the result of a positive error in the estimate of value by buyer management.
James and Weir 1987	Found evidence in support of positive target shareholders returns and negative bidding shareholder returns.
Cheng, Gup, and Wall 1989	Concluded that target bank profitability, capital adequacy, management efficiency, size, diversification, and leverage are collectively significant in explaining the premium paid by the acquirer bank.
Servacs 1991	Found that the takeover gains were larger if the target company is performing poorly and the buying company is performing well.
Healy, Palepu, and Ruback 1992	Found significant improvements in operating cash flows from increased asset productivity resulting from business combinations.
Cornett and Tehranian 1992	Found improved returns and cash flow for a sample of bank acquisitions resulting from attracting more loans, more deposits, improving productivity, and increasing assets.
Palia 1993	Concluded that merger premiums were associated with the regulatory environments for both acquirer and target banks as well as the characteristics of both the acquirer and target banks (inefficient management, synergy, and new business opportunities).

Exhibit 3.8 *(Continued)*

Studies	Findings
Gart and Al-jafari 1993	Found that banks' core deposits, leverage, return on assets, state deposit cap restrictions, and non-performing assets as well as the method of accounting (pooling versus purchase) are statistically significant in explaining the premium paid by the acquirer bank to the target bank.
Hadlock, Houston, and Ryngaert 1999	Found that banks with higher levels of management ownership are less likely to be acquired, especially in a situation where target managers depart from their jobs following the acquisition.
Brewer, Jackson, Juliani, and Nguyen 2000	Provided evidence that indicates that the passage of the Riegle-Neal Interstate Act has increased the demand for target banks as the number of potential bidders increases, resulting in higher M & A prices.

Rose (1988a)[33] analyzed data for all U.S. commercial banks that completed mergers between 1970 and 1980 and concluded that: (1) acquiring banks had a larger market share of deposits and loans as well as faster growth and less efficiency in comparison with non-merging banks; and (2) target banks showed larger market shares, faster growth in deposits and loans, and more efficiency than non-merging banks.

Fraser and Kolari (1988)[34] found a positive relationship between merger premiums defined as the market-to-book ratio and target banks' financial ratios measured as net income/total assets, demand deposits/time deposits, and leverage. Hunter & Wall (1989)[35] concluded that profitability measured by return on equity and core-deposit growth of acquired banks had consistently important effects on a merger premium. Cheng et al. (1989)[36] found a significant positive relationship between a target bank's profitability, core-deposit growth, loan quality, and a merger premium and negative association between the total asset growth of the acquiring bank, the relative ratio of the asset sizes (e.g., the total assets of the acquired/the total assets of the acquiring bank), and a merger premium.

O'Keefe (1996)[37] analyzed merger-related data for U.S. commercial and savings banks between 1984 and 1995 and found that: (1) acquired banks, in general, had lower earnings and higher liquid asset portfolios than non-merging banks; and (2) the probability of becoming a target increases when the regulator rate on earnings is poor measured by capital adequacy, asset quality, management quality, earnings, and liquidity.

Several recent studies examined the effect of certain variables, such as interest rates, interest-rate exposures, management incentives, corporate governance, and performance on the level of M & A activities. Esty et al. (1999) concluded that (1) the level of M & A activity is more positively associated with equity indices and more negatively correlated with interest rates for banks than non-banks; and (2) merger pricing is a function of the interest-rate environment in the sense that acquirers are paying higher prices and earning lower returns when rates are low. Hadlock et al. (1999)[39] found that (1) banks with higher levels of management ownership are less likely to be acquired, especially in a situation where target managers depart from their jobs following the acquisition; (2) high rates of management turnover follow bank acquisition; and (3) corporate governance or performance variables are not systematically related to the probability a bank is acquired.

Brewer et al. (2000)[40] investigated whether (1) prices offered to target banks have been increased over time; (2) increased prices encourage bank owners to sell; and (3) prices are correlated with the financial characteristics of target banks and their market structure. They concluded that, prior to the Riegle-Neal Interstate Banking and Branching Efficiency Act of 1994, the number of potential bidders for a given target bank was limited by laws governing intrastate and interstate M & A activities. The passage of the Riegle-Neal Act has increased the demand for target banks as the number of potential bidders increases, resulting in higher M & A prices. Brewer et al. (2000) found (1) higher performance targets, as measured by both return on assets and return on equity, receive higher bids; (2) the lower the capital-to-deposit ratio, the larger the bid the acquiring bank is willing to offer; (3) larger targets' loan-to-assets ratios are associated with larger bid premiums; (4) bank size is positively correlated with bid premiums; (5) market concentration is not related to bid premiums; (6) changes in state and federal banking regulations have a significant impact on both bank merger activity and prices; (7) there are higher bid premiums in Southeast compact states relative to other parts of the country; and (8) when target banks are large, but not megamergers of equals, there is a greater stock market reaction to the merger announcement than for other target banks, indicating that large banks are using their increased freedom to merge in a way intended to increase the value of their deposit insurance.

3.10   MERGERS AND ACQUISITIONS PROCESS

Exhibit 3.9 summarizes the ten phases of a typical M & A process. Although every M & A transaction is unique, this ten-step process provides an overview of most M & A transactions and describes many of the various aspects of a carefully-planned M & A deal. Chapter 12 describes the M & A process in more depth from banks' point of view. The chronology of M & A activities in financial institutions consists of the following:

- Developing M & A strategy.
- Identifying and selecting the potential M & A target(s).
- Identifying key issues.
- Structuring the transaction.
- Starting the due diligence process of dialogue with the target.
- Negotiating the transaction.
- Discussing financial issues including pricing the transaction.
- Assessing all relevant M & A risks.
- Closing the transaction.
- Designing and implementing integration.

Exhibit 3.9 M & A Process

Phase	Description
1. Strategy Development	Establish M & A strategy consistent with your organization's overall mission, goals, and needs to grow through business combinations.
2. Target Identification and Selection	Identify, screen, and select potential targets based on the criteria designed to achieve M & A strategy and to minimize M & A risk.
3. Risk Assessment	Identify all related M & A risks including: (1) operating risk that the combined business does not perform as expected at the time the M & A was approved; (2) overpayment risk of paying too much premium to the target entity; and (3) financial risk of not having adequate financial resources to meet debt service requirements of the combined entity. These risks should be assessed and then minimized in order for an M & A transaction to be a successful one.
4. Key Issues Identification	Identify key relevant issues and trends and incorporate them into the due diligence team.
5. Transaction Structure	Schedule the initial meeting between two parties (the potential target and acquirer). Key issues such as negotiating strategies, financing options, deal structure, and price should be discussed in the initial meeting. Structure the M & A transaction in such a way that is good for both buyer and seller.
6. Due Diligence Process	Identify and evaluate potential deal breakers and gather information that can be used to determine the purchase price and transaction structure reflected in the non-binding letter of intent. Ensure that functional specialists (e.g., accountants, appraisers, arbitragers, attorneys, risk management consultants) all get involved in this due diligence process. Analyze the target's historical operations, products, profitability, capital spending, and working capital sensitivity.
7. Negotiation	Negotiate the final M & A transaction by addressing issues such as the purchase price, the structure, and other key important issues and considerations including accounting, tax, and employee benefits.
8. Financial Structure	The financial structure depends on the size of the transaction and the nature and quality of both the target and acquirer organization. Incorporate the following factors in the financial structure: estimated purchase price, the maximum amount of equity needed; the projected amount of cash flow needed; and the method of financing the required cash flow (e.g., debt, equity).
9. Closing	Consummate the M & A transaction by completing the due diligence, reviewing all of the closing documents, exchanging financial consideration, and distributing all necessary documents to the proper authorities.
10. Integration	Design and implement the changes necessary to integrate a new acquisition into an existing business. Consider relevant actions such as downsizing, eliminating duplicated overhead, developing new cash management/treasury systems, consolidating accounting and management information systems, and transitioning new employee benefits plans.

3.10.1 Strategy Development

The first consideration in developing M & A strategy is to decide whether or not an acquisition or even a merger is an appropriate strategy for growth. The M & A strategy should be consistent with the acquirer's overall mission, objectives, and goals to grow through business combinations. The M & A strategy should clearly define financial objectives, acquisition criteria, and acquisition budget. Financial objectives including purchase price will vary depending on the unique characteristics of a target entity and its industry. The acquisition criteria should specify the objective(s) of acquisition as: (1) diversification of products, services, and related business risk; (2) expansion of market share by acquiring competitors; and (3) vertical integration by acquiring suppliers and distributors. The acquisition budget should specify qualifications, talents, and plans of management for post-acquisition integration, risk profile of management (e.g., high risk target with a greater potential for high returns versus low risk probability of lower returns), and the required cash flow including the method of financing the purchase price (e.g., debt, equity, or a combination of both). The M & A strategy should also specify the types of financial advisor(s) and intermediaries needed for M & A consultations. Advisors and intermediaries include: accountants, attorneys, business brokers, investment bankers, lending sources (e.g., commercial bankers), and M & A specialized consultants. Exhibit 3.10 provides a list of financial advisors, ranked by number of deals and total deal value in 1999 and the first quarter of 2000.

3.10.2 Target Identification and Selection

Identification and selection of acquisition target(s) should be done according to the established acquisition criteria. The first step in searching for target(s) is to select the industry or industries that the acquirer wishes to consider. The industry candidate(s) can be the industry in which the acquirer has business experience with the intention of acquiring potential competitors, suppliers, or customers. The other approach is to consider other industries that have growth potential. The acquirer's acquisition criteria, strengths, and experience should be matched with the particular characteristics of the industry under consideration. The second consideration in target selection is the size and price of the target. The acquisition strategy should specify the minimum and maximum price the acquirer is willing and able to pay for the target. Searching for the potential target(s) can be handled in several ways, including through: intermediaries; personal contacts; professional referral sources such as lawyers, bankers, accountants, and appraisers; industry contacts; and business or M & A publications. The screening process should be based on sound screening criteria of incorporating marketing, production, financing, management, and administrative issues into the consideration. The screening criteria should be consistently and unbiasedly used to reduce the broad universe of potential acquisition candidates to a handful of manageable, likely candidates. The reduced pool of candidates then should be prioritized according to the established screening criteria. The acquirer should obtain adequate relevant information regarding the pool of candidates for acquisition. Exhibit 3.11 provides a sample list of M & A information sources, which should be of great interest to acquirers.

Exhibit 3.10　Top Financial Advisers

Top Financial Advisers, Mid-Atlantic

2000 Q1 Rank	1999 Rank	Firm	Number of Deals	Total Deal Value* ($M)
1	1	McConnell, Budd & Downes, Inc.	3	171.9
2	11	PR Financial LC	2	83.6
2	2	Ryan, Beck & Company	2	187.0
2	4	Sander O'Neill & Partners L.P.	2	136.8
5	11	Advest, Inc.	1	179.5
5	NR	Alex Sheshunoff & Co	1	19.9
5	11	Capital Resources Group, Inc.	1	41.6
5	11	Credit Suisse First Boston Corp.	1	2,618.6
5	4	Danielson Associates	1	179.5
5	NR	The Endicott Group	1	80.3
5	11	Finpro Inc.	1	7.5
5	11	Garland Mc Pherson & Assoc, Inc.	1	97.1
5	6	Goldman, Sachs & Co.	1	2,618.6
5	6	Tucker Anthony Cleary Gull	1	70.2

Top Financial Advisers, Midwest

2000 Q1 Rank	1999 Rank	Firm	Number of Deals	Total Deal Value* ($M)
1	1	Keefe, Bruyette & Woods, Inc.[2]	4	162.1
1	11	RP Financial LC[1]	4	140.2
3	3	GRA, Thompson, White & Co. P.C.	3	6.2
4	2	McDonald Investments Inc.[3]	2	51.7
5	7	Austin Associates, Inc.	1	33.3
%	11	McConnell, Budd, & Downes, Inc.	1	138.7
5	22	Merrill Lynch & Co.	1	479.5
5	NR	Northland Bank Investments	1	12.0
5	NR	Raymond James & Associates Inc.[5]	1	33.3
5	NR	Renninger & Associates, LLC	1	33.4
5	NR	Ryan, Beck, & Company	1	133.4
5	6	Sander O'Neill & Partners L.P.	1	33.8
5	7	Stifel Nicolaus & Co.	1	34.8

Top Financial Advisers, New England

2000 Q1 Rank	1999 Rank	Firm	Number of Deals	Total Deal Value* ($M)
1	2	HAS Associates[1]	1	NA
1	5	McConnell, Budd & Downes, Inc.	1	16.1
1	NR	McDonald Investments Inc.[3]	1	12.1
1	2	Merrill Lynch & Co.	1	16.1
1	NR	New England Business Adviser Inc.	1	12.1

Top Financial Advisers, Southeast

2000 Q1 Rank	1999 Rank	Firm	Number of Deals	Total Deal Value* ($M)
1	19	Sander O'Neill & Partners L.P.	2	1,279.2
2	NR	Austin Associates, Inc.	1	40.0
2	19	Austin Financial Services, Inc.	1	13.4

Exhibit 3.10 *(Continued)*

Top Financial Advisers, Southeast *(continued)*

2000 Q1 Rank	1999 Rank	Firm	Number of Deals	Total Deal Value* ($M)
2	19	Chaffe & Associates, Inc.[1]	1	NA
2	NR	Credit Suisse First Boston Corp.	1	1,930.1
2	NR	J.P. Morgan & Co.	1	1,930.1
2	1	McDonald Investments Inc.[3]	1	77.0
2	14	McKinnon & Company	1	5.8
2	14	Merrill Lynch & Co.	1	1,202.2
2	NR	Morgan Stanley Dean Witter	1	1,930.1
2	19	National Capital Corporation[1]	1	NA
2	NR	Nesbitt Burns	1	13.4
2	19	Orr Management Company	1	303.7
2	2	Robinson-Humphrey[4]	1	303.7
2	19	RP Financial LC	1	77.0
2	NR	Salomon Smith Barney Holdings Inc.	1	303.7

Top Financial Advisers, Southwest

2000 Q1 Rank	1999 Rank	Firm	Number of Deals	Total Deal Value* ($M)
1	4	Alex Sheshunoff & Co.[1]	1	NA
1	NR	Belle Plaine Financial LLC	1	45.5
1	NR	GRA, Thompson, White & Co. P.C.	1	6.1
1	2	Hoefer & Amett, Inc.	1	4.9
1	3	SAMCO Capital Markets[1]	1	NA
1	NR	Stifel Nicolaus & Co.	1	45.5
1	7	The Wallach Company[1]	1	NA

Top Financial Advisers, West

2000 Q1 Rank	1999 Rank	Firm	Number of Deals	Total Deal Value* ($M)
1	3	Hoefer & Amett, Inc.	4	189.9
2	5	Baxter Fentriss and Company	2	46.1
3	7	Alex Sheshunoff & Co.[1]	1	NA
3	NR	Austin Associates, Inc.	1	3.6
3	17	Carpenter & Company	1	6.5
3	NR	Dain Rauscher Corp.	1	40.2
3	1	First Security Van Kasper Inc.	1	89.5
3	NR	SAMCO Capital Markets	1	15.0
3	2	The Findley Companies	1	16.7

[1] Deal value not included for at least one transaction
[2] Includes deals for Charles Webb & Co., a subsidiary of Keefe, Bruyette & Woods
[3] Includes deals for Trident Securities, a subsidiary of McDonald Investments Inc.
[4] Robinson-Humphrey is an affiliate of Salomon Smith Barney Holdings
[5] Includes deals for Roney Capital Markets, a subsidiary of Raymond James & Associates Inc.
*Deal Value at Announcement
NR = Not Ranked
NA = Not Available
Note: 1999 rankings are recalculated as of April 5, 2000.
Source: SNL Bank M&A DataSource

Exhibit 3.11   A Sample List of M & A Information Sources

Source	Information
Online Services	
America Online	Financial information on public companies including stock prices.
Bureau of Labor Statistics	Economic data.
Business Profiler	
Daily Stocks	Public company information.
Dailog Web	Over 1,000 databases.
Disclosure Online	SEC filings and annual reports.
Disclosure/Spectrum Ownership	Corporate ownership information.
D & B Credit Reports	Financial information on more than 700,000 U.S. businesses.
Dow Jones Interactive	Financial information, stock quotes, articles from more than 3,000 periodicals. Stock analyst's reports.
Investex	Investment data links.
Investing	Financial information, analysis, full text of general and business news.
Lexis/Nexis	M & A database.
Mergers & Acquisitions	M & A database.
Mergerstat	Public company information
Microsoft Investor	News and background on U.S. companies.
Moody's Corporate Profiles	
One Source.com Business Browser	
SEC Filings	SEC, NYU, Edgar Online, FreeEDGAR. M & A database.
SNL Securities	M & A database.
Securities Data Corporation	Corporate information, financial information, news, executive biographies,
Standard & Poor's	Public company information.
Wall Street Journal Interactive Edition	Public company information.
Wall Street Research Net	
Worldwide Mergers, Acquisitions & Alliances	
Yahoo Finance	

Other M & A Related Periodicals are:
1. Corporate Growth Report
2. Directory of M & A Intermediaries
3. Encyclopedia of Business Information Sources
4. Mergers & Acquisitions
5. Mergers & Acquisitions Report
6. Mergers & Corporate Policy

3.10.3 Identifying Key Issues and Contacting Targets

Once a group of potential candidates has been carefully selected, they should be contacted and presented with a range of prices in order to create price competition and to maximize shareholder value. The potential candidates are selected by identifying and considering a number of key issues and factors unique to the acquirer such as industry, location, marketing, products, management, size, earnings potential, and operating results. The acquirer should ensure that these candidates are genuinely interested in engaging in merger or sale discussion. The price range presented to potential candidates is typically driven by the acquirer's ability to reduce the operating expenses of candidates through downsizing, which may pose significant risk to candidates' employees and management. This process should assist the acquirer in selecting the appropriate and suitable target that meets the established acquisition criteria and insure that its initial valuation fits the previously defined criteria.

3.10.4 Structuring the Acquisition Transaction

Structuring the acquisition transaction starts with scheduling the initial meeting between the acquirer and the target. Key issues discussed are negotiating strategy, valuation of the acquisition transaction, and financing options. Determining the value of the target is probably one of the most difficult aspects of the M & A transaction primarily because every business is unique, and it is difficult to set the worth of the target at a single figure. The best way of structuring and specifying terms of a transaction is to reach an agreement that is suitable and acceptable to both the target and the acquirer. The following issues should be addressed when structuring the transaction:

- The needs expressed by the target.
- The requirements of the acquirer.
- Considerations exchanged between the target and the buyer (e.g., cash, capital, combination of cash and equity).
- Income or estate tax situation of both parties.
- Accounting method used for the transaction.
- The role of the target and its management in the operations after the transaction is completed.
- Compensation and employment issues for the target and key members of its management.
- Financial structure of the purchase price.
- The valuation methods used in establishing purchase price.
- Post-closing issues (e.g., responsibility and obligation of the target, ownership of real estate or other fixed assets).

3.10.5 Due Diligence Process

Due diligence is the process of examining thoroughly the information provided by the target to determine the accuracy and reliability of the information, the acquirer's final decision to buy the target, the purchase price, and how to finance the M & A transaction. The primary objectives of this process are to: (1) examine all relevant information; (2) evaluate the key issues and potential areas of the business including financial, operational, legal, and contractual activities; (3) assess the potential risks of the M & A transaction; and (4) decide the purchase price and the methods of financing the transaction. The due diligence process consists of financial, operational, and legal due diligence. The due diligence process is a very important and time-consuming process requiring participation of key members of the management team as well as other professionals such as attorneys, accountants, insurance experts, investment bankers, business brokers, operational and marketing consultants, and environmental specialists. This due diligence team should gather relevant and reliable information about the target by:

- Interviewing all key management personnel to determine the target's strengths and weaknesses of each functional area and the target's future prospects.
- Identifying and resolving deal breakers, which could delay or preclude pursuing the transaction any further.
- Determine the integrity and competence of all key personnel of the target organization especially those who are going to stay after the transaction is completed.
- Obtaining a thorough knowledge and understanding of the target's business and industry by reviewing the target's industry specifications as well as corporate records (e.g., articles of incorporation, bylaws, minutes, stock records), material and continuous contracts, loan agreements, pending and potential litigation, employment contracts, stockholder agreements, royalty agreements, environmental liability, labor agreements, and any other important legal documents.
- Examining the financial information and representations received from the target to: (a) evaluate the target's financial strengths and weaknesses including historical earnings, cash flows, financial position, and earnings potential; (b) corroborate assertions made through interviews and other sources; and (c) provide a basis for determining financial projections and forecasts.
- Selecting valuation method(s) in determining the purchase price.
- Considering all possible financial methods to finance the transaction.

The due diligence process should be completed before finalizing the financial terms of the M & A deal. Due diligence, consisting of an extensive due diligence checklist, should be prepared by the acquirer and can be scheduled at different stages of the acquisition process. It is usually in the best interest of both the target and the acquirer to schedule due diligence before final price negotiation and before any letter of intent or definitive agreements are signed. This gives the acquirer plenty of time to review the information and representations received from the target and allows the acquirer to put forth its best and highest offer price and reduce the risks of subsequent acquisition price changes. The target should sign a mutual confidentiality agreement before exchanging information with any potential acquirers.

3.10.6   Risk Assessment

A number of benefits can be derived from M & A deals including: (1) the potential reduction in costs resulting from the adoption of more economical and efficient technology (synergy); (2) expanding territory by creating better market for products or services; (3) combining managerial positions and removing inefficient management; (4) economies of scale; (5) strengthening financial position; and (6) stabilizing a cyclical or seasonal business. However, growing through business combinations is a decision fraught with risk which may cause failure of M & A transactions. The acquisition team should identify, assess, and minimize all relevant M & A risks to a prudent, rational, and intelligent business risk. This risk assessment consists of identifying all relevant M & A risk, quantifying the risk, determining the probability of risk occurrence, and minimizing the M & A risk to the acceptable prudent business risk. Relevant M & A risks, in addition to the typical business uncertainties of competition, demand and supply changes, pricing volatility, and technological changes, are operating, legal, overpayment, and financial risks.

Operating risk is the failure of the business combination to perform as intended and expected when the M & A transaction was completed. Factors that may cause occurrence of an excessive operating risk are insufficient understanding and knowledge of the target business and industry, lack of a sound post-acquisition integration plan, inexperienced management team in conducting a post-integration plan, mistakes in proper execution of the integration plan, and unrealistic expectations of the target's prospects.

Legal risk is the probability that the legal due diligence fails to: (1) provide adequate and relevant information on legal issues and contingencies of the target; (2) investigate the affairs of the target; (3) uncover potential liabilities; (4) ensure compliance with applicable laws and regulations; (5) ensure the legality of the transaction; and (6) determine properly the target's capability to convey agreed-upon assets, liabilities, and other attributes of the business.

Overpayment risk is the risk of paying too much premium to the target. Many factors can contribute to the overpayment risk including:

- Undefined objectives for the valuation.
- Use of inappropriate valuation methods.
- Overestimating the market potential of the target's products.
- Inadequate and ineffective analysis of financial position and results of operations of the target.
- Mistakes in forecasting prospects of the target.
- Underestimating the impact of competition.
- Overestimating the potential benefits of the integration (e.g., synergies, cost saving, economies of scale).

Financial risk is the risk of not having adequate financial resources to meet debt service requirements of the combined entity. Factors that increase the financial risk are:

- Underestimation of the purchase price.
- Inability to raise the projected amount of equity.
- Mistakes in calculating the target's assets and cash flow in determining the financing gap to be filled by additional debt or equity.
- Ignoring the effect of changes in key variables (e.g., competition, economy, marketing, products, interest rates, revenue, operating margin) on the proposed financial structure.
- Inability to generate sufficient cash flow to fund not only operations subsequent to integration but also the incurred significant debt service.

Exhibit 3.12   A Sample of Definitive Purchase Agreement

1. Description of the M & A transaction structure.
2. The types of consideration used in the M & A transaction.
3. Warranties by both the potential acquirer and the target.
4. The purchase price and what is being purchased.
5. Descriptions of any specific conditions that should be met at or before closing the M & A deal.
6. Provisions regarding the operation of the target between the date of the agreement and closing of the M & A deal.
7. Applicable law of specifying which state laws will govern the agreements.
8. Descriptions of other terms of agreement such as general information relating to closing procedures, expenses, indemnification, and termination of the deal.
9. Provisions for "lock-up" agreements, limiting the target's ability to negotiate with other acquirers.
10. A statement pertaining to truthfulness and accuracy of the target's information, representations, and warranties.
11. Any agreed "break-up" fee.
12. Provision for signature.

3.10.7   Negotiation

Negotiations play a crucial role throughout the M & A process. Continuous effective negotiations addressing key issues should be conducted at every step of the process especially when new information becomes available. The acquisition team should get all key personnel in both the target and the acquirer organization involved in developing a negotiating strategy. The outside experts should also be consulted when establishing an effective negotiating strategy. The negotiating strategy should be flexible enough to consider the needs, objectives, strengths, and weaknesses of both the target and the acquirer.

The negotiation of M & A transactions consists of two phases: (1) preparing the letter of intent; and (2) finalizing the acquisition agreement. The purpose of the letter of intent is to confirm in writing the interests of the two parties (target and acquirer) and to document the basic terms and conditions of the M & A transaction that have been agreed upon in the initial phase of negotiation. Legal counsels should be advised in preparing the letter of intent to ensure the non-binding aspects of the letter. Although the letter of intent is not legally binding, it brings the parties closer to agreement by spelling out the interests of the two parties and reducing the possibility that other buyers will make an offer.

The definitive purchase agreement should be drafted by the acquirer's attorney to address the new issues that may arise during the due diligence process and to confirm terms and conditions of the acquisition. The content of a definitive purchase agreement depends on the structure of the M & A transaction. Exhibit 3.12, however, presents a typical definitive purchase agreement. After the agreements are signed and publicized, the acquirer and the target should work together to satisfy the provisions and terms of the agreement. Specifically, the acquirer should closely monitor the operations of the target to ensure that: (1) the representations and warranties from the definitive agreement are true and accurate; and (2) there are no material adverse changes in the operations or policies of the target.

3.10.8 Financial Structure

The financial structure depends on the size of the transaction, purchase price, and the nature and quality of both the target and the acquirer. The first step in the financial structure is to determine the purchase price. The valuation methods constitute a starting point for establishing purchase price. Valuation methods typically being used for M & A transactions are: industry "rules of thumb," comparable company methods, comparable acquisition methods, asset-based methods, capitalization methods, discounted cash flow analysis, and leveraged buyout methods. These valuation methods are discussed thoroughly in Chapter 6. After the long process of finding a good target company, performing due diligence, negotiating a fair purchase price, and structuring the transaction, the acquirer should find a means of financing the deal.

The amount of financing is determined based on the following formula:

Established Purchase Price	XXXX
Add: Transaction Expenses	XX
Total Funds Needed	XXXX
Less: Equity that can be raised	(XX)
Assets that can be converted to cash	(XX)
Financing needed through additional debt or equity	XXX

Sensitivity analysis should be performed to determine the possible impact of changes in key variables (revenue, operating margins, interest rates, economy, competition) on the amount of financing. The transaction can be financed using equity, debt, or a combination of equity and debt. There are a variety of funding resources that may consider equity investments (e.g., common or preferred stocks). Examples are business corporations, banks, investment companies, individual investors, institutional investors, insurance companies, domestic and multi-national corporations. Unlike debt, there are no scheduled payments for equity funding; however, equity investors have residual interests in the company and may exercise their controlling rights. Sources of debt financing are: (1) asset-based borrowings against the assets of the acquired company; (2) cash flow leveraged buyouts, which are financed, in part, by a lender who is willing to lend based on future cash flows; (3) long-term debt (bonds); and (4) sale/leaseback transactions.

M & A transactions should be executed according to the applicable tax laws and rules. This requires examination of both the target's and the acquirer's financial reports and tax returns. Tax returns of the past eight to ten years should be reviewed to provide information on potential tax attributes, business relationships, tax-sharing agreements, accounting for loan fees, income taxes, M & A expenses, and projected liabilities. M & A transactions can be in the form of stock or assets, and depending on their specifications they can be taxable or nontaxable. If the target bank will be taxed upon receipt of stock or cash, it will ask for higher premiums for the M & A deal. However, under the existing IRS guidelines, the merger may be considered tax-free when target shareholders receive stock equal to 50 percent of what they have given up.

3.10.9 Closing the Deal

The letter of intent and the purchase agreements usually specify a timetable to ensure that both parties move expeditiously and prudently to close the deal after a long process of finding the target, conducting due diligence, structuring the transaction, negotiating the purchase price, and securing financing. Several procedures should be performed to professionally and legally close the transaction. Among these procedures are:

- Completing the due diligence process particularly the legal due diligence of reviewing all important legal documents, complying with the terms of the purchase agreement, and other applicable laws and regulations.
- Obtaining a tax ruling if necessary.
- Receiving financing commitments
- Completing the purchase agreement
- Receiving audited financial statements.
- Complying with applicable laws and regulations.
- Securing key employment agreements.
- Resolving tax accounting issues of the transaction (tax and accounting issues of M & A transactions will be discussed in depth in Chapters 4 and 7).
- Maintaining minimum net worth requirements.
- Obtaining of third-party consents on the transfer of material agreements, licenses, or rights.
- Consummating the deal of distributing all necessary documents to the proper parties.
- Preparing for integration.

3.10.10   Integration

Subsequent to successful closing of the transaction, the acquirer should design and implement the changes necessary to integrate a new acquisition into an existing business. An effective integration plan, which specifies all appropriate post-closing decisions and actions, plays an important role in making the M & A deal a success. The integration plan is typically prepared by the acquirer's management; however, participation of the target's key personnel in finalizing the plan can tremendously improve its success. The integration plan should clearly define the organizational structure of the newly-merged entity including appropriate functional responsibilities (e.g., manufacturing, marketing, accounting), their proper authority and responsibility, and their required human and capital resources.

Merger integration is a long-term process with a number of planned activities such as downsizing, eliminating duplicated overhead, developing new cash management/treasury systems, consolidating accounting and management information systems, and transitioning new employee benefit plans. The human resources aspect of post-merger integration is very crucial to the success of the combined entity. Merger announcements typically cause anxieties on the part of employees who are wondering about the future of the merged entity and their role, if any, in that future.

It is inevitable that not all employees, both in managerial and non-managerial positions in both the acquirer and the target, will be offered positions with the combined entity. In this case, it is advantageous to the combined entity to be generous with compensation and severance packages in order to improve new management's reputation, morale of the retained employees, and future alliances, as well as to create goodwill among customers and employees. Employee compensation plans to compensate or protect the target's employees should be properly designed in advance, even before the preparation of the letter of intent, primarily because of the following reasons:

- Any stock option, severance, or other similar arrangements with employees should be negotiated with employees, discussed with legal, accounting, tax, and professional advisors, and finally approved by the board of directors.
- Employees' compensation packets are often priced in the M & A transaction, especially any payments in excess of normal compensation.
- The acquirer typically considers any excess compensation in calculating the purchase price, which in turn may reduce the amount received by the target's shareholders.

The integration plan should consider all important issues and processes of the combined entity's human resources, capital resources, organization structure, and business processes such as sales, manufacturing, supply chain, and distribution. The integration plan should also have provisions for an annual post-merger audit for the primary purpose of determining whether the merged entity has achieved its intended goals and is continuously working toward achievement of objectives of broadening product lines, increasing market share, strengthening financial position, and increasing shareholder's value. After the integration, the acquirer and the target (the combined entity) should work together to achieve their organization's goals.

3.11 CONCLUSION

M & A within the financial services industry have continued with varying levels of intensity since the end of World War II. Prior to the Riegle-Neal Act, the number of M & A was limited by state law governing interstate and intrastate acquisitions. During the late 1970s and the early 1980s, some states formed regional banking pacts to permit banks to combine with or acquire target banks in pact states. The past two decades have witnessed substantial increases in M & A deals in the banking industry. Ever-increasing bank consolidation has been motivated by a favorable regulatory environment, opportunities for market expansion, greater efficiency following M & A, strong stock market, favorable stock prices, economies of scale, and technological advancements.

The wave of bank consolidation during the 1990s has significantly changed the characteristics and structure of the banking industry in the United States. The number of banks has substantially decreased with far fewer local and small banks and more large and regional or national banks. The market shares of large banks have also increased as a result of megamergers. This rapid pace of bank M & A is likely to continue into the future and possibly accelerate in the financial services industry as a result of the passage of the Gramm-Leach-Bliley Act of 1999.

Regulators typically consider three fundamental factors of motives, value to society, and optimal response when assessing an M & A deal. Motives refer to the reasons for consideration and the expectations of the acquirer from the M & A deal such as achieving economies of scale, gaining larger market share, spreading best-management and practice techniques, and decreasing competition. Value to society is a trade-off between potential social benefits of increases in effectiveness, efficiency, and diversification and possible social costs of concentration, influence, and monopoly power. Optimal response refers to M & A activities undertaken to minimize undesirable effects of the deal such as employee compensation, branch divestitures, increasing quality and quantity of products.

Recent bank M & A studies have investigated two important issues of M & A deals: (1) what bank(s) are potential targets for acquisition; and (2) what prices were paid for acquired banks. The issue of which banks chose to acquire or merge is fundamentally motivated and determined by value maximization factors such as profitability, sales, and earnings growth. For example, Palepu (1986)[41] found that nonfinancial firms that were acquired had lower growth, liquidity, and leverage than did firms that were not acquired. Morek, Schleifer, and Vishny (1988)[42] found that banks were more likely to be acquired when their executives owned larger percentages of the outstanding shares. Studies of the prices paid (premiums) in bank M & A (e.g., Cheng, Gup, and Wall, 1989[43]; Rhoades, 1987[44]) found that the price-to-book paid for a bank increased with the profitability of the acquired and decreased with the acquired bank's capital-to-asset ratio and return on assets.

Empirical studies of M & A transactions discussed in this chapter found evidence in support of the hypothesis that: (1) target shareholders incur positive abnormal returns while acquirer (bidding) shareholders experience negative abnormal returns; (2) banks that make larger acquisitions perform better than banks making small acquisitions; (3) cash tenders are more significant than stock transactions in determining premiums paid to targets (e.g., price to book-value); (4) bank takeover valuations (price-to-book) have increased; (5) number of banks has declined; (6) size of M & A deals has increased; and (7) number of M & A deals has substantially increased.

The decision to expand through consolidation or even sell the company that is a strong acquisition candidate is one that should be made by management and owners of the company. However, a professional, competent, and experienced appraiser or valuation firm can provide valuable valuation services in determining the appropriate asking price based upon market forces. Consulting and using an experienced appraiser or valuation firm can make the tedious M & A process, explained in this chapter, easier and the M & A deal more profitable to shareholders of the target company. Acquirers, especially public consolidators, often pay for their acquisitions with their own publicly traded shares, which are typically restricted. Restricted shares obtained through the M & A deal cannot be sold to third parties for some period of time, often one to two years or more. Thus, owners of the acquired company should have reasonable assurance and confidence that the acquiring company will be as strong as it is now in one or two years, otherwise, their restricted stock may be worth much less. A professional, competent, and experienced appraiser can assist the target company in determining the market value of restricted stocks and provide reasonable assurance that the stock is appropriately discounted from its currently stated market value.

Empirical studies reviewed in this chapter find evidence that indicates that changes in state and federal banking regulations have an important effect on M & A prices and activities in the banking industry. The passage of the GLB Act of 1999 repealed the 66-year-old Glass-Steagall Act by allowing banks to form financial holding companies (FHCs) under which they can engage in a variety of financial services including selling insurance and securities products. The GLB Act also permits business combinations between banking organizations, insurance companies, brokerage firms, and mutual funds which will increase M & A activities in the financial services industry. This Act created a number of challenges for financial services organizations to protect consumer privacy, disclose costs, and ensure reinvestment within the communities. It is expected that the GLB Act will cause a substantial increase in M & A activities in the financial industry. Thus, the due diligence process presented in this chapter provides a basic understanding of the M & A process from the standpoints of both the target and the acquirer.

Typical problems with most M & A deals are overpayment, lack of proper assessment of M & A risks presented in this chapter, and improper implementation and integration. Successful M & A deals, on the other hand, are those involving consolidation of closely related entities, small premiums, and participation and retention of acquired management. M & A decisions involve proper analysis and assessment of strategic, financial, and integration factors discussed in this chapter. The strategic review determines whether growth, especially through M & A, is a desirable choice. Financial institutions should perform financial analysis to determine whether the M & A deal increases shareholder value creation and reduces the risk of overpayment. Finally, the integration review determines the ability of the acquirer to successfully integrate the acquired financial institution into its own organization. Empirical studies show that ultimate success of M & A deals is measured in terms of the creation of shareholder value. To be considered a successful M & A deal, the merger should be effective operationally, and it should also create value for acquiring shareholders.

ENDNOTES

1. Spiegel, J., and A. Gart, "What Lies Behind the Bank Merger and Acquisition Frenzy?" *Business Economics* (April 1996): 47–52.

2. RHI Management Resources, 1999. Press Releases. *www.rhimr.com/news/press122099.html*.

3. Marcial, Gene G., 1998. "That Was Just the Warm-Up." *Business Week* (December 28): 151.

4. Ibid.

5. U.S. Department of Justice, 1984. "Merger Guidelines" (June 14) p. 4.

6. Rhoades, Stephen A., 1996. "Competition and Bank Mergers: Directions for Analysis from Available Evidence." *The Antitrust Bulletin,* Vol. 41, No. 2 (Summer): 339–364.

7. Humphrey, David B., 1990. "Why Do Estimates of Bank Scale Economies Differ?" *Economic Review* (Federal Reserve Bank of Richmond), (Vol. 76, No. 5, September/October): 38–50.

8. Kwast, Myron L., 1999. "Bank Mergers: What Should Policymakers Do?" *Journal of Banking and Finance* (Vol. 23): 629–636.

9. Humphrey, David B., 1990. "Why Do Estimates of Bank Scale Economies Differ?" *Economic Review* (Federal Reserve Bank of Richmond), (Vol. 76, No. 5, September/October): 38–50.

10. See order Denying Acquisition of First State Bancshares of Blakely, Inc. Federal Reserve Bulletin, Vol. 82, No. 10 (October 1996): 953–958; and Order Denying Acquisition of Banc-Security Corporation, Marshalltown, Iowa. *Federal Reserve Bulletin,* Vol. 83, No. 2 (February 1997): 122–126.

11. Stephen A. Rhoades, 1993. "The Herfindahl-Hirshman Index." *Federal Reserve Bulletin,* (Vol. 79, March): 188–189.

12. Werden, G.J., Joskow, A.S., and Johnson, R.L., 1989. "The Effects of Mergers on Economic Performance: Two Case Studies from the Airline Industry," Economic Analysis Group, Department of Justice, Working Paper, EAG 89–15.

13. Borenstein, S., 1990. "Airline Mergers, Airport Dominance and Market Power," *American Economic Review,* Vol. 80, pp. 400–404.

14. Kim E.H. and Singal, V., 1993. "Mergers and Market Power: Evidence from the Airline Industry," *American Economic Review,* Vol. 83, pp. 549–569.

15. Akhavein, J.O, Berger, A.N. and Humphrey, D.B., 1997. "The Effects of Megamergers on Efficiency and Prices: Evidence from a Bank Profit Function," *Review of Industrial Organization,* Vol. 12, pp. 95–139.

16. Prager, R.A., Hannan, T.H. 1998. "Do Substantial Horizontal Mergers Generate Significant Price Effects? Evidence From the Banking Industry." *Journal of Industrial Economics* (December) Vol. 46, pp. 433–452.

17. Barancik, Scott, 1999. "Big Mergers Change Fund's Risk Calculation." *The American Banker* (September 8).

18. Broaddus, J. Alfred, Jr., 1998. "The Bank Merger Wave: Causes and Consequences," *Economic Quarterly* (Summer) v84 i3: 1.

19. Ibid.

20. Strahan, Phillip F. and J.P. Weston. 1996. "Small Business Lending and Bank Consolidation: Is There Cause for Concern?" *Current Issues in Economics and Finance* 2. Federal Reserve Bank of New York, 1–6.

21. Berger, Allen N., Joseph M. Scalise, and Anil K. Kushyup. 1995. The Transformation of the U.S. Banking Industry: What a Long, Strange Trip It's Been." *Brookings Papers on Economic Activity* 2:55–218.

22. Berger, Allen N., Anthony Saunders, Joseph M. Scalise, and Gregory F. Udell. 1998. "The Effects of Bank Mergers and Acquisitions on Small Business Lending." *Journal of Financial Economics* 50: 187–229.

23. Prager, Robin A., and Timothy H. Hannan. 1998. "Do Substantial Horizontal Mergers Generate Significant Price Effects? Evidence from the Banking Industry." *Journal of Industrial Economics* 46: 433–452.

24. Smith, D., 1971. "The Performance of Merging Banks." *Journal of Business* (Vol. 44, April): 184–192.

25. Piper, T.R. and S.J. Weiss, 1971. "The Profitability of Multibank Holding Company Acquisitions." *Journal of Finance* (Vol. 29): 163–174.

26. James, C. and P. Weir, 1987. "Returns to Acquirers and Competition in the Acquisition Market: The Case of Banking." *Journal of Political Economy* (Vol. 95, No. 2): 355–357.

27. Palia, D., 1993. "The Managerial, Regulatory and Financial Determinants of Bank Merger Premiums." *Journal of Industrial Economics* (Vol. 41, No. 1): 91–102.

28. Gart, A., and M.K. Al-jafari, 1998. "Revisiting the Determinants of Large Bank Merger and Acquisition Premiums." *Journal of Applied Management and Entrepreneurship* (Vol. 4, No. 2): 76–86.

29. Rose, Peter S. 1988b. "Bank Mergers in a Deregulated Environment." Rolling Meadows: Bank Administration Institute.

30. Curry, Timothy J. 1981. "The Pre-Acquisition Characteristics of Banks Acquired by Multibank Holding Companies." *Journal of Bank Research* (Summer): 82–89.

31. Hannan, T.H., and S.A. Rhoades, 1987. "Acquisition Targets and Motives: The Case of the Banking Industry." *Review of Economics and Statistics* (February): 67–74.

32. Beatty, Randolph P., Anthony M. Santomera, and Michael L. Smirlock. 1987. "Bank Merger Premiums: Analysis and Evidence." Monograph Series in Finance and Economics, New York University.

33. Rose, Peter S. 1988a. "Characteristics of Merging Banks in the United States: Theory, Empirical Results, and Implications for Public Policy." *Review of Business and Economic Research* 24 (Fall): 1–19.

34. Fraser, Donald R., and James W. Kolari. 1988. "Pricing Small Bank Acquisitions." *Journal of Retail Banking* 10 (Winter): 23–28.

35. Hunter, William C., and Larry O. Wall. 1989. "Bank Merger Motivations: A Review of the Evidence and an Examination of Key Target Bank Characteristics." *Economic Review* 74 (September/October 1989): 2–19.

36. Cheng, S., L. Gup, and R. Wall, 1989. "Financial Determinants of Bank Takeovers." *Journal of Money, Credit and Banking* (Vol. 21, No. 4): 524–536.

37. O'Keefe, John P. 1996. "Banking Industry Consolidation: Financial Attributes of Merging Banks." *The FDIC Banking Review* 9 (December): 18–37.

38. Esty, Benjamin, Bhanu Narasimhan, and Peter Tufano, 1999. "Interest-rate Exposure and Bank Mergers." *Journal of Banking and Finance* (Vol. 23): 255–285.

39. Hadlock, Charles, Joel Houston, and Michael Ryngaert, 1999. "The Role of Managerial Incentives in Bank Acquisitions." *Journal of Banking and Finance* (Vol. 23): 255–285.

40. Brewer, Elijah, III; William E. Jackson, III; Julapa A. Jagtiani; and Thong Nguyen, 2000. "The Price of Bank Mergers in the 1990s." *Economic Perspectives* (Federal Reserve Bank of Chicago, first quarter): 2–23.

41. Palepu, K. 1986. "Predicting Takeover Targets: A Methodology and Empirical Analysis." *Journal of Accounting and Economics* 8: 3–35.

42. Morch, R., A. Schleifer, and R.W. Vishny. 1988. "Management Ownership and Market Valuation." *Journal of Financial Economics* 20: 293–315.

43. Cheng, S., L. Gup, and R. Wall, 1989. "Financial Determinants of Bank Takeovers." *Journal of Money, Credit and Banking* (Vol. 21, No. 4): 524–536.

44. Rhoades, S.A. 1987. "Determinants of Premiums Paid in Bank Acquisition." *Atlantic Economics Journal* 15: 20–30.

REFERENCES

Asquith, P.R. and E.H. Kim, 1982. "The Impact of Merger Bids on the Participating Firm's Security Holders." Journal of Finance (Vol. 37, December): 1209–1228.

Berger, Allen N., Rebecca S. Demsetz, and Phillip E. Strahan. 1999. "The Consolidation of the Financial Services Industry: Causes, Consequences, and Implications for the Future." *Journal of Banking and Finance* 23: 135–194.

Cornett, M. and H. Tehranian, 1992. "Changes in Corporate Performance Associated with Bank Acquisitions." Journal of Financial Economics (Vol. 31): 211–234.

DeAngelo, H., L. DeAngelo, and E. Rice, 1984. "Going Private: Minority Freezeouts and Stockholder Wealth." Journal of Law and Economics (Vol. 24): 367–402.

Dodd, P., 1980. "Merger Proposals, Management Discretion and Stockholder Wealth." Journal of Financial Economics (December, Volume 8): 105–137.

Firth, M., 1980. "Takeovers, Shareholder Return and the Theory of the Firm." Quarterly Journal of Economics (March): 235–260.

Healy, P.M., K. Palepu, and R. Ruback, 1992. "Does Corporate Performance Improve After Mergers?" Journal of Financial Economics (Vol. 31): 135–175.

Jensen, M.C. and R.S. Ruback, 1983. The Market for Corporate Control: The Scientific Evidence." Journal of Financial Economics (Vol. 11): 586–631.

Lev, B. and G. Mandelker, 1972. "The Microeconomic Consequences of Corporate Mergers." Journal of Business (Vol. 45): 85–104.

Mueller, D.C., 1980. "The Determinants and Effects of Mergers: An International Comparison." Gunn and Hain, Publishers, Inc.

Phillips, D. and C. Pavel, 1986. "Interstate Banking Game Plans: Implications for the Midwest." Economic Perspectives (Federal Reserve Bank of Chicago) (March/April): 23–39.

Roll, R., 1986. "The Hubris Hypothesis of Corporate Takeovers." *Journal of Business* (Vol. 59): 197–216.

Servaes, H., 1991. "Tobin's Q and the Gains from Takeovers." *Journal of Finance* (Vol. 46, No. 1): 409–426.

Singleton, John P. 1994. "The Technology and the Role it Should Play." Edited by John B. McCoy, Larry A. Frieder, and Robert B. Hedges, Jr. Bottomline Banking. Chicago: Probus Publishing Company.

Varaiya, N., 1986. "An Empirical Investigation of the Bidding Firms' Gains for Corporate Takeovers." Research in Finance (Vol. 6): 149–178.

Regulatory Environment and Financial Reporting Process of Financial Institutions

4.1 INTRODUCTION

The safety, soundness, efficiency, and effectiveness of the U.S. banking system is best served by: (1) a stable monetary policy; (2) effective market discipline; (3) adoptive regulatory environment; and (4) vigilant financial reporting process. Given the significant changes that are taking place in financial institutions, the purpose of this chapter is to discuss the banking regulatory and financial reporting environment. This chapter examines the three most fundamental public policy issues facing the financial services industry including consolidation, regulatory reform, and financial reporting.

4.2 CONSOLIDATION

The recent wave of consolidations in the banking industry has resulted in fewer but bigger banking organizations. Exhibit 4.1 lists the top 50 banks, by total assets as of the end of 1999, in the United States. Consolidations have been viewed positively in the sense that they enhance the value of the combined institution to its owners by reducing the number of financial services organizations chasing marginal business and running up the cost of funds. Consolidations are also considered as effective vehicles for reducing overhead costs and creating economies of scale and scope, which in turn would benefit customers seeking desirable financial services.

As geographic and activity deregulations are occurring in the financial services industry, consolidations can be very beneficial to the financial services organizations and their customers as the industry attempts to take advantage of economies of scale and scope and risk-reduction opportunities offered by geographical diversification. The financial services industry consolidation could be the result of natural global market forces driving the industry toward bigger organizations to achieve lower costs, higher profitability, and ability to compete effectively in the global market. Several factors have played important roles in promoting the current wave of

Exhibit 4.1 Top 50 Banks by Total Assets as of 12/31/1999 in the United States

Rank	Name	City	State	Total Assets(K)
1	Bank of America, National Association	Charlotte	NC	571,732,000
2	Chase Manhattan Bank, The	New York	NY	332,198,000
3	Citibank, N.A.	New York	NY	327,899,000
4	First Union National Bank	Charlotte	NC	229,272,000
5	Morgan Guaranty Trust Company of New York	New York	NY	167,665,788
6	Wells Fargo Bank, National Association	San Francisco	CA	96,316,000
7	Bank One, National Association	Chicago	IL	93,893,688
8	Fleet National Bank	Providence	RI	87,741,000
9	HSBC Bank USA	Buffalo	NY	79,619,379
10	Bankboston, National Association	Boston	MA	78,334,990
11	U.S. Bank National Association	Minneapolis	MN	75,384,963
12	Keybank National Association	Cleveland	OH	75,032,116
13	Bank of New York, The	New York	NY	71,794,790
14	PNC Bank, National Association	Pittsburgh	PA	68,187,311
15	Wachovia Bank, National Association	Winston-Salem	NC	63,557,835
16	State Street Bank and Trust Company	Boston	MA	56,226,197
17	Bankers Trust Company	New York	NY	51,156,000
18	Southtrust Bank, N.A.	Birmingham	AL	43,203,109
19	Amsouth Bank	Birmingham	AL	43,189,937
20	Regions Bank	Birmingham	AL	42,237,958
21	Firstar Bank, National Association	Cincinnati	OH	40,164,088
22	Mellon Bank, N.A.	Pittsburgh	PA	39,619,161
23	Norwest Bank Minnesota, National Association	Minneapolis	MN	36,529,999
24	Chase Manhattan Bank USA, National Association	Wilmington	DE	35,397,783
25	Washington Mutual Bank	Seattle	WA	35,036,229
26	National City Bank	Cleveland	OH	34,003,107
27	Bank One, National Association	Columbus	OH	33,856,142
28	Union Bank of California, National Association	San Francisco	CA	33,354,513
29	Union Planters Bank, National Association	Memphis	TN	32,684,807
30	Comerica Bank	Detroit	MI	31,242,731
31	Summit Bank	Hackensack	NJ	31,208,437
32	Bank One, Texas, National Association	Dallas	TX	30,664,622
33	Lasalle Bank, National Association	Chicago	IL	30,302,664
34	Branch Banking and Trust Company	Winston-Salem	NC	29,631,391
35	MBNA America Bank, National Association	Wilmington	DE	29,000,906
36	Huntington National Bank, The	Columbus	OH	28,760,019
37	Crestar Bank	Richmond	VA	27,301,368
38	Fleet Bank, National Association	Jersey City	NJ	25,778,000
39	Chase Bank of Texas, National Association	Houston	TX	25,435,803
40	Northern Trust Company, The	Chicago	IL	23,500,051
41	Bank One, Arizona, National Association	Phoenix	AZ	23,347,658

Exhibit 4.1   *(Continued)*

Rank	Name	City	State	Total Assets(K)
42	Suntrust Bank, Atlanta	Atlanta	GA	23,326,136
43	Greenwood Trust Company	Greenwood	DE	22,581,304
44	Manufacturers and Traders Trust Company	Buffalo	NY	21,623,497
45	Bank One, Michigan	Detroit	MI	21,122,317
46	Harris Trust and Savings Bank	Chicago	IL	20,210,599
47	Mercantile Bank, National Association	Saint Louis	MO	20,026,610
48	National City Bank of Michigan/Illinois	Bannockburn	IL	18,348,993
49	Banco Popular De Puerto Rico	San Juan	PR	18,258,000
50	Compass Bank	Birmingham	AL	18,183,920

Source: http://www.ffiec.gov/NIC/default.htm

consolidation in the financial services industry. Among these factors are technological innovations, geographical diversifications, and global competition.

Government regulations have traditionally affected consolidation in the financial services industry in two different ways. First, the McFadden Act of 1927, by vesting states with authority to limit branch banking and to prohibit interstate banking, placed limitations on geographic expansion of banks. Second, the Glass-Steagall Act of 1933 prohibited the line of business expansion for banks expanding into fields such as insurance and securities underwriting. Two important acts passed in the early 1980s have effectively nullified the McFadden Act. These are the Depository Institutions Deregulation and Monetary Control Act (DIDMCA) of 1980 and the Garn-St. Germain Depository Institutions Act (GSGDIA) of 1982. The passage of the DIDMC and GSGDI Acts and the corresponding changes in state banking laws have encouraged a substantial consolidation and expansion in the banking industry during the 1980s. For example, in 1980 there were 12,679 banking organizations (including 14,737 banks). These numbers decreased to 9,688 organizations (including 12,526 banks) by 1990, indicating a 24 percent decline in organizations and a 15 percent decline in the number of banks.[1] The passage of the Riegle-Neal Interstate Banking and Branching Efficiency Act (RNIBBEA) of 1994 permits a bank holding company (BHC) to acquire target banks located in any other state. The RNIBBEA by allowing national and state bank mergers across state lines, has lowered the previous interstate banking barriers and has had a significant impact in stimulating the ongoing M & A activities in the banking industry. The Glass-Steagall Act was reversed in 1999 by the GLB Act, which permits line of business expansion combinations between banks, insurance companies, investment firms, and mutual funds.

4.2.1   Technological Innovations

Technology (e.g., Internet banking, visual and audio communication systems, e-commerce) is crucial to providing financial services effectively and efficiently. Technological innovations have made it possible to reduce the cost and to increase the speed of providing financial services across distances, including national and cross-border boundaries. It is assumed that bigger financial services organizations have higher potential to expand the scale and scope of technology in which they can invest and spread over a larger customer base. If enhanced technology lowers the cost of offering financial services, then the bigger financial services organizations may have economies of scale and scope advantage over small organizations. Thus, the cost and ability to afford investment in technological innovations can be viewed as a relevant factor in explaining consolidation in the financial industry.

The new technology has facilitated mergers in the financial services industry by enabling financial institutions to take advantage of economies of scale and related cost reduction. The use of information technology has created opportunities for financial institutions to develop more sophisticated computerized financial instruments (e.g., derivatives) by unbundling risks and reallocating them to parties willing and able to take the risk. The new technology has also fostered full development of e-commerce and Internet banking. The new information technology has made universal banking possible which enhances global competition in the financial services industry. Technological advances are viewed as an important impetus toward consolidation because they have made it more efficient for banks to grow larger and consolidate their operations.

4.2.2 Geographical and Activity Diversification

Prior to 1970, interstate banking was not practiced. In the late 1970s and 1980s, some states established regional banking pacts as other states allowed even nation-wide banking systems with reciprocal arrangements.[2] Exhibit 4.2 presents interstate banking laws prior to the Riegle-Neal Act of 1994. The Riegle-Neal Interstate Banking and Branch Efficiency Act allowed banks to expand across state lines and branch interstate by: (1) combining existing out-of-state bank subsidiaries; and/or (2) acquiring banks or individual branches through M & A. The Act also permitted bank holding companies (BHC) to: (1) acquire banks in any states effective September 29, 1995; and (2) merge with other banks located in different states beginning June 1, 1997.

Empirical studies (e.g., Adkisson and Fraser, 1990[3]; Brewer et al., 2000[4]) present two competing hypotheses regarding the impact of geographic expansion and deregulation on consolidation, in general, and prices paid for bank acquisitions in particular. The first hypothesis states that prices of acquisitions increase as restrictions on geographic expansion are reduced primarily because the number of potential bidders for a target bank increases. The second hypothesis asserts that M & A prices decrease as restrictions on geographic expansion are reduced primarily because target banks are not protected with a market niche to earn excess profits. Any reductions in the opportunities to earn excess returns by target banks lower merger prices. Brewer et al. (2000)[5] found empirical evidence in support of the first hypothesis in that the removal of geographic restrictions, caused by the Riegel-Neal Act, increased the demand for target banks as the number of potential bidders increases, resulting in higher M & A prices.

Consolidation can provide financial services with the opportunity and potential to diversify across products (financial services) and geographical regions. For example, large banks can offer a greater variety of loans to a variety of customers in a variety of geographical areas through branching networks and specialized loan production officers.

4.2.3 National and Global Competition

The current banking crisis in East Asia is caused, in most part, by the excessive build-up of short-term debt. The excessive level of short-term debt systematically increases the risks of

Exhibit 4.2   Interstate Banking Laws Prior to Riegle-Neal Act

State	Area Covered and Reciprocity
Alabama	Reciprocal, 13 states (AR, FL, GA, KY, LA, MD, MS, NC, SC, TN, TX, VA, WV)
Alaska	National, no reciprocity
Arizona	National, no reciprocity
Arkansas	Reciprocal, 16 states (AL, FL, GA, KY, LA, MD, MO, MS, NC, NE, OK, SC, TN, TX, VA, WV)
California	National, reciprocal
Colorado	National, no reciprocity
Connecticut	National, reciprocal
Delaware	National, reciprocal
District of Columbia	Reciprocal, 11 states (AL, FL, GA, LA, MD, MS, NC, SC, TN, VA, WV)
Florida	Reciprocal, 11 states (AL, AR, GA, LA, MD, MS, NC, SC, TN, VA, WV) and DC
Georgia	Reciprocal, 11 states (AL, FL, KY, LA, MD, MS, NC, SC, TN, VA, WV) and DC
Idaho	National, no reciprocity
Illinois	National, reciprocal
Indiana	National, reciprocal
Iowa	Reciprocal, 6 states (IL, MN, MO, NE, SD, WI)
Kansas	Reciprocal, 6 states (AR, CO, IA, MO, NE, OK)
Kentucky	National, reciprocal
Louisiana	National, reciprocal
Maine	National, no reciprocity
Maryland	Reciprocal, 14 states (AL, AR, DE, FL, GA, KY, LA, MS, NC, PA, SC, TN, VA, WV) and DC
Massachusetts	National, reciprocal
Michigan	National, reciprocal
Minnesota	Reciprocal, 16 states (CO, IA, ID, IL, IN, KS, MI, MO, MT, ND, NE, OH, SC, WA, WI, WY)
Mississippi	Reciprocal, 13 states (AL, AR, FL, GA, KY, LA, MO, NC, SC, TN, TX, VA, WV)
Missouri	Reciprocal, 8 states (AR, IA, IL, KS, KY, NE, OK, TN)
Montana	Reciprocal, 7 states (CO, ID, MN, ND, SD, WI, WY)
Nebraska	National, reciprocal
Nevada	National, no reciprocity
New Hampshire	National, no reciprocity
New Jersey	National, reciprocal
New Mexico	National, no reciprocity
New York	National, reciprocal
North Carolina	Reciprocal, 13 states (AL, AR, FL, GA, KY, LA, MD, MS, SC, TN, TX, VA, WV) and DC
North Dakota	National, reciprocal
Ohio	National, reciprocal
Oklahoma	National, no reciprocity for initial entry; after initial entry, bank holding company must be from state offering reciprocity or wait 4 years to expand
Oregon	National, no reciprocity
Pennsylvania	National, reciprocal

Exhibit 4.2 *(Continued)*

State	Area Covered and Reciprocity
South Carolina	Reciprocal, 12 states (AL, AR, FL, GA, KY, LA, MD, MS, NC, TN, VA, WV) and DC
Rhode Island	National, reciprocal
South Dakota	National, reciprocal
Tennessee	National, reciprocal
Texas	National, no reciprocity
Utah	National, no reciprocity
Vermont	National, reciprocal
Virginia	Reciprocal, 12 states (AL, AR, FL, GA, KY, LA, MD, MS, NC, SC, TN, WV) and DC
Washington	National, reciprocal
West Virginia	National, reciprocal
Wisconsin	Reciprocal, 8 states (IA, IL, IN, KY, MI, MN, MO, OH)
Wyoming	National, no reciprocity

Source: Savage, Donald T., 1993. "Interstate Banking: A Status Report." *Federal Reserve Bulletin* (Vol. 73, December): 1075–1099.

a financial crisis and causes recessions. Thus, the stability of the international financial system is important. The 1997 Asian crisis proved: (1) that the minimum Basel capital adequacy ratio of eight percent was not sufficient to compensate the systematic risk that was taken by banks in these countries; and (2) that there was no adequate and effective risk management system. Thus, the need for sound and consistent global banking policies and procedures became more important as the financial services industry and financial institutions are integrating worldwide. The widespread effect of the Asian Crisis of 1997 demonstrated the growing integration of the global financial markets and the need for the global supervisory requirements, capital adequacy, and risk management assessments.

Economies of scale and scope as well as the potential cost reductions and geographical and activity diversification of consolidations should enable financial services to compete more effectively in the national and global markets. Consolidation in the financial services industry may serve the public interest by creating social benefits if competition is maintained and consumer convenience of one-stop shopping is enhanced. U.S. laws governing bank acquisitions are neutral regarding the nationality of the acquirers. Indeed, banks and banking organizations in the United States have been open to foreign acquisitions in line with the U.S. government's commitment to free flow of capital among nations. However, studies reveal that the United States has the most liberal policies on foreign bank acquisitions compared to other countries.[6]

4.3   REGULATORY ENVIRONMENT

There are several sources of bank supervision and regulation. Exhibit 4.3 reveals regulations pertaining to financial institutions. A bank or a savings and loan association (S & L) may operate under a state or federal charter. National banks: (1) operate under federal charter; (2) are supervised by the Office of the Comptroller of the Currency (OCC); (3) are required to be

Exhibit 4.3 Regulations Related to Financial Institutions

Year	Regulation	Provisions
1927	McFadden Act	Restricts geographic expansion of banks by limiting branch banking and prohibiting interstate banking.
1933	The Glass-Steagall Act	1. Separates commercial banking from investment banking to ensure financial safety. 2. Bars banks from paying interest on deposits. 3. Restricts the types of assets banks could own. 4. Prohibits bank distribution of mutual funds. 5. Prohibits the line of business expansion for banks expanding into fields such as insurance and security underwriting.
1933	The SEC Act	1. Protects initial investors' rights. 2. Requires full disclosure of all the relevant information needed to make a decision about investing in corporate securities including banks' stock.
1934	The SEC Act	1. Protects the right of investors who trade securities. 2. Requires full disclosure and audited annual financial statements of publicly-traded corporations. 3. Regulates all national securities' exchanges.
1940	Investment Company Act	1. Separates fund management from other financial services. 2. Establishes rules for selling practices, capital structure, and accounting.
1956	Bank Holding Company Act	1. Puts the Federal Reserve Board in charge of multibank holding companies. 2. Grants the Federal Reserve Board to review the effects of consolidation in the banking industry.
1960	Bank Merger Act	Requires the Federal Reserve Board to review the impacts of merger in the banking industry by applying the competitive standards of the Sherman Act and Clayton Antitrust Acts on bank mergers.
1970	Securities Investor Protection Act	Indemnifies brokerage customers against losses from a failed broker/dealer.
1980	Depository Institutions Deregulation and Monetary Control Act	1. Nullifies the McFadden Act. 2. Permits branch-banking and interstate banking.
1982	Garn-St. Germain Depository Institution Act	1. Encourages substantial consolidation and expansion in the banking industry. 2. Permits branch-banking and interstate banking.
1994	Riegle-Neal Interstate Banking and Branching Efficiency Act	1. Permits a bank holding company (BHC) to acquire target banks located in any other state. 2. Allows national and state bank consolidations across state lines.
1999	Gramm-Leach-Bliley Act or Financial Services Modernization Act (GLB)	1. Repeals Glass-Steagall Act. 2. Permits banks, securities firms, insurance companies, mutual funds, brokerage firms, and asset managers to freely enter each others' business or merger. 3. Creates financial holding companies that may conduct a broad number of financial services including insurance and securities underwriting, commercial banking, investment banking, merchant banking, asset management and distribution, and even real estate development and investment typically under separate subsidiaries.

members of the Federal Reserve Board System; and (4) are required to have their deposits insured by the Federal Deposit Insurance Corporation (FDIC). Federal S & L are: (1) chartered by the Office of Thrift Supervision (OTS); and (2) insured through the Savings Association Insurance Fund (SAIF) and the FDIC. Banks and federally insured mutual savings are insured by the Bank Insurance Fund (BIF) of the FDIC. Exhibit 4.4 outlines a typical national bank's supervisory and regulatory services.

4.4 BANK SUPERVISION

The Federal Reserve and other U.S. and foreign bank supervisory agencies through the Basel Committee have developed an approach for measuring and managing bank risk based on three so-called pillars: capital standards, supervision, and market discipline.[7] To supervise large, complex, and globally-active banks effectively, U.S. regulators (e.g., the Federal Reserve) have developed a special supervisory program for large and complex banking organizations which focuses on continuous risk-assessment approach. Market discipline can provide oversight functions more closely to business practice by: (1) linking banks' funding costs of both debt and equity more closely to their risk-taking; and (2) providing a supplementary reliable and objective source of information to the examination process.

Chairman Greenspan (1999) suggested a multi-track approach to bank supervision and prudential oversight by seeking to strengthen market discipline, supervision, and minimum capital regulation.[8]

4.4.1 Market Discipline

Market discipline now plays an important role in banking behavior and supervision through disclosing adequate and relevant disclosures to market participants. This market discipline is more important and evident when a large portion of bank assets are funded by non-insured liabilities. An effective market discipline requires: (1) the enhancement in the amount and kind of public disclosure that uninsured claimants need about bank activities and on-and-off balance sheet assets; and (2) the establishment of new disclosure standards to uniformize and improve banks' public disclosure and risk-management practices.

Effective market discipline can be achieved when market participants including investors, financial intermediaries, and policymakers receive timely, reliable, and relevant information. This requires that financial reporting of financial institutions properly disclose the distribution of the institutions' internal ratings, asset quality, risk management, and management practices. Lack of existence of uniform international accounting standards based on fair value and ineffective enforcement of these accounting standards hamper the quality of information being received by the global market participants. Improper financial disclosure can cause bad decision making and poor risk management assessment which may result in ineffective market discipline.

There should also be effective and comprehensive procedures for monitoring the performance of banks worldwide in meeting the established international banking standards (e.g., Basel Committee) as well as international accounting standards in reporting compliance with banking standards. Finally, failure to require fair value accounting for financial reporting purposes of financial institutions worldwide can induce serious distortions in the financial reports because there is always an incentive to realize gains on assets whose value has increased and retain assets whose value has declined.

4.4.2 Supervision

The most effective and efficient approach to bank supervision is to examine the safety and soundness of the overall structure and operation of banks' risk-management systems. Proper emphasis and reliance on banks' internal risk-management systems can also be used to enhance prudential assessment of a bank's capital adequacy. Indeed, the Federal Reserve, in June 1999, issued new examination guidance encouraging banks to perform self-assessment of their capital adequacy in light of objective and quantifiable measurement of risk. This internal self-assessment will be evaluated during on-site examinations and will be considered in assigning supervisory ratings.

According to the provisions of the Gramm-Leach-Bliley (GLB) Act and the amendment to Regulation Y issued by the Federal Reserve Board, banking organizations can elect to become financial holding companies and perform a variety of financial services now allowed under the GLB Act. The Board also applies capital and managerial standards to foreign banks wishing to establish financial holding companies comparable to those pertaining to U.S. banking organizations. The U.S. bank risk-based capital standards of six percent Tier 1 capital and 10 percent total capital are also applied to foreign banks becoming financial holding companies. In supervising FHCs, especially global FHCs, the Federal Reserve considers provisions of the GLB Act and relies on the Basel Committee to continue coordinating banking supervisory policies and practices worldwide. The global capital adequacy, determined based on the level of underlying systematic and economic risk, is an essential supervisory tool for fostering the safety and soundness of banks worldwide.

Reform of the supervisory role for the Federal Reserve and regulatory structure for financial institutions is needed to keep pace with the ever-changing characteristics and environment of the financial services industry. The passage of the Bank Holding Company Act Amendments of 1970 increased the role of the Federal Reserve in bank supervision and regulations. There has been debate in the financial community around the issues of whether there is a conflict of interest in this dual role of the Federal Reserve as related to monetary policy objectives, on one hand, and the supervision and regulation role on the other hand. Other countries (e.g., United Kingdom) have addressed the issue of reforming regulatory structures to better deal with the current changes in the financial services industry. Indeed, the new Financial Services Authority (FSA) established in the United Kingdom to authorize, supervise, and regulate all forms of financial services including banks.[9] The primary reason for transferring bank supervision to the FSA was the current changes in "financial innovation and globalization." This important issue of separating central banking and bank regulation has received considerable attention in the United States and has been addressed by the Shadow Financial Regulatory Committee.[10] The Committee made the following observations and recommendations regarding the Federal Reserve perceived conflict of interest problems:

> There is at times a clear conflict of interest inherent in the Fed's carrying on roles as both a promoter of stability in the domestic and international financial markets and as a supervisor of banking organizations. . . . The authority to supervise national banks and their holding companies should rest with the Comptroller of the Currency,

Exhibit 4.4 Bank Supervisory and Regulatory Environment

Source	Date of Establishment	Mission	Applicability	Provisions
Federal Deposit Insurance Corporation (FDIC)	1933 as part of the Federal Reserve Act and in 1950 under the Federal Deposit Insurance Act.	1. To promote and preserve public confidence in financial institutions. 2. To project the money supply through insurance coverage for deposits.	1. Insures deposits of up to $100,000 in: (1) national banks; (2) state banks that apply for federal deposit insurance; and (3) federally insured S & Ls.	1. Maintains separate insurance funds to insure financial institutions: (a) Bank Insurance Fund (BIF); and (b) the Savings Association Insurance Fund (SAIF). 2. Requires regular financial reporting on the part of insured banks.
Resolution Trust Corporation (RTC)	1989 Financial Institutions Reform, Recovery & Enforcement Act	1. To manage and resolve financially troubled thrift institutions. 2. Dispose of residual assets in a manner that: (a) maximizes returns and minimizes losses to the FDIC Insurance fund; (b) minimizes the impact on local real estate and financial markets; and (c) maximizes the preservation of the availability and affordability of residential property for low- and moderate-income individuals.	1. Acts as conservator or receiver for savings associations that are under the direct control of the government or that have failed.	1. Develops policies and programs for the management and disposition of all the real property assets under its jurisdiction. 2. Its funding comes from three sources: (1) the Resolution Funding Corporation; (2) a line of credit from the U.S. Treasury; and (3) unsecured obligations issued by the RTC.

Institution	Established	Purpose	Supervises/Insures	Functions
Federal Financial Institutions Examination Council	In 1978 by Congress	1. To provide consistency and progress in federal examination and supervision of financial institutions.	1. Insured bank.	1. The authority to establish principles, standards, reporting forms, and systems.
Federal Reserve System	In 1913 by the Federal Reserve Act	1. To perform as the central bank of the United States. 2. To assume responsibility for administering and making policy for the nation's credit and monetary affairs. 3. To act as fiscal agent, legal depository, and custodian of funds for the U.S. government. 4. Oversee the safety and soundness of state-chartered banks that choose to become members of the Federal Reserve System.	1. State member insured banks (other than DC). 2. Bank holding companies and their subsidiaries.	1. Holding the legal reserves of banks and other depository institutions. 2. Providing write transfers of funds. 3. Facilitating clearance and collection of checks. 4. Examining and supervising state-chartered member banks and bank holding companies. 5. Collecting and disseminating economic data.
Federal Home Loan Bank System	In 1932 by the Federal Home Loan Bank Act	1. To provide a flexible credit reserve for member savings institutions engaged in home mortgage lending.	1. Savings associations, insured banks, and insured credit unions with at least 10% of their assets in residential mortgage loans.	1. Provides advances to its members as a supplement to savings flows in meeting recurring variations in the supply and demand for residential mortgage credit.

Exhibit 4.4 *(Continued)*

Source	Date of Establishment	Mission	Applicability	Provisions
Offices of the Comptroller of the Currency (OCC)	1863 as part of the national banking system.	1. The Comptroller of the Currency is: (a) the Chief Regulatory Officer for national banks; and (b) responsbile for governing the operations of national banks. 2. The OCC has authority to charter national banks.	1. Examines all national banks to determine their financial condition, soundness of operations, quality of management, and compliance with federal regulations. 2. Oversees the regulation of federally licensed branches and agencies of foreign banks.	1. Operates as an independent unit within the Department of the Treasury.
Office of Thrift Supervision (OTS)	1986 as part of the FIRREA.	1. Has responsibility for chartering and regulating federal savings associations and their holding companies. 2. Supervising state-chartered savings associations.	1. Assures the safety and soundness of federally chartered S & Ls and federal savings banks.	1. Operates as an independent unit within the Department of the Treasury.
State Banking Departments		1. Every state has an agency that supervises and monitors state-chartered banks.	1. Many state-chartered banks are also: (1) members of the Federal Reserve System; (2) insured by the FDIC; and (3) subject to the regulation of those agencies.	

while similar responsibility for state chartered banks and their holding companies should be transferred to the Federal Deposit Insurance Corporation. (Shadow Committee, Statement #153, December 7, 1998.)

Effective bank supervision in the twenty-first century according to Spillenkothen (1999) depends on the proper development and implementation of the following strategies:

- Enhanced supervisory focus on the quality of internal systems and processes for identifying, measuring, monitoring, and controlling risks.
- Active encouragement of banks to continually develop, reassess, and upgrade sound risk management policies and practices.
- Substantial improvements in public disclosure by banks and greater reliance on financial markets to discipline and "regulate" bank risk taking.[11]

4.4.3 Minimum Capital Regulation

The regulatory capital requirements can be viewed as the third pillar of bank supervision and prudential oversight. The 1988 Basel Accord, in an attempt to create a level playing field for international banks, for the first time, provides a common international definition of bank capital. The regulatory capital requirements should be linked to banks' internal risk ratings to ensure the adequacy of capital. During the past decade, banks and bank hold companies worldwide have been subject to a set of regulatory capital guidelines that define minimum amounts of capital to be held against various categories of on-and off balance sheet position. The guidelines are established based on the 1988 "Basel Accord" adopted by the Basel Committee on Banking Supervision, comprised of bank supervisors from the G-10 countries (see Wagster, 1996 for a thorough discussion of the Basel Accord).[12] Other countries have also adopted bank capital standards based on the Basel Accord that specify which debt and equity instruments on a bank's balance sheet qualify as regulatory capital. The U.S. risk-based capital standards conform to the guidelines of the Basel Accord.

The initial Basel Accord and U.S. risk-based capital guidelines focused primarily on a bank's credit risk exposure in suggesting minimum capital standards. The primary purposes of the risk-based capital measure according to the Basel Committee on Banking Supervision and as implemented by the Federal Reserve are to:

1. ensure that regulatory capital requirements are sensitive to differences in risk profiles among banking organizations;
2. achieve greater uniformity and consistency in the assessment of the capital adequacy of major banks worldwide;
3. factor off-balance-sheet exposures (e.g., derivatives) into the measurement of capital adequacy; and
4. minimize disincentives to holding liquid, low-risk assets.

The above risk-based capital measure is intended to evaluate the credit risk associated with the nature of banking organizations and provides a definition of capital and a framework for determining risk-weighted assets by relating assets and off-balance-sheet items to broad categories of credit risk. A bank's risk-based capital ratio is then calculated by dividing its qualifying capital by its risk-weighted assets. This risk-based capital ration establishes minimum supervisory capital standards that apply to all banking organizations on a consolidated basis. This ratio focuses primarily on credit risk and its impact on capital adequacy. Thus, for overall assessment purposes of capital adequacy, the other components of risk, including interest rate, liquidity, funding, and market risks should be taken into consideration.

The two elements of the risk-based capital ratio are the qualifying capital and risk-weighted assets. Banking organizations' capital consists of two major components: core capital and supplementary capital. Core capital elements, also known as tier 1 capital, consist of common equity (e.g., common stock and retained earnings), qualifying noncumulative perpetual preferred stock, and minority interest in the equity accounts of consolidated subsidiaries. Supplementary capital elements, also known as tier 2 capital, include a limited amount of the allowance for loan and lease losses, perpetual preferred stock that does not qualify as tier 2 (e.g., perpetual preferred stock of bank holding companies exceeding the 25 percent cap of tier 1 capital), mandatory convertible securities and other hybrid capital instruments, long-term preferred stock, intermediate preferred stock, limited amounts of subordinated debt, and unrealized holding gains on qualifying equity securities. The qualifying capital for the purpose of calculating the risk-based capital ratio is the sum of tier 1 and tier 2 capital less any deductions.

The denominator of the risk-based capital ratio is the risk-weighted assets which are calculated by assigning one of four broad risk categories (e.g., 0, 20, 50, and 100 percent) to each asset and off-balance-sheet items. The four broad risk categories are determined based on the obligor, guarantor, or type of collateral. However, the standard risk category most often used for the majority of assets is 100 percent. The risk-weighted assets are calculated by multiplying dollar value of the amount in each category by associated risk and then adding together to determine the risk-weighted assets. Nevertheless, in 1996, both the U.S. risk-based capital guidelines and the Basel Accord were amended to incorporate minimum capital standards for a bank's exposure to market risk.[13] Market risk is broadly defined as the risk of loss from an adverse movement in the market value of an asset, liability, or off-balance sheet position. Market risk is determined by the volatility of underlying risk factors such as interest rates, exchange rates, equity prices, or commodity prices as well as the sensitivity of the bank's portfolio to movements in these risk factors.

Currently, capital standards focus on the market risk resulting from a bank's trading activities as well as its overall exposure to interest risk. The market risk capital standards require both a quantitative minimum capital charge based on the output of a bank's internal risk-management model and a number of qualitative standards for the measurement and management of market risk. The qualitative standards incorporate some of the basic principles of sound risk management into the capital requirement and consists of:

- A risk measurement system that is conceptually sound and adequate and is implemented effectively with integrity.
- Periodic stress tests of its portfolio to assess the impact of extreme market conditions.
- An independent risk control unit that is separate from the business units that generate market risk exposure.
- An independent review of the bank's risk management and measurement process conducted by internal and/or external auditors.

The qualitative capital requirements consist of separate capital charges for general market risk and specific risk. General market risk is defined in the capital standards as the risk resulting from movements in the general level of underlying risk factors such as interest rates, exchange rates, and equity prices and commodity prices. Specific risk is defined as the risk of an adverse movement in the price of an individual security due to factors related to the individual insurer which is intended to cover even the credit risk.

The Federal Reserve amended its risk-based capital framework in August 1996 to incorporate a measure of market risk. Financial institutions with $1 billion or more trading activity or global trading activity greater than 10 percent of their total assets should assess their market risk using their internal value-at-risk (VAR). Financial institutions may calculate VAR using an internal model based on variance-covariance matrices, historical simulations, Monte Carlo simulations, or other statistical approaches.

The 1996 market-risk amendment requires that a supervisor request the following quarterly market-risk related information:[14]

- Total trading gain or loss for the quarter;
- Average risk-based capital charge for market risk during the quarter;
- Market-risk capital charge for general risk during the quarter;
- Average one-day VAR for the quarter;
- Maximum one-day VAR for the quarter;
- Larger one-day loss during the quarter and the VAR for the preceding day;
- The number of times the loss exceeded the one-day VAR during the quarter, and for each occurrence, the amount of the loss and the prior day's VAR;
- The cause of back-testing exceptions, either by portfolio or major risk factor;
- The market-risk multiplier currently in use.

An institution's VAR measures must also meet the following quantitative requirements:

- The VAR methodology must be commensurate with the nature and size of the institution's trading activities and risk profile.
- VAR measures must be computed each business day based on a 99 percent (one-tailed) confidence level of estimated maximum loss.
- VAR measures must be based on a price shock equivalent to a 10-day movement in rates and prices.
- VAR measures must be based on a minimum historical observation period of one year for estimating future price and rate changes.
- VAR model data must be updated at least once every three months and more frequently if market conditions warrant.
- VAR measures may incorporate empirical correlations both within and across broad risk categories.
- VAR measures must be reviewed for aggregating VAR estimates across the entire portfolio.

The general market risk charge is based on the bank's internal value-at-risk model, which determines an estimate of the maximum amount that the bank can lose on a particular portfolio over a given holding period with a given degree of statistical confidence level and precision. A number of empirical approaches have been used to calculate value-at-risk estimates based on the behavior and movements of underlying risk factors (e.g., interest rates, exchange rates).[15] For the purposes of the supervisory standard, these value-at-risk estimates are calculated on a daily basis using a minimum historical observation period of one year, or the equivalent of one year if observations are weighted over time. The capital charge for general market risk is equal to the average value-at-risk estimate over the previous sixty trading days (approximately one quarter) times a "multiplication factor," typically equal to three (3) calibrated to a ten-day, 99th percentile standard. This common supervisory standard is required to ensure that the capital charge entails a consistent prudential level across banks. For example, if the ten-day, 99th percentile value-at-risk is calculated to be $100, it means that the bank would expect to lose more than $100 on only 1 out of 100 ten-day periods. The purpose of this supervisory minimum capital standard is to ensure that banks hold adequate capital to withstand the impacts of prolonged and/or severe adverse movements in the market rates and prices that affect the value of their trading portfolios.

The specific risk capital charges are intended to cover the risks of adverse price movements related to factors pertaining to the issuer of an individual security and are applicable to long- and short-term debt and equity positions in the bank's trading portfolio. Under the initial risk-based capital guidelines, long-term debt and equity positions in the trading portfolio were subject to capital charges ranging from zero percent (for government securities) to eight percent (for corporate debt and equity) of the book value of the positions (see Dimson and Marsh, 1995 for an in-depth discussion of regulatory capital requirements for securities firms).[16]

4.4.4   Safety and Soundness

The three core components of capital requirements as discussed by Estrella (1995) are: (1) a definition of capital; (2) a measure of the bank's exposure to risk that the capital is intended to cover; and (3) a required relationship between the two amounts.[17] Approximately once every 12 to 18 months, federal or state supervisors examine each U.S. commercial bank to assess its safety and soundness. This examination reveals the CAMELS rating measuring the bank's *C*apital adequacy, *A*sset quality, *M*anagement, *E*arnings, *L*iquidity, and *S*ensitivity to market risk determined by the supervisor. Each bank is rated from 1, the highest, to 5, the lowest, on each of the component categories and given a composite rating. Banks with a rating of 1 (sound in every respect) or 2 (fundamentally sound) are not likely to be constrained in any way by supervisory oversight. Banks with a CAMELS rating of 3 (flawed performance) are likely to have potential problems addressed by the examiners that are considered to be correctable. Banks with a 4 rating (potential of failure, impaired viability) are viewed to incur a significant risk of failure. Finally, banks with a CAMELS rating of 5 (high probability of failure, severely deficient performance) are those banks with the most severe problems. These ratings are determined by the examination of a combination of publicly-available information (e.g., financial statements, audit reports) and private information produced by bank examiners during their investigation (e.g., the quality of individual loans).

These CAMELS ratings on individual institutions are viewed as extremely confidential by each of the bank regulators. Until recently, the Federal Deposit Insurance Corporation

(FDIC) had a policy of not disclosing the CAMELS rating even to bank management. Recently, supervisors report these ratings only to top management of the bank, who may not reveal them to employees, customers, or financial market participants. Therefore, neither the public nor any financial market participants (e.g., financial analysts) have access to CAMELS rating data on individual banks. It is assumed that the public release of such data can be very detrimental to a bank, particularly if it became widely known that examiners determined a bank had a very high probability of failure. Even though the CAMELS ratings are not publicly available, banks prefer to have a good rating because it can affect the extent of their minimum capital requirements, the frequency and nature of future supervisory examinations, the types of activities undertaken, and the amount a bank pays for deposit insurance. Berger and Davies (1994) found that the CAMELS ratings are value-relevant containing useful private information uncovered during the course of bank exams that is not known to the public.[18]

4.5   FINANCIAL MODERNIZATION: THE GRAMM-LEACH-BLILEY ACT

Mergers and acquisitions among U.S. banks and thrifts, which trailed off in 1999 (total M & A deals of 349) compared to a booming 1998 (total M & A deals of 506) are expected to substantially increase for several reasons, including improvements in banks' profitability, the expected elimination of pooling of interest accounting, the implication of the Gramm-Leach-Bliley Act, and increases in the number of prime acquisition targets. The 1990s have experienced an unpredictable pace of bank mergers and acquisitions. Number of bank M & A deals grew from 170 in 1990 to 413 in 1998. As a result of M & A activities, the number of banks operating in the United States has declined over 30 percent since 1990.

On November 12, 1999, President Clinton signed the Gramm-Leach-Bliley Act known as the Financial Services Modernization Act allowing banks to merge with securities firms and insurance companies within financial holding companies. The Act makes banking regulations more consistent with marketplace realities and financial services more aligned with the needs of consumers. This Act will further expand the merger opportunities for banking organizations and may tend towards a new wave of convergence in the financial services industry. The provisions of the Act are as follows:

- Permits commercial banks to affiliate with investment banks by repealing provisions of the Glass Steagall Act of 1933.
- Allows companies that own commercial banks to offer any type of financial services by modifying the Bank Holding Company Act of 1956.
- Permits subsidiaries of banks to offer a broad range of financial services that are not allowed for banks themselves.
- Removes remaining statutory limitations on the financial activities allowable in banking organizations for qualified bank holding companies.
- Creates "financial holding companies" that may conduct a broad range of financial activities including insurance and securities underwriting, merchant banking, real estate development and investment.

- Delays approval of cross-industry mergers until 120 days after enactment (mid-March 2000.)

- Establishes restrictions on the locations of the new or expanded nonbank financial activities within the banking organization.

- Blends functional supervision of the component entities with umbrella supervision of consolidated financial holding companies by requiring that: (a) the Federal Reserve supervises the consolidated organization; (b) bank regulators regulate and supervise the banking subsidiaries; and (c) functional regulators supervise and regulate selected nonbank components.

- Improves privacy protections on disseminating information about customer accounts to third parties.

- Affects the implementation of the Community Reinvestment Act of 1977 (CRA) including the requirement that a bank holding company cannot become a financial holding company unless all the company's insured depository institutions have a CRA rating of at least satisfactory. The CRA requires banks that take deposits in a community to also make a certain level of loans available to that community including low- and moderate-income areas. Banks are regularly examined for compliance with the CRA on their lending investments and community development activities in particular areas and can obtain one of four ratings: outstanding, satisfactory, needs to improve, and substantial noncompliance.

Proponents of the Act argue that the act will benefit consumers by allowing "one-stop-shopping" for all of their financial services and will enable U.S. financial services providers to compete more effectively in the global market. Critics of the Act argue that the Act's implementation will lead to unhealthy concentration of financial services, will weaken requirements that banks reinvest funds in local communities, and inadequately protect consumers' private financial information. The banking industry would benefit from the provisions of the Act in the following ways:

- National banks including community banks through their established subsidiaries will be able to offer their financial services without geographical limitations.

- Community banks under $500 million in assets obtain much greater access to Federal Home Loan Bank advances which expands their ability to obtain lendable funds and meet other liquidity needs.

- National and state banks remain protected from discriminatory state rules on the sale of insurance and other financial services.

- Banks of all sizes are able to offer a wide range of financial products and services without the costly restraints of outdated laws (e.g., the "town of 5000" provision).

- Banking organizations and other financial services companies (e.g., securities, insurance, financial technology) are able to combine much more readily.

The GLB Act of 1999 will affect the Community Reinvestment Act (CRA) in three ways: (1) qualification process; (2) examination process; and (3) sunshine provisions:

1. Qualification process: Based on the provisions of the GLB Act, all subsidiaries and affiliates of banking organizations should have CRA ratings of at least satisfactory to qualify for establishing financial holding companies (FHC) or converting the existing

bank holding companies to FHCs. These provisions of the GLB Act further extend the review of CRA performance to transactions involving nonbanking financial activities.

2. Examination process: Currently small insured depository institutions are examined on a three-year cycle for compliance with applicable laws and regulations including CRA, Equal Credit Opportunity, and Truth in Lending. The GLB Act changed this three-year cycle, for small institutions only, to a four-year interval or a five-year cycle if the institution's last CRA rating was "satisfactory" or "outstanding," respectively.

3. Sunshine provisions: Sunshine provisions of the GLB Act require financial institutions to provide new data on their lending agreements with community groups. If these lending agreements involve loans of $50,000 or above a year and payment of $10,000 or above per year, then both the institution and the community groups must publicly disclose the agreements and make annual reports to the institution's regulator. Even though institutions' regulators do not influence these lending agreements with community groups, they enforce compliance with their reporting requirements under the GLB Act.

The GLB Act permits creation of new types of regulated institutions namely "financial holding companies" that are authorized to offer a broad range of financial products and services. A financial holding company is a bank holding company whose depository institutions are well capitalized and well managed. The GLB Act and the Federal Reserve Board have established rules that specify conditions that must be met for a bank holding company or a foreign bank to become a financial holding company authorized to engage in expanded activities. The Federal Reserve Board has approved 362 financial holding companies, as of August 2000, in the 11 regulatory federal reserve districts. To become a financial holding company, a domestic bank holding company must file with the appropriate Reserve Board a written declaration that contains the following information:

1. a statement that the bank holding company elects to be a financial holding company,
2. the name and head office address of the company and of each depository institution controlled by the company,
3. a certification that all depository institutions controlled by the company are well capitalized,
4. the capital ratios for all relevant capital measures, and
5. a certification that all depository institutions controlled by the company are well managed.

The GLB Act authorizes a financial holding company to engage in the following activities:

1. activities pertaining to banking under the Bank Holding Company Act (e.g., lending, leasing, investment advice),
2. normal activities in connection with the transaction of banking abroad (e.g., management consulting),
3. financial activities such as underwriting and dealing in securities, insurance underwriting, and merchant banking,
4. any other activities that are financial in nature, incidental to financial activities, or complementary to financial activities. Prior Federal Reserve Board approval is required for the cases of being incidental to financial activities and complementary to financial activities.

4.6 FINANCIAL REPORTING PROCESS OF FINANCIAL INSTITUTIONS

Current financial statements of banks are combinations of values derived from fair-value, cost-basis, depreciation, amortization, impairment, and other accounting standards. The 1980s and early 1990s witnessed the greatest number of financial institution failures in U.S. history. The savings and loan association crisis of the 1980s and banking organization financial problems of the early 1990s caused many to question the usefulness and relevance of historical cost financial reporting in reflecting the true economic net worth of troubled financial institutions. Many troubled financial institutions had negative economic net worth, even though based on historical cost accounting, they reported positive net worth in excess of regulatory requirements.

The highly publicized crisis in the S & L industry has been attributed to a number of causes including economic downturn, deregulation, fraud, changes in tax laws, problems in real estate markets, and lax lending standards. Mandated accounting standards have also been criticized for their tendency to overstate financial institutions' earnings, net worth, and underlying asset values. There is no evidence that indicates that the use of historical cost accounting caused financial institutions to fail; however, many argue that fair value accounting would have provided warning signals of possible financial difficulties and led regulators, bank supervisors, and other financial statement users to address the institutions' financial difficulties earlier.

During the S & L crisis, many S & Ls had a negative spread between the asset yields and cost of funds that resulted in both a negative cash flow and a decrease in the value of the loans. These decreases in S & L net worth encouraged financial institutions to use Regulatory Accounting Principles (RAP) as a means of meeting government-mandated minimum capital requirements. During the S & L crisis, the Federal Home Loan Bank Board (FHLBB) permitted S & Ls to deviate from generally-accepted accounting principles (GAAP) in certain ways as part of a program of regulatory forbearance. There are several differences between RAP and GAAP used by business firms. For example, under RAP, financial institutions could deter losses of sales of assets with below-market yield. This practice allowed the write-off of loans over the life of the loan rather than when the loss occurred (as GAAP required). Another example of following RAP in violation of GAAP was that regulators permitted an increase to the capital account of S & Ls for the appraisal value of owned property, which helped boost the S & Ls net worth above the minimum capital requirements. Brewer (1989) stated that "GAAP reveals that many of the currently insolvent S & Ls have been insolvent for quite some time. In contrast, RAP suggests that the problem is more recent."[19]

The S & L debacle has demonstrated the insufficiency and irrelevancy of historical costs in reflecting economic reality of business. The lack of fair value accounting encouraged S & Ls to recognize transactions that were not in the best interest of the institution. For example, S & Ls often recognized the increase in value of the bonds sold as income or net worth, while any decline in the value of bonds were ignored or not written down. The seriousness of problems facing the S & L industry led to the passage of the Financial Institutions Reform, Recovery, and Enforcement Act (FIRREA) in August 1989. Furthermore, in 1991, the Federal Deposit Insurance Corporation Improvement Act (FDICIA) introduced mandatory procedures called prompt correction action (PCA), which requires regulators to promptly close depository institutions when their capital falls below predetermined quantitative standards. The FDICIA also required that RAP be no less conservative than GAAP in determining the regulatory capital requirements.

During the past two decades, there has been considerable interest in the reporting by financial institutions of the fair values of their financial instruments either as complements or substitutes for historical book values. Traditionally, the financial community, regulatory bodies, standard-setting authorities, and the accounting profession have continued to express conflicting views of the desirability and feasibility of using the fair value accounting (FVA) approach for financial reporting purposes. The accounting profession and legislators have not fully confronted the issue of FVA with historical cost accounting (HCA); however, the new accounting standards indicate that they are heading in this direction. Fair value, market value-based, mark-to-market, and market-value accounting are frequently used interchangeably as synonyms.

The adoption of FMV for financial reporting purposes has long been a subject of controversy, both in the financial community and the accounting professions. Proponents of FVA (e.g., Morris and Sellon, 1991[20]; Mondschean, 1992[21]) assert that its use in financial reporting provides more useful and reliable financial information and reduces the alleged gain-trading problems of selling high-quality assets to recognize gains while retaining poor-quality assets to avoid realizing related losses. Advocates of FVA also believe that fair value provides more relevant and useful measures of assets, liability, and earnings than the use of historical cost. Opponents of FVA (e.g., Mergh, 1990[22]; Sulton and Johnson, 1993[23]) take the position that it is not justifiable nor reasonable to report intermediate fluctuations in investment value until it is realized. In addition, the major arguments against fair market value (FMV) center around the possible volatility in reported earnings and owner's equity resulting from the use of FMV and the lack of reliability and objectivity in determining FMV of items that are not publicly traded. Nevertheless, disclosure of objectivity-measured and reliable fair values could improve the effectiveness of market and regulatory discipline and to the extent that the use of FVA improves the measurement of capital, it could call for more timely supervision action of capital-impaired institutions.

The financial services industry has been depicted as strongly opposed to any move toward the use of FVA. KPMG Peat Marwick[24] (KPMG Coopers now, 1992) conducted a survey in 1992 which shows that 90 percent of the participating bankers, analysts, and users of financial statements in the United States opposes the use of fair value accounting. Ninety-five percent of the respondents prefer historical cost accounting, with supplemental fair value disclosures. The survey found that users of financial statements (e.g., investors, analysts) were less opposed to their use of FVA than preparers of financial statements. Even though the fair value accounting debates relate to all financial items of all entities (e.g., assets, liabilities, owner's equity items) the focus has been on the use of FVA for assets and liabilities of financial institutions, especially banks' investment securities.

The usefulness of historical cost-based financial statements is extensively debated in the literature. Historical balance sheet measurements are viewed as irrelevant, and more useful concepts such as fair value are suggested as measurement attributes. If the purpose of financial institutions is to increase shareholder's value, the existing historical financial reporting fails to properly report changes in shareholder value. Currently, Pricewaterhouse Coopers, one of the big five CPA firms, has developed an approach called ValueReporting, which focuses on cash and nonfinancial measures driving shareholder value creation.[25]

ValueReporting is a comprehensive set of financial and other nonfinancial performance benchmarks tailored to the company that provide both historical and predictive indicators of shareholder value creation. It focuses on value creation and the underlying activities that are crucial to the company's ability to generate sustainable shareholder value.

The main theme of ValueReporting is that management should compile and report relevant, reliable, and timely information regarding the company's value derivers and factors that increase the shareholder's value. Factors that are driving the change in corporate reporting are changes in the capital market and the internal characteristics of the company. Changes in the capital market consist of (1) ever-increasing globalization of capital markets; (2) growing interest in the concept of shareholder value; (3) consolidation and convergence in most industries, especially the financial services industry; (4) greater use of technology and sophisticated valuation models; and (5) investors' investment strategies of holding stock on a long-term basis to create value. Changes in the internal characteristics of companies include (1) shareholder value orientation (greater focus on cash flow); (2) increasing use of balanced scorecards linking performance to shareholder value creation; and (3) embedding of value-based management systems and procedures. This ValueReporting can be used as supplementary reporting to the existing financial reports to provide additional relevant information to users of financial reports, especially investors. The ValueReporting approach provides fair value information for all financial items that can be useful as the global economy and business shift away from industrial and move toward a more service-based business and economy. For example, it is easier to determine the value of manufacturing inventory than the value of the user base of an Internet shopping site. Thus, as intangible assets grow, more value-relevant information on these assets should be disclosed on a timely basis.

Theoretically, there are three possible approaches to the implementation of FVA for financial reporting purposes: (1) adopt FVA for certain assets, with an objectively determinable fair market value (e.g., trade investments); (2) piecemeal adoption of FMV for selected assets and liabilities (e.g., match funds with liabilities of similar duration); and (3) adopt a comprehensive FVA system to determine and disclose fair value of all on-and-off balance sheet assets, liabilities, and owner's equity. The Financial Accounting Standards Board (FASB) has eventually moved toward the possible requirements of a comprehensive FVA system for financial institutions during the past 20 years by issuing a number of Statements of Financial Accounting Standards (SFAS) pertaining to the fair value of financial instruments. The FASB has issued several SFAS on disclosure of the fair value of financial instruments including loans, equity securities, and derivatives. They are as follows:

- SFAS No. 105, "Disclosure of Information about Financial Instruments with Off-Balance Sheet Risk and Financial Instruments with Concentration of Credit Risk," in March 1990.
- SFAS No. 107, "Disclosure about Fair Value of Financial Instruments," in December 1991.
- SFAS No. 114, "Accounting by Creditors for Impairment of a Loan," in May 1993.
- SFAS No. 118, "Accounting by Creditors for Impairment of a Loan—Income Recognition and Disclosure," in August 1994.
- SFAS No. 119, "Disclosure about Derivative Financial Instruments and Fair Value of Financial Instruments," in October 1994.

These SFAS require additional disclosures of the fair value information on both assets and liabilities as well as the accounting treatment for loan impairment. A loan is impaired when it is probable that the creditor cannot collect all amounts due according to the loan agreements.

One major difficulty with these standards is that they permit a wide variety of approaches which may impair comparability of financial statements. Another concern with these standards is that the valuation exercise often takes place at the end of the reporting period and management has a variety of options in determining fair value. Since market information at the year end is the key criterion in most valuation methods, and a variety of methods can be used, year-end valuation estimations may not properly reflect the performance of the bank's secured or unsecured loans during the fiscal year. Although SFAS Nos. 105, 107, and 118 were steps in the right direction, fair values suggested in these standards did not address the risk aspect of loan types or asset composition. Finally, the FASB has issued SFAS Nos. 115 and 133, which establish guidelines for the measurement, recognition, and reporting of fair values of investment in debt and equity securities as well as derivatives, respectively.

4.7 STATEMENT OF FINANCIAL ACCOUNTING STANDARDS (SFAS) NO. 115

The FASB issued SFAS No. 115, "Accounting for Certain Investment in Debt and Equity Securities" in May 1993. SFAS No. 115 is one of the challenging accounting standards pertaining to financial institutions. SFAS No. 115 intended to: (1) provide better uniformity in the financial reporting process of financial institutions; (2) standardize portfolio accounting practices across industry lines; (3) establish guidelines for the fair value measurement, recognition, and reporting of investments in debt and equity securities; and (4) discourage financial institutions from selectively selling securities recorded at historical cost in an attempt to manage their reported earnings (gains trading). SFAS No. 115 has generated widespread interest and criticism by requiring the use of fair value accounting for certain investments in debt and equity securities. SFAS No. 115 defined the following terms:

- Financial Instruments. SFAS No. 115 defines a financial instrument as a debt or equity security that evidences an ownership interest in an entity or a contract that: (1) contractually obligates an entity to transfer cash or another financial instrument to a second entity or exchange financial instruments on potentially unfavorable terms with the second entity; and (2) provides that second entity a contractual right to receive cash or other financial instruments from the first entity or exchange other financial instruments on potentially unfavorable terms with the first entity.

- Security. SFAS No. 115 defines a security as a share, participation, or other interest in property or in the issuer's enterprise that is represented by a financial instrument that can be divisible into classes of shares, participations, interests, or obligations. Securities include debt securities (also called credit instruments) and equity instruments, which represent ownership interests in a company.

- Fair value. SFAS No. 115 retains SFAS No. 107's definition of fair value as the amount at which buyers and sellers are willing, not forced as in a liquidation sale, to exchange financial instruments. Management should determine these values from the most active stock exchanges as possible using quoted market prices. For example, auction markets (e.g., the New York Stock Exchange) would be preferable to dealer markets that usually contain buy-sell "spreads" (e.g., the over-the-counter markets). Similarly, broker markets, where buyers and sellers often do not know each other's needs (e.g., private placements) are preferable to principal-to-principal markets, where buyers and sellers exchange securities for cash using intermediaries' services. Techniques now available to measure fair value include closing prices for auction markets, the average of closing bid and asked prices for dealer markets, using broker prices or quoted values of "similar" financial instruments to ascertain the value of certain not-readily-available fair values, and relying on "valid" mathematical models (e.g., capital pricing, binomial pricing, or Black-Sholes models) for certain types of financial instruments.

- Debt securities include U.S. Treasury bonds, U.S. agency securities, municipal securities, convertible debt, corporate bonds, commercial paper and secured debt instruments, such as collateralized mortgage obligations, but not unsecured trade accounts receivable and consumer loans payable.

- Equity securities consist of an entity's ownership interest in another entity or right to acquire or dispose of such an interest at a fixed or determinable price, including common stock, stock rights and warrants, and put and call options. Financial instruments also include foreign currency forward contracts, loan agreements, financial options and guarantees, loan commitments and letters of credit, but not convertible debt or redeemable preferred stock.

- SFAS No. 115 specifies that fair values of equity securities are readily determinable if they are traded on a securities exchange registered with the Securities and Exchange Commission or in the over-the-counter market, provided that sales prices or bid-and-asked quotations are currently determinable (i.e., if they are published and based on current transactions). However, SFAS No. 115 does not apply to investments in equity securities that were accounted for under the equity method or financial statement consolidation.

SFAS No. 115 classifies securities into three categories: held-to-maturity, trading, and available-for-sale. It also establishes different financial reporting treatments for each category of securities.

1. Held-to-maturity
   A financial institution should carry, at amortized cost, all debt securities that it has both the positive intent and ability to hold to maturity. Thus, management may not include securities in this category that it plans to hold for an indefinite amount of time or lacks a specific intent to sell or redeem by a specific date. Since the fair market value of such securities will normally reverse in the long-term, management should recognize no gains and losses on such debt instruments until the financial instruments mature.

2. Trading
   Entities purchase trading debt and equity securities for resale purposes, primarily to make short-term profits rather than holding them for longer-term capital appreciation. Financial institutions should thus carry at market value and include in income all unrealized gains and losses of such securities that were bought and held for the purpose of selling them in the near-term (e.g., within the entity's operating cycle). Trading securities also include mortgage-backed securities held for sale in conjunction with mortgage banking activities. Portfolio managers often continually trade financial instruments in this category.

Exhibit 4.5   Reporting Requirements of SFAS No. 115

	Held-to Maturity	Trading Securities	Available for Sale
Basis for Measurement	Amortized Cost	Fair Value	Fair Value
Recognition of Unrealized Gains and Losses	No recognition. Footnote disclosure only.	Recognize in Earnings.	Recognize in Stockholders' Equity.

3. Available-for-sale
   Entities should classify all securities that are not classified in the held-to-maturity or trading categories as available-for-sale. This catch-all category includes debt securities that do not meet the "intent-to-hold" criteria and equity securities that are not classified as trading securities. Financial institutions should carry these investments at market value and include unrealized gains and losses as a separate component of stockholders' equity without first going through the income statement, thereby minimizing earnings fluctuations on changes in the market values of such debt and equity securities. Management should defer recognizing in income unrealized gains and losses until realizing the revenues from these financial instruments. Exhibit 4.5 reveals reporting requirements of SFAS No. 115 for each securities category.

4.8   AUDITING PROPER CLASSIFICATIONS OF MARKETABLE SECURITIES

SFAS No. 115 in establishing accounting for certain investment securities relies heavily on management's intent and the entity's ability to hold the investment, but auditors needed some guidance to help "verify" this "ability." Thus, Statement on Auditing Standards (SAS) No. 81, "Auditing Investments," which becomes effective for periods ending on or after December 15, 1997 provides further guidance to auditors to evaluate such intent and ability. When evaluating management's intent, auditors should consider if actual investment activities are consistent with management's stated intent, which ordinarily requires examining records of investment strategies, records of investment activities, instructions to portfolio managers, and minutes of meetings of the board of directors or the investment committee. In evaluating an entity's ability to hold a debt security to maturity, auditors should consider factors such as the entity's financial position, working capital needs, operating results, debt agreements, and other relevant contractual obligations as well as laws and regulations.

SAS No. 81 also provides guidance regarding valuation of investments and evaluation of other-than-temporary impairment conditions. SAS No. 81 discusses various circumstances that may require differing auditing procedures ranging from testing quoted market prices for marketable securities to the need to consider the use of a specialist when a fair value estimate is based on a complex valuation model. The SAS also gives examples of factors to consider when an other-than-temporary impairment condition exists.

When auditing an entity's investments, auditors should be familiar with applicable accounting guidance and with the rules that apply both to the particular type of entity and to the types of investments it holds. SAS No. 81 discusses the evidence needed to corroborate assertions related to debt and equity securities investments primarily since the FASB now requires greater use of management's intent and ability to hold financial instruments and the related measuring of FMV. Since valid approaches to determine fair value can vary with the type of investment, auditors should determine if the entity's fair value is consistent with the approach specific in SFAS No. 115. For example, the use of market value quotations as opposed to estimation techniques is required when measuring the fair value of equity securities accounted for under SFAS No. 115.

4.9 TAX CONSIDERATION OF FAIR VALUE

The Revenue Reconciliation Act of 1993 expressed the position of the U.S. Congress on FVA for the financial services industry. Section 13223 of the 1993 Act requires the use of FVA for securities dealers and added Section 475 to the Internal Revenue Code. Section 475 affects the tax treatment of banks and other financial institutions that qualify as "dealers in securities" and provides a new boost toward the ultimate adoption of FVA for financial reporting and tax purposes. Exhibit 4.6 compares the provisions of SFAS No. 115 and Section 475.[26] The major similarities between Section 475 and SFAS No. 115 are: (1) the requirement of the use of FVA for securities reported for 1994 and thereafter; (2) establishment of more uniformity for certain investments in debt and equity securities; and (3) changes in managerial and financial activities of affected entities. The major differences are: (1) in the application of FVA rules; (2) classification of securities; (3) definition and nature of affected entities (dealers in securities); and (4) timing and character of gain or loss recognition for financial reporting and tax purposes.

Under Section 475: (1) securities dealers are required to use the mark-to-market method with respect to securities held in inventory; (2) a security may be any stock, bond, or other evidence of indebtedness; a beneficial interest in a widely-held partnership or trust; various notional principal contracts; and any option, forward, contract, currency, short position, or other derivative financial interest in the above securities; and (3) the mark-to-market rules do not apply to: (a) any security held for investment; (b) any evidence of indebtedness that dealers acquire or originate in the normal course of their business provided they are not held for sale to customers; and (c) any security that is issued as a hedge for another security that is not subject to the mark-to-market rules or as a hedge for a position, income right, or liability that is not a security in the taxpayer's hands; and (4) a dealer in securities is defined as any taxpayer who: (a) regularly purchases securities from or sells securities to customers in the ordinary course of a trade or business; or (b) regularly offers to enter into, assume, offset, assign, or otherwise terminate positions in securities with customers in the ordinary course of a trade or business.

The mark-to-market tax rules complement SFAS No. 115 and force financial institutions to report their earnings and investment portfolios on a more timely and realistic basis. The adoption of Section 475 significantly affects asset/liability management strategies of many financial institutions that have not traditionally been considered as securities dealers. Under Section 475, a community bank, thrift, or any other taxpayer that makes and then sells loans may be a dealer in securities. The implementation of SFAS No. 115 and Section 475 can: (1) reduce gains trading which is the practice of selling appreciated securities to recognize gains while retaining those that have fallen in value as long-term investments; (2) cause financial institutions to manage their investment portfolios more cautiously by requiring disclosure of fair value which better reflects the true economic value of assets and liabilities; and (3) provide early warning signals of financial difficulties by reflecting the fair value of assets and liabilities.

4.10   RECENT DEVELOPMENT OF FAIR VALUE ACCOUNTING

Many in the financial community believe that the existing financial reporting model, based on historical cost, is not keeping up with rapid changes in information technology, the global economy, and business. The FASB issued a proposal to make fair value accounting mandatory for virtually the entire bank balance sheet. The release of preliminary views suggesting fair value accounting has moved the FASB a step closer to adopting this controversial method of valuing assets and liabilities. Fair value accounting would present investors with relevant and useful information on the true current value of a loan, derivative, security, or deposit.

In December 1999, the FASB issued its Preliminary Views (PV) entitled, "Reporting Financial Instruments and Certain Related Assets and Liabilities at Fair Value."[27] The objective of the PV is to solicit comments on the Board's views regarding issues pertaining to reporting financial instruments at fair value. The FASB has reached preliminary decisions about: (1) the definition of fair value; (2) the definition of a financial instrument; and (3) general guidance for determining fair value. The FASB, however, has not yet decided when, if ever, it will be appropriate and feasible to report fair values of all financial instruments in the basic financial statements.

The FASB states that a financial instrument is one of the following: "(1) cash; (2) an ownership interest in an entity; (3) a contractual obligation of one entity to deliver a financial instrument to a second entity and a corresponding contractor's right of the second entity to receive that financial instrument in exchange for no consideration other than release from the obligation; and (4) a contractual obligation of one entity to exchange financial instruments with a second entity and a contractual right of the second entity to require an exchange of financial instruments with the first entity." To further clarify this broad definition of a financial instrument, the FASB provided examples of the types of financial instruments as well as items that are considered as financial instruments and items that are not financial instruments. These items are summarized in Exhibit 4.7.

The FASB defines fair value as "an estimate of the price an entity would have realized if it had sold an asset or paid if it had been relieved of a liability on the reporting date in an arm's length exchange motivated by normal business considerations. That is, it is an estimate of an exit price determined by market interactions." The FASB is in favor of exit prices as a proxy for fair value. The exit price for an asset or a liability is the price at which it could be sold or settled at present, which is determined by the market's estimate of the present value of its expected future cash flows. The exit price should reflect the amount, timing, and uncertainty of future cash flows of the entity that owns the asset or owes the liability. The estimated market exit price for a financial instrument can be determined as follows:

- Based on the price of the identical instrument, if it is available and traded in the same active market.
- Based on prices in observed transactions. If more than one active market exists for the particular instrument and if a similar instrument is traded more recently than the identical

Exhibit 4.6 Comparison of Provisions of SFAS No. 115 and IRC Section 475

Provisions	SFAS No 115	IRC Section 475
1. Application	Any entities holding certain investments in debt and equity securities	Any taxpayer that is a dealer in securities
2. Purpose	Establish guidelines for the recognition and measurement of investment in debt and equity securities by requiring a piecemeal adoption of market value accounting (MVA) for certain securities	Use the market-to-market accounting method for any securities held in inventory for U.S. tax purposes
3. Reporting Requirements	Market value adjustments of any realized or unrealized holding gains or losses of "trading securities" and realized gains and losses of "available-for-sales securities" should be included in the determination of net income. Any market adjustments of unrealized holding gains or losses of "available-for-sales securities" should be reported as a net amount in a separate component of shareholders' equity until realized.	Any non-exempted market adjustment gains or losses on securities held in inventory should be included in taxable income. Any sales of securities during the tax year are recognized as ordinary income or losses. A security may be stock, bond, or other evidence of indebtedness.
4. Security Classifications	Trading: Any securities bought and sold to make short-term profits rather than to realize long-term gains from capital appreciation. Held to maturity: Debt securities with positive intent and ability to hold to maturity. Available for sale: Any debt and equity securities not assigned to the above categories which may be sold prior to maturity.	Held for investment: any security that is not held by the taxpayer primarily for sale to customers in the ordinary course of the taxpayer's trade or business. Held in inventory: any securities for sales.

5. Possible Impacts	Changes in asset/liability management strategies and funding decisions. Fluctuations in reported earnings and equity due to market adjustments for securities. Reclassification of securities.	Recording of earnings and investment portfolio on a more timely and realistic bases. Taxpayers who make or sell loans may consider dealers in securities.
6. Effective Dates	Effective for fiscal years beginning after December 15, 1993.	Effective for tax years ending on or after December 31, 1993.
7. Implementation	Obtain a complete knowledge and understanding of the provisions of SFAS No. 115 including circumstances in which debt and equity are reported at amortized cost. Establish policies and procedures regarding securities classification into the three suggested categories Evaluate (1) how investment securities should be recorded, measured, and adjusted for market value; (2) how securities should be transferred between categories; (3) how earnings and capital volatility resulting from market adjustments can be minimized; and (4) how to manage a securities portfolio to minimize negative impacts on cash flows. Establish an adequate and effective internal control system for investment securities to assure compliance with provisions of SFAS No. 115.	Maintain proper records on an ongoing basis to determine which accountants (securities) are subject to or excepted from the market-to-market requirements. Planning: monitor new transactions and activities using the identification procedures outlined in Reg. 1.1236-a(d). Identify exempted securities in records before the close of the day on which they were acquired, originated, and entered into. Evaluate tax planning opportunities to minimize the possible negative impacts on income tax liability. Avoid an IRS investigation or an enforcement action by complying with all tax rules and regulations on MVA.

Source: Leung and Rezaee, 1995.

Exhibit 4.7   Contractual Rights and Obligations that Are/Are Not Financial Instruments

Contractual Rights and Obligations that Are Financial Instruments

Contractual obligations to deliver financial instruments and corresponding rights to require delivery of financial instruments.

- Obligations to pay and the corresponding rights to require payment, for example, accounts, notes, and loans payable and receivable, debt securities, demand and time deposits, insurance claims payable and receivable, and derivative settlements after the settlement amount is fixed.
- Obligations to return borrowed securities, obligations to deliver financial instruments for which payment has been received, and the corresponding rights to require return or delivery.
- Insurance policies and warranty contracts that will be settled in cash.
- Reinsurance contracts that will be settled in cash.
- Derivatives that require net settlement in cash or other financial instruments.
- Contracts excluded from Statement 133 in paragraph 10(e), that is, "weather derivatives."
- Financial guarantees.

Contractual obligations to exchange financial instruments and corresponding rights to require exchange of financial instruments.

- Cardholder's options in credit card contracts.
- Loan commitments.
- Lines of credit.
- Securities options.
- Forward exchanges of securities.

Similar Contractual Rights and Obligations that Are Not Financial Instruments

Contractual obligations to deliver items other than financial instruments and corresponding rights to require deliveries of those items.

- Obligations to deliver goods or services that have been prepaid.
- Obligations to return a borrowed item other than a financial instrument.
- Warranty guarantees that provide for repair or replacement of the warranted items.
- Insurance policies that provide for services or property replacement.

Contractual obligations to exchange financial instruments for items other than financial instruments and corresponding rights to require those exchanges.

- Forward exchanges or optional exchanges of services or goods other than financial instruments, for example, purchase orders and sales orders, whether or not they are considered "normal purchases and normal sales" under paragraph 10(b) of Statement 133 and commodity contracts that are required to be settled by deliveries of commodities.

Other Similar Assets and Liabilities that Are Not Financial Instruments

- Taxes payable.
- Tax refunds receivable.
- Deferred taxes.
- Legal (other than contractual) requirements to issue or renew insurance policies.
- Certain accruals of revenues and expenses, for example, obligations to repair environmental damage that are not yet liabilities to a particular entity.

instrument, the price of the identical instrument should be adjusted for changes in market factors since the date of the last transaction.

- Estimates based on actual transactions should be used if they are available. In some cases, transaction prices require adjustment especially when: (a) the observable transactions are not recent and there is compelling evidence that a current price would be different; (b) two parties to the transaction are affiliates (e.g., related parties transactions); and (c) one party to the transaction is subject to financial or regulatory difficulties.

- When there is more than one market for certain instruments, the portfolio of items can be used in estimating the exit price. The exit price of the portfolio might be higher than the total of the exit prices of the individual instruments. In this case, the fair value should be based on the market with the most advantageous price which is the optimum accessible market price. The most advantageous price would be a higher exit price for an asset and a lower exit price for a liability.

- The market exit price is considered to be the best evidence of the fair value of an asset or liability when it is obtainable in a market to which the entity has reasonable access.

- The market exit price may not be obtainable on which to base fair value when: (a) a current exchange is not possible or readily available; (b) the instrument is unique or highly unusual; and (c) market participants do not disclose prices or valuation models regarding similar instruments. Under these circumstances, the exit price must be determined based on a combination of general market information (e.g., interest rates, exchange rates) and internally developed estimates and assumptions based on the present value of future cash flows.

- The present value calculations should be based on the projected cash flows for a financial instrument including contractual rights and obligations and cash expected to be delivered or exchanged under the contract.

- The projected cash flows should be adjusted for the following items: (a) the time value of money (e.g., discount rate); (b) expectations and changes in future conditions about possible variations in the amount or timing of these cash flows; (c) the risk premium which is the price marketplace participants expect to receive for bearing the uncertainty inherent in the asset or liability; and (d) other factors such as market imperfections, anticipated profit margins, and illiquidity.

Under GAAP the best evidence of fair value is quoted market price in an active market. However, in the absence of quoted market prices, the fair value should be estimated based on reasonable, justifiable, and relevant assumptions. For example, in valuing the interests retained from the sale of the higher risk assets (for example, subprime and high loan-to-value assets.) The fair value of these expected future cash flows should be recorded on balance sheets as assets under retained interests. The fundamental assumptions in the valuation of these retained interests, among others, include default rates, loss severity factors, discount rates, prepayment or payment rates.

The FASB's long-term goal is to eventually have all financial items (assets and liabilities) recognized and reported at their fair values in financial statements. The major conceptual advantages of fair value over historical costs as a measurement attribute are that fair value: (1) does not depend on the date or cost at which an asset or liability was acquired or incurred; (2) is the same for all entities having access to the same markets in determining

Exhibit 4.8   Pertinent Features of Fair-Value-Based and Historical-Cost-Based Measures of Financial Assets and Liabilities

Fair Value	Historical Cost
Improves comparability by making like things look alike and unlike things look different.	Impairs comparability by making like things look different and different things look alike.
Provides information about benefits expected from assets and burdens imposed by liabilities under current economic conditions.	Provides information about benefits expected from assets and burdens imposed by liabilities under the economic conditions when they were acquired or incurred.
Reflects effect on entity performance of management's decisions to continue to hold assets or owe liabilities, as well as decisions to acquire or sell assets and to incur or settle liabilities.	Reflects effect on entity performance only of decisions to acquire or sell assets or to incur or settle liabilities. Ignores effects of decisions to continue to hold or to owe.
Reports gains and losses from price changes when they occur.	Reports gains and losses from price changes only when they are realized by sale or settlement, even though sale or settlement is not the event that caused the gain or loss.
Requires current market prices to determine reported amounts, which may require estimation and can lead to reliability problems.	Reported amounts can be computed based on internally available information about prices in past transactions, without reference to outside market data.
Easily reflects the effects of most risk-management strategies.	Requires complex rules to attempt to reflect the effect of most risk-management strategies.

the market exit price of assets or liabilities; (3) does not depend on the intended disposition of an asset or liability; and (4) provides relevant information about assets and liabilities that is more useful than historical cost information. The changes in fair value should be reported in earnings when they occur whether or not they are realized. Exhibit 4.8 summarizes the conceptual advantages of fair value information over historical cost information.

The FASB has been considering the issue of fair value as a measurement attribute for all financial items including assets, liabilities, and instruments for over a decade. Its ultimate goal is to require measurement of all financial assets and liabilities at fair value in the basic financial statements. Other alternatives such as the requirement for improved disclosure of fair value of financial items or a separate supplementary set of fair value financial statements are also being considered. The FASB issued the statement of Financial Accounting Concept (SFAC) No. 7, entitled "Using Cash Flow Information and Present Value in Accounting Measurements" in February 2000. SFAC emphasized present-value accounting for assets and liabilities through a pure balance sheet approach. This SFAC establishes a framework for using future cash flows as the basis for accounting measurements at initial recognition or fresh-start measurements and for the interest method of amortization. It is based on the concept that a true present value of future cash flow is unknown, and the next closest measurement is current (market) value or fair value. The fair value is defined as the amount at which an asset could be bought or sold or a liability could be incurred or settled in a current transaction between willing parties in the normal course of business.

4.11 FINANCIAL REPORTING REQUIREMENTS OF FINANCIAL INSTITUTIONS

Financial institutions should maintain sound accounting and reporting procedures and systems to prepare regulatory reports in conformity with generally accepted accounting principles (GAAP) or U.S. regulatory accounting principles (RAP). Financial institutions should also maintain clear and concise records with special emphasis on documenting adjustments and reconciliation when converting foreign accounting principles to either GAAP or RAP. Domestic and foreign financial institutions are required to file timely and accurate regulatory reports with the Federal Reserve System. Financial information compiled in the regulatory reports can serve several purposes: (1) facilitating early identification and signaling of problem situations that can threaten the safety and soundness of reporting institutions; (2) ensuring timely implementation of the prompt-corrective-action provisions required by banking legislation; and (3) assessing the financial conditions and position of the reporting institution by the public, including investors, depositors, and creditors. The Consolidated Reports of Condition and Income (known as call reports) are used to prepare the Uniform Bank Performance Report (UBPR), which uses ration analysis and analytical procedures to detect unusual or abnormal (red flag) changes in an institution's financial condition and position.

The Financial Institutions Reform, Recovery, and Enforcement Act of 1989 (FIRREA) and the Federal Deposit Insurance Corporation Improvement Act of 1991 (FDICIA) have given authority to the Federal Reserve to assess civil money penalties against state member banks, bank holding companies, and foreign institutions that file late, false, and misleading regulatory reports. The civil money penalties can also be assessed against individuals including outside auditors who cause or participate in filing late, false, or misleading regulatory reports. These reports should be reviewed by the assigned examiner for verification of the accuracy of the reports and assurance that they meet statutory and regulatory requirements. National banks, state member banks, and insured state non-member banks are required to file Consolidated Reports of Condition and Income (known as call reports) as of the close of business on the last calendar day of each calendar quarter. Call reports should be received by the appropriate supervisory agencies (e.g., national banks and state non-member banks submit the reports to the FDIC, state member banks submit the reports to the appropriate Federal Reserve Bank) no more than 30 calendar days after the report date. The nature and extent of financial reports and disclosures depend upon the size and characteristics of the financial institution (e.g., total assets of less than $100 million, global operations.) The call report plays an important role in ensuring customizing the bank supervisory approach to the activities and risks undertaken by financial institutions. The regulatory requirements of the call report are in the process of revision and modernization to ensure the elimination of many financial items that are not relevant to today's banking environment and to reflect the kinds of activities that banks are undertaking today such as securitization and venture capital.

The Report of Condition provides consolidated and detailed information on:

1. assets, liabilities, capital, and off-balance-sheet activity; and
2. certain aggregated information and figures on loans to executive officers, directors, principal shareholders, and their related interests.

The Report of Income provides information on : (1) consolidated earnings; (2) changes in capital accounts; (3) the allowance for loan and lease losses; and (4) charge-offs and recoveries. Call reports typically contain financial reports and supplement disclosures of the following major financial attributes and items:

- Statement of financial position (bsalance sheet).
- Statement of income.
- Statement of changes in owner's equity.
- Applicable income taxes by taxing authorities.
- Charge-offs and recoveries and changes in allowance for loan and lease losses.
- Loans and lease-financing receivables.
- Deposit liabilities.
- Cash and balances due from depository institutions.
- Securities.
- Quarterly average balances.
- Past-due and non-accrual loans and leases.
- Risk-based capital.
- Off-balance sheet items.
- Supplemental disclosure on significant non-recurring items or changes of accounting method.

Call reports are filed with the appropriate agency and are generally made available to the public upon request by the federal bank supervisory agencies. State member banks are no longer required to publish their report of condition according to Section 308 of the Riegle Community Development and Regulatory Improvement Act of 1994. However, they may still be required to publish their report of condition under state law. Savings and loan associations (S & Ls) are required to file less extensive call reports with the Office of Thrift Supervision.

4.11.1 Reports Required Under Regulation H and the SEC Act of 1934

Financial institutions under the Securities and Exchange Commission (SEC) jurisdiction (e.g., publicly traded banks) must file quarterly (Form 10-Q) and annual (Form 10-K) reports and proxies with the SEC. Section 208.16(a) of regulation H requires that state member banks whose securities are subject to registration under the SEC Act of 1934 file special reports with the Federal Reserve Board and the SEC including the following:

1. Form 8-A, which is the registration of certain classes of securities, pursuant to section 12(b) or 12(g) of the 1934 act, especially those listings on national securities exchanges;
2. Form 8-B, which is the registration of securities of certain successor issuers pursuant to section 1s(b) or 12(g) of the 1934 act;
3. Form 10, which is the general form for registration of securities pursuant to section 12(b) or 12(g) of the 1934 act for classes of securities of issuers for which no other form is prescribed;

4. Form 8-K, which must be filed within 15 days after the occurrence of the earliest of one or more specified events such as changes in control of registrant or acquisition of disposition of significant assets;

5. Form 10-Q, which is for quarterly and transition reports and must be filed within 45 days after the end of each of the first three fiscal quarters;

6. Form 10-K, which is for annual and transition reports that must be filed within 90 calendar days after the end of the registrant's fiscal year;

7. Form 3, which is an initial statement of beneficial ownership of registered companies, including securities of the bank;

8. Form 4, which is a statement of charges of beneficial ownership of registered companies, including the securities of the bank;

9. The Financial and Operational Combined Uniform Single (FOCUS) report, required by the SEC, which discloses the details of securities revenue and capitalization information of financial institutions.

4.11.2 Reporting Requirement for International Activities

The following reports should be filed with the Federal Financial Institutions Examination. Council (FFIEC) for banks that conduct or intend to conduct international activities through either foreign branches or Edge Act or agreement corporations. Exhibit 4.9 presents regulatory reports of banks including types, description, frequency, and content. The reports are:

1. FFIEC 009—Country Exposure Report, which should be filed quarterly by all U.S. banks and bank holding companies that meet certain ownership criteria and have total consolidated outstanding claims on foreign residents in excess of $30 million.

2. FFIEC 009—Country Exposure Information Report, which is a quarterly supplement to the FFIEC 009 that provides public disclosure of significant country exposures of U.S. banking institutions.

3. FFIEC 030—Foreign Branch Report of condition, which should be filed by every insured commercial bank with one or more branch offices in a foreign country as of December 31 of each year. Significant branches with either total assets of at least $2 billion or commitments to purchase foreign currencies and U.S. dollar exchange of at least $5 billion should submit this report quarterly.

4. FFIEC 035—Monthly consolidated Foreign Currency Report of Banks in the United States, which should be filed by U.S. financial institutions that have greater than $1 billion in commitments to purchase foreign currencies. This report consists of monthly data on institutions' gross assets, gross liabilities, and positions in foreign currencies, on a fully consolidated basis.

5. FR 2058—Notification of Foreign Branch Status. This report should be filed within 30 days of the opening, closing, or relocation of a foreign branch of that U.S. organization or of its foreign subsidiary(ies).

6. FR 2064—Report of Changes in Investment Made under Regulation K, Subparts A and C, for the acquisition or disposition of reportable investment.

Exhibit 4.9 Bank Regulatory Reports

Type	Description	Frequency	Content
FFIEC 031	Consolidated reports of condition and income for a bank with domestic and foreign offices	Quarterly	This report contains several schedules RC-B and RC-D, which capture all types of securities, and Schedule RC-L, which shows off-balance-sheet financial instruments.
FIEC 030	Report of condition for foreign branch of U.S. bank	Annually for all overseas branch offices, quarterly for significant branches	This report captures information on balance-sheet data and selected off-balance-sheet instruments.
FFIEC 035	Monthly consolidated foreign-currency report of banks in the United States	Last business day of each month	This report captures information on foreign-exchange transactions.
FFIEC 002	Reports of assets and liabilities of U.S. branches and agencies of foreign banks	Quarterly	This report shows information pertaining to balance-sheet and off-balance sheet transactions reported by all branches and agencies.
FFIEC 069	Weekly report of assets and liabilities for large U.S. branches and agencies of foreign banks	As of the close of business every Wednesday	All on-balance-sheet and off-balance-sheet instruments are included in this report.
FFIEC 019	Country exposure for U.S. branches and agencies of foreign banks	Quarterly	This report presents country distribution of foreign claims held by branches and agencies.
FR 2314a	Report of condition for foreign subsidiaries of U.S. banking organizations	Annually	This report should be filed annually by banks with total assets exceeding U.S. $100 million and quarterly for significant subsidiaries.
1a.FR 2314b	Report of condition for foreign subsidiaries of U.S. banking organizations	Annually	This report should be filed by banking organizations with total assets between U.S. $50-100 million of the report date.
1b.FR 2314C	Report of condition for foreign subsidiaries of U.S. banking organizations	Annually	For banking organizations with total assets less than $50 million.
FR 2886b	Report of condition for Edge Act and agreement corporations	Quarterly	This report reflects the consolidation of all Edge and agreement operations, except for those majority-owned Edge or agreement subsidiaries.

Source: *Trading and Capital Markets Activities Manual*. 1998. Section 2130-5. www.federalreserve.gov

7. FR 2314—Annual Report of Condition for foreign subsidiaries of U.S. banking organizations that should be filed as of December 31 of each year by foreign companies.

8. FR 25029—Quarterly Report of Assets and liabilities of large foreign offices of U.S. branches. This report represents large foreign branches of U.S. banking institutions and large foreign bank subsidiaries.

9. FR 2886b—Report of condition and income for Edge Act and Agreement corporations. This report represents the operations of the reporting corporation including any international banking facilities of the reporter.

10. FR 2915—Report of Foreign Currency deposits. This report collects seven-day averages of the amounts outstanding of foreign currency.

Bank holding companies, owning stock of one or more banks, established according to the Federal Regulation Y, can engage in a number of activities considered closely related to and a proper incident to banking (e.g., insurance, brokerage, discount stock brokerage, third party fee appraisals, third party data processing). BHCs are chartered as corporations under the laws of their home states and, therefore, must file a registration statement and an annual report of operations with their district Federal Reserve Bank and the Board of Governors. Exhibit 4.10 presents regulatory reports of BHCs including types, description, frequency, and content. BHCs should file the following reports:

- Y-6 Annual Report. This report contains Parent's consolidated financial statements and must be filed by all domestic BHCs.

- Y-7 Annual Report of Foreign Banking Organizations. This report must be filed by BHCs that are established under the laws of a foreign country.

- Y-9 Financial Supplement. This report must be filed by BHCs with consolidated assets of $50 million or more.

The review of the required regulatory reports is aimed toward achievement of three goals of determining whether the (1) required reports are being filed on time; (2) content of reports is accurate; and (3) corrective actions are being taken when official reporting, practices, policies, or procedures are deficient. Thus, the examiner's primary purpose when reviewing the regulatory-reporting function is to vouch for the timeliness, accuracy, and consistency of reporting requirements.

4.12 CORPORATE GOVERNANCE OF FINANCIAL INSTITUTIONS

This past decade has witnessed significant improvement in the financial reporting process and corporate governance activities of financial institutions. The final rule of the Federal Deposit Insurance Corporation (FDIC) implementing Section 112 of the FDIC Improvement Act of 1991 (FDICIA) was approved in May 1993.[28] The final rule required state member banks and other insured depository institutions with $500 million or more in total assets, for their fiscal years beginning after December 31, 1992, to submit to their regulatory agencies, within 90 days after the end of their fiscal year, a copy of: (1) an annual

Exhibit 4.10 Regulatory Reports (Bank Holding Companies, BHC)

Type	Description	Frequency	Content
FR-Y-9C	Consolidated financial statements for (1) top-tier BHC with total consolidated assets of $150 million or more; (2) lower-tier BHC with total consolidated assets of $1 billion or more; and (3) other multibank BHC with debt outstanding to the general public or that are engaged in certain nonbank activities.	Quarterly	Schedule HC-A securities including U.S. Treasuries, municipal mortgage-backed, foreign governments, corporations, IDC debt, equities. Schedule HC-F instruments including futures and forwards, forward rate agreements, interest-rate swaps, foreign exchange, currency swaps, options commodities, hybrids, index-linked activities.
FR-Y-9SR	Parent company only financial statements for one BHC with total consolidated assets of less than $150 million	Semi-annually	No off-balance-sheet items are captured in this report, only securities are included.
FR-Y-9LP	Parent company only financial statements for each BHC that files the FR-Y-9C	Quarterly	Only securities transactions are reviewed by the examiners. No off-balance-sheet items are captured in this report.
FR-Y-8	Report of BHC intercompany transactions and balances	Semi-annually and on an interim basis	BHC with consolidated assets of $300 million or more are required to file this report of large asset transfers.
FR-Y-8f	Report of intercompany transactions for foreign banking organizations and their U.S. bank subsidiaries	Semi-annually and on an interim basis	This report presents intercompany asset transfers (loans and securities) and foreign exchange transactions for foreign banking organizations).

FR-Y-20	Financial statement for a bank holding company subsidiary engaged in ineligible securities underwriting and dealing	Quarterly	Schedules SUD and SUD-A capture securities transactions and transactions involving equities, futures, forwards, and options.
FR-Y-11Q	Financial statements for each individual nonbank subsidiary of a BHC with total consolidated assets of $150 million or more	Quarterly	Both balance-sheet securities and off-balance-sheet instruments are captured on this report.
FR-Y-11I	Financial statements for each individual nonbank subsidiary that is owned or controlled by a BHC subject-size consideration	Annually	Both balance-sheet securities and off-balance-sheet instruments are captured on this report.
FEIEC035	Monthly consolidated foreign-currency report of banks in the United States	Last business day of each month	This report shows information on foreign-exchange transactions (spot, forwards, futures), cross-currency interest-rate swamps, and options for a BCH that files an FR Y-9 and has foreign-exchange commitments in excess of U.S. $100 million.
FFIEC 009	Country exposure information report	Quarterly	This report is filed by U.S. commercial banks and/or BHC that meet certain ownership criteria.
FFIEC 009a	Country exposure information report supplements to the FFIEC 009	Quarterly	This report provides public disclosure of significant country exposures of U.S. BHC.
X-17A-5	Focus report	Quarterly	This report captures data on securities and spot commodities owned by broker-dealers.

Source: *Trading and Capital-Markets Activities Manual*. 1998. Section 2130-2. www.federalreserve.gov.

report; (2) a management report; and (3) an auditor's attestation report. Furthermore, affected institutions are required to establish and maintain audit committees consisting of outside, non-executive, and independent directors. The final rule will affect all aspects of financial institutions' financial reporting, internal control, and audit committees ensuring corporate governance and accountability. This section examines these three areas which are most affected by the new rule.

4.12.1   Financial Reporting

Traditionally, financial institutions have prepared annual reports in response to the needs and wants of shareholders as well as in compliance with requirements of regulatory agencies. Recently, an institution's annual report has become more of a compliance document to satisfy regulatory requirements than a communication vehicle for providing relevant, reliable, and useful financial information to shareholders. The FDIC rule (Section 363.2) requires affected institutions to submit their annual reports to the Federal Reserve Bank, the FDIC, and their state regulatory agency within 90 days after the end of their fiscal year.

The submitted annual reports should contain: (1) comparative financial statements including balance sheets, income statements, statements of cash flows, and statements of changes in owners' equity and related footnote disclosures prepared in accordance with generally accepted accounting principles (GAAP); (2) a report indicating management's responsibility for preparing the submitted annual financial statements; and (3) an independent auditor's report on the institution's annual financial statements audited in accordance with generally accepted auditing standards (GAAS). The final rule does not mandate any additional reporting requirements for covered institutions. Management is primarily responsible for the fair presentation of an institution's financial statements in accordance with GAAP by establishing and maintaining a sound accounting information system and an adequate and effective internal control structure. The independent auditor lends credibility, objectivity, and reliability to an institution's financial statements by expressing an opinion regarding the fair presentation of the financial statements in conformity with GAAP.

14.12.2   Internal Control Structure

Recently, the challenges of globalization, rapid technological advancements, business failure, and fraudulent financial activities (e.g., savings and loan crisis) have sharpened the ever-increasing attention of internal controls. Internal control is a widely used concept and its importance to the business community and banking industry has grown significantly. Yet, until recently, there was no common view of what internal control encompasses and what it should achieve. Management and internal auditors typically view internal control very broadly to cover both internal administrative control; ensuring achievement of the organization's goals and compliance with applicable laws and regulations; and internal accounting control, ensuring reliability of financial statements and safeguarding economic resources. On the other hand, external auditors and regulators consider internal control for a narrow perspective as being primarily internal accounting controls. While the final FDIC rule did not attempt to determine a common definition and standards for internal controls, it clearly sets forth additional responsibility for management as well as internal and external auditors.

(i) Management Responsibility for Internal Control

The new FDIC rule requires a statement of management's responsibility in the institution's annual report for: (1) establishing and maintaining adequate internal controls over financial reporting and for complying with applicable laws and regulations; and (2) management's assessment of the effectiveness of internal controls and the institutions's compliance with the designated laws and regulations. Traditionally, management has been responsible for establishing and maintaining adequate and effective internal controls to ensure: (1) achievement of the organization's goals; (2) adherence to managerial policies and procedures; (3) safeguarding of economic resources; (4) enhancement of the reliability of financial statements; and (5) compliance with applicable laws and regulations. Thus, the new rule for covered institutions reemphasizes the importance of an adequate internal control structure to ensure reliable financial reporting and responsible corporate governance.

The idea of a management report on the effectiveness of internal controls to external parties and an independent auditor's report on management's assertions regarding the effectiveness of internal controls over financial reporting has been debated in the accounting profession and authorization bodies (e.g., AICPA and SEC) since the passage of the Foreign Corrupt Practice Act (FCPA) of 1977.[29] Subsequently, the National Commission of Fraudulent Financial Reporting (Treadway Commission, 1987)[30] stated that accounting controls set forth by the FCPA are not sufficient to reduce the incidence of fraudulent financial reporting. Furthermore, the Treadway Commission recommended that the SEC be required to publicly report its responsibility for the establishment and maintenance of an adequate internal control system and its assessment of the effectiveness of such a system in achieving established internal control objectives. However, the SEC has yet to make the Treadway Commission's recommendations requirements for publicly traded companies. The Treadway Commission also recommended that its Committee of Sponsoring Organizations (COSO) work to integrate the various internal control concepts and definitions and to develop a common reference point.

The COSO issued its report entitled "Internal Control: Integrated Framework," in September 1992.[31] The provisions of the COSO report help: (1) businesses and interested users understand the value and use of internal controls; (2) establish a common definition for internal control; and (3) provide a criterion against which all entities can assess their internal control systems. Since the FDIC regulations do not establish standards for internal controls and determine the criterion against which institutions can assess the effectiveness of their internal control systems, this is management's responsibility. However, the COSO report can be used as a source of guidelines by management of affected institutions to comply with the FDIC rule.

The COSO report consists of four volumes. The first volume is the executive summary, which is a high-level overview of the internal control framework. It gives a broad outline of the nature of internal control structures, defines internal control, and discusses what internal control can do. The second volume describes internal control components and provides criteria against which management, board of directors, internal auditors, and external auditors can assess the effectiveness of internal control systems. The third volume provides guidance for reporting publicly on the effectiveness of internal control. Finally, the fourth volume provides guidance and evaluation tools that management and auditors can use in evaluating the effectiveness of internal control systems.

To comply with the requirements of the FDIC rule, the banking industry is using the COSO framework in creating or modifying their internal control structure (e.g., Banc One

Corp. in Columbus, OH; Continental Bank in Chicago).[32] The COSO report defines internal control objectives for achieving effectiveness and efficiency in operations, reliability of financial reporting, and compliance with applicable laws and regulations. These internal control objectives are similar to those suggested in the FDIC rule. The COSO report defines the five components of an adequate internal control structure as: control environment, risk assessment, control activities, information and communication, and monitoring. These five components can help an institution's management establish and maintain an adequate internal control structure and establish procedures for financial reporting and compliance with designated laws and regulations relating to the bank's safety and soundness as required by Section 363.2(b) of the FDIC rule.

The third and fourth volumes of the COSO report should help an institution's management evaluate the effectiveness of an internal control system and report on the effectiveness of such a system to external parties. While the COSO report takes no position on whether entities should issue a management report, currently about 25 percent of publicly-traded companies and approximately 60 percent of the Fortune 500 companies include in their annual reports a management report discussing some aspects of internal control.[33] The COSO report provides a framework for those companies that are required to report on internal control.

For the first time, the FDIC regulations require an institution's management to make a public statement regarding its responsibilities for the effectiveness of internal controls over financial reporting, operating activities, and compliance requirements. This reporting requirement necessitates adequate documentation of understanding, determination, and assessment of deficiencies in internal controls on financial reporting as well as the degree of compliance with applicable laws and regulations. The COSO report should help management with such documentation. However, the COSO report focuses only on those internal controls that relate to the effectiveness of internal controls assessment regarding the reliability of published financial statements.

Although the definition of internal control includes controls over financial reporting, operations, and compliance with applicable laws and regulations, the scope of external reporting on internal control, in the COSO report, volume three, is not extended to operations and compliance objectives. Therefore, the affected institutions should establish their own reporting format for management reporting on internal controls over compliance with applicable laws and regulations. The management-required report on the assessment of the effectiveness of the internal control structure over financial reporting should document deficiencies in internal control at the end of the fiscal year, while documentation of the assessment of compliance with applicable laws and regulations is required for the entire fiscal year. The proper documentation assists independent auditors in ascertaining management's assertions on the internal control structure.

Management's report on internal controls should include the following: (1) an assessment of the effectiveness of internal controls over the reliability of the financial statements and compliance with applicable laws and regulations; (2) a statement regarding the existence of mechanisms for monitoring and reporting on identified financial control deficiencies and noncompliance with applicable laws and regulations; (3) a statement regarding the inherent limitations of internal control systems; (4) the criteria against which the internal control structure is evaluated; (5) a description of any material deficiencies or weaknesses that exist at year end and all matters of noncompliance found throughout the year that come to the attention of management; and (6) the date of the report and proper signatures.

(ii)   Auditor's Involvement with Internal Controls

The FDIC regulations have a tremendous impact on the independent auditor's consideration of institutions' internal control structure. Traditionally, independent auditors have been
concerned more with the adequacy and effectiveness of their clients' internal control system in safeguarding assets and enhancing the reliability of financial information. Thus, independent auditors have not concentrated much on the assessment of compliance with applicable laws and regulations. The FDIC regulations require that the independent auditor
attest to and report separately on the assertions in the management report concerning the
institution's internal control structure and procedures for financial reporting. The independent auditor should also perform agreed-upon procedures to test compliance with the
specified laws and regulations.

Independent auditors' reports on management's assertions regarding the effectiveness of
internal control over financial reporting and compliance with laws and regulations are considered attestation reports and accordingly are governed by the Statement of Standards for
Attestation Engagement (SSAE) issued by the Auditing Standards Board of the American
Institute of Certified Public Accountants (AICPA).[34] These attestation standards are different from generally accepted auditing standards followed in the audit of financial statements.
The SSAE No. 1 provides guidance for performing examinations and reporting on management's written assertions about the effectiveness of internal controls over compliance with
laws and regulations. The independent auditor's attestation report on the agreed-upon procedures covering compliance with specified laws and regulations is due annually and is limited to use by management, the specified regulatory agency, and/or specified third parties.

The SSAE No. 2 provides guidance for the examination and report on management's
written assertions regarding the effectiveness of an entity's internal control structure and
procedures over financial reporting. The independent auditor's attestation report on internal control over financial reporting of affected institutions is due annually within 90 days
after the end of the fiscal year and is a public document. Thus, no restriction is placed upon
the distribution of this type of report. The purpose of the independent auditor's report is to
express an opinion on whether management's assertions regarding the effectiveness of the
institution's internal control structure is fairly stated, in all material aspects, based upon the
control criteria.

The FDIC regulations also encourage and promote the role of institutions' internal auditors from the traditional reactive role of just investigating internal control systems to the new
proactive role of participating in all aspects of the institution's internal control structure. The
proactive role of internal auditors is to assist and participate with management in: (1) defining internal control and related objectives over the financial reporting process and compliance with certain laws and regulations; (2) establishing and maintaining an adequate internal
control structure and its components; (3) determining appropriate evaluation tools in measuring the adequacy and effectiveness of established internal controls; (4) monitoring internal
control continuously and periodically to ensure its objectives are being achieved; (5) preparing and reporting on the effectiveness of the internal control structure and procedures for financial reporting, and (6) assessing the institution's compliance with the specified safety and
soundness laws and regulations. Internal auditors may also provide direct assistance to the independent auditors in auditing financial statements and the internal control attestation. Internal auditors can provide a variety of accounting and non-accounting services to the institution's audit committee in fulfilling its responsibilities as stated in the FDIC regulations.

4.12.3 Independent Audit Committee

The credibility and usefulness of published financial statements is currently being challenged. To regain confidence in the financial reporting process, corporations have established audit committees to provide an oversight function and to act as a liaison between the board of directors and the external and internal auditors. The Treadway Commission has suggested the expansion of responsibilities for audit committees to ensure a reliable financial reporting process, responsible corporate governance, and management commitment to adequate and effective internal control systems.

The Treadway Commission has called on the Securities and Exchange Commission (SEC) to require all public companies to establish audit committees composed solely of independent, outside board members. The SEC has long advocated the adoption of the audit committee, but has yet to make it a requirement for publicly-traded companies. The United States General Accounting Office (GAO)[35] in its report of April 1991, suggested that banks establish independent audit committees to enhance reliability on the financial reporting process and ensure responsible corporate governance and accountability. Furthermore, in October 1991, the GAO[36] issued another report which made several recommendations regarding the relevance and importance of banks' audit committees in strengthening their internal control structure and procedures.

The GAO report argued that many bank audit committees are composed of non-independent or unqualified members with no adequate support to effectively perform their assigned functions. Thus, the report made several suggestions regarding the formation, structure, and functions of audit committees. The FDIC regulations (Section 363.5) require affected institutions to establish an independent audit committee of outside, non-executive board members. The board of directors is responsible for determining: (1) whether its audit committee meets the independence requirements of the FDIC rules and (2) whether a member of the audit committee has the necessary experience and is not a large customer.

The board of directors, in complying with the requirements of the FDIC rule establishing an institution's independent audit committee, should take into considerations the 11 recommendations made by the Treadway Commission regarding the structure and role of audit committees. These recommendations increase the responsibility of the audit committee and place more demands on audit committees. Both the Treadway Commission and the FDIC regulations recognize the value and importance of audit committees in enhancing the reliability of the financial reporting process, in promoting greater corporate accountability, and in securing responsible corporate governance.

The Treadway Commission recommended that: (1) the SEC require all public companies to establish audit committees composed solely of independent directors; (2) public companies develop a written charter for the audit committee describing its mission, objectives, authority, and responsibilities. The board of directors should approve the charter, review it periodically, and modify it as necessary; and (3) ensure audit committees have adequate resources and authority to discharge their responsibilities. While the FDIC rule requires affected institutions to establish an independent audit committee, it has placed the responsibility of determining independence, necessary experience, expertise, qualifications, and duties of members of audit committees with the institution's board of directors. Perhaps the Treadway Commission recommendations pertaining to the role, responsibility, and function of audit committees are relevant and applicable for covered institutions under the FDIC regulations. The relevant recommendations for duties of affected institutions' audit committees are to: (1) prepare a letter for inclusion in the annual reports describing the committee's responsibilities, functions, and accomplishments during the years; (2) oversee quarterly and annual financial reports, the institution's internal control structure and procedures as well as compliance with specified laws and regulations; (3) serve as a liaison between the board of directors and both the external and internal auditors to ensure the independence of auditors; (4) advise management when it seeks a second opinion on the institution's policies, rules, regulations, or accounting procedures; and (5) review management's report and the auditors' report on the internal control structure as well as financial reporting or reports on any other attestation and consultation services performed by auditors including the scope of both internal and external auditors.

An effective audit committee should be independent from management and understand the institution's business, economic, social, and political environment. The audit committee has the responsibility to obtain from management and internal and external auditors facts pertaining to the institution's financial, investment, operating, and business activities; financial reporting; internal controls; and compliance with laws and regulations. Auditors and management should inform the audit committee about significant changes in the institution's business activities and financial and nonfinancial policies and procedures. Regarding the qualifications of audit committee members, the FDIC rule requires audit committees of institutions to include at least two members with banking or financial management expertise. Other members can have educational, professional, or regulatory experience in accounting, auditing, or financial backgrounds. FDIC regulations also require very large institutions' audit committees to have access to their own outside counsel.

4.12.4 Functions of Audit Committees

Functions typically performed by audit committees vary in accordance with their mission statement or charter granted to them by the board of directors. Audit committees normally assist the board of directors in discharging its responsibility as it relates to: (1) corporate governance and accountability; (2) the financial reporting process; (3) the assessment of internal control structure; and (4) the relationship with internal and external auditors.

1. **Corporate Governance and Accountability.** Corporate governance includes the institution's board of directors and its overall organization structure, management, and audit committee. Audit committee functions, including relationships with management, auditors, regulators, and other outside agencies, are very relevant to the overall issue of corporate governance and accountability. Ever-increasing concerns over corporate governance and accountability (e.g., S & L crises) have encouraged financial institutions to take actions to improve the role, structure, and responsibility of audit committees.

2. **Business Activities.** The role of the audit committee has evolved to accommodate the ever-changing business environment. The audit committee should pay attention to critical business issues and should ensure that management and external auditors have identified, understood, and considered the areas of greater risk to the entity. Failure in internal control systems and financial information risks are often directly related to the business risks and corporate problems. Thus, members of the audit committee should have a sufficient understanding of all external and internal functions and issues affecting the entity's business and operation. These factors are: (1) the entity's products

and/or major services; (2) competitive position and market share; (3) the entity's related applicable roles and regulations; (4) globalization challenges; (5) the nature of industry-wide economic trends; and (6) accounting and auditing problems.

3. Financial Reporting. Management is primarily responsible for the fair presentation of financial information by setting "the tone at the top" and by establishing a reliable financial reporting process and control environment. The audit committee should understand this process and environment in order to exercise effective oversight. The audit committee should ensure that the financial reporting process produces relevant, useful, and reliable information to manage the entity and properly report on its results of operations and financial position. As an overseer of the financial reporting process, the audit committee assists in objective and fair presentation of the entity's operations.

The independent auditor, by performing a financial audit, lends more credibility to published financial statements. The external auditors by virtue of their independence and knowledge are expected to bring to the financial reporting process technical competence, professional judgment, objectivity, and integrity. The audit committee is responsible for communicating with independent auditors regarding important audit matters. This communication should be free and open to ensure the audit committee is informed of potential misstatements in the financial statements, alternative accounting treatments, any significant deficiencies in internal control structure, other significant audit findings, and the scope of the audit engagement.

4. Internal Controls. An adequate and effective internal control system enables management to be in control. Management is primarily responsible for establishing and maintaining an adequate and effective internal control system to achieve organizational goals. However, internal auditors usually evaluate such a system. Internal auditors can assist audit committees by providing them with an objective assessment of the adequacy and effectiveness of the entity's internal control system. The audit committee, by ensuring the existence of an adequate and effective internal control structure, helps to prevent and detect fraud and misappropriation of shareholders' assets.

5. Risk Assessment. The audit committee should conform to the top management consideration of tone and atmosphere of ethical behavior and the corporate code of conduct. The audit committee in an attempt to reduce the risk of fraudulent financial reporting should consider the following factors: (1) business environment; (2) financial stability and liquidity; (3) organizational complexity and control; (4) management philosophy, style, reputation; (5) basis for management compensation and rewards; and (6) existence of aggressive or unusual policies.

6. Safeguarding Assets and Compliance. The audit committee should have open communication with management regarding policies to protect the entity's assets from waste and inefficient use of resources. The audit committee should have direct access to the internal auditors in order to receive input on the adequacy and effectiveness of internal control systems in safeguarding business assets.

The Securities and Exchange Commission, in 1999, proposed some rules to improve disclosure about the functioning of audit committees and to enhance the reliability and credibility of published financial statements of public companies including financial institutions. In response to the proposed SEC rules, the Blue Ribbon Committee on Improving the Effectiveness of Corporate Audit Committees issued a report in February

1999. This report made 10 recommendations for strengthening the independence of the audit committee and making it more effective in ensuring responsible corporate governance and reliable financial reporting problems.[37] Exhibit 4.11 summarizes the recommendations of the Blue Ribbon Committee pertaining to audit committees' independence, qualifications, composition, and charter.

4.13 CONCLUSION

This chapter examined three fundamental issues of consolidation, regulatory environment, and financial reporting pertaining to the financial services industry, in general, and banking organizations in particular. Banks and banking organizations in the United States have reported nine consecutive years of record earnings showing financial health and strength in rebounding from the financial difficulties of the late 1980s and the early 1990s. Low interest, optimistic earning power, excess profitability, high price shares, deregulation, and especially the passage of the Financial Modernization Act (the Gramm-Leach-Bliley Act of 1999) have encouraged the number and volume of M & A activities to increase significantly in the financial services industry. This current M & A mania is going to continue, which, in turn, will result in a reduction in the number of banks that provide full financial services.

Technological advances coupled with the demand by customers for a broad range of financial services (e.g., banking, insurance, securities) have encouraged financial institutions to expand their territory and assets to effectively compete in the global market. By the late 1990s, banks realized that to compete successfully in a global market, they had to move away from traditional commercial services into investment and asset-management businesses. Thus, distinctions in financial services including banking, insurance, and securities in the financial industry are vanishing. Today, financial institutions may enter and exit distant markets more freely, they may provide a variety of financial services (e.g., loans, mutual funds, insurance, investment, financing, credit cards), and their customers may also receive financial services from a dozen institutions. Thus, financial institutions' financial reporting should properly disclose the distribution of their internal ratings, asset quality, risk measurement, and management practices. Large banks should also strengthen their supervisory information systems. It is becoming more difficult to properly value an institution because branch networks and bricks and mortar do not count for as much as they used to.

The accounting profession has addressed fair value accounting (FVA) for financial reporting purposes during the past two decades. Regulatory agencies and bank examiners have also been considering the use of FVA for financial institutions since the savings and loan disaster of the 1980s to prevent similar crises in the industry. The issuance of SFAS No. 115 by the FASB was an important step in the evolutionary process toward the adoption of a comprehensive FVA system for financial institutions. IRS Section 475 has also provided a new boost toward the ultimate adoption of FVA for financial reporting and tax purposes.

The implementation of both SFAS No. 115 and Section 475 has improved the financial reporting process of financial institutions by: (1) providing more uniformity in financial reporting; (2) presenting fair value information about assets and liabilities of financial institutions which better reflect the true economic value of their net worth; (3) providing early warning signals of those financial institutions whose capital is impaired; (4) discouraging

Exhibit 4.11   1999 Blue Ribbon Committee's Recommendations for Corporate Audit Committees

Attribute	Recommendations	Description
1. Audit committee member independence	Recommendation 1: Both the NYSE and the NASD/AMEX adopt the recommended definition of independence for purposes of service on the audit committee for listed companies with a market capitalization above $200 million.	Members of the audit committee should be considered independent if they are free of any relationship that would interfere with impartial judgment in carrying out their responsibilities. For example, an employee of the company or any affiliate in the current year or any of the past three years generally is prohibited from serving on the audit committee. A member of the immediate family of an executive officer is also precluded from serving on an audit committee.
	Recommendation 2: The NYSE and the NASD/AMEX require that listed companies with a market capitalization above $200 million have an audit committee composed solely of independent directors.	The NYSE and the NASD/AMEX maintain their respective current audit committee independence requirements and their respective definitions of independence for listed companies with a market capitalization of $200 million or below.
2. Qualifications and composition	Recommendation: Large listed companies (a market capitalization above $200 million) to have an audit committee composed of a minimum of three directors who are financially literate or become financially literate within a reasonable time after appointment.	The small listed companies (market capitalization of $200 or below should maintain their respective current audit committee size and membership requirements.
3. Audit committees' activities	Recommendation 1: The audit committee (1) adopts a formal written charter provided by the board, which specifies its scope, responsibilities, structure, processes, and membership requirements; and (2) reviews and evaluates its adequacy on an annual basis.	The effect, however, of the audit committee depends on its diligence in defining its role, function, responsibilities, structure, and process. The audit committee must review and reasses the charter's adequacy annually.
	Recommendation 2: The SEC requires companies under its jurisdiction to establish the audit committee and companies to disclose in their proxy statement whether their audit committee has adopted a formal written charter and has satisfied its responsibilities during the year in compliance with its charter.	The SEC rules contain "safe harbor" provisions regarding all disclosures about the audit committee charter and report.

4. Mechanisms for accountability of audit committees	Recommendation 1: The audit committee charter should specify that the outside auditor is ultimately accountable to the board of directors and the audit committee.	The board of directors and the audit committee as representatives of shareholders have the ultimate authority and responsibility to select, evaluate, and, where appropriate, replace the outside auditor.
	Recommendation 2: The audit committee charter should specify that the audit committee receive a formal written statement from outside auditors delineating all relationships between the auditor and the company.	The audit committee should discuss with the auditor any disclosed relationships or services that may affect the objectivity and independence of the auditor.
	Recommendation 3: Generally Accepted Auditing Standards (GAAS) require that the outside auditor discuss with the audit committee the auditor's judgments about the quality, not just the acceptability, of the company's accounting principles.	This requirement should address many concerns about the "quality" of financial reporting and should be written in such a way as to encourage open, frank discussion and to avoid boilerplate.
	Recommendation 4: The SEC requires a letter from the audit committee in the annual report indicating that (1) management has reviewed the audited financial statements with the audit committee; (2) the outside auditors have discussed with the audit committee the outside auditors' judgements of the quality of accounting principles used; and (3) the audit committee discussed the information received from both management and outside auditors without them present.	The audit committee should review the entire audit process and do more than just rely upon information it receives. SEC registrants must (1) have independent audit review of interim financial information; (2) comply with the new disclosure requirements, including the audit committee report, committee charter, and disclosure regarding member independence.
	Recommendation 5: The SEC requires that a reporting company's outside auditor conduct a SAS No. 71 Interim Financial Review prior to the company's filing of its Form 10-Q.	To increase the level and effectiveness of monitoring of the interim reporting process, the audit committee should discuss interim financial reports with the outside auditor and management.

financial institutions from engaging in cosmetic transactions intended primarily to manage reported earnings (e.g., gains trading by selling appreciated assets while retaining depreciated assets;) (5) standardizing portfolio accounting practices across financial institutions; (6) changing financial institutions' asset/liability management strategies and funding decisions; (7) restricting the circumstances in which debt and equity are reported at amortized costs; and (8) presenting a number of tax-planning opportunities which should be considered carefully before any mergers and acquisitions in the financial services industry.

The savings and loan association crisis in the late 1980s, capital inadequacy problems, failures of many banks during the late 1980s and early 1990s, and inefficiency in huge mergers and consolidations of banks during the 1980s raised some serious doubt about the credibility and relevance of institutions' financial reporting processes as well as governance and accountability. The Federal Deposit Insurance Corporation Improvement Act (FDICIA) of 1991 attempted to reform the banking industry by introducing new financial reporting, internal control reporting, and auditing requirements. These new requirements are designed to enhance the reliability of financial statements; improve the accountability and corporate governance of the affected institutions; and to secure compliance with certain laws and regulations by affected institutions.

Although the regulations explicitly exclude institutions with less than $500 million in total assets, almost all depository institutions are implicitly required to: (1) report to the FDIC and other regulatory agencies on internal control and compliance with certain laws and regulations; (2) have an audit committee composed of independent outside directors; and (3) prepare and disseminate audited financial statements. This section examines financial reporting, internal controls, and corporate governance and accountability requirements of affected institutions under the new FDIC regulations as well as providing some guidance and implementation suggestions for covered institutions to better comply with the provisions of the new FDIC regulations.

The audit committee should perform its role with diligence to underscore the institution's commitment to the highest standards of corporate governance and financial reporting. The audit committee's activities will clearly add value to responsible corporate governance and the reliable financial reporting process by reducing the business risk, misuse of assets, corporate misconduct, or material misstatement of financial condition. The role of the audit committee has received considerable attention in recent years in ensuring responsible corporate governance and reliable financial reporting process.

ENDNOTES

1. LaWare, John, 1991, Member, Board of Governors of the Federal Reserve System. Statement before Committee on Banking, Finance, and Urban Affairs, U.S. House of Representatives (September 24). As reported in the *Federal Reserve Bulletin,* November 1991.

2. Savage, Donald T., 1993. "Interstate Banking: A Status Report." *Federal Reserve Bulletin* (Vol. 73, December): 1075–1089.

3. Adkisson, J. Amanda, and Donald R. Fraser, 1990. "The Effect of Geographical Deregulation on Bank Acquisition Premium." *Journal of Financial Services* (Vol. 4, July): 145–155.

4. Brewer, Elijah, III, William E. III, Jackson, Jagliani, Julapa A., and Nguyen, Thong, 2000. "The Price of Bank Mergers in the 1990s." *Economic Perspectives,* Federal Reserve Bank of Chicago (First Quarter): 2–23.

5. Ibid.

6. Weiss, Steven J., (1999). "National Policies on Foreign Acquisitions of Banks." *The Bankers Magazine* (March): 25–29.

7. The Federal Reserve Board, 1999. Remarks by Vice Chairman Roger W. Ferguson, Jr., Before the Bond Market Association, New York, New York (October 28).

8. Remarks by Chairman Alan Greenspan, 1999. The Evolution of Bank Supervision. Before the American Bankers Association, Phoenix, Arizona (October 11).

9. Golembe, Carter H., 1999. "Global Financial Crises: Implications for Banking and Regulation." Conference on Bank Structure and Competition, Federal Reserve Bank of Chicago (Chicago, Illinois, May 6–7).

10. Ibid.

11. The Federal Reserve Board, 1999. Remarks by Richard Spillenkothen, Director, Division of Supervision and Regulation. At the New York State Banking Department, New York, New York, October 25.

12. Wagster, J.D., 1996. "Impact of the 1988 Basel Accord on International Banks." *Journal of Finance* (Vol. 51): 1321–1346.

13. Basel Committee on Banking Supervision, 1996. "Amendment to the Capital Accord to Incorporate Market Risks" (January).

14. Department of the Treasury (Office of the Comptroller of the Currency), Federal Reserve System and Federal Deposit Insurance Corporation, 1996. "Risk-Based Capital Standards: Market Risk." (August). Federal Reserve. 1996. "The Market-Risk Amendment." Commercial Bank Examination Manual. Regulation H (12CFR 208, Appendix E, and 12CFR 225, Appendix E).

15. Hendricks, Darryll, 1996, "Evaluation of Value at Risk Models Using Historical Data." Federal Reserve Bank of New York, *Economic Policy Review* (April): 36–69.

16. Dimson, E. and Marsh, P., 1995. "Capital Requirements for Securities Firms." *Journal of Finance* (Vol. 50): 821–851.

17. Estrella, Arturo, 1995. "A Prolegomenon to Future Capital Requirements." Federal Reserve Bank of New York, *Economic Policy Review* (July): 1–12.

18. Berger, Allen N. and Sally M. Davies, 1994. "The Information Content of Bank Exams." Bank Structure and Rating Position, Federal Reserve Bank of Chicago (May).

19. Brewer, Elijah III, 1989. "Full-Blown Crisis, Half-Measure Cure." Federal Reserve Bank of Chicago, Economic Perspectives (November/December): 2–17.

20. Morris, Charles S. and Gordon H. Sellon, Jr., 1991. "Market Value Accounting for Bankers: Pros and Cons." *Economic Review,* Federal Reserve Bank of Kansas City (March/April): 5–19.

21. Mondschean, Thomas, 1992. "Market Value Accounting May Cure Banking Net Worth Distortions." Business Credit (June): 14.

22. Mergh, David L., 1990. "Market Value Accounting and the Bank Balance Sheet." Contemporary Policy Issues (April): 82–94.

23. Sulton, Michael H. and James A. Johnson, 1993. "Current Value: Finding a Way Forward." Financial Executives (January/February): 39–43.

24. KPMG Peat Marwick, 1992. Fair Value of Financial Instruments—An Insurance Industry Survey: The Views of Preparers and Users of Insurance Company Financial Statements and Fair Value Disclosure Implementations (November.)

25. Pricewaterhouse Coopers, 2000. Audit Committee Update 2000: Current Financial Reporting Model and Meeting User's Needs: 37.

26. Leung, Cecilia and Zabihollah Rezaee, 1995. "Interactions Between Financial and Tax Rules on Market Value Accounting." Journal of Taxation of Investments (Winter 1997): 132–151.

27. Financial Accounting Standard Board (FASB). 1999. Preliminary Views: Report Financial Instruments and Certain Related Assets and Liabilities at Fair Value (FASB, Norwalk, Connecticut, December 14).

28. Supervisory Guidance on the Implementation of Section 112 of the Federal Deposit Insurance Corporation Improvement Act, 1991, *The Board of Directors of the FDIC* (May 11, 1993).

29. Foreign Corrupt Practice Act (FCPA), pp. 95–213, Title 1; 91 Stat. 1494, December 19, 1977.

30. National Commission on Fraudulent Financial Reporting, "Report of the National Commission on Fraudulent Financial Reporting," (October 1987).

31. Committee of Sponsoring Organizations of the Treadway Commission (COSO), "Internal Control—Integrated Framework," *Coopers and Lybrand* (September 1992): Volume 1–4.

32. Mary Colby, "New Audit and Reporting Rule Generates Yet More Paperwork," *Bank Management* (August 1993) pp. 47–49.

33. COSO Report, op. cit.

34. American Institute of Certified Public Accountants (AICPA), "Statement on Standards for Attestation Engagements," Nos. 1 and 2 *The Auditing Standards Board of AICPA* (May 1993).

35. Failed Banks: Accounting and Auditing Reform Urgently Needed (U.S. General Accounting Office (GAO)/AFMD 91–43) April 22, 1991.

36. New York Stock Exchange and National Association of Securities Dealers. 1999. Audit Committees: Legislation Needed to Strengthen Bank Controls (U.S. General Accounting Office (GAO/AFMD 92–19)) October 21, 1991.

37. Report and Recommendations on the Blue Ribbon Committee on Improving the Effectiveness of Corporate Audit Committees, February 1999.

PART II

Fundamentals of Valuations: Concepts, Standards, and Techniques

CHAPTER 5

Value and Valuation: A Conceptual Foundation

The concept of *value* is not as straightforward as many people believe. The value of any asset depends on several factors: the party for whom the valuation is made; the type of value being measured; the point in time at which the value is being estimated; and the purpose of the valuation. This chapter presents key concepts and definitions of value and valuation that are important to understand when applying the various valuation approaches described in Chapter 6.

5.1 THE NATURE OF VALUE

In the context of valuation for bank mergers and acquisitions, value means *economic value*. Such value is an amount, expressed in dollar terms, that would be paid in exchange for an asset or the right to receive future benefits from the use of that asset. Economic value is, therefore, the monetary worth of an asset.[1]

Value is not a static or homogeneous concept. The value of any asset depends on many factors which can change over time, such as:

- total economic environment;
- potential use of the asset;
- timing of the value estimate;
- location of the asset;
- relative scarcity and values of substitutes;
- extent of ownership involved;
- liquidity of and market for the asset; and
- physical condition of the asset.

The concept of value is different from *price* or *cost*. Price is the actual amount spent to acquire an asset. Cost typically means the dollar value of the factors of production (land, labor, capital, and management) required to create an asset. The expression "He overpaid for that house" indicates a difference between the price someone paid for the house and the value someone else placed on it. A similar difference exists between value and cost. The cost of developing a shopping center, for example, may not reflect its value if it is located in a community which loses its largest employer the day after the shopping center opens. In this case the cost could far exceed the value.

Value, price, and cost are different concepts and seldom are of equal monetary amounts. The discussion in this and other chapters focuses on value. Where price and cost come into play, they are explicitly identified.

5.2 TWELVE CONCEPTS OF VALUE

A Chinese proverb states "Wisdom begins with calling things by their right names." This saying has direct applicability to valuation, where different concepts of value have very different definitions, uses, and interpretations. It often is surprising to bankers and other professionals when they hear that the meaning of value is more complex than "what something is worth." As discussed in the preceding section, value depends on the person assessing it, the purpose, the timing, and a host of other factors. In other words, there is no one *right* value. Consequently, it is important to define the various concepts of value that can be used to establish a bank's value for a merger or acquisition.

1. Fair Market Value
The most common type of value definition is the *fair market value method,* also known as market value or cash value. The generally accepted definition of fair market value is:

> The amount, expressed in cash or equivalent, at which a property (or any other asset) would exchange between a willing buyer and willing seller, each having a reasonable knowledge of all pertinent facts, neither being under compulsion to buy or sell and with equity to both.

This definition of value applies to virtually all federal and state tax matters, as well as to many other valuation situations.

It is important to remember that the willing buyer and willing seller described in the definition are not "particular" buyer and seller. They are hypothetical parties in an arm's length transaction. Consequently, if the price paid for an asset reflects factors that are atypical to the hypothetical willing buyer and willing seller, then that price reflects something other than fair market value. For example, the developer of a parcel of real estate may have more interest than anyone else in an adjoining strip of land because it would round out a total development. This unique situation of one particular buyer should not be taken into account when establishing a fair market value of that adjoining strip of land.

The concept of a hypothetical willing buyer and willing seller is sometimes difficult to grasp, because no one considers himself or herself as hypothetical. An alternate way of viewing this concept is to consider the hypothetical willing buyer and willing seller as the "most likely" buyer or seller. Therefore, fair market value could be considered the "most likely" transaction price. This value would reflect consensus of assumptions of typical or likely buyers of the asset.

Fair market value is determined as of a specific date based on the price that a willing buyer would pay a willing seller with all relevant knowledge. The general public may confuse fair market value with fairness. Fair market value is not about fairness, but rather what a willing buyer would pay a willing seller at a specific date based on the best educated guess and judgment using all of the knowledge available on that date.

Fair market value assumes a continuation in the general pattern of the property being valued. In other words, fair market value is, more or less, an *as is* value, without improvements that a particular buyer may be able to implement. The buyer, in the process of establishing a price to offer for a particular asset, often considers the potential impact of improvements to the property. The results of such "value creation" efforts are not (and should not be) reflected in fair market value. In the real world of buying and selling assets, however, it is very common for a seller to benefit from at least some of the *value creation potential* in the form of a price higher than a theoretically "pure" fair market value. In a competitive market, more than one buyer will be bidding for the property of the seller, and the ultimate price paid may reflect the fair market value plus some portion of the value creation opportunity the buyer believes it can realize. The price ultimately paid by a particular buyer is usually attributable to *investment value,* an extremely important merger and acquisition value concept described below.

2. Investment Value

The most familiar type of value to professionals involved in mergers and acquisitions is *investment value.* This type of value is usually thought of as the value of the future benefits of ownership of an asset to a particular buyer. Investment value is often a more easily understood concept, because it is the value of a specific asset to a specific buyer.

The investment value can differ significantly from one potential buyer to another for a variety of valid reasons. Some factors that can affect a particular buyer's estimate of investment value in, say, a business include:

- perceived synergy and value creation opportunities;
- desire on the part of the buyer to enter a new market;
- perception of riskiness and/or volatility of the asset's earning power;
- tax status of buyer; and
- optimism of buyer.

All of these factors influence the particular buyer's estimate of the future earning power of the business, and therefore that buyer's estimation of value.

Fair market value and investment value are related but seldom equal. If all potential buyers had the same assumptions and situations, the two types of values would be equal. As this is an improbable situation, it will always be the case that some buyers are willing to pay more for an asset than others. The techniques and approaches used to estimate fair market value and investment value are essentially the same; it is the assumptions that differ.

3. Fair Value

The concept of fair value has recently received considerable attention from standard-setting bodies (e.g., Financial Accounting Standards Board) and judicial process through case laws. Fair value is the statutory standard of value that has evolved from case laws and applies to certain specific transactions. The concept of fair value has developed by case laws, and, accordingly, states have different interpretations of fair value with almost no consensus about its definition and application. However, in most court cases, the concept of fair value is equated to fair market value and applied primarily in dissenting or oppressed shareholder actions in mergers or sell-outs. In cases when the fair value concept should be used, the appraiser must obtain a definition of fair value by consulting local case law, statutes, and attorneys in the jurisdiction in which the case would be filed.

In the current accounting standards, the FASB defines fair value as "an estimate of the price an entity would have realized if it had sold an asset or paid if it had been relieved of a liability on the reporting date in an arm's length exchange motivated by normal business considerations. That is, it is an estimate of an exit price determined by market interactions."[2] In this definition, the FASB equates fair value with exit price, that is, the price at which an asset or liability could be sold or settled. The exit price is determined by the market's estimate of the present value of the expected future cash flows of the entity that owns the asset or owes the liability. Thus, based on the above definition, the fair value is the amount at which (1) an asset could be bought or sold between willing parties in a normal course of business, or (2) a liability could be incurred or settled in a current transaction between willing parties.

4. Intrinsic Value

Intrinsic value, also known as fundamental value, is the concept used frequently by financial analysts to estimate the value of stocks based on all of the facts and circumstances of the business or the investment. Intrinsic value of an investment (e.g., security) is determined based on both the earning power and earnings quality of the investment. Earning power is measured in terms of the entity's capability to constantly increase profitability and rate of return in light of plausible assumptions including both internal sources and external economic and benchmark data. Earnings quality is assessed by factors such as customer base, profitability, customer satisfaction, employee satisfaction, relative risk, competitiveness, and steadiness of earnings forecasts.

The intrinsic value is the present value of the future earnings stream discounted at the current market yield. Intrinsic value of an investment is a function of estimated discounted periodic earnings stream, market gains or losses, and time horizon of earnings stream. If the market value of a stock is above its calculated intrinsic value, the stock is a good "sell," and investors will be able to earn excess return. Conversely, if the market price of a stock is below its predicted intrinsic value, the stock is a good "buy." The term intrinsic value is often used incorrectly and interchangeably with the concept of investment value. Investment value commonly refers to the value perceived by a specific buyer in light of a specific set of circumstances at a specific point of time. Intrinsic value, on the other hand, is typically viewed as the value of a going concern to a particular owner, regardless of the marketability of a business or a business interest under consideration.

5. Value-In-Use/Value-In-Exchange

Value-in-use is not a type of value, but a condition under which certain assumptions are made in valuing assets. It is associated with assets that are in productive use and can be described as the value of an asset, for a particular use or to a particular user, as part of an operating enterprise. There is no official definition of value-in-use by professional valuation societies or the Internal Revenue Service (IRS). It is, however, important to understand the concept since the value of acquired assets (especially furniture, fixtures, equipment, and premises) in most bank mergers and acquisitions is influenced significantly by their use as part of the bank. When specific assets used by any ongoing business are valued, it is usually assumed that those assets will remain in their most productive use.

Value-in-exchange is essentially the opposite of value-in-use. The concept of value-in-exchange relates to the value of a property or asset as exchanged by itself separate from an operating entity. Typically, the value-in-exchange is less than the value-in-use of an asset in an ongoing business enterprise. For example, the teller counters in a bank branch have less value if sold separately than if sold as part of a total branch sale.

6. Goodwill Value

Goodwill is a specific type of intangible asset that arises when a business as a whole has value greater than the value of its tangible and specifically identified intangible assets. A 1960 court case defined goodwill as:

> The sum total of imponderable qualities which attract the customers to a business; in essence it is the expectancy of continued patronage for whatever reason.[3]

From a merger and acquisition perspective, the value of goodwill is calculated as the difference between the price paid for an acquired business and the fair market value of the assets acquired (both tangible and separately identified intangible) net of the liabilities. The concept of goodwill value has important applicability to banks for tax, financial reporting, and regulatory reasons.

7. Going Concern Value

Going concern value is somewhat of a misnomer since it is not a standard of value as is fair market value or investment value. In other words, it would be incorrect to state that "the going concern value of XYZ Bank is $100 million." A proper statement would be "the fair market value of XYZ Bank *as a going concern* is $100 million." This distinction appears to be a minor semantic difference, but the subtle differences in terminology is one key to understanding valuation.

The concept of going concern value is typically brought into play when a business (such as a bank) is being valued as a viable operating unit, with no immediate threat of discontinuance of operations. In tax situations, however, going concern value carries a somewhat different connotation. The IRS has taken the position that going concern value is a nonamortizable (for tax purposes) intangible asset acquired by a buyer of a business, a value that reflects the fact that the purchased entity has staff and management in place, a sales and marketing organization, established customer and supplier relationships, and so on. The IRS has used this concept when the existence of goodwill was difficult to demonstrate or was nonexistent. A number of court cases admitted that no specific guidelines exist to measure going concern value in the absence of goodwill.[4] Nonetheless, the IRS has been able to argue successfully that even without the goodwill, some assets of a business that are acquired have intangible value because they are in place and part of a "going concern." The real controversy, however, is not whether going concern value exists or not, but whether or not it is amortizable for tax purposes. The IRS generally has been successful in having at least some part of the purchase price of a business allocated to nonamortizable going concern value when goodwill is difficult or impossible to measure. (Chapter 8 specifically addresses intangible assets and the related valuation issues.)

8. Book Value

One of the most misleading uses of the term value is in conjunction with *book value*. It is an accounting and tax concept only, not a valuational or economic one. For a particular asset (such as a piece of equipment) book value is simply the historical cost of that asset less accumulated depreciation.[5] For a business enterprise, book value is the total book values of all individual assets less the book value of individual liabilities. In an accounting sense, this is also called *net worth* or *book equity*.

An extremely important concept to bear in mind when valuing merger and acquisition candidates is that book value may or may not have any relation to fair market value or investment value of a bank, and consequently valuing a bank using a multiple of book value is an unreliable technique. A real life example illustrates the difference between book value and measures of economic value such as fair market value.

The financial statistics in Exhibit 5.1 represent a bank that is being valued as a potential acquisition candidate. The adjustments from book value to fair market value of all assets and liabilities would be based on in-depth analysis of the underlying loans, securities, premises, and deposits. The book equity was $6,271,000 whereas the fair market value of the equity was $5,509,000; a 12.2 percent decline and over $750,000 difference. Using book value to gauge any type of valuation estimate would be, at best, misleading.

Despite the failings of book value, it is used extensively in bank acquisitions as a means to gauge the appropriateness of a price paid. It is important to keep in mind the weaknesses inherent in book value and the potentially misleading information it can generate.

Exhibit 5.1   Illustration of Equity Valuation—Book Value Versus Fair Market Value ($000)

Assets	Book Value	Fair Market Value*
Cash and due froms	$ 11,694	$ 11,694
Investments	34,369	31,812
Total loans	56,718	52,892
(Loan loss reserves)	(780)	(780)
Net loans	55,938	52,112
Premises and fixed assets	3,517	4,703
Real estate owned	810	525
Other assets	2,860	2,487
Core deposit intangible	—	4,646
Total assets	$109,188	$107,979
Liabilities		
Customer deposits	$ 99,261	$ 98,814
Fed funds purchased	2,125	2,125
Other liabilities	1,531	1,531
Total liabilities	$102,917	$102,470
Equity	$ 6,271	$ 5,509

*Fair market value is derived by valuing the financial, tangible, and identifiable intangible assets and liabilities individually.

9. Liquidation Value

Liquidation value is not, by itself, a separate type of value, but a condition under which value is estimated. It is the net amount that can be realized if a business is terminated, its assets sold individually, and liabilities satisfied. As with going concern value described earlier, it would be incorrect to state "the liquidation value of asset X is $100." The correct statement would be "the value of asset X in liquidation is $100." In practice, however, the term liquidation value is used for simplicity.

Liquidation can be *forced* or *orderly,* with the major difference being the time allowed to find a buyer. The generally accepted definitions are:

- *Forced Liquidation:* The net amount that an asset will bring if exposed for immediate sale on the open market, both buyer and seller having knowledge of the uses and purposes to which it is adapted and for which it is capable of being used, the seller being compelled to sell and the buyer being willing, but not compelled, to buy.
- *Orderly Liquidation:* The net amount that an asset will bring if exposed for sale on the open market with a *reasonable time* allowed to find a purchaser, both buyer and seller having knowledge of the uses and purposes to which it is adapted and for which it is capable of being used, the seller being compelled to sell and the buyer being willing, but not compelled, to buy.

The *net amount,* as used in the definitions above, is the price, less any commissions and administrative cost associated with the liquidation.

From the standpoint of the value of a business, the lowest value possible is its liquidation value.[6] In other words, the worst scenario from a value perspective is to terminate the business, liquidate its assets, and satisfy its liabilities with the remaining balance being distributed to the stockholders.

The liquidation value concept is involved when the Federal Deposit Insurance Corporation (FDIC) does not accept bids for failed banks. In such cases, the agency has determined that the failed bank's value is higher (or its losses are less) if the FDIC liquidates the bank, pays depositors, and collects loans as best as possible. In other words, the bank had less value as an ongoing business than the value of the individual assets (net of liabilities) of that bank.

10. Insurable Value

Insurable value is very straightforward; it is simply the dollar value of destructible portions of an asset that will be insured to indemnify the owner in the event of loss. This type of value has little relevance to bank mergers and acquisitions, except possibly in a post-acquisition review of insurance coverage of premises and equipment.

11. Replacement Value

The replacement value of an asset is simply the cost of acquiring a new asset of equal utility. An estimate of replacement cost takes into account how an asset would be replaced with newer materials and current technology. Replacement value is not the same as reproduction value. The latter is the cost of a duplicate asset based on current prices. Replacement value and reproduction cost are used mostly in the valuation of tangible assets that do not produce income directly, such as furniture, equipment, and fixtures.

12. Salvage Value

Salvage value is the amount realizable upon sale or other disposition of an asset after it is no longer useful to the current owner and is to be taken out of service. This is different from the concept of *scrap value,* which assumes the asset is no longer useful to anyone for any purpose.

During a bank merger or acquisition, salvage value may be involved if the combined banks will have excess equipment (for example, computers or proof machines). It may be useful to the buyer to know the salvage value of such equipment.

5.3 TYPES OF PROPERTY THAT CAN BE VALUED

Valuation is an economic concept closely aligned with the legal concept of *property.* When involved in valuation, the term property usually means the rights and benefits associated with ownership. The legal concept of property and ownership is very complex, but a few points are beneficial in providing a better understanding of valuations for bank mergers and acquisitions.

The most obvious type of property is a *tangible asset,* such as buildings, equipment, and furniture. These are "hard" assets that have physical shape and substance. Ownership of tangible assets is secured through titles and deeds. In a bank, the bulk of the physical tangible assets are shown on the balance sheet under *premises and fixed assets* and *other real estate owned.*

In a bank, loans and investments are considered tangible financial assets. While not having true physical substance, loans and investments represent a contractual claim on future income at a stated rate and for a specified period of time. The fair market value of a loan or investment is the net present value of the income stream based on the timing and riskiness of that income stream.

Property can also be *intangible.* Such property, in the context of an ongoing business, includes those assets that have no physical substance, but are important contributors to the success of the business. The benefits of ownership of intangible assets are usually measured by the financial return from those assets. Typical intangible assets in a banking environment include:

- core deposit base;
- loan servicing contracts;
- safe deposit box contracts;
- proprietary computer software;
- leasehold interests;
- assembled work force;
- name recognition; and
- goodwill.

Each of these types of intangible assets can be valued.

The third type of property which can be valued is the business in total, a combination of the tangible and intangible property. To understand the concept of a business as a property to be valued, distinct from the value of the underlying tangible and intangible assets, it is useful to understand the legal concept of *unity of use.*

Any combination of tangible and intangible assets, integrated so that they function as a unit, are considered to have unity of use. When valuing a bank as an ongoing business, it is being valued as a combination of tangible and intangible assets functioning with unity of use.

5.4 RELATIONSHIP AMONG DIFFERENT TYPES OF VALUE

Within the context of total business (or total enterprise) value, the relationship among the various types of value described earlier can be seen. Exhibit 5.2 illustrates how different levels of future income of a business affect the various types of value.

The lowest conceivable value of a business is the scrap value of the tangible assets, which is the same no matter what the income level is of the enterprise. For example, the scrap value of a piece of equipment is constant, at a given point in time, irrespective of the earnings of the business that owns it.

Forced liquidation value is the second lowest potential value, but from a practical perspective this is probably the lowest value a business as a whole would bring. Like scrap value, the forced liquidation value is the same no matter what the income of the enterprise. Orderly liquidation value is conceptually identical to forced liquidation, except that a higher value is usually received because more time is allowed to find a buyer.

Value-in-use of the tangible assets typically increases with the income of the business (up to the point at which the value-in-use equals the replacement value of the asset). At zero income, the value-in-use and orderly liquidation value are theoretically equivalent, but as the business becomes more successful, the importance of the tangible assets becomes more significant; thus value-in-use exceeds orderly liquidation value.

Exhibit 5.2 Illustration of Relationship Among Various Types of Business Value and the Future Income of That Business

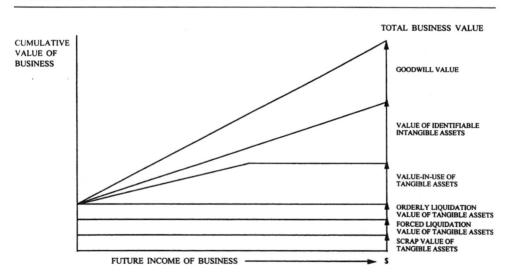

Value of identifiable intangible assets also tends to increase as the income of the business grows. As with tangible assets, the importance of the identifiable intangibles grows along with the income of the business.

Goodwill value will nearly always increase with the earnings of the business because goodwill is computed as the difference between the value of the total business and the value of the tangible and identified intangible assets. Consequently, as the earnings of the business grow, so does its total goodwill and enterprise value.

The cumulative result is the total business value. This is the value of the tangible and intangible assets, and it increases along with the future income prospects of the business. Most valuations of a business are measuring total business value.

5.5 PRINCIPLES OF VALUATION THEORY

Basic economic principles—such as supply and demand—affect the value of a property or asset. There are, however, four specific economic principles that affect valuation in important ways. These principles are described below.

5.5.1 Principle of Alternatives

The *principle of alternatives* states that in any contemplated transfer of ownership, both the buyer and the seller have alternatives to consummation of the transaction. This principle does not mean that all alternatives are equally desirable. It simply means that a seller is not forced to sell to a given buyer, and a buyer is not forced to buy from a given seller. If this were not the case, the market mechanism would be distorted and a fair market value could not be established. A normal valuation assumes that the principle of alternatives is satisfied.

5.5.2 Principle of Replacement

The *principle of replacement* states that a prudent buyer will pay no more for a property or asset than the cost necessary to reproduce it with one of equal utility. The simplest illustration of this principle is in the value of used machinery and equipment. A prudent buyer would not pay more for a used piece of equipment than for a new one that performs the same functions. The application of this principle to a total business enterprise is much more difficult, since the estimation of costs required to replace a business would be very complex. The *cost approach* to valuation (described in Chapter 6) is based on the principle of replacement.

5.5.3 Principle of Substitution

The *principle of substitution* is an extremely important concept of valuation. It states that the value of a property or asset tends to be determined by the cost that would be incurred to acquire an equally desirable substitute. An example, although somewhat improbable, illustrates this principle. Consider two banks of the same size, same staff, same earnings, same spreads, and so on. Common sense and valuation science would conclude that both banks are of equal or very nearly equal value because they are equally desirable substitutes (and in this case identical substitutes).

A more realistic example would be an investor group considering the acquisition of a bank. As prudent investors, they would not only examine the target bank itself, but also the prices paid for comparable banks (that is, for equally desirable substitutes). The principle of substitution is the theoretical basis for the *market approach* to valuation, which is described in Chapter 6.

5.5.4 Principle of Future Benefits

The *principle of future benefits,* which is particularly important in a merger and acquisition context, states that the value of a property or asset reflects anticipated future economic benefits from ownership or control of that property or asset. From this perspective, the value of a bank, or any business, is the net present value of all future economic benefits attained as a result of the ownership of that bank or business. In a theoretical sense, what a bank has accomplished in the past has no relevance to value. From a practical standpoint, however, past performance is usually one good indicator of future performance, unless unusual outside events have distorted past trends.

The application of the future benefits principle is very complex and requires numerous assumptions about the future of the business. Nonetheless, the net present value of future economic benefits is often the best indicator of value.[7] The principle of future benefits is the foundation for the *income approach* to value, described in Chapter 6.

5.6 PRICING VALUE VERSUS REPORTING VALUE

As mentioned previously in this chapter, one factor affecting value estimates is the purpose for the valuation. Different valuation purposes influence the value assumptions and the type of value to be measured. Often, different people assess the value of a property or business for different reasons and from different perspectives. In general, the points of view usually fall into two categories: pricing and reporting.

The pricing point of view is taken by an investor who is assessing a company for purposes of acquisition. From this perspective, measures of earnings, cash flow, tax benefits, discount rates, synergy potential, and value creation opportunities are important. These types of considerations are crucial to an assessment for pricing and economic return analysis.

The reporting point of view, on the other hand, is concerned with supporting an estimate of value for tax or accounting purposes. To provide the requisite support, it is necessary to use techniques that satisfy taxing and regulatory bodies. Such techniques may, or may not, coincide with those used for pricing.

The distinction between these two points of view is sometimes difficult to understand, but provides one way of reconciling seemingly disparate approaches to, and estimates of, value. Consider the acquisition of a bank. To the buyer, the sole determinant of price may be the future dividend potential—the future economic benefits of ownership. The buyer may have little or no concern for the prices other similar banks have brought. For tax or accounting reporting purposes, however, that same buyer would have to follow certain guidelines that require consideration of prices paid for comparable banks as a basis of establishing value. The buyer is not being inconsistent, but is simply reflecting different valuation needs at different points in time for different purposes.

5.7   LIMITATIONS OF THE VALUATION PROCESS

Valuation is an inexact science. It requires judgment, assumptions, and opinion. Consequently, two equally qualified appraisers could easily derive two different, yet equally supportable, value estimates for the same asset or property.

It is important to remember that a value estimate is an opinion of value. If prepared by a competent valuation professional, it is an informed opinion based on accepted analyses and techniques. It is, however, still an opinion.

ENDNOTES

1. Throughout this book, the term "value" is synonymous with "economic value," and "asset" is used interchangeably with "property."
2. Financial Accounting Standards Board (FASB). 2000. Preliminary Views on Reporting Financial Instruments and Certain Related Assets and Liabilities at Fair Value." (May 31), p. 47.
3. *Boe v. Comr.,* 35 T.C. 1038 (1960), aff'd 287 F.2d 1 (2nd cir. 1961).
4. For example *Concord Control, Inc. v. Comr.,* T.C. Memo 1976-301, aff'd and rem'd, 615-F.2d 1153 (6th Cir. 1980) and *Northern Natural Gas v. U.S.* 420 F.2d, 1107 (8th Cir. 1973).
5. Book value can be either accounting or tax book, but the basic principles are the same.
6. One scenario where liquidation value may not be the lowest value is a business that has assets that are of no use at all, and would have only scrap value. This is, however, an unlikely possibility.
7. Situations often arise where the estimate of value by means of calculating the net present value of future income is much more, or less than what the market seems to be paying for equally desirable substitutes. Such situations require judgment by the appraiser to reconcile the differences and determine which is the more reasonable approach, or if a combination of approaches is appropriate.

CHAPTER 6

Approaches to Measuring Value

This chapter addresses specific approaches used to value property. Such property can be real estate, machinery, equipment, stock of a company, a privately held business, or an intangible asset. These techniques of valuation are conceptually the same irrespective of the particular type of property being appraised. Specific applications of these techniques to valuing a bank are described in Chapter 14.

There are three primary approaches to valuation:

1. the cost approach;
2. the market approach; and
3. the income approach.

Each approach is discussed in this chapter, along with special topics relating to valuation of intangible assets and businesses.

6.1 OVERVIEW OF THE VALUATION PROCESS

Regardless of which particular approach to valuation is appropriate in a given circumstance, there is a basic process to any value estimation undertaking. A valuation professional will normally use five major steps in the process of conducting the assignment.

1. The first step is to define what is to be valued, the date of the value, the purpose of the valuation, and the means by which the results will be communicated. It is important to all parties concerned that these issues be addressed. The subsequent research, analysis, and approach will be determined by the answers.
2. The second step is to analyze carefully the property being appraised; whether it is a business, a parcel of real estate, equipment, or machinery. The types of analysis will differ significantly depending on the property being valued. Nonetheless, the asset must be analyzed thoroughly.
3. The third major step is to gather data which will be input to the valuation of the subject property. To value a business, data on other companies would be gathered. For real estate, reproduction costs of similar properties and comparable sales would be gathered.

4. The fourth step is to use the information generated in steps two and three, and apply the appropriate valuation techniques in order to arrive at a conclusion of value.

5. The last step is the preparation of a written report of the valuation. All valuation estimates should be in writing. The form of the report may be brief and simple or long and complex, depending on the situation. In addition to the value estimate, the report should identify the purpose of the appraisal, the date of the value, assumptions underlying the value estimate, and limiting conditions.

The elapsed time to complete these steps can range from a few days for a simple property to months for a complex assignment with multiple properties and/or locations.

The discussions in this chapter focus on the application of valuation techniques once the valuation assignment has been defined and information on the subject asset and any other relevant data have been gathered. In other words, the focus of the balance of this chapter is step four of the valuation process.

6.2   THE COST APPROACH TO VALUATION

The cost approach to valuation is based on a comparison of the property being appraised with the cost of replacing it. This approach makes intuitive sense because a property should be worth the cost of another one of similar utility, with appropriate adjustments for any physical, functional, and economic obsolescence.

The cost approach to valuation is most frequently applied to the valuation of nonincome-producing machinery, equipment, and real estate that are part of a business. Valuations of businesses in total are seldom made using this approach. Typically, only when specific underlying assets of the business are being appraised is the cost approach applicable. The cost approach, using improved real estate as an example, determines the property's value by estimating the cost to reproduce the improvements (for example, buildings, parking, landscaping) deducting for physical, functional, and/or economic obsolescence; then adding the market value of the land. (The land must be valued separately because the cost approach is not a valid valuation technique for land—every parcel of land is, by definition, unique because of location and cannot be "replaced" by one exactly like it.)

In order to estimate the cost to reproduce the improvements, a thorough analysis of those improvements must be undertaken. Then, using current local prices for each item, the cost to reproduce the improvements is calculated. Exhibit 6.1 illustrates the results of the cost approach to valuing an apartment complex after in-depth analysis of the property and current costs to reproduce each improvement are determined. Obsolescence is then calculated to derive market value.

A critical element in applying the cost approach is the obsolescence factor. Obsolescence measures the true decline in utility of an asset from one, two, or all three potential sources.

1. *Physical Obsolescence:* This is the actual physical deterioration of a property through wear and tear. Under normal circumstances, this is the source of most obsolescence in physical assets.

Exhibit 6.1 Illustration of Cost Approach to Valuation (Apartment Complex as Example)

Item	Reproduction Cost	Obsolescence	Market Value
• Building			
(235,000 sq. ft. @ $42.00/sq.ft.)	$ 9,870,000	10%	$ 8,883,000
• Appliances and interior fixtures			
(350 units @ $2,200/unit)	$ 770,000	20%	$ 616.00
• Yard improvements			
Asphalt paving	$ 250,000	15%	$ 212,500
Concrete walks	275,000	10%	247,500
Maintenance shed	7,500	25%	5,625
Street lights	80,000	10%	72,000
Landscaping	110,000	15%	93,500
Swimming pool	80,000	20%	64,000
Other	10,000	10%	9,000
Total	$ 812,500		$ 704,125
Total reproduction costs	$11,452,500		$10,203,125
Value of land*	N/A	N/A	$ 897,000
		Total value (rounded)	$11,100,000

*Valued by the market approach. Land cannot be valued by the cost approach.

2. *Functional Obsolescence:* This source of obsolescence is a result of "defects" in design of the property. Such defects are not physical, but functional in nature, such as obsolete materials or design. Functional obsolescence, which can be curable or incurable
depending on the situation, is usually a result of either size (too large or too small) or
outdated design (requires modernization). An example of functional obsolescence in a
banking situation is a "superadequate" branch—one that is too large or too opulent to
be justified economically in today's environment. Because of ATMs and other electronic delivery systems, many older bank branches suffer from some functional obsolescence due to superadequacy.

3. *Economic Obsolescence:* This type of obsolescence is a result of the diminished utility of a property due to external factors. For example, a piece of equipment that man-
ufactures Beta videotapes has suffered economic obsolescence through the evolution
of VHS as the standard. By definition, economic obsolescence is always incurable.

The estimates of the extent of the obsolescence are a major factor in determining the value
of a property and are often very subjective.

In the context of valuations as part of bank mergers and acquisitions, it is likely that the
cost approach will only be used to value individual tangible assets. When pricing an acquisition target or evaluating a purchase offer, the cost approach is seldom, if ever, used. The
exception might be the case in which the bank has significantly undervalued fixed assets on
its books that could be sold for a substantial profit after the transaction is complete. Chapter 8 discusses valuation of individual tangible assets of a bank in more detail.

6.3   THE MARKET APPROACH TO VALUATION

The second major technique of valuation is the market approach. In its simplest form, this approach states that a property's value is equal to the cost of acquiring an equally desirable substitute.[1] The process requires a comparison and correlation between the subject property and similar properties being exchanged in the current market with appropriate adjustments as necessary. The market approach entails using comparative valuation techniques according to specific guidelines in similar industries, for similar business interests, in similar publicly traded companies. This approach is most appropriate in determining the value of a marketable minority interest.

The market approach is relatively easy to understand but can be difficult to apply unless there is a reasonably active market for properties similar to the one being valued. For example, it is difficult to use the market approach to value a nuclear power plant, since there is, for all intents and purposes, no historical transaction data for these types of properties. Conversely, the market approach is very valid when the comparable property types, such as office buildings in major cities or common stock of businesses, are actively traded.

The market approach is widely applied to bank mergers and acquisitions. Because of the reporting requirements of the industry, there is an abundance of information available on sales of banks, as well as information on trades of widely held bank stock. This excellent base of information allows for the application of the market approach in most cases.

Even with an abundance of market transaction data, the use of the market approach requires thorough and thoughtful analysis. There are two key challenges in applying the market approach:

1.   Comparable transactions must be identified; and
2.   Adjustments to those comparables must be made.

Each of these issues is discussed below.

6.3.1   Identifying Comparables

The first issue is the identification of comparable properties. Such comparables (*comps* in valuation jargon) must meet two basic requirements:

1.   The comparables must be generally desirable substitutes for the property being appraised; and
2.   The terms and conditions of the comparable transaction must reflect meaningful market conditions and "arm's length" criteria.

These two requirements mean that the comparables should be as similar as possible to the subject property, and sales data (terms, conditions, financing, etc.) should reflect open market conditions. Within the general limitation of these requirements, there are four basic considerations used when identifying comparables.

The first of these considerations is the *availability of data on actual transactions.* (Offers which were not consummated are not valid because they do not reflect market actions.) The information on the transaction must be reliable and reasonably complete. Fortunately, in the banking industry the information about change of control prices available through regulatory agencies and private sources usually meets both these criteria.

The second consideration is the *number of comparable transactions* that can be identified. Information may be reliable and complete, but if statistics on only one or two transactions are available, use of the market approach is effectively eliminated. Normally, four or five truly comparable transactions are the minimum number necessary for a valid application of the market approach. In general, it is desirable to have as many comparable transactions as possible.

The *degree of similarity between the subject property and the comparables* is the third consideration. Ideally, all comparables would be identical, not just similar, to the subject property. In the real world, however, this will never happen. Nonetheless, the greater the degree of similarity between the subject property and the comparables, the more meaningful the information on the transaction. In the context of a bank valuation, this means the comparable transaction should involve a bank of roughly the same size, market type, and balance sheet composition.

The fourth consideration in identifying comparables are the *conditions and terms of the transaction*. The transaction must reflect arm's length negotiations and sale, with no insider influence. Also, the form of payment must be known. Prices can vary significantly with different forms of payment—for example, all cash, cash and notes, or stock.

Once comparable transactions are identified and they meet the four considerations above, it is necessary to adjust the comparables to match the subject property. The factors considered when making these adjustments are described below.

6.3.2 Adjusting for Lack of Comparability

Comparables are never identical to the subject property; therefore, adjustments are nearly always necessary. Such adjustments can be made either to the actual sales price of the comparable, or to a meaningful financial ratio. For example, using comparable bank sale data, the selling price could be adjusted up or down, depending on the situation, or adjustments could be made to ratios, such as price-to-earnings or price-to-book.[2] In either case, the adjustments are based on the informed opinion of the valuation professional.

With respect to a single tangible asset, the types of factors for which adjustments might be required include:

- age of the asset;
- timing of sale;
- physical condition;
- functional obsolescence; and
- possible amenities or extra features.

When estimating the value of an entire business, the factors that usually lead to adjustments in sales transaction data include:

- size of the business;
- form of ownership (for example, closely held versus publicly held);

- degree of liquidity and marketability;
- degree of profitability;
- liability and capital structure;
- market position and location;
- fixed assets; and
- past growth rates.

Whether adjustments to the comparables are made up or down will depend on the particular situation. Ideally, the comparables used should require a minimal amount of adjustment.

6.4   THE INCOME APPROACH TO VALUATION

The income approach to valuation is based on the principle that the worth of a property is equal to the net present value of future economic benefits—the income—it will bring to the owner. This approach views a property in terms of its ability to generate income. Consequently, it is applicable only for income-producing assets (e.g., a business, rental property, etc.). Nonincome-producing assets such as special use property, furniture, and fixtures cannot be valued properly by the income approach. In the context of bank mergers and acquisitions, the income approach can be used effectively to value a bank as a total business. It can also be used to value selected individual assets of the bank, such as loans, investments, core deposit base, loan servicing rights, and safe deposit box contracts.

The income approach is most relevant when valuing a business as an acquisition target. This approach examines the particular business, its unique circumstances, and its ability to generate income in the future. As described in Chapter 5, value can be defined as the dollar amount that would be paid for a property or the right to receive future benefits from use of such property. The income approach bases value on these future economic benefits.

The income approach estimates the future income generated by a property, determines the appropriate relation between future income and value, then converts that future income to an estimate of value. As with the other approaches to valuation, the concept is fairly straightforward, but the application can be difficult.

Mathematically, the income approach is derived from the simple concept that the amount of income from an investment is equal to the invested amount multiplied by the rate of return; or in equation form:

$$\text{annual income} = \text{invested amount} \times \text{Annual Rate of Return}$$

For example, if $12,500 is invested at 8 percent, the annual income is $1,000 ($12,500 × .08).

The equation can be rewritten as:

$$\text{invested amount} = \text{annual income}^3/\text{Annual Rate of Return}$$

If the annual income is again $1,000, and the annual rate of return is 8 percent, the amount invested would be $12,500, calculated as $1,000/.08. In terms of valuation, this formula can be interpreted as answering the question: *"What is the value of a property gener-*

ating $1,000 annually to an investor requiring an 8 percent annual return?" The value of that property to that investor would be $12,500. This process is known as *capitalization* and is simply the conversion of a stream of future income to a single value. In equation form, capitalization is:

$$\text{value of a property} =$$
$$\text{annual income from property/appropriate capitalization rate}$$

The mathematics of capitalization are simple. The difficulty of applying the approach lies in determining the future annual income and identifying the appropriate capitalization rate. To use the income approach properly, these two inputs must be determined carefully and only after thorough analysis.[4]

The selection of a capitalization rate can be especially difficult, as it must reflect the riskiness of the future income as well as the long-term growth of that income. Therefore, the capitalization rate and required rate of return are not necessarily equivalent, as would be implied by the example shown. The differences are discussed later in this chapter along with techniques for the selection of the capitalization rate.

Two variations of the income approach are typically used. They differ only in complexity, not in concept. The two variations are:

- the stabilized income method
- the discounted future income method

6.4.1 The Stabilized Income Method

The *stabilized income* approach uses a single measure of annual income (that is, the stabilized income) and a single capitalization rate to determine value. The example used previously—in which income was $1,000, rate was 8 percent, and value was $12,500—is an application of the stabilized income approach.

To use this approach, a level of stabilized income that is *representative* of the asset is estimated. The term *stabilized* does not mean that income is stagnant and will not increase in the future. The projected annual growth of the income is reflected in the capitalization rate, as discussed in the next section of this chapter.

One common method used to estimate the stabilized income level is to compute a *weighted average* of the last five years' income, with more recent years' income weighted most heavily. An example is shown in Exhibit 6.2. In this example, the stabilized level of income to be used in the valuation process would be $631.

The next requirement is the selection of the appropriate capitalization rate. This rate reflects the return a prudent investor would expect on an investment in the property, given its risk characteristics and the long-term income growth prospects of the property. For example, assume that the appropriate capitalization rate is 11 percent. The value would then be:

$$\text{value} = \text{stabilized income/capitalization rate}$$
$$\text{or}$$
$$\$631/.11$$
$$= \$5,736$$

Exhibit 6.2   Calculation of Weighted Historical Income

Year	Historical Income	Weight	Weighted Income
1995	$500	1	$ 500
1996	580	2	1,160
1997	620	3	1,860
1998	620	4	2,440
1999	700	5	3,500
		Total 15	9,460
		Weighted Average: (9,460/15)	$ 631

Exhibit 6.3   Projected Income for Five-Year Asset

Year	Income
1	$ 900
2	1,050
3	1,200
4	1,450
5	1,600

The process used to determine the stabilized level of income in this example is just one of a number of possibilities. Other ways to determine income and techniques used to select a capitalization rate are described in detail later in this chapter.

6.4.2   The Discounted Future Income Method

The second variation of the income approach involves projecting income and converting the income to a present value through the process of *discounting*. This process is central to the application of the discounted future income approach. A simple example will illustrate the technique.

Assume an income-producing asset with a five-year life, at which time it will be worth zero (that is, it will have no scrap or salvage value) with projected income as shown in Exhibit 6.3. The value of this asset can be computed as:

$$
\begin{aligned}
\text{value of asset} = \\
\text{year 1 income} \times \text{year 1 discount factor} \\
+ \text{ year 2 income} \times \text{year 2 discount factor} \\
+ \text{ year 3 income} \times \text{year 3 discount factor} \\
+ \text{ year 4 income} \times \text{year 4 discount factor} \\
+ \text{ year 5 income} \times \text{year 5 discount factor}
\end{aligned}
$$

The computation of the discount factor is accomplished by the following formula:

$$\text{discount factor for year "N"} = 1/(1 + \text{discount rate})^{N}$$

Exhibit 6.4   Calculation of Discount Factor

Discount Formula	Factor
Year 1: $1/(1 + 1.3)^1$	.885
Year 2: $1/(1 + .13)^2$	.783
Year 3: $1/(1 + .13)^3$	.693
Year 4: $1/(1 + .13)^4$	.613
Year 5: $1/(1 + .13)^5$	.543

Exhibit 6.5   Calculation of Present Value of Future Income

Year	Income	Discount Factor	Present Value of Income
1	$ 900	.885	$ 796.5
2	1,050	.783	822.2
3	1,200	.693	831.6
4	1,450	.613	888.9
5	1,600	.543	868.8
			$4,208.0

The discount rate is a percentage that reflects the yield a prudent investor would require to purchase the asset, given that asset's risk characteristics. (As discussed later in this chapter, discount rate and capitalization rate are *not* the same.)

If the discount rate was assumed to be 13 percent, the discount factor for each year would be as shown in Exhibit 6.4. Under these assumptions, the value of the asset would be about $4,200, calculated as shown in Exhibit 6.5.

The preceding example has the unrealistic assumption that the income will be produced by the asset over a finite *and* predictable period of time, and then will be worth nothing. Such conditions rarely exist. More typically, income is produced over a long period, the extent of which is not known exactly at the date of the valuation.

A business is a good example of this situation. The life of a business is unknown and with proper management can exist, for all intents and purposes, into perpetuity. Valuation in this circumstance is accomplished using the discounted future income approach for a defined period of time (usually five to ten years) then using the stabilized income method to compute the *residual* value of the business at the end of the finite period.

Continuing with the preceding example, suppose that the stabilized level of future earnings after Year Five is estimated to be $1,750 and a capitalization rate of 11 percent is determined to be appropriate. The value of the asset would then be about $11,850, calculated as shown in Exhibit 6.6.

6.4.3   Discounted Cash Earnings

Discounted cash earnings stream is a commonly used method of determining the value of financial institutions. This method assesses an institution's value as a function of two

Exhibit 6.6   Calculation of Present Value of Future Income with Residual

Year	Income	Discount Factor	Present Value of Income
1	$ 900	.885	$ 796.5
2	1,050	.783	822.2
3	1,200	.693	831.6
4	1,450	.613	888.9
5	1,600	.543	868.8
Residual	$1,750	.480	$ 7,636.4*
		Total	$11,844.44

*Assumes residual income is capitalized at 11%, then discounted to present value.

variables: (1) an estimate of continuous cash earning power, and (2) a discounted rate, usually the weighted average cost of capital (WACC) to capitalize cash flow earnings. Assessment of cash flow earning power is the most essential and difficult component in the valuation process because it is a function of a number of internal and external factors. Internal factors that may influence the cash flow earning power are, among others, (1) the mix of assets and liabilities; (2) management's philosophy and operating style regarding composition, maturity, yield, and costs of debt and equity instruments; (3) the credit, business, and financing risks inherent in the loan portfolio; and (4) the institution's ability to generate fee income determined by customer base as well as products and services offered. External factors are industry specifications, competitive environment, fluctuations in interest rates, regulatory laws and regulations, market conditions, and general economic conditions.

Most recently (February 2000), the Financial Accounting Standards Board (FASB) issued the Statement of Financial Accounting Concepts No. 7 (SFAC), which provides a framework for using present value to estimate fair value of assets and liabilities.[5]

SFAC No. 7 establishes guidelines for using future cash flows as the basis for accounting measurements at initial recognition or fresh-start measurements and for the interest method of amortization. SFAC No. 7 provides a framework for using present value, especially when the amount of future cash flows, their timing, or both are uncertain. Present value captures the economic difference between sets of estimated future cash flows by reflecting the uncertainties inherent in the estimated cash flows. If a price for an asset or liability or identical one can be determined in the marketplace, there is no need to use present value primarily because the marketplace assessment of present value is already embodied in such prices. However, in most cases, the present value of expected future cash flows can be used to estimate fair value. The present value formula [$P_v = F_v/(1 + I)^n$, where $P_v =$ present value, $F_v =$ future value, i = interest rate, and n = number of periods] is a tool used to incorporate the time value of money in a measurement to capture the present value of the amount that will be received in the future.

6.4.4   Selecting the Type of Income to Use

In the preceding examples it was assumed, for purposes of illustrating the concept, that the type of income, the income levels, and capitalization and discount rates all were known.

These are the essential elements in using the income approach, and in real life must be computed *before* applying the income approach.

In the context of a bank valuation analysis, the most appropriate type of income measure to use is *available cash flow*. This is the amount of cash that is available each year to the owner in the form of dividends. In the context of bank valuations, available cash flow usually means the cash which can be distributed to owners as dividends or proceeds of a sale. The accounting definition of cash flow is not as meaningful for valuation purposes. Calculation of available cash flow from dividends is discussed in detail in Chapter 14.

For purposes of presenting the concept and mechanics of the income approach to valuation, the term *income* is used.

6.4.5 Estimating the Stabilized Level of Income

Once the type of income is selected, it is necessary to determine the stabilized level of income and/or to project that income for a five- to ten-year period. There are four basic characteristics of the income which need to be considered in the projection process.

1. *Amount of Income:* The first consideration examines the amount of past income, carefully assessing whether the amounts are realistic compared with the size of the property or business, the market environment, and competitive conditions. The major factor is whether abnormal circumstances have skewed historical income performance so that it is not indicative of the future.

2. *Regularity of Income:* In this case, the pattern of income must be considered. The critical aspect is the volatility of past income trends. If a property, especially a business, exhibits excessive income variations, it is more difficult to forecast the income, unless those variations were a result of predictable market phenomena (for example, it might be a seasonal business). Occasionally, the volatility of income is so great that the income approach to valuation is not appropriate, and other approaches are required.

3. *Duration of Income:* Occasionally, the income will have a known and finite life. An office building leased at a fixed rate for a fixed term is an example of such a situation. In such a case, the stabilized income approach would not be the valid valuation technique. In cases of a business enterprise valuation, it is not necessary to assume that income goes on forever, but only that it will continue for a substantial number of years. This is a reasonable expectation with most healthy banking institutions.

4. *Certainty of Income:* Future income is never certain, but some sources of income have greater certainty than others. In most cases, the greater the degree of certainty, the less risk involved (a factor that affects the discount and capitalization rates).

When determining a stabilized income level or when projecting future income levels, the process and results will be influenced by the four above-mentioned characteristics of the income. To assess these characteristics, the historical income of the subject property or business must be analyzed carefully. Depending on the situation, it may be necessary to adjust the actual reported income if it has extraneous or unusual elements. For example, a business may have had an unusual, one-time event that raised or lowered income (sale of property, legal costs, and so on) or excessive salaries may have been paid that would not continue into the future under prudent management. In certain cases it may be necessary to adjust past earnings to gain a true picture of the past. In the examples used in this chapter, the income figures exclude any abnormal occurrences.

A stabilized income level to be capitalized into value can be determined by way of analysis of past income trends. There are typically three patterns that historical income trends can follow, each affecting the way that stabilized income level is estimated.

The *steady trend* pattern is the easiest method. In such a circumstance, income is increasing (or decreasing) at a more or less steady rate, in either dollar or percentage terms. The most straightforward way to deal with this situation is to use the latest year's income as being a representative, stabilized level of income. For example, if the income pattern shown in Exhibit 6.7 is being valued, the 1999 income could be considered a stabilized level of income.

The appropriate level of stabilized income to use in this example would be $1,216. (The 5 percent annual increase in earnings, which is expected to continue, will be reflected in the value estimate through the selected capitalization rate, as discussed in the next section of this chapter.)

The next type of income pattern is the *growing erratic trend,* which is typical of businesses in a cyclical but expanding market. In this case, the best way to determine the stabilized level of income is usually a simple average of historical income as in Exhibit 6.8. In this example, a stabilized income level of $1,164 would be appropriate. (Again, the growth rate and instability of earnings will be reflected in the selected capitalization rate.)

The third type of income is the *erratic trend.* In this case, a careful assessment must be made of whether the income is too erratic to use. If so, it may not be possible to use the income approach. Otherwise, the simple average techniques used in the growing erratic case may be appropriate.

Exhibit 6.7   Stabilized Income Trend Example

Year	Income	Percent Change
1995	$1,000	—
1996	1,050	5%
1997	1,103	5%
1998	1,158	5%
1999	1,216	5%

Exhibit 6.8   Erratic Income Trend Example

Year	Income	Percent Change
1995	$1,000	—
1996	1,200	20.0%
1997	1,080	(10.0%)
1998	1,290	19.0%
1999	1,250	(3.0%)
Average	$1,164	

6.4.6   Projecting Future Income Levels

Projecting income for use in the discounted future income approach requires an in-depth analysis of past financial trends to identify the steadiness or instability of the income and the reasons for the pattern.[6] The income is usually projected for a five- to ten-year period, and can be forecasted in one of three ways.

The most straightforward method to forecast income is the development of a time series equation of past income, then assuming a continuation of the time series. Exhibit 6.9 illustrates a time series calculation and the resulting equation used to forecast income. The statistical technique *regression analysis* is used to compute the equation based on historical income data. That equation is then used to calculate the unknown variable, future income, based on the known variable, the year. The time series approach is appropriate when past income has exhibited a reasonably steady growth pattern.

A second method to forecast total income is to project the individual components of income, then aggregate to a total. This approach is appropriate when the subject property has more than one major source of income, such as a business with multiple product lines. Each such source may have different growth characteristics and future potential. If each income source is reasonably steady, the time series technique could be used on each individual source.

Exhibit 6.10 illustrates the forecasting of total income for a business that has three product lines. The approach is the same as forecasting total income, except that each component is analyzed separately. In the example, Product A is a small, slow growth product and has more risk. Product B is a rapidly growing product and has more opportunity. Product C is the large, modestly growing cash cow, which is more stable and predictable. The advantage of separating the components is in the identification of the different opportunity and risk characteristics associated with each source of income.

The third method is an indirect way to forecast income. Underlying drivers of income and expenses are first identified, then the quantitative relationships between income and those drivers are established, the income drivers are forecasted, and finally income based on the future levels of the drivers is estimated. In a bank, the principal drivers of net income include loans and investments (which create interest income), deposits (which create interest expense), loan loss provision, operating expenses, and noninterest income. It is usually more accurate to project loans, investments, and other income drivers (based, for example, on market potential) than it is to project income directly. The relationship among loans, investments, deposits, and the associated income and expenses is then calculated to derive income for valuation purposes.

This indirect approach to forecasting income is probably the most difficult because it requires an in-depth analysis of income and expense drivers. In the application of valuation techniques to bank mergers and acquisitions described in Chapter 14, this indirect approach is used as it is a more realistic basis of estimating future income levels.

6.4.7   Selecting the Capitalization and Discount Rates

The second crucial area of decision making in the income approach is the selection of capitalization and discount rates. It should be noted that these rates are related, *but they are not the same.*

Exhibit 6.9   Using Time Series Equation to Forecast Total Income of a Business

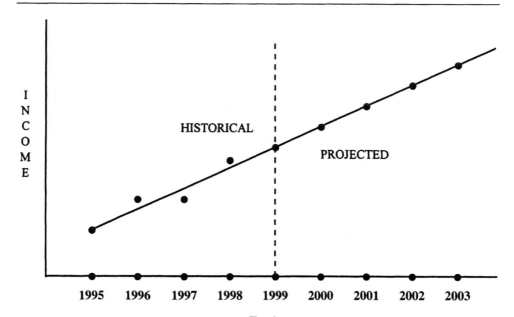

Year	Total Income
1995	$1,000
1996	1,150
1997	1,210
1998	1,300
1999	1,340

CALCULATED TIME SERIES
REGRESSION EQUATION:
Total income = (year × 83) − 163,638

Year	Projected Total Income
2000	$1,532
2001	1,615
2002	1,698
2003	1,781
2004	1,864

Exhibit 6.10   Using Time Series Equations to Forecast Components of Total Income of a Business

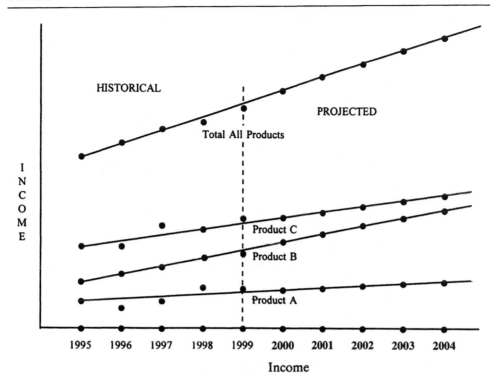

Income

Year	Product A	Product B	Product C	Total
1995	$500	$600	$1,000	$2,100
1996	500	780	950	2,230
1997	490	810	1,050	2,350
1998	520	900	1,040	2,460
1999	518	920	1,060	2,498

CALCULATED TIME SERIES EQUATION

Product A income = (year × 6.0) − 11,412
\+ Product B income = (year × 76.0) − 150,134
\+ Product C income = (year × 21.0) − 40,686
= Total income

Projected Income

Year	Product A	Product B	Product C	Total
2000	$528	$1,106	$1,104	$2,738
2001	534	1,182	1,125	2,744
2002	539	1,258	1,146	2,943
2003	545	1,334	1,167	3,046
2004	551	1,410	1,188	3,149

The mathematical relationship between the discount rate and the capitalization rate is:

$$\text{capitalization rate} =$$
$$\text{discount rate} - \text{annual future growth of income}$$

The capitalization rate converts a single estimate of annual income into a current capitalized value of that income, whereas the discount rate converts a flow of future income to present value.

Future income flows must be converted to present value because "a dollar tomorrow is worth less than a dollar today," and the farther into the future one projects, the less that dollar is worth in today's terms. This is the fundamental principle of the *time value of money*. If income is received today, it can be invested in an interest-bearing asset, resulting in interest plus the original balance. This basic financial concept has a significant impact on valuation. Since the valuation date is normally at the present, and the income is in the future, it is necessary to compensate for the *time value* of that income. This compensation is accomplished through the process of discounting. The calculations of discounting are shown below:

$$\text{present value of income to be received in year N} =$$
$$\text{income to be received in year N} \times [1/(1 + \text{year N discount rate})^N]$$

where year N is the future year corresponding to the receipt of the income. The fraction $1/(1 + \text{discount rate})^N$ is the discount factor used previously in the illustration of the income approach. For example, if \$500 is to be received in three years, its present value, discounted at 9 percent, is \$386, calculated as:

$$\$500 \times [1/(1 + .09)^3] = \$386$$

Income that is to be received in multiple years is discounted in exactly the same way. The income in each year is converted to present value, then the individual results are totaled. For example, if \$400 is to be received in one year, \$550 in two years, and \$775 in three years, the present value of that stream of income discounted at 9 percent is \$1,386, calculated as:

$$[\$400 \times 1/(1 + .09)^1] + [\$500 \times 1/(1 + .09)^2] + [\$775 \times 1/(1 + .09)^3] = \$1,386$$

The discount rate can be thought of as the rate of return required to invest in the income flow, taking into account alternative investments and the riskiness and uncertainty of the income. The following two components constitute a discount rate:

- *A risk-free rate of return:* The return an investor could earn without risk. (All investments have risk, but a risk-free rate reflects the safest investment possible, usually a United States Government security.)
- *A risk premium:* The additional return an investor would require to invest in the particular property being valued.

The capitalization rate also reflects the risk-free rate and a risk premium. In addition, however, the capitalization rate reflects the long-term income growth prospects of the asset. The mathematical comparison between the discount rate and the capitalization rate is shown as:

$$\text{discount rate} = \text{risk-free return} + \text{risk premium}$$
$$\text{capitalization rate} = \text{discount rate} - \text{annual growth rate}$$

The annual growth rate of income is subtracted because faster growth, all other things being equal, has higher value (that is, a lower capitalization rate). The only time the discount rate equals the capitalization rate is when the long-term growth of income is expected to be zero.

Theoretically, a potential problem can exist if the growth rate exceeds the risk-free rate plus the risk premium. In practice, however, this problem will not be encountered for two reasons. First, it is unlikely that any business can be expected to sustain very rapid income growth into perpetuity. Second, faster growth usually implies greater risk, thus requiring an increase in the risk premium.

An illustration of the discount rate and capitalization rate is shown below. Assume the risk-free return is 7 percent, the risk premium for the particular investment is 8 percent, and the long-term growth is 4 percent per year. The calculations would be:

$$\text{discount rate} = .07 + .08 = .15$$
$$\text{capitalization rate} = .15 - .04 = .11$$

If the stabilized income method is used, the single measure of income is capitalized at 11 percent. If estimates of future income—the discounted future income method—are used, those estimates are discounted at 15 percent.

The critical step is to select the proper discount rate, which can then be used as a basis to calculate the capitalization rate. There are three principal approaches which can be used to determine an appropriate discount rate:

1. summation;
2. weighted cost of capital, and
3. market comparison

The summation approach builds up the discount rate by component parts. The weighted cost of the capital approach creates a discount rate based on the costs of debt and equity, which is based on the capital structure associated with the subject property. The market comparison approach estimates the discount rate in total by comparing the subject property with other similar investments.

The *summation method* is based on the view that a discount rate can be thought of as comprising two parts, the risk-free rate of return and a risk premium. Each component can be dealt with separately, then they can be added together to arrive at the discount rate. A risk-free rate is the return an investor can be more or less certain to receive on an investment that has a ready market. United States Government securities are typically used as a proxy for measuring a risk-free return. These rates are reported in a variety of business publications and are easily obtainable. Rates for United States Government securities in late 2000 are shown in Exhibit 6.11. Short-term United States Government securities (for example, three-month T-bills) are often viewed as the most risk-free investment. However, for purposes of valuation, it is normally better to use the rate on government securities of longer maturities (one year or more) as a base rate. Long-term securities have greater risk of not selling at par, but because valuations usually involve value based on long-term income

Exhibit 6.11   Yields on Selected U.S. Government Securities

(As of October 30, 2000)	
3-month treasury bill	6.31
6-month treasury bill	6.35
1-year treasury bill	6.12
Long-term treasury securities	5.73

Exhibit 6.12   Factors Impacting Level of Risk Premium

Risks Associated with Subject Property*

- Type of product/service
- Size of business
- Financial condition
- Quality of management
- Quality and quantity of income
- Market position
- Liquidity of investment in business
- Location

*Using a business as an example.

Risk Associated with Market

- General outlook for industry
- Conditions of overall economy
- Availability/cost of credit
- Condition of local economy
- Outlook for customers of the business
- Legal or regulatory restrictions

trends, the rate on longer maturity securities is often a more comparable and relevant proxy for a risk-free rate.

The risk premium portion of the discount rate must reflect the risk associated with the particular property or business being appraised and the risk associated with the market. Some factors that should be considered in the risk premium are shown in Exhibit 6.12.

The actual determination of the risk premium, after due consideration of the above-mentioned factors, can be a difficult process and will differ among various potential buyers. To establish a starting point, it is useful to analyze the rates on various investments less the risk-free rate, the difference being the risk premium. A good starting point is the rate charged by a commercial bank for a loan on a similar asset. For example, if a bank will charge 13 percent to finance the purchase of a property similar to that being appraised and the risk-free rate is 8 percent, then a starting point for the risk premium would be 5 percent. Additional risk with a particular property may require additional risk premium.

Another technique that can be used to quantify the risk premium portion of the discount rate is the *Capital Asset Pricing Model*. This model is an analytical approach that uses ac-

Exhibit 6.13   Calculation of Weighted Cost of Capital

Component of Capital	Percent of Capital	Pre-tax Cost	After-tax Cost
Senior debt	30%	11%	7.15%
Subordinated debt	20%	13%	8.45%
Equity	50%	20%*	20.00%
Weighted Cost of Capital			13.84%

*Often estimated using the capital asset pricing model described above.

tual data on publicly traded equity instruments to describe the way prices of individual assets are determined in efficient markets. The Capital Asset Pricing Model theorizes that the expected rate of return on an asset is equal to the risk-free return *plus* an overall risk premium that reflects risk associated with the specific industry and the specific company. In equation form, the Capital Asset Pricing Model is applied to discount rate determination as:

$$\text{discount rate} = \text{risk-free rate} + (\text{risk premium} \times \text{beta factor})$$

where the risk premium equals the systematic market risk for all businesses in the industry, and the "beta" factor reflects the risk associated with the specific business being valued relative to all other businesses. This model is most applicable to businesses that have widely traded stocks. A good history of stock sales is usually necessary to have an historical basis for estimation of the beta factor.

Essentially, use of the Capital Asset Pricing Model to determine a discount rate is a variation of the summation approach. An added enhancement of this approach is that it reflects the historical volatility of the specific business being valued. Practically speaking, however, this methodology is applicable only for fairly actively traded, publicly held businesses.

A second technique used to establish a discount rate is the *weighted cost of capital approach*. A weighted average of the cost of debt and required return on equity is computed as in the example shown in Exhibit 6.13. In this illustration, an investor requires 20 percent pretax return on equity, with debt costs at 11 percent for senior debt and 13 percent for subordinated debt, resulting in a discount rate of 13.84 percent. This figure is simply a weighted average based on the mix and cost of capital.

The third technique used to establish an appropriate discount rate is the *market comparison approach*. With this technique, discount rates are examined for situations similar to the subject asset, in terms of type of sale, income levels, riskiness, and liquidity. A rate is then selected, as opposed to the summation method where the rate is built up from components.

For business valuations, data on publicly traded stocks provide a surrogate measure of a discount rate, assuming the publicly traded businesses are similar to the one being valued. The widely reported price/earnings (P/E) ratios provide a general idea of the yield the market requires. The deficiencies of the P/E ratio are, unfortunately, substantial: price reflects investors' expectations for the future while earnings are historical; the P/E is for one particular company which may or may not be comparable to the business being valued; and the quoted price used in the P/E is usually for a minority position.

Notwithstanding these deficiencies, the P/E ratio can be a useful way to begin the determination of a discount rate. The P/E ratio is based on reported earnings; therefore, it cannot be applied directly to cash flow measures. The best way to apply the P/E is to use an average P/E for a sample of comparable businesses. The calculations would be as shown below.

$$\text{initial discount rate estimate} =$$
$$(1 + \text{control premium})/\text{average P/E for companies}$$
$$+ \text{projected income growth rate for companies}$$

The control premium factor must be applied to the inverse of the P/E ratio because the P/E reflects a minority position in the company. The expected growth of the sample companies must be added because the inverse of the P/E actually computes a capitalization rate and, as described earlier, the discount rate is the capitalization rate plus annual growth. An example of the P/E method is shown as follows. Assume that:

Average P/E for sample companies: 13
Control premium: 37%
Projected growth of sample companies: 4% annually

Initial discount rate estimate is:

$$(1 + .37)/13 + .04 = .105 + .04 = 14.5\%$$

The business being valued may have unusual risk characteristics, which would require an increase in the initial 14.5 percent rate estimate. This is a subjective factor based on a case-by-case analysis.

Public company P/Es should be used very cautiously in deriving an initial discount rate estimate. The problem with using public companies is somewhat theoretical, but valid nonetheless. The control premium percentage is used to adjust the P/E to a majority position that is then used as a proxy for the required rate of return. Such a relationship implies that greater control allows greater influence over the systematic risks of the business. This is probably not true because systematic risks are, by definition, beyond the control of the owner. Control premium is more directly related to the ability of the majority owner to influence future cash flow and earnings.

One solution to this problem is to use acquisition P/Es rather than stock trade P/Es. This approach avoids the control premium adjustment problem. The formula to use is:

$$\text{discount rate estimate} =$$
$$\text{earnings of sample companies}/\text{price paid for companies}$$
$$+ \text{projected growth rate of companies}$$

An example of the calculations is shown below.

Average earnings of sample companies: $3,100,000
Average price paid for sample companies: $30,000,000
Projected annual growth of sample companies: 4.0%

Exhibit 6.14 Valuation of an Income Stream to Illustrate Discount, Capitalization, and Growth Rates

	Year 1	Year 2	Year 3	Year 4	Year 5	Residual
Income						
(rounded)	$1,000	$ 1,050	$1,180	$1,300	$1,400	$ 1,500
Annual growth	—	5.0%	12.4%	10.2%	7.7%	5.0%
Discount rate	15%	15%	15%	15%	15%	15%
Discount factor	.870	.756	.657	.571	.497	.432
Capitalization						
rate	—	—	—	—	—	10%*
Capitalized value						
(rounded)	—	—	—	—	—	$15,000
Present value	$ 870	$ 794	$ 775	$ 742	$ 696	$ 6,480
Sum of present						
values		$10,357				

The income stream for years one through five is converted to present value by multiplying the income in a given year by the discount factor for that year (e.g., for Year 3, the income of $1,180 is multiplied by the discount factor of .657 to equal $775). The residual income level is capitalized at 10% (to equal $15,000), then converted to present value by multiplying by the discount factor of .432 (to equal $6,480). The individual present value figures are summed to arrive at a value estimate.

*15% discount rate less 5% expected growth of the $1,500 level of residual income.

Initial discount rate estimate is:

$$\$3,100,000/\$30,000,000 + .04 = .103 + .04 = 14.3\%$$

As before, the business being valued may have more or less risk associated with it, resulting in the need to adjust the 14.3 percent upward or downward.

Once the discount rate has been estimated, by one or more of the techniques described above, it is possible to calculate the capitalization rate. To reiterate the formula:

$$\text{capitalization rate} = \text{discount rate} - \text{growth rate of income}$$

The expected annual growth rate of the income stream of the property being valued is subtracted from the discount rate to arrive at the appropriate capitalization rate. Exhibit 6.14 illustrates how the discount, capitalization, and growth rates work together to value a projected income stream.

6.4.8 Dividend Capitalization Model

A variant of the income approach that can be used to value businesses is the dividend capitalization model. This approach can be used whether or not the business actually pays dividends to stockholders. The easiest case is valuation of a business which has a record of paying dividends. Instead of capitalizing total income, income per share is capitalized to derive a per share value. This value is on a minority basis, with a majority position determined by

Exhibit 6.15   Valuation of a Business Using Dividend Capitalization Model

Dividends per share*	$2.50
Capitalization rate**	15%
Control premium	40%
Shares outstanding	100,000
Per share value on minority basis	
(Dividends per share/capitalization rate)	
($2.50/.15)	$16.67
Aggregate minority value	
(Per share value on minority	
basis × shares outstanding)	
($16.67 × 100,000 shares)	$1,667,000
Per share value on control basis	
(Per share value on minority	
basis × control premium)	
($16.67 × 1.4)	$23.34
Value of business on control basis	$2,334,000

*A "stabilized" level of dividends, analogous to stabilized income used earlier.

**Selected using techniques described earlier, with consideration of dividend yields on stocks of comparable risk.

adding a control premium. An example is shown in Exhibit 6.15. This approach can be used to value publicly held, widely traded stock.

The dividend capitalization model can also be used when the business does not pay dividends, but has the financial capacity to do so. This is often the case with closely held businesses. The key is to evaluate comparable companies to determine the industry average for dividends (expressed as a percent of net income or as a return on book value of equity). The next step is to assess whether the business being appraised has the financial capacity to pay the industry average dividends. If so, the dividends can be imputed, and value assessed as if the company had actually paid dividends.

The dividend paying capacity concept plays an extremely important role in the valuation of a bank for acquisition purposes. The basis of the income approach described in Chapter 14 is that the available cash flow to the owner of a bank is equal to the bank's dividend paying capacity.

6.4.9   The Effects of Inflation

As every businessperson knows, inflation can have a devastating and uncontrollable effect on the value of a property. Consequently, it would seem logical to value an income-producing property using estimates of *real* future income, excluding any inflationary growth. If real income is used, however, the capitalization and discount rates would have to be reduced by an amount equal to the expected rate of inflation. This adjustment is needed because the various measures of return on investment already reflect the *market's consensus* on expected inflation. Therefore, if *real* income is to be used, *real* rates of return must be the basis for discounting. Valuations by the income approach usually are made with projected income (including whatever level of inflation is expected) and discounted by a rate that includes the market's assessment of inflation.

6.5 SPECIAL TOPICS—APPROACHES TO INTANGIBLE ASSET VALUATION

Intangible assets are those that have no physical substance, but are positive contributors to the success of a business.[7] Such intangibles include among others customer lists, patents, proprietary computer software, assembled work force, copyrights, brand names, and goodwill. Intangible assets often constitute a large portion of the total value of a business, which by definition is:

$$
\begin{aligned}
&\text{total value of a business} = \\
&\quad\text{tangible asset value} \\
&+ \text{intangible asset value} \\
&- \text{liabilities assumed}
\end{aligned}
$$

Intangible asset value, in turn, is made up of several components:

$$
\begin{aligned}
&\text{intangible asset value} = \\
&\quad\text{amortizable identified asset value} \\
&+ \text{nonamortizable identified asset value} \\
&+ \text{goodwill}
\end{aligned}
$$

The segregation of the three components of intangible assets is important for tax reasons rather than for pricing, except if tax attributes will have a significant impact on cash flows. The term *amortizable* means that the intangible asset is allowed a deduction from taxable income, similar to the way tangible assets are depreciated. An identified intangible asset is one that can be valued separately. Goodwill and other intangibles are part of important tax issues and are discussed in Chapter 8. General approaches to intangible asset valuation are described below.

6.5.1 Cost of Replacement of Intangible Asset

The cost of replacement approach to valuing an intangible asset is based upon the current costs that would be incurred to replace the asset with one of comparable utility. An example of an intangible that can be valued by this technique is proprietary computer software. The person-hours required to create the software are multiplied by an hourly rate (salary, consultant's fees, etc.) to arrive at a replacement cost. This approach does not consider any income benefit to the business as a result of having the intangible asset.

6.5.2 Income from Intangible Asset

If an intangible asset generates income, the various income approaches described in the preceding section can be used. Copyrights and patents are examples of intangible assets that

Exhibit 6.16   Valuation of a Patent with Income

Year	Income	Discount Rate	Discount Factor	Present Value
1	$500,000	10%	.909	$454,500
2	540,000	10%	.826	446,040
3	583,200	10%	.751	437,983
4	629,856	10%	.683	430,192
5	680,244	10%	.621	422,432
6	734,664	10%	.564	414.351
7	793,437	10%	.513	407,033
			Value of patent =	$3,012,531

can be valued based on the income generated to the owner. For example, assume a business owns a special process patent that it has licensed to other companies, the income (fees, net of administrative expenses) from which is $500,000 annually and increasing at 8 percent per year. Also assume the patent has seven years remaining on its seventeen year life. The value of that patent can be calculated as shown in Exhibit 6.16.

This approach is applicable if the intangible has a known and finite life. For intangibles without a definite life, or a life so long it is virtually indefinite (such as a copyright that runs for the author's life plus 50 years), the capitalization of income approach may be more appropriate. This technique estimates the stabilized income from the intangible asset, and capitalizes it to a value (exactly as described earlier in the Income Approach to Valuation). For example, assume that the income from a copyright is estimated at $750,000 annually and projected to increase at 5 percent per year. If the risk-free return and the risk premium total 14 percent (the discount rate), the capitalization rate is 9 percent (14 percent minus 5 percent). Therefore, the value of the copyright is $8,333,333 ($750,000/.09).

If ownership of an intangible asset results in tax benefits from amortization, the value should also reflect the net present value of those tax savings. The calculations become very complex because the value of the intangible is influenced by the tax savings, but the tax savings are influenced by the value. The value of the intangible including tax benefits of amortization can be estimated by this formula:

present value of cash flow/[1 − (tax rate × annuity factor)/remaining life]

The present value of cash flow factor excludes amortization. The tax rate is the marginal tax rate of the business owning the intangible. The annuity factor is based on an interest rate equal to the cost of capital and a term equal to the remaining life of the asset. This formula provides for the valuation of the intangible based on income and tax savings from amortization.

6.5.3   Cost Savings from Intangible Asset

Occasionally, a business is able to avoid costs because it owns an intangible asset. The cost savings approach can be illustrated using the patent process example again. If the company not only licenses the process, but also uses it, the value of that patent would be the income received plus the savings to the company from not having to pay a license fee to someone else. If this were the case, the valuation would be as shown in Exhibit 6.17. The cost sav-

Exhibit 6.17   Valuation of a Patent with Income and Cost Savings

Year	Income	Cost Savings	Discount Rate	Discount Factor	Present Value
1	$500,000	$55,000	10%	.909	$504,495
2	540,000	60,000	10%	.826	495,000
3	583,200	64,800	10%	.751	486,648
4	629,856	69,984	10%	.683	477,991
5	680,244	75,580	10%	.621	469,367
6	734,663	81,629	10%	.563	459,573
7	793,437	88,160	10%	.513	452,259
				Value of patent =	$3,345,933

ings adds about 11 percent to the value of the patent compared to the valuation under an assumption of income only.

6.5.4 Excess Earnings Method

The excess earnings method is a technique that was originally used by the IRS to estimate the value of the goodwill of a business. The technique has evolved, however, into one way to estimate the value of the total business by valuing net tangible assets and calculating the value of excess earnings attributable to intangibles.

The excess earnings method requires the following five steps.

1. Value net tangible assets of the business (that is, the market value of tangible assets less market value of liabilities of the business).
2. Determine a stabilized total income level.
3. Select a rate of return on net tangible assets and compute income attributable to net tangible assets.
4. Subtract income attributable to tangible assets from stabilized total income, and capitalize the difference, which equals the value of excess earnings (the value of the intangible assets).
5. Add net tangible asset value to the value of "excess" earnings to estimate total value of the business.

An example of the excess earnings method is shown below.

Net tangible asset value	$1,000,000
Stabilized total income	$ 200,000
Rate of return on net tangible assets	13%[8]
Earnings attributable to net tangible assets (.13 × $1,000,000)	$ 130,000
Excess earnings ($200,000 − $130,000)	$ 70,000
Capitalization rate on excess earnings	20%
Value of excess earnings ($70,000/.20)	$ 350,000
Value of business ($1,000,000 + $350,000)	$1,350,000

The excess earnings method generally is not used in determining the value of intangible assets.

6.6 SPECIAL TOPICS—BUSINESS VALUATION

Most property types can be valued by using one, two, or all three of the approaches to valuation. Businesses, whether publicly or privately held, can also be valued using the three basic approaches. There are, however, some special aspects of business valuations that would not apply to other types of property. These special aspects are discussed on the following pages.

6.6.1 Market-to-Book Value Method

The ratio of market-to-book value method is another method that can be utilized to assess the value of financial institutions. The excess capital or equity should be taken into consideration when using the market-to-book value method. Typically, during favorable economic periods (e.g., 1990s) financial institutions may generate favorable return, which if retained (e.g., no increase in dividends, no stock buy-backs, no expansion or acquisition) can result in higher than the industry norm or benchmark for equity-to-asset ratio. Investors do not typically capitalize excess equity, but they are willing to pay dollar-for-dollar for it.

6.6.2 Total Enterprise Value Versus Value of Equity

From a technical standpoint, the phrase *value of a business* is somewhat ambiguous. What is usually meant is the "fair market value of the equity of the business as a going concern." Another term commonly used is *total enterprise value*. This term is often erroneously used interchangeably with *value of a business* and *value of equity*. The difference is that total enterprise value is based upon a debt-free financial structure, while value of equity is based upon the income considering the debt structure. The relation between total enterprise value and value of equity is shown below:

$$\text{value of equity} = \text{total enterprise value} - \text{long-term debt}$$

Or conversely:

$$\text{total enterprise value} = \text{value of equity} + \text{long-term debt}$$

Throughout this book, value of a *business* means the value of the *equity* of that business. The objective in most business valuations is to value the equity. This can be accomplished directly or indirectly.

The direct approach to valuing equity uses historical financial performance as it actually exists for a business, given whatever long-term debt structure was in place during the period under analysis. Determination of future income and selection of comparable transactions for use in the valuation are done directly. This approach is appropriate in two main instances:

- when the company has little long-term debt relative to equity; or
- when most comparable businesses have very similar long-term debt/equity structure.

Exhibit 6.18 Illustration of Direct and Indirect Approaches to Valuing Equity of a Business

	Direct Valuation of Equity					
	Year 1	Year 2	Year 3	Year 4	Year 5	Residual
Income (after debt service)*	$1,000	$1,075	$1,200	$1,350	$1,525	$1,650
Capitalization rate	—	—	—	—	—	.11%
Discount rate	15%	15%	15%	15%	15%	15%
Discount factor	.870	.756	.657	.571	.497	.432
Present value (rounded)	$ 870	$ 813	$ 788	$ 771	$ 758	$6,480

Value of Equity by Direct Approach = $10,480

	Indirect Valuation of Equity					
	Year 1	Year 2	Year 3	Year 4	Year 5	Residual
Debt-free income*	$1,045	$1,120	$1,245	$1,395	$1,570	$ 1,695
Capitalization rate	—	—	—	—	—	11%
Discount rate	15%	15%	15%	15%	15%	15%
Discount factor	.870	.756	.657	.571	.497	.432
Present value (rounded)	$ 909	$ 847	$ 818	$ 797	$ 780	$ 6,656

Enterprise Value $10,807
− Long-term Debt − 500
= Value of Equity by Indirect Approach = $10.307

* Assumes business had $500 in long-term debt at 9 percent annual interest cost.

The other method to valuing equity, the indirect approach, uses historical financial performance without cost of long-term debt, and projects future income without debt. This calculation provides the value of the business on a debt-free basis. Subtraction of any long-term debt produces the value of the equity. Exhibit 6.18 illustrates the calculation of the value of equity directly and indirectly. These examples illustrate that slightly different results will be obtained depending on which method is used.

A situation where the total enterprise value rather than the value of equity would be of more interest is when a business is being acquired but long-term debt is *not* to be assumed by the buyer. If that debt is not to be assumed and is a substantial part of the capital structure, it is usually more appropriate to value the entity on a debt-free basis and then subtract the long-term debt to arrive at value of the equity.

6.6.3 Existence of Preferred Stock

When the equity of a company consists only of common stock, the value of the stock is synonymous with the value of the equity of a business. When preferred stock is involved, the value of the business consists of the value of both types of stock. The equation below illustrates the relationship:

$$\text{value of the equity of business} =$$
$$\text{value of common stock} + \text{value of preferred stock}$$

When the objective is to value the common stock only, it is necessary first to value the business in total and then to value the preferred stock, with the difference being the value of the common stock. Under most circumstances, ownership of preferred stock does not entail control. Therefore, when the value of preferred stock is subtracted from the total value of the business (by definition a majority position value), the result is the value of the common stock on a majority basis.

Preferred stock represents a portion of ownership of a company, and therefore is similar to common stock. Preferred stock can also be like perpetual debt if it is not convertible to common stock. Basically, preferred stock is a security that generates income (that is, a yield) to the holder. Consequently, it can be valued as an entity separate from the total business or the common stock. The income approach, specifically the capitalization of expected dividends, is normally used to value preferred stock. The formula for the value of a preferred issue with a fixed-rate dividend is:

$$\text{per share value of preferred stock} =$$
$$(\text{dividend rate} \times \text{par value})/\text{capitalization rate}$$

The equation becomes more complex with adjustable dividend rates, but is conceptually the same.

The most significant factor in preferred stock valuation is the selection of the capitalization rate. The usual way to estimate this rate is to examine the current yields on similar types of preferred stock. These yields, which can be thought of as proxies of capitalization rates, reflect the dividends of the stock, the current market price, and investors' expectations of the issuing company's growth and performance. The key is to analyze preferred stock issues that are comparable to the issue being valued. Factors that indicate comparability of preferred stock issues are described below:

1. *Similarity of Businesses:* If possible, the preferred stock should be issued by a company in the same line(s) of business as the company being valued. Preferred stock yields are driven by the credit worthiness of the issuing company as well as the overall risk associated with the industry. Therefore, companies in different industries of comparable risks could be used. Assessing such industry risk can be difficult. Consequently, selecting companies in the same industry can provide for a more certain selection of equal risk companies.

2. *Rating:* The assessment of risk provided by a rating agency such as Moody's or Standard & Poors should be similar. If, however, the preferred issue being valued is not rated, it is necessary to focus on leverage ratios, fixed charge coverage ratios, business risk levels, and other measures of creditworthiness to determine appropriate yields.

3. *Cumulative versus Noncumulative:* If a preferred issue is cumulative, all dividends owed to date must be paid to preferred shareholders prior to any common stock dividends. The cumulative provision is a protective device that ensures preferred stockholders will be paid before any common stock dividends are declared. If the preferred stock is noncumulative and a dividend was omitted in a quarter (or year), the holder has no priority claim to that omitted dividend. Few, if any, preferred stock issues are noncumulative.

4. *Dividend Policy:* A major comparison factor is whether the dividend is a fixed percentage of par or a variable based upon some market index. All other things being equal, yields on variable rate preferred stock are typically less than fixed rate issues.

5. *Convertibility:* If preferred stock can be exchanged for common stock at a preset formula, it is a convertible issue.

6. *Participation:* This refers to the right of preferred stockholders to participate in the profits of the company, usually based on a formula.

7. *Call Provision:* This is the right given to the company to require preferred stockholders to redeem their shares for par value plus a stated call premium.

8. *Voting Rights:* Occasionally, preferred stockholders have limited voting rights, typically activated when preferred dividends have not been paid for a stated period of time. These voting rights usually have little impact on value on a minority basis.

Other types of comparisons could include the size of the issue (hence its marketability), redemption provisions, and whether it is listed on an exchange or traded over the counter. Once the preferred stocks have been identified which generally are comparable to the stock being appraised, the yields can be analyzed to compute a capitalization rate for the subject preferred stock. Exhibit 6.19 illustrates the valuation of a preferred stock issue. In this par-

Exhibit 6.19 Illustration of Preferred Stock Valuation
(All comparable preferred issues are cumulative, adjustable rate, nonconvertible, nonparticipating, perpetual, nonvoting.)

Company	S&P Rating*	Yield
Comparable A	A+	5.3%
Comparable B	A+	6.2%
Comparable C	AA−	9.3%
Comparable D	BBB	9.0%
Comparable E	NR	6.5%
Comparable F	A+	7.1%
Comparable G	A−	7.5%
Comparable H	NR	5.9%
Comparable I	NR	8.2%
Comparable J	NR	7.1%
Average		7.2%
Par value of subject preferred stock		$100.00/share
Stated dividend rate		7%
Expected annual dividend		$7.00/share
Capitalization rate		8%**
Value per share ($7.00/0.8)		$87.50/share
Total value of preferred stock (500,000 shares)		$43,750,000

* The assessment of the capacity and willingness of an issuer to pay preferred stock dividends and any applicable sinking fund obligations as provided by Standard & Poors Corporation. These ratings range from AAA 1 to BBB 2 for investment grade preferred issues, BB 1 to CCC 2 for speculative grade issues, and CC 1 to D 2 for issues in arrears or default.

** Used rate higher than the 7.2% average to illustrate situation where subject preferred stock is felt to be slightly riskier on average than comparables.

ticular example, the value of the preferred stock is $43,750,000. If the total value of the business was calculated to be $90,000,000, the value of the common stock would be $46,250,000 ($90,000,000 − $43,750,000).

6.6.4 Adjusted Book Value to Compute Market Value of Equity

Another way to value the equity of a business is to calculate its adjusted book value (sometimes called net asset value). This approach adjusts the tangible assets from book value to fair market value, values the intangible assets, then subtracts liabilities. The result is the fair market value of equity. This approach is useful for valuing a business that has had very erratic earnings, or has had successive years of losses, both situations that could render the income approach inapplicable. It is also used when market comparables are unavailable.

To compute the adjusted book value, it is necessary to convert the value of each asset from its book value to its fair market value. Technically, this process requires that each asset of the company be appraised individually, which is rarely done. More often, the substantial assets are individually valued, the market values of minor assets are estimated, the values of any intangible assets are established, and the liabilities are subtracted. Exhibit 6.20 illustrates the adjustments to book value of each asset to compute fair market value of the equity of a bank. The adjusted book value approach as applied to banks is discussed more fully in Chapter 14.

6.6.5 Liquidation of Business

Occasionally, a business is worth more as a collection of assets to be sold individually than as an ongoing entity. In this case, valuation of the business would require the liquidation approach.

Exhibit 6.20   Illustration of Adjustments to Book Value of a Bank to Compute Market Value of Equity (Off-Balance Sheet Items Excluded for Simplicity, $000)

Assets	December 31, 1999 Book Value	December 31, 1999 Fair Market Value
Cash and due forms	$ 4,190	$ 4,190
Investments	6,000	6,000
Fed funds sold	9,250	9,250
Total loans	46,940	44,950
(Loan loss reserves)	(6,520)	(6,520)
Net loans	40,420	38,430
Premises & fixed assets	5,710	7,520
Real estate owned	10,490	9,210
Other assets	1,050	1,050
Core deposit base	—	3,040
Total assets	$77,110	$78,690
Liabilities		
Deposits	$75,970	$75,970
Other liabilities	770	770
Total liabilities	$76,740	$76,740
Equity	$ 370	$ 1,950

Conceptually, the liquidation value whether orderly or forced is simple:

$$\text{liquidation value of a business} =$$
$$\text{liquidation value of tangible assets} - \text{liabilities}$$

This is virtually identical to the adjusted book value approach just described, except that adjustments are made from book value to liquidation value, not to market value. The liquidation value of the assets should reflect the costs associated with the liquidation such as broker's fees and legal costs. Estimating liquidation value can be useful even when there is no immediate danger of actual liquidation. The liquidation value provides a lower limit of the company's value. With respect to a bank acquisition, the liquidation value approach may have relevance if a bank is considering a regulatory assisted takeover.

6.7   VALUATION AND BUSINESS CONCENTRATIONS

Business concentration is an important factor that should be considered during the valuation process. It is typically determined in terms of the institutions' dependence on (1) a single customer or a small group of customers for all or a major portion of offered financial products and services; (2) customers within a narrow industry segment for all or a major portion of financial products and services provided; (3) operations within a narrowly defined geographic territory; or (4) domination by a small group of management with no adequate oversight board or audit committee. Concentrations adversely affect the institution's value in two ways: (1) increased risk of potential decline in earning-generating power resulting from the possible inability to provide financial services or substantial decrease in demand for financial services, and (2) perception of a possible limit on future earnings growth due to lack of ability to satisfy customers' financial services needs. Appraisers should identify all relevant business concentrations and examine their impact on valuation by adjusting the discount rate, capitalization factor, and future earnings growth.

6.8   SPECIAL TOPICS—CLOSELY HELD STOCK

Companies that are closely held generally have a number of recognizable characteristics:

- They are privately held by a few stockholders, sometimes all members of the same family.
- There is a close relationship between ownership and management.
- There is little, if any, trading and that is usually among existing stockholders.
- The entity is publicly held, but with very narrow ownership, and it is thinly traded.

Closely held corporations (CHC, also known as close corporations, family corporations, or incorporated partnerships), while enjoying many advantages of corporations such as limited liability and tax benefits, maintain the internal attributes of a non-incorporated business. Stock of a CHC is held by a relatively small group of people, a family, or a single individual and is not available to the public. Thus, there is normally no established market for the CHC's stock. The valuation of a CHC's stock is a challenge when it is sold, exchanged, liquidated, or involved in mergers, buy-sell agreements, or stock options, and especially when the stock is held for estate and gift tax purposes. Since stock of a CHC is not publicly traded and has no readily available trading value, there is often conflict between the IRS and taxpayers in determining its fair market value.

The Congress and the Treasury Department have addressed the issue of determining fair market value for CHCs' stock by issuing Revenue Ruling 59-60, 1959-1 CB 237, code Section 2031. Revenue Ruling 59-60 states that the valuation process is distinctly different for sales/service companies than for holding/investment companies. The valuation standard often used in appraising stock in closely held corporations for estate and gift tax purposes is "fair market value."

Reg. Sec. 20.2031-1 states:

> The fair market value is the price at which the property would change hands between a willing buyer and a willing seller, neither being under any compulsion to buy or sell and both having reasonable knowledge of relevant facts.

The application of this definition in valuing stock of CHCs involves at least two problems. First, stock of CHCs is not easily traded because often no rules have occurred and any change that may have occurred was probably within a family relationship. Second, the criterion of objective and independent willing buyer, willing seller does not exist in estate and gift tax situations. Exhibit 6.21 shows relevant estate and gift tax regulations.

It is important to understand special aspects of closely held stock when undertaking a valuation. Several of these aspects are described below.

6.8.1   Revenue Ruling 59-60

The Internal Revenue Service originally issued Revenue Ruling 59-60 to be the guideline in the valuation of closely held capital stock for estate and gift tax purposes. The considerations in that ruling have subsequently been extended to cover all types of business interests for all income and other tax purposes. Revenue Ruling 59-60 defines fair market value and suggests that all relevant factors and available financial information should be considered in determining fair market value. More specifically, Revenue Ruling 59-60 describes eight general factors which should be used in calculating the value of stock for which market quotations are either unavailable or are so scarce that they would not be useful in determining value. The eight specified factors outlined in Revenue Ruling 59-60 are almost applicable to all valuation assignments requiring determination of fair market value. These eight factors have been considered in official opinions of the tax court while some factors (e.g., earnings, book value, dividend-paying capacity) are emphasized more than others.

The eight factors listed in Revenue Ruling 59-60 that should be taken into account when valuing closely held business interests are:

1. the nature of the business and the history of the enterprise from its inception;
2. the economic outlook in general, and the condition and outlook of the specific industry in particular;
3. the book value and the financial condition of the business;

Exhibit 6.21 Estate and Gift Tax Regulations

Regulations	Description
Estate Tax	
1. Reg. § 20.3031-1(b)	Defines fair market value as the value a willing buyer and willing seller would agree upon given both parties have a reasonable knowledge of the relevant facts.
2. Reg. § 20.2031-2(a)	States that the fair market value is determined on the applicable valuation date.
3. Reg. § 20.2031-2(c)	Explains how to value securities when selling prices or bid and ask prices do not reflect fair market value.
4. Reg. § 20.2031-2(f)	Describes salient factors for determining stock value for unlisted securities where selling prices or bid and asked prices are unavailable.
5. Reg. § 20.2031-2(h)	States that restrictive agreements (e.g. option or contract to purchase stock at a stated price) may not be given any tax effect.
6. Reg. § 20.2031-3	Emphasizes the importance of valuing all assets both tangible and intangible and other relevant factors (e.g. earning capacity) to determine fair market value.

Regulations	Description
Gift Tax	
1. Reg. § 25.2512-1	Specifies that the value of a gift is determined as the date of the gift the same as for estate taxes which is the fair market value that a willing buyer and a willing seller would agree upon, both having a reasonable knowledge of the relevant facts.
2. Reg. § 25.2512-2(c)	Provides information for valuing securities when the selling prices or bid and asked prices do not represent a true fair market value (e.g., sale between family members).
3. Reg. § 25.2512-2(f)	Describes important factors for determining value of the gift.

4. the earning capacity of the company;
5. the dividend-paying capacity;
6. whether or not the enterprise has goodwill or other intangible value;
7. sales of the stock and the size of the block of stock to be valued; and
8. the market price of stocks of corporations engaged in the same or a similar line of business having their stocks actively traded in a free and open market.

6.8.2 Discounts for Minority Position/Premium for Control

Currently, business owners have created a new class of non-voting recapitalizations in Subchapter S corporations for use in succession and estate planning by giving away this class of non-voting shares and taking valuation discounts for minority interest status, lack of voting rights, and lack of marketability. Non-voting recapitalizations enable the founder (owner) of the company to remain in control until successors (e.g., next generation) are ready, willing, and able to effectively operate the business. The following discounting opportunities may be available for these types of non-voting shares.

1. Minority Discount. Minority interest is typically discounted for lack of control.
2. Non-voting Discount. Non-voting shares generally are worth significantly less than the equivalent voting shares.
3. Lack of Marketability Discount. Non-readily tradable and marketable shares are often discounted for lack of marketability and liquidity.

Minority and marketability discount is often available for a small, limited partner interest in the Family Limited Partnership (FLP). The person buying the limited partner interest in FLP does not have the assurance or expectation to get at the underlying value of the assets in FLP. When family members hold minority interests, the value of such shares may be discounted for lack of control.

A fundamental principle of valuation is that a single share of stock is not worth its pro rata value of the total company. In other words, if a company in total is valued at $1,000,000, and it has 100,000 shares of common stock, the value of a single share is less than $10.00. Conversely, the total value of a company is worth more than the price of a single share of stock multiplied by the shares outstanding. The reason for this anomaly is that control positions command a premium (and conversely minority positions require a discount). Control commands premiums because controlling interest involves such prerogatives as the power to:

- acquire or liquidate;
- select management;
- guide policy;
- declare and pay dividends; and
- set compensation.

Normally when a business is valued, it is on a 100 percent ownership basis; that is, the value of the company if 100 percent interest is purchased. Once the total value is known, the discount for a minority position is applied to arrive at the aggregate minority value. This figure then is divided by the shares outstanding to derive per share value on a minority basis. Mathematically, the calculation is:

$$\text{minority value per share} =$$
$$[\text{total value of business} \times (1 - \text{minority discount \%})]/\text{shares outstanding}$$

For example, if the total value of the business on a control basis is $1,000,000, there are 100,000 shares outstanding, and a minority discount of 40 percent is appropriate, the value per share on a minority basis is:

$$\text{minority value per share} =$$
$$[\$1,000,000 \times (1 - .40)]/100,000 =$$
$$\$6.00$$

This calculation also determines the premium for control, which is the percent increase from per share minority value to per share control value; in this example 66.7 percent. In general, the premium for control and minority discount are related as:

$$\text{control premium } \% =$$
$$[1/(1 - \text{minority discount } \%)] - 1$$
$$\text{minority discount } \% =$$
$$1 - [1/(1 + \text{control premium } \%)]$$

The minority value of the stock also can be estimated directly if data on minority position sales are available. Also, quoted stock prices for comparable companies can be used since by definition they reflect minority positions.

6.8.3 Discount for Lack of Marketability

Closely held stocks are not as readily marketable as shares of widely held, actively traded stocks. This lack of marketability and resulting lower liquidity has an adverse effect on the value of the stock, especially if it is a minority position. Consequently, a minority position in a closely held company would be valued with both minority and marketability discounts. Marketability discounts as high as 30 percent to 40 percent are not uncommon for minority positions in small corporations.

6.9 SPECIAL TOPICS—VALUING WIDELY TRADED COMPANIES

An entire field of study has developed around the valuation of widely traded stock and other equity instruments. This area of finance often involves the use of complex mathematical and economic models to simulate the behavior of public equity markets.

When a widely traded bank holding company is an acquisition target, its quoted stock price represents the per share value of the institution on a minority basis. The premium offered for controlling interest will depend on the buyer's assessment of the investment value of the target. Therefore, when a widely traded bank is being targeted for acquisition, the value measure relevant to the buyer is the value of a 100 percent interest. The market price of a share of stock is of secondary importance. Consequently, the types of analyses and valuation approaches described in this chapter are essentially the same, irrespective of whether the target is closely or widely held.

ENDNOTES

1. This is essentially the same as the principle of substitution described in Chapter 5.
2. The deficiencies inherent in using book value are discussed in Chapter 5.
3. If the income is received each year into perpetuity, or over a long period of time.
4. In discussing the income approach, the term income can apply to any measure of monetary receipts: earnings, cash flow, dividend capacity, and so on. The specific type of income used in a given situation does not affect the conceptual basis. From a practical standpoint, however, proper application of the income approach requires careful consideration of the type of income to be used. The different types are discussed later in this chapter.
5. Financial Accounting Standards Board. 2000. "Statement of Financial Accounting Concepts No. 7: Using Cash Flow Information and Present Value in Accounting Measurement (FASB, Norwalk, CT).

6. As mentioned at the beginning of this chapter, it was assumed for the sake of discussion of valuation principles that appropriate information on the subject asset and other data as necessary have been gathered.

7. Chapter 7 contains a more thorough discussion of the legal, tax, and accounting aspects of intangible assets.

8. The rate of return on net tangible assets must reflect a return on capital as well as a return of capital. The return on capital would be analogous to the discount rate. The return of capital would be analogous to a sinking fund contribution to return the capital (less any salvage value). If the net tangible assets are those that tend to increase in value, then return of capital is not a factor. Depreciating and wasting assets, however, need to be reflected as a higher rate of return.

Valuations for Tax and Accounting Purposes

Various tax and accounting requirements drive the need for valuations. Valuations can provide both a basis for depreciation or amortization and a means to revalue the balance sheet for purchase accounting transactions. This chapter addresses the pertinent tax and accounting aspects of mergers and acquisitions, and the role valuation can play.

7.1 TAX ASPECTS OF MERGERS AND ACQUISITIONS

A merger or acquisition will be either a taxable or a nontaxable transaction. In a nontaxable transaction, the seller receives payment in a form that will not result in taxes paid on any gain realized. In a taxable transaction, conversely, the seller is liable for tax on the gain. Valuations can be an important part of either transaction type. Before addressing the valuation issues, it is beneficial to describe some of the basic characteristics of nontaxable and taxable transactions. This discussion is not intended to provide a comprehensive examination of the tax attributes of various transactions. It is an overview of the basic tax nature of bank merger and acquisition transactions.

7.1.1 Nontaxable Transactions

A common type of nontaxable transaction is the *Type A* reorganization (called a statutory merger). In this type of transaction, the seller receives stock, cash, and/or securities of the buyer equal to the purchase price. The seller's shareholders can receive different types of consideration (for example, one may receive stock, another cash) and still qualify as nontaxable,[1] so long as the continuity of interest test is met. This test requires that the seller's shareholders must have an equity position in the surviving company equal to at least 50 percent of the value of their formerly outstanding stock. Any boot received is taxable to the seller's shareholders only to the extent of the value of the boot.[2] In the case of a Type A reorganization, boot is usually cash received by those shareholders who do not want stock or debt.

The *Type B* transaction (stock-for-stock) is one in which the seller's shareholders receive *voting* stock of the buyer in exchange for their shares. The buyer must acquire at least 80 percent of the voting and other classes of stock of the seller. No other consideration can be paid to the seller's shareholders (except cash for fractional shares) and still qualify as a Type B nontaxable transaction.

A *Type C* transaction (stock-for-assets) is similar to a Type B except that the buyer is exchanging voting stock for the assets of the seller. Under a Type C reorganization, the buyer may give the seller a limited amount of property in addition to voting stock; up to 20 percent of the fair market value of the net assets received.

The *Type D* reorganization involves the transfer of the assets of one company to another, and immediately thereafter the transferor and/or its shareholders are in control of the transferee. The Type D reorganization is most commonly used for spin-offs, split-offs, and split-ups. The requirements are extremely complex, but it can be a useful tool when a bank desires to transfer certain of its assets to a new, separate company.

A *Type E* reorganization is a recapitalization and involves only one corporation. A recapitalization occurs when a corporation issues a new type of debt or equity in exchange for its current debt or equity.

The last type of reorganization is a *Type F* and involves a change in identity, form, or place of a corporation. This type of reorganization is used when banks desire to change their legal status. It is not generally applicable to a merger transaction.

7.1.2 Taxable Transactions

Taxable transactions are relatively straightforward in their process: the stock or assets of a corporation are acquired for cash or its equivalent. The seller of the stock or assets is subject to tax at the time of the sale on the excess of the purchase price received over their tax basis in the stock or assets sold.

In a sale of assets, there are two layers of tax. The selling corporation recognizes any gain on the sale, and pays tax on that gain. Then, when the net proceeds of the sale are paid to shareholders, they will be taxed on the gain of the receipts over their basis in the stock. Prior to the Tax Reform Act of 1986, the first layer of tax (at the corporate level of the seller) could be avoided by adopting a complete plan of liquidation under Section 337. The result of such a liquidation was that no tax at the corporate level was paid, except for certain tax recapture items. However, under the rules established by the 1986 tax law, the so-called General Utilities doctrine, which allowed the avoidance of double taxation, was repealed. Now, double taxation is the rule rather than the exception. Additionally, if the buyer steps up the tax basis, it is subject to recapture of depreciation on real and personal property and investment tax credits. Although these recaptures were required under the old law, these, along with repeal of General Utilities, has made a Section 337 asset acquisition even less desirable.

In a taxable sale of assets, their tax attributes do not generally survive the transaction. The buyer's new tax basis in the assets will equal the purchase price. In a taxable sale of stock, however, the tax attributes of the purchased company's assets will survive. In other words, the tax basis of the seller's assets would not change after the transaction and would carry over to the buyer.

Section 338 of the Internal Revenue Code allows a stock acquisition to be treated, for tax purposes, as an asset acquisition if a corporation acquires 80 percent or more of the stock of another corporation. The buyer elects to take this approach to step up the tax basis of the acquired assets, thus generating higher depreciation to reduce future tax liabilities. Unfortunately, under the 1986 tax law, the gain on the assets (that is, the purchase price over tax basis) becomes a cost to the buyer because of the mechanics of a 338 election and repeal of *General Utilities* described previously. To understand why the buyer of the assets becomes liable for taxes on the gain in a sale, it is necessary to clarify the process of a 338 election.

1. On the day of the stock sale, the selling corporation is treated (for tax purposes) as having sold all its assets at the close of business in a single transaction to a hypothetical new corporation.

2. On the day after the stock sale, the selling corporation is treated (again, for tax purposes) as the hypothetical new corporation which purchases the same assets. The gain on the sale is now the responsibility of this new corporation.

3. This hypothetical new corporation is then liquidated into the buying corporation with the tax attributes and liabilities of the new corporation becoming those of the buyer. Consequently, the buyer now has responsibility for tax on the gain of the assets' values.

The 338 election allows the buyer to achieve the tax objective of allocating the price paid for stock to the underlying assets (that is, to step up the tax basis) without actual transfer of assets or liquidation.

Prior to the 1986 tax law, Section 338 elections were very common in taxable bank acquisitions. The buyer could acquire stock, step up the tax basis of depreciable assets, and reduce future tax liabilities. Under General Utilities, the buyer could establish a new tax basis without incurring a tax liability on the gain. The 1986 law, however, makes this a much less desirable alternative. In order for a 338 election to be economically sound, the net present value of future tax savings from higher depreciation and amortization must be greater than the immediate tax liability payable on the gain. For all practical purposes, the benefits of a 338 election evaporated with the repeal of General Utilities.

7.2 TYPICAL TAX-ORIENTED VALUATIONS

Virtually all tax-related valuation requirements are driven by the need to establish a new tax basis of an asset: for computing taxable gain, for determining depreciation, for allocating purchase price among various assets, or for new property taxes. Even in nontaxable transactions, however, there are often tax-oriented valuation requirements. For example, in a Type A reorganization (statutory merger) it may be necessary to value the seller's (mergee's) stock to confirm that the 50 percent continuity of interest test is met. Additionally, if the buyer (mergor) is issuing new securities or a new class of stock, it may be necessary to value them to determine the taxable gain of the seller.

Valuations can also be critical in the success of a Type C reorganization (stock-for-assets). If the parties of the transaction seek to exchange boot, the parties must be very certain of their valuations. Items which must be valued include those listed below:

- the stock of the buyer;
- the boot if it is property other than cash;
- the property acquired; and
- the seller's property that is not acquired.

Exhibit 7.1   Tax-oriented Purchase Price Allocation ($000,000)

	Tax Basis	Fair Market Value* Basis	Difference
Assets of Selling Bank			
Cash	$ 10	$ 10	$ 0
Investments	50	52	2
Loans (net)	100	98	(2)
Premises	30	34	4
Other	10	11	1
Core deposit intangible	—	5	5
Total	$200	$210	$10
Liabilities of Selling Bank			
Deposits	$175	$180	$ 5
Other	10	10	0
Total	$185	$190	$ 5
Net Asset Value	$ 15	$ 20	$ 5
Total Liabilities and Net Asset Value	$200	$210	$10

Transaction:
  Buyer agreed to pay $28 million for 100% of seller's stock. The assets and liabilities are revalued to market value. Identified assets less liabilities equals $20 million, leaving $8 million ($28 million purchase price less $20 million net identifiable assets) to be "allocated" to goodwill. After the transaction, the buyer will have an $8 million intangible asset called goodwill on its balance sheet.

The last item can be a problem if the seller has widely scattered assets of which the buyer has little knowledge. This can be a problem because the 80 percent voting stock requirement means 80 percent of the *total value of all property* of the seller, not just 80 percent of the value of property acquired. If retained property is found to be such that less than 80 percent of total value was exchanged, the transaction would be denied nontaxable treatment.

Valuation requirements are far more common and visible with taxable transactions, particularly cash-for-assets and cash-for-stock with a Section 338 election. In either of these types of transactions a new basis in the assets must be established, thus requiring an estimate of fair market value of the assets for determining future depreciation or amortization.

The most common reason for valuation in a taxable transaction is for *purchase price allocation*. This is the process of allocating—distributing—the total purchase price paid among the acquired net assets. Exhibit 7.1 illustrates how a purchase price allocation would proceed in a bank acquisition.

In this example, the total fair market value of acquired assets is $210 million. Subtracting the market value liabilities of $190 million, the net asset value is $20 million. Since the buyer is paying $28 million for the stock, $20 million is allocated to the identified net assets, with the balance of $8 million allocated to goodwill. The identified assets and liabilities are put on the buyer's books at their respective market values. The $8 million difference is put on the buyer's books as goodwill. This allocation to goodwill has significant tax ramifications for the buyer because goodwill is a nonamortizable asset, thus no tax benefit is realized, whereas other assets can be expensed against taxable income (through depreciation or amortization) over their useful life. Consequently, it is important that accurate and supportable valuations be made of all assets of the seller.

7.3 ACCOUNTING ASPECTS OF MERGERS AND ACQUISITIONS

When two banks are combined, the transaction can be reflected, from an accounting perspective, as either a *pooling of interests* (*pooling* for short) or a *purchase.*

7.3.1 Pooling Versus Purchase Accounting

An acquisition that qualifies for pooling allows the balance sheets of the two banks to be combined without adjustments to the values of assets or liabilities. In this type of transaction, it is assumed that two shareholder groups mutually accept the risks and rewards of combining their banks and agree to an exchange of their ownership interests. Exhibit 7.2 illustrates how the pooling of interest results in a new balance sheet and income statement.

The other method of merger and acquisition accounting, the purchase method, is more complex. Under purchase accounting rules, a new balance sheet is created that reflects the current value of assets and liabilities of the seller rather than their historical book values. The effect of this method on the resulting balance sheet, especially capital, can be significant. Exhibit 7.3 illustrates the results of purchase method accounting on the balance sheet, using the same facts as in Exhibit 7.2. In the purchase accounting example (an all cash sale), the equity-to-asset ratio falls significantly, from 7.41 percent to 5.48 percent. If the transaction had been less than all cash (some stocks and notes), the effect on equity ratios would not be quite as dramatic, but relative capital levels would still decline.

The only time purchase accounting does not cause a lower equity-to-asset ratio is when the seller receives only equity instruments of the buyer as payment. In general, the greater the percent of purchase price that is in cash and the higher the premium over book, the greater the decline in the capital ratio.

7.3.2 Requirements for Use of Pooling Accounting

The determination of whether to use pooling or purchase accounting is not an option of the bank. There are twelve very clear requirements that must *all* be met in order for the buying bank to use pooling to account for an acquisition.

These twelve requirements are spelled out in paragraphs 46–48 of Accounting Principles Board (APB) Opinion No. 16. The essence of these twelve requirements is summarized below:

1. Each of the entities must be autonomous and may not have been a subsidiary or division of another company within two years before the plan of consolidation is initiated.

2. Each of the combining companies must be independent of each other from initiation to consummation of the transaction. Independence means that the companies can hold no more than 10 percent of each other's stock.

3. The combination must be effected in a single transaction or in accordance with a specific plan within one year after the acquisition is initiated.

Exhibit 7.2   Example of Pooling of Interest Accounting Where Bank "A" is Acquirer, Bank "B" is Target ($000, Except Book Value Per Share)

	Bank A	Bank B	Adjustments	Combined
Assets				
Cash and due froms	$ 15,000	$ 6,000	—	$ 21,000
Investments	75,000	45,000	—	120,000
Net loans	160,000	42,000	—	202,000
Premises & equipment	9,000	5,000	—	14,000
Other assets	11,000	2,000	—	13,000
Total Assets	$270,000	$100,000	—	$370,000
Liabilities				
Deposits	$200,000	$ 80,000	—	$280,000
Short-term debt	30,000	10,000	—	40,000
Other liabilities	17,000	5,000	—	22,000
Long-term debt	3,000	0	—	3,000
Total Liabilities	$250,000	$ 95,000		$345,000
Shareholders Equity				
Common stock	$ 5,000	$ 1,000	($2,440)[1]	$ 3,560
Surplus	6,000	1,000	2,440[1]	9,440
Retained earnings	9,000	3,000	—	12,000
Total Equity	$ 20,000	$ 5,000	—	$ 25,000
Total Liabilities and Equity	$270,000	$100,000	—	$370,000
Common shares outstanding	150,000	40,000	—	206,000[1]
Book value/share	$ 133	$ 125	—	$ 121.36
Equity/assets	7.41%	5.00%	—	6.76%

[1] Assumes an exchange ratio of 1.4:1 (about 1.5 times B's book value), therefore Bank A must issue 56,000 shares at $133 to issue to Bank B shareholders to redeem their 40,000 shares. Because Bank A is "buying" shares worth $125 for 1.4 of its shares which are worth $186, there must be offsetting adjustments to common stock and surplus equal to the difference in book value ($61) times shares redeemed (40,000). These entries do not affect the total equity, only the relative composition of the equity account.

4. One of the corporations offers and issues only common stock with rights identical to those of the majority of its outstanding voting common stock in exchange for substantially all (90 percent or more) of the voting common stock interest of the other company.

5. None of the combining entities may have changed the equity interest of the voting common stock in contemplation of effecting the combination either within two years before the plan of combination is initiated, or between the dates the combination is initiated and consummated.

6. Each of the combining companies reacquires shares of voting common stock only for purposes other than business combinations, and no company reacquires more than a normal number of shares between the date the plan of combination is initiated and the date it is consummated. Acquisitions of voting common stock of the issuing corporation by any of the combining corporations or their subsidiaries are treated as reacquisitions by the issuing company.

Valuations for accounting purposes are usually required when a transaction is treated as a purchase. When purchase accounting is used, the seller's assets are restated to current fair market values. Liabilities assumed are recorded at their present value under current interest rates. The value of the payment made (whether in cash, stock, or debt) becomes the basis of the transaction.

The purpose of the purchase accounting valuation is to allocate the price paid to the net assets purchased (that is, to the net value of the acquired tangible and intangible assets less liabilities assumed). The concept is similar to the tax-oriented valuations for a Section 338 election described earlier in this chapter.

The concept of allocating acquisition cost (including fees and expenses) to acquired net assets is fairly straightforward: the fair market value of all assets acquired (both tangible and intangible) less liabilities assumed must equal the acquisition cost. The basic steps in this process are described below.

First, the tangible assets must be valued. Then the intangible assets are valued. This topic is addressed in general in Chapter 8 and specifically for core deposits in Chapter 16. Then, liabilities are valued. The bulk of a bank's liabilities are in customer deposits. Short-term, variable rate, or noninterest-bearing deposits are usually valued at their current levels. Deposits that are long-term (over one year) and at fixed rates should be revalued to reflect a premium, if current market rates exceed the deposit instrument's rate, or to reflect a discount if current rates are below the deposit instrument's rates.

If the acquisition cost exceeds the value of tangible and identified intangible assets net of liabilities, the difference is accounted for on the buyer's balance sheet as goodwill. Accounting Principles Board Opinions Nos. 16 and 17, and Statement of Financial Accounting Standards No. 72 deal with the accounting treatment of goodwill.

Exhibit 7.5 illustrates conceptually how various values interrelate to form the basis of a purchase price allocation for accounting purposes. In this example, the composition of the book assets and liabilities is shown on the left. On a book basis, the net asset book value (the book value of equity) is $8 million. After the valuation, asset values total $108 million. Liabilities are revalued from $92 million book to $93 million market. Therefore, the net asset value is $15 million. This example has a $20 million acquisition cost. Consequently, there will be $5 million of goodwill (the $20 million purchase price less $15 million of market value of net assets).

The valuation of acquired assets and assumed liabilities has a substantial impact on the economics of the transaction. First, goodwill will be amortized in accordance with APB 17, thus reducing future reported income. Second, goodwill cannot be used to reduce taxable income (as discussed previously). Third, goodwill is excluded from calculation of Tier 1 capital. In general, a buyer usually wants to minimize the amount of the purchase price allocated to goodwill. Consequently, a thorough identification and valuation of all assets, both tangible and intangible, becomes critically important.

ENDNOTES

1. The overall transaction would be considered nontaxable, although shareholders receiving cash would be taxed on their gain.

2. Boot is the designation for property which, transferred in an otherwise nontaxable transaction, gives rise to taxable income.

7.3 Accounting Aspe...

Exhibit 7.3 Example of Purchase Accounting—100% Cash Acquisition Where Bank "A" is Acquirer, Bank "..." Target ($000, except book value per share)

	Bank A	Bank B	Adjustments	Combined
Assets				
	$ 15,000	$ 6,000		$ 21,000
	75,000	45,000	($1,000)[1]	119,000
	160,000	42,000	(2,000)[2]	200,000
...rrent	9,000	5,000	440 [3]	14,440
	11,000	2,000		13,000
...ngible	—	—	4,000 [4]	4,000
	—	—	1,000 [5]	1,000
	$270,000	$100,000	($5,000)	$372,400
	$200,000	$ 80,000	—	$280,000
	30,000	10,000	—	40,000
...ies	17,000	5,000	—	22,000
Long-term debt	3,000	0	$7,440 [6]	10,440
Total Liabilities	$250,000	$ 95,000	$7,440	$352,440
Shareholders Equity				
Common stock	$ 5,000	$ 1,000	($1,000)[7]	$ 5,000
Surplus	6,000	1,000	(1,000)[7]	6,000
Retained earnings	9,000	3,000	($3,000)[7]	$ 9,000
Total Equity	$ 20,000	$ 5,000	($5,000)[7]	$ 20,000
Total Liabilities and Equity	$270,000	$100,000	($5,000)	$365,000
Common shares outstanding	150,000	40,000	(40,000)[8]	150,000
Book value/share	$ 133	$ 125	—	$ 133
Equity/assets	7.41%	5.00%	—	5.48%

[1] Assumed market value of investments $1,000,000 less than book value.
[2] Assumed market value of loans $2,000,000 less than book value.
[3] Assumed market value of premises $440,000 more than book value.
[4] Value of core deposit base (described in Chapter 16).
[5] Excess of purchase price ($7,440,000) over market value of Bank B's assets ($6,000,000 cash, $44,000,000 in investments, $40,000,000 in loans, $5,440,000 in premises, $2,000,000 in other assets, and $4,000,000 core deposit value) less liabilities ($95,000,000).
[6] Debt incurred of $7,440,000 (equal to $186 per share as in pooling example in preceding exhibit).
[7] Since Bank B ceases to exist, the equity account is completely distributed and also ceases to exist.
[8] All of Bank B's stock acquired for cash.

7. The ratio of the interest of an individual common stockholder to those of other common stockholders in a combining company must remain the same as a result of the exchange of common stock to effect the combination.

8. The voting rights to which the common stock ownership interests in the resulting combined corporation are entitled must be exercisable by the stockholders; the stockholders may neither be deprived of nor restricted in exercising those rights for a specified period.

9. The combination must be resolved at the date the plan is consummated and no provisions relating to the issue of securities or other terms of consideration may be pending.

Exhibit 7.4   Pooling and Purchasing Accounting: Advantages and Disadvantages

	Pooling Accounting	Purchasing
Advantages	Straightforward from an accounting perspective	Negotiations usual...
	No borrowing or debt issuance	Ownership dilution ...
	Avoids potential regulatory concerns relating to debt issuance or goodwill	Opportunity to revalue ...
	Capital of both entities survives transaction	Opportunity to sell off n...
Disadvantages	Hard to qualify for (the twelve strict rules)	Accounting more complex
	Less flexibility in negotiations	Can adversely impact capital ratios and future earnings
	Stock issuance can dilute earnings	Goodwill and intangible asset considerations
	Historical asset values retained	Reduces capital ratios in most cases
	Merger costs are expensed in year of transaction	

10. The combined corporation may not agree directly or indirectly to retire or reacquire all or part of the common stock issued to effect the combination.

11. The combined corporation may not enter into other financial arrangements for the benefit of the former stockholders of a combining company, such as guaranty of loans secured by stock issued in the combination, which, in effect, negates the exchange of equity.

12. The combined corporation may not intend or plan to dispose of a significant part of the assets of the combining companies within two years after the combination, other than disposals in the ordinary course of business of the formerly separated companies to eliminate duplicate facilities or excess capacity.

The requirements for pooling are complex and strictly enforced. If the transaction does not pass all the tests, it will be accounted for as a purchase. If a bank is contemplating a transaction that is to be accounted for as a pooling, competent accounting and legal advice should be sought.

7.3.3   Advantages and Disadvantages of Purchase and Pooling Accounting

The two methods of accounting for mergers and acquisitions each have their advantages and disadvantages, some of which are summarized in Exhibit 7.4.

7.4   TYPICAL ACCOUNTING-ORIENTED VALUATIONS

If a transaction qualifies for pooling accounting, there are no accounting requirements for valuation of assets. The balance sheets and income statements of the banks are combined at their book values without adjustment.

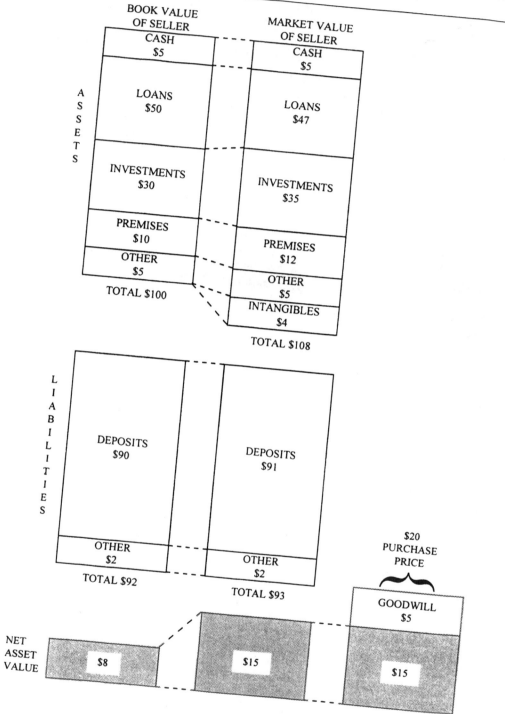

Exhibit 7.5   Relationship Among Book Value, Market Value, Purchase Price, and Goodwill ($Millions)

Intangible Asset Valuation

Often it is necessary for tax and accounting purposes, as described in Chapter 7, to value the intangible assets of an acquired company. This chapter addresses the unique characteristics of intangible assets and their role in the acquisition process. Specific examples of bank intangible assets are used where appropriate.

8.1 NATURE AND TYPES OF INTANGIBLE ASSETS

Intangible assets do not have physical substance, but are, nonetheless, integral components of the overall value of a business. The value of an intangible asset is usually a result of economic benefits that accrue to the owner. The fact that the purchase price of a business exceeds the net value of tangible assets confirms that intangible assets have benefits and the buyer perceives them to have value.

8.1.1 Criteria for Defining Intangible Assets

By standards of common law, assets such as stocks, bonds, and loans are considered intangible. For tax and accounting purposes in acquisitions, however, these types of assets are not considered intangible. For tax and accounting purposes, an asset is intangible if it possesses two key characteristics:

1. *Immateriality*[1]: This criterion distinguishes an intangible asset from a nontangible asset. Intangible assets are considered immaterial noncurrent assets, which means they have a relatively permanent nature and are not intended for sale. Nontangible assets, however, are claims against other parties, such as notes and receivables, and could be sold individually. It is for this reason that the loans of a bank are not considered intangible assets even though they are incorporeal property. In the preceding chapter, these were referred to as tangible financial assets.

2. *Inseparability:* Assets are considered intangible if they are inseparable from the active business. In other words, the intangible asset, separated from the business, is usually worthless or meaningless.

Under most circumstances, it is necessary to identify and value intangible assets only for tax and accounting reasons. Substantial tax benefits can be derived from valuing the intangible assets, and there are financial reporting requirements that need to be met. The common types of intangible assets likely to be found in an acquired bank are described below. Not all of these will or can be amortizable for tax purposes. Nonetheless it is useful to consider their value when analyzing an acquisition.

8.1.2   Core Deposit Base

The core deposit base of a bank is composed of the funds associated with stable customer deposit relationships. An intangible asset is created because the bank has a source of funding that is usually less costly than the market rate of alternative funds on the open market.

Deposits are a liability of a bank, and for many this has negative implications: How can a liability be an asset? To understand this seemingly contradictory statement, it is necessary to view deposits as the raw materials of banks. With them, banks invest in earning assets at a spread to generate a profit. Deposits are so beneficial that banks are willing to pay to attract them through branches, advertising, and premiums in addition to interest paid. Consequently, when a bank and its deposits are acquired there is a definite economic benefit to the buyer. Chapter 16 addresses the core deposit base as an intangible asset in detail because it is such a crucial part of bank acquisition valuation.

8.1.3   Loan Servicing Contracts

Often a bank will sell a loan it has made but retain the right to service it—take payments, keep records, and so on—for a fee. The buyer of the loan receives the interest and principal payments without the responsibilities and costs of operations. The fee the bank receives for servicing the loan in excess of the operations costs incurred is the economic benefit, and an intangible asset.

8.1.4   Safe Deposit Box Contracts

Banks that have safe deposit boxes rent these boxes to customers for specified monthly fees. Often the book value of the boxes is minimal or nonexistent—the boxes have long since been depreciated. Because they still have economic utility they continue to generate income. The value of this future income stream in excess of the expenses associated with the safe deposit boxes is an intangible asset.

8.1.5   Proprietary Computer Software

When a bank develops computer software for its own use, it does so at considerable expense and consequently creates an asset that has value. The extent of that value is usually based on the cost necessary to acquire similar software, or on the time that was required to develop it originally. With the proliferation of packaged banking software, proprietary programs are becoming less common, especially in smaller community banks.

8.1.6   Trust Accounts

Banks that maintain trust departments manage assets for customers for a fee. Like a loan servicing contract, the fees received for managing trust accounts, in excess of costs, create an intangible asset.

8.1.7 Leasehold Interests

Often, banks will operate branches in leased quarters or on leased ground. These leases are often long-term in nature and sometimes at rental rates below the market for similar properties. The difference between the lease rate paid by the bank and the current market rate over the life of the lease, discounted to present value, is an intangible asset.

8.1.8 Assembled Work Force

When a bank is acquired, the in-place staff represents an intangible asset. The costs to attract, recruit, and train an equivalent staff—their replacement cost—would be substantial. Consequently, there is value in the staff of the acquired bank.

8.1.9 Goodwill

Goodwill is a catch-all intangible asset. It reflects the difference between the price paid for a bank (or any business) and the bank's value of the tangible and identified intangible assets, less the liabilities assumed. From a strategic valuation standpoint, separating goodwill from other intangibles is not that critical. From a tactical standpoint, however, the separation can be very important for tax and accounting reasons as discussed in Chapter 7.

8.2 AMORTIZABLE VERSUS NONAMORTIZABLE INTANGIBLE ASSETS

As discussed in Chapter 6, the total value of a business is the sum of the tangible and intangible asset values less liabilities assumed. The intangible assets can be identified intangibles (such as core deposit base and loan service contracts) or unidentified intangibles (goodwill). Moreover, the identified intangibles can be either amortizable (enabling a depreciation-like deduction against taxable income to be taken) or nonamortizable (not eligible for the deduction). Consequently, the total value of a business could be described as:

> total value of a business =
>   tangible asset value
> +   amortizable intangible asset value
> +   nonamortizable intangible asset value
> +   goodwill
> −   liabilities assumed

The ability to first identify an intangible asset and then prove it amortizable can yield significant tax savings and result in increased postacquisition cash flow.

8.2.1 Benefits of Amortization

Amortization refers to the depreciation of an intangible asset. It is based on the concept of the wasting or exhaustible asset, although an intangible asset does not waste away as a physical asset does. The wasting away of an intangible asset is a legal fiction, but is necessary to consider in order to spread the recovery of a payment for that intangible asset over its fixed or useful life.

If an intangible asset can be amortized, significant tax savings often can be realized. The potential tax savings is equal to the amortization amount multiplied by the marginal tax rate. For example, if intangible assets valued at $10 million are amortizable over, say, ten years, and the marginal tax rate is 35 percent, annual tax savings to the acquiror of $350,000 ($10 million ÷ 10 years × 35%) are possible.

8.2.2 Requirements for Amortization

The IRS has issued several rulings that relate to the issue of intangible assets amortization. The two most significant are Revenue Ruling 68-483 and Revenue Ruling 74-456. In general these rulings held that in order for an intangible asset to be amortizable for federal income tax purposes, it must meet three tests:

1. it must be separated and isolated from goodwill; that is, it must be separately identifiable;
2. it must have a limited useful life; and
3. that limited life must be measurable with reasonable accuracy.

Separating intangible assets from nonamortizable goodwill should never be considered easy. In general, the IRS has been very aggressive in its interpretation of goodwill, and tends to allocate as many intangible assets as possible to that category. However, separate identification of intangible assets historically has not been the main cause for denial of the amortization deduction. The more common reason for disallowance is the inability to establish and measure a limited useful life. Consequently, it may be possible to identify an intangible asset, but not be able to life it (that is, to establish and measure its useful life). Then it is classified as a nonamortizable identified intangible asset, and treated no differently than goodwill for tax purposes.

The ability to life an intangible asset depends on first proving the asset has a limited life, and second, on measuring that life. In determining whether an intangible has a limited life, it is useful to ask these two questions.

1. Does the asset's value to the business diminish progressively over time?
2. Is the availability of the asset to the business limited, irrespective of that asset's current or future value?

The first question applies to intangible assets that do not regenerate naturally. Core deposit accounts tend to be viewed as nonregenerative intangibles. In other words, over time core deposit relationships will naturally dwindle as customers move and businesses close.

An example of the second question is the intangible asset created by a below-market lease rate on a branch. The value may actually increase if market lease rates escalate, but if the lease is in effect for only five years, its availability to the bank is limited and so it has a limited useful life.

The second key aspect in lifing an intangible asset is measuring the length of that useful life. Unless the intangible asset has a clear duration (like the branch lease example used above), estimating the life is usually the most difficult aspect of proving it to be amortizable. The courts have indicated in numerous cases that the life need only be determined with *reasonable,* not *perfect,* accuracy. In practice, the most supportable lives are based on in-depth, comprehensive analysis of the experiences of the business owning the asset.

8.3 MEASURING THE USEFUL LIFE OF AN INTANGIBLE ASSET

Measuring the life of an intangible asset is relatively straightforward if there is a contractual life without renewal possibilities. Unfortunately, few intangible assets as part of a bank acquisition are this clear-cut. Most have lives that can be determined only by experience, such as being based on the historical pattern of the availability and usefulness of the intangible asset to the bank. For example, the core deposit base of a bank is composed of individual customer relationships and could theoretically stay active in perpetuity. In reality, however, the deposit base acquired at a given time has a finite life and eventually will diminish through the natural process of customers moving and businesses closing. This same concept can be applied to many other bank-related intangibles, such as safe deposit box contracts and trust accounts.

Intangibles without a stated contractual life are those most vulnerable to IRS attack and potential disallowance of amortization deduction. Consequently, it is essential that the life of intangible assets to be amortized be established from thorough, objective analysis. Two factors appear to improve the supportability of a useful life calculation:

1. using the unique experience of the business being acquired relative to the intangible asset being lifed—in other words, not using industry averages or other businesses' experiences as the basis for the life; and
2. where possible, lifing each component of the intangible asset base or as small a component as possible—for example with loan servicing contracts, estimating the average life of each contract based on its characteristics, rather than an overall average.

Both of the factors are discussed below in more detail.

8.3.1 Unique Experience

The *unique experience* aspect necessitates a detailed analysis of the historical data of the bank being acquired. This requirement often results in tedious data collection, especially in smaller banks where historical records are not always in machine-readable form. The investment in such data gathering, however, is often justified by the potential tax savings.

The types of historical data to be gathered to measure useful life will vary depending on the nature of the particular intangible asset. In most cases, however, it is desirable to determine a start date (when the account was opened or the contract started) and an end date (when the account was closed or the contract terminated) for the various components of the intangible asset. If these two dates can be identified for each component for a significant historical time period (say, five years), the historical attrition rates can be gauged and an overall average useful life measured.

Very few banks maintain the meticulous records necessary to determine the start and end dates for each component of an intangible asset over a five-year historical period. This information is especially difficult for components that are not active at the time of analysis but are needed to establish the statistical base. For example, if the life of a core deposit base is being measured, it is necessary to retrieve data on accounts opened and already closed, as well as accounts opened and still active. It is the closed accounts that can be difficult to analyze, since most banks purge them from their automated systems.

One technique used to compensate for this lack of data involves first identifying the active accounts at the end of each year for, say, the past five years and at the date of the acquisition. Then, starting with the first year, the account numbers (or contract numbers) are tracked through each successive year to determine if it was still active at the end of the second year, at the end of the third year, and so on to the time of acquisition. At some point, the account or contract may disappear from the list, showing that its closing date was during that year. This is not perfect accuracy because the exact end date is not known, but if applied properly, this technique usually achieves the reasonable accuracy criterion for the courts. A detailed discussion of the use of a bank's unique experience to establish core deposit life is included in Chapter 16.

8.3.2 Individual Component Analysis

Tax law surrounding intangible assets involves a concept known as the *mass asset rule*. The courts have defined a mass asset to be a group of intangible assets grouped together for the convenience of the owner of the business. If one mass asset is acquired, and not a group of individual intangible assets, the amortization deduction will not be allowed. The courts have reasoned that a mass asset does not have a determinable or measurable useful life, even though some of the individual components do. Consequently, to support an amortization deduction, it is necessary to prevent intangible assets from being classified as *mass assets.*

The mass asset rule was first applied in a 1925 court case when a buyer of a newspaper subscription list was denied amortization of the list's value.[2] This case and a number of others through the mid-1960s took a hard line on mass assets being in the nature of goodwill and therefore nonamortizable. This rule was typically invoked when the intangible asset in question was some type of customer or subscription list.

The first break in the hard line application of the mass asset rule came in the *Seaboard* case.[3] The taxpayer was allowed an amortization of the premium paid for loan servicing contracts. The aggregate premium was valued based on an analysis of each loan and its unique characteristics. In this case, the methodology led the court to conclude that each loan contract had a separately identified value to the taxpayer and, therefore, the taxpayer acquired separate loan contracts and not a mass asset.

After the *Seaboard* case, it appeared that amortization required each component to be lifed and valued individually. This made the practical application difficult and expensive. In 1969, however, in the *Western Mortgage* case, the taxpayer was allowed an amortization deduction on mortgage loan servicing rights even though each loan was not lifed and valued individually.[4] The court held that the taxpayer properly measured an *average* service life of the acquired mortgage portfolio. This important case expanded the practical applicability of supporting intangible asset lives. The IRS was, however, still arguing that intangible assets were inseparable from goodwill.

The most crucial case in the erosion of the mass asset rule was the *First Pennsylvania* case.[5] This 1971 case also involved loan servicing contracts and the estimate of the useful life of these contracts which varied due to prepayment and refinancings by borrowers. The arguments in the case centered on the useful life estimate, not on whether the loan servicing contracts represented an intangible asset separable from goodwill. The potential amortization of the asset was conceded by the IRS by virtue of the fact that the IRS introduced witnesses to dispute the taxpayer's estimate of useful life. If the intangible asset had been no different from goodwill there would have been no need to dispute the life estimate. Revenue Ruling 68-483 (issued in 1968) stated "whether or not an intangible asset, or a tangible asset, is depreciable for Federal income tax purposes depends on the determination that the asset is actually exhausting, and that such exhaustion is susceptible to measurement." Here the IRS explicitly states that if the intangible asset can be proven to be wasting (that is, having a measurable and finite useful life), it can be amortized.

Revenue Ruling 74-456 (issued in 1974) stated that certain intangible assets, such as customer and subscription lists, generally have indeterminable useful lives and are not amortizable, except in unusual cases where the asset's life can be measured and its value determined. The IRS, therefore, is on record as stating that unusual circumstances may exist to justify intangible asset amortization even where the useful life is not known with certainty.

In general, given the history of the mass asset rule and the IRS position of requiring unusual circumstances, it is best to have a detailed analysis of the individual intangible assets. The useful life estimation will be on more solid foundation with a detailed analysis.

8.4   ESTABLISHING VALUE OF INTANGIBLE ASSETS

Once the intangible asset has been identified (thus being separable from goodwill) and lifed (avoiding the mass asset problem), it needs to be valued. Identifying and lifing an intangible asset establishes it as amortizable. The value is needed to arrive at the dollar amount of that amortization deduction.

The general techniques used to value intangible assets are the same as those used to value any asset: the *cost, market,* and *income* approaches. The particular situation and nature of the asset will determine the best approach.

8.4.1   The Cost Approach

The cost approach values an intangible asset based on the cost necessary to replace it with one of comparable utility. This approach can be used, for example, to value proprietary software based on the cost to purchase or develop similar software. The cost approach could also be applied to such intangible assets as the core deposit base, based on the cost to create an equal level of deposits. This particular technique, however, is rarely applied to core deposits because other techniques are available that are more supportable.

In general, in order to use the cost approach to value an intangible asset it is necessary to estimate with reasonable accuracy the cost to purchase, develop, or create a similar asset. It is this requirement that causes the cost approach to be difficult to apply to many intangible assets.

8.4.2   The Market Approach

The market approach to valuation requires comparable transaction data. Due to the nature of intangible assets, especially their inseparability from the total business, they are rarely sold individually. Consequently, direct market comparables are virtually nonexistent. Even indirect comparables are usually not available. Publicly reported data might show total premium paid for an acquisition, but the allocation of that premium among various intangible assets is not reported. Only in unusual circumstances can the market approach be used to value an intangible asset.

8.4.3   The Income Approach

The most common technique used to value intangible assets is the income approach. This technique is directly applicable because most intangible assets result from an economic benefit (some level of income) that accrues to the asset's owner. In simplest terms, the value of an intangible asset is the income stream (less related expenses) over the useful life of the asset, discounted to present value. A simple example using safe deposit box contracts can illustrate the calculation. (For this illustration, tax benefits are assumed to be zero. As described earlier in Chapter 7, however, when amortization of an intangible results in tax savings, those future tax savings should be reflected in the value.)

Assume that the average life of a safe deposit box contract is five years, the total safe deposit income to a bank is $100,000 a year, and annual costs associated with the safe deposit boxes (depreciation, maintenance, salary for clerk, and so on) total $60,000. The value of these safe deposit contracts is calculated as shown in Exhibit 8.1. The value of the safe deposit box contracts in force on the date of acquisition is about $155,000.

A variation of the income approach is the cost savings method. This method is used when the intangible asset does not produce income but allows the owner to avoid costs that otherwise might be incurred. The value is equal to the cost savings over the life of the asset, discounted to present value. A favorable lease can be valued using the cost savings method. For example, suppose that a bank has a 2,500 square foot branch in the lobby of an office building leased at a rate of $15 per square foot per year, but market rates for comparable space are $20 per square foot each year. Also, suppose the lease has seven years remaining before the bank must renew at market rates. The value of the intangible asset created by a below-market rate leasehold interest is calculated as shown in Exhibit 8.2. The value of the intangible asset created by the lease, because of cost savings, is about $64,000.

8.5   AMORTIZATION METHODS

Once the intangible asset has been valued, the annual deduction for taxes must be calculated to determine the annual amortization. The most common way to ascertain the annual amortization deduction of an intangible asset is the *time method*. This method computes the deduction as follows:

$$\text{annual amortization deduction} =$$
$$\text{value of intangible} \div \text{useful life in years}$$

This method is analogous to straight-line depreciation used for tangible assets.

Another approach is the *income forecast method,* which measures the amortization in a given year based on the percent of total income or cost savings from the asset likely to be

Exhibit 8.1 Valuation of Safe Deposit Box Contracts

Year	Safe Deposit Boxes Net Income	Discount Factor @ 8.5%	Present Value
1	$40,000	.9217	$ 36,868
2	40,000	.8495	33,980
3	40,000	.7829	33,316
4	40,000	.6650	26,600
5	40,000	.6129	24,516
	Net Present Value		$155,280

Exhibit 8.2 Valuation of a Below-Market Rate Lease

Year	Market Rent*	Lease Rate Rent**	Cost Savings	Discount Factor @ 13%	Present Value
1	$50,000	$37,500	$12,500	.885	$11,025
2	50,000	37,500	12,500	.783	9,728
3	50,000	37,500	12,500	.693	8,663
4	50,000	37,500	12,500	.613	7,663
5	50,000	37,500	12,500	.543	6,788
6	50,000	37,500	12,500	.480	6,000
7	50,000	37,500	12,500	.425	5,313
			Net Present Value		$55,340

* 2,500 square feet multiplied by $20, for simplicity, assumes market rate does not increase over lease period.
** 2,500 square feet multiplied by $15.

generated in that year. This approach is used when the total benefit of an intangible asset is not evenly distributed over its useful life. A good example, outside of banking, is film rights. Typically the income from a film is higher in the first few years because it is most likely to be popular when it is new. Consequently, the owner of the film rights would amortize more of the value in early years than in later years of the useful life. Tax court rulings, especially the C&S case (Citizens & Southern Bancorporation) described in Chapter 16, give support to the possibility of using the income forecast method for core deposit base amortization.

The *cost recovery method* is a third technique of determining amortization deduction. This approach uses the actual experience during a taxable year to determine the decline in value of an asset. This method has been used to amortize magazine subscription lists based upon the actual number of lost subscribers during a year.

8.6 SUPPORTING INTANGIBLE ASSET VALUATION AND AMORTIZATION

Intangible asset valuation should not be an afterthought, but an integral part of the negotiations and acquisition agreement.[6] To improve the supportability of intangible asset amortization, it is beneficial to follow these seven key guidelines.

1. *Be familiar with the latest IRS rulings.* The acquiring bank and its counsel should become familiar with cases involving intangible assets, especially financial institution related cases. Understanding the reasoning of the courts and the IRS positions is helpful in designing a more supportable acquisition tax plan.

2. *Include intangible asset value in acquisition agreement.* The binding acquisition agreement should state the classes of tangible and intangible assets being acquired and the allocation of the purchase price among them. This will help support the separability of amortizable intangible assets from goodwill and nonamortizable intangible assets.

3. *Avoid the temptation to eliminate goodwill completely.* Very seldom is there a bank acquisition that does not involve some element of goodwill. Consequently, a portion of the purchase price should be allocated to goodwill, and included in the contract.

4. *Be meticulous when establishing useful lives.* The establishment of a useful life is the area the IRS is likely to find fault. Consequently, the best techniques, using the bank's own unique data and experiences when possible, should be employed. Perfect accuracy is not required, only reasonable accuracy. In general, however, the closer to perfect, the better it can be supported.

5. *Establish intangible asset values professionally.* The supportability of value is strengthened when independent, qualified valuation professionals are used. Their experience and objectivity strengthen the taxpayer's evidence if called upon to defend the amortization deduction. Moreover, professionals will be aware of the best techniques to use in a given situation.

6. *Maintain good records.* From the first step in the acquisition process, the buyer should maintain complete records, especially related to the assets purchased and their value. Consequently, it is often beneficial to have preliminary valuations of major intangible assets early in the process.

7. *Be reasonable and logical.* Once all the research and analysis is completed, it should be checked for reasonableness and logic. Consider how the IRS might attack assumptions and techniques used.

By following these seven guidelines, the likelihood increases that intangible asset amortization will be supportable.

ENDNOTES

1. Immateriality as used here is a legal term meaning the assets do not have material—physical—substance. It does not mean immaterial in the economic or accounting sense.
2. *Danville Press Inc. v. Comr.,* 1 B.T.A. 1171 (1925).
3. *Comr. v Seaboard Finance Co.,* 367 F.2d 646 (9th cir. 1966), cert. denied, 372 U.S. 935 (1963).
4. *Western Mortgage Corporation v. Comr.,* 308 F.Supp. 333 (C.D. Cal. 1969).
5. *First Pennsylvania Banking & Trust Co. v. Comr.,* 56 T.C. 677 (1971), acq. 1972-1 C.B. 2.
6. See discussion of C&S case for core deposit amortization in Chapter 16.

PART III

Assessment of Financial Institutions

CHAPTER 9

Financial Analysis of Banks and Bank Holding Companies

The analysis of the financial performance of a bank to be valued is one of the most essential parts of the valuation research process. The financial performance, however, is only the quantified reflection of the management of the institution. In other words, the financial statistics are not the bank, but they represent a scorecard of how well the bank is organized and operated. Consequently, a thorough analysis of the financials provides an objective assessment of performance.

9.1 TYPES AND SOURCES OF FINANCIAL DATA

Banks, because of their regulated nature, are required to submit substantial amounts of financial data to regulators. Much of the financial information is made available to the public. The format of reporting is identical, which allows for apples-to-apples comparisons across banks of different sizes and in different locations with the knowledge that the information is probably 99 percent consistent.

Financial information on banks and bank holding companies is available on an individual basis, or in total for various peer groups. In a typical valuation, information at both levels is beneficial; it is then possible to analyze the bank directly and to compare it with its peer group.

9.1.1 The Uniform Bank Performance Report

One of the more useful reports available is the Uniform Bank Performance Report (UBPR) prepared by the Federal Financial Institutions Examination Council. This report presents a comprehensive profile of a bank for a five-year period, along with comparisons to peer groups. The statistics presented in a UBPR for a given bank are divided into four broad sections.

The first section of the UBPR presents summary ratios that provide an overview of the bank. Key ratios are shown in the areas of income and expenses as percents of average assets, nonperforming loans, liquidity and rate sensitivity, capitalization, and overall growth rates. Ratios for banks in the peer group are also shown. This allows for easy comparison between Example Bank and its peers.

The second section of the UBPR presents a wide variety of statistics relative to income performance. A summary five-year income statement is shown, along with ratios of expenses to assets, margins, yields on earning assets, cost of funds, noninterest income, and overhead expenses as a percent of both assets and total income.

The UBPR's third section is a dissection of the bank's balance sheet. A detailed breakdown of loans and investments is shown, along with nonearning assets. The liabilities are also shown, with core and noncore deposits listed separately. The capital levels and composition are analyzed in great detail. This section also presents in-depth statistics on loans and loan losses, asset/liability management, and liquidity.

The fourth and final section of the UBPR presents a variety of ratios for banks in the same state as the subject bank, and those in the same peer group. Also presented are statistics on any foreign offices of the subject bank.

9.1.2   The Bank Holding Company Performance Report

A report similar to the UBPR is the Bank Holding Company Performance Report (BHCPR). This is an essential report if the banking organization being analyzed is a holding company. The Federal Reserve System provides this report to the public.

The BHCPR contains four major sections. The first section contains various ratios of profitability, loan losses, liquidity, and debt and equity on a consolidated basis (that is, for the parent company and all subsidiaries). The ratios for the peer group are also shown.

The second section is a summary of various income and expense levels and ratios. Income and expenses are shown as a percent of assets, with margins and yields also computed. These statistics are presented on a consolidated basis.

The third section is a detailed balance sheet analysis, including a five-year summary of assets, liabilities, and capital, along with a multitude of balance sheet ratios. Special tables are produced for loan losses, liquidity, and capital. As in the preceding two sections, the statistics are presented on a consolidated basis.

The last section presents the balance sheet and income statement of the parent company only, and selected ratios with peer group comparisons. Unless the holding company has significant nonbanking activities, the parent company statistics should be relatively minor in relation to the consolidated total.

9.1.3   Other Public Sources

The UBPR and BHCPR are invaluable sources of financial data on a bank or bank holding company. If specific call reports—the financial statements banks submit to regulators—are desired, these can be obtained from the National Information Center (NIC) Web site (http://www.ffiec.gov/nic/). The NIC provides comprehensive information on banks and other financial institutions including both domestic and foreign institutions operating in the United States in which the Federal Reserve has a supervisory, regulatory, or research interest.

In recent years, the various regulatory agencies have used the same format for every bank and bank holding company irrespective of whether it is state, national, Federal Reserve System member, or non-Fed member. There are, however, degrees of detail in the call reports depending on the size of the bank and whether it has non-U.S. offices. For banks, there are four call reports:

- *FFIEC 031*—for banks with domestic and foreign offices;
- *FFIEC 032*—for banks with assets over $300 million, and domestic offices only;
- *FFIEC 033*—for banks with assets between $100 million and $300 million, and domestic offices only; and
- *FFIEC 034*—for banks with assets below $100 million and domestic offices only.

These reports are all in the same basic format, with slightly less detailed reporting requirements for smaller banks.

Bank holding companies, which report consolidated and parent company financial data to the Federal Reserve, also have several different forms:

- *FR Y-9C*—consolidated financial statements for bank holding companies with more than $150 million in assets, and all bank holding companies with two or more subsidiary banks;
- *FR Y-9LP*—parent only financial statements for bank holding companies with more than $150 million assets and all bank holding companies with two or more subsidiary banks; and
- *FR Y-9SP*—financial statements for one-bank holding companies with assets less than $150 million.

If stock of the bank or bank holding company is widely traded, a copy of its annual report can provide a wealth of financial data as well as other information on operations. If the institution is registered with the SEC, a copy of its 10-K report provides extremely beneficial information.

9.1.4 Private Sources

A number of private companies have been preparing and marketing specialized reports, using the public data as input. Most of these private sources are quite good and prepare a product that is often more readable than data from public sources. Two such sources of data are Sheshunoff Information Services, Inc. of Austin, Texas, and the investment banking firm of Keefe, Bruyette & Woods. These companies also offer bank data on computer disk that allows for easy manipulation and analysis.

9.1.5 Internal Data Sources

If access to the subject bank's internal records is possible, there is a wealth of potential data. However, reports produced by banks differ widely. Some banks are very sophisticated and generate excellent management reports in a wide variety of areas. Others produce very minimal data. Consequently, each situation must be assessed individually. Nonetheless, there are some basic reports that are likely to exist in every bank.

The most common is the "daily statement of condition," which is a detailed balance sheet and income statement created after the close of every business day. This report is useful because of its detailed nature, but it rarely follows the same format as the regulatory reports. Therefore, some rearranging of the daily statement is usually necessary if comparison with historical call reports is desired.

The delinquent (past due) loan report should also be reviewed. This report will usually show the loans which have not received payment within seven days of the due date. The report will segregate the loans by length of delinquency (for example, 7–30 days, 31–60 days, 61–90 days, and so on).

The bank should also have records regarding the loans charged off and those that have had reserves established but not yet completely charged off. This information provides detail with respect to the recognition of problem loans and any possible future losses likely to surface.

Another excellent source of information, financial and otherwise, is the bank's examination report. The report issued by the bank's regulatory agency will contain detailed analyses of nonperforming loans, foreclosed property, investment risks, and a wide variety of insights into the operations and organization. This report is highly confidential and is not available through public sources. If, however, the bank is cooperating in the valuation, it may be possible to view this report.

The annual budgets of the bank can also be beneficial. Depending on the sophistication of the institution, the budget can be a detailed forecast of financial performance based on strategic plans or it can be a simplistic extrapolation of the preceding year's performance. The particular situation will determine the usefulness of budgets in the valuation research process.

Asset/liability (A/L) management reports are also beneficial if the bank has a formal A/L system. Such a system monitors the repricing opportunities for all interest-earning assets and interest-bearing liabilities. From these reports it is possible to assess the interest rate risk the bank faces. For example, a bank may have $500 million in commercial loans, with some adjustable at 30 days, some at 60 days and some at 90 days. Consequently, the $500 million would be allocated into time groups depending on their "rollover" date. This is called a repricing opportunity because the bank can adjust the interest rate (that is, reprice it) during that time period. The same process is undertaken on the liability side, except that repricing is based on the deposits or other funding sources' maturity dates.

The internal information sources described here are just a few of those likely to be available in any given bank or bank holding company. Each situation must be assessed individually to determine the applicability and availability of financial data beyond the basic reports.

9.2 OVERVIEW OF FINANCIAL STATEMENTS

Banks and bank holding companies are required to maintain financial records and reports for regulators, in addition to the normal financial information kept by any prudent business. The format and level of detail of various financial reports will differ from bank to bank. The conceptual framework, however, will be similar. This framework is described below.

9.2.1 Income Generation and Income Statement

Exhibit 9.1 illustrates how income is created by a bank. The major source of income is interest, which is generated mainly by loans and investments. Subtracted from that figure is the interest expense (mostly interest paid on deposits). The resulting difference is called "net interest income." The noninterest income (mostly from service charges and fees) is

Exhibit 9.1   Schematic of Bank Income Generation

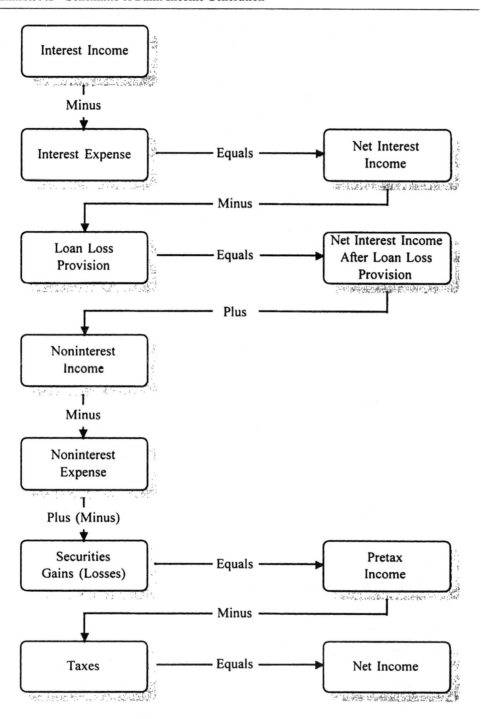

added, which results in total income. Overhead expenses include such costs as personnel, office occupancy, data processing supplies, utilities, and insurance. The provision for loan losses is a charge against income to reflect bad loans. The resulting figure, after subtracting operating expenses and loan loss provision, is pretax income. With taxes subtracted, the final figure is net income.

The internal financial reports and/or annual reports of a bank or bank holding company may not be in the same format as regulatory reports. Occasionally, the income statement will be in the general format shown below.

$$
\begin{array}{rl}
   & \text{interest income} \\
- & \underline{\text{interest expense}} \\
= & \text{net interest income} \\
- & \underline{\text{loan loss provision}} \\
= & \text{net interest income after loan loss provision} \\
+ & \text{noninterest income} \\
- & \text{noninterest expense} \\
+ & \underline{\text{securities gains (or minus losses)}} \\
= & \text{pretax income} \\
- & \underline{\text{taxes}} \\
= & \text{net income}
\end{array}
$$

Consequently, it is sometimes necessary to rearrange either the internal or regulatory reports to allow comparison between the two types.

9.2.2 Balance Sheet

The major items shown on a bank or bank holding company balance sheet are listed below:

- cash, cash balances at other depository institutions, and due from accounts
- securities (investments) held by the bank
- fed funds sold (short-term loans to other banks) and securities purchased under agreement to resell (also called "reverse repos")
- total loans and lease financing receivables (net of unearned income)
- loan loss reserves
- net loans (total loans less loan loss reserves)
- assets held in bank's own trading account
- bank premises and fixed assets
- other real estate owned (property temporarily owned by the bank, usually as a result of loan foreclosure)
- investment in subsidiaries or other companies not consolidated in financial statements
- customer liabilities on acceptances outstanding
- intangible assets (as a result of acquisitions)
- other assets

Assets can be either earning or nonearning. Earning assets are principally the loans and investments held by the bank, with Fed funds sold and interest-bearing balances at other banks usually being a smaller part. Earning assets are about 91 percent of the total assets of all banks. Of the earning assets, loans comprise about 57 percent, investments about 34 percent, Fed funds sold about 6 percent, and interest-bearing balances at other banks about 3 percent. Of the nonearning assets, most were in noninterest balances at other banks and due from accounts. About one-fifth of nonearning assets were in premises and equipment.

The liability side of the balance sheet is arranged in order of priority claim on the bank's assets (from highest to lowest). The categories typically listed include:

- customer deposits;
- Fed funds purchased (short-term borrowings from other banks) and securities sold under agreement to repurchase ("repos");
- demand notes issued to the U.S. Treasury;
- miscellaneous borrowed funds;
- mortgages and capitalized leases;
- the bank's liability on customer acceptances outstanding
- notes and debentures subordinated to depositors; and
- other liabilities.

Deposits account for about 97 percent of banks' liabilities.

Another entry on the liability side of the balance sheet is limited-life preferred stock. This type of preferred stock has a stated maturity (or it is redeemed at the option of the holder, not the bank) and is *not* convertible to perpetual preferred or common stock. Limited-life preferred stock is technically not debt, therefore not a liability, but it is not counted fully as equity. Limited-life preferred stock is addressed in greater detail later in this chapter as part of the discussion of bank capital.

The equity portion of the balance sheet represents the owners' interest in the bank. Equity consists of:

- perpetual preferred stock;
- common stock;
- surplus;
- undivided profits and capital reserves; and
- cumulative foreign currency translation adjustment.

Equity is about 8 to 9 percent of assets at all U.S. banks.

9.3 COMPOSITION OF BANK ASSETS

The assets of a bank represent the uses of funds. Each major category of assets is discussed on the following pages. Unless otherwise noted, the asset items are equivalent for a bank or bank holding company.

9.3.1 Cash and Due Froms

The cash and due froms category accounts for about 8 percent of all assets. There are five major types of assets in this category:

- actual vault cash;
- cash items (usually checks) in process of collection;
- deposits at banks in the United States;
- deposits at foreign banks; and
- deposits at the Federal Reserve Bank.

Cash items in process of collection is usually the largest component of the cash and due from total. This represents the value of checks that have been deposited by customers but not yet collected from the bank on which those funds are drawn.

9.3.2 Investment Securities

Investment securities comprise about 29 percent of all bank assets. Banks hold a variety of investment securities, the most common of which are:

- Treasury Securities such as T-Bills, Treasury Notes, and Treasury Bonds;
- obligations of U.S. Government agencies and corporations; and
- securities issued by states and municipalities.

Historically, banks were able to record the value of investments at the purchase price, adjusted for amortization of premiums and accretion of discounts. Two new accounting rules, Statement of Financial Accounting Standards (SFAS) 107 and SFAS 115, impact how banks report the value of investments on their balance sheets.

SFAS 107 requires business entities, including financial institutions, to disclose the fair value of investments where it is practicable to estimate such fair value. The definition of fair value for SFAS 107 is "the amount at which the instrument could be exchanged in a current transaction between willing parties other than in a forced or liquidation sale." From a practical standpoint, most investments held by banks have quoted market prices. Therefore, the estimation of fair value is reliable and consistent.

SFAS 115 requires banks to classify each investment security into one of three types: trading account, held to maturity (HTM), and available for sale (AFS). Most banks will have a very small portion of their portfolio, if any, in the trading account category. This new reporting gives greater insights into the nature of the bank's balance sheet.

9.3.3 Fed Funds Sold and Reverse Repos

Fed funds sold are excess reserves of the bank which are loaned to other banks on a short-term basis, usually overnight. Reverse repurchase agreements (or reverse repos) provide another use for excess funds. To create a reverse repo, the bank purchases an investment security from another bank for a short period of time under an agreement to resell. At the end of that time period, it sells the investment back to the bank from which it was purchased. This action allows the bank to earn a market rate of interest, or close to it, on excess funds that may be available only for a day or two. About 5 percent of total bank assets are in Fed funds and reverse repos.

9.3.4 Loans and Lease Financing Receivables

Loans and lease financing receivables are extensions of credit made directly to bank customers, or the purchase of such assets from other financial institutions. Loans, net of reserves, constitute approximately 52 percent of total assets of all banks.

Total loans, as reported by banks, is not the aggregate face value of those loans. The difference between the amount reported as total loans and the face value of all loans is the unearned income of those loans. A simple example illustrates the difference.

If an individual borrows $10,000 for three years at 11 percent annual interest with monthly payments, the total payback will be $11,786. The actual note amount (the total loan) is $11,786, but that figure includes unearned income of $1,786 at the beginning of the loan. Consequently the amount recorded at the inception of the loan is $10,000, not the $11,786 note amount. As the borrower makes payments, the principal owed is reduced as is the amount reported in the balance sheet. Not all loan types are structured like a consumer loan. Some loans, most commonly real estate, do not include future income in the note amount. For example, a $10,000 real estate loan has a face value of $10,000 and is reported as such. As the principal is repaid, the face value and reported amount decreases.

Loans and leases are generally reported in these categories:

- secured by real estate;
- to depository institutions;
- agricultural;
- commercial and industrial;
- acceptances from other banks;
- to individuals;
- to foreign governments;
- to state and local governments; and
- other loans.

The allowance for loan and lease losses is subtracted from total loans and lease financing receivables. This is a reserve account to cover anticipated losses on loans and leases.

Another subtraction from loans is the *allocated transfer risk reserve.* This is a special reserve account used by banks that have loans to specific countries which have not been able to make payments on external debt and where no definite prospects exist for orderly restoration of debt service. This is a minor amount in virtually all nonmoney center banks.

Loans and lease financing receivables less the reserves (both loss and allocated transfer risk) results in *net loans and lease financing receivables.* For simplicity, throughout this book the term *loans* is used for this asset group unless otherwise stated. Also, the term *loan loss reserves* is used for all types of loan, lease, and allocated transfer risk reserves.

9.3.5   Assets Held in Trading Accounts

Securities and other investments held by banks for their own trading account are recorded on the balance sheet at market value. Trading account assets include most of the same types of investments banks hold for the securities portion of their balance sheet. This asset type is found almost exclusively in larger banks with full-time trading departments that regularly deal in securities. Banks with over $10 billion in assets have about 1.5 percent of their assets in trading account securities. The figure was 0.26 percent for banks with $3 to $10 billion of assets, 0.2 percent for banks with $1 to $3 billion, and virtually none for banks under $1 billion.

9.3.6   Premises and Fixed Assets

This asset category includes the buildings, furniture, fixtures, and equipment used by the bank in its normal business. Overall, less than 2 percent of the total assets of all banks is made up of premises and fixed assets. These assets are reported at original cost less accumulated depreciation. Included in this category are any loans to, or investments in, groups that will purchase premises and lease them back to the bank. Other leased premises and/or equipment are carried at their capitalized value net of depreciation. The requirements for a capitalized lease are complex; they are specified in Financial Accounting Standards Board Statement Number 13 (FASB 13). Essentially, most arm's length long-term leases are capitalized. The bank's assets appear as if the bank purchased the premises with the corresponding liability being obligations for capitalized leases.

Specifically excluded from the premises and fixed assets account are valuable art objects (recorded as other assets) and favorable leases (recorded as intangible assets).

9.3.7   Other Real Estate Owned

Real estate owned by the bank, but not used in its normal business, is part of the ORE portfolio (also called OREO, or REO). It is usually property the bank has acquired through foreclosure, although there are other reasons for ORE (for example, there may be closed but unsold branches or land originally purchased for expansion but no longer needed). Overall, about 0.5 percent of banking assets are in ORE.

ORE is reported at book value (not to exceed fair market value) less accumulated depreciation and any loss reserves established for the properties. If a bank owns only a portion of a property (perhaps as a result of participation loan foreclosure) its pro rata share of the property's value is recorded as ORE.

9.3.8   Investments in Unconsolidated Subsidiaries and Associated Companies

This asset category is a minor entry on most banks' balance sheets. It includes the amount of a bank's investment in the stock of all subsidiaries that have not been consolidated into the financial statements.

9.3.9   Customer Liabilities to Bank on Acceptances Outstanding

This asset category includes the full amount of customers' liabilities to the bank for the bank's guarantee of certain drafts and bills of exchange, usually for financing of imports and exports. There is an offsetting liability entry for the bank's obligation to honor the acceptance, usually for the same amount as the asset. The liability is called a *bankers acceptance* and is a marketable investment for the holder, much like a large certificate of deposit issued by a bank would be marketable.

9.3.10 Intangible Assets

Intangible assets are recorded on a buying bank's balance sheet as a result of a business combination under the purchase method of accounting. The typical types of *identified* intangible assets in a bank are:

- core deposit base;
- computer software;
- mortgage servicing rights; and
- favorable leases.

The primary *unidentified* intangible is goodwill.

When intangible assets, especially goodwill, are high it usually means that the bank or bank holding company has acquired another institution at a significant premium over book value. Since most acquisitions are by bank holding companies, intangibles are usually found on their books, rather than on the books of individual banks.

9.3.11 Other Assets

Other assets is a catchall category for assets that do not fit the other categories and are not large enough to warrant a separate line item.

9.4 COMPOSITION OF BANK LIABILITIES

The liabilities of the bank represent the sources of funds used to invest in assets. The major liability groups of a bank are described below. These liabilities are virtually the same for both banks and bank holding companies.

9.4.1 Deposits

The most prevalent liabilities of a bank are customer deposits. Overall, deposits represent about 97 percent of all bank liabilities. The types of deposits reported are shown in Exhibit 9.2. Deposit levels are also segregated by IPC (Individuals, Partnerships and Corporations) and public funds.

One other deposit segregation reported in the UBPR is a core versus noncore deposit. The core deposits of a bank are generally considered to be those that are the result of a stable customer relationship and are not likely to be volatile. About 75 to 80 percent of banking deposits are usually in the core deposits category. Noncore deposits are usually considered to be certificates of deposit of $100,000 or more (called jumbo CDs), public funds, and brokered deposits.

Exhibit 9.2   Deposits by Type in U.S. Banks—1999

Deposit Type	Approximate % of All Deposits
Demand	9%
Savings, NOWs	16%
CDs under $100,000	41%
CDs over $100,000	11%
Super NOW/MMDAs	16%
Foreign Office Deposits	7%
Total	100%

9.4.2   Fed Funds Purchased and Repos

Fed funds purchased are the opposite of Fed funds sold. The bank that "purchases" Fed funds—borrows excess reserves from another bank—is satisfying a temporary deficiency in its reserve position. By using Fed funds, the bank is able to satisfy its reserve needs without liquidating part of its security holdings. (If the Fed funds transaction involves funds that are immediately available but mature in more than one business day, they are called *term Fed funds* and are recorded as other borrowings.)

Repos serve the same basic purpose as Fed funds purchased; the bank sells a security to a third party with the agreement to repurchase it within a short period of time, sometimes overnight. The selling bank receives needed short-term funds without actually liquidating securities.

9.4.3   Demand Notes Issued to U.S. Treasury

Banks involved with the Treasury Tax and Loan note program from time to time receive funds that are to be credited to the U.S. Government. The day after such funds are received, they are recorded as demand notes of the U.S. Treasury and constitute a liability of the bank. This liability is essentially a special type of deposit.

9.4.4   Other Borrowed Money

Banks and bank holding companies have a variety of techniques for borrowing money for short-term or long-term needs. A bank can borrow funds:

- on its promissory notes (if it is a holding company);
- on notes and bills rediscounted (including commodity drafts rediscounted);
- through loans sold with agreement to repurchase;
- by creation of due bills (an obligation that results when a bank sells a security or asset and receives payment, but does not deliver the security or asset);
- from the Federal Reserve Bank;
- by overdrawing correspondent accounts;
- on purchase of term Fed funds;

- by selling assets short (in other words, selling an asset it does not actually own); and/or
- by issuing notes and debentures.

The liability category "all other borrowed money" comprises only one-tenth of one percent of total liabilities.

9.4.5 Mortgage Indebtedness/Capitalized Leases

This liability encompasses the debt a bank has incurred for purposes of building or acquiring premises and fixed assets. This category also includes any obligations for long-term capitalized leases.

9.4.6 Bank's Liability on Acceptances Executed and Outstanding

This balance sheet category reflects the bank's liability from customers' drafts and bills of exchange which the bank has agreed to pay. This liability is an offset of the customers' liability to the bank on acceptances outstanding asset described in the preceding section.

9.4.7 Subordinated Notes and Debentures

A subordinated note or debenture is a type of debt issued by a bank or bank holding company which is subordinate to depositors' claims on the bank's assets. When issued by a bank directly, a subordinated note or debenture is not insured and matures in seven or more years. When issued by a bank holding company, it is considered unsecured long-term debt. Banks report mandatory convertible securities with subordinated notes and debentures, while holding companies record them separately.

9.4.8 Other Liabilities

The last liability group includes all miscellaneous liabilities of the bank, including:

- accrued but unpaid expenses;
- deferred income taxes;
- dividends payable;
- accounts payable; and
- deferred gains.

9.5 OFF-BALANCE SHEET ITEMS

In addition to items that are recorded on the balance sheet of a bank, there are *off-balance sheet* items. These are contingent liabilities such as letters of credit and interest rate swaps. In large money center banks, off-balance sheet commitments can be substantial, sometimes more than the value of recorded assets. Most of these commitments are related to futures and options contracts and foreign exchange dealings.

The area of off-balance sheet commitments, and the risk associated with such commitments, is very complex. Risk-based capital guidelines discussed later in this chapter attempt to factor in that risk in determining capital adequacy. Where off-balance sheet commitments are substantial, in-depth research by a knowledgeable professional is necessary.

9.6   COMPOSITION OF BANK CAPITAL

The capital of a bank or any other business serves three basic purposes:

- to absorb unanticipated losses;
- to provide operating funds; and
- to measure ownership.

Banks are unique in that they have *equity capital* and *regulatory capital*. The equity capital of a bank is measured the same way as the equity of any business—assets less liabilities. The principal components of equity capital are:

- par value of stock (common, limited life preferred and/or perpetual preferred);
- surplus;
- undivided profits; and
- capital reserves.

Regulatory capital is a measure used by regulatory agencies to assess the financial condition of a bank under their supervision. The components of equity capital are described in this section, and regulatory capital definitions and guidelines in the following section.

9.6.1   Par Value of Stock

The aggregate par value of common, limited life preferred, and/or perpetual preferred stock is simply the par (or stated) value of the stock multiplied by the number of shares outstanding. Par value bears no relation to the market value of the stock.

9.6.2   Surplus

Surplus is the net amount of funds that have been formally transferred to this account as a result of capital contributions and any amount received for common stock and perpetual preferred stock in excess of par value. The allocation to the surplus account is a bookkeeping entry and does not affect financial performance. This capital account is more pertinent for various legal and accounting requirements than for understanding the capital base of the bank. For example, the surplus account is considered part of permanent or legal capital in virtually all states and is not returned to owners through cash dividends or purchase of their shares unless creditor claims are adequately protected. In order to provide some measure of protection to creditors, most states designate a minimum level of permanent capital. From an accounting standpoint, the surplus account is used to keep track of this permanent capital and to meet various state incorporation laws. From a valuation and financial analysis standpoint, the delineation between aggregate par value and surplus is not important.

9.6.3 Undivided Profits

The undivided profits of a bank are the accumulated net income, gains, and losses less dividend distributions to shareholders and amounts transferred to the surplus account. The undivided profits account increases through net income, including any extraordinary gains. This account can decrease through net losses, including extraordinary losses, and dividends paid to shareholders. The issuance or retirement of stock does not affect the undivided profits accounts. These transactions affect the surplus account as described above.

9.6.4 Capital Reserves

The last component of equity capital is capital reserves or accounts established to prepare for future uses such as:

- reserves for undeclared dividends, either stock or cash (although each would have a separate reserve account);
- retirement of limited life preferred stock or notes and debentures subordinated to deposits, if the issues called for such a reserve; and
- reserves for contingencies such as lawsuits or other claims against the bank.

Capital reserves are in reality segregations of the retained earnings account and normally do not show on publicly available financial data as separate items. Therefore, without access to a bank's internal records, it may be hard to determine the existence of special capital reserves. From a valuation standpoint, separating out capital reserves is not of critical importance.

9.7 REGULATORY CAPITAL COMPONENTS

Banking regulators take a much more complex view of capital than the simple accounting definition described above. The details of regulatory capital and definitions of components vary from time to time, but the major elements are consistent. The discussion below is based on regulations in effect as of April 2000.

Regulators categorize bank and bank holding company capital as core capital elements (Tier 1), supplement capital elements (Tier 2), and total capital (Tier 1 plus Tier 2) for risk-based capital purposes described in Chapter 4. The components of each tier differ slightly between banks and bank holding companies. Each is discussed below separately.

9.7.1 Capital Components—Banks

The foundation components for banks to use for Tier 1 capital are the following:

- Common stock
- Surplus

- Undivided profits (also called retained earnings)
- Capital reserves
- Cumulative foreign currency translation adjustments
- Minority interest in consolidated subsidiaries
- Perpetual preferred stock that is noncumulative (means that if dividends are not paid they do not accumulate to the next period)
- Mortgage servicing rights up to 50 percent of Tier 1 capital
- Purchased credit card relationships up to 25 percent of Tier 1 capital
- Intangible assets that have been grandfathered for regulatory capital purposes

Items that must be subtracted from the above components to calculate Tier 1 capital are:

- Intangible assets
- Unrealized holding losses in the available-for-sale equity portfolio
- Deferred tax assets disallowed for regulatory capital purposes

Tier 1 capital represents the highest form of capital and is generally defined as the sum of core capital elements less intangible assets including goodwill, unrealized holding losses in the available-for-sale equity portfolio, and any investment in subsidiaries that the Federal Reserve determines should be deducted from Tier 1 capital.

Tier 2 capital includes these components:

- Allowance for loan and lease losses, up to 1.25 percent of gross risk-weighted assets
- Perpetual preferred stock not qualifying as Tier 1 capital
- Mandatory convertible debt, net of common or preferred stock, set aside to redeem such debt
- Subordinated debt, intermediate term preferred stock, and other limited-life capital instruments with value qualifying as Tier 2 capital based upon remaining maturity:

Over five years:	100% qualifies
Four to five years:	80% qualifies
Three to four years:	60% qualifies
Two to three years:	40% qualifies
One to two years:	20% qualifies
Under one year:	0% qualifies

- Intermediate-term preferred stock
- Unrealized holding gains on qualifying equity securities

Total regulatory capital in a bank is simply Tier 1 plus Tier 2 capital, with the restriction that Tier 2 may account for no more than 50 percent of total capital. The sum of Tier 1 and Tier 2 capital less any deductions makes up total capital, which is the numerator of the risk-based capital ratio discussed in Chapter 4. Bank's risk-based capital ratio is the ratio of qualifying capital to assets and off-balance-sheet items that have been "risk weighted" based on perceived credit risk.

9.7.2 Capital Components—Bank Holding Companies

For a bank holding company (BHC), the foundation components of Tier 1 capital are these:

- Total equity capital
- Minority interests in consolidated subsidiaries
- Intangible assets recorded before February 19, 1992, except goodwill, purchased mortgage servicing rights, and purchased credit card relationships

From these amounts, the following items must be subtracted to calculate Tier 1 capital for a BHC:

- Auction rate preferred stock and any other perpetual preferred stock deemed by the Federal Reserve to be eligible for Tier 2 capital only
- Cumulative preferred stock in excess of 25 percent of Tier 1 capital
- Goodwill
- Identified intangible assets recorded February 19, 1992 or later
- Purchased credit card relationships in excess of 25 percent of Tier 1 capital
- Mortgage servicing rights plus purchased credit card relationships in excess of 50 percent of Tier 1 capital

Components eligible for Tier 2 regulatory capital in a BHC include:

- Intermediate preferred stock with a weighted average maturity of five years or more, subordinated debt with a weighted average maturity of five years or more, and subordinated debt with an original maturity of five years or more based on the remaining term of the instrument:

Over five years:	100% qualifies
Four to five years:	80% qualifies
Three to four years:	60% qualifies
Two to three years:	40% qualifies
One to two years:	20% qualifies
Under one year:	0% qualifies

- Unsecured long-term debt issued by the BHC prior to March 12, 1988, with the remaining time to maturity impacting the percent that qualifies as Tier 2 capital:

Over five years to maturity:	100% qualifies
Four to five years to maturity:	80% qualifies
Three to four years to maturity:	60% qualifies
Two to three years to maturity:	40% qualifies
One to two years to maturity:	20% qualifies
Under one year to maturity:	0% qualifies

- Auction rate preferred stock and any other perpetual preferred stock deemed by the Federal Reserve to be eligible for Tier 2 capital only

- Cumulative perpetual preferred stock in excess of 25 percent of core capital
- Total perpetual debt
- Mandatory convertible securities, both equity contract notes and equity commitment notes
- Long-term preferred stock based upon remaining term to maturity:

Over five years:	100% qualifies
Four to five years:	80% qualifies
Three to four years:	60% qualifies
Two to three years:	40% qualifies
One to two years:	20% qualifies
Under one year:	0% qualifies

- Allowance for loan and lease losses, up to 1.25 percent of gross risk-weighted assets, limited to 100% of Tier 1 capital amount

From these Tier 2 qualifying amounts for BHCs, these must be subtracted:

- Common or perpetual preferred stock set aside to retire or redeem outstanding equity contract notes or equity commitment notes
- Capital investments in unconsolidated companies controlled by the BHC
- Reciprocal holdings of banking organizations' capital instruments

9.8 RISK-BASED CAPITAL

In evaluating the financial strength of a bank or bank holding company, regulators evaluate the capital level (Tier 1 and Tier 2 as described above) relative to risk-weighted assets. The calculation of risk-weighted assets is done to reflect the fact that not all assets are of the same risk of loss and, therefore, do not need the same capital cushion.

In calculating risk-weighted assets, the "true" assets on the balance sheet and off-balance sheet items are assigned a risk weight of 100 percent, 50 percent, 20 percent, or zero percent. Total risk-weighted assets is the sum of all assets and off-balance sheet asset equivalents times their respective risk weight.

The major balance sheet items that have a zero percent risk weighting (that is, riskless and not requiring capital) are:

- Cash
- Federal Reserve Bank balances
- U.S. Government guaranteed debt
- U.S. Government securities
- Book value of paid-in-stock at the Federal Reserve Bank

Significant items that have a 20 percent risk weight are:

- Cash items in process of collection
- Claims on domestic and OECD banks
- Claims on any other bank maturing in less than one year
- Claims guaranteed by U.S. financial institutions
- Securities issued or guaranteed by U.S. Government agencies, and state and local governments
- Portions of loans or other assets collateralized by securities issued by U.S. Government agencies, U.S. Treasury, OECD countries, or cash
- Local currency claims on foreign central governments up to value of local liabilities in that country
- Privately issued mortgage-backed securities representing indirect ownership or mortgage-related U.S. Government agency or U.S. Government sponsored agency
- Portion of securities and loans conditionally guaranteed by the U.S. Government

The 50 percent risk-weight assets are:

- U.S. state or local government revenue bonds or similar securities
- Residential real estate mortgage loans representing first liens on 1–4 family dwellings
- Credit equivalent amounts on interest rate and foreign exchange rate contracts, unless assigned to a lower risk-weighting category

The 100 percent risk-weight assets are:

- Loans and other claims on private obligors except residential real estate first liens
- Claims on non-OECD banks with over one year maturity
- Claims on foreign central governments not included elsewhere
- Obligations of state and local governments repayable solely by a private party or enterprise
- Fixed assets
- Investments in unconsolidated subsidiaries, joint ventures, or associated companies (if not deducted from capital)
- Instruments used by other banking organizations that qualify as capital
- All other tangible or intangible assets not deducted from capital

Off-balance sheet items are also taken into account in calculating regulatory capital requirements. These off-balance sheet items also carry a 100 percent, 50 percent, 20 percent, or zero percent weighting.

The off-balance sheet items with a zero percent risk weight are unused commitments with original maturity under one year or which can be unconditionally cancelled at any time.

The only 20 percent weighted items are short-term, self-liquidating, trade-related contingencies which arise from the movement of goods.

Exhibit 9.3   Illustration of Calculation of Risk-Weighted Assets

Balance Sheet	Book Value	Weight	Risk-Weighted Amount
Cash and Equivalents	$ 100	0%	$ 0
Cash Items	200	20%	40
Securities	700	20%	140
Revenue Bonds	50	50%	25
Residential Mortgage Loans	500	50%	250
Other Loans	2,000	100%	2,000
Revenues and Fixed Assets	60	100%	60
Other Real Estate Owned	12	100%	12
Other Assets	78	100%	78
	$3,700		$2,605

Off-Balance Sheet	Notional Value	Conversion Factor	Balance Sheet Equivalent
Loan Commitments			
(under 1 year)	$ 100	100%	$ 100
Standby Commitments	160	100%	160
Loan Commitments			
(over 1 year)	80	50%	40
	$ 340		$ 300
	Total Risk-Weighted Assets		$2,905

The 50 percent weighted items are:

- Transaction-related contingencies
- Unused commitments with original maturity over one year
- Revolving underwriting facilities and not issuance facilities where the borrower can issue short-term paper in its own name on a revolving basis and the underwriting banks have a legally binding commitment to either purchase notes not sold by the borrower or to advance funds to the borrower

The 100 percent weighted items are:

- Direct credit substitutes
- Sales and repurchase agreements and asset sales with recourse not already on the balance sheet
- Principal amount of assets to be purchased as part of forward agreements
- Securities lent where bank is at risk

An example of calculating risk-weighted assets is shown in Exhibit 9.3.

In determining the capital adequacy of a bank or BHC, the risk-adjusted capital ratio is calculated. In general, regulators look for at least an eight percent total risk-adjusted capital ratio. The ratio is calculated as:

- Bank total risk-adjusted capital ratio:

$$\frac{\text{Total capital (Tier 1 and Tier 2)}}{\begin{array}{l}\text{Gross risk-weighted assets—loan and}\\ \text{lease loss allowance over 1.25\% of risk-weighted}\\ \text{assets—allocated transfer risk reserve}\end{array}}$$

- BHC total risk-adjusted capital ratio:

$$\frac{\text{Total capital (Tier 1 and Tier 2)}}{\begin{array}{l}\text{Gross risk-weighted assets—mortgage servicing}\\ \text{rights over 50\% of Tier 1 capital—purchased credit}\\ \text{card relationships over 25\% of Tier 1 capital—}\\ \text{all other identified intangible assets—goodwill—loan}\\ \text{and lease loss allowance over 1.25\% of risk-weighted}\\ \text{assets—allocated transfer risk reserve}\end{array}}$$

The valuation implications of these capital requirements is that the required annual contribution of capital from earnings must be sufficient enough to maintain at least the regulatory minimums.

9.9 VALUE-AT-RISK (VAR) MODELS

Banks' regulatory capital changes and requirements for the market risk exposure in the United States are in conformity with an amendment to the 1988 Basle Capital Accord. Currently, the three methods employed in determining regulatory capital changes for market risk exposure[1] are: standardized approach, precommitment approach, and internal models. The standardized approach is based on standard risk management procedures consistent with regulatory rules that assign capital charges to specific assets in estimating the selected portfolio effect on banks' risk exposure. The precommitment approach suggested by the Federal Reserve Board of Governors is another method that can be used. The third method is based on banks' internal models utilizing the standardized regulatory parameters of a ten-day holding period and 99 percent coverage.

Recently commercial banks have used time-series Value-at-Risk (VAR) models to determine their regulatory capital requirements for market exposure.[2] VAR estimates, generated by banks' internal VAR models, are forecasts of the maximum portfolio value that could be lost over the specified time horizon with a specified precision and confidence level. VAR estimates are crucial and relevant to banks and their regulators in assessing regulatory capital requirements. Thus, the reliability of these forecasts and the accuracy of their underlying VAR models are essential.

Bank regulators have utilized four statistical methods, suggested in the literature[3,4] for assessing the accuracy and reliability of VAR models. Banks often report their specified VAR internal estimates to the regulators who assess whether the trading losses are less than or greater than these estimates. This regulatory assessment is conducted by evaluating VAR estimates based on (1) the binomial distribution; (2) internal forecasts; (3) distribution forecasts; and/or (4) probability forecasts. These statistical assessment methods determine whether the VAR forecasts in question exhibit a specified property of accurate VAR forecasts using a hypothesis-testing concept. The binomial distribution assessment method is based on the assumption that the VAR estimates are independent across time and determined from independent binomial random variables. The VAR interval forecasts valuation method considers VAR estimates as interval forecasts of the lower left-hand interval at a specified probability level. The VAR distribution forecasts assessment method determines whether the observed quantities derived under the interval model's distribution forecasts exhibit the properties of observed quantities from accurate distribution forecasts. The VAR probability forecasts evaluation method is based on standard forecast evaluation tools that measure the accuracy of VAR interval models in terms of how well their generated probability forecasts of specified regulatory actions minimize a loss function relevant to regulators. The loss functions relevant to regulators are determined based on proper scoring rules of probability forecasts.

9.10   COMPOSITION OF BANK INCOME

The income of a bank is primarily derived from interest and fees. Interest income is earned from various earning assets (for example, loans and investments) while fee income can be a result of many different activities (such as service charges, safe deposit box rental, foreign exchange transactions, and trust fees). Larger banks can also generate significant income through trading gains.

9.10.1   Interest Income

Interest income represents about 90 percent of gross income of all banks in the United States and about 85 percent of bank holding company income. Nearly two-thirds of that amount is derived from loans. The bank call reports identify interest income from these sources:

- loans to businesses, individuals, and governments;
- lease financing receivables;
- deposit accounts at other financial institutions;
- treasury and U.S. agencies securities;
- other municipal securities;
- other domestic securities (debt and equity);
- foreign securities;
- assets held in trading accounts; and
- Fed funds sold and securities purchased under agreements to resell.

Every earning asset on the balance sheet generates some level of income. In general, the income associated with an earning asset is equal to:

$$\text{interest income from earning asset} =$$
$$\text{average balance of earning asset} \times \text{interest rate on earning asset}$$

If an earning asset has an average balance during the year of $1,000 at a rate of 9 percent, about $90 in income for the year would result. It is "about" $90 because there are different techniques of accruing interest income, especially on loans. For example, the "rule of 78s" is a technique for recognizing interest income that gives slightly greater interest in the early periods. Therefore, if the example used above is a $1,000 loan at 9 percent that is being accrued by the rule of 78s, the income earned may be slightly over $90 in the early years, and slightly less than $90 later on. On average, however, the formula used above is a good approximation of interest income based on the level of earning assets.

9.10.2 Noninterest Income

The noninterest income of a bank is reported in these categories:

- income from fiduciary (trust) activities;
- service charges on deposit accounts;
- securities gains and losses;
- trading gains and fees from foreign exchange transactions;
- other foreign transaction gains (or losses);
- gains (or losses) and fees from assets held in trading accounts; and
- other noninterest income.

The last category, other noninterest income, covers a wide variety of income generating activities including:

- fees for services provided to others (such as data and correspondent services);
- safe deposit box rentals;
- gains on sale of assets;
- all service charges, commissions, and fees not related to deposit accounts and foreign exchange transactions;
- rental income;
- credit card fees; and
- teller overages.

The relationship is indirect between the magnitude of noninterest income and the size of the balance sheet. Some banks are more fee-oriented than others. On average, noninterest income represents about 8 percent of gross income (interest income plus all other income) of all U.S. banks. In the largest banks (with over $10 billion in assets), noninterest income represents over 15 percent of gross income. In general, smaller banks have greater reliance on interest income rather than fees and service charges.

The area of securities gains (or losses) is one that should be examined carefully in a bank, especially in times of volatile investment markets. Because banks hold securities in their investment portfolio, there is buying and selling of such securities as a normal part of the financial management of the institution. When securities are bought there is always the possibility that a gain (or loss) over the carrying value will be realized if the security is ultimately sold. This can be a relatively unpredictable part of the bank's income, especially if it holds long-term investments in its portfolio. In general, however, securities gains represent a very small portion of a bank's gross income.

9.10.3 Extraordinary Gains (Losses)

Like any business, banks can realize nonrecurring gains or losses on transactions that are unusual and infrequent. Both the unusual and infrequent criteria must be met for a transaction to be classified as extraordinary. To be unusual, an event or transaction must be highly abnormal or obviously unrelated to the normal operations of the bank. To be infrequent, the event or transaction should not be reasonably expected to recur in the foreseeable future.

The rules are very strict for reporting a gain or loss as extraordinary. If a bank sells an asset, for example a branch office, and realizes a gain (that is, if sales proceeds exceed book value), the amount would not be considered an extraordinary gain even if the bank had never before sold a branch. Such a transaction would not pass the unusual test because banks buy and sell branches routinely, even though that particular bank had not done so in the past. If, however, a natural disaster destroyed a branch, thus causing a net loss, this amount would be an extraordinary loss and would be reported as such. Such an occurrence would be defined as both unusual and infrequent.

As would be expected, extraordinary items are an insignificant portion of all bank incomes, less than 0.1 percent of total income. However, for a given bank during a given year the impact can be significant.

9.11 COMPOSITION OF BANK EXPENSES

The expenses incurred by a bank or bank holding company usually fall into four main categories:

1. interest expense—paid on deposits and other sources of funds;
2. noninterest expense—normal expenditures for personnel, facilities and other overhead, amortization expense, and all other functional expenses which are not related to interest, loan losses or taxes;
3. provision for loan and lease losses and allocated transfer risk—set aside in anticipation of losses from loans; and
4. taxes—on income at federal, state, and local level as applicable.

Interest expense constitutes about 54 percent of total expenses; noninterest expenses, 38 percent; provisions for loan and lease losses and allocated transfer risk, 4 percent; and taxes, 4 percent.

9.11.1 Interest Expense

The interest expenses of a bank reflect the price paid to attract and keep funds. The annual interest expense associated with a liability is equal to the average balance of that liability during a year multiplied by the annual interest rate. The most significant funding source is customer deposits, which represent about 97 percent of all bank liabilities. The expenses associated with these deposits are segregated into two groups:

- interest on certificates of deposit of $100,000 or more (jumbo CDs), and public funds; and
- interest on other deposits.

This separation is made because jumbo CDs and public funds usually are not considered to be core deposits, and it is beneficial to separate the cost of attracting these more volatile funds.

The next major interest expense category is expenses of Fed funds purchased and securities sold under agreements to repurchase. Expenses in this category reflect the cost of borrowing short-term funds from other banks to meet reserve requirements.

Interest on demand notes issued to U.S. Treasury and other borrowed money is the third category of interest expense. The costs in this area are a result of normal borrowings of a bank that do not fall into other categories, as well as the cost of demand notes (part of the Treasury Tax and Loan program described earlier in this chapter).

Any interest paid by the bank on mortgage indebtedness and capitalized leases is also shown separately on the income statement. The interest portion of a mortgage payment (for example on funds borrowed to build a branch) would be determined by the amortization schedule of the debt. On a capitalized lease, the interest payment is imputed from the total lease payment. In other words, the capitalized lease is viewed as financing and is reported as such, with a portion of the lease payment imputed to interest and a portion to equivalent principal reduction.

The last category of interest expense is interest on notes and debentures subordinated to deposits. These costs reflect the issuance of such debt instruments by the bank. Included with these costs are the fees incurred to issue the notes, amortized over the life of the note.

9.11.2 Noninterest Expense

The noninterest expenses of a bank include operating and overhead expenses. The major classification of expenses are salary and employee benefits, premises and fixed asset expense, and other noninterest expenses.

The expense category of salary and employee benefits includes virtually all costs associated with the staff: salaries, overtime pay, bonuses, social security, unemployment tax, insurance, pension plans, and other direct employee benefits. The only employee-related expenses not included are training and professional organization dues, which are both included in other noninterest expense.

Premises and fixed asset expenses include the costs associated with the operation and maintenance of facilities, equipment, vehicles, furniture, and fixtures used by the bank in the normal course of business. Both direct out-of-pocket costs and depreciation expenses are included in this category. Expenses associated with property owned by the bank, but not used in the normal course of business, such as foreclosed real estate, are included in other noninterest expenses.

Other noninterest expense is a catchall category for expenses not applicable elsewhere. Examples of expenses in this category include:

- director fees;
- fidelity insurance premiums;
- regulatory assessment fees;
- legal and other professional fees;
- net losses on sale of assets;
- expenses associated with ORE;
- management fees paid to parent bank holding company;
- intangible asset amortization;
- advertising and public relations fees;
- office supplies and telephone; and
- data processing.

9.11.3   Provision for Loan and Lease Losses and Allocated Transfer Risk

The provision for loan and lease losses and allocated transfer risk is an expense item in that it is a charge against current income. The allocated transfer risk is a reserve for bad loans made to certain countries that appear unable to resume debt repayment. This is a minor expense item even for large international banks.

The amount of the provision for normal loans and leases is based on anticipated losses on loans, including any accrued, but unpaid, interest. When a provision for a loan loss is made, the destination of the expense is the loan loss reserve described earlier in this chapter in the asset discussion. Any subsequent actual loan charge-off is applied against the loan loss reserve, never directly against retained earnings. Conversely, recoveries of loans previously charged off are credited to the loan loss reserve.

The provision for loan loss expense is an item that is reported differently for accounting and income tax purposes (where it is called reserve for bad debts). The difference is referred to as a *timing difference*. The tax effect of such a timing difference is accounted for and reported as a deferred income tax credit or debit on the income statement, and in the balance sheet as an other liability (if a credit balance) or an other asset (if a debit balance). Any difference between the bank's loan loss reserve and its reserve for bad debts for tax purposes can be eliminated only through subsequent differences between the bad debt deduction for taxes and the provision for loan losses.

9.11.4   Income Taxes

The last category of expenses is income tax at federal, state, and local levels. The income tax expense shown in a bank's call report is the applicable income tax of the bank based on the reported income. The calculation of the actual income tax liability to be paid is based on rules prescribed in the regulations of the various taxing authorities. These rules are usually different from those used to prepare call reports. Therefore, the tax liability arising from the pretax income on a call report will probably be different from the actual taxes paid. The differences arise from two primary sources:

- *Timing differences* caused when a bank reports an item of income or expense in one period for call report purposes but in another period for income tax purposes. An example is a bank that uses straight-line depreciation for book purposes and accelerated depreciation for tax purposes. The total depreciation is the same, but the reported amount in any one period will be different because of timing.
- *Permanent differences* caused when a bank reports an item of income or expense for call report purposes that will never be reported for tax purposes. An example is goodwill amortization, which is an expense for book purposes but not for tax purposes.

The income tax figures reported in a bank's call report are generally determined by these steps:

1. Determine income before taxes and extraordinary items and other adjustments (equal to total bank income less interest expense less noninterest expenses less provision for loan loss).
2. Adjust for any permanent differences in book versus tax income by adding back expense items not eligible for tax deductions (e.g., amortization of goodwill and premiums paid on officer life insurance where the bank is the beneficiary) and subtracting income not taxable (e.g., qualifying municipal bond interest and 85 percent of cash dividends received on the stock of U.S. corporations).
3. Apply the combined federal, state, and local income tax rates to the results of steps one and two.
4. Reduce the amount from step three by any tax credits expected to be taken on the bank's tax return.

The resulting figure in step four is the applicable income tax line on a bank's call report. If this figure is different from the actual taxes to be paid by the bank during the year, the difference is shown as deferred portion of applicable income taxes. If applicable taxes are less than actual taxes, the deferred portion is a debit balance and is carried in other assets, subject to certain limitations. If the applicable taxes are greater, it is a credit balance and carried as an other liability.

9.12   BALANCE SHEET ANALYSIS ILLUSTRATION

A key component in the understanding of a bank for valuation purposes is the analysis of historical balance sheet trends. This is an important part of the financial analysis and is essential to establishing value accurately. The primary sources of balance sheet data are the call reports, the UBPR, and other internal reports as available.

Exhibit 9.4 shows the balance sheet items and selected ratios for *Example Bank*. The analysis described in the balance of this chapter is based on these statistics. These statistics were used in the example of valuation by the income approach described in Chapter 14.

Exhibit 9.4 Example Bank Balance Sheet Summary ($000)

	1999	1998	1997	1996	1995	1994
Assets						
Cash & Due Froms						
Noninterest Bearing	$ 26,992	$ 20,991	$ 24,096	$ 22,122	$ 19,577	$ 18,306
Interest Bearing	8,972	6,390	2,509	10,120	2,450	1,309
Subtotal Cash & Due Froms	35,964	27,381	26,605	32,242	22,027	21,615
Securities	70,309	58,345	52,700	38,264	36,658	32,129
Fed Funds Sold & Securities Purchased	2,786	2,596	7,189	18,609	14,709	12,064
Total Loans	266,235	243,665	214,201	171,553	143,707	121,350
(Loan Loss Reserve)	2,879	2,559	2,180	1,554	1,398	998
Net Loans	263,356	241,106	212,021	169,999	142,309	120,352
Trading Account Assets	0	0	0	0	0	0
Premises & Fixed Assets	5,885	6,214	5,816	5,131	4,718	5,237
Other Real Estate Owned	854	332	529	450	717	834
Intangible Assets	2,423	2,524	2,971	3,321	3,488	2,888
Other Assets	6,629	4,587	6,805	3,794	3,409	4,117
Total Assets	$388,206	$343,085	$314,636	$271,810	$228,035	$197,236
Liabilities						
Deposit of Customers						
Demand Deposits	$ 67,947	$ 67,264	$ 78,121	$ 62,271	$ 59,974	$ 45,677
Other Transaction Deposits	21,330	18,475	17,606	11,780	12,030	21,223
MMDA Savings	60,699	47,827	54,573	47,541	27,623	15,083
Other Savings	14,617	12,659	10,565	8,413	8,669	7,328
CDs Under $100,000	53,302	44,937	34,679	34,863	32,258	29,853
Subtotal Core Deposits	217,895	191,162	195,544	164,868	140,554	119,164
Other Deposits	54,538	45,149	35,018	33,364	30,586	27,851
Total Deposits	272,433	236,311	230,562	198,232	171,140	147,015

Fed Funds Purchased & Securities Sold	85,491	78,047	50,240	39,478	33,845	28,650
Other Borrowed Money	132	141	3,403	4,569	160	113
Mortgages & Capitalized Leases	1,249	1,269	1,299	1,304	1,271	1,195
Subordinated Notes & Debentures	798	827	935	960	1,010	1,123
Other Liabilities	6,530	7,001	10,662	10,878	7,186	6,903
Total Liabilities	$366,633	$323,596	$297,061	$255,691	$214,612	$184,999
Limited Life Preferred Stock	0	0	0	0	0	0
Equity Capital	21,573	19,489	17,575	16,119	13,423	12,237
Total Liabilities and Equity Capital	$388,206	$343,085	$314,636	$271,810	$228,035	$197,236
As Percent of Assets						
Net Loans						
Bank	67.8%	70.3%	67.4%	62.5%	62.4%	61.0%
Peer	55.0%	54.2%	56.2%	54.6%	52.1%	52.7%
Investments						
Bank	21.1%	19.6%	19.8%	24.7%	23.6%	25.1%
Peer	21.9%	22.2%	23.0%	24.3%	26.4%	26.0%
Premises and Fixed Assets						
Bank	1.5%	1.8%	1.9%	1.9%	2.0%	2.2%
Peer	1.8%	1.8%	1.8%	1.8%	1.9%	2.0%
Other Real Estate Owned						
Bank	0.22%	0.10%	0.17%	0.17%	0.31%	0.42%
Peer	0.55%	0.51%	0.39%	0.28%	0.25%	0.18%
Earning Assets						
Bank	89.9%	87.2%	87.2%	86.0%	86.1%	84.1%
Peer	89.5%	89.4%	89.5%	89.5%	89.0%	88.6%
Loan Loss Reserve						
Bank	0.74%	0.75%	0.69%	0.57%	0.61%	0.51%
Peer	0.71%	0.70%	0.70%	0.61%	0.61%	0.60%

Exhibit 9.4 (*Continued*)

	1999	1998	1997	1996	1995	1994
Core Deposits						
Bank	56.3%	55.7%	62.2%	60.6%	61.6%	60.4%
Peer	69.8%	70.9%	70.5%	69.1%	69.8%	65.1%
Demand and Transaction Deposits						
Bank	23.0%	25.0%	30.4%	27.2%	31.6%	33.9%
Peer	23.2%	24.4%	26.0%	26.5%	26.2%	26.4%
MMDA and Other Savings						
Bank	19.4%	17.0%	20.7%	20.6%	15.9%	11.4%
Peer	24.9%	23.0%	21.3%	19.6%	19.7%	11.8%
CDs < $100,000						
Bank	13.7%	13.1%	11.0%	12.8%	14.2%	15.1%
Peer	21.0%	21.8%	23.2%	23.5%	23.7%	26.3%
Capital Composition						
Common Equity	$21,573	$19,489	$17,575	$16,119	$13,423	$12,237
Loan Loss Reserve	2,879	2,559	2,180	1,554	1,398	998
Permanent and Conv. Preferred	0	0	0	0	0	0
Total Primary Capital	$24,452	$22,048	$19,755	$17,673	$14,821	$13,235
Changes in Common Equity						
Balance-Beginning of Year	$19,489	$17,575	$16,119	$13,423	$12,237	$10,953

Net Income	3,007	2,729	2,394	1,605	1,142	1,724
(Cash Dividends)	(923)	(815)	(938)	(409)	(456)	(440)
Other Changes (New Capital)	0	0	0	1,500	500	0
Balance-End of Year	$21,573	$19,489	$17,575	$16,119	$13,423	$12,237

Capital Ratios

Primary Capital/Assets

Bank	6.3%	6.4%	6.3%	6.5%	6.5%	6.7%
Peer	8.0%	8.0%	8.1%	7.9%	7.9%	8.1%

Equity/Assets

Bank	5.6%	5.7%	5.6%	5.9%	5.9%	6.2%
Peer	7.0%	7.1%	7.5%	7.5%	7.5%	7.7%

Net Income/Average Equity

Bank	14.7%	14.7%	14.2%	10.9%	8.9%	15.6%
Peer	10.1%	9.9%	13.9%	14.6%	14.5%	14.7%

Dividends/Average Equity

Bank	4.5%	4.4%	5.6%	2.8%	3.6%	3.8%
Peer	6.1%	6.5%	7.2%	6.4%	6.4%	6.2%

Dividends/Net Income

Bank	30.7%	29.9%	39.2%	25.5%	39.9%	25.5%
Peer	55.2%	65.6%	51.8%	43.8%	44.1%	42.1%

Exhibit 9.5   Example Bank Asset Growth Rates

	Change in Total Assets
1994–1995	15.6%
1995–1996	19.2%
1996–1997	15.7%
1997–1998	9.0%
1998–1999	13.1%
Compounded 1994–1999	14.5%

9.12.1   Asset Growth Rates

Example Bank's total assets have grown rapidly from $197 million at year end 1994 to over $388 million at year end 1999. The year-to-year increases are shown in Exhibit 9.5. This rate of growth has generally been consistent with the bank's aggressive philosophy, especially in the lending areas. While asset growth averaged 14.5 percent compounded annually, loans grew at over 17 percent each year. When valuing Example Bank it would probably be overly optimistic to assume such growth could continue. This is especially true given the fact that much of the asset growth was supported by funding other than core deposits (as discussed later).

9.12.2   Asset Composition

From 1994 to 1999 loans consistently increased as a percent of total assets; from 61.0 percent to 70.3 percent. In 1999, however, that ratio declined to 67.8 percent reflecting a more conservative balance sheet management policy. Also, Example Bank has improved on its noninterest bearing cash and due froms, reducing to 6.9 percent of assets in 1999 from 8.3 percent in 1994. In general Example Bank has significantly reduced its level of nonearning assets relative to total assets between 1994 and 1999, from 13.9 percent of assets to 11.0 percent.

9.12.3   Asset Composition—Peer Group Comparison

Also shown in Exhibit 9.4 are various ratios for Example Bank and a peer comparison. From these statistics it is clear that the bank is an aggressive lender; 68 percent of its assets are in loans versus 55 percent for peers. Most of the other asset categories are generally consistent with the peer group, except Example Bank appears to have less of an REO problem.

The one area where Example Bank compares unfavorably is in its funding base; core deposits are significantly lower than its peers on a percentage of deposits basis, as are smaller CDs. The danger sign is that the bank may be susceptible to volatile funding costs. The rapid growth in assets was funded by a variety of liabilities which are not necessarily stable.

This potential weakness in the balance sheet must be considered in the valuation process.

9.12.4   Liability Growth Rates

Between 1994 and 1999, liabilities at Example Bank grew at a 14.7 percent compounded annual rate. Core deposits grew at a 12.8 percent rate, while other deposits increased at 14.4 percent per year on average. Other interest-bearing liabilities grew at a 23 percent rate, further indicating the bank's reliance on volatile funding sources.

9.12.5   Liability Composition

Example Bank's liabilities are clearly oriented toward customer deposits, although that orientation has decreased in recent years. At year end 1999, 74.3 percent of all the bank's liabilities were in customer deposits, and 59.4 percent in core deposits. The other major category of liabilities is Fed Funds Purchased and Securities Sold with Repurchase Agreements, accounting for 23.3 percent of liabilities in 1999 versus 15.5 percent in 1994.

9.12.6   Liability Composition—Peer Group Comparison

Example Bank has relied more on volatile funding sources during the past few years than has its peers. This is evidenced by the fact that core deposits are lower as a percent of assets at the bank than for the peer group. Within the core deposit base, Example Bank tends to have a much lower small CD base than its peers.

9.12.7   Capital Levels and Trends

Despite fairly good levels of net income, Example Bank's equity and primary capital position declined slightly between 1994 and 1999. This has been a direct result of the rapid growth in the asset base, which has made it more difficult to grow capital at the same rate.

In general, Example Bank has been adequately capitalized since 1994, but below peer group averages on a capital ratio basis. However, good income growth has enabled the bank to grow the absolute level of capital at an impressive rate; 12 percent per year between 1994 and 1999. Net income to average equity has been above peer group averages, except for down years in 1995 and 1996. The price for internal generation of capital has been a low level of dividends. Dividends paid have been below peer averages, measured by both dividends to average equity and dividends as a percent of net income. From 1994 to 1999, Example Bank paid dividends equal to 31.7 percent of net income, whereas peer groups averaged 50.4 percent of net income—60 percent more.

9.13   INCOME STATEMENT AND PROFITABILITY ANALYSIS ILLUSTRATION

Once the trends and composition of the balance sheet have been analyzed, the next analysis focuses on the income statement and related measures of profitability. The purpose of this analysis is to understand fully the sources and nature of all income and expenses. Each major type of analysis needed for valuation is described below. Exhibit 9.6 presents income statement components and summaries.

Exhibit 9.6 Example Bank Income and Expense Summary ($000s)

	1999	1998	1997	1996	1995	1994
Interest & Fees-Loans & Leases						
Real Estate Loans	$11,207	$8,883	$6,627	$4,690	$3,654	$3,590
Loans to Individuals	5,088	5,119	5,868	5,658	5,532	5,426
Commercial Loans	14,027	11,989	10,411	9,913	9,114	8,920
All Other Loans	0	0	0	0	0	0
Leases	393	368	217	278	237	331
Subtotal Loans & Leases	$30,714	$26,358	$23,124	$20,539	$18,537	$18,267
Interest & Fees-Investments						
Balances at Other Institutions	$483	$207	$233	$376	$345	$233
Securities	4,636	4,247	3,240	2,790	2,767	2,234
Fed Funds Sold	69	206	597	895	693	503
Other Investments	92	77	75	73	160	94
Subtotal Investments	$5,280	$4,737	$4,145	$4,134	$3,965	$3,054
Interest Income-Other	$0	$0	$0	$0	$0	$0
Total Interest Income:						
Actual As Reported	$35,994	$31,095	$27,269	$24,673	$22,502	$21,321
Memo: Tax Equivalent (TE)	$36,401	$31,561	$27,990	$25,618	$23,589	$22,119
Interest Expense—Deposits						
Transaction Accounts	$1,445	$1,385	$1,304	$1,248	$1,148	$1,031
MMDAs	5,109	4,205	3,960	3,792	3,485	3,232
Other Savings	1,109	957	902	863	794	713
CDs Under $100,000	5,843	4,443	4,986	4,763	4,077	3,492
CDs Over $100,000	3,724	3,160	2,521	2,420	2,395	2,307
Other Deposits	0	0	0	0	0	0
Subtotal Deposits	$17,229	$14,149	$13,672	$13,085	$11,897	$10,774

Interest Expense-Other					
Fed Funds Purchased	$ 5,672	$ 2,678	$ 2,541	$ 3,077	$ 2,911
Other Borrowed Money	42	137	32	18	23
Mortgages & Capitalized Leases	109	108	101	71	55
Subordinated Notes/Debentures	59	71	74	75	69
Subtotal Others	$ 5,882	$ 2,994	$ 2,748	$ 3,241	$ 3,058
Total Interest Expense	$23,111	$16,666	$15,833	$15,138	$13,832
Net Interest Income:					
Actual As Reported	$12,883	$10,603	$ 8,840	$ 7,364	$ 7,489
Memo: Tax Equivalent (TE)	$13,290	$11,324	$ 9,785	$ 8,451	$ 8,287
Loan Loss Provision	$ 1,377	$ 1,251	$ 809	$ 400	$ 539
Net Interest Income After Loan Loss Provision					
Actual As Reported	$11,506	$ 9,352	$ 8,031	$ 6,964	$ 6,950
Memo: Tax Equivalent (TE)	11,913	10,073	8,976	8,051	7,748
Noninterest Income					
Fiduciary Activities	$ 599	$ 441	$ 356	$ 293	$ 204
Service Charges	2,427	1,796	1,595	1,367	1,123
Trading Gains (Losses)	0	0	0	0	0
Other Noninterest Income	2,648	2,349	1,995	1,098	683
Total Noninterest Income	$ 5,193	$ 4,586	$ 3,946	$ 2,758	$ 2,010
Total Income Before Loan Loss Provision					
Actual As Reported	$18,690	$15,189	$12,786	$10,122	$ 9,499
Memo: Tax Equivalent (TE)	19,097	15,910	13,731	11,209	10,099

Exhibit 9.6 *(Continued)*

	1999	1998	1997	1996	1995	1994
Total Income After Loan						
Loss Provision						
Actual As Reported	$17,313	$15,503	$13,938	$11,977	$ 9,722	$ 8,960
Memo: Tax Equivalent (TE)	17,720	15,969	14,659	12,922	10,809	9,758
Noninterest (Operating) Expenses						
Salaries & Benefits	$ 5,734	$ 5,495	$ 5,026	$ 4,539	$ 3,747	$ 2,994
Premises & Fixed Assets	2,777	2,522	2,320	1,987	1,514	1,007
Other Noninterest Expenses	4,973	4,785	4,353	3,821	3,280	2,886
Total Noninterest Expenses	$13,484	$12,802	$11,699	$10,347	$ 8,541	$ 6,887
Securities Gains (Losses)	$ 28	$ 80	$ 373	$ 365	$ 10	($65)
Pre-Tax Income						
Actual As Reported	$ 3,857	$ 2,781	$ 2,612	$ 1,995	$ 1,191	$ 2,008
Memo: Tax Equivalent (TE)	$ 4,208	$ 3,087	$ 2,587	$ 2,210	$ 2,258	$ 2,738
Income Tax Liability (Credit)	$ 850	$ 52	$ 218	$ 390	$ 49	$ 284
Net Income	$ 3,007	$ 2,729	$ 2,394	$ 1,605	$ 1,142	$ 1,724
(Memo: Dividends Paid)	$ 923	$ 815	$ 938	$ 409	$ 456	$ 440

Net Interest Margin on Average Earnings Assets*					
Bank	4.03%	4.34%	4.40%	4.49%	4.59%
Peers	4.77%	4.89%	5.01%	5.01%	5.02%
Noninterest Income to Total Income					
Bank	30.4%	28.9%	28.8%	28.7%	24.6%
Peers	18.1%	17.3%	15.1%	14.2%	13.7%
Operating Expenses to Total Income					
Bank	70.6%	71.0%	73.5%	75.3%	76.2%
Peers	65.1%	63.5%	63.0%	61.1%	62.9%
Loan Loss Provision to Average Total Loans					
Bank	0.54%	0.86%	0.65%	0.51%	0.30%
Peers	0.78%	1.15%	0.78%	0.61%	0.53%
Net Income to Average Total Assets					
Bank	0.82%	0.83%	0.82%	0.64%	0.54%
Peers	0.97%	0.71%	1.00%	1.05%	1.04%

*Tax Equivalent

9.13.1   Overall Income and Expenses

Along with assets, income and expenses at Example Bank have grown rapidly. Total interest income on a tax equivalent basis grew at an annual rate of 9.17 percent between 1994 and 1999. Over the same period, interest expense grew at an 8.8 percent rate. Tax equivalent net interest income increased at a 9.5 percent annual rate. Noninterest income increased at a 16.1 percent annual rate, and increased from 24.6 percent of total tax equivalent income in 1994 to 30.4 percent in 1999. Total income increased at an annual rate of 11.2 percent.

Overhead expenses grew at a 9.6 percent annual rate, slower than asset increases and total income. It appears that Example Bank is improving its cost effectiveness.

The expenses associated with loan losses were extremely high in 1998, reflecting a cleaning up of the loan portfolio. Before that time and in 1999, loan loss provision expense has generally been a relatively constant percent of loans.

Net income has been strong except for a decline in 1995. Since then, however, Example Bank has achieved returns on equity above its peers. As discussed below, the higher return on equity is due more to higher leverage than to stronger earnings.

9.13.2   Sources of Profitability

The best way to examine the sources of profitability is to calculate the performance of the bank in the key areas that drive income. There are four key measures examined for Example Bank:

- *Net interest margin* (usually expressed as a percent of average earning assets, sometimes shown after loan loss provision to arrive at a "loss-adjusted" margin).
- *Noninterest income to total income* (the proportion of total income accounted for by noninterest sources).
- *Operating expenses per dollar of total income* (the outlays made by the bank to generate a dollar of income).
- *Loan loss provision to average loans* (measures the credit quality and risks).

Clearly, there are other measures that can be used to assess performance. A focus on these four, however, provides an excellent overview of a bank's performance.

Example Bank's net interest margin has been declining since 1994 (as has those of its peers), reflecting the overall squeeze on margins felt by all depository institutions. Of more concern, however, is the fact that Example Bank's margins are much smaller than those of its peers, and the gap appears to be widening. Much of this is due to the fact that Example Bank is using higher cost noncore deposits as a significant source of funding.

On the other hand, Example Bank is doing an excellent job of generating noninterest income. Over 30 percent of total income in 1999 was from noninterest sources, versus 18.1 percent for its peers. Moreover, the proportion of income from noninterest sources has increased from 1994.

A major weakness of Example Bank is operating expense control, although it has improved in that area. In 1999, the bank required nearly 71 cents to generate one dollar of income, versus 65 cents for peers. Example Bank has improved dramatically since 1995 when it required 76 cents, but improvement is still needed, particularly because margins are low and declining.

The last area, loan loss provision to average loans, is something that Example Bank does very well. Despite aggressive loan growth, its rate of losses (measured by the provision made to loan loss reserves) has been consistently below that of its peers.

The end result is that Example Bank has had a return on assets below its peer group every year except 1998. The major cause of this low level of profit is the small margins on earning assets. High operating expenses have compounded the problem.

9.14   LOAN RISK ANALYSIS ILLUSTRATION

The analysis of the loan position of a bank being valued is of critical importance. Loans are usually the major source of income and potentially the major source of losses. The danger to a buyer who is valuing a bank for acquisition purposes is that the loan portfolio may not be as strong as historical financial statements would indicate. In other words, substantial and abnormal losses may be looming on loans already on the books. A bank with expected future loan losses of, say, $500,000 is clearly valued higher than if those loan losses were $1 million.

Like many other aspects of valuation, estimating future loan losses requires judgment. Determining the percent of a loan that ultimately will be collected is difficult, especially with turbulent domestic and international economic conditions.

Before discussing strategies to assess a loan portfolio, it is beneficial to demonstrate why an accurate estimate of loan quality is essential. The analysis below illustrates how loan losses dramatically affect future income and consequently value.

9.14.1   The Magnified Impact of Loan Losses

Using Example Bank as an illustration, consider its 1999 income under two scenarios: actual conditions and with an additional and unexpected one-half of one percent of loans going bad. This would result in a loan loss provision of $830,000 more than the actual level as shown in Exhibit 9.7. With just an additional 0.5 percent of the loan portfolio going bad, income declined by nearly 35 percent.

Exhibit 9.7   Illustration of Impact of Loan Losses on Net Income: Example Bank—1999 Income ($000)

	Actual	With Additional 1/2 of 1% Loans Going Bad
Total interest income	$35,994	$35,994
Total interest expense	23,111	23,111
Net interest income	12,883	12,883
Provision for loan losses	1,377	2,708
Noninterest income	5,807	5,807
Total operating expenses	13,484	13,484
Securities gains (losses)	28	28
Pretax income	3,857	2,526
Taxes	850	557
Net income	3,007	1,969

Another way to view the impact of loan losses is to calculate the new good loans Example Bank must make to offset the impact of the unexpected additional one-half of one percent of the portfolio going bad—in other words, the dollars in new loans needed to replace the $1,038,000 decrease in pretax income. Example Bank would need to make just over $12 million in new good loans to equal $1,038,000 pretax income. Stated alternatively, about $19 in new loans are needed to generate sufficient income to offset $1 of loans that go bad.

Clearly, the future level of loan losses has a substantial impact on financial performance. It is imperative that these losses be quantified as accurately as possible before a valuation of the bank is made. One systematic technique to quantify future loan losses is described in the following section.

9.14.2 Delinquent and Classified Loan Analysis

When a loan portfolio is being analyzed as part of an overall bank valuation, the loans of particular interest are those that are delinquent and those that are classified. Delinquent loans are late in payment (anywhere from a few days to a few months), whereas classified loans are those that are beyond delinquent and are no longer accruing income. Depending on the bank's and the regulatory examiner's judgment, reserves may be established to cover losses for a given classified loan, at a rate of 10 to as much as 90 percent. When a loan is charged off, this is, in effect, reserving 100 percent of the outstanding balance.

There are two alternatives to projecting the loss level on delinquent and classified loans. The easiest way is to use the historical experience of the bank to estimate future losses on a group of loans. For example, the bank's experience may indicate that 75 percent of the principal balance of delinquent loans and 25 percent of the principal balance of classified loans eventually are recovered. These rates could be applied to loans in those categories as of the date of valuation. This approach works reasonably well when there are large numbers of fairly small loans, such as auto loans and credit card receivables.

The more difficult approach is to assess each delinquent and classified loan individually. This can be a tedious process, but often appropriate where the loans are large and complex. For most banks, larger commercial and real estate loans would fit these criteria.

Exhibit 9.8 presents a tabular format that can be used to analyze individual delinquent loans. This tabular format lists the loan (by name, number or other relevant description), the amount outstanding, the days past due, reserves established to date (if any), any comments on the loan's outlook, the future loss percentage on book value, and the dollar amount of loss. The total dollar amount of loss for all delinquent loans is the figure of interest in the valuation process.

Exhibit 9.9 illustrates a format that can be used to analyze classified loans. This form is slightly different from that used for delinquent loans. The reason is that classified loans usually have some reserves already established—that is, some loss has been recognized and reflected in past net income. For example, a $100,000 original balance loan may have already had a 25 percent reserve established. Therefore, on date of valuation $75,000 is the potential loss amount. A $25,000 expense item to loan loss reserves is already reflected in past net income figures.

Another difference in the form is in accrued but unpaid interest. This situation occurs when a borrower stops payments but the bank continues to accrue the interest income and reverse income accrued but not received. After ninety days, most banks will discontinue the accrual of interest-income. If the loan eventually becomes a total loss, the principal must be charged off, as well as whatever interest income was accrued but never actually received.

olio Summary

	1996	1995	1994
	107.3%	103.2%	102.6%
	81.4%	76.1%	80.1%
	100.0%	69.3%	46.0%
	33.0%	30.2%	26.5%
	0%	5.3%	30.2%
	41.3%	42.2%	30.2%
	0%	25.4%	23.8%
	25.7%	27.6%	43.3%

EALM MODEL)

ct changes in market value of port-
scenarios would affect the market
rrently being used by some banks
veloped by Chase Financial Tech-
aking a proactive approach to their
e impact of different interest-rate
ALM enables banks to download all
he model rather than using aggre-
ctuations in interest rates on each

Y CONSIDERATIONS

The financial statements of a holding
pects. First, the holding company re-
s that the financial statements of the
re added together along with any as-
ompany level. Second, because non-
e of the income and expenses will be
. Third, because the holding company
d debt and intangible assets are nor-

t and content of holding company fi-
s of valuation, establishing value of a
ases, involve the same types of analy-
fferences.

Exhibit 9.8   Format for Delinquent Loan Analysis

Loan Name/Number	Amount Outstanding on Date of Valuation*	Days Past Due	Loss Provisions to Date	Outlook for Loan	Estimated Loss%	Estimated Loss Amount

* Includes principal balance and any accrued but unpaid interest.

Exhibit 9.9   Format for Classified Loan Analysis

Loan Name/Number	Amount Outstanding on Date of Valuation*	Loss Provisions to Date	Accrued but Unpaid Interest	Status as of Date of Valuation	Additional Future Losses

* Includes princi...

Exhibit 9.11   Example Bank Liquidity and Investment Port...

	1999	1998	1997
Loans/core deposits			
Bank	122.1%	124.7%	118.4%
Peer	84.9%	85.2%	85.8%
% of securities < 1 year			
Bank	88.2%	86.4%	86.6%
Peer	32.7%	30.1%	33.6%
% of securities 1 to 5 years			
Bank	6.0%	7.2%	6.5%
Peer	40.4%	42.7%	41.1%
% of securities > 5 years			
Bank	5.8%	6.4%	6.9%
Peer	26.9%	27.2%	25.3%

9.16   PORTFOLIO EQUITIES ANALYSIS (R

REALM is a duration-analysis model designed to predi
folio equities by determining how different interest-rate
value of an institution's portfolio equity. REALM is cu
such as Easter Bank in Boston and was originally de
nologies.[5] REALM can assist financial institutions in t
asset/liability management process by determining th
scenarios on the market value of equity portfolio. REA
their loan-and-deposit portfolios, item by item, into
gated information and then analyze the effect of flu
asset/liability item.

9.17   SPECIAL BANK HOLDING COMPA

Many banks are owned by bank holding companies.
company can differ from those of a bank in several res
ports its financials on a consolidated basis. This mea
individual banks, and any other owned businesses, a
sets, liabilities, income, and expenses at the parent
bank entities can be part of a holding company, som
attributable to activities other than traditional banking
is usually the vehicle for acquisitions, any associate
mally found at the holding company level.

In most cases, the difference between the forma
nancials and bank financials will be minor. In term
bank or a bank holding company will, in nearly all
ses. It is useful, however, to understand the major di

The consolidated financial statements of a holding company reflect all the subsidiaries added together, plus any assets, liabilities, income, and expenses at the parent company level. The parent in a bank holding company structure is usually just a legal entity that is not directly engaged in income-generating businesses. The income of the parent is mainly the dividends paid by the subsidiaries. Miscellaneous parent company income might include interest income from miscellaneous investments owned by the holding company or interest-bearing deposits it has. In general, the income reported on a consolidated basis will be the aggregate of the subsidiaries' incomes.

Expenses of the holding company can vary widely. Some holding companies are shells and have no expenses outside of miscellaneous legal and accounting fees for filing regulatory statements, and preparing annual reports. Other holding companies, conversely, are complete service centers for their subsidiaries, offering diverse services such as operations, audit, courier, data processing, check clearing, and investment management. In this case, expenses are incurred at the holding company level which would otherwise be incurred by the bank. The bank is charged a management fee for these services.

With assets, the main difference between a bank holding company and a bank is in the area of intangible assets. In nearly all instances, intangibles created by an acquisition are "booked" at the parent company. Also, the stock of the subsidiaries is an asset of the parent company. These two assets account for 90 to 95 percent of the assets of the parent company in a typical bank holding company structure.

For most parent companies the only liability of any consequence is debt, usually incurred to acquire subsidiaries. The stockholders' equity account of the parent is essentially the same as a bank—that is, stock, surplus, and retained earnings.

In general, the existence of a holding company as owner of a bank does not complicate the financial analysis. There are a few differences, as described above, which are useful to bear in mind during the analysis. The techniques of analysis and eventual valuation of a holding company are essentially the same as those for an individual bank. The exception would be a holding company that has many nonbank businesses. Such a situation would require different valuation research, analysis, and techniques.

ENDNOTES

1. Kupiec, P., and J. M. O'Brien. 1995. "A Pre-Commitment approach to capital Requirements of Market Risk." Manuscript. Division of Research and Statistics, Board of Governors of the Federal Reserve System.
2. Hendricks, D. 1995. "Evaluation of Value-at-Risk Models Using Historical Data." *Federal Reserve Bank of New York Economics Policy Review* 2: 39–69.
3. Lopez, Jose A. 1997. "Regulatory Evaluation of Value-at-Risk Models." Research Paper #9710. Federal Reserve Bank of New York.
4. Kupiec, P. 1995. "Techniques for verifying the accuracy of risk measurement models." *Journal of Derivatives,* 3: 73–84.
5. Fassett, Wayne S. 1991. "REALM Improves Interest-rate Risk Reading." *Bank Management* (August): 54–55.

CHAPTER 10

Internal Characteristics Assessment

The financial analysis described in the preceding chapter provides extensive insight into the characteristics of the banking company being valued. The numbers, however, do not tell the full story. To understand the bank completely, it is necessary to analyze the internal characteristics of the institution. It is these internal characteristics that create the financial performance. Consequently, an assessment of the business behind the numbers is essential to a thorough and accurate valuation.

The requirements for a proper internal characteristics assessment are fairly easy to identify but more difficult to achieve. They are:

- *A complete financial profile:* Based on publicly available data, a financial profile (as described in the preceding chapter) should be developed prior to internal investigation.

- *Access to the bank being analyzed:* Proper analysis cannot be undertaken without access to staff and records. Consequently, it is unlikely that the assessment can be undertaken much before the due diligence review.

- *A work plan to follow:* Because acquisitions are time-critical, it is necessary to have a definite plan of action including: areas to be analyzed, priorities, responsibilities, data required, and schedules.

- *Knowledge analysts:* Banks are unique types of businesses, and the people undertaking an internal characteristics assessment should be experienced in bank analysis and terminology. The pressured time of an acquisition is not the proper forum for training.

Assessing the internal characteristics is a more difficult task than analyzing the financial performance. With financial data, there are rules and definitions that allow an objective comparison of a bank over time and with its peers. Internal characteristics, however, are often less objective and require greater creativity and intuition. There are some techniques that can be used to organize the research and ensure that important internal characteristics are not overlooked.

10.1   OBJECTIVES AND BENEFITS OF AN INTERNAL CHARACTERISTICS ASSESSMENT

The primary reason for undertaking an assessment of internal characteristics of a bank is to provide a greater understanding of the institution, thus allowing better assumptions to be made in the valuation process. As discussed in Chapter 5, valuation is an inexact science at best, and requires a variety of assumptions about future performance. The more background information considered, the more accurate are the assumptions of future performance. Consequently, the main benefit of a thorough internal characteristics assessment is a better estimate of the bank's value.

Another reason for an internal characteristics assessment is a more complete due diligence review. Too often, due diligence reviews focus on the loan and investment portfolio, almost to the exclusion of other critical factors. Obviously, loans and investments are extremely important aspects of the bank, but other aspects should also be analyzed carefully. The internal characteristics assessment described in this chapter helps provide for a more complete due diligence review.

Identifying potential integration problems is a third reason for a thorough internal characteristics assessment. Knowledge gained during the analysis often uncovers weaknesses that must be addressed in order to integrate the two entities. Executives who have been involved with acquisitions say that 80 percent of the value is created *after* the transaction is closed during the integration period. The most creative, well-priced acquisition usually will not realize its full benefit potential without proper integration. The earlier problems are identified, the easier it will be to resolve them with minimum disruption.

The fourth reason for an internal characteristics assessment is profit improvement. In every bank there are opportunities to increase income and/or decrease expenses. If undertaken properly, the assessment of internal characteristics can result in ideas for improving profits after the acquisition.

10.2   THE "TEN P FACTOR" FRAMEWORK

Because banks are complex business entities, it is useful to have a framework for assessing the internal characteristics. Such a framework allows better organization of the analysis and delegation of blocks of research to appropriate staff and outside consultants.

For a complete assessment, research should be undertaken in ten areas labeled the *Ten P Factors* for convenience. Each of these factors covers a relatively distinct portion of a complete internal characteristics analysis. The Ten P Factors are:

1. Profits
2. People
3. Personality
4. Physical Distribution

5. Portfolio
6. Products
7. Processes
8. Property
9. Planning
10. Potential

The types of analyses appropriate in each of these ten areas are described below and on the next several pages.

10.2.1 Profits

The financial analysis described in Chapter 9 addressed in great detail the *quantity* of the profits. The *Profit Factor* considers the *quality* of the profits. Quality refers to the likelihood of the profits continuing or growing from historic levels. To assess quality, it is necessary to go beyond the financial statements. The nature and sources of profit performance must be assessed. It is critically important to determine whether abnormal business conditions affected past profits. The publicly available financial statistics are seldom sufficient to make this assessment. Some key factors to consider when assessing profit quality include sources of net interest income, sources of noninterest income, importance of nontraditional activities, and expenses.

The basis of interest income should be investigated to determine whether the sources are stable over the long term. For example, interest income may be abnormally high due to high risk loans made by the bank. Also, the basis of interest expense should be identified, particularly any reliance upon purchased funds, which may indicate a need to replace those funds at an even higher cost.

The noninterest income generated by fees, service charges, and trading gains can provide significant revenue to the bank without a corresponding increase in overhead. To a buyer, it is essential to determine whether those sources of noninterest income can continue. Service charges on deposit accounts are relatively stable and predictable, as are service charges and commissions on such routine items as money orders, credit life insurance, and safe deposit boxes. However, other gains are transitory, such as sale of assets, trading account activities, and foreign currency transactions. If the bank generates income from nontraditional activities, it is important to assess the stability of that income and of the outlook for the future.

Expense trends should also be scrutinized. The most likely area of potential window dressing by a seller is expenses. It is important to analyze the type of expenses to identify any category of expenses that has grown much faster or slower than others. For example, lower equipment expenses may be a sign of deferred maintenance. Decreasing personnel expenses may be the result of wholesale, short-term layoffs rather than structural improvements in operational efficiency. Many expense reductions are, in reality, expense deferrals for which payment will eventually be incurred by the buyer. These types of reductions do not truly increase a bank's performance or long-term value.

10.2.2 People

The *People Factor* considers the impact of the staff on the bank's future success. To effect a successful integration, it is crucial to understand the unique nature of the acquired bank's staff.

The first area of analysis is the organizational structure. This can be a complex topic requiring a creative analysis in order to judge the organization's strengths and weaknesses. There are, however, six common organizational characteristics that a buyer should investigate for potential problems:

1. *Lack of a reasonably accurate organization chart:* Having one does not imply there is a good organization, but lack of one suggests there is a poor organizational structure.

2. *Unclear lines of authority:* When the authority (and derivatively, the responsibility) is unclear, there are likely to be organizational problems.

3. *Multiple reporting relationships:* If some staff report to more than one superior, this is a sign of potential weakness in the organization.

4. *Excessive spans of control:* The number of subordinates to which a manager can effectively provide functional and technical direction is limited. A very common situation, indicative of potential organizational weaknesses, is the assignment of too many direct reports to one manager, and too few to others. This type of imbalance indicates poor use of managerial talent. The right number of subordinates depends on the variety and complexity of tasks being performed. Typically, however, more than six or seven direct reports per manager is excessive.

5. *Inappropriate reporting relationships:* In weak organizations, there are likely to be numerous instances of staff reporting to a superior unrelated to their functions. This is a symptom of an organization that just happened rather than one that has been planned.

6. *Mismatched positions and responsibilities:* Another sign of an unplanned organization is the lack of relationship between a person's position and his or her responsibility. Some vice presidents may be glorified clerks while key staff are in lower positions.

Evaluating organizational structure is a very subjective exercise. If, however, the organization is analyzed in relation to the six factors described above, major potential problems and weaknesses are likely to be observed.

The next aspect of the People Factor is management depth. Successful integration requires competent, motivated staff on both the buyer's and seller's side. It is important to evaluate the depth and breadth of management talent at the bank. Frequently, especially in smaller banks, a small number of key people run the bank. If these people leave after the acquisition, which can happen after a change of ownership, there will be few replacements and a disproportionate share of the acquirer's management resources would be necessary to fill the void.

The actual level of staffing is another important People Factor concern. Overstaffing is a problem for many banks and can reduce the potential value of an acquisition target. Unfortunately, it is not possible to make a judgment about overstaffing using simple rules of thumb, such as "one employee for every two million in assets." The proper staffing level is dependent on a multitude of factors unrelated to size, such as number of branches, types of operational systems, location, loan mix, liability mix, and lines of business. Determining

Exhibit 10.1

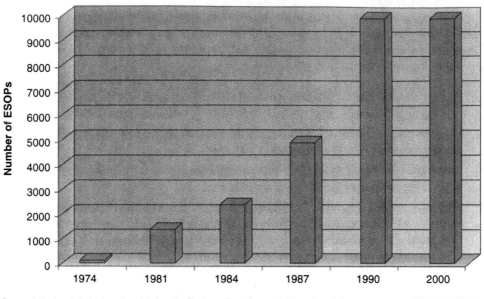

Growth of Employee Stock Ownership Plans (ESOPs) in the United States

Source: Author's calculation based on data from the Employee Stock Ownership Plans Association.

whether or not a bank is staffed properly requires an analysis of the workload and operations of each department.

Another aspect of the People Factor is the existence of employee stock ownership plans (ESOPs). An ESOP is defined by the Employee Retirement Income Security Act of 1974 (ERISA) as a qualified retirement plan designed to invest primarily in the employer's securities. An ESOP provides a means for employees to have an ownership interest in the employee corporation. There are a number of organizational, financial, and taxation benefits to ESOPs, including (1) providing a means for employees to invest in the employer's securities; (2) generating liquidity for closely held corporation shareholders by purchasing stock directly from shareholders and creating a partial market for corporate stock; (3) providing income tax benefits for employers; and (4) creating motivations for employees, improved employee rations, and employee productivity. Exhibit 10.1 shows the growth of ESOPs during the past two decades, resulting from the perceived benefits of such plans.

Many companies created leveraged employee stock ownership plans by borrowing funds to purchase company stocks in the late 1980s. ESOPs were originally created in 1974 when Congress permitted the establishment of ESOPs by the enactment of ERISA. In 1984, Congress added an exclusion from gross income for 50 percent of the interest a qualified lender receives on a securities acquisition loan. Furthermore, in 1986 Congress made dividends paid on ESOP shares deductible when they were used to repay exempt loans. The use of ESOPs grew substantially during the 1990s primarily because of (1) a rising stock market;

(2) the increased tax advantages; (3) hostile takeover activities; and (4) the availability of high yield debt to purchase companies.

The current ESOPs are created to finance leveraged buyouts, known as ESOPLBO, for the purpose of purchasing part of a company being taken private. The ESOP issues debt to third parties to generate funds necessary to buy a substantial portion of the shares. The company is allowed to deduct dividends on ESOP shares used to repay the exempt loan, and a qualified lender is permitted to exclude from gross income 50 percent of the interest earned on certain loans. As the loan is being paid, the purchase shares are allocated to participating employees under the ESOPs. This ownership granted to employees under the ESOPs can create better incentives for employees to be more effective and efficient and lead to loyalty and increased productivity.

Family-owned businesses can use ESOPs as devices to sell the business through tax-advantaged Section 1042 sales. Small businesses can utilize ESOPs to reduce taxes through the use of ESOP-owned S corporations. The AICPA issued Statement of Position (SOP) 93-9, Employers' Accounting for Employee Stock Ownership Plans in 1993. The SOP requires that when a company allocates shares to participants' ESOP accounts, a compensation expense measured by the fair market value of the stock on the allocation date should be recognized. Any dividends on stock held in an ESOP should be treated the same as dividends on non-ESOP shares, which should reduce retained earnings.

The Section 133 interest exclusion for qualified ESOP lenders was restricted by the Revenue Reconciliation Act of 1989 (RRA). The RRA limited loans to 15 years and also required that for loans made after July 10, 1989, the ESOP owns more than 50 percent of each class and of the total value of all of the corporation's outstanding stock. This exclusion was repealed by Section 1602(a) of the Small Business Job Protection Act of 1996, which allowed loans in existence on or before August 10, 1996, to be grandfathered.

The last aspect of the People Factor is personnel administration. It is essential that a buyer review the system in place for the personnel-related functions such as salary administration, benefits, performance reviews, grade structure, payroll system, recruitment, pension, and general employment practices. It is beneficial to know of any discrepancies between the buyer's and seller's personnel administration policies as early as possible.

10.2.3   Personality

Every organization has a personality, or culture, that has evolved over the years. The *Personality Factor* considers this aspect of the organization. An organization's personality has a powerful influence on the actions of individuals within that organization. Some personalities are clear and obvious, while others nearly defy description. Some different types of organizational personalities that might be found in an acquisition target could include profit-oriented, growth-oriented, participatory, autocratic, informal, process-oriented, results-driven, or conservative. However, when assessing an organization's personality, it is far more important to examine actions than words.

The Personality Factor is related to the People Factor, but the personality of an organization outlives staff and is carried on through successive generations of personnel. Consequently, it can be extremely difficult to change an organization's personality or to merge two different ones. The more divergent the buyer's and seller's organizational personalities, the greater the risk that integration after acquisition will be difficult.

10.2.4 Physical Distribution

The *Physical Distribution Factor* considers all means by which services are delivered to customers, such as branches, automated teller machines (ATMs), automated clearing-house (ACH), audio response, point-of-sale (POS), and home banking. These physical distribution components usually represent a significant financial investment and can create a basis for future growth. There are four key factors to analyze with respect to the physical distribution system: location, costs, technology, and synergy opportunities.

The location is a critical factor for branches and ATMs. If they are well located they can provide a significant competitive advantage, but if they are poorly located they can be a drain on income. Factors to consider include the desirability of the market served, growth prospects, nearby competition, site characteristics, traffic flows, visibility, accessibility, and exposure.

Costs are another key concern. The cost effectiveness of the physical distribution system components must be addressed on the basis of expenses incurred relative to benefits derived. If the bank has a reasonably accurate cost allocation system, it is useful to develop a comparison table for branches, such as the one shown in Exhibit 10.2. In this example, Branches C and D are far more cost effective than the other three, even though Branch C has the second lowest transaction volume and branch D has the highest costs. This type of analysis can also be applied to gauge the effectiveness of other components of the physical distribution system.

The third element is technology. The sophistication of the physical distribution system is an important concern, because if it is used properly technology can lead to lower transaction costs. The situation to be aware of is one of over-technology, where the investment has been made in hardware and software but is not being utilized fully because of lack of training, customer resistance, or poor vendor support.

The fourth point of analysis is synergy opportunities in the physical distribution system. Often, a principal objective in an acquisition is the expansion of the market in geographic and/or market segment terms. A physical distribution system that complements the buyer's own system has greater potential value than one that results in overlapping markets and duplicate coverage.

Exhibit 10.2 Example of Branch Cost-Effectiveness Comparison

Branch	Fully Allocated Monthly Expenses[1]	Transactions[2]	Cost-Effectiveness Ratio[3]
A	$150,000	70,000	.92
B	200,000	75,000	.74
C	75,000	62,000	1.63
D	300,000	175,000	1.15
E	100,000	38,000	.75

[1]Includes direct operating expenses and pro rata share of indirect expenses based on consistent allocation formula.
[2]Teller transactions, used as a surrogate measure of benefits derived by the branch. Other measures could be used, such as accounts opened, deposits, or loans made.
[3]Ratio is computed as the percent of total transactions at the branch divided by percent of expenses incurred by the branch (i.e., the five branch average would equal 1.0).

10.2.5   Portfolio

The *Portfolio Factor* addresses the mix of earning assets and interest liabilities in the bank's portfolio. Much of the financial analysis of the portfolio was described in Chapter 9. This assessment expands on that analysis and provides qualitative input.

The loan part of a bank's portfolio typically receives the most attention during an acquisition, which is appropriate because unanticipated loan losses have a potentially devastating impact on value. In addition to the financial-oriented analysis of loans detailed in the preceding chapter, it is beneficial to evaluate the quality of the credit systems, including credit approvals, documentation, audits, collateral appraisal, funds disbursement procedures, and undue concentrations in certain industries. It may be necessary to investigate the underlying physical collateral on large loans to ensure that realistic values are assigned and that potential problems will not surface after the acquisition.

The investment part of the portfolio is usually fairly easy to analyze from safekeeping records. These records normally list the type of security, rate, yield, maturity, book value, and market value. It is prudent, however, to verify the actual existence of the securities.

On the liability side, the Portfolio Factor considers the deposit base funding the assets, especially the mix of stable core deposits versus other more volatile sources of funds. Within the core deposit base it is useful to assess:

- concentrations of deposits from a limited number of customers;
- the cost of the deposits;
- the maturity dates of the accounts; and
- the trend in deposit mix over the last five years.

This analysis complements and enhances the financial analysis described in Chapter 9.

10.2.6   Products

Another key aspect is the *Product Factor,* which addresses what products the bank offers and how they fit in the competitive environment. For example, the range of products may be too limited to meet market needs, thus necessitating significant investment by the buyer for development and promotion of new products. Conversely, the target bank's range of products may be adequate but incompatible with the buyer's, for strategic and/or operational reasons.

When analyzing the products of a bank, these five criteria are relevant:

1. *Features:* the characteristics of the product that make it successful or unsuccessful;
2. *Support:* the back room systems in place to support the products, including hardware, software, and staff;
3. *Pricing:* the fee structure, including both implicit and explicit charges;
4. *Promotion:* programs and approaches used to promote the product in the marketplace; and
5. *Competitive Comparison:* how the quality, range, and price of services compares with competition.

These five criteria allow for a thorough analysis of the products of the bank.

10.2.7   Processes

The *Processes Factor* addresses the procedural aspects of the bank, which can include all functions but normally focuses on high volume, labor-intensive activities due to the limited time available during an acquisition analysis.

The purpose of the analysis is to understand the operational strengths and weaknesses of the bank to the greatest extent possible. The high priority functional areas to be analyzed should, at a minimum, include:

- loan processing;
- proof and transit;
- bookkeeping and tellers; and
- data processing.

The types of analyses useful to undertake in each area include:

- staff scheduling relative to volume requirements;
- equipment utilization;
- inter- and intradepartmental work flow;
- methods and procedures; and
- automation opportunities.

A thorough analysis can identify weakness in the current processes, potential integration problems, and profit improvement opportunities in addition to providing a better base of information for valuation.

10.2.8   Property

Banking is a labor-intensive business, but significant amounts of capital are invested in property. The *Property Factor* addresses the fixed assets owned and leased by the bank being valued, and the potential contribution of these properties to the future success of the institution.

The bank's facilities should be analyzed from four principal perspectives:

- physical;
- functional;
- locational; and
- financial.

A review of the physical aspects of the facilities will uncover deferred maintenance and the need to invest in repairs in order to bring the structures to standard. When a bank is to be sold, maintenance and repair expenditures can be delayed to improve earnings. A relatively quick analysis, performed by a knowledgeable architect or engineer, can uncover potentially significant future expenditure requirements.

The functional characteristics of the facilities relate to the suitability of size, layout, and configuration. For example, large, opulent branches may constitute the bulk of a bank's branch system, but they may be functionally inefficient and/or obsolete.[1] In such a case, the appraised value of the branches may overstate the true value of the branch network to the buyer. Conversely, a system of efficient, functional branches may have value to the buyer far in excess of the appraised real estate value (due to enhanced market position and locational advantage).

The locational aspects of the facilities should also be analyzed carefully. If buildings (especially branches) are well located, they can be invaluable in maintaining and expanding the bank's market reach. Conversely, if the facilities are poorly located in declining areas, there may be negative value in the buildings—that is, they may detract from the overall value of the bank. The locational analysis requires input from professionals who have experience analyzing both the market and the placement of bank facilities based on market potential.

The last aspect of the property analysis is the financial aspect. In this analysis, the costs of operating the facilities are evaluated, including utilities, maintenance, insurance, and taxes. The purpose is to understand the facilities costs as well as to identify any abnormal expenditures.

Depending on the stage of the acquisition process, a full appraisal of the premises may or may not be necessary. During the early acquisition stages, an overall review is normally sufficient. Later, when specific points are being negotiated or tax allocations are being made, a full appraisal of all property may be necessary. This appraisal may also point out significant gains possible from sale of facilities. If any such facilities could be sold after acquisition, this could enhance the investment value of the bank.

The fixtures of the bank should also be examined. Furniture, teller counters, and other routine equipment are not likely to have a substantial impact on value. There are, however, instances of valuable objects in the fixtures category—for example, art or coin collections. In such a case, sale of those items may result in gain unanticipated from a review of the financial statements.

The equipment used by the bank is important to analyze. Banks have a substantial amount of equipment such as computers, terminals, and item processors. The important aspect from a buyer's perspective is the compatibility of equipment. For example, if the seller's computer equipment does not interface with the buyer's, it may be necessary to acquire a completely new system that can accommodate the new, larger bank. This situation can affect how a target bank's value is viewed by the buyer.

10.2.9 Planning

The quality of the preparation and implementation of the strategic plan is indicative of the bank's overall approach to its business. The *Planning Factor* assesses whether the bank has established a defensible market position or is wandering aimlessly with no particular direction. The results of the bank's planning efforts are major influences on the strength of the bank's franchise value. This banking franchise concept reflects the correct observation that a buyer is purchasing a current and future market position, as well as physical and financial assets, when it buys another bank.[2] How well the bank has planned (and subsequently executed the plan) often is the crucial element in determining its position in the market, and derivatively its franchise value.

From a practical standpoint, very few banks have done a particularly good job at strategic planning. If they go through the exercise at all, many view it as a waste of time that detracts from real work. In many cases, the unique franchise a bank has developed (if any) is a result of location or luck. When valuing such a bank, it is essential to consider the uniqueness of the franchise, how it developed, and the likelihood of sustaining and improving it.

10.2.10   Potential

The *Potential Factor* considers the future opportunity available to the bank and the level of resources necessary to capitalize on those opportunities. To a great extent, the true value of a bank is determined by the potential. As described in Chapter 5, value is the net present value of the future benefits of ownership. Because the future is so critical to value, it is essential that the potential of the bank's market be analyzed carefully.

Potential can be measured a number of ways. For a retail-oriented community or regional bank, the key measures may be future population and income growth, which measure future deposit and loan potential. For a global money center bank, the measures of potential become far more complex as they are based on worldwide economic conditions, conditions within targeted market segments, and a host of other macro factors. Nonetheless, some measure of potential should be quantified.

The direct impact of potential can be illustrated by a simple example. Assume two banks of identical size and profitability, equal in all respects except that one is located in a growing, dynamic metropolitan area, and the other in a stable rural community. Using the stabilized income approach as described in Chapter 6 for simplicity and illustration, the value of each of the two banks would be calculated as:

$$\text{value} = \text{stabilized income/capitalization rate}$$

Suppose "stabilized income" at each bank is $5 million, then value is:

$$\text{value} = (\$5,000,000)/\text{capitalization rate}$$

As discussed in Chapter 6, the capitalization rate is the discount rate *minus* the expected growth rate of income. Assume the risk structures of both banks would require a 15 percent discount rate. Therefore, the value of either bank would be:

$$\text{value} = \$5,000,000/(.15 - \text{growth rate})$$

Only the growth rate differentiates the two banks. If the metropolitan bank can expect growth of 8 percent, its value would be:

$$\text{value of metropolitan bank} = \$5,000,000/(.15 - .07)$$
$$= \$62.5 \text{ million}$$

If the rural bank can expect growth of only 4 percent, its value would be:

$$\text{value of rural bank} = \$5,000,000/(.15 - .05)$$
$$= \$50.0 \text{ million}$$

The lower growth potential resulted in a 20 percent decrease in value. Clearly, the future income growth potential of the bank has a substantial bearing on its value.

10.3 SHAREHOLDER VALUE CREATION

Shareholder value creation should be one of the most important goals of financial institutions. Indeed, any consolidation and convergence in the financial services industry is executed in an attempt to improve shareholders' value creation of the combined organization. Several internal performance measurement techniques can be used by financial institutions in assessing shareholder value creation. These techniques are (1) risk assessment; (2) economic value added; and (3) balanced scorecard.

10.3.1 Risk Assessment

The risk assessment method focuses on the risk assessment and risk management units to measure shareholder value creation. This method entails identification of all types of risk, including credit, market, strategy, operation, and political risks. Financial institutions should incorporate all types of potential risks into their internal value-at-risk model which determines an estimate of the maximum loss amount of a particular portfolio over a given holding period. The value-at-risk estimates are determined based on the behavior and movements of underlying risk factors (e.g., credit risk, market risk, liquidity risk). Financial institutions should measure and manage the interrelated nature of all of their risks and minimize them to a prudent acceptable business risk in order to enhance their shareholder value creation.

10.3.2 Economic Value Added

The economic value added (EVA) can be used to assess shareholder value creation through a set of matrices that determines whether the actual reported net income exceeds the predetermined expected earnings. The EVA equals the difference between the reported net income and the dollar cost of capital charged to earnings [EVA = net income − (cost of capital) (investment)]. When the EVA is positive, it indicates value creation, and when the EVA is negative, it measures that shareholder value is destroyed.

The concept of EVA implies that an investment must generate returns equivalent to at least cost of capital to be considered profitable and economically justified. Cost of capital is the weighted average cost of debt and equity and is the return that both shareholders and bondholders could have earned by investing in equally risky investments. EVA measures the combined banks' performance based on its return on capital, both equity and debt. It measures how well shareholders of the merged banks are rewarded for investing in the combined banks rather than another. Traditional income measurement only considers one type of capital cost, namely the "interest" on debt, while ignoring the cost of equity finance. The external financial reporting process does not measure the cost of finance provided by the entity's shareholders because these costs, like all opportunity costs, cannot be easily and directly observed. However, this cost should be estimated and considered in performance measurement to properly assess how successful a bank has been, after the merger, in creating value for its shareholders.

Mergers and acquisitions deals can be considered successful in improving shareholder value creation when they increase the combined banks' market value added (MVA). MVA is the difference between the market value of the merged bank and its invested capital (including both equity and debt).

MVA   = market value of the merged bank − invested capital
MVA   = present value of expected future EVAs
EVA   = reported accounting income − capital charges
capital charges   = (weighted average cost of capital)(invested capital, including both
                             equity and debt)

To ensure the success of the combined bank in creating shareholder value, management should measure EVA for all of the provided services and products. The use of EVA as a performance benchmark encourages managers and even employees to think and act more like shareholders in an attempt to create shareholder value.

10.3.3 Balanced Scorecard (BSC)

The balanced scorecard (BSC) method is the most commonly used technique of assessing shareholder value creation. The BSC is a relatively new measurement tool developed originally by Kaplan and Norton in 1992.[3] The BSC approach suggests a balance between financial measures (e.g., net income, profitability, return on investment) and nonfinancial measures (e.g., service quality, customer satisfaction and retention, innovativeness, employee satisfaction), in assessing shareholder value creation. The key distinction of the BSC is that it measures both financial and nonfinancial factors, including financial indicators, customer satisfaction, internal operations, and employee growth and learning. Financial measures including net income, operating margin, earnings per share, and new product revenue are ultimately used to assess shareholder value creation. Operational measures consist of productivity, operational efficiency and effectiveness, product innovations, technological advances, and safety. The customer perspective measures used to assess customer satisfaction indices with information such as repeat business or results from customer surveys. These measures enable financial institutions to assess the quality of their products and services by improving customer satisfaction and meeting the needs of customers. The learning and growth measures determine how well a work force is prepared for and motivated to be creative and innovative. These measures include in-house and on-the-job training, continuing professional education, certifications, designations, and other credentials of employees. An effective BSC should balance between performance drivers (leading indicators) and outcome measures (lagging indicators). Examples of banks that are currently using the BSC are Citicorp, Chase, BancOne, and Wachovia. Financial institutions should use the BSC to ensure that their goals are being achieved by providing answers to the following questions: (1) how do their customers see them; (2) how do they look to their shareholders; (3) how can they improve quality and be more efficient and effective; and (4) can they continue to improve and create value? Answers to these questions should provide adequate input to the BSC method to customize an appropriate mix of outcomes (lagging indicators) and performance drivers (leading indicators) into the institutions' strategy. This strategy should include the following steps to ensure the institution's success in using the balanced scorecard:

- top management's establishment of vision for the institution and define mission, goals, and strategies to achieve them;
- communication of the BSC to all affected personnel and the requirement of feedback from them;

- alignment of the BSC with the institution's business units;
- utilization of a rewards system that links performance measures to key success factors;
- implementation of the BSC into the institution's planning and budgeting systems;
- utilization of the BSC as an everyday management tool in creating an appropriate balance between performance and outcome indicators;
- continuous improvement of the BSC approach by finding better performance drivers (leading indicators) and outcomes (lagging indicators).

The balanced scorecard approach is becoming a very popular performance measure system in assessing shareholder value creation. Financial institutions should be aware of and utilize the BSC approach in order to compete effectively in today's global market.

ENDNOTES

1. This problem of superadequacy of branches was discussed in Chapter 6 as a form of functional obsolescence.
2. The concepts of franchise and franchise value are discussed in Chapter 14.
3. Kaplan, Robert S., and David P. Norton. 1992. "The Balanced Scorecard—Measures that Drive Performance." *Harvard Business Review* (January/February 1992): 71.

CHAPTER 11

External Environment Assessment

The analyses described in Chapters 9 and 10 provide important insight into the bank being valued. They are, however, inwardly focused analyses. To complete the analysis, it is essential that an assessment be made of the external environment in which the bank operates.

This chapter reviews techniques that can be used to determine the viability and future prospects of the market served by the bank. Each situation will be different, but there are certain basic measures that are indicative of market potential and banking opportunity. These key measures are the focus of this chapter.

11.1   IMPACT OF EXTERNAL ENVIRONMENT ON VALUE

The condition and viability of the external environment has an important bearing on a bank's value. All other things being equal, the better the market, the higher the value of a bank operating in that market. In an active, growing market there tends to be greater opportunity, less price competition, and more customers. Growing, vibrant markets create opportunity and, if capitalized upon, create value.

In the preceding chapter, the tenth P Factor, Potential, addressed the issue of opportunity and how well the bank seizes upon this opportunity as a contributor to value. The degree of success is a result of internal factors, such as marketing, pricing, and strategic planning. No matter how well the bank seizes opportunity, however, that opportunity first must exist. A bank in a stagnant economy may not be able to maintain growth at the rate of inflation, no matter how well it is managed. Consequently, it is imperative that the future potential of the market be assessed and wherever possible quantified.

11.2   SOURCES OF DATA

There are a variety of sources for data useful to the external environment assessment. The most widely used is the U.S. Department of Commerce, which gathers and publishes an enormous amount of economic and demographic data. The Census of Population and Housing, an important data source, contains detailed data on virtually every aspect of demographics at a small area level—data by township, census tract, and even block. *The disadvantage of the census is that it is undertaken only every decade, most recently in 2000,* with updates only in selected areas. The 1990 census fell 4.7 million people short by missing 1.8 percent of the population. This undercount was not spread evenly across the nation, as children and minorities were disproportionately undercounted. However, the Census Bureau's goal in Census 2000 is to improve the accuracy of its census data. The 2000 census can be obtained by visiting the U.S. Census Bureau's home page (http://www.census.gov/). Nonetheless, the census is the most complete and authoritative demographic database available.[1]

Local data sources include planning agencies and chambers of commerce. Planning agencies are usually excellent sources of information on a variety of demographic and economic trends. Many agencies are well staffed and maintain sophisticated, up-to-date databases. A directory of planning agencies is available from the National Association of Regional Councils in Washington, D.C. Chambers of commerce provide a variety of information, especially regarding local business activity. Like planning agencies, however, the range of sophistication is wide. In general, the larger urban areas tend to have more complete and timely data available from their chambers of commerce.

There are a number of private sources that offer demographic and economic data on hardcopy, computer disk, or via on-line computer connections. Most of these sources offer updates to census data and provide customized reports at a county, city, census tract, or zip code level.

Data on financial institution competitors can be gathered from a variety of public and private sources. If detailed financial statistics on competing banks are desired, the Uniform Bank Performance Reports provide a complete database. Deposit statistics at bank and savings and loan branches are available from the Federal Deposit Insurance Corporation (FDIC) and Office of Thrift Supervision (OTS) respectively, as well as from a number of private companies.

11.3 MARKET-WIDE VERSUS SMALL AREA ANALYSIS

There are two potential levels of external environment analysis. The market-wide level analysis considers the broad trend of demographic and economic characteristics at, for example, a regional or county level. A small area analysis examines these characteristics at a census tract, zip code, or city level.

The nature of the market and bank being valued determines whether a market-wide analysis or small area analysis is needed. For example, if a bank being valued operates county-wide, an analysis with county level data is probably sufficient. Conversely, if a bank is located in only one section of a city or county, it may be necessary to analyze that small area, in addition to the market-wide characteristics.

Unless small area data are clearly required, it is usually necessary to undertake only a market-wide analysis. Demographic and economic statistics at a county or regional level are easier to gather, usually more accurate, and updated more often. Small area information, such as at a census tract level, is more difficult to gather and, unless it is taken from the census, has a greater potential for error. The discussions in this chapter focus on external environment assessment at a market-wide level.

Exhibit 11.1   Population Trends By County 1980–2005 (Projected)

	Actual		Estimated		Projected
	1980	1990	1999	2000	2005
County A	42,540	44,950	45,500	46,000	45,000
County B	59,380	60,125	63,520	65,000	70,000
County C	18,760	20,175	24,350	29,000	35,000
Total	120,680	125,250	133,100	140,000	150,000

11.4   DEMOGRAPHIC ANALYSIS

In most cases, the success of local businesses is related to the local population. Therefore, demographic characteristics of the population in the market served by the bank should be analyzed first. To determine the future viability of the market, it is essential that the nature of the people living and working there is analyzed. Even if the bank being valued does not primarily serve consumers, but serves businesses, it is essential to examine demographics.

The most basic assessment is a look at the number of people in the market, how that number has changed over time, and projected changes if available. A summary population table might be constructed as shown in Exhibit 11.1, which was drawn up for a bank with a market area of three counties. From these statistics a wide variety of percentage increases and growth rates can be computed.

The same type of analysis can be undertaken for the number of households, which will not necessarily show the same pattern as the population analysis. Because of declining average household sizes (due in part to more divorces and fewer children), population often increases at rates less than household growth.

Income is the next major area of analysis. There is a strong correlation between the income of households in a market and the banking potential (as measured by deposits and loans). There are a variety of ways to measure income—the two most common are:

- *Per Capita Income:* the average income of all people in an area; and
- *Median Household or Family Income:* the income level where half the households or families make less, and half make more.

Normally, median income is a more useful figure and should be used where possible.

To analyze income trends, a table like the one shown in Exhibit 11.2 might be constructed. The annual increases in income can then be compared to the rate of inflation to determine whether or not real income growth has occurred.

Another demographic measure of interest is the age distribution of the population. The pattern of age can have an impact on whether the market is deposit-oriented, loan-oriented, or a mix of the two. In general, markets with a greater proportion of middle-aged and older residents tend to be deposit-intensive. Conversely, younger residents tend to generate greater loan demand.

The median age figure is not a good measure of the age distribution. A better measure is the percent of residents within various age groups. By comparing the percent of residents

Exhibit 11.2   Median Household Income by County 1980–2005 (Projected)

	Actual		Estimated		Projected
	1980	1990	1999	2000	2005
County A	$ 8,500	$17,500	$22,000	$29,000	$33,000
County B	10,000	21,000	26,500	30,500	35,000
County C	9,500	10,000	12,000	14,000	27,000
Weighted Average	$ 9,393	$17,972	$22,308	$26,590	$32,533

age 18 to 34 or 45 to 64 in the market and in the state, a hypothesis can be made about whether the market will be more loan- or deposit-oriented, or whether it will be both.

Education level is another indicator of market viability. Higher levels of education normally are associated with greater earning power and more banking potential. The percent of residents with four or more years of college should be compared with regional or state figures.

The combination of population, households, income, age, and education provides a sound basis for understanding the nature of the residents in a market and the future viability of the area. Wherever possible, it is beneficial to examine historical trends and projections as well as comparisons to a larger region or the state.

11.5   ECONOMIC ANALYSIS

The next broad type of analysis of the external environment is economic, which considers the business and employment activity in a market and assesses its future potential. Examining the economic characteristics of a market is an essential adjunct to the demographic analysis. Jobs and business opportunity are the principal factors that retain existing residents and attract new ones.

The most basic measure of economic activity is employment. It is important to examine the trend in employment over the last five to ten years and to analyze the levels of employment by industry. These statistics are normally gathered by the state employment service. The breakdown by industry can highlight potential weaknesses in the local or regional economy. This analysis can also indicate whether the market is overly dependent on one industry or employer.

Another good indicator of economic health is the level and trend in retail sales. In a growing market the trend in retail sales is usually upward and at a rate exceeding inflation—usually there is real growth in retail sales. The level of retail sales can be assessed by comparing the sales per person in the market versus the sales per person in the state overall. If the market average is higher than the state average, it means that residents are better off on average and/or that the market is an economic and service center for a larger region, one which draws people from outside the immediate area. Either situation is indicative of above normal banking market potential.

A third important gauge of economic health is the number and type of business firms in a market. The *County Business Patterns* report (U.S. Department of Commerce) provides a detailed listing of the number of businesses by SIC (Standard Industrial Classification) Code in every United States county.

Depending on the size, type, and sophistication of the market being analyzed, there may be a wide variety of other economic statistics available that provide greater insight into the economy. Such measures might include:

- building permits;
- office vacancy rates;
- industrial productions;
- tonnages shipped; and
- tourists.

Each market should be approached as a unique entity, with different types of data indicative of economic health analyzed as appropriate.

11.6 COMPETITIVE ANALYSIS

Reviewing the performance of competitors provides excellent information on the general economy and how the bank being valued fits into the competitive landscape. All the information needed for this analysis is available from the FDIC, the Uniform Bank Performance Reports, OTS (for savings and loans), or National Credit Union Administration (for credit unions).

The first type of competitive analysis is to review the deposit trends for all banks, savings and loans, and credit unions in the market. It is usually best to examine deposits of individuals, partnerships, and corporations (IPC deposits). The difference between total deposits and IPC deposits is public funds. Distortions in deposit trends can result from public funds since these are usually attracted by a bidding process and do not necessarily reflect market forces. Exhibit 11.3 shows a useful way to organize basic deposit data.

This same type of table could also be constructed for each type of deposit (demand, savings, time) as well as for loans.

It is also beneficial to evaluate the strengths of the different types of institutions. In the example above, banks dominate the market with 67 percent of 1999 deposits, but that is down from 71 percent in 1995. Credit unions are almost inconsequential in this particular

Exhibit 11.3   Example-Regional IPC Deposit Trends ($000,000)

	1999	1998	1997	1996	1995
Banks	$1,025	$1,007	$ 989	$ 975	$ 949
S&Ls	482	465	440	409	382
Credit Unions	18	15	14	12	10
Total	$1,525	$1,487	$1,443	$1,396	$1,341
Subject Bank	$ 372	$ 350	$ 307	$ 281	$ 259
Share	24.4%	23.5%	21.3%	20.1%	19.3%

Exhibit 11.4   Gauge of Competitive Intensity

	Market	State
Number of offices		
Banks	43	901
S&Ls	16	194
Credit Union	2	30
Households-number	56,300	880,300
Households per office		
Bank	1,309	977
S&L	3,519	4,538
Credit Union	28,152	29,343
All	923	782

market. The savings and loans are a little stronger with nearly 32 percent of deposits in 1999, up from 28 percent in 1995.

When evaluating deposits it is important that deposit figures be gathered only for branches located in the market being analyzed. For example, suppose the market being analyzed is one county, and one branch of a statewide bank is located in that county. It would be erroneous to include all that bank's deposits in the analysis, since only one branch is represented in the market. Consequently, only the deposits for that one branch should be included. The FDIC reports branch deposit data for banks, as does the OTS for savings and loans. Credit unions do not report branch data, but they usually have few branches or are so small that their effect is negligible.

No information, except for deposits, is publicly reported by branch office. Assets, income, and expenses are reported by the entire institution only. Therefore, if the market being studied has branches of out-of-market institutions, the local area competitive market share analysis will probably be limited to deposits. Wherever possible, however, the relative standing of the subject bank in terms of loans, income, and expenses should be analyzed.

The intensity of financial institution activity is another useful analysis. The intensity can be measured by the ratio of households per financial institution office. When this ratio is compared to other markets, it provides an assessment as to the overbanked or underbanked nature of the market. This information can give some clue as to the opportunity to expand market share, which is likely to be easier in an underbanked market. Exhibit 11.4 can be used to organize the analysis. The statistics indicate that the market being analyzed is slightly underbanked relative to the state average (because the market tends to have more people per financial institution office).

There are many other ways in which a bank can be compared with its competitors:

- locations of facilities and ATMs;
- services offered;
- interest rates and fees;
- profitability measures; and
- markets served.

By analyzing the competition thoroughly, a clear picture of the bank's standing relative to the competition evolves. This can be important input to the assessment of the future opportunity of the bank being valued.

ENDNOTE

1. Other U.S. Department of Commerce publications can be secured at most public and university libraries. This source should be investigated to determine the availability of special reports for the market area being analyzed.

PART IV

Valuation of Mergers and Acquisitions

CHAPTER 12

The Bank Merger and Acquisition Process

The process of merging or acquiring two banking organizations is extremely complex; it requires a great deal of time and effort from both buyer and seller. The business, legal, operational, organizational, accounting, and tax issues must all be addressed if the merger or acquisition is to be successful. Throughout the process, valuation can be an important input to the decision-making process, from initial target analysis through integration of the entities.

The merger and acquisition process, shown graphically in Exhibit 12.1, can be viewed as having three broad phases:

- Strategy Phase
- Negotiation and Investigation Phase
- Finalization and Integration Phase

This chapter reviews the three broad phases of a merger or acquisition and describes the steps normally undertaken. These are not necessarily the steps that would be taken in every situation. They represent, however, the general process that could be undertaken to ensure a successful merger and acquisition program.

12.1 STRATEGY PHASE

The first phase of any merger or acquisition is the development of a *strategy,* which defines the direction of the bank and establishes the long-range goals to be pursued. There are typically seven parts to the first phase:

- Overall strategic plan;
- Merger and acquisition team;
- Merger and acquisition plan;
- Candidate criteria;
- Candidate identification;

Exhibit 12.1   The Merger and Acquisition Process

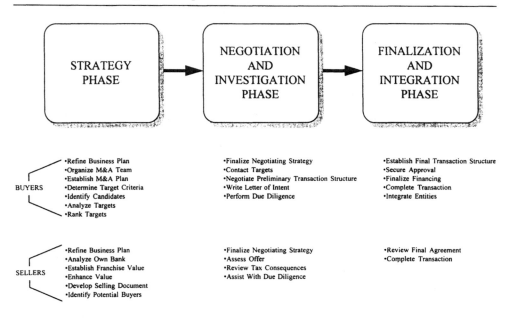

* Candidate analysis; and
* Preliminary valuation and financial feasibility.

This process tends to be oriented to buyers, but sellers should plan just as thoroughly as buyers. Sellers should be prepared for unexpected offers, and possibly even unwanted suitors. A seller should have an overall business strategy defined and know the value of the bank, based on the way a buyer would view it. A selling bank should expend as much effort in the strategy phase as will the buyer.

12.1.1   Overall Strategic Plan

It is essential that a bank establish an overall strategic plan. This overall plan outlines the focus, direction, and objectives of the bank, usually over a three- to five-year time horizon. Such a plan specifies how and where the bank will compete, and identifies markets to be served, resources required, products, pricing, delivery systems, financial structure, growth objectives, and a host of other management variables. Any decision on mergers and acquisitions, whether as buyer or seller, should be made only after broader business direction and goals have been established.

The overall strategic planning process must begin with an honest assessment of the bank's strengths and weaknesses in all areas: finance, management, operations, organization, productivity, market position, delivery systems, and so on. An objective and occasionally overcritical analysis of the bank is absolutely essential for the development of a realistic business plan.

It is then necessary to analyze the market and competitive environment facing the bank thoroughly. Such factors as economic activity, population growth, demographic characteristics, commercial activity, market shares, and legal restrictions are all factors that are external to the bank but have an impact on its strategic alternatives.

Once the bank understands itself and the external environment it faces, major strategic objectives can be identified. Strategic objectives are long term in nature and define the major thrust and direction of the organization, as opposed to specific quantified targets (which come later in the process). Examples of possible strategic objectives include:

- expanding geographic trade area into an adjacent market;
- improving operational capabilities in loan processing;
- enhancing product lines to include more sophisticated credit products; and
- broadening management capabilities in middle-market commercial lending.

In the normal strategic planning process there may be hundreds of objectives. The next task is to identify which objectives are most critical and therefore deserve priority attention.

Strategic objectives do not define the means by which they will be accomplished. There can be several alternative approaches to meet a given objective. For example, a merger or acquisition could be one way to accomplish any one of the four strategic objectives listed above. There are, however, other ways that could be used to achieve these objectives. In other words, *merger/acquisition is not an objective, but a way to achieve other business objectives.* This is a critical distinction because it places mergers and acquisitions in proper perspective; a means to an end, not an end in itself.

Once the strategic objectives of the bank have been identified and ranked, the next task is to establish approaches to achieve the objectives. For any given objective, there can be a variety of alternative approaches. For example, consider the objective of *expanding a geographic trade area into an adjacent market.* There are a number of approaches that could achieve that objective: an acquisition, branches, or a new charter bank. Each alternative approach must be evaluated on its own risks and merits, and the one selected should best meet the needs of the bank. It is usually in this stage of the strategic planning process that the buy/sell/stay independent decisions are made.

After the preferred approach to achieve an objective is selected, the tactical operating plans that will be used to implement the approach can be developed. These tactical plans detail the actions, time frames, responsibilities, resource requirements, and output of the multitude of tasks required to implement a broad program.

The tactical plans can be in a variety of areas such as finance, organization, operations, human resources, marketing, delivery systems, products, and mergers/acquisitions. All the individual plans are related in the sense that they help in achieving the overall objectives of the bank. The merger/acquisition plan, whether the bank will be a buyer or seller, should be developed only within the context of the bank's overall objectives.

12.1.2 Merger and Acquisition Team

If a merger or acquisition is part of the overall plan, the next step in the strategy phase is to organize the merger and acquisition team. It should consist of key bank staff in areas such as lending, administration, finance, operations, marketing, and human resources. The team leaders should be sufficiently senior executives to ensure that extremely critical decisions receive the attention they deserve.

Outside assistance can be valuable throughout the merger and acquisition process. Specialists involved with the merger and acquisition team usually include lawyers, accountants, strategy consultants, appraisers, investment bankers, operational consultants, public relations experts, and special examiners. The input from specialists throughout the process can be crucial to a successful merger or acquisition.

The formation of a merger and acquisition team usually is thought of as the buyer's responsibility. A seller, however, should also have a team. As one of the most important decisions in the life of a bank, the decision to sell and the planning for it should not be taken lightly. The team organized by the seller would have the following types of functions:

- Improve the operational and financial condition of the bank as much as possible.
- Quantify the value of the bank's franchise as is as well as from the perspective of potential buyers.
- Prepare a profile of the bank for potential buyers.
- Determine optimal transaction structure from a tax standpoint.
- Identify potential buyers, and determine the potential value of the bank to each of these buyers.

As with the buyer, the seller's team should consist of key staff and outside experts. Sellers must plan as carefully and prepare just as thoroughly as buyers.

12.1.3   Merger and Acquisition Plan

With the overall business strategy developed and the team identified, the next task is to develop a merger and acquisition plan. The elements of this plan should include:

- timing of activities;
- preparing for sale (if seller);
- desired structure of transaction;
- financial and tax ramifications; and
- negotiating strategy.

The plan developed at this point in the merger and acquisition sequence provides a framework for the remainder of the process.

12.1.4   Candidate Criteria

The bank that intends to buy must establish the criteria to select potential acquisition candidates. These criteria define what kind of institution will be considered by the buyer. The range of possible criteria is almost endless; however, they usually include:

- size, usually measured by level of assets or deposits;
- location;
- quality of loan portfolio;

- asset mix;
- liability structure;
- type of customer or market served;
- market position;
- capital levels; and
- extent of delivery system.

Any given buyer will have its own list of specifications for acquisition candidates. Whatever those criteria are, they should be established early, so that subsequent work is focused in areas where the objectives of the bank will best be met.

12.1.5 Candidate Identification

The acquisition criteria provide the framework from which a list of potential candidates can be developed. At this point, the analysis is usually undertaken using data available from public and private sources. Unless inside information is available, it will be difficult to assess many of the selected candidates on the nonfinancial criteria. Nonetheless, publicly available financial data and information can reveal much about a target institution. Review of the financial data often can reveal strategies, such as retail versus commercial orientation (from loan mix) and degree of aggressiveness (loan-to-deposit ratios and market shares). Field research can help in the evaluation of the target's service delivery system, pricing philosophies, product mix, and marketing programs. Direct consumer research can yield insights about the candidate's image in the marketplace.

After thorough review of the financial data and sound field research, the list of potential candidates can be reduced to a few high priority targets. Frequently, a priority ranking of the candidates will also emerge. While this first cut will not yield all required information, it does reduce the possibilities and thereby facilitates more detailed analysis of the remaining banks. The buyer's management and staff time is, therefore, used more effectively in the subsequent stages of the acquisition process.

12.1.6 Candidate Analysis

With the list of potential targets reduced to a select few, a more thorough analysis can be undertaken. The first analysis is a detailed review of the banks' financial conditions. An examination of five-year trends can be beneficial in identifying strengths and weaknesses of the banks. (Chapter 9 addresses the financial analysis in detail.)

The market and competitive environments should also be analyzed. The economic activity and demographic patterns in the target's market area should be investigated to determine the future growth and expansion opportunities for each target. Part of this review should also be an assessment of competitive activity, especially relative market shares of financial institutions. (Chapter 11 discusses market and competitive analyses.)

12.1.7 Preliminary Valuation and Financial Feasibility

With information from the preceding step, it is possible to place a preliminary value on each candidate. This value estimate is based on information available from public sources and the buyer's market research, and provides a general guideline to the value of each candidate bank. These preliminary valuations are undertaken using the same basic approaches as any other valuation, but the input assumptions are not as complete at this stage as they may be later in the process.

It is also useful to simulate the financial impact on the buying bank assuming various prices and transaction structures. Computer models allow a variety of acquisition assumptions to be assessed in terms of impact on earnings, dilution, and capital levels. From the range of alternatives, it is possible to identify the preferable transaction structures. This does not mean that the seller will necessarily agree to the proposed structure, but the buyer should know the impact of other options.

12.2 NEGOTIATION AND INVESTIGATION PHASE

The second broad phase in the merger and acquisition process is *negotiation and investigation*. This phase covers the activities from initial contact between buyer and seller to the point where the final merger or acquisition agreement can be prepared. There are four major aspects of this phase of the merger and acquisition process:

- Negotiation strategy
- Candidate contact and preliminary negotiations
- Letter of intent
- Due diligence

12.2.1 Negotiation Strategy

The first step is to decide how the initial contact with the target will be made, who will be contacted at the target, who from the buyer will do the contacting, and the general approach to the negotiations. This part of the merger and acquisition process does not lend itself to generalizations. There is an infinite variety of potential strategies. The best approach depends on the unique nature and personality of buyer and seller.

12.2.2 Candidate Contact and Preliminary Negotiations

The first contact with a target is usually made with the chair or president. There are situations, however, where a large shareholder may be the appropriate initial contact. Identifying that shareholder may be difficult; consequently, in any first meeting one should attempt to identify key shareholders.

During the preliminary negotiations the buyer and seller typically discuss their respective goals and objectives in general terms. The basic structure of the proposed transaction is discussed, but price usually is not addressed until the preliminary negotiations are underway. The objective of the preliminary negotiations is for both parties to come to a meeting of the minds.

Obviously, price must be addressed at some time in the preliminary negotiations. At this point, however, the buyer does not have sufficient information to establish a firm price.

Consequently, the price is usually discussed as a *range,* either in dollars or as the stock exchange ratio in a stock-for-stock transaction.

12.2.3 Letter of Intent

If the preliminary negotiations yield positive results, a *letter of intent* should be sent by the buyer to the seller. Such a letter is an agreement in principle to acquire or be acquired, but it is usually not a legally binding commitment. The letter of intent provides the approval for a close inspection by the buyer, and should protect both parties. The letter of intent should cover these points:

- The purchase price range and consideration to be paid
- Approval to provide access to necessary information and staff
- Commitment to maintain confidentiality
- A date by which the transaction is either completed or canceled
- Conditions under which either buyer or seller can escape (usually unforeseen events that could impact the value of the seller significantly, or events that cause a decline in the buyer's stock below a specified level)
- Prohibition of seller from soliciting other offers (to avoid price shopping)

The letter of intent can address as many issues as necessary based on the buyer's and seller's circumstances and needs. At a minimum, however, the six areas described above should be covered.

12.2.4 Due Diligence

Possibly the most critical step in the merger and acquisition process is the *due diligence review.* This is the in-depth analysis of the selling bank by the buyer to ensure that initial assumptions of performance and value are valid. This review is essential to ensure that the underlying business is sound. A thorough due diligence review also can be valuable in identifying weaknesses that will have to be addressed if the acquisition is consummated. Areas normally covered during the due diligence period include:

- Asset quality, especially loan portfolio
- Investments
- Organization, personnel, and staffing
- Delivery systems and facility locations
- Future loan losses and adequacy of existing reserves
- Data processing
- Operations
- Management depth
- Physical plant and property
- Asset/liability management

- Customer base
- Market position
- Interest rate risk exposure
- Concentration of risk
- Contingent liabilities
- Other real estate owned portfolio
- Tax liabilities
- Cash management

Also, an extremely detailed analysis of the financial statements of the bank is appropriate to ensure that all reported financial data are compiled in accordance with generally accepted accounting principles, regulatory requirements, and sound business practices.

A team approach is usually taken in the due diligence review. In addition to the buyer's staff, outside auditors, consultants, lawyers, valuation experts, and investment bankers can play an important role in ensuring that all relevant facts are uncovered. Once the due diligence review is completed, there should be no surprises after the transaction is consummated.

The four elements of negotiation and investigation described above take a buyer's perspective, but the seller must also play an active role. To negotiate effectively, the seller must have a negotiation strategy. Once the letter of intent is received, the preliminary price and deal structure must be analyzed, especially the tax consequences.

One important element that is often not given adequate attention by sellers is the value of the *currency* to be used as payment in a stock-for-stock transaction. In this context, the currency is the stock of the buyer's bank or bank holding company. If the stock received in the transaction is not worth the value the buyer established in the letter of intent, the price actually received by the seller is reduced. This can be a particularly important concern when the buyer's stock is not widely traded. In this case, a prudent seller values the buyer's stock to ensure that a fair exchange ratio is established. Even if the buyer is widely traded, a seller should still have an independent valuation of the buyer's stock.

The seller should also assist in the due diligence review by providing reasonable access to information and staff. The more helpful the seller, the less time the buyer's due diligence team will spend, thereby reducing disruptions to normal activities.

12.3 FINALIZATION AND INTEGRATION PHASE

The last broad phase in the merger and acquisition process is *finalization and integration.* In this phase, the transaction terms are finalized, the transaction is consummated, and the task of integrating the entities begins. The five major aspects of this phase are:

- Final agreement;
- Regulator and shareholder approval;
- Final review;

- Transaction finalization; and
- Integration.

12.3.1 Final Agreement

The *final agreement* is the formal, detailed document that specifies the exact conditions of the transaction. The agreement is a complex legal document that should be prepared and reviewed by both the buyer's and seller's legal counsel. A merger/acquisition agreement usually includes these significant items:

- Description of transaction and closing
- Determination of price and means and conditions for adjustment from initially agreed upon price
- Representations and warranties of the seller—for example, existence of authority to sell, capitalization, approvals/consents, undisclosed liabilities, taxes, litigation, contracts/commitments, and title
- Covenants of the seller—for example, access provision, conduct of business, cooperation, shareholder approval, and avoidance of inconsistent activities
- Covenants of the buyer—for example, filing of regulatory forms, shareholder approval and confidentiality
- Special agreements—for example, management contracts, purchase/sale of assets, and tax sharing
- Employee benefits
- Allocation of purchase price to net assets acquired including intangible assets such as core deposits[1]
- Conditions of closing
- Termination of contract
- Any other special agreements as necessary

No two final agreements are the same, as each transaction has different requirements. These areas listed above, however, typically are found in most agreements.

12.3.2 Regulator and Shareholder Approval

All changes in bank control, whether merger or acquisition, require some type of regulatory approval. The regulatory authorities for various types of banking organizations are:

- *Federal Reserve Bank:* Holding companies
- *Comptroller of the Currency:* National banks
- *Federal Reserve Banks and State Banking Department:* State banks that are Federal Reserve System members
- *FDIC and State Banking Department:* State banks that are not Federal Reserve System members

Usually, the criteria used to evaluate a merger or acquisition are similar for all regulators. The most important criterion is the *safety and soundness* of the combined banks. This criterion considers the resulting financial condition of the combined banks, specifically the so-called *CAMEL* factors—Capital, Asset quality, Management, Earnings, and Liquidity. The regulators search for evidence that indicates that the transaction would weaken the financial condition of the buyer, especially post-merger capital levels.

The second regulatory criterion is *antitrust,* which considers the effect on competition and concentration of economic power. Until 1980, this was the most common reason for denial of a bank merger or acquisition. Since that time, however, the application of antitrust guidelines has been less stringent. One major difference has been in the definition of competition. Heretofore, only commercial banks were counted in calculation of antitrust concentration ratios (the Herfindahl-Hirshmann Index measure of market concentration was the most widely used of these ratios). Regulators now include competition from other financial institutions in their calculations. Consequently, many mergers and acquisitions that would have been denied before 1980 are routinely approved.

The third area of regulatory consideration is *community impact,* especially compliance with the Community Reinvestment Act. Regulators do not look favorably on mergers or acquisitions that would reduce service and convenience to the community. Community activists have been successful in holding up mergers and gaining certain commitments from the parties for low-income housing loans.

Shareholder approval also must be received. The seller's shareholders must always approve the transaction. Moreover, in certain financing arrangements the buyer's shareholders must also approve the transaction. The proxy statements sent to shareholders, which must be approved by regulators, normally include information on the transaction in these areas:

- The reason for the transaction
- The structure of the transaction, including complete description of consideration to be received
- Historical financial data of seller
- Historical financial data of buyer and pro forma presentation of combined historical results if buyer is issuing securities as part of transaction
- Pertinent information about directors and senior management of buyer and seller
- Explanation of dissenting shareholder rights
- Copy of merger agreement

The process of securing regulatory and shareholder approval is extremely complex. The advice of legal, financial, and accounting counsel is required to avoid problems that can delay the transaction.

12.3.3 Final Review

Because bank acquisitions are complicated transactions, the length of time between the due diligence review and all approvals may be six months or more. Often it is beneficial to conduct another brief review of the seller to ensure that there have not been any material changes during that period.

the accounting method used in M & A deals, cash flows of the combined companies remain the same and, accordingly, the cosmetic dilution of earnings and EPS under the purchase method reflects artificial accounting differences rather than real economic consequences.

13.1 ACCOUNTING FOR BUSINESS COMBINATIONS

Business combinations are a fact of life, and M & A activities are happening at a record pace in the global business community. Accounting for business combinations has also emerged as a hot topic in the international standard-setting community. However, the currently used accounting methods for M & A deals have been controversial primarily for several reasons. First, under the current accounting standards [Accounting Principles Board (APB) Opinion No. 16], on business combinations, determination of whether a merger should be accounted as a pooling or a purchase method can be difficult.[3] Twelve relatively subjective criteria must be met for the combination to be accounted for as a pooling method. These twelve criteria are classified into three categories: (1) attribute of combining entities; (2) manner of combining interest; and (3) absence of planned transactions. Exhibit 13.1 shows the three categories and related criteria.

To use the pooling method a bank should comply in advance of an acquisition with the 12 criteria listed in APB Opinion No. 16 as well as with additional Securities and Exchange Commission (SEC) conditions. Most importantly: (1) the acquiring company must issue common stock with rights identical to the majority class for substantially all the shares of the acquired company; (2) cash can be used only for dissenting shareholders and cannot exceed ten percent of the total transaction; (3) only separate and totally independent banks can be pooled; and (4) the combination should be treated as if the two banks had always been combined by simply adding together their historical balance sheets and income statements.

Exhibit 13.1   12 Criteria for Pooling-of-Interests Method of Business Combinations

Group I: Attributes of Combining Entities
1. Autonomous (two-year rule, each of the combining entities may not have been a subsidiary or division of another entity).
2. Independence (10 percent rule, no combining entity may own more than 10 percent of the voting common stock).

Group II: Manner of Combining Interest
. Single transaction (fully completed within one year after plan initiated).
   Exchange of common stock for common stock (90 percent test).
   No equity changes in contemplation of combination (two-year rule).
   Shares reacquired only for purposes other than combination.
   No change in proportionate equity interest.
   Voting rights immediately exercisable.
   Combination resolved at consummation (no pending or conditional provisions).

   p III: Absence of Planned Transactions
   uing entity does not agree to reacquire shares.
   uing entity does not enter into agreements to benefit former shareholders.
   uing company does not plan to dispose of assets within two years of combination.

12.3.4   Transaction Finalization

Once all necessary approvals have been received, the transaction can be closed. The financing is completed and the change of ownership is made. It is at this point that many believe that the process is over. The final task, however, is the most crucial and probably the most difficult.

12.3.5   Integration

To realize the potential benefits of a merger or acquisition, successful integration of the two entities is usually required. Integration management has become a critical component in the overall merger and acquisition process. Integration is not glamorous, but without it all the preceding effort may be wasted.

Early in the process, usually during the due diligence period, a fundamental decision should be made by the buyer. This decision involves the degree of integration to apply after the deal is closed. In other words, how far and how fast will the buyer move in combining the entities? The answer depends on the unique situation and objectives of the buyer, but the options normally fall into one of four categories.

1. *Hands-off:* The seller retains its operations and organization as before the transaction, with the only integration being financial statement consolidation.

2. *Coordinate Activities:* An option that combines the straightforward and easy elements (for example, property insurance, employee benefits, and auditing), but retains separate major operational and organizational systems.

3. *Back Room Consolidation:* An option that combines virtually all the activities not involved with customer contact (for example, data processing, proof, and investments) in addition to the straightforward functions.

4. *Intervention:* The total integration of the seller into the buyer's organization. Under this approach, the seller essentially becomes a branch of the buyer.

Each type of integration approach has been used with varying degrees of success. The buyer should decide early on which level is appropriate for a given transaction.

Irrespective of which approach is to be used, the first important task is to appoint an integration project manager. This function should be considered full time, at least for the duration of the integration. The person should be a high level executive (but not the chief executive officer, as a full-time commitment is unlikely) who has a good understanding of the various aspects of a bank. This position should be given high status and direct access to executive management.

The integration manager should select the team that will work full time to formulate the integration strategy and identify the priority projects needed to integrate the entities successfully. These staff members should be quality people drawn from both the buyer and the seller. Also, it is often beneficial to utilize outside resources as necessary to facilitate the integration and provide objective viewpoints. Consultants in a variety of disciplines can be of assistance on an as-needed basis.

With the required projects identified, the integration team forms task forces of staff to assist on a given project. The members of the task force will not be full-time integration team members, but they will be drawn from the appropriate operational and functional areas.

The integration manager and team have the responsibility of reporting results and ensuring that progress is made according to plan. They also have responsibility to communicate to the task forces the feedback from other areas and senior management. Timely and open communications are essential in successful integration.

ENDNOTE

1. Chapters 8 and 16 discuss the importance of stating value of intangible assets, such as core deposit base, in the merger agreement.

CHAPTER 13

Accounting Standards on Mergers and Acquisitions

Mergers and acquisitions are occurring at a fast pace as companies worldwide look for new ways to improve their efficiency and effectiveness. During the past decade, the volume of mergers and acquisitions has grown substantially and the total value of business combinations, in 1998, mounted to over $1 trillion worldwide.[1] Furthermore, the Gramm-Leach-Bliley Financial Modernization Act (FMA) of 1999, by allowing combinations between banks and other financial services companies including insurance companies, mutual fund and stock brokerages, encourages more mergers and acquisitions (M & A) in the finan services industry. Thus, the need for globally uniform accounting standards for busi combinations is gaining momentum since there is a significant difference in merg counting standards between the United States and the international accounting comr To narrow this gap, the Financial Accounting Standards Board (FASB), on Septe 1999, issued its Exposure Draft (ED) entitled, "Proposed Statement of Financial ing Standards: Business Combinations and Intangible Assets."

The pace of mergers and acquisitions escalated rapidly during the 1990s and to continue in the current century. Together, the combined companies shou greater rate of return on investment regardless of the accounting method used business combinations. Nevertheless, the pooling of interests method (p makes earnings look more attractive in the short run than the purchase meth gained more popularity in the business community. Indeed, in 1998, for t total value of all pooling deals (882.9 billion) exceeds the 773.9 billion purchase transactions.[2]

The ED would change the accounting treatment of M & A transac eliminating the use of the pooling method and requiring that all busir accounted for utilizing the purchase method. The ED would also req imum goodwill amortization period from 40 years currently being The use of the purchase method which results in goodwill recognit quirement of reducing the goodwill amortization period, would ported earnings and the related earnings per share (EPS) for futu mitigate the potential earnings' dilution effects of using the pur allow companies to present in their financial statements a s number which excludes goodwill charges in addition to the

Failure to follow any of these rules precludes the use of the pooling method and, thus, the purchase method should be employed.

Under the purchase method: (1) the purchase price paid plus assumed liabilities (at their fair value) should be allocated to the various acquired assets according to the fair value of those assets; and (2) any purchase price plus other assumed liabilities in excess of these assets' fair value should be treated as goodwill and must be amortized over a period of up to 40 years. The use of the purchase method will normally result in lower reported future net income than a pooling method primarily because of depreciation of the acquired assets and amortization of the recognized goodwill. Although the use of the pooling method may result in higher profits through lower asset values and no recorded goodwill, it may cause dilution in EPS resulting from the issuance of additional common shares for the acquisition of the target company. However, the EPS of the acquiring company will increase upon the acquisition of a company with a lower price-to-earnings multiple (P/E).

The second difficulty is in the proper implementation of the provisions of APB Opinion No. 16. A great portion of the time of regulators is not spent on business combination issues. For example, it is estimated that more than 50 percent of the SEC staff's time is spent on business combinations issues, especially the application of the pooling method.[4] The third controversy is that the existing accounting standards affecting business combinations in the United States are not congruent with those of other countries. In 1997, the G4+1 group, the coalition of standard setters from the United States (FASB), United Kingdom, Australia, Canada, and New Zealand, and the International Accounting Standards Committee (IASC), issued the Exposure Draft (E61) on business combinations.[5]

The IASC, in 1998, revised its IAS 22 by incorporating the provisions of E61 to accounting standards.[6] The revised IAS 22 recognizes two basic types of business combinations: (1) utility of interests in which the acquirer cannot be identified and, thus, such combinations must be accounted for by using the pooling method; and (2) acquisitions in which combinations must be accounted for by using the purchase method. The pooling method should be used only in rare and unusual business combinations in which neither party can be truly identified as the acquirer. To resolve the above controversy and to narrow the gap between the U.S. accounting standards on business combinations and the rest of the world, the FASB, on September 7, 1999, issued its Exposure Draft (ED) on business combinations.[7]

13.2 ALTERNATIVE PROPOSALS TO ED

As an alternative to the FASB's ED which would require the elimination of the pooling-of-interest method, the FASB could opt for restricting the use of the pooling-of-interest method to a standard consistent with International Accounting Standards (IAS.) IAS No. 22 is adopted by G4+1 member organizations (United Kingdom, Canada, Australia, New Zealand) and other countries. These countries permit the pooling method when an acquirer cannot be identified in situations when: (1) the significant majority of voting common shares of the combining entities are exchanged or pooled; (2) the fair value of one entity is not materially different from that of the other combined entity; and (3) the shareholders of each entity maintain substantially the same voting rights and interest in the combined entity. Under the pooling of interest method: (1) carrying amounts on the books of the combining entities should be carried forward; (2) no goodwill should be recognized; and (3) prior financial statements should be restated as if the combining entity had always been combined.

The purchase method of accounting should be used for a business combination in which one of the entities (the acquirer) obtains control over the net assets and operations of another entity (the acquiree) in exchange for the transfer of assets, incurrence of a liability, or issuance of equity. Under the purchase method for business combinations: (1) assets and liabilities of the combined entities should be recognized when it is probable that an economic benefit will flow and if there is a reliable measure of cost or fair value; (2) assets and liabilities of the acquired entity should be valued at the fair value (acquirer purchase price) and be included in the consolidated financial statements of the acquirer's entity; (3) the amount of goodwill for the difference between the cost of the purchase and the fair value of the net assets should be recognized; (4) goodwill should be (a) amortized over its useful life, but not more than five years unless longer (up to 20 years) can be justified; (b) reviewed each year for impairment; (c) written down for impairment with no reverse of the writedown; and (5) no negative goodwill should be recognized, instead the non-monetary assets should proportionately be reduced for negative goodwill; any remaining balance should be treated as deferred income. The revised IAS 22 is effective for annual financial statements beginning on or after July 1, 1999 with earlier application being encouraged.

The ED, which would only apply to profit-oriented entities including financial institutions, consists of two parts. The first part, which is an amendment of APB Opinion No. 16, addresses the accounting method for business combinations. The second part addresses the accounting for intangible assets including goodwill and supersedes APB Opinion No. 17, Intangible Assets. The ED would eliminate the use of the pooling method and require that all business combinations be accounted for using the purchase method. The ED would also require: (1) the amount of goodwill (the excess of the cost of the acquisition price over the fair value of acquired net assets) to be recognized as an asset, and, subsequently, to be amortized on a straight-line basis over its useful economic life, which may not extend 20 years; (2) all goodwill to be reviewed for impairment in accordance with SFAS No. 121; (3) goodwill and identifiable intangible assets to be presented as separate line items on the balance sheet; and (4) goodwill charges (e.g., amortization, impairment) net of tax to be presented in the income statement as a separate line item between income from "continuing operations" and "discontinued operations and extraordinary items." ED would require that goodwill amortization and impairment charges should be disclosed on a net-of-tax basis as a separate line item after income from continuing operations. ED would also require that a per-share amount should be disclosed on the face of the income statement for goodwill charges.

Currently, M & A transactions may be recorded using either the pooling or purchase method. The two methods yield very different financial statement results. Under the pooling method, merging banks simply combine their assets and liabilities as if they had always operated as one without recognizing goodwill or subsequently amortizing goodwill or writing it off against future earnings. Under the pooling method, there is no cash to change hands, only exchange of stock, no assets to write up or write down, no goodwill to drag on future earnings. Thus, the use of the pooling method adds no economic value to merger transactions. It only gives cosmetic boost to EPS. However, the popularity of the pooling method is evident in the growing volume and value of the pooling as a percentage of all acquisitions. The number of M & A transactions using the pooling method has been growing during the past two years as depicted in Exhibit 13.2 and the value of all pooling transactions in 1998 hit a record $850 billion, more than half of the $1.6 trillion value of all U.S. M & A deals.[8] Exhibit 13.2 clearly shows a trend toward a growing number of M & A deals in recent years including Daimler Benz AG and Chrysler Corp; Exxon and Mobil; Travelers and Citicorp;

Exhibit 13.2 Business Combinations

Accounting Method	Year and Number of Combinations				
	1994	1995	1996	1997	Total
	215	244	256	278	993
Purchase Method					
Pooling Method					
a. Prior year financial statements restated.	7	19	17	20	63
b. Prior year financial statements not restated.	12	13	15	18	58
Total Pooling Method	19	32	32	38	121
Total Pooling Combinations	234	276	288	316	

Total I Institute of Certified Public Accountants. 1998. Accounting Trends & Techniques (Fifty-
——67.
Sou
se

...rica and Nations Bank, that have used the pooling method. However, the ED has
...significant concern in merger-minded executives who favor the pooling method to
...ognizing the full market value of the target's assets and the related goodwill on their
...'s financial statements. Financial executives typically favor the pooling method be-
...treats a merger as the combination of two businesses, rather than as one business ac-
...another.

...purchase method has traditionally been applied to business combinations in which
...the consideration is given in cash, other assets, debt, equity shares, or a combination
...of by viewing one of the combining companies as the acquirer and the other as the ac-
...ed or target company. Under the purchase method, the assumption is that the acquirer
...rchases assets and liabilities of the acquired bank in exchange for consideration in the form
of cash or cash equivalent (e.g., other assets, debt instruments, equity shares). The use of the
purchase method to account for M & A transactions normally results in lower reported future net income and dilution of EPS than a pooling method primarily because of the recognition of goodwill charges and higher depreciation of the acquired assets. However, the purchase method should provide management with much greater flexibility in structuring M &
A transactions by: (1) incorporating the use of earn-outs with subsequent payments based on
performance; (2) suggesting new alternatives to corporations such as stock buybacks prohibited by the pooling before and immediately after acquisitions; and (3) recording assets of
the acquired company at their fair value rather than unrealistic historical costs.

13.3 POTENTIAL IMPACTS OF NEW ACCOUNTING STANDARDS ON M & A DEALS

The new ED would practically eliminate the use of the pooling method and require that all
M & A transactions be accounted for by using the purchase method. The FASB initially intended to issue the final statement on accounting for business combinations and intangible
assets by January 2001. However, the FASB is currently (as of October 2000) in the process
of researching and discussing the various alternatives proposed by constituents, the best
method of accounting for goodwill, and other issues related to business combinations.
Thus, the board has decided to delay final deliberations on accounting methods for business

combinations until the year 2002. The ED, by suggesting the possible elimination of the
pooling method, thereby reducing the amortization period to maximum 20 years; and allowing companies to display in their financial statements a second EPS further excluding
goodwill charges (cash flow EPS) may have the following effects on M & A transactions: (1) increasing number of M&A deals before the adoption of the statement on
business combinations (e.g., 2002); (2) more acceptance of cash flow EPS; more efficient M & A deals.

13.3.1 Effect on M & A Deals

One possible impact of the ED in suggesting the elimination of the pooling for all
deals after 2002 would be a significant increase in the numbers of M & A transac-
advance of the final statement by the FASB on business combinations. Companies
crease their willingness to make acquisitions, using the pooling method, during the tim
riod before having to use the purchase method. It is expected that M & A deals will incr
up until 2002 (when the Statement on Business Combinations will be adopted) for prin
rily two reasons. First, the acquirers have the option of using the pooling method which w
prevent dilution of EPS by not recognizing goodwill charges, avoid recognizing goodwill
charges, and avoid recognition of the full market value of the target's assets.

Second, the target banks are in a better bargaining position to ask for higher prices. Indeed, the annotative evidence indicates that acquirers typically pay a higher price to target
companies if they can manage the M & A deals by using the pooling method. For example,
Kimelman (1999, p. 22A) reports that "Banks Under $1 billion in assets went for 2.59 times
book value in pooling deals, a 53 percent premium over the ratio for small banks that were
purchased using purchase accounting."[9] Banks using the pooling method in aggregate pay
much larger premiums (up to 200 percent higher) over fair values than banks that use the
purchase method. Corry [1999, p. 4(A)2] reports that "pooling allowed a company to give
more value in stock than they would in cash."[10] Thus, a boom in M & A deals is expected
through the end of 2000. However, even the elimination of the pooling method should not
slow down the pace of M & A deals because the economic advantages of M & A (e.g.,
economies of scale and scope, increasing efficiency by eliminating duplication of resources
and improving effectiveness by sharing fixed costs of production, marketing, and administration) should far outweigh the cosmetic effects of accounting methods. Nevertheless, the
use of two accounting methods for M & A transactions not only undermines generally accepted accounting principles (GAAP), but also ruins comparability of financial statements
and is not in alignment with accounting standards in the rest of the world.

13.3.2 Cash Flow

The FASB's rationale in eliminating the use of the pooling method is to make earnings more
comparable among companies. Goodwill charges recognized under the purchase method
create a dilution in EPS compared to the pooling method. However, regardless of the accounting method used for M & A transactions, cash flows remain the same and, accordingly,
the dilution of earnings and EPS under the purchase method reflects artificial accounting differences rather than real economic consequences. Indeed, cash flows under the purchase
method for years post-combination can be higher than those under the pooling method for
taxable M & A transactions of goodwill amortization. To mitigate the perceived disadvan-

ASSETS		LIABILITIES & EQUITY	
Cash and due from banks	100	Liabilities:	
Investments	2500	Deposits	8000
Loans & Lease Financing	7500	Borrowings	2000
Premises & equipment (net)	800	Other Liability	500
Other Assets	1100	Total Liability	10500
		Equity:	
		Paid-In Capital	1000
		Retained Earnings	500
		Total Equity	1500
Total Assets	12000	Total Liabs & Equity	12000

ASSETS		LIABILITIES & EQUITY	
Cash and due...			
Investments			
Loans & Lease Financing		Other Liability	
Premises & equipment (net)	90	Total Liability	
Other Assets	85	Equity:	
		Paid-In Capital	100
		Retained Earnings	50
		Total Equity	150
Total Assets	1200	Total Liabs & Equity	1200

Pooling Method
Combined Banks - Statement of Financial Position
At the Date of the Acquisition
($000,000s)

ASSETS		LIABILITIES & EQUITY	
Cash and due from banks	115	Liabilities:	
Investments	2750	Deposits	8770
Loans & Lease Financing	8260	Borrowings	2210
Premises & equipment (net)	890	Other Liability	570
Other Assets	1185	Total Liability	11550
		Equity:	
		Paid-In Capital	1100
		Retained Earnings	550
		Total Equity	1650
Total Assets	13200	Total Liabs & Equity	13200

Purchase Method
Combined Banks - Statement of Financial Position
At the Date of the Acquisition
($000,000s)

ASSETS		LIABILITIES & EQUITY	
Cash and due from banks	115	Liabilities:	
Investments	2750	Deposits	8770
Loans & Lease Financing	8260	Borrowings	2210
Premises & equipment (net)	890	Other Liability	570
Other Assets	1185	Total Liability	11550
Goodwill	450	Equity:	
		Paid-In Capital	1600
		Retained Earnings	500
		Total Equity	2100
Total Assets	13650	Total Liabs & Equity	13650

tage of
r
gc
con
O.
metho
tions, tc
in additic
and cash fr
ment) and, t.
ings. Financi
cash flow earn
analysts to use c

13.3.3 More E.

The use of the poolin
wise would be paid in
ing method would redu
higher prices in order to s.
No. 16 and by the SEC. Sin
ily for future M & A deals, m
binations. The pooling metho
amortization of goodwill, may
discipline in negotiation can be lc
purchase method) to account for
combinations. Especially companie
consummate more efficient M & A
(FMA) of 1999. The passage of the F\
to banks and other types of financial co.
and stock brokerages) that should be add

EPS typically plays an important role i
pooling has favorable impact on EPS, it ma
However, cash flows of the combined banks r
of the merged companies should not be affecte
& A deal. In addition, the pooling method treats
nesses rather than one business acquiring another,
actions consummated through the issuance of stoc.
process than cash transactions which may cause th
price for the target company under the pooling methoo
stock to obtain tax-free treatment of a merger while th
stock to utilize the pooling method to avoid dilution of
goodwill charges. If banks start presenting cash flow earn
in the ED, the market price would decline in the short-ten.
market pricing would improve as cash EPS becomes widel)
pants, especially analysts. Indeed, Kimelman (1999) reports t.
ing will have an impact on the pricing of banks for at least one

Accounting Methods for Business Combinations

A (Acquirer)
al position

Bank B (Target) Financial Position
Statement of Financial Position
December 12, 20X1
($000,000's)

LIABILITIES & EQUITY

Liabilities:
Deposits
Borrowings
Liability

1050
710
210
70
15
250

from banks

	Bank A (Acquirer) Income Statement For the Year Ended 12/31/20X1 (000,000s)	Bank B (Target) Income Statement For the Year Ended 12/31/20X1 (000,000s)	Pooling Method Combined Banks—Income Statement For the First Year of Combination (000,000s)	Purchase Method Combined Banks—Income Statement For the First Year of Combination (000,000s)
Interest Income	1200	125	1325	1325
Interest Expense	(450)	(42)	(497)	(497)
New Interest Revenue	750	78	828	828
Non-Interest Income (Fees & Commissions)	320	33	353	353 (F & C)
Non-Interest Expense (Operating Expense)	(780)	(80)	(860)	(860)
Income Before Inc Tax	290	31	321	321
Taxes, etc.	(150)	(16)	(166)	(166)
Income before Goodwill (GW)				155
GW (Net of $9 tax benefit)				(21)
Net Income	140	15	155	134
ROA	= 1.17%	= 1.25%	= 1.17%	= .98%
ROE	= 9.3%	= 10%	= 9.4%	= 6.4%

*$450 GW is amortized over 15 years.

structuring of the financial transactions; and, finally, establishing revised procedures for negotiating future mergers and acquisitions. Organizations in the financial services industry should also consider how the provisions of the GLB Act will affect their future M & A deals under the new standards. The GLB Act, which was signed by President Clinton on November 12, 1999, permits combinations between banks, insurance firms, and mutual funds. Its passage presents new challenges (e.g., reshaping banks) to banks and other types of financial companies, including insurance firms, mutual funds, and stock brokerages that should be addressed before the GLB Act is implemented by the industry's regulators.

13.5.2   Examine the Risks Inherent in Mergers

Reassess the risk areas in proposed merger and acquisition transactions to minimize the risk of disappointing results. Identify off-balance-sheet contingencies which may affect such mergers under the proposed accounting standards. The risks associated with future mergers and acquisitions that should be re-examined include: (1) operating risk—the likelihood that the business combination does not achieve the intended operational performance; (2) overpayment risk—the risk of overestimating the market value and potential benefit of acquiring another company; and (3) the financial risk of not being able to meet the debt and equity service requirements expected from the proposed business combination.

13.5.3   Determine How the Proposed Accounting Standards Will Affect Bank Mergers, Before and After Their Adoption

Under the proposed accounting standards, banks would be required to use the purchase method, which would force them to amortize any goodwill that was created as a result of a merger or acquisition, which would in turn reduce the merged bank's future reported net income. Indeed, a study by Merrill Lynch (1991)[21] concludes that: (1) fast growing firms in the information technology, financial services, and pharmaceutical sectors which recognize goodwill resulting from the valuation of intangible assets such as intellectual assets, customer base, reputation, or brand name would be most likely affected; and (2) implementation of the proposed accounting standards would discourage productive mergers, mislead investors, and distort the earnings power of the combined firm.

The example presented in Exhibit 13.3 indicates that the pooling method is typically preferred by banks when goodwill is involved because of the negative impact which goodwill amortization has on reported future net income under the purchase method. In addition, banks may favor the pooling method over the purchase method in an attempt to reduce the likelihood of falling out of the minimum regulatory capital requirements. This goodwill amortization also sharply reduces the return on equity of the merged entity for future financial reporting periods. If banks can achieve economic benefits without creating goodwill, they have a strong incentive to initiate business combinations and to offer targets substantial premiums over the book value of their net assets to complete these transactions. Another likely managerial impact of the proposed accounting standards on business combinations would be to encourage a substantial increase in the number of business combinations in the time remaining before the issuance and adoption of new accounting standards (e.g., end of the year 2001). This may also create incentives for management to make acquisitions before the new standards apply based on what looks good financially rather than on substance. The adoption of the proposed standards may also encourage management to negotiate the purchase price of acquired entities much closer to the book value of their assets and assumed liabilities, thereby creating less goodwill.

13.5.4 Consider the Appropriate Accounting Treatment of the Business Combination Transaction

Currently, the merger transaction may be recorded using either the pooling or purchase method. Exhibit 13.4 presents transaction specifications and their effects on the financial statements under both methods. The two methods yield very different financial statement results than those depicted in Exhibit 13.3. Thus, the selected method will affect the future reported earnings per share, and returns on equity significantly. According to APB Opinion No. 16, a pooling method should be used if the shareholders of the two independent banks agree to combine in a joint risk-taking effort while the former shareholders of each company continue to share in the rights and risks of the combined bank. Under APB Opinion No. 16, the twelve specific criteria should be met for a business combination to be treated as a pooling-of-interests method. Most importantly: (1) the acquiring bank must issue common stock with rights identical to the majority class for substantially all the shares of the other entity; (2) cash can be used only for dissenting shareholders and cannot exceed ten percent of the total transaction; (3) only separate entities can be pooled—any divisions or subsidiaries spun off for a combination violate the pooling concept; and (4) the combination should be treated as if the two entities had always been combined by simply adding together the historical balance sheet and income statements of the two banks. Under the pooling method, merging entities simply combine their assets and liabilities as if they had always operated as one without recognizing goodwill or subsequently amortizing goodwill or writing it off against future earnings.

The purchase method of business combinations should be used for any transaction that fails to meet the 12 specific requirements of a pooling method. Under the purchase method; (1) the purchase price paid plus assumed liabilities (at their fair value) should be allocated to the various acquired assets according to the fair value of those assets, and (2) any purchase price plus other assumed liabilities in excess of these assets' fair value should be treated as goodwill and must be amortized over a period of up to 20 years (15 years for tax purposes). The use of the purchase method will normally result in lower reported future net income than a pooling method primarily because of depreciation of the acquired assets and amortization of the recognized goodwill. The ED, however, would eliminate the pooling method to account for business combinations and require the purchase method to be used to account for all business combinations. Under the purchase method, the amount of goodwill should be recognized for the excess of the cost of the acquisition price over the fair value of acquired net assets. The goodwill should be amortized over its useful economic life, not exceeding 20 years. All goodwill and other intangible assets should be aggregated and presented as a separate line item in the balance sheet. Goodwill charges (e.g., amortization, impairment losses) should be presented on a net-of-tax basis as a separate line item in the income statement as shown in Exhibit 13.3.

13.5.5 Consider the Cash Flow Implications of the Proposed Accounting Standards

The FASB's rationale in eliminating the use of the pooling method is to make earnings more comparable among companies. Goodwill charges recognized under the purchase method

Exhibit 13.4 Methods of Accounting for Business Combinations

Transaction Specifications	Pooling	Purchase
1. Assets and liabilities of the predecessor bank are valued at fair value derived from transaction price.	No	Yes (those of the acquired)
2. Goodwill implicit in the transaction price is initially recognized and subsequently amortized.	No	Yes
3. Retained earnings of the predecessor bank are carried over.	Yes (all)	Yes (those of the acquirer)
4. Earnings of the merged banks are combined prior to the date of combination.	Yes	No
5. Ownership groups remain intact.	Yes	No
6. The combined bank is viewed as a continuation of its predecessors.	Yes	No (only that of the acquirer)
7. Combining companies are considered parties in the business combination.	No (shareholders only)	Yes
8. New bank is created as a result of the business combination.	No (predecessors survive in combined form)	No (dominant party survives)
9. There is a change in control of some or all of the assets and liabilities of the combining banks.	No	Yes (those of the acquirer)

create a dilution in EPS compared to the pooling method. However, regardless of the accounting method used for M & A transactions, cash flows remain the same and, accordingly, the dilution of earnings and EPS under the purchase method reflects artificial accounting differences rather than real economic consequences. Indeed, cash flows under the purchase method for post-combination years can be higher than those of the pooling method for taxable M & A transactions because of tax benefits of the goodwill amortization. To mitigate the perceived disadvantage of the purchase method, the ED allows companies to present cash flow EPS that does not include goodwill charges (e.g., impairment and amortization). The ED suggests that goodwill charges be presented in the income statement as a separate line item between income from "continuing operations" and "discontinued operations and extraordinary items."

One alternative method of eliminating the cosmetic disadvantage of the purchase method over the pooling method is to encourage companies' reported cash earnings and cash flow earnings per share in addition to commonly reported accrual earnings per share. The reported cash earnings and cash flow earnings per share exclude goodwill charges (e.g., amortization and impairment) and therefore, mitigate the cosmetic negative effects of the purchase method on earnings. Companies and their executives (e.g., top level management) should use cash flow earnings in forecasting future earnings and encourage and educate their financial analysts to use cash flow earnings per share in their forecasts and subsequent revisions.

13.5.6 Recalculate the Tax Implications of Mergers Under the New Proposed Accounting Standards

As always, the business objective here is to structure a tax strategy that minimizes the total taxes paid on the business combination transaction by both acquired and acquiring entities. By minimizing the combined taxes, value will be added to the transaction that should be shared by both the buyer and seller. The buyer should manage the merger and acquisition under the new standards so as to reduce the after-tax cost of acquiring the business by: (1) maximizing the business tax assets after the purchase, and (2) allocating the purchase price to assets that can be expensed or depreciated quickly for tax purposes. The seller should try to structure the sale in such a way as to maximize the after-tax proceeds from the sale by managing the timing and recognition of any taxable gains in an optimal manner to minimize taxes paid on such gains. The ED would require that goodwill charges (e.g., amortization, impairment) be presented on a net-of-tax basis. Goodwill charges may be deductible for tax purposes in taxable business combinations. Whenever goodwill charges are recognized, pretax income or loss from continuing operations should include goodwill charges on a pretax basis and should be calculated by applying a "with and without" computation as suggested in the ED.

13.5.7 Review All of the Above with Independent Bank Accounting Firms and Tax Advisors

Consult with bank independent public accountants prior to, during, and after future mergers and acquisitions because they should have the knowledge and expertise to help assess the accounting, auditing, taxation, and operating system aspects of business combinations under the proposed accounting standards. Indeed, all Big Five CPA firms now provide mergers and acquisitions advisory and due diligence services, which are gearing up to address such issues. If you are utilizing a smaller firm, ask them to indicate if they are up to speed on the critical merger issues discussed above, as they are affected by the new proposed accounting standards.

13.5.8   Provide Full Disclosure of Merger and Acquisition Transactions

The ED will require two relatively different sets of financial disclosures for material business combinations and individually immaterial business combinations. For material business combinations, the ED would require: (1) the name and a brief description of the acquired enterprise and the percentage of voting shares acquired; (2) the consolidation period; (3) the cost of the acquired enterprise; (4) any contingent payments, options, or commitments agreed upon; and (5) a condensed balance sheet disclosing the book value and fair value of major assets of the acquired enterprise at the date of acquisition. The ED would require practically the same aforementioned disclosures for individually immaterial business combinations if such combinations are material in the aggregate.

13.5.9   Inform Financial Statement Users About Bank Business Combinations

Communicate merger and acquisition strategies including their possible financial and managerial impacts to all interested parties, including executive management, directors, the audit committee, shareholders, creditors, and regulators. Shareholders and creditors may overreact to the perceived negative financial effects of the proposed mandatory use of the purchase method and the elimination of the pooling method. The bank's secretary should be involved to ensure that key shareholders and financial analysts are informed about the nature, complexity, and transaction impacts of new mergers and acquisitions and their accounting and reporting requirements under the ED. The assumption is that sophisticated investors and analysts look through mere accounting numbers in assessing economic consequences of corporate actions. Thus, while the pooling of interests method may be favored by corporate officers to avoid the apparent negative effect of goodwill amortization under the purchase method, the real economic consequences of the ED to investors and analysts is less clear.

13.6   CONCLUSION

The high profile of recent merger and acquisition announcements has placed accounting for business combinations on the front burner of standard-setting bodies worldwide. The FASB is rapidly moving toward mandating the purchase method of accounting for future business combinations and the elimination of the pooling of interests method. This deliberation process will take about a year to finalize, and it is expected that the FASB will issue its final statement on business combinations in 2002. Therefore, the differences in accounting methods for business combinations will continue to exist for several quarters, which makes it difficult to assess the comparability of financial statements of enterprises that are active in mergers and acquisitions. Exhibit 13.3 illustrates how the differences in accounting between the two most commonly used methods (pooling, purchase) for business combinations affect the combined entities' financial statements. It clearly shows that there are significant differences in both balance sheets and income statements between the two methods.

When the FASB mandates accounting standards that require the use of purchase accounting as the only generally accepted method for business combinations, it will force significant changes in financial reporting and managerial decision making. The balance sheet impact of using the purchase method is an increase in the size of the balance sheet because of the recognition of goodwill and the excess of fair value over book value of identifiable assets. The income statement effect is the dilutive earnings per share effect of goodwill charges (e.g., amortization, impairment). Even though the use of the accounting method (pooling versus purchase) may not have a direct impact on future cash flows, management should pay a great deal of attention to the true economic consequences of merger transactions. Furthermore, the complexity of the proposed accounting standards on business combinations will make the implementation process difficult. Therefore banks should move now to ensure timely establishment of the proper managerial strategies for assessing future business combinations.

ENDNOTES

1. Marcial, Gene G. 1998. "That Was Just the "Warm-up." *Business Week* (December 29): 151.
2. MacDonald, E. 1999a. Accounting Rule Makers Vote to End Popular Poolings of Interest in Mergers. *The Wall Street Journal* (April 22): C23.
3. Accounting Principles Board. 1970. "APB Opinion No. 16, Business Combinations" (August).
4. Munter, P. 1999. New Proposals Planned for Business Combinations, Consolidations, and Stock Compensation Plans. *Journal of Corporate Accounting & Finance* (Spring): 159–164.
5. International Accounting Standards Committee. 1997. "Proposed International Accounting Standards: Business Combinations." (E61, August).
6. International Accounting Standards Committee. 1998, "ISA22." *Business Combinations.*
7. Financial Accounting Standards Board. 1999. Proposed Statement of Financial Accounting Standards: Business Combinations and Intangible Assets (December 7, FASB, Norwalk, CT).
8. MacDonald, E. 1999b. Accounting Rule Makers Unveil Plan to Abolish Poolings of Interest for M&A. *Wall Street Journal* (September 9): A4(W).
9. Kimelman, J. 1999. Plan to End Pooling-of-Interests Accounting Will Impact Merger Plans. *American Banker* (September 14): 22A.
10. Corry, C. 1999. M&A Accounting Raises Concerns. *Business News* (September 17): P4(A)2.
11. loct. Kimmelman. 1999.
12. Franks, J., R. Harris, and S. Titman. 1991. The Post-merger Share-price Performance of Acquiring Firms. *Journal of Financial Economics* (Vol. 29): 81–96.
13. Agrawal, A., J.F. Jaffe, and G.N. Mondelker. 1992. The Post-merger Performance of Acquiring Firms: A Re-examination of an Anomaly. *Journal of Finance* (Vol. 47): 1605–1622.
14. Larcker, D.F., and J.E. Balkcom. 1984. Executive Compensation Contracts and Investment Behavior: An Analysis of Mergers. Manuscript. Northwestern University.
15. Robinson, J., and P. Shane. 1990. Acquisition Accounting Method and Bid Premium for Target Firms. *The Accounting Review* (January): 25–48.

16. Lys, T. and L. Vincent. 1995. An Analysis of Value Destruction in AT&T's Acquisition of NCR. *Journal of Financial Economics* (Vol. 39): 353–378.

17. Vincent, L. 1997. Equity Valuation Implications of Purchase versus Pooling Accounting. *The Journal of Financial Statement Analysis* (Summer): 5–19.

18. Ibid.

19. Crawford, D. 1987. The Structure of Corporate Mergers: Accounting, Tax, and Form-of-payment Choices. Dissertation, University of Rochester.

20. loct. Larcker and Balkcom. 1984.

21. Merrill Lynch. 1999. Valuing the New Economy. A White Paper presented by the Merrill Lynch Forum (June).

CHAPTER 14

Valuing a Bank as a Business Enterprise

Valuing a bank or bank holding company is one of the more crucial and highly visible aspects of valuation as part of a merger or acquisition. A mistake at this point can be very costly. Overestimate value and a buyer is left with a difficult premium to earn back; underestimate value and the seller does not realize the best price or maximize shareholder value.

This chapter presents techniques that can be used to establish the value of a bank as an ongoing business entity. To examine the process, Example Bank is used to illustrate specific application of the valuation principles. The financial history of Example Bank is discussed in Chapter 9. The discussion in this chapter focuses on the process of valuing the bank rather than the research necessary to develop the required base of information. The research required for a thorough bank valuation is the subject of Part III of this book, Chapters 9, 10, and 11.

The Example Bank referred to in this chapter is not a particular bank. It is a composite of several real banks with characteristics that allow illustration of a straightforward valuation. Conditions that can make a valuation more complex and difficult are addressed in Chapter 18.

14.1 BUSINESS ENTERPRISE VERSUS A COLLECTION OF ASSETS

When establishing the value of a bank as a business enterprise, the assets owned by the bank need not be valued individually except in unusual circumstances. The relevant value estimate is based on the future income-generating capabilities of the bank as a whole operating unit, not on the specific assets it happens to own. At this level of analysis, the individual assets are important only to the extent that they help explain the basis for future income. For example, understanding the overall mix and quality of loans and investments is essential to forecasting future income levels. It is usually not necessary, however, to know the value of each individual loan and investment, except in cases where large losses are possible or unrealized on the balance sheet.

There are instances where individual assets may need to be examined, even within the context of the valuation of the total business enterprise. Situations where nonperforming loans or other real estate (ORE) are a substantial part of the asset base may require a special analysis. Individual assets are also more important when recent earnings have been poor and the outlook is not good. In such a case, a more accurate indicator of the bank's overall value may be its net asset value rather than future earnings potential.

In this chapter, it is assumed that the Example Bank is a profitable institution with favorable prospects for continued profitability. Chapter 18 discusses approaches to situations different from this one.

14.2   THE CONCEPT OF THE BANKING FRANCHISE

Valuation of a bank as a business enterprise is essentially the valuation of its *franchise*. This term is used frequently in merger and acquisitions, but there seems to be a range of opinion as to exactly what franchise means.

When people speak of a banking franchise they usually are referring to the composite nature of all the bank's individual characteristics that make it an economically viable entity. These individual characteristics can include:

- Customer base
- Deposit insurance as part of charter
- Management and staff
- Office locations
- Operational systems
- Technological capabilities
- Financial acumen
- Delivery systems
- Image
- Market share

These and many other individual characteristics combine and work together to form the franchise. The stronger these characteristics are and the more effectively they work together, the more valuable the franchise.

Theoretically, a buyer should pay no more for a bank than its current franchise value. In other words, the buyer should not pay the seller for value the buyer may create in the future through better management and planning. This was the difference between fair market value and investment value discussed in Chapter 5. In reality, however, the market for banks, especially sound and healthy ones, is competitive, with multiple buyers usually bidding for one seller. Consequently, the price paid will almost always reflect a sharing of the value creation opportunities the buyer expects to bring. For example, suppose a selling bank's as is franchise is valued at $100 million.[1] Two buyers are bidding, with one projecting a value creation potential of $20 million over current franchise value, the other an additional $10 million. Each of these buyers believes it can bring skills that will lead to enhanced value of the selling bank. If each buyer has a great desire to own the seller, the eventual price is likely to be over $110 million. The first buyer was willing to share value creation potential with the seller up to the point of outbidding the second buyer. The problem arises if the buyer overestimates its ability to add value. If the buyer does not add $10 to $20 million of value, its shareholders suffer the consequences.

The entire subject of franchise value, both current and potential, is critical to the proper valuation of an acquisition target. An astute buyer will usually value a target bank given its current franchise, analogous to the value if purchased and left alone. This provides a starting point for further valuation based on various value creation assumptions: that is, a "buy and improve" value. The smart buyer knows to walk away when the price to be paid requires too much sharing of value creation potential with the seller.

14.3 DIFFERENCE BETWEEN STRATEGIC AND TACTICAL VALUATIONS

The types of valuation thought of most often during a merger and acquisition are those at a *strategic* level. These types of valuations are critical to the overall decision-making process, especially in assessing franchise value, quantifying value creation potential, pricing a target, or evaluating an offer.

The stated objective in virtually all mergers and acquisitions is the enhancement of shareholder value. Given this objective, the postcombination earnings, return on equity, and/or stock price should be higher than before the combination. For these conditions to be met, the transaction price must reflect a realistic value of the selling bank to that buyer. Consequently, the most critical valuation task at a strategic level is establishing a value of the target bank's franchise, both as is and potential, as discussed above. This is especially important to the buyer (so as not to overpay) but it is also important to the seller (to ensure a fair price is received).

In the early stages of the merger and acquisition process it is possible to value an institution from the outside as a freestanding entity. For this type of valuation, the needed information is publicly available. This value is not as accurate as it would be after full access to the subject bank, but it provides a general starting point. The buyer's financial analysts and tax advisors can then simulate the impact on the buyer of various combinations of payment, price, and transaction structures. Also, the effect on value creation of different assumptions about the target's growth rates, future loan losses, spreads, and expenses can be quantified. It is essential that a range of values be established for a target early in the process, and the effect on the buyer's financial structure and performance be quantified. This knowledge allows the buyer to negotiate with a better understanding of the impact of different assumptions on key financial variables.

The seller should also have a valuation of its own franchise to provide a basis for assessing an offer price. The value of the franchise can be assessed on an as is basis, and from the perspective of specific potential buyers. Early on, the seller should also have a review of tangible asset value, as well as potential intangible assets.

Once buyer and seller agree to proceed, strategic valuation requirements still exist. From the buyer's perspective, a more detailed valuation is required based upon full access to the seller's internal records. The additional information will allow for better assumptions on which to estimate value. The internal information will also allow for identification of intangible assets that may exist. (The early identification of intangibles, and their inclusion in the final acquisition agreement, can be useful in supporting certain tax allocations and deductions.)

The seller should also value the buyer's stock if such stock is part of the consideration received. This ensures that the stock exchange ratio is appropriate relative to the values of the two banks. The valuation of the buyer's stock is especially important if it is a closely held bank with a limited market for the stock.

While the strategic level valuations are the well known type, the *tactical level* valuations usually require the most effort and are necessary to meet a variety of regulatory, legal, tax, and/or accounting purposes. From the buyer's perspective, detailed valuations of premises and other tangible assets are required for accounting and tax reasons, especially if purchase accounting is used. Moreover, the valuation of intangible assets can have tax advantages under certain transaction structures. The buyer should also value the major components of the seller's loan portfolio and underlying collateral of substantial book value. This type of valuation can provide valuable input for making decisions on the structure of the transaction, as well as strategic moves after the acquisition.

14.4 WHY THE COST APPROACH IS NOT USED FOR STRATEGIC BANK VALUATIONS

The cost approach values a property based on the expenses incurred to replace it, less any physical, functional, and economic obsolescence. From a practical standpoint, this approach is very difficult to use when valuing a bank (or any type of business) as an operating entity, especially where significant intangible assets are involved.

The cost approach is better suited for valuation of the individual tangible assets of a bank, such as its building and equipment. The value of the bank's franchise, as mentioned previously, is more than the collective value of the assets. Consequently, the cost approach is generally not used to value a bank at a strategic level.

14.5 APPLICATION OF THE MARKET APPROACH TO VALUING A BANK

The market approach values a bank based on the prices paid to acquire similar banks, with adjustments as necessary to compensate for the lack of direct comparability. This valuation approach must be used very carefully, as every acquisition situation is different and the prices paid in other transactions must be assessed thoroughly. Since each situation is unique, the exact same circumstances of buyer and seller will not be replicated. Consequently, great care must be taken when selecting comparable transactions and using the data as a basis for determining the value of a bank.

The previous discussion of value creation potential and its impact on price is the reason that the market approach must be used carefully. Because the market for financially solid banks is relatively competitive, buyers often bid up prices based on value creation possibilities (either real or perceived). Consequently, the prices reported often reflect as is value and a value creation factor. This is the *investment value* described in Chapter 5. By using these prices to value another bank, it must be realized that something above as is or stand-alone value is being measured. Notwithstanding these problems, the market approach is used widely in pricing bank acquisitions.

14.5.1 Identification of Comparable Transactions

The first task in applying the market approach is to gather data on similar bank acquisition transactions. There are public and private data sources on banking acquisitions. The Federal Reserve Bank or State Banking Department with jurisdiction over the proposed acquisition should be able to assist in identifying comparable transactions.

The result of this research should yield a chart similar to that shown in Exhibit 14.1. These ten bank sales fit the general characteristics of Example Bank—they are all roughly the same asset size and historically profitable. Information that is not shown on the exhibit but should be analyzed nonetheless includes other characteristics such as asset/liability mix, capital levels, market area, and general lines of business.

14.5.2   Basis of Comparability

No two transactions will be comparable in every way. Consequently, the identified transactions may have to be adjusted to be more comparable to the bank being valued. Although there is an infinite number of variables that can affect the purchase price, the six key factors shown below are the most significant.

1. *Type of Market:* Comparable transactions should be in similar types of businesses and sizes of markets. This factor should also reflect the various market risks associated with the comparable bank sales.
2. *Sales Dates:* Sales within the last two years are preferred, because changing economic and competitive conditions can alter the acquisition environment.
3. *Asset Size:* Comparables should be of approximately the same size, preferably no smaller than half the size and no larger than twice the size.
4. *Five-Year Asset Growth:* Because asset growth is positively correlated with value in many cases, it is best to compare banks that have grown at about the same rate.
5. *Five-Year Return on Assets:* Because profitability has a direct influence on value, the nearer the return on assets, the more comparable the transaction. Also, the degree of volatility of income should be considered.
6. *Form of Payment:* Because form of payment affects tax and liquidity issues, it can affect price paid. Consequently it is better to have transactions which involved the same payment medium.

No transaction will be identical to another, but if the six factors described previously are used as a basis, transactions that are sufficiently similar to allow valid comparison or that can be adjusted to reflect the conditions of the proposed transaction can be selected.

14.5.3   Publicly Traded Companies As Comparables

If the bank or bank holding company being valued is publicly traded, then other such banks can be used as comparables. Market price per share plus a control premium provides a basis for a value estimate.

Great care must be taken, however, when using data on publicly traded banks as a basis for establishing value of a closely held bank. The dynamics and economics of their respective markets are quite different. Also, the types of institutions are usually dissimilar—with different lines of businesses, leverage, debt structure, markets, and so on. It can be useful to investigate the price-earnings ratios for publicly traded bank stocks to gauge, in general,

Exhibit 14.1 Bank Sales Comparable to Example Bank ($000)

Name	Sales Date	Asset Size	5 yr. Annual Asset Growth	5 yr. avg. Return on Assets	Form of Payment	Price to Book Equity	Price to Recent Year's Earnings
Bank 1	4/12/98	$316,129	12.7%	0.95%	Cash/Stock	1.25	18.1
Bank 2	6/19/98	369,178	18.2%	1.22%	Cash	1.47	9.2
Bank 3	8/1/98	558,496	9.7%	0.94%	Cash	1.03	11.7
Bank 4	8/10/98	423,048	13.1%	1.15%	Stock	1.35	12.3
Bank 5	9/27/98	341,911	6.8%	1.32%	Stock	1.78	13.8
Bank 6	1/17/99	534,715	15.2%	0.78%	Cash	0.95	9.2
Bank 7	3/15/99	478,776	12.9%	1.17%	Cash	1.17	13.1
Bank 8	5/19/99	310,160	16.1%	0.80%	Cash/Stock	1.51	14.4
Bank 9	6/12/99	322,399	7.9%	1.20%	Cash	1.33	12.7
Bank 10	8/28/99	412,315	13.7%	1.04%	Cash	1.14	10.5
Average $ (Unweighted)	—	$406,713	12.6%	1.06%	—	1.30	12.5
Example Bank	12/31/99	$388,206	14.5%	0.73%	Cash	—	—

what other investors are paying for an income stream. Reliance upon that information alone for value estimation of a closely held bank is risky. In general, it is advisable to avoid exclusive or predominant use of data on publicly traded banks when valuing a closely held one. Other techniques and data sources that involve greater certainty are usually available.

14.5.4 Value Estimation by Market Approach—An Example

The data in Exhibit 14.1 show the price paid for the ten comparable transactions as a multiple of book equity and earnings. The average for the comparables is also shown. The application of these statistics to the proposed transaction requires careful judgment, as the publicly available data may mask underlying factors and conditions that affected the purchase price, including adverse market conditions, unusual loan losses, or any number of other unique circumstances.

The ten comparable banks are slightly larger in asset size, slower growing, and more profitable than Example Bank. How these factors interrelate to form value is a subjective measure. In the Example Bank case, faster asset growth is a positive factor only if profitability can support the higher capital requirements, but the somewhat lower profitability is negative. Based on an in-depth analysis of Example Bank and its market, it is known that such asset growth is unlikely to continue, given changes in its market served, and that future asset growth will be nearer or less than the ten bank average.

The profitability of Example Bank has been increasing slightly, but is still well below the ten bank sample for a five-year average. A thorough analysis of Example Bank indicated that a 0.9 to 1.0 percent return on average assets is a reasonable long-term expectation.

Two measures are used to compute the value of Example Bank by the market approach: price to book equity and price to earnings.[2] Because Example Bank is expected to be less profitable than the ten comparables, a price to earnings ratio of 10 is reasonable, resulting in a value estimate of $30.7 million. Because of expected future performance, a price to equity multiple of 1.1 was used, resulting in a value estimate of $23.7 million. Averaging the results yields an estimate of value of Example Bank using the market approach of $27.0 million.

14.5.5 Advantages and Disadvantages of Market Approach

The market approach has one overriding advantage: it considers real transactions. In other words, it reflects actual conditions in the marketplace. The disadvantages, however, are significant, especially if the bank being valued and the comparables are closely held.

Price paid reflects much more than book value of equity or last year's earnings. As described in Chapter 5, book value has little or no relevance to market value. Consequently, relating a market price to a nonmarket measure is comparing apples to oranges. Moreover, value is a reflection of future benefits, whereas last year's earnings are historical.

The most significant disadvantage, however, is that comparable prices often reflect more than the current franchise value of the selling bank. As discussed earlier in this chapter, the eventual price will, in all probability, reflect current franchise value plus the level of value creation potential the buyer is willing to share with the seller. The relation between price and value depends on the unique circumstances and perceptions of buyer and seller. The value of a bank established by comparing it to other transactions is likely to be higher than its current franchise value. Therefore, the market approach must be used very carefully with full awareness of what is, and what is not, included in comparable sales data.

Notwithstanding the disadvantages of the market approach, this technique can be a good check on values derived by other approaches if used properly. Also, because the information on bank transactions is reported widely, the data needed to utilize this approach are fairly easy to gather.

14.6   APPLICATION OF THE INCOME APPROACH TO VALUING A BANK

The income approach values a bank based on the net present value of future income (best measured by available cash flow) generated by the bank. This future income has two components:

1. Actual cash available to owners each year after meeting all expenses, reserves, and capital requirements necessary to sustain and grow the bank

2. The residual value of the bank at the end of a specified projection period (ten years is typical)

The first component, cash available to the owners, can be thought of as the dividend paying capacity of the business. The second component, residual value, is analogous to the value of the bank's franchise if it were sold at the end of the projection period. The bank need not be sold, but a residual value must be computed as part of the valuation mathematics. These two sources of income are comparable to the potential benefits of any investment: current income and future income from appreciation of the asset.

14.6.1   Measuring Available Cash Flow

Available cash flow in the context of a bank acquisition is the amount of cash available to the owners at the end of an accounting period. This is true cash flow because it quantifies the monetary amounts that can be paid to owners. This is not the same as cash flow in an accounting sense as reported by banks in their annual reports.

Available cash flow is driven by the net income of the bank after it adds to capital the amounts necessary to meet regulatory requirements. As a formula:

$$\text{available cash flow} =$$
$$\text{net income} - \text{required additions to equity capital}$$

This is also the formula for potential dividends. Therefore, the available cash flow from a bank to owners can be thought of as the potential dividends the bank could pay.

This formula is consistent in every bank because all regulated banks come under specific rules with respect to dividends and capital:

- Banks have very specific minimum capital requirements that cannot be violated (at least beyond short periods of time).
- Dividends can be paid only to the extent that capital is not reduced (except with special permission).
- Net income is the basis for determining allowable/potential dividends.

14.6.2   Overview of Income Approach Model

The general form of the income approach model that can be used to value a bank is shown below:

value of bank by income approach =
present value of available cash flow for 10 years
+ present value of residual value after tenth year

The most crucial aspect of the valuation is the forecast of available cash flows. To arrive at that figure, it is necessary to project the balance sheet and income statement of the bank being valued. Techniques to project these variables are discussed in the next two sections of this chapter.

14.6.3   Projection of Key Balance Sheet Items

The first step in projecting available cash flows is to project the key balance sheet items of the bank. The balance sheet contains the "drivers" of income and expenses such as loans, investments, deposits and so on. Estimating future income based on "drivers" is a more complex approach than simply extrapolating historical income and expenses. Use of this approach is justified, however, because it is a more accurate reflection of the way income is actually generated at a bank.

Exhibit 14.2 illustrates some key balance sheet items and techniques that can be used to forecast each item. As with any projection, judgment and analysis must interact to form a reasonable, informed estimate.

There are a number of techniques that could be used to project a bank's balance sheet. The one used in this book requires these seven steps:

1. Project the year-end asset levels for the next ten years and the residual period, based on a percentage increase over the preceding year.
2. Project earning and nonearning assets as a percent of year-end total assets.
3. Project total loans as a percent of earning assets, and net loans based on a target loan loss reserve to total loans ratio.
4. Project investments and other earning assets as the difference between total earning assets and net loans.
5. Project total liabilities as the difference between total assets and equity.
6. Project core deposits, noncore deposits, and other interest-bearing liabilities as a percent of total liabilities.
7. Project capital requirements under new risk-weighted rules, given the projected asset mix.

The assumptions used to project the balance sheet of Example Bank are summarized in Exhibit 14.3. The resulting projected balance sheet is shown in Exhibit 14.4.

Exhibit 14.2   Possible Approaches to Projecting Key Balance Sheet Items

Item	Alternative Projection Techniques
Loans	• Market share • Percentage change from preceding year • Percent of total assets • Absolute value
Loan Loss Reserves	• Target percent of total loans • Absolute levels
Investments	• Percentage change from preceding year • Percent of total assets • Absolute value • Difference between total earning assets and net loans
Other Earning Assets	• Percentage change from preceding year • Percent of total assets
Nonearning Assets	• Difference between total assets and earning assets • Percent of total assets • Percent change from preceding year • Absolute value
Total Assets	• Percentage change from preceding year • Summation of individual asset values • Absolute value
Core Deposits	• Market share • Percentage change from preceding year • Percent of total liabilities • Absolute value
Other Deposits	• Percentage change from preceding year • Percent of total liabilities • Absolute value
Other Liabilities	• Percentage change from preceding year • Percent of total liabilities • Absolute value • Difference between total liabilities and deposits
Total Liabilities	• Difference between total assets and equity • Summation of individual liability values

14.6.4   Projection of Income, Expenses, and Available Cash Flow

Simultaneously with the projection of the key balance sheet items, the future income, expenses, and cash flows can be estimated based on a variety of assumptions. The derivations of the income assumptions are summarized below:

• *Net Interest Income.* This is total interest income minus total interest expense. Rather than attempt to project each individually (which requires a forecast of interest rates), it is more reasonable to project the interest spread that is achievable over a base cost of funds. The base cost of funds used in the valuation of Example Bank is the cost of interest-bearing

Exhibit 14.3   Assumptions to Project Balance Sheet of Example Bank

Variable	Assumptions
Asset Growth Per Year	8% in year 1, 7% in year 2, 5% thereafter.
Nonearning Assets	11% of total assets in year 1, 10% in year 2, 9% thereafter.
Total Loans	69% of total assets in year 1, 70% in year 2, 71% in year 3, 72% thereafter.
Loan Loss Reserves	1.0% of total loans in year 1, 0.9% in year 2, 0.8% in year 3, 0.7% thereafter.
Investments and Other Earning Assets	Balance of total assets minus total loans minus loan loss reserves minus nonearning assets.
Total Deposits	80% of liabilities in year 1, 85% in year 2, 90% in year 3, 95% in year 4.
Noninterest Bearing Core Deposits	23% of total deposits in year 1, dropping by 2% per year and stabilizing at 11% in year 7.
Interest Bearing Core Deposits	75% of total deposits in year 1, increasing by 2% per year to 80% in year 6.
Noncore Deposits	2% of total deposits all years.

core deposits during the last year. The yield on loans, investments, and other earning assets is expressed as a *spread* over the base cost of funds. Similarly, the cost of noncore deposits is expressed as a premium over the cost of core deposits. This approach does not require a projection of absolute interest rates, just the difference—the spread—between them.

- *Noninterest Income.* The income from sources other than interest (including trust fees, service charges, and so on) is forecast as a percent of total income.

These two sources of income are added to derive Total Income.

Forecasting operating expenses can be as detailed as appropriate for a given situation. Normally, the categories described below are sufficient.

- *Personnel Expenses:* This expense category includes all salaries, benefits, payroll taxes, and other costs related to staff. The most straightforward way is to express personnel expenses as a percent of total income.
- *Premises and Fixed Asset Expenses:* This expense category includes all occupancy and related fixed asset costs. These expenses can also be projected as a percent of total income.
- *Other Operating Expenses:* This category includes all other costs and can be expressed as a percent of total income.

The tax rate must also be projected. Because the model projects tax equivalent income, the maximum marginal rate for that tax bracket should be used as a starting point. The actual effective rate may be lower due to loss carryforwards, accelerated depreciation, and so on. This is a judgment call, and must be made on a case-by-case basis.

The last projection assumption is the minimum capital-to-asset ratio required under risk-based capital rules. This is a critical assumption as it has an impact on the levels of available cash flow used in the valuation process. Capital rules spell out clearly the minimum level of

Exhibit 14.4 Projected Balance Sheet of Example Bank ($000)

	Year 1	Year 2	Year 3	Year 4	Year 5	Year 6	Year 7	Year 8	Year 8	Year 10	Residual
Assets											
Net Loans	$286,398	$310,887	$331,095	$352,546	$370,174	$388,682	$408,116	$428,552	$449,948	$472,446	$496,068
Investments & Other Earnings Assets	86,745	92,862	97,533	97,534	102,411	107,531	112,908	118,553	124,481	130,705	137,240
Total Earning Assets	373,144	403,750	428,648	450,080	472,584	496,213	521,024	547,075	574,429	603,150	633,308
Nonearning Assets	46,119	44,861	42,394	44,513	46,739	49,076	51,530	54,106	56,812	59,652	62,635
Total Assets	$419,262	$448,611	$471,041	$494,593	$519,323	$545,289	$572,554	$601,181	$631,241	$662,803	$695,943
Liabilities											
Noninterest Bearing Core Deposits	$ 73,175	$ 76,007	$ 76,449	$ 75,458	$ 69,992	$ 63,734	$ 56,607	$ 59,420	$ 62,373	$ 65,474	$ 68,730
Interest Bearing Core Deposits	238,614	278,692	317,868	359,535	387,287	416,722	447,713	469,958	493,315	517,842	543,595
Noncore Deposits	6,363	7,239	8,047	8,877	9,332	9,805	10,292	10,804	11,341	11,904	12,496
Total Deposits	318,152	361,938	402,364	443,871	466,611	490,261	514,612	540,181	567,029	595,220	624,822
Other Liabilities	79,538	63,871	44,707	23,362	24,558	25,803	27,085	28,431	29,844	31,327	32,885
Total Liabilities	$397,689	$425,809	$447,071	$467,232	$491,169	$516,065	$541,697	$568,612	$596,873	$626,548	$657,707
Total Equity	$ 21,573	$ 22,801	$ 23,970	$ 27,361	$ 28,154	$ 29,225	$ 30,857	$ 32,570	$ 34,368	$ 36,225	$ 38,235
Total Liabilities & Equity	$419,262	$448,611	$471,041	$494,593	$519,323	$545,289	$572,554	$601,181	$631,241	$662,803	$695,943

Note: Historical financial data for Example Bank presented and analyzed in Chapter 9.

Exhibit 14.5   Assumptions Used to Project Income Statement of Example Bank

Variable	Assumptions
Spread Over Cost of Interest Bearing Core Deposits	For loans: 550 basis points, all years. For investments: 75 basis points, all years. For other earning assets: 75 basis points, all years.
Premium Paid Over Core Deposits	For noncore deposits: 100 basis points, all years. For other interest bearing liabilities: 125 basis points, all years.
Noninterest Income	31% of total income in year 1, increasing by 1% per year to 40%.
Operating Expenses	Salaries & Benefits: 28% of total income, all years. Occupancy & Fixed Assets: 13% of total income, all years. Other operating expenses: 25% of total income, all years.
Loan Loss Provision	Provision is set so as to maintain a 1.0% reserve to total loan ratio, and assuming net chargeoffs equal 0.3% of total loans.
Securities Gain/Losses	None.
Taxes	30% on fully tax-equivalent income.

capital that must be maintained. As is often the case, however, the bank being valued has excess capital. The projection model should not, however, assume that capital in excess of regulatory minimum can be dividended out. In fact, banking regulators normally do not allow dividends to be paid if those dividends reduce the absolute level of capital. Consequently, if there is excess capital in the bank being valued for acquisition, it means that the new owner may have greater flexibility in paying dividends as long as the capital ratios are adequate.

The assumptions used in projecting the income and available cash flow of Example Bank are summarized in Exhibit 14.5. The resulting projected income and cash flow statement is shown in Exhibit 14.6.

14.6.5   Value Estimation By Income Approach—An Example

With the total and available cash flows projected, the valuation process can be completed. The future available cash flows are discounted to present value, the residual value is determined, and they are added together. The key elements are the discount rates used to convert future cash flows into present value and the residual value of the bank after the end of the tenth year.

The discount rates used in the valuation of Example Bank are shown in Exhibit 14.7. These rates were derived using the techniques described in Chapter 6. The discount rate of 14 percent reflects the risk-free rate plus an appropriate risk premium.

The residual value of Example Bank was calculated based on the capitalization of its residual available cash flow.[3] It was assumed that a 3 percent long-term growth of income was reasonable. Therefore, a capitalization rate of 11 percent was used (discount rate of 14 percent minus growth rate of 3 percent).

Given all the assumptions of balance sheet growth and composition, income expenses, capital needs, and discount rates, the value of Example Bank using the income approach is $25.2 million, about 1.17 times 1999 book value.

Exhibit 14.6 Projected Income Statement and Available Cash Flow of Example Bank (000)

	Year 1	Year 2	Year 3	Year 4	Year 5	Year 6	Year 7	Year 8	Year 10	Residual
Net Interest Income (Tax Equivalent)	$14,590	$15,026	$16,171	$15,759	$15,911	$16,039	$16,140	$16,947	$18,684	$19,618
Noninterest Income	6,555	7,071	7,965	8,118	8,567	9,022	9,479	10,387	12,465	13,079
Total Income (Tax Equivalent)	$21,145	$22,098	$24,136	$23,877	$24,478	$25,061	$25,619	$27,334	$31,140	$32,697
Operating Expenses										
Salaries & Benefits	$ 5,920	$ 6,187	$ 6,758	$ 6,686	$ 6,854	$ 7,017	$ 7,173	$ 7,654	$ 8,719	$ 9,155
Premises & Fixed Assets	2,749	2,873	3,138	3,104	3,182	3,258	3,331	3,553	4,048	4,251
Other Operating Expenses	5,286	5,524	6,034	5,969	6,120	6,265	6,405	6,834	7,785	8,174
Total Operating Expenses	$13,956	$14,584	$15,930	$15,759	$16,156	$16,540	$16,909	$18,040	$20,553	$21,580
Provision for Loan Losses	882	1,189	1,207	1,285	1,300	1,365	1,433	1,505	1,659	1,742
Securities Gains (Losses)	0	0	0	0	0	0	0	0	0	0
Pre-Tax Income	6,308	6,324	6,999	6,833	7,023	7,156	7,278	7,789	8,929	9,375
Taxes	1,892	1,897	2,100	2,050	2,107	2,147	2,183	2,337	2,679	2,813
Net Income	$ 4,415	$ 4,427	$ 4,899	$ 4,783	$ 4,916	$ 5,009	$ 5,094	$ 5,452	$ 6,250	$ 6,563
ROA	1.09%	1.02%	1.07%	.99%	.97%	.94%	.91%	.93%	.97%	.97%
Required Additions to Capital	$ 1,713	$ 1,653	$ 3,876	$ 1,278	$ 1,555	$ 1,632	$ 1,713	$ 1,798	$ 1,981	$ 2,079
Available Cash Flow	$ 2,702	$ 2,773	$ 1,024	$ 3,506	$ 3,361	$ 3,377	$ 3,381	$ 3,654	$ 4,270	$ 4,484

NOTE: Historical financial data for Example Bank presented and analyzed in Chapter 9.

Exhibit 14.7 Valuation of Example Bank Using Income Approach (000)

	Year 1	Year 2	Year 3	Year 4	Year 5	Year 6	Year 7	Year 8	Year 9	Year 10	Residual
Available Cash Flow	$2,702	$2,773	$1,024	$3,506	$3,361	$3,377	$3,381	$3,654	$3,950	$4,270	$ 4,484
Discount Rate	14%	14%	14%	14%	14%	14%	14%	14%	14%	14%	14%
Present Value of Available Cash Flow	$2,370	$2,134	$691	$2,076	$1,746	$1,539	$1,351	$1,281	$1,215	$1,152	—
Growth Rate of Available Cash Flow in Perpetuity	—	—	—	—	—	—	—	—	—	—	3.0%
Capitalization Rate On Residual Available Cash Flow	—	—	—	—	—	—	—	—	—	—	11%
Capitalized Value of Cash Flows	—	—	—	—	—	—	—	—	—	—	$42,828
Net Present Value of Available Cash Flows (Years 1–10)						$15,555					
Present Value of Capitalized Cash Flows						$ 9,645					
Value of Example Bank (rounded)							$25,200,000				

14.7 SENSITIVITY OF VALUE ESTIMATE TO ASSUMPTION CHANGES

The discounted cash flow (DCF) should be used in valuing M & A deals with great caution given the dynamic and uncertain nature of the market. The more sophisticated methods such as the capital asset pricing model and option pricing model are superior to DCF primarily because they (1) capture the full value of financial engineering—such as lowering the cost of capital, gaining tax and accounting advantages, reducing unnecessary regulatory costs, and restructuring particular assets through securitization; and (2) measure unique synergies in distribution and product lines. The acquirer can create value in the following ways: (1) universal synergies, which are often fully reflected in the M & A price, can be created by improving the yield on investments, eliminating excess cost, or improving productivity and pricing; (2) endemic synergies, which are less reflected in M & A deal pricing, can be achieved by selling the products of a new company; and (3) unique synergies are distinctive and the deciding factor in most M & A deals, achieved through earning revenue from special skills or assets, leveraging an entity's base to create new business opportunities, and restructuring to gain a distinct competitive advantage.

In general, the final estimates of value are very sensitive to changes in assumptions. It is for this reason that two prospective buyers could value a selling bank completely differently, yet still both be justified. Consequently it is essential that valuation assumptions be selected very carefully and only after thorough analysis of the target bank.

There are many different assumptions that can affect value, but some cause more changes in the final value estimate than others. The more critical assumption areas are:

- Net interest margin
- Operating expenses
- Loan loss provision
- Discount rate on available cash flows
- Capitalization rate on residual available cash flow

Exhibit 14.8 summarizes the impact on Example Bank's value of a 10 percent change in the six key assumptions. Each assumption was altered 10 percent in the direction that normally would increase value. From the data it is clear that net interest margin and operating expenses have the largest magnifying impact on value. Therefore, the assumptions in these two areas need to be considered very carefully when establishing value.

14.8 VALUE CREATION OPPORTUNITIES AND THE ACQUISITION PRICE

The value just estimated by the income approach is the franchise value of Example Bank as a stand-alone entity on an as is basis to a hypothetical buyer. Consequently, it is a starting point in establishing a purchase price. As a passive investment, Example Bank is worth about $25.2 million given the assumptions used. To a particular buyer, however, Example Bank may be worth more for a variety of value creation reasons. For example, a particular

Exhibit 14.8 Sensitivity of Value Estimates to Changes in Key Assumptions $000,000

Assumption Area	Base Assumptions	Revised Assumptions[1]	Original Value	Revised Value	Percentage Change in Value
Net Interest Margin on Average Earning Assets	3.91% in year 1, 3.87% in year 2, 3.89% in year 3, 3.59% in year 4, 3.45% in year 5, 3.31% in year 6, 3.17% thereafter	4.30% in year 1, 4.26% in year 2, 4.28% in year 3, 3.95% in year 4, 3.80% in year 5, 3.64% in year 6, 3.49% thereafter	$25.2	$29.9	+18.5%
Operating Expenses	66% of total income all years	59.4% of income all years	$25.2	$34.2	+35.8%
Loan Loss Provision	Target loan loss reserve to total loans of 1%, with charge-offs equalling 0.3% of loans	Charge-offs equal 0.27% of loans, same reserve balance	$25.2	$25.8	+ 2.4%
Discount Rate on Cash Flow	14% all years	12.6% all years	$25.2	$29.4	+16.5%
Growth Rate of Available Cash Flow in Perpetuity	3.0% annually	3.3% annually	$25.2	$25.5	+ 1.2%

[1]Revised assumptions equal base assumptions changed by 10 percent in direction that would tend to increase value.

buyer may be able to reduce operating expenses by combining facilities and staff. Another buyer may be able to increase the net interest margin due to sophisticated financial management and loan-pricing capabilities. There are any number of reasons why the price a particular buyer is willing to offer for Example Bank may be higher than its value as a stand-alone entity.

The information below illustrates how three different types of buyers might offer different yet equally justifiable prices for Example Bank. Different buyer situations and assumptions significantly influence their perceptions of value, and the price each believes would be justified.

- *Cost Cutter Buyer:* Able to reduce operating expenses to total income by 20 percent over four years—Resulting value would be $40.8 million (+ 62 percent).

- *Money-Manager Buyer:* Able to sustain 3.91 percent margin on earning assets—Resulting value would be $32.5 million (+ 29 percent).

- *Expansion Buyer:* Able to grow assets at rate two percentage points higher—Resulting value would be $23.6 million (− 6.3 percent).[4]

From these scenarios it is clear that different assumptions and situations of buyers can have a significant impact on the perceived value of a target.

The figures shown above quantify the impact of different value creation scenarios. Actually achieving enhanced shareholder value through a merger or acquisition depends on the distinctive benefits the buyer can bring.[5] To justify the premiums paid for many banks, the buyer must be able to improve the performance of the seller and/or the combined entities. If not, shareholder value will be diminished, not enhanced.

The first area of potential improvement is through enhancement of the operations of buyer and seller so that each is better than before the merger. Enhancements can be in the areas of processing (lowering per unit costs through economies of scale), personnel (bringing needed skills to the seller), and asset utilization (putting assets to more profitable use). Describing these enhancement areas is easy; implementing plans to achieve them is very difficult. There seems to be mounting evidence that many buyers of banks do not realize sufficient benefits to justify the premiums paid.

The second area is market benefits. Through merger, the combined entities may have a stronger position in a market, reach the critical mass needed to enter certain businesses, and be able to develop and deliver services more efficiently. Like operational enhancements, however, market benefits can be extremely difficult to realize.

A third area of potential improvement is financial. Typically, the types of benefits include diversification of the types of businesses in which the bank is engaged to reduce cyclical risk, lower borrowing costs, and increase debt capacity. These benefits are mentioned infrequently in bank acquisitions. The market has tended not to reward these potential benefits with higher stock prices. Investors do not pay a premium for diversified firms and in fact seem to discount them. (Diversification as used here means the variety of types of businesses, not diversification of customer types within a certain line of business. In fact, there does seem to be some advantage to, for example, a diversified commercial loan portfolio.) Moreover, lower borrowing costs and increased debt capacity are difficult to associate with enhanced shareholder value.

The fourth area of benefit potential is tax. Many acquisitions have been motivated by the opportunity to use net operating loss carryforwards and to step up the tax basis of assets to get higher depreciation. Since the Tax Reform Act of 1986, virtually all the benefits that used to motivate certain acquisitions have been eliminated. There are, however, potential benefits to reduce future tax liability through amortization of some acquired intangible assets.

A fifth area is the buyer's ability to collect loans that have been charged off. Some buyers have the staff skills and support systems to do a better job in collecting bad assets. If loans already charged off are included in the acquisition, any collections on them fall to the bottom line and increase available cash flow, thus value.

In the final analysis, the most straightforward way to enhance shareholder value is to improve the earnings. Under normal circumstances, a bank earning 1.2 percent on assets after an acquisition, compared with 1.1 percent before, will have enhanced its shareholders' value.

14.9   VALUATION METHODS FOR MERGERS AND ACQUISITIONS

Valuation can be one of the most tedious but crucial steps in the entire mergers and acquisitions process. A wide variety of valuation methods for M & A can be used, ranging from simplistic rules of thumb to highly sophisticated mathematical models. The primary purpose of any valuation process is to determine the price or a range of reasonable prices for an M & A deal. In an acquisition deal, the acquirer tries to estimate the target's intrinsic value and the synergistic value that the combined entity will create.

The intrinsic value is determined based on the earning power and earnings quality. Earning power is measured in terms of the entity's capability to constantly increase profitability and rate of return in light of plausible assumptions based on both internal sources and external economic and benchmark data. Earnings quality is assessed by factors such as customer base, profitability, customer satisfaction, employee satisfaction, and relative risk. Synergistic value is determined based on the perceived synergy in the form of economies of scale, risk reduction, increased power, lower funding or capital costs, increased sales, improved management efficiency, or improved productivity. The acquirer should assess these values in determining and negotiating a price for the M & A deal. Although the price is actually determined in the negotiation process, considerations are given to the valuation assumptions and estimates.

To maximize shareholders' value under the arm's-length dealing concept, the acquiring company attempts to negotiate the lowest possible price below the sum of the target's intrinsic value and the acquisition's synergistic value. The target, on the other hand, tries to obtain the highest price possible. Within this framework, there is typically a range of acceptable prices to both the acquirer and the target. Present value of an entity can be measured as the total current wealth enjoyed by the owners of the entity. The current wealth consists of

1.   the current market value of the shares purchased; and
2.   the total cash dividends received.

A business combination can be considered successful if it results in increases in the total current wealth of the owners of the combined entity. The three most commonly used valuation approaches in determining a bank's intrinsic value are (1) income approach (earnings/cash flow); (2) asset approach (balance sheet); and (3) market approach (market valuations).

14.9.1   Income Approach

The income approach estimates the target bank's value based on its historical and projected earnings and cash flows. Under the income approach the acquirer bank must (1) determine the target's core accrual earnings; (2) estimate the synergies and costs arising from the combination; (3) make adjustment for noncash earnings to estimate cash earnings; and (4) discount the estimated cash earnings at a rate appropriate to reflect risk. The core earnings are income from continuing and normal operations (e.g., services and products) not affected by nonrecurring events such as the sales of assets, extraordinary loan loss provisions, or any income from real estate activities or other abnormal/nonrecurring events. The acquirer should estimate both the synergistic gains and transaction costs resulting from the combination. Estimating synergistic gains and transaction costs resulting from economies of scale, revenue enhancement opportunities, and regulatory and legal needs is perhaps the most difficult task in determining the value of the target bank.

Synergies can be achieved through economies of scale and scope, risk reductions, lowering funding or capital costs, and increased sales. Thus, examples of synergistic gains resulting from revenue enhancements and economies of scale are:

1. increased net interest margin from improving loan yield and/or reducing deposit costs;
2. increased fee income provided from opportunities to offer new financial products and services previously unavailable;
3. cost savings resulting from consolidating overlapping branches, administrative, marketing, accounting, and operating activities, and personnel expenses; and
4. other related revenue enhancements or cost reductions.

Transaction or incremental costs are estimated according to the M & A strategies. Examples of incremental costs are:

1. increased loan loss provisions;
2. possible increases in deposit insurance premiums;
3. early retirement and severance costs resulting from consolidating management and personnel; and
4. other incremental costs resulting from the combination.

Two calculations are often used to determine normalized earnings and cash flows: (1) capitalization of historical earnings/cash flow and (2) discounted projected earnings/ cash flow. Under the capitalization of historical cash earnings approach, normalized historical cash earnings are viewed as an indication of an institution's future capacity to provide returns to both debt and equity holders. The capitalization approach requires the determination of normalized historical cash earnings and the calculation of a capitalization rate that is appropriate for the particular cash earnings base. The normalized cash earnings are determined using an appropriate rate of return that reflects the risk associated with the cash earnings stream and the market's required rate of return for an investment in the bank. The capitalization rate is the weighted average cost of capital calculated based on both cost of debt and cost of equity capital.

The normalized cash earnings for each year are calculated as follows:

Item	Amount
Core earnings from normal operations	$1,000,000
+ Synergistic benefits	200,000
− Incremental costs	100,000
Accrual-adjusted earnings	1,100,000
+ noncash charges (e.g., depreciation, goodwill)	150,000
Cash earnings (CE)	$1,250,000

The most commonly used formula for the capitalization of historical cash earnings is:

$$P_t = \frac{CE(1 + g)}{r - g}$$

where:

P_t = present value of the target bank (long-term debt and equity)
CE = normalized cash earnings ($1,250,000 as calculated above)
g = long-term annual growth rate (assumed five percent)
r = weighted average cost of capital (WACC) representing the required rate of return on cash earnings (assumed 15 percent)

Thus,

$$P_t = \frac{\$1,250,000(1 + .05)}{.15 - .05} = \$13,125,000$$

P_t ($13,125,000) is the estimate of fair market value of the target's capital (long-term debt and equity). If the fair market value long-term debt is estimated to be $3,000,000, then the target's fair market value of equity will be $10,125,000 ($13,125,000−3,000,000).

The discounted net cash flow methodology determines the value of the target bank based on the present value of the future economic benefits to both debt and equity holders. The future economic income is measured by the projected net cash flows which are then discounted using the WACC as a discount rate. The sum of the discounted projected cash flows represents the fair market value of the target bank based on the following formula:

$$P_v = CF_0 + \frac{CF_1}{(1 + r)^1} + \frac{CF_2}{(1 + r)^2} + \ldots + \frac{CF_n}{(1 + r)^n}$$

where:

P_v = present value of cash flows representing the fair market value
CF = the net cash flow for a given period
r = the discount rate using weighted average cost of capital

The precision of the present value analysis depends on the accuracy of forecasted cash flows, selected discount rates, time periods, and terminal value. To accurately forecast reasonable cash flows expected from an M & A deal, the appraiser must develop a projected balance sheet and income statement for the target on the relevant time horizon (e.g., five years). Using the above formula in calculating present value of future cash flows indefinitely is a meaningless exercise primarily because the present value effect of distant cash flows is immaterial. To shorten the time horizon, the appraiser must incorporate a terminal cash flow for the final year, which could be thought of as a sale or liquidation of the investment, determined based on a market value multiple such as P/E or price/book.

Using the present value method, the value of the target bank under the following assumptions is determined as follows:

1. total assets are $5,000 million and are expected to grow at 8 percent per year;
2. equity is $375 million and desired equity/assets ratio is 7 percent;
3. return on assets (ROA) is 1 percent each year;
4. terminal value in year 6 is projected at 10 percent year five averages assets; and
5. the discount rate is 12 percent.

The results presented in Exhibit 14.9 show that under these assumptions the bank has an intrinsic value of $610.1 million. This acquisition value is determined based on the given assumption. The appraiser can use sensitivity analysis and simulation analysis to determine the effect of changes of these assumptions on the present value. Although present value analysis requires a number of projections and assumptions, it can produce relevant valuation estimates for acquisition analysis.

14.9.2   Balance Sheet Approach

The underlying premise of the asset approach is that the value of the target bank equals the current value of its net assets (assets − liabilities) plus a premium to account for its intangible value such as goodwill. Using this approach the value of the target bank is determined by estimating the fair market value of its assets and liabilities. The asset approach assesses the fair market value of all types of assets and liabilities including:

1. current assets (cash, deposits, loans, securities, receivables);
2. property, plants, and equipment;
3. intangible assets (e.g., core deposits, customer lists, goodwill);
4. current liabilities; and
5. long-term liabilities.

One of the most commonly used methods to estimate the net assets valuation is to assess deposit valuation. The deposit valuation method is appropriate when estimating the value of a branch or a failed bank acquisition. Deposit valuation requires information regarding the amount and types of deposits, estimated lives, interest and operating costs, discount rate,

Exhibit 14.9 Present Value Analysis ($ in Millions)

Year	Average Assets	Earnings	Required Equity	Actual Equity	Cash Flow	Discount Factor	Present Value
0 (Acquisition Date)	$5,100	$50	$350	$375	$ 25	1.0	$ 25
1	5,200	52	362	405	43	.8929	38.4
2	5,400	54	378	437.4	59.4	.7972	47.4
3	5,624.3	56.2	393.7	472.4	78.7	.7118	56.1
4	5,849.3	58.5	409.5	510.2	100.7	.6355	64.0
5	6,083.3	60.8	425.8	551.0	125.2	.5674	71.1
6	608.1					.5066	
Terminal value							308.1
Total present value							610.1

fee income, and marginal earnings rate for the deposits. The balance sheet approach to valuation of the target bank is determined by this simple formula:

1. Recorded historical value of net assets (assets − liabilities)   xxxx
2. Add:
    *   Premiums for undervalued assets and/or overstated liabilities   xx
    *   Fair market value of off-balance sheet assets   xx
    *   Fair market value of intangibles (e.g., goodwill)   xx
3. Total: xxxx
4. Subtract
    *   Discounts for overvalued assets and/or undervalued liabilities   (xx)
    *   Value of off-balance-sheet liabilities   (xx)
5. Value of the target bank   xxx

14.9.3   Market Approach

The market approach is based on two concepts. The first premise is that the value of the target bank should be determined according to how its stock is being valued in the market where it is traded. The second concept is to compare prices of similar acquisitions with the target bank to estimate the acquisition market value for the target. The market valuation approach based on the comparable bank market multiple and comparable bank transactions relies on analyzing financial data, ratios, and price multiples obtained from publicly traded banks. The following measurements or price multiples from the comparable bank data can be used to estimate fair market value of the target bank:

1. $\text{Premium to Market} = \dfrac{\text{merger price per share}}{\text{market price per share before announcement}}$

2. $\text{Price/Earnings} = \dfrac{\text{merger price per share}}{\text{earnings per share}}$

3. $\text{Price/Book} = \dfrac{\text{merger price per share}}{\text{book value per share}}$

4. $\text{Premium to Deposits} = \dfrac{\text{merger price per share}}{\text{total deposits}}$

5. $\text{Invested Capital/Assets} = \dfrac{\substack{\text{market value of invested capital} \\ \text{(market value of long-term debt and equity)}}}{\text{total assets}}$

Using a bank stock's trading value to estimate acquisition valuation has several limitations. First, the majority of bank shares traded are not within the organized stock exchanges (e.g., NYSE, AMSE) or even regional over-the-counter markets. Thus, the trading price may not represent an objective and relevant valuation. Second, if the acquiring bank attempts to gain control through "open market" purchases, the price would rise to reflect an acquisition premium or to induce others to sell. Finally, capital markets fluctuate based on economic and capital market forces rather than just the intrinsic value of individual stocks.

Compiling relevant data on previously comparable M & A deals and comparing them to the target is not without problems. Each M & A deal has its own attributes and characteristics distinguishable from other deals. However, the usefulness of comparable merger market analysis depends on how the sample M & A transactions are selected (e.g., size, location, market position, performance in market, market extension). These limitations of the market approach should be considered when using this approach to estimate the intrinsic value of the target bank. If the intrinsic value is below the suggested merger price for other similar banks, the acquirer should not attempt to negotiate the price. Conversely, if the intrinsic value is above previous merger prices for comparable banks, then the acquirer has more room to negotiate the price.

14.10 SOPHISTICATED VALUATION TECHNIQUES FOR MERGERS AND ACQUISITIONS

Appraisers most often use the valuation approaches discussed in the previous section (e.g., income approach, balance sheet approach, market approach) when valuing the acquisition under consideration. Although these approaches can be useful in estimating the intrinsic value of the target bank, a more sophisticated valuation method presented in this section can improve the precision and accuracy of valuation. The sophisticated valuation techniques can be empirically estimated with a high degree of reliability.

The valuation of mergers and acquisitions has received much attention in finance and accounting literature during the past five decades. A number of valuation techniques have been employed to assess the value and results of M & A transactions. Early empirical studies of M & A[6,7] utilized a portfolio or paired sample technique of calculating the differences in return to the sample of acquiring firms and the return on a portfolio of like firms or a paired sample of comparable firms. Thus, differences in the returns of the paired samples indicate the impact of M & A deals. These studies used different versions of the following return equation:

$$\Delta R_n = \frac{P_n \sum_{t=0}^{N} D_t}{P_0} - \frac{P_n' \sum_{t=0}^{N} D_t'}{P_0}$$

where

ΔR_n = Differences in return to shareholders
P_n = Price of share at time period n
P_0 = Price of share at time 0 (merger announcement or completion)
D_t = Dividend at time t

$P_n = \dfrac{\sum_{t=0}^{N} D_t}{P_0}$ = $\left(\begin{array}{l}\text{the return to the investor who purchased a share of the merging firm at} \\ \text{time 0 and held this share until time } n\end{array}\right)$

$P_n' = \dfrac{\sum_{t_0}^{N} D_t'}{P_0}$ = $\left(\begin{array}{l}\text{the return to an investor of no merging firms or an investor based on an} \\ \text{estimation of the price and dividend stream had no merger occurred}\end{array}\right)$

The empirical results of early studies of M & A transactions are inconsistent and inconclusive. Some mergers showed positive benefits, and other mergers were not deemed successful or there were no significant differences between the merged firms and the non-merged firms in risk, growth rate, or financial structure.

Recent studies of M & A transactions have used the capital market event methodology to measure market returns to M & A deals. Dodd (1980)[8] investigated both completed and canceled mergers by employing the market model to assess market reactions to merger announcements and found that shareholders of target firms earn large positive abnormal returns. Merger-related event methodology is based on three underlying M & A theories. The first theory refers to non-value maximizing behavior by management of acquiring firms and implies that acquisitions are attempts by acquiring management to maximize growth in sales or assets or to control a large firm. Acquisition of this type would have no real economic impact on the combined business, indicating that any positive gains made by the target shareholders would be offset by a loss to the acquiring firms' stockholders. Empirical studies in support of this theory of M & A are Trits and Scanlon (1987)[9] and Hannan and Rhoades (1987),[10] which found that target banks gain positive returns while acquiring banks accrue a negative return surrounding the merger announcement day.

The second theory of M & A refers to value maximization motivations of increasing the value of acquiring firms' shareholders. Current merger studies found evidence in support of the value maximization theory. Desai and Stover (1985)[11] employed event study methodology for measuring returns and found a positive average abnormal return for shareholders of acquiring banks during the two days surrounding the merger announcement and on the date the Federal Reserve Board approved the acquisition.

14.10.1   The Capital Asset Pricing Model (CAPM)

The capital asset pricing model is based on capital market theory, which describes how investors must behave when selecting a particular security (e.g., common stocks) for their portfolios under a given set of assumptions. The CAPM has been used in the literature to evaluate capital market reactions to M & A announcements and changes in market participants' (e.g., investors') behavior resulting from the M & A deal. The CAPM is calculated based on the following formula;

$$R_{it} = \alpha_i + \beta_i R_{mt} + e_{it}$$
$$e_{it} = R_{it} - (\alpha_i + \beta_i R_{mt})$$

where:

R_{it} = return on security i for period t
R_{mt} = return on the market portfolio for period t
α_i = constant for security i
β_i = systematic risk of security i
e_{it} = residual of abnormal return for security

The capital asset pricing model (CAPM) commonly used in the finance literature is typically utilized to calculate average abnormal return and cumulative abnormal return.

$$\text{Average Residual} = \overline{e}t_t = \frac{\sum_{i=1}^{N} e_{it}}{N}$$

$$\text{Cumulative Average Residual} = CART = \sum_{T+t}^{T-t} \overline{e}_t$$

$\overline{e}_i$ = Average of all residuals for period t_i
e_{it} = Firm i residual at time t
N = Number of firms within group
T = Number of periods aggregated

The abnormal residuals can be used in measuring the synergistic benefits of M & A deals. CAPM is used to estimate the fair rate of return on capital market investment securities of M & A transactions. Another use of CAPM in the valuation process is to estimate the cost of equity capital component of an overall income capitalization value. CAPM explains rational investment decision making, which is relevant to any business valuation, especially valuation of M & A deals.

14.10.2 Accounting-Based Valuation Approach (Ohlson Model)

The Ohlson model utilizes the noncontroversial dividend discount model to measure stock price in terms of current book value and future residual income.[12] The model is based on the assumption that the accounting system is an effective means of recognizing and accumulating wealth by business entities. More specifically, recorded book value serves as a static measure of firm value at a given point in time, while earnings measures the increment to shareholder wealth over a specified period of time. The theoretical framework of the model is that book value and earnings are relevant valuation attributes. Book value represents a stock measure of value, while earnings measure increments to book value and are indicators of future dividend-paying ability of an entity.

The Ohlson model is based on the noncontroversial assumption that the market value of an entity's equity P_t is equal to the present value of current and future dividend payments, d_{t+j}

$$P_t = \sum_{j=1}^{\infty} (1 + r)^{-j} E_t[d + j],$$

where
P_t = market value of equity
r = the discount rate or cost of equity capital
E_t = expected future earnings
D_{t+j} = future dividend payments.

This model also assumes that the accounting data follow the clean surplus relation:

$$b_{vt} = bv_{t-1} + x_t - d_t,$$

where:

b_{vt} = net book value

x_t = earnings for period t.

This clean surplus relation implies that the current book value is a function of previous book value, future earnings, and dividends. The payment of dividends at time t reduces future-period earnings due to the reduction in the firm's asset base rather than reducing current earnings. The clean surplus assumption allows the rewriting of the dividend discount model in terms of accounting data:

$$P_t = b_{vt} + \sum_{j=1}^{\infty}(1 + r)^{-j}E_t[x_{t+j}^a],$$

where

x_t^a = residual income or abnormal earnings.

The above formula indicates that the estimated value of a firm's equity is determined by discounting its future abnormal earnings or residual income and adding it to the current book value of the firm. The practical implementation of the Ohlson model requires: (1) the prediction of future earnings; (2) determination of the appropriate forecast horizon; and (3) selection of the appropriate discount rate. The implication of this discounted residual income model for assessing an M & A deal is that the book value provides an important beginning reference point in the valuation process.

14.11   RELATION BETWEEN PRICE AND VALUE AND EFFECT ON STOCKHOLDERS

This chapter has focused on the determination of a banking company's value. As described in Chapter 5, however, there is a difference between price and value. The price that one bank pays to acquire another usually reflects the value the particular buyer placed on an acquisition (the investment value concept), not necessarily the as is or consensus value (the fair market value concept). Consequently, any given acquisition price reflects individual negotiations between buyer and seller. Depending on the competitive situation, the buyer's willingness to share future value creation potential with the seller could vary substantially. High multiples for interstate acquisitions reflect, in part, the desire for banks to expand their franchise and their willingness to pay the price while the window of opportunity is open. In other words, to ensure entry into the market, buyers were willing to share with the seller a substantial portion of the value creation potential.

The price paid reflects the buyer's perception of the value of the target, based on future expectations of the performance of that target and the added value the buyer can bring. More frequently, buyers examine the price–value relationship in terms of the effect on stockholders, and what levels of earnings and growth are needed to justify the price paid relative to value received by stockholders. Buyers are also looking much more carefully at the strategic actions necessary to achieve the added value.

The most common measure of impact on shareholders is *earnings dilution,* which is the reduction in earnings per share after an acquisition. Dilution occurs because the earnings of

Exhibit 14.10 Illustration of Earnings per Share Dilution Resulting from Stock-for-Stock Acquisition (Assumes pooling of interest accounting)

	Buyer	Seller	Combined
Earnings (latest year)	$ 2,000,000	$ 500,000	$ 2,500,000
Shares outstanding	1,500,000	—	—
Equity (book value)	$14,000,000	$3,000,000	$17,000,000
Purchase price	$ 4,500,000	—	—
Market price of stock/book value	80%	—	—
Market price/share	$7.47	—	—
Number of new shares issued to seller's shareholders	602,410	—	—
Total shares outstanding	—	—	2,102,410
Earnings/share	$1.33	—	$1.19
Dilution percentage	—	—	10.5%

the combined entities are not sufficient to offset the increased stock issued (if a stock-for-stock transaction) or the interest on acquisition debt (if a cash-for-stock transaction with debt). Exhibit 14.10 illustrates the dilution resulting from a stock-for-stock acquisition. In this example, dilution of over 10 percent will be experienced by shareholders of the buying bank. This particular bank may believe a 10 percent dilution is acceptable and be willing to pay $4.5 million for the selling bank. Another bank, however, may face different circumstances. For example, if the buyer's stock sold for 60 percent of book (instead of the 80 percent shown in the exhibit), the dilution would be over 18 percent. A potential buyer in this situation may find this level of dilution unacceptable.

In general, dilution of the buyer's earnings per share will occur during a stock-for-stock acquisition when the purchase price, as a multiple of the selling bank's earnings, is greater than the market price of the buyer's stock as a multiple of its earnings. In the example described above, the purchase price is nine times the seller's earnings, while the buyer's stock price is less than six times earnings. For there to be no dilution, the buying bank's stock would have to be priced at a 28 percent premium over book ($11.95), rather than the 20 percent discount ($7.47).

The same type of dilution analysis can be undertaken in a cash-for-stock acquisition, except the price is evaluated based on debt costs (or the opportunity cost of an earning asset liquidated to fund the acquisition) instead of stock. Exhibit 14.11 illustrates the dilution in a cash-for-stock acquisition. In this case, the buyer experienced an earnings per share dilution of about 1 percent. In a cash acquisition, dilution will occur if the interest expense on acquisition debt and goodwill amortization exceed the selling bank's earnings.

The key point is that the price paid for one particular acquired bank reflects value to that buyer, not necessarily to other banks. The final price of an acquisition is the combination of the value of the bank as a stand-alone investment *plus* its value to the particular buyer as a result of synergies and franchise expansion opportunities. The ultimate test of the appropriateness of price paid is the extent to which shareholder value is enhanced, and this may not be evident until several years after the transaction. Consequently, some of the high premiums are justified by the unique circumstances and strategies of a particular buyer. However, if the perceived opportunities of value creation do not materialize, then the high premiums will not be justified.

Exhibit 14.11   Illustration of Earnings per Share Dilution Resulting from Cash-for-Stock Acquisition (Assumes purchase accounting)

	Buyer	Seller	Combined
Earnings	$ 2,000,00	$ 500,000	$2,500,000
Share outstanding	1,500,000	—	1,500,000
Equity (book value)	$14,000,000	$3,000,000	—
Purchase price	$ 5,500,000	—	—
Interest rate on acquisition debt	12%	—	—
Goodwill	—	$2,000,000	—
Goodwill amortization	—	25 years	—
Tax rate	35%	—	—
Acquisition debt interest expense (after tax)	—	—	$ 439,000
Goodwill amortization	—	—	$ 80,000
Earnings	—	—	$1,981,000
Earnings/share	$1.33	—	$1.32
Dilution percentage	—	—	0.8%

ENDNOTES

1. The term "as is" means the bank with its current strategies, markets, financial structures, and so on.

2. Deficiencies in these measures were described in Chapter 5, but application of the market approach is very difficult without using these two widely reported figures.

3. There are alternative ways of computing residual value, such as multiple of earnings and book value. Use of these measures to determine residual value suffers from the same deficiencies as using these measures to determine total value.

4. Faster asset growth results in lower value because a greater proportion of income must be allocated to capital to meet regulatory requirements. Consequently, this buyer would "destroy" value if it did nothing else but increase the bank's assets at a faster rate.

5. For an excellent discussion see Alfred Rappaport, "Converting Merger Benefits to Shareholder Value," *Mergers & Acquisitions,* March/April, 1987, pp. 49–55.

6. Hogarty, Thomas. 1970. "Profits from Mergers: The Evidence of Fifty Years." *St. John's Law Review,* special edition, 44:378–391.

7. Lev, B., and G. Mandelker. 1972. "The Microeconomic Consequences of Corporate Mergers." *Journal of Business* (Vol. 45): 85–104.

8. Dodd, P. 1980. "Merger Proposals, Management Discretion and Stockholder Wealth." *Journal of Financial Economics* (December, Vol. 8): 105–137.

9. Thrifs, J. W., and K. P. Scanlon. 1987. "Interstate Bank Mergers: The Early Evidence." *Journal of Financial Research* (Vol. 10, No. 4): 67–74.

10. Hannan, T. H., and S. A. Rhoades. 1987. "Acquisition Targets and Motives: The Case of the Banking Industry." *Review of Economics and Statistics* (February): 67–74.

11. Desai, Anand, and R. D. Stover. 1995. "Bank Holding Company Acquisitions, Stockholder Returns, and Regulatory Uncertainty." *Journal of Financial Research* (Vol. 8, No. 2): 145–156.

12. Ohlson, J. A. 1995. "Earnings, Book Values, and Dividend in Equity Valuation." *Contemporary Accounting Research* 11: 661–687.

CHAPTER 15

Valuation of Tangible Bank Assets

Valuing a bank as a business enterprise (as discussed in the preceding chapter) does not necessarily require the valuation of each individual tangible asset owned by the bank. Nonetheless, it is appropriate in some situations to value some or all of the tangible assets. Three primary reasons to value specific tangible assets are to:

1. determine a new taxable basis in a merger that uses purchase accounting rules (discussed in Chapter 7);

2. compute the portion of the purchase price that is attributable to goodwill (also discussed in Chapter 7); and

3. gauge the extent of unrealized gains or losses on the balance sheet that could impact future earnings potential of the bank, particularly in loans and investments (a real world complication discussed in Chapter 18).

Tangible assets to be valued fall into two categories: physical and financial. Physical tangible assets are those with true physical substance such as furniture, fixtures, equipment, and premises. Financial tangible assets are those that involve a clear legal claim on future income or underlying assets, such as loans and investments.

The context in which tangible bank assets are valued is usually the fair market value in the current productive use of the asset—value-in-use. This is an important distinction because it assumes continuation of the current use of the property or asset. This value-in-use is not necessarily the theoretically highest value of the asset. For example, a bank that maintains a branch at a major intersection may have a locational advantage for new and existing customers. This particular site, however, might be worth far more to the developer of a fast food restaurant. At some point in the future, the bank may decide that the sale of the branch would yield a profit substantial enough to warrant such action, but current valuation cannot presume such future actions.

This chapter addresses the valuation of both physical and financial tangible assets in the context of their value-in-use. The extent to which a theoretically higher value exists in some other use is outside the scope of this discussion.

15.1 TANGIBLE PHYSICAL ASSETS

The physical assets of a bank include primarily the premises, furniture, fixtures, and equipment—the assets the bank uses in its daily operations. Depending on the size and complexity of the bank, identifying all the physical assets may be difficult or impossible. Some banks maintain excellent fixed asset management systems; others do not. Nonetheless, unless the internal records are grossly inadequate, it usually is possible to identify the major assets that will account for 90 to 95 percent of the total physical asset value. Listed below are many of the physical assets likely to be found at a typical bank:

- Buildings
- Vacant land for expansion
- Leasehold improvements
- Vaults
- Parking lots
- Furniture and fixtures
- Computers and peripherals
- Automated teller machines
- Automobiles
- Computer software
- Art objects and decorations
- Item processing equipment

Even with an accurate inventory of physical assets, it is worthwhile to conduct an investigation to identify and verify the major physical assets in the bank.

Placing a value on a bank's physical assets nearly always requires the cost rather than the market or income approaches. The cost approach is applicable because it values a physical asset based on the cost to replace it with one of equal utility, less any physical, functional, and/or economic obsolescence. Because the bank's property is used in the course of business and does not generate income directly, the income approach is not applicable. Also, because bank property is often very specialized (it includes vaults, teller counters, and proof machines) it is difficult to apply the market approach, which requires comparison with recent sales of similar properties. There is not a sufficiently large market for used bank physical assets to generate the comparable sales data. The discussion of approaches to value in Chapter 6 describes the cost approach in detail.

The overall value of a bank's balance sheet is unlikely to be significantly impacted by the difference between market value and book value of tangible physical assets because they account for such a small percentage of total assets. Tangible financial assets are the real drivers of asset value, as discussed below.

15.2 TANGIBLE FINANCIAL ASSETS

Normally, one thinks of tangible assets as those with physical substance, such as buildings, machinery, or inventory. The majority of many businesses' assets fits this description. In a bank, however, the bulk of the assets are financial, such as loans and investments. These assets are not truly physical but are tangible in that they are usually marketable and involve a legal claim to property and/or future income.

Valuing the tangible financial assets of a bank typically requires the discounted future income approach. Since the loans and investments of a bank represent rights to future income, the values of these instruments are equal to that future income, discounted to present value at a rate commensurate with the risks.

Two major categories of tangible financial assets are important to value for merger or acquisition: investment securities and the loan portfolio. These two categories account for over 90 percent of a typical bank's total assets.

15.2.1 Investment Securities Valuation

Valuing the investments of a bank can be very simple if the types of investments are such plain vanilla as U.S. Treasury Securities or municipal bonds. Because of the depth of the market for these types of investments, daily price quotes provide the best, most reliable guide to market value.

If the bank has a significant exposure to more exotic investments such as derivatives or Collateralized Mortgage Obligations (CMOs), the valuation can be extraordinarily complex. Many of these types of investment activities are off-balance-sheet items, which affect the earnings of the bank but do not show up on the balance sheet.

The majority of banks do not have substantial exposure to exotic investment vehicles and off-balance-sheet activities. Consequently, the discussion in this chapter focuses on more traditional investments made by banks: U.S. Treasury Securities, Government Agency Securities, and municipal bonds. As mentioned above, price quotes are easily obtained, but it is useful to understand how the market determines values for these types of investments.

All valuation models for investment securities are based upon the income approach— that is, the current market value of the particular investment is equal to the net present value of the cash flows to be received by the owner of that investment. The primary parameters needed to value an investment security are the cash flows to be received, time to maturity, and the discount rate. Exhibit 15.1 illustrates a simple valuation of a bond with known cash flows for a defined time period.

The current market value of the investment generating this cash flow stream, with an annual discount rate of 8.5 percent, is $2,386.29.

Exhibit 15.1   Valuation of a Bond Paying $100 Semiannually for Three Years, $2,500 Face Value

Payment #	Payment	Maturity Value	Discount Factor @ 8.5%/yr	Present Value
1	$100	—	.9593	$ 95.93
2	100	—	.9203	92.03
3	100	—	.8826	88.26
4	100	—	.8467	84.67
5	100	2,500	.7790	2,025.40
				2,386.29

From a practical standpoint, a bank is able to track the value of its investment portfolio better than it can track most other assets on the balance sheet. Most banks, or their safe-keeping agents, frequently revalue the investment portfolio—often it is done daily. A report is generated showing, among other things, the type of security, its par value, maturity date, coupon rate, yield to maturity, book value, and market value. In most cases, this is the best source of investment portfolio market value amounts. Very seldom is there a need to establish value independently of the normal types of investments most banks hold.

15.2.2 Loan Portfolio Valuation

Loans can present a much more difficult valuation problem, even though the mathematical approach is similar to that used for investments. The difference is that most types of bank loans do not have an active, organized market with a free exchange of information. Therefore, a bank is not able to value its loan portfolio each day based on the input of the market. This situation is changing somewhat with active secondary mortgage markets and loan securitization. For the most part, however, the loan portfolio of a bank must be valued on a case-by-case basis. Much of the valuation process is subjective and open to disagreement. There are numerous assumptions that must be made about timing of payments, prepayments, default risk, and future interest rates. Nonetheless, it is important that the value of the loan portfolio be carefully considered.

A good starting point for the loan valuation is the book value of the portfolio. The book value of a loan is the original balance of the loan less the reduction in principal from payments made through day of the value plus loan charge-offs, if any. The book value is usually easy to determine from the information carried in the loan systems of the bank. Most computerized loan systems carry previous day book values.

The market value of a loan is the net present value of the future income stream generated by that loan discounted at a rate that reflects current interest rates, and the timing and risk of the future income. There are two primary reasons why book value and market value are unlikely to be the same for a given loan:

1. The current interest rate that would be charged on a similar loan made today is different from the rate actually charged on the loan. For example, if the interest rate charged on a loan is 8 percent, but the current rate on a similar loan is 10 percent, the market value of the loan would be less than its book value, all other things being equal.

2. The loan is nonperforming—interest payments are not being made—and the collateral value does not cover the outstanding principal balance and unpaid interest due. In this case the market value would be less than book value.

For performing loans, the valuation is virtually identical in approach to the valuation of an investment security—the net present value of the future income stream discounted by an appropriate rate of interest.

When valuing performing loans, the rate used to discount future income to present value is the rate that would be charged for an equivalent loan at the time of the valuation, *not* the interest rate stated on the loan. As with investments, current rates determine the value of an income-generating asset, not the rate stated on that asset.

Nonperforming loans cannot be valued by calculating the net present value of future income, because there is no income, and there may never be. The valuation of a nonperform-

ing loan is a more subjective process that must consider the likelihood of payments beginning again and/or the value of any underlying collateral. If a loan is nonperforming, it does
not mean that its market value is necessarily less than its book value. If a loan is well collateralized with marketable property, the liquidation value of the collateral may cover the
debt sufficiently.

When valuing the loan portfolio of a bank, it is useful to assign each loan being valued
to one of five categories:

1. Commercial loans
2. Consumer loans
3. Mortgage loans
4. Lease financing
5. Nonperforming loans

15.2.3 Commercial Loans

Because commercial loans are larger and more complex, they can have a disproportionate
impact on the overall value of the bank's assets. Consequently, these types of loans must be
examined very carefully. The value of these loans depends on the timing of repayments, assumptions about prepayment, and prevailing interest rates. The approach is similar to that
used for investment securities, except that cash flow (payments) for commercial loans can
be irregular. Consequently, it is often necessary to project the future cash flow of the loan
until its maturity date, then apply the discount rate to calculate net present value.

For example, a commercial loan with book value of $500,000 at 10 percent, one year re-
maining life, and interest-only payments for six months with bullet payments in months six,
nine, and twelve has cash flow and valuation as shown in Exhibit 15.2. Because the loan is
paying a 10 percent rate in an environment where an 8.5 percent discount rate is appropriate, market value is somewhat higher than current book value.

Exhibit 15.2   Valuation of a Commercial Loan

Month	Cash Flow	Discount Factor @ 8.5%	Present Value of Cash Flow
1	$ 4,167	.993	$ 4,138
2	4,167	.986	4,109
3	4,167	.979	4,079
4	4,167	.972	4,050
5	4,167	.965	4,022
6	170,834	.959	163,398
7	4,167	.952	3,967
8	4,167	.945	3,938
9	170,834	.938	159,820
10	4,167	.932	3,884
11	4,167	.925	3,954
12	170,834	.919	156,583
			$515,842

This type of valuation analysis, while time consuming, may be justified for the larger commercial loans. It is not unusual to find 4 or 5 percent of loans constituting a third to a half of dollar volume. Clearly, an in-depth valuation of these larger loans is worthwhile.

15.2.4 Consumer Loans

Consumer loans are relatively easy to value, because they usually have fixed payments for a specified period of time. There is some prepayment risk with consumer loans, but it is typically less of a problem than with other types of loans, particularly mortgage loans.

A straightforward formula can be used to calculate the value of a portfolio of fixed payment consumer loans that share the same number of remaining payments and contractual interest rate:

$$
\frac{\left(\dfrac{1}{DR}\right) \times \left(1 - \dfrac{1}{(1 + DR)^n}\right)}{\left(\dfrac{1}{IR}\right) \times \left(1 - \dfrac{1}{(1 + IR)^n}\right)} \times \text{Loan Amount}
$$

where IR is the contractual interest rate per payment period on the loans, DR is the discount rate per payment period, and n is the number of payment periods remaining.

An example illustrates the use of this formula. Suppose a portfolio of auto loans with a book value of $20 million is to be valued. These loans are all four year auto loans at 13 percent (1.083 percent per month) with 27 months remaining on their original 48 month life. An annual discount rate of 12 percent is being used, resulting in a 1 percent rate per payment period.

$$
\frac{\left(\dfrac{1}{.01}\right) \times \left(1 - \dfrac{1}{(1 + .01)^{27}}\right)}{\left(\dfrac{1}{.01083}\right) \times \left(1 - \dfrac{1}{(1 + .01083)^{27}}\right)} \times \$20{,}000{,}000
$$

$$
= \frac{23.56}{23.30} \times \$20{,}000{,}000
$$

$$
= \$20{,}223{,}176
$$

This portfolio of loans has a value of about $20.22 million.

To account for potential prepayment risk, this same formula could be used with a different assumption of remaining periods n. For example, if the remaining life is assumed to be 20 periods instead of 27, (that is, if early payoffs bring down average life), the value of the portfolio declines slightly to $20.17 million.

15.2.5 Mortgage Loans

Mortgage loans present a particularly difficult valuation challenge because of the variety of payment streams and the general availability of no-penalty prepayment options. Because mortgage borrowers are very rate sensitive, the slightest decrease in rates causes massive prepayments and refinancing, as was experienced in 1992 and 1993. Also, the widespread success of adjustable and graduated payment mortgages with caps, collars, and floors gives even more uncertainty to the value of a mortgage.

In its simplest form, a mortgage loan with fixed payments over a known remaining time period can be valued exactly like a consumer loan or a bond. In the case where mortgage rates are expected to fall, thus creating prepayments, the calculated value of a mortgage portfolio can change dramatically. For example, a $150 million portfolio of 30 year monthly-pay, fixed rate loans at 7 percent with 26 years remaining (312 months) discounted at 8 percent has a value of $137 million. If the assumption of remaining life changes to, for example, 13 years (156 months), the value of the portfolio is $142 million. In this particular example the value is higher with a shorter life because the prevailing interest rate environment (the discount rate of 8 percent) is higher than the interest rate of 7 percent on the portfolio.

15.2.6   Lease Financing

Lease financing loans are similar to normal loans with regular payments, except that a residual value of the collateral exists at the end of the lease term. During the term of the lease, the payment stream can be valued exactly as a consumer loan. The driver of the valuation of the lease portfolio, however, is the residual value of the assets being financed. Therefore, careful attention must be paid to the collateral underlying the lease and the assumptions of residual value.

15.2.7   Nonperforming Loans

Nonperforming loans need to be evaluated on a case-by-case basis because there is no cash flow to value. An examination of the underlying collateral can gauge the liquidation value of the loan. This provides a worst-case scenario of the value. Individual analysis may lead to assumptions of resumed payments that can be valued through discounting.

15.3   TANGIBLE ASSETS IN BANK MERGERS AND ACQUISITIONS

When banks are acquired, the acquisition is seldom a case of a purchase of individual assets. The buyer is interested in the future income-generating capabilities of the bank as a business entity (the franchise). The quality of the individual assets, however, can be a primary determinant of that future income. A clean loan portfolio, a well-balanced investment mix, and efficient fixed assets are all signs of a profitable bank. Consequently, from a business decision-making perspective, the value—and corresponding quality of the tangible assets—are important factors.

From a tax and accounting perspective, the individual assets and their values are also important. Purchase price allocations and establishing new depreciable basis of assets are both critical factors affecting tangible assets in a bank merger or acquisition. These issues are addressed in Chapter 7.

CHAPTER 16

Core Deposits as a Special Type of Intangible Asset Valuation

The core deposit base is an intangible asset unique to banks. It is usually the single largest potentially amortizable intangible asset associated with a bank acquisition. Recent tax court and Supreme Court rulings have made the amortization deduction opportunities clearer, but the whole issue must still be approached carefully. This chapter presents a variety of issues related to core deposits as an intangible asset, and some different points of view on definition and measurement of their value.

16.1 THE CONCEPT OF CORE DEPOSIT BASE AS AN INTANGIBLE ASSET

Deposits are a liability of a bank, but their existence may create an intangible asset. On the surface this can appear to be a contradiction, but it is not. Deposits are the lifeblood of a bank, without which there would be no funds for loans and investments. When a bank is acquired, the buyer receives a built-in base of usually stable customer relationships. This customer base has demonstrable economic benefits to the buyer.

Clearly, bankers place value on deposits and depositors. In order to attract depositors, branches are built and staffed, premiums are offered, and advertising is undertaken. These activities are all evidence that deposits have value and banks are willing to pay more than just the interest cost to attract them.

The critical issues associated with core deposits are not related to whether they have economic benefit, which they clearly do, but to the measurement of that economic benefit and determination of whether the customer relationship is a wasting asset—that is, whether it has a measurable, finite life.

16.2 INTERNAL REVENUE SERVICE POSITION ON CORE DEPOSITS

The IRS historically has challenged the concept that core deposits represent an intangible asset separate and distinct from goodwill. The IRS concedes that stable customer relationships have economic value, but it has historically put forth the theory that they are part of the over-all goodwill of the bank. In the past, all amortization deductions of core deposits for federal income tax purposes have been challenged. The IRS has spent a great deal of effort attempting to invalidate the deduction of core deposit value amortization for federal income tax purposes. Typically, the IRS has focused on these areas to deny the deduction of core deposit value:

- inappropriate deposit types included in core deposit base;
- incorrect alternative funds rates used in cost-savings approaches; and
- faulty statistical data.

The implications of the IRS's strategy is that buyers who plan to amortize and deduct the core deposit base premium for federal income tax purposes must have a thorough, well-documented core deposit valuation methodology and statistical basis.

16.3 IMPORTANT CORE DEPOSIT TAX COURT CASES

For many years, the idea has been put forth that the core deposit base of an acquired bank is an intangible asset that could be amortized for federal income tax purposes. The IRS has challenged such efforts, with the result being a number of cases that give insight into the thought process and direction of the courts. There are five cases in particular that are important. Each of these cases is discussed in this section.

16.3.1 The Midlantic Case

The first case, *Midlantic*,[1] involved a purchase and assumption of a failed bank. The tax-payer argued that the premium paid to acquire a failed bank should not be considered good-will or going concern value, because the bank was failing. Only the right to solicit depositors of the former bank should be considered an intangible asset. The tax court held that this right to solicit was an intangible asset with a limited useful life and was, therefore, amortizable. *Midlantic* was not definitive because it involved a failed bank and was not considered applicable to voluntary combinations of healthy banks.

16.3.2 The Banc One Case

The second important case, *Banc One*,[2] was a 1985 case involving several issues that affected the purchase price allocation, some of which were related to core deposit value. Other issues involved the valuing of goodwill and other unrecorded intangible assets. Although the ruling went against the taxpayer, the tax court's reasoning offered positive indications that it believed that core deposits could exist as an amortizable intangible asset.

In 1973 and 1974, through cash transactions Banc One Corporation acquired the assets and assumed the liabilities of two banks. In both cases, the purchase price was allocated to the acquired net assets using a second tier approach (a technique that is no longer available for tax valuations). Initially, Banc One did not value the deposit base but did allocate a portion of the purchase price to a loan premium. During litigation in 1984, Banc One amended its petition in order to claim that it acquired an amortizable deposit premium. The IRS agreed that core deposits possessed a value, but argued that the value was inseparable from nonamortizable goodwill and that the deposit base is self-regenerative—that it is not a wasting asset—and thus its useful life could not be determined.

The important aspect of this case, with respect to core deposits, is the reason for the court's ruling against Banc One. Amortization for tax purposes was denied not because the tax court believed core deposits were, across the board, inseparable from goodwill, but because the court believed the methodology used by Banc One's appraiser to establish useful life was improper. Facts after the date of acquisition were used to establish the life of the deposits acquired in 1973 and 1974. The tax court stated that because the life of the deposit base was established based on data after the close of the tax year in which the acquisition occurred (and therefore improperly established), there was no need to rule whether the value of deposits were or were not separable from goodwill. The court's reasoning was such that the issue of whether or not a definite life existed was not decided. Some observers felt that had the court believed core deposit value was not separable from goodwill, it would have based its ruling on that determination.

16.3.3 The AmSouth Case

The third important case, *AmSouth,*[3] was decided in favor of the IRS on February 25, 1988. The court held that AmSouth had not demonstrated that the value of the acquired core deposit was separate and distinct from goodwill. Therefore, the value of the core deposit relationship was not amortizable and thus not deductible for federal income tax purposes.

In February 1979, AmSouth Bancorporation acquired the assets and assumed the liabilities of the Bank of East Alabama (BEA), with a premium paid of $4.8 million. At the time of the acquisition, BEA was having financial difficulties and capital adequacy problems. Nonetheless, BEA was not in immediate danger of failing nor had it experienced a deposit outflow. In fact, deposits were still growing at a modest rate.

In 1977, the Board of Directors of BEA decided to sell the bank, and on December 30, 1977, it was announced that AmSouth agreed to purchase the assets and assume the liabilities of BEA. The acquisition was finalized in February 1979.

On June 12, 1978, BEA signed the merger agreement with AmSouth. This agreement contained the purchase price, but did not allocate that price to specific assets or liabilities. An Agreement of Purchase was signed on August 25, 1978, which allocated to goodwill $1.7 million of the $4.8 million purchase price. On February 25, 1979 the final purchase agreement was signed, which assigned $1,679,045 of the purchase price to customer deposit base with no allocation to goodwill.

The $1,679,045 customer deposit base figure was arrived at by the residual method. AmSouth first allocated the purchase price to the fixed assets, the loan portfolio, the investment portfolio, cash, and other assets. The amount of liabilities assumed was then deducted from the value of the assets to arrive at a net tangible asset figure of $3,120,955. The entire excess of $1,679,045 (the residual) of the purchase price ($4,800,000) over the value of net tangible assets ($3,120,955) was assigned to core deposit value. To arrive at net tangible asset value, the book values of loans were used; no fair market value calculations were made. Moreover, it is not clear whether any assets were revalued to market or if only the book values were used. AmSouth did not perform, or have performed, a valuation of the core deposit base prior to or at the time of the acquisition. After the amortization deduction was challenged, AmSouth retained two appraisal firms to value the customer deposit base independently. The results of these valuations were used in the AmSouth case.

One appraisal firm valued the deposit base at $3.1 million as of December 31, 1987 (rather than the February 28, 1979 acquisition date) with a remaining life of 40 years for the business customers and 25 years for individual customers. All deposits were valued, including jumbo CDs (those over $100,000). The appraisal firm determined the value of the deposits by calculating the difference in the marginal cost of deposits for AmSouth and the actual cost of deposits for BEA. This difference was multiplied by the projected average balances of the customer deposit base over its estimated remaining useful life.

The second appraisal firm estimated the deposit base value at $3.0 million (also as of December 31, 1987) with a useful life of 40 years. This value was derived by calculating the present value of the projected net income to be obtained from that part of the acquired deposit base that remained in each successive year over its useful life. This net income was determined to be the difference between the cost of the deposits and the income derived from investing those deposits in typical bank assets.

Both appraisal firms estimated the remaining useful life by analyzing closed account history. Also, both used a "snapshot" approach that assumed that all deposits remain at their current balances until closed, and that deposit relationships do not provide value in the form of cross-selling opportunities.

AmSouth presented several arguments to support its amortization claim. The major one, however, was the assertion that BEA had no goodwill because it was in financial difficulty at the time of the acquisition and there had been negative publicity about certain activities of its past president. AmSouth cited the Midlantic case as support. The court disagreed because BEA did not fail (as was the situation in the Midlantic case) and, in fact, had continued to experience deposit growth. Although the court decided the AmSouth case on fairly narrow grounds, a number of aspects of the case, summarized below, probably diminished AmSouth's position.

- In the final purchase agreement, AmSouth allocated nothing to goodwill even though BEA was solvent and had continual deposit growth.

- The purchase agreement included a value for core deposits, but this value was not supported by any valuation procedure undertaken before the acquisition. The core deposit value was not part of the determination of purchase price, but was the leftover between price and net tangible asset value (the residual method).

- AmSouth used two appraisal firms that employed substantially different approaches yet arrived at approximately the same values after several revisions. The credibility of these valuations was suspect.

- All deposits, not just core deposits, were included in the valuation.

- AmSouth failed to revise the values of all assets as required by APB 16 and 17—instead, the bank used book values for all acquired assets.

- The two appraisal firms' values were much higher than AmSouth's original core deposits value estimate. AmSouth should have proportionately reduced the value of other assets to ensure no negative goodwill.

In the end, the court did not explicitly state that core deposits in general do not have value separate from goodwill. It only held that AmSouth had not demonstrated that the deposits of BEA it acquired had value separate and distinct from goodwill. The conclusion from a number of observers was that the unsupported valuation and less-than-comprehensive documentation were the main reasons for the unfavorable ruling.

16.3.4 The Citizens & Southern Case

The fourth major case related to core deposits is *Citizens & Southern* (C&S).[4] In this case, the court ruled on September 6, 1988 that C&S had demonstrated that the value of acquired core deposits was separate and distinct from goodwill, thereby permitting C&S to amortize the cost of the core deposits.

Beginning in the late 1950s, C&S developed close relationships with a number of banks located throughout Georgia. These correspondent associates, as they were known, utilized certain operational and banking services of C&S, and in some cases they used the C&S name. During 1981 and 1982 C&S acquired nine of these correspondent associates, and after the acquisition conducted business in substantially the same manner as before. C&S paid a premium of $52 million (for all nine banks) of which $42 million was allocated to the core deposit base and $10 million to goodwill.

To establish the purchase price, C&S used a computer acquisition model developed by its finance staff. This model projected future dividend potential, then discounted those dividends to present value to arrive at acquisition value. An integral part of the projections was the funding provided by core deposits, which was shown separately in the model. While the model did not explicitly value the core deposits, when assumptions of greater core deposit funding were made the model did produce higher value estimates, all other assumptions being the same.

C&S acquired the nine banks in taxable mergers or stock purchases that constituted taxable asset purchases for federal income tax purposes. C&S allocated the purchase price of the acquired banks in a manner consistent with generally accepted accounting principles (GAAP). The fair market values of the loan and investment portfolios were determined, the intangible assets other than core deposits were valued at cost, and the deposit base was valued and classified as a separately identifiable intangible asset. Goodwill was calculated as the excess of the purchase price over the value of net tangible and identifiable intangible assets.

The valuation of the core deposit base was thoroughly prepared and became crucial to the favorable ruling C&S received. C&S included only transaction accounts (DDA and NOWs), regular savings, and time deposit open accounts (TDOAs). All of these accounts represented deposits that were relatively low cost funds, reasonably stable over time, and more or less insensitive to interest rate changes.

The C&S valuation considered only those accounts that existed at the time of valuation, and reflected market information and conditions at the time. These valuations were completed prior to the acquisition date.

An income approach was used by C&S to value the core deposits (described in detail later in this chapter). The steps C&S used were:

- Determine account survival probabilities by examining the past rate of closure of deposit accounts. (C&S used actual account closure data, for each type of account, for each acquired bank.)

- Project net investable balances (net of reserves and float) of each type of account open at each year into the future.

- Calculate expected income on deposits by multiplying the spread (interest earnings and service charge income less interest and operating cost on the deposits) by the net investable balances. The interest earnings assumed the funds would be invested in loans. Service charge income was estimated based on the acquired banks' records and Federal Reserve Functional Cost Analysis data. The cost of deposits included both the interest expense if any and the overhead costs required to service accounts.

- Discount projected income to present value. (C&S used the yield on the acquired banks' loan portfolios as the discount rate, a relatively conservative approach.)

The appraiser retained by C&S also used the cost savings approach to core deposit value estimation. This approach measured the value of an asset as the present value of the difference between the ongoing cost of the asset and its market rate alternative. The appraiser used the rate on insured CDs as the market alternative, another conservative approach. The value of the core deposit base using the cost savings approach was $34 million (versus the $42 million using the income approach).

To derive the annual depreciation deduction, C&S computed the present value at the acquisition date of the projected income for the taxable year. Since deposit accounts tend to run off faster in early years, the net effect is that C&S was able to take greater deductions in early years than would be possible with straight-line amortization.

C&S presented a number of circumstances and facts that led to the ruling in its favor, and that made the case substantially different from AmSouth or Banc One.

- C&S made it clear through documentation that its primary motivation for the acquisition was to garner deposits.

- C&S contended that under GAAP, deposit base is recognized as being separate from goodwill (APB Opinion No. 17 and FASB 72).

- C&S claimed that there were reliable techniques to value core deposits and estimate their useful life.

- Allocations to core deposits were made prior to the acquisitions and became an integral part of the pricing process (and there was ample evidence to prove this).

- C&S used only true core deposits in its valuation.

- All core deposit accounts were examined in the valuation, not just a sample of accounts.

- The life of the core deposit base at each acquired bank was estimated based on the actual history of that bank. Moreover, C&S used an independent competent statistician to establish the deposit lines and conducted follow-up studies that corroborated the projections.

In general, the process used by C&S was thoroughly documented and well thought out, and these facts were essential in the favorable ruling it received.

One important issue that was decided by the court in the C&S case was that of valuation methodology. Both an income and cost savings approach were used to value the acquired core deposits. The IRS claimed that by using the income approach to value the core deposit intangible asset, C&S allocated the purchase price to the earning assets twice. The IRS's reasoning was as follows:

- C&S valued the loans and investments (the earning assets) of the nine acquired banks based on the present value of the income stream they were expected to generate—interest income from the earning assets less cost of funding.
- C&S calculated the value of the deposit base as the present value of the income stream the deposits could generate by being invested in earning assets.
- C&S assumed that all core deposits were immediately available for investment, but in reality C&S could only invest the core deposits already funding earning assets only when those earning assets matured or rolled off.
- Therefore, C&S should have adjusted the core deposit base by that portion that was invested in earning assets it had previously valued.

The court agreed with this logic and held that the income approach was not proper, and that the cost savings approach was the correct valuation method to be used.

Another key issue decided in the C&S case was the basis of the amortization deduction. IRC Section 167(c) indicates that straight-line depreciation is the only method available for intangible assets. In the C&S case, however, the court held that the evidence supported an accelerated method because it was shown that the deposit base does decline more rapidly in the early years after an acquisition. The court agreed that the amount of depreciation is equal to the present value, on the acquisition date, of the projected cost savings for each taxable year.

16.3.5 The Newark Morning Ledger Case

Another recent case applicable to core deposit valuation is the *Newark Morning Ledger.*[5] On April 20, 1993, the Supreme Court overturned an appeals court ruling that assets such as customer lists should be classified as goodwill and not be deductible for tax purposes. In a 5–4 ruling the court reaffirmed that an intangible asset can be depreciated for federal income tax purposes if it can be valued and has a limited useful life that can be measured with reasonable accuracy.

In 1976 The Herald Company (later acquired by the Newark Morning Ledger Company) purchased the outstanding shares of Booth Newspapers, Inc. As a taxable transaction, The Herald Company allocated its adjusted income tax basis in the Booth shares among the assets that were acquired. Among the assets identified and valued was the "paid subscriber" list, valued at $67.8 million based on the estimate of future value derived from the identified subscribers of Booth's eight newspapers. The IRS denied the claimed depreciation deduction on the ground that the concept of a paid subscriber was indistinguishable from goodwill, and therefore not depreciable.

The IRS did not contest the estimate of useful life or the assumptions underlying The Herald Company's estimate of value using the income approach (the present value of subscription revenue stream less the cost of collecting those subscriptions). The IRS claimed that the value of an acquired paid subscriber list is only the cost of replacing them with an equal number of new subscribers (estimated by the IRS at $3 million), and that asset is still indistinguishable from goodwill.

The Supreme Court held for the Newark Morning Ledger (as successor to The Herald Company) by stating that the company proved that a paid subscriber list is an intangible asset with an ascertainable value and a limited useful life that can be measured with reasonable accuracy. The court also stated that The Herald Company proved that the asset is not self-regenerating; rather, it wastes as a finite number of subscriptions are canceled.

The importance of this case cannot be overstated as a foundation to deduct core deposit value for tax purposes. Nonetheless, the case did not relieve the taxpayer of the responsibility to properly value the intangible asset and estimate its useful life with reasonable accuracy. In fact it reemphasized the need for solid, well-documented valuation work.

Another aspect of *Newark Morning Ledger* that is relevant to bank core deposit valuations is the court's implied support of the income approach. While it did not explicitly rule for this particular method, it did state that the value was more than the cost of generating new customer names. Had the method of valuation been in question, the court could have allowed a deduction on just the $3 million value the government placed on the "paid subscriber" list.

16.4   DEPOSITS TO BE INCLUDED IN VALUATION

There appears to be less than complete agreement among regulators as to which deposit accounts should be considered core. The Office of the Comptroller of the Currency (OCC) defines core deposits as the base of demand and savings accounts that—while usually not legally restricted—the bank can expect to maintain for an extended period of years because of generally stable relationships. While CDs are not explicitly listed, the Citizens & Southern case seems to support the exclusion of CDs in the core deposit base. The specific types of deposit accounts to be considered core at a given bank should be evaluated on an individual basis. The safest approach appears to be to include only noninterest-bearing DDA, NOWs, and savings in the core deposit base value calculations.

16.5   ALTERNATIVE APPROACHES TO VALUING A CORE DEPOSIT BASE

As with other types of assets, there are several ways to approach the valuation of a core deposit base. Each approach has advantages and disadvantages, as well as practical limitations. Moreover, the Citizens & Southern and Newark Morning Ledger cases demonstrated that the court favored the cost savings approach over others. Nonetheless, three possible approaches to core deposit valuation are described below. Applications of the techniques are described later in this chapter.

16.5.1   Historical Development Cost Approach

One possible way to establish the value of a core deposit base is to determine the costs actually incurred to attract those deposits—the amount spent, for example, on branches, advertising, and so on. This approach is analogous to the cost approach to valuing assets described in Chapter 6.

The historical development cost approach presents some very serious practical difficulties. Assigning historical costs incurred to attract core deposits, as opposed to the attraction of other types of business, is virtually impossible. Even for banks that have excellent cost accounting and management information systems, identifying the relationship between certain costs and resulting depositor relationships would be suspect at best. Consequently, establishing core deposit value based on historical development costs is rarely, if ever, used.

Another problem with the historical development cost approach is that a bank has already deducted, for tax purposes, the cost of acquiring deposits as part of normal operating expenses. Therefore, to reflect those acquisition costs in determining core deposit value for tax purposes may imply double counting of those expenses. In general, the valuation of a core deposit base using historical costs should be avoided.

16.5.2 Cost Savings Approach

Conceptually, the cost savings approach to core deposit valuation is based on the premise that the deposits being acquired have value because the cost of alternative funding is higher. The most supportable alternative funding to use to make this comparison is usually retail CDs (as was used in the successful Citizens & Southern case). The alternative funding rate would include the interest cost and maintenance expenses of CDs.

The cost savings approach to valuing the core deposit base is approached in much the same way that an investment is valued, except that when an investment is valued, cash *inflows* are discounted to present value, whereas when a deposit base is valued the cash *outflows* are discounted. These cash outflows associated with the deposits include the interest costs on the deposits, the maintenance costs (net of any fees), and the runoff of the deposits themselves. These future outflows are discounted at a market rate of interest that reflects the yield curve for the alternative source of funds (for example, CDs) at the time of the valuation. The difference between the actual level of the deposits acquired and the net present value of discounted future cash outflows is the value benefit of the deposit base.

A practical problem arises in that a yield curve on retail CDs is normally not available. A reasonable assumption to make is that the shape of the CD yield curve is the same as the shape of the yield curve of zero-coupon Treasury instruments. Another reasonable assumption is that the difference in the rates between zero-coupon Treasury instruments and CDs at any point on the yield curve is equal to the maintenance cost of those CDs.[6] Therefore, the total of CD interest and maintenance costs would equal the rate on zero-coupon Treasury instruments. Consequently, using this yield curve to discount future cash outflows from the acquired deposit base is a reasonable and supportable assumption.

16.5.3 Future Income Approach

A third technique of core deposit valuation is the future income approach. This technique establishes value based on the difference between the cost of deposits (both interest and maintenance) and the income generated by using those deposits to make loans and investments, as well as fees from deposit accounts. The weakness in this approach, as shown in the Citizens & Southern case, is the potential for double counting of value.

The future income approach starts with the interest income generated by earning assets (mostly loans and investments), minus the interest costs associated with the deposits funding those earning assets. The result is *net interest income*. Any fee and service charge income associated with the deposits is added, then the maintenance expenses associated with the deposits are subtracted. Finally, taxes are subtracted. The net income for each year is then discounted to present value. The resulting figure is the value of the core deposit base to the owner.

The discount rate used to convert future income flows to present value must reflect the riskiness of the business of taking deposits and making loans. Consequently, there are risks with the deposits and the loans. The selection of a discount rate would follow the procedures described in Chapter 6 and would be analogous to discounting the future income of a business as described in Chapter 14.

Establishing value based on future income is often the most complex and difficult approach, because various operations and maintenance expenses must be assigned to earning assets and deposits. Without a good cost accounting or product profitability system, this cost assignment can be difficult.

It should be noted that the future income approach may not be the most supportable technique for establishing a tax basis, but it can be a good way to establish acquisition value. When a bank is considering the acquisition of a branch, the better way to establish the economic value of the deposits to be assumed (as opposed to the tax value) is probably the income approach.

16.6   CORE DEPOSIT BASE LIFE ESTIMATION

Irrespective of which approach to valuation is used, establishing a life of the core deposit base is the most essential element of the valuation process if this asset is to be considered as an amortizable intangible asset by the IRS. Without an accurate estimate of useful life, the value of the core deposit base may be treated no differently, for tax purposes, than goodwill. Consequently, it is very important that the life of the deposit base be established with reasonable accuracy.

In general, to establish the life of the acquired deposit base it is best to use the actual experience of the bank being acquired. Use of industry or peer group averages may be reasonable, but it is less supportable if challenged by the IRS. The completeness and accuracy of records maintained by the bank will, to a great extent, determine how much reliance must be placed on industry data. For the discussion that follows, it is assumed that the necessary information is available from automated and/or manual sources at the bank.

16.6.1   Historical Retention

The initial step in lifing a core deposit base is to quantify the historical retention rate for each type of core deposit account (DDA, savings, and so on). This retention rate, sometimes called a survival rate, can be defined as the percent of accounts for each deposit type open at the beginning of a year that will still be open at the end of that year.

One method to quantify historical retention rates is to construct a table similar to that shown in Exhibit 16.1. The first step in constructing such a table is to start with a base year (1995 in this example) and find the number of accounts active at year end (1,000 in this example). These are the *base year* accounts. The next step is to determine the number of base year accounts that were still open one year later, two years later, three years later, and so on.

Exhibit 16.1 Illustration of Historical Retention Rate Calculation

Age of Account (yrs.)	Number of Accounts Open at Date					Retention Rate	
	12/31/95	12/31/96	12/31/97	12/31/98	12/31/99	Age of Account (yrs.)	Probability of Account Remaining Open in Next Year
0–1	1,000	360	548	429	419	0–1	67.9%[1]*
1–2	—	690	234	370	300	1–2	76.8%[2]**
2–3	—	—	518	176	296	2–3	77.0%[3]***
3–4	—	—	—	400	135	3–4	87.5%[4]****
4–5	—	—	—	—	350		
Total	1,000	1,050	1,300	1,375	1,500		

Notes:

$$*(1) \quad \left(\frac{690}{1,000} + \frac{234}{360} + \frac{370}{548} + \frac{300}{429} \right) \div 4 = 67.9\%$$

$$**(2) \quad \left(\frac{518}{690} + \frac{176}{234} + \frac{296}{370} \right) \div 3 = 76.8\%$$

$$***(3) \quad \left(\frac{400}{518} + \frac{135}{176} \right) \div 2 = 77.0\%$$

$$****(4) \quad \frac{350}{400} = 87.5\%$$

In the example, of the 1,000 base year accounts, 690 were still active one year later, 518 two years later, 400 three years later, and 350 four years later. In 1996, 360 accounts were opened during the year and remained open at year end. Of those 360, 234 were still open one year later, 176 two years later, and 135 three years later. A similar pattern can be developed for the 548 accounts opened in 1997, the 429 opened in 1998, and the 419 opened in 1999.

Using this table, the retention rate for first year accounts can be computed (it is 67.9 percent in this example with the calculations shown at the bottom of the exhibit). This figure means that if an account is open less than one year, there is a 67.9 percent chance it will stay open another year. If an account has been open between one and two years, there is a 76.8 percent chance it will stay open another year. If an account has been open between two and three years, the chance that it will stay open an additional year increases to 77.0 percent. Over three years, the retention rate is 87.5 percent. A higher retention rate as an account ages is common. Bankers have long recognized that the longer a customer has been with the bank, the less likely it is that he or she will leave during a given year.

If historical records are available in automated form, it is easier to apply this technique. Special computer programs may be necessary to extract the data from historical records, but basic data should be available. The problem arises when records are in manual form or nonexistent. Such situations must be assessed on a case-by-case basis to determine if a sampling of accounts is possible or if less historical information provides a sufficient basis for estimating retention rates.

There are several typical deficiencies in data availability likely to be found. The most common among smaller banks is the lack of historical account data in machine-readable form. Normally, the information on active accounts is available. The problem arises in tracking accounts that have been opened and already closed during the four- or five-year-long historical period being studied.

One technique to determine the active or closed status of accounts is to examine the year-end trial balances for each account type. If accounts are opened and numbered sequentially (that is, if the latest account has the highest account number), it is relatively easy to determine the number of accounts opened during a year:

$$\text{new accounts during year}^7 =$$
$$\text{last account no. this year } - \text{ first account no. this year}$$

This figure is then subtracted from the number of active accounts at the end of the year. The difference is the number of accounts retained. For example, suppose there were 1,000 accounts active at the beginning of a year, and through examination of account number sequence it is found that 400 new accounts were opened, and from the trial balance report it is known that there were 1,090 accounts active at the end of the year. The number of the original 1,000 accounts retained would be 690 (1,090 − 400).

The second and subsequent years become somewhat more complex because multiple years and multiple groups of account numbers are tracked. The basic approach, however, is the same.

Another common data deficiency occurs when a bank has changed data processing systems. Occasionally, the data can be reconstructed using various conversion programs. If not, it may be necessary to take a sample of accounts and track manually, or use less historical data.

There are a number of ways to establish the life of a core deposit base. The method described is one of those ways. If the historical information is available, construction of a table showing the accounts open by age group is an excellent technique to establish the retention rates for the bank being analyzed. This analysis provides a basis for estimating the likely retention of the acquired deposit accounts.

16.6.2   Projected Lifing of Acquired Core Deposit Accounts

Based on the retention rates computed from historical data, it is possible to project the run-off of the acquired deposit accounts. The age distribution of those acquired accounts is determined based on account opening dates. The number of accounts in each age group (0 to 1 years, 1 to 2, and so on) form the beginning of the account retention projection.

As shown in Exhibit 16.2, the 1,500 accounts acquired in 1999 are distributed in five age groups; 419 were under a year old, 300 were 1 to 2 years old, 296 were 2 to 3 years old, 135 were 3 to 4 years old, and 350 were over 5 years old. At the end of 2000, the projected number of accounts that will be retained is computed based on the historical retention rates. For example, of the 419 acquired accounts that were less than one year old, at year end 1999, 67.9 percent (285) will be retained to year end 2000. During 2001, those 285 accounts that will then be one to two years old will be retained at a rate of 76.8 percent (ending with 219). During 2002, those 219 accounts which are now two to three years old will be retained at a rate of 77 percent (ending with 169). During 2003, the 169 accounts will be retained at a rate of 87.5 percent (ending 1998 with 148 accounts). The retention rate then stabilizes at 87.5 percent.

The same process is undertaken for each account age group, except that acquired deposit accounts that are one to two years old begin with the 76.8 percent retention rate, accounts two to three years old begin at 77.0 percent, and accounts over three years old begin at 87.5 percent.

The net result of these calculations is a projection of the number of acquired accounts remaining active at the end of each year (the column titled Total Acquired Accounts in Exhibit 16.2). When the number of accounts still open reaches about 5 percent of the original group (in this example, 75 accounts) it is assumed that the next year the remaining accounts run off.

The final step is to compute the average number of accounts open during each future year. This average is calculated as the midpoint between two year-end figures. This method of calculating the average implicitly assumes accounts are closed at a fairly constant rate during a year. Under most conditions this is a reasonable assumption.

16.7   APPLICATION OF THE COST SAVINGS APPROACH

As described previously, the most supportable way to measure the value of a core deposit base is to gauge the differential between the costs associated with the core deposits and the costs of alternative funding at market rates. The discussion below uses the data from the preceding example to illustrate how the cost savings approach can be applied.

The cost savings approach is similar in concept to the valuation of a bond, except that in the case of deposits, the amount of the deposit base originally acquired is compared with the future cash outflows (principal, interest and maintenance costs net of fees) associated with that deposit base. Exhibit 16.3 shows an illustration of the calculations.

The first step is to determine the volume of the originally acquired deposits retained at the end of each year through the life of that deposit base. This is based on the average num-

Exhibit 16.2 Calculations of Projected Balances of Acquired Deposit Accounts (Acquisition date is 12/31/94)

	Age of Acquired Deposit Accounts					Total Acquired Accounts	Avg. No. of Accts.	Average Balance*
	0–1	1–2	2–3	3–4	5+			
12/31/99 (actual/acquired)	419	300	296	135	350	1,500	—	$2,000
12/31/00	285	230	228	113	306	1,167	1,334	2,040
12/31/01	219	177	199	103	268	966	1,067	2,080
12/31/02	169	155	175	90	235	824	895	2,125
12/31/03	148	136	153	79	205	721	773	2,175
12/31/04	130	119	133	69	180	631	676	2,200
12/31/05	113	104	117	60	158	552	592	2,250
12/31/06	99	91	102	53	138	483	518	2,300
12/31/07	87	80	90	46	120	423	453	2,350
12/31/08	76	70	78	41	105	370	397	2,400
12/31/09	66	61	69	35	92	323	347	2,440
12/31/10	58	53	60	31	81	283	303	2,490
12/31/11	51	47	52	27	71	248	266	2,535
12/31/12	44	41	46	24	61	216	232	2,590
12/31/13	39	36	40	21	54	190	203	2,640
12/31/14	34	31	35	18	48	166	178	2,690
12/31/15	30	27	31	15	41	145	156	2,750
12/31/16	26	24	27	14	36	127	136	2,800
12/31/17	23	21	24	12	31	111	119	2,860
12/31/18	20	18	21	10	28	97	104	2,920
12/31/19	17	16	18	9	25	85	91	2,970
12/31/20	15	14	16	8	21	74	80	3,030
12/31/21	13	12	14	7	16	0**	37	3,100

*5% annual increase.

**It is assumed that when the remaining accounts reach 5% of original number acquired (75 in this example), all accounts run off the next year.

Exhibit 16.3   Illustration of Cost Savings Approach to Valuation of Core Deposit Base (Rounded to $000, using data from Exhibit 16.2)

Year	Average Deposits During Year From Acquired Accts[1]	Interest[2]	Mainte-nance[3]	Runoff	Total	Discount Rate[4]	Discounted Value of Cash Outflow
			Cash Outflows Associated Deposits				
2000	$2,721	$177	$54	$279	$510	7.85%	$ 472
2001	2,219	144	44	502	690	8.05%	591
2002	1,902	124	38	317	479	8.16%	379
2003	1,681	109	34	221	368	8.17%	269
2004	1,487	97	30	194	321	8.17%	217
2005	1,332	87	27	155	269	8.23%	167
2006	1,191	77	24	141	242	8.26%	139
2007	1,065	69	21	126	216	8.30%	114
2008	953	62	19	112	193	8.34%	94
2009	847	55	17	106	178	8.35%	80
2010	754	49	15	93	157	8.37%	65
2011	674	44	13	80	137	8.39%	52
2012	601	39	12	73	124	8.40%	43
2013	536	35	11	65	111	8.41%	36
2014	479	31	10	57	98	8.41%	29
2015	429	28	9	50	87	8.40%	24
2016	381	25	8	48	81	8.41%	21
2017	340	22	7	41	70	8.41%	16
2018	304	20	6	36	69	8.39%	15
2019	271	18	5	33	56	8.35%	11
2020	242	16	5	29	50	8.35%	9
2021	115	7	2	127	136	8.33%	23
						TOTAL	$2,866

CORE DEPOSIT VALUE =
DEPOSITS ACQUIRED ($3,000) − DISCOUNTED VALUE OF OUTFLOW ($2,866) = $134 (4.5% PREMIUM).

[1]Average number of accounts that were open during year times average balance (from Exhibit 16.2).
[2]At 6.5%.
[3]At 2% of balances, per Fed Functional Cost Analysis, for regular savings.
[4]Using a yield curve on zero-coupon 30-year U.S. Government instruments.

ber of accounts open during the year multiplied by the average balances (Results of that calculation are shown in column one of Exhibit 16.3, using the data from Exhibit 16.2.)

The next step is to determine the cash outflows associated with the deposits. The interest costs in this example are assumed to be 6.5 percent of deposits during the year (results shown in column 2). Maintenance costs are based on Federal Reserves Functional Cost Analysis figures at 200 basis points (2 percent) of deposits (results shown in column 3). Runoff is simply the reduction in deposit balances during the year (balances during preceding year less balances during current year, results in column 4). The total outflows (column 5) are discounted at the rate on zero-coupon Treasury instruments (usually the average of the four quarterly rates for the year being discounted). The sum of these discounted values ($2,866,000) is subtracted from the deposits acquired ($3,000,000) to arrive at the deposit base value ($134,000).

The cost savings approach to core deposit base valuation can be difficult to understand. To address this difficulty, it is useful to think of two streams of cash that a bank will have to pay out over some period of time. The first stream of cash outflow is that which the bank will pay to the depositors who own the deposits being acquired (column 5 in Exhibit 16.3). The bank has acquired a liability with a book value of $3,000,000, but because the payout occurs over time the value of the liability is less than $3,000,000 even considering interest and maintenance costs.

The second stream of cash outflow to think of is one associated with the payout on a portfolio of CDs paying market rates and having the exact same runoff characteristics as the deposit base which was acquired. Since it is assumed that the cost of alternative funding at market rates is equal to the cost of CDs, the net present value of that portfolio of CDs (including interest and maintenance) will be enough to replace the acquired deposits ($3,000,000).

Returning to the first stream of cash, those future outflows are discounted to present value at a rate that reflects only the risk of the future cash outflows. The yields on zero-coupon Treasury instruments are an excellent proxy for the market's assessment of future investment income risk at a specific point in time. Using these rates, the net present value of the future cash outflows can be computed (in the example, $2,866,000).

The present value of the future liability of the bank for the deposits it acquired is $2,866,000. The present value of an alternative source of funding liabilities at market rates is $3,000,000. The difference between these two represents the advantage to the bank of being able to use core deposits instead of market rate alternatives. Consequently, the value of those core deposits is equal to that advantage, or $134,000.

16.8 APPLICATION OF THE FUTURE INCOME APPROACH

The future income approach to valuing a core deposit base requires three steps:

1. Determine the earnings per acquired account based on the interest expense and operating costs associated with each account.
2. Project the total earnings from all acquired accounts as they run off over the average life of the account base.
3. Compute the value of the deposit base by discounting the future earnings to present value.

Each of these three steps is described below.

16.8.1 Earnings Per Account Calculation

The fundamental basis of the future income approach is that deposits are invested in interest-bearing assets. Consequently, the first step is to calculate how much is earned from each dollar of deposit that is invested. The procedure below explains the after-tax earnings generated by one hundred dollars of deposits (assuming same type of savings deposit base as in the cost savings example).

Exhibit 16.4   Calculation of Core Deposit Base Value Using Income Approach (Rounded to $000, using data from Exhibit 16.2)

Year	Average Deposits During Year From Acquired Accts[1]	After Tax Income[2]	Discount Rate[3]	Discounted Value of Income
2000	$2,721	$34	12%	$ 30
2001	2,219	28	12%	22
2002	1,902	24	12%	17
2003	1,681	21	12%	13
2004	1,487	19	12%	11
2005	1,332	17	12%	9
2006	1,191	15	12%	7
2007	1,065	14	12%	6
2008	953	12	12%	4
2009	847	11	12%	4
2010	754	10	12%	3
2011	674	9	12%	2
2012	601	8	12%	2
2013	536	7	12%	1
2014	479	6	12%	1
2015	429	5	12%	1
2016	381	4	12%	1
2017	340	4	12%	1
2018	304	4	12%	.5
2019	271	3	12%	.3
2020	242	3	12%	.3
2021	115	1	12%	.1
				$136

[1]Average number of accounts open during year times average balance (from Exhibit 16.2).
[2]At 1.27%, as described in text.
[3]The 12% discount rate reflects what a bank would expect to apply to a comparable business that takes deposits and makes loans. This is fundamentally different from the discount rate used in the cost savings approach to valuation, and will not be the same.

1.   Gross deposit received of $100.00
2.   Minus reserves and float of $5.00
3.   Equals net investable deposits of $95.00
4.   Multiplied by yield on earning assets of 8.16 percent equals $7.75
5.   Minus interest expense on gross deposit of 4.0 percent equals $3.95
6.   Minus operations costs of $2.00 equals $1.95
7.   Minus taxes of $.68
8.   Equals after-tax earnings on deposit of $1.27 (1.27 percent)

The foundation of the future income approach becomes the 1.27 percent after-tax earnings rate on deposits.

16.8.2   Projection of Earnings from Acquired Deposit Base

Once the percent return from each deposit account type is calculated, the future earnings of the acquired deposit base can be computed. Exhibit 16.4 illustrates the earnings calculation. The average number of accounts is multiplied by the average balance (which results in total deposit balances). The after-tax income percent (1.27 percent) is applied, resulting in the earnings attributable to the acquired deposits each year over the life of the deposit base.

16.8.3   Computation of Deposit Base Value

The value of the deposit base under the future income approach is the net present value of the after-tax income attributable to the acquired deposits. Applying a 12 percent discount rate, the net present value of all after-tax income shown in Exhibit 16.4 is about $136,000—a 4.5 percent premium. This is the value of the acquired deposit accounts (for that one type of account) to the buyer.

Notice that in the income approach a discount rate of 12 percent was used, but for the cost savings the discount rate used was based on the yield curve for zero-coupon Treasury securities. The main difference is that the 12 percent reflects what a bank would apply to a comparable business taking deposits. Consequently, there is a risk factor associated with the business activity in addition to the normal time value of money reflected in the yield curve of zero-coupon Treasury securities.

The core deposit value by the cost savings approach was $134,000. By the future income approach, the value was estimated at $136,000. As with the valuation of any asset, different approaches will yield different results. In general, it is unlikely that two different approaches to core deposit value will result in estimates that are this close to one another.

ENDNOTES

1. *Midlantic National Bank v. Comr.,* T.C. Memo 1983–58.
2. *Banc One Corp. v. Comr.,* T.C. Memo 1983–35.
3. *AmSouth Bancorporation v. United States,* 88–1, U.S.T.C.
4. *Citizens & Southern Bancorporation & Subs v. Commissioner,* 91 T.C. No. 35 (1988).
5. *Newark Morning Ledger Co., as successor to the Herald Company, petitioner v. United States.* Supreme Court of the United States; 91–1135, 4/20/93, 113 set 1670.
6. The economic argument underlying this assumption is based on the principle of substitution. If CDs plus maintenance cost yielded a rate higher than zero-coupon Treasury instruments, the bank would substitute open market funding for CDs. Admittedly, this ignores potential relationships with the customer for other product sales, but it is a supportable and reasonable assumption.
7. If account numbers are assigned sequentially.

CHAPTER 17

Derivative Financial Instruments

Derivative financial instruments have grown rapidly because of the dynamics of the global financial markets, the ever-lasting fluctuation in interest and currency exchange rates, the complexity of financial engineering, and their potential profitability. Commercial banks in the United States reported outstanding derivatives contracts with a national value of $33 trillion in 1999. The trend in derivatives transactions shows a steady growth of about 20 percent compound annual rate increase since 1990. Of the $33 trillion reported outstanding derivatives national value, only four trillion were exchange-traded derivatives, and the remainder were off-exchange or over-the-counter (OTC) derivatives.[1] Derivatives are defined as any financial instruments or other contracts (e.g, futures, forwards, options, swaptions, caps, collars, and floors) with one or more underlyings (e.g., interest rate, index security price, commodity price, foreign exchange rate, or some other variables) with one or more notional amounts or payment provisions or both (e.g., face amount expressed in currency units, number of shares, bushels, pounds, or other units specified in the contract). Key elements of this definition are "underlying," "notional amount," and "payment provision." An underlying is a specified interest rate, security price, commodity price, foreign exchange rate, or some other variable or index whose market movements cause the fair market value or cash flows of a derivative to fluctuate. A notional amount is a number of currency units, shares, bushels, pounds, or other units specified in the contract that determines the size of the change caused by the movement of the underlying. The underlying and notional amount typically determine the amount of settlement and whether or not a settlement is required in most cases. A payment provision determines a fixed or determinable settlement that is to be made if the underlying behaves in a certain manner. A net settlement indicates that a derivative can be settled in cash rather than the delivery of the underlying item.

Derivatives typically derive their value from underlying traditional financial instruments. Participants in derivative markets (e.g., dealers, financial institutions, business firms, mutual and pension funds, state and local governments) use derivatives for a number of reasons, including risk management purposes and speculation activities. The widespread use of derivatives, coupled with the concerns raised by the financial community regarding complexities, risks, failures, and insufficient measurement, recognition, and disclosures of derivative transactions, has caused regulators and the accounting profession to issue authoritative guidelines on derivatives.

Derivatives have been used for: (1) managing financial risks; (2) speculating on the price of financial instruments; (3) reducing the cost of raising capital; (4) earning higher investment returns; (5) adjusting investment portfolios to take advantage of miss-pricing between stock baskets and stock index futures; and (6) combining derivatives with other financial instruments to create new and more powerful financial products. Most commonly, active end-users of derivatives are financial institutions, mutual funds, pension funds, and commercial firms. Derivatives are being traded through both organized exchanges and over-the-counter and their "notional value" exceeds the estimated total value of the world's bonds and stocks. Exchange-traded derivatives are typically more standardized and offer greater liquidity than OTC derivatives which are individually arranged contracts. Most of the risk associated with exchange-traded derivatives is market risk rather than credit risk. OTC derivatives are privately-traded instruments which are customized to meet specific needs and for which the counterparty is not an organized exchange.

Derivative transactions have grown significantly in volume and complexity from the traditional interest rate and currency swaps to more sophisticated, computer-driven risk management derivatives. This ever-increasing use of derivatives and recent losses by some derivatives end-users have raised numerous issues of concern among regulators, the financial community, and the accounting profession as to the appropriate use, proper risk assessment, and adequate disclosures of derivative transactions by both issuers and end-users of these financial products. Improved oversight by regulators and new accounting standards by the accounting profession have been suggested as a means of addressing these issues.

The global financial community is concerned with the frequency and magnitude of derivatives losses suffered by public companies (e.g., Gibson Greetings, Proctor & Gamble, Air Products & Chemicals, and Eastman Kodak), mutual funds and municipal governments (e.g., Orange County, California), and Barings PLC (e.g., British Merchant Bank). These well publicized derivative losses focused on renewed attention on OTC derivatives sold by banks and brokers. As a result, several congressional and private initiatives have been taken to address derivatives issues.

17.1 AUTHORITATIVE GUIDELINES ON DERIVATIVES

A number of reports (GAO, 1994; The Group of Thirty, 1993)[2,3] studied derivatives and made recommendations to Congress, financial regulators, the SECs, and the FASBs to take proper actions to: (1) close the perceived regulatory gaps related to dealers of derivatives; (2) establish new regulations for derivatives brokers, dealers, and end-users to ensure investors' protection; (3) issue new accounting standards and guidelines for proper disclosures of derivatives; and (4) require reasonable capital requirements for derivatives dealers and brokers to mitigate unexpected derivatives losses or failures. The GAO report places the responsibility for managing derivatives on a strong system of corporate governance consisting of responsible boards of directors, independent audit committees, and effective internal and external auditors.

The Federal Financial Institutions Examination Council (FFIEC), in April 1998, published a new rule that affects financial institutions' investment activities entitled, "The Supervisory Policy Statement on Investment Securities and End-User Derivatives Activities."[4] The FFIEC consists of the main five regulatory agencies, the Federal Reserve System, the Federal Deposit Insurance Corporation, the National Credit Union Administration, the Office of Thrift Supervision, and the Office of the Comptroller of the Currency who oversees financial institutions. This policy statement states that management should establish and maintain appropriate risk management practices to continuously assess the risks of investment securities and derivatives activities for the entire institution in the context of the portfolio as a whole. The policy statement describes five types of risk associated with investment securities and derivatives transactions. These are market or interest risk, credit risk, liquidity risk, operational or transaction risk, and legal risk. These risks and their related control activities will be discussed in section 17.4 and Exhibit 17.2.

17.2   DERIVATIVE MARKETS

Derivative markets are markets for contractual financial instruments whose value is determined based on the value of underlying assets or instruments, and their performance is measured by how underlying assets or instruments perform. Like any other contracts, derivatives are agreements between two parties (buyer and seller) dealing on an arm's length basis. The price of these contracts is determined based on bargaining power of the two involved parties, when the buyer tries to purchase as cheaply as possible and the seller attempts to sell as dearly as possible. Like any other investment market, the derivatives market determines the prices of the derivatives trading therein which theoretically should reflect their fair values or true economic values to investors. In efficient derivatives markets, prices are determined by using investment models (e.g., the Capital Asset Pricing Model, the Arbitrage Pricing Theory, or the Black-Scholes Option Pricing Model) in such a way that prices fluctuate randomly as investors cannot consistently earn abnormal returns (returns above those that would compensate them for the level of risk they assume). Return measures investment performance which represents the percentage increase in the investor's wealth resulting from making the investment (for stock this is the percentage change in price plus the dividend yield). Risk is the uncertainty of future returns.

To increase their wealth, investors attempt to maximize their return subject to minimum level of risk. However, in an investment market, there is a positive correlation between risk and return, known as the risk-return trade-off. Derivative prices (e.g., options, forwards) are based on the prices of the underlying traditional financial instruments (e.g., stocks, bonds) traded in capital markets. Derivatives are often used for hedging purposes to manage the risk of investing in the underlying instruments. Derivatives can also be utilized for speculation purposes of trading derivative contracts rather than the underlying securities. Nevertheless, derivative markets typically offer several advantages over security markets. First, commissions and other trading costs of derivative markets are much lower than transaction costs of spot markets. Second, derivative markets (e.g., options and futures) typically have greater liquidity than the underlying securities market. Finally, short selling is readily available and possible in derivative markets but not in securities markets. Derivative markets allow the speculators willing to assume risk to accommodate the hedgers wishing to reduce it and, thus, help financial markets become more efficient which provides better opportunities to managing risk.

OTC derivatives are often traded based on the system of telephones and voice brokers. Some firms use on-line systems through which traders can assess the availability of credit lines for the counterparty and within overall trading limits. Automation of trading has been traditionally limited in the OTC derivatives market which makes it difficult to determine the on-line fair value of OTC derivative transactions. Brokers are being utilized to locate counterparties who are willing to transact at the quoted price. After counterparties have been identified, they determine for themselves whether each other's credit quality is acceptable and whether the exposure can be accommodated within credit limits. Foreign exchange dealers, especially bank dealers, have developed electronic trading facilities such as Web sites that allow their customers to trade electronically. Therefore, the on-line fair value quotations are easily available for foreign exchange derivatives.

Forward foreign exchange and forward foreign agreements are the two derivative products that have attracted significant volumes. Development of electronic trading systems for swaps has facilitated execution of online swap tradings between dealers. Participants in this system electronically express their desire to enter into specific swap transactions, while other participants (e.g., dealers) accept the transaction as offered or suggest possible changes in terms. The credit limits of all participants (dealers) are also loaded into the system prior to trading. These electronic systems allow on-line, accurate capture of data especially fair value for swap transactions. The rapid growth and widespread acceptance of electronic on-line brokering of derivatives has made the pricing process of determining fair value more accurate and timely.

The rapid growth and increasing use of derivatives by many large banks has concerned banking authorities and regulators and has provided sufficient incentives for market participants and policymakers to re-evaluate derivatives risk management procedures, especially the risk assessment and management of counterparty credit risk and the probability that a counterparty will not settle an obligation for full value, either when the obligation is due or at any time thereafter.

17.3 DERIVATIVES RISK MANAGEMENT

The collapse of long-term capital management prompted several professional groups to study derivatives and their related risk. The President's Working Group on Financial Markets (PWGFM), Counterparty Risk Management Policy Group (CRMPG), and the International Swaps and Derivatives Association (ISDA) are the most active groups which have suggested ways to strengthen risk management for derivatives.[5] The PWGFM issued its report that evaluates the regulatory framework for over-the-counter derivatives and suggests policies, procedures, and techniques by which individual firms measure and manage counterparty risk associated with derivatives. The CRMPG and the ISDA called for important cooperative efforts related to collateral programs to strengthen market infrastructure to reduce derivative risk. The ISDA has developed templates for confirmations that market participants use for many derivative products. The confirmation lists both the economic features and legal terms of derivative transactions.

Banks involved in derivative transactions should establish and maintain an adequate and effective risk management system which promotes risk-management policies and procedures, develops effective risk-assessment and monitoring systems, and requires both internal and external audits and sound accounting systems in properly measuring, recognizing, and disclosing fair value of derivatives. Banks should establish an adequate and effective derivatives risk management system consisting of: (1) appropriate board of directors, audit committee, and management oversight; (2) sufficient risk-management policies and procedures; (3) adequate and effective risk-measurement and monitoring systems; (4) adequate and effective internal controls; and (5) independent external audit.

Derivatives can be utilized to manage (e.g., increase or decrease) the risk of investing in the spot items (underlying instruments) primarily because the value of derivatives is related to the prices of the underlying spot market goods. Derivative markets enable investors to manage their risk to their tolerant and preferable level by transferring risk from those wishing to reduce the risk to those willing to increase it. Thus, risk management is essential to the valuation and long-term performance of derivatives. Financial institutions are facing significant risks of changes in interest rates, foreign currency value, equity, and commodity prices as well as loan defaults and changes in market conditions. Therefore, financial institutions often use derivatives to manage, transfer, or hedge such risks. Indeed, one study reveals that 80 percent of private sector entities consider derivatives as critical or imperative risk management strategies.[6]

The Committee of Sponsoring Organizations of the Treadway Commission better known as the COSO, in 1996, issued a report entitled "Internal Control Issues in Derivatives Usage—An Information Tool for Considering the COSO Internal Control-Integrates Framework in Derivatives Applications." The COSO report suggests the application of the COSO framework control principles to derivatives in their overall risk management processes. These risk management processes, depending on the nature and extent of derivatives used, should consist of the following (COSO, p. 4):

1. Understanding operations and entity-wide objectives.

2. Identifying, measuring, assessing, and modifying business risk.

3. Evaluating the use of derivatives to control market risk and link use to entity-wide and activity-level objectives.

4. Defining risk management activities and terms relating to derivatives to provide a clear understanding of their intended use.

5. Assessing the appropriateness of specified activities and strategies relating to the use of derivatives.

6. Establishing procedures for obtaining and communicating information and analyzing and monitoring risk management activities and their results.[7]

The COSO report also suggests that entities, including financial institutions and their boards of directors, senior management, and others involved with derivatives, consider a number of actions to manage the use of their derivatives. These suggested actions are (COSO, p. 6):

1. Initiating a self-assessment of entity-wide control systems, directing attention specifically to areas of derivative operations that are of primary importance.

2. Fully integrating management of derivative activities into the enterprises' overall risk management system by developing and implementing a comprehensive risk management policy.

3. Ensuring that policy objectives specifying the use of derivatives are clearly articulated and documented.

4. Requiring that any use of derivatives be clearly linked with entity-wide and activity-level objectives.

17.4 DERIVATIVES RISK MANAGEMENT POLICY

An appropriate risk management policy for derivatives should address all aspects and issues pertaining to derivatives including their purposes, risks, and accounting methods to measure their fair value. Such a risk management policy should become part of the risk management process which addresses all aspects and key considerations of the use of derivatives. This process is described in the following sections.

17.4.1 The Extent of Derivatives' Use

Recently, derivatives have grown rapidly because of the dynamic state of financial markets, the volatility in interest and currency exchange rates, the complexity of financial engineering, and the impact of derivatives on profitability and risk management. The extent of the use of derivatives should be considered because it determines the degree to which the institution is affected by fair value measurement and recognition requirements of accounting standards (e.g., SFAS No. 133).[8]

17.4.2 Identification and Analysis of All Types of Derivatives

Derivatives are generally classified into: (1) stand-alone (freestanding) derivatives; (2) compound derivatives (derivatives combined with other derivatives); and (3) embedded derivatives (derivatives that are bifurcated from the instrument in which they are embedded). The proper classification of derivatives is important because SFAS No. 133 requires that accounting for and reporting of gains and losses resulting from changes in fair value depend on the purpose and reasons for holding derivatives as well as their intended use and the resulting designation. For financial reporting purposes, derivatives should be designated as: (1) a fair value hedge of an existing asset, liability, or firm commitment; (2) a cash flow hedge of a forecasted transaction; (3) a hedge of a foreign operation; or (4) not intended as a hedge.

The description, examples, and accounting for each of these four categories are summarized in Exhibit 17.1. The basic premise of the three types of hedges (cash flow, fair value, foreign currency) is that a derivative must be expected to be "highly effective" in offsetting exposure due to changes in fair value attributable to the risk of being hedged. Derivatives, in terms of their contract, can be described as either forward-based, option-based, or hybrid. A forward-based derivative (e.g., futures, forward, swap) is a two-sided contract in which each party can incur a favorable or unfavorable outcome resulting from changes in the value of the underlying instrument or the amount of the underlying reference factor. An option-based derivative (e.g., options, interest-rate caps, interest-rate floors) is only a one-sided contract in which the holder of such derivative has an option to exercise the right, which would result in a favorable outcome for the holder and an unfavorable outcome for the buyer. However, if market conditions would result in an unfavorable outcome for the holder, the holder can leave the right to expire unexercised.

17.4.3 Identification and Assessment of Derivative Risk

Derivatives typically expose issuers, holders, and investors to various types of risk. Financial institutions should establish adequate and effective internal control structure and procedures

Exhibit 17.1 Derivatives Categories, Description, Examples, and Their Accounting Treatment Under SFAS No. 133

Type	Description	Example	Accounting
Fair Value Hedge	The hedge of an exposure to changes in the fair value of an asset, liability, or an unrecognized firm commitment that is attributable to a particular risk.	a. The use of an interest-rate swap to change fixed-rate debt into floating-rate debt. b. The use of futures contracts to hedge the fair value of copper or other types of inventory. c. The use of a derivative to hedge the fair value of a firm commitment (e.g., to sell crude oil at a fixed price).	a. The derivatives should be measured at their fair value and reported as assets or liabilities. b. Any changes in fair value (gains or losses) of the hedged items attributable to the risk being hedged should be recognized in earnings in the period of change and as an adjustment to the carrying amount of the item. c. Any changes in fair value (gains or losses) of a derivative designated as a fair value hedge must be recognized in income.
Cash Flow Hedge	The hedge of an exposure to variability in cash flows of recognized assets, liabilities, or forecasted transactions that is attributable to a particular risk.	a. The hedge of a forecasted sale or purchase of natural gas (or another commodity) with futures contracts. b. The hedge of variable interest payments using an interest-rate swap to convert the variable payments into fixed payments.	a. These derivatives should be measured at their fair value and reported as assets or liabilities. b. The effective portion of derivatives' gains or losses (changes in fair value) should be initially reported as a component of other comprehensive income (outside earnings) and subsequently reclassified into earnings when the forecasted transaction affects earnings. c. The ineffective portion of gains or losses (unrealized) should be reported in earnings immediately when derivative transactions are expected to occur.

Foreign Currency Hedge	The hedge of the foreign-currency exposures of a net investment in foreign operations that are attributable to a particular risk.	The hedge of the foreign-currency exposure of: a. An unrecognized firm commitment (a fair value hedge). b. An available-for-sale security (a fair value hedge). c. A forecasted transaction (a cash flow hedge), or d. A net investment in a foreign operation.	a. These derivatives should be measured at fair value and recognized as assets or liabilities. b. Any changes in fair value (gains or losses) should be reported in other comprehensive income (outside earnings) as part of the cumulative translation adjustment to the extent of the offsetting translation gain or loss recorded in other comprehensive income. c. Any ineffective portion of a derivative gain or loss may not be included in the cumulative translation adjustment account in other comprehensive income. d. Translation gains or losses should be reported in other comprehensive income (outside earnings).
Derivatives Not Intended to Hedge			a. These derivatives should be reported at their fair value. b. Any changes in fair value should be recognized in earnings in the period of change.

to manage derivative risks by: (1) identifying and classifying derivative risks; (2) measuring the effects of these risks on the institutions' value and reputation; (3) determining the likelihood of risk occurrence and magnitude of their expected losses and unfavorable outcomes; and (4) managing derivative risks to an acceptable prudent risk. Derivative risks are: (1) market risk; (2) credit risk; (3) liquidity risk; (4) operational risk; (5) legal risk; (6) control risk; (7) basis or correlation risk; (8) systematic risk; (9) settlement risk; and (10) valuation or model risk. Many of these risks and their related control activities described in this section were derived from the following sources:

- Deloitte & Touche LLP, 1996. "Internal Control Issues in Derivatives Usage." The Committee of Sponsoring Organizations of the Treadway Commission.
- American Institute of Certified Public Accountants, 1994. "Derivatives—Current Accounting and Auditing Literature." The Financial Instruments Task Force of the Accounting Standards Executive Committee.
- The Federal Financial Institutions Examination Council (FFIEC), 1998. "The Supervisory Policy Statement on Investment Securities and End-User Derivatives Activities (April)."

Exhibit 17.2 presents these ten types of derivative risks and their related attributes and control activities.

(i) Market Risk
This risk is defined as the exposure to an institution's financial condition causing economic losses resulted from adverse changes in the fair value of the derivative. Any significant and unexpected movements in interest rates, foreign exchange rates, equity prices, commodity prices, and other factors related to market volatilities of the rate, index, or price underlying the derivative can increase the derivative market risk.

(ii) Credit Risk
With this risk, an end user would incur economic losses if the counterparty fails to meet its financial obligations under the contract. The derivative credit risk is positively correlated with the derivative's market value which is the economic benefit that can be lost if the counterparty fails to fulfill its obligation.

(iii) Liquidity Risk
This risk is related to the institution's failure to achieve its cash flow projections and liquidity characteristics of derivatives used in accomplishing institutional objectives. The institution should identify the types and sources of funding liquidity risk of all derivatives and consider the effects that market risk can have on liquidity for different types of instruments.

(iv) Operational Risk
This risk is defined as the failure of the institution to: (1) establish appropriate risk-management policy consistent with derivative objectives set for the board of directors authorization; (2) develop adequate and effective control activities to ensure that only authorized derivative transactions take place and that unauthorized derivative transactions are detected and corrected; (3) ensure that the magnitude, complexity, and risks of derivatives are commensurate with the purposes established for derivatives activities; (4) maintain appropriate source documents to support management intent as well as justification regarding issuing, holding, and classifying derivatives; (5) keep accurate subsidiary ledgers for all de-

rivatives; and (6) periodically reconcile all derivatives on the general ledger to the supporting subsidiary ledgers.

(v) Legal Risk

This risk is the failure of the institution to comply with applicable rules, laws, and regulations pertaining to derivatives which may cause losses due to legal or regulatory actions taken against the institution. Legal risk can arise from: (1) misunderstanding of terms of derivative contracts; (2) insufficient documentation of the contract; (3) adverse changes in applicable laws and regulations including tax laws and regulatory requirements that prohibit the institution from investing in or even holding certain types of derivatives; and (4) inability to enforce a netting arrangement in bankruptcy.

(vi) Control Risk

This risk is defined as the failure of the institution's internal control structure pertaining to derivatives to prevent, detect, and correct errors, irregularities, and fraud that negatively affect the institution's ability to achieve its derivatives' operational, financial, and compliance objectives. Control risk could arise from: (1) absence of an adequate and effective derivatives' internal control structure; (2) lack of appropriate managerial policies and procedures to continuously monitor derivative transactions; (3) noncompliance with applicable laws, regulations, and contract requirements; and (4) noncompliance with derivatives' financial reporting requirements.

(vii) Basis or Correlation Risk

This risk mostly relates to hedging contracts and measures the differing effects market forces have on the performance or value of two or more distinct instruments used in a combination. Basis risk is determined by calculating the difference between the cash market price of the derivative being hedged and the price of the related hedging contract. This risk indicates the lack of proper correlation between hedging contract prices and the price movement in the cash market when the basis changes while the hedging contract is open.

(viii) Systematic or Interconnection Risk

This risk relates to the institution's particular risk resulting from operating in a particular market segment, across specific markets or borders, and/or to a settlement system.

(ix) Settlement Risk

This risk is defined as the institution's inability to settle derivative contracts in cash or other assets that are readily convertible into cash such as treasury securities or marketable equity securities rather than the delivery of the underlying items on an appropriately timely basis.

(x) Valuation and Model Risk

This risk relates to the imperfection and subjectivity of models and the associated assumptions used to value derivatives. Valuation model is the failure of the utilized derivative models to determine the true fair value of derivatives. This risk will be further discussed in Section 17.9.

17.5 ACCOUNTING OF DERIVATIVES

Financial derivatives have grown rapidly during the past decade primarily because of fundamental changes in global financial markets, advancements in computer technology, and fluctuations in interest and currency exchange rates. Derivatives have become increasingly

Exhibit 17.2 Derivatives Risks, Attributes, and Control Activities

Risk	Attributes	Control Activities
Market	1. Market risk measurement system addressing capital at risk and value at risk. 2. Ongoing mark-to-market valuation of derivative positions. 3. Sensitivity and simulation analysis of derivative portfolios in determining their performance under stress conditions (e.g., abnormal volatility of market, market shocks). 4. Determination of overall market risk limits (e.g., net and/or gross position, stop-loss, rate change, options, value-at-risk). 5. Selection of appropriate model estimations of market values.	1. Board-approved limits (e.g., trade, counterparty position, levels of unhedged market exposure, stop-loss, open position by product type). 2. Market-to-market derivatives. 3. Incorporation of stress testing, sensitivity analysis and scenario analysis into derivative model estimates. 4. Continuous assessment of board-approved limits. 5. Review model estimations of market values especially when market values are not readily available.
Credit	Appropriate credit risk management which: 1. Addresses complexity of derivative transactions. 2. Identification of the various types and sources of credit risk. 3. Policy provisions for counterparty default, settlement, and pre-settlement credit risk. 4. Proper credit risk limits on individual and counterparty exposure. 5. Mechanism for monitoring credit risk on an ongoing basis. 6. Establishment and documentation of credit risk policies and procedures.	1. Assessing the creditworthiness of the issuer or counterparty. 2. Third party verification of counterparty credit. 3. Continuous monitoring of counterparty credit. 4. Ongoing monitoring of credit risk limits. 5. Procedures for monitoring of credit exposure on the institution-wide basis. 6. Review and re-approval of credit risk policies, procedures, and limits.
Liquidity	1. Identification of the types and sources of market liquidity risk. 2. Participation in OTC markets. 3. Pre-approval of the liquidity characteristics of derivatives. 4. Board-approved liquidity limits.	1. Reviewing the types and sources of market liquidity risk. 2. Close monitoring of OTC market in which the institution participates. 3. Continuously monitoring liquidity limits and characteristics of derivatives.
Operational	1. Proper authorization of derivative transactions. 2. Effective execution of derivative transactions. 3. Establishment of adequate and effective internal control structure for derivatives. 4. Operational policies and procedures to ensure proper pricing and valuation of derivatives. 5. Sound accounting information systems which gather, classify, measure, recognize, and report derivative transactions.	1. Approving every derivative transaction according to the established authorization policies and procedures. 2. Evaluating and monitoring the derivative's internal control structure on an ongoing basis. 3. Continuous monitoring of valuation and pricing models. 4. Ensuring that derivative's information system conforms to applicable accounting and reporting standards.

Category		
Legal	1. Identification of different types and sources of legal risk. 2. Involvement of legal counsel for derivative activities. 3. Enforceable procedures for derivative transactions. 4. Adequate legal documents of derivative contracts. 5. Due diligence contract enforcement activities.	1. Continuous assessment of the nature of derivatives and the authority of counterparties. 2. Use of standard contract or master agreement. 3. Continuous monitoring by legal counsel.
Control	1. Risk-management policy consistent with derivative objectives set forth by the board of directors. 2. Existence of adequate and effective internal control system for derivatives. 3. Achievement of internal operational goals. 4. External financial reporting requirements. 5. Compliance with all applicable laws and regulations.	1. Ensuring that only authorized derivative transactions take place and that unauthorized transactions are detected and corrected. 2. Ensuring that the magnitude, complexity, and risks of derivatives are commensurate with the purpose established for derivative activities. 3. Maintaining appropriate source documents to support management intent for issuing, holding, and classifying derivatives. 4. Keeping accurate subsidiary ledgers for all derivatives and periodically reconciling all derivatives on the general ledger to the supporting subsidiary ledgers.
Basis or Correlation	1. Identification of the types and sources of derivative basis or correlation risk. 2. Board-approved correlation limits. 3. Methodology of correlation measurements.	1. Assessing the correlation between derivative instruments priced off of different yield curves. 2. Measuring and evaluating the correlation coefficient. 3. Ensuring that correlation limits are within the approved level.
Systematic	1. Identification of the different types and sources of systematic risk. 2. Effective risk management system. 3. Existence of contingency plans to minimize losses when market disruptions occur.	1. Continuous monitoring of systematic risk. 2. Taking appropriate action based on the approved contingency plans when market disruptions occur.
Settlement	1. Identification of the different types and sources of settlement risk. 2. Board-approved maximum settlement risk limits.	1. Monitoring payments on an appropriately timely basis. 2. Closely monitoring unsettled items.
Valuation or Model	1. Identification of all appropriate valuation models of pricing all types of derivatives. 2. Use of value-at-risk methodology to measure market risk.	1. Assessing different valuation models. 2. Continuously monitoring variable of valuation models. 3. Using value-at-risk methodology in measuring market risk.

important and widely used in global business. They have been utilized for a variety of purposes, including risks management, financing schemes, tax planning, earnings management, and speculation activities. However, the nature and risks associated with derivatives and how entities use them are not well understood by many users of published financial statements (e.g., investors, creditors, customers). The financial community and standard-setting bodies are concerned with complexities, risks, lack of uniform accounting practices for derivatives, and insufficient disclosures of their fair values. Thus, the Financial Accounting Standards Board (FASB) issued its Statement of Financial Accounting Standards (SFAS) No. 133 'Accounting for Derivative Instruments and Hedging Activities' in June 1998 to standardize accounting for derivative transactions.

SFAS No. 133 establishes accounting and reporting standards for derivative instruments and hedging activities by requiring that affected entities recognize all derivatives as either assets or liabilities in financial statements and measure them at fair value. The adoption of SFAS No. 133 provides for the first mandated source of public information about fair value of derivatives. The fair value measurement and recognition requirements of the Statement provide some detailed information about previously unreported derivatives extensively used by all entities including not-for-profit organizations.

Derivatives are commonly defined as financial products such as swaps, options, futures, forwards, and unstructured receivables, which derive their value from underlying financial instruments such as stocks, bonds, and foreign currencies. SFAS No. 133 (Paragraph 6) defines a derivative instrument as "a financial instrument or other contract with all three of the following characteristics: (a) It has (1) one or more underlyings and (2) one or more notional amounts of payment provisions or both . . .; (b) it requires no initial net investment or an initial net investment that is smaller than would be required for other types of contracts . . . ; (c) Its terms require or permit net settlement . . . ." These derivatives have been used for: (1) managing financial risks; (2) speculating on the price of financial instruments; (3) reducing the cost of raising capital; (4) earning higher investment returns; (5) adjusting investment portfolios to take advantage of miss-pricing between stock baskets and stock index futures; and (6) combining derivatives with other financial instruments to create new and more powerful financial products. The most common active end-users of derivatives are financial institutions, mutual funds, pension funds, and commercial firms. Derivatives are being traded through both organized exchanges and over-the-counter and their "notional value" exceeds the estimated total value of the world's bonds and stocks.[9] Exchanged traded derivatives are typically more standardized and offer greater liquidity than OTC derivatives which are individually arranged contracts.

Derivative transactions have grown significantly in volume and complexity from the traditional interest-rate and currency swaps to more sophisticated computer-driven risk management derivatives. This ever-increasing use of derivatives and recent losses by some derivatives end-users has raised numerous issues of concern among regulators, the financial community, and the accounting profession as to the appropriate use, proper risk assessment, and adequate disclosures of derivative transactions by both issuers and end-users of these financial products. Improved oversight by regulators and new accounting standards by the accounting profession have been suggested as a means of addressing these issues. SFAS No. 119 provides more guidance for proper disclosures of derivatives than SFAS Nos. 105 and 107. However, SFAS No. 119 only deals with disclosures of derivatives, not their measurement and recognition, and is only considered as a step in the right direction for providing better and more adequate guidance for companies to present quantified disclosure of the risks they face from on-and-off book financial instruments. SFAS No. 119 intended to improve the quality of disclosures about derivatives instruments while SFAS No. 133 addressed accounting for recognition and measurement of derivative transactions.

SFAS No. 133 requires all derivative instruments to be measured at fair market value and be reported on the balance sheet as assets or liabilities. The accounting method and reporting of the change in fair values depend on the reason for holding derivatives, their intended use, and the resulting designation. The FASB rationales in issuing SFAS No. 133 (Paragraph 3) were: (1) derivatives represent rights or obligations that meet the definitions of assets or liabilities and, accordingly, should be reported in financial statements; (2) fair value is the only relevant measure for derivatives and hedging activities and, therefore, they should be measured at fair value; (3) only derivatives and hedged items that are considered either assets or liabilities should be reported as such in financial statements; and (4) special accounting for hedging activities should be provided only for qualified hedged items that are attributable to the risk being hedged.

Other initiatives by the SEC and Congress have been introduced that would eventually require more quantitative disclosures about derivative risks and risk management activities of companies under the SEC's jurisdiction. In response to derivatives concerns, six of Wall Street's biggest securities firms have voluntarily agreed to impose more controls over their derivatives activities.[10] The firms have agreed to provide adequate disclosures to the SEC and Commodity Futures Trading Commission (CFTC) about: (1) how they manage their internal derivative risks; and (2) their capital standards and reporting requirements. These standards are intended to avoid direct legislative action on derivatives by Congress. These standards address four derivatives issues: (1) adequate and effective internal controls for monitoring derivatives risks; (2) proper disclosure and reporting of derivatives activities to regulators; (3) sufficiency of the firm's capital standards in terms of the risks involved; and (4) counterparty relationships in dealing with the firm's customers. The SEC (1997) has amended and expanded the disclosure requirement for derivatives under SFAS No. 119 in Release No. 33-7386.[11] The amendments require enhanced disclosure of accounting policies for derivatives as well as quantitative and qualitative information about market risk inherent in market risk sensitive instruments.

17.5.1   Financial and Managerial Impacts of SFAS No. 133

Adoption of SFAS No. 133 provides the first mandated source of public information about fair value of derivatives. The fair value recognition requirements of SFAS No. 133 provide some details of these previously unreported derivatives used extensively by financial companies to service customers and generate income and by other entities to manage risk including interest rate and foreign currency exposures. Thus, issuers and end-users of derivatives are affected by the fair value recognition of the statement. The FASB has addressed several problems associated with current accounting practices for derivatives. These problems include inconsistent, incomplete, and complex accounting guidance for derivatives and the fact that the effect of derivatives is not transparent in the financial statements. As a result, under current accounting practices, derivative transactions are not properly recognized in the financial statements, making it difficult for users to determine the nature, extent, and effects of derivatives on a firm's financial positions and results of operations.

SFAS No. 133 is intended to address and resolve the perceived problems of lack of visibility, completeness, and consistency of accounting practices for derivative transactions.

All derivatives should be reported in the statement of financial position at fair value and their related changes in fair value should be recognized in income when they occur. There is one exception which is for derivatives that qualify as hedges. Depending on the nature of the exposure, changes in the fair value can be reported in other comprehensive income (via shareholders' equity). The requirement of recognition of changes in fair value would, depending on the accounting method used (hedge or non-hedge accounting), create volatility in either income or equity. Thus, under the current accounting standards, all derivatives would be reported on the balance sheet at fair value. The accounting for gains or losses that result from changes in fair value depends on the reasons for holding the instrument, its intended use, and whether it qualifies for designation as a hedge of a fair value exposure, a cash flow exposure, or a net investment in a foreign entity.

The FASB rationales for issuing SFAS No. 133 were: (1) derivatives represent rights or obligations that meet the definition of asset or liabilities and, therefore, should be reported as such in financial statements; (2) like other financial instruments, derivatives should be measured at fair value because fair value is the only relevant measure for derivatives; (3) any adjustments to the carrying amount of hedged items should reflect changes in their fair value (gains or losses) associated with the risk being hedged; (4) only hedged items that are qualified as assets or liabilities should be reported in financial statements; and (5) special accounting for items designated as being hedged should be provided only for qualifying items. SFAS No. 133 requires matching the timing of gain or loss recognition on the hedging instrument with the recognition of: (1) the changes in the fair value of the exposure-hedged asset or liability; and (2) the earnings effect of the hedged-forecasted transaction.

Adoption of SFAS No. 133 may increase volatility in earnings and equity through comprehensive income. The degree of volatility, however, depends on the entity's intended use of derivatives and their nature and the type and extent of derivatives and hedging activities. The increased volatility results primarily from the requirement for recognition of any changes in fair value (gains or losses) in either earnings or components of other comprehensive income depending on the reason for holding derivatives or hedging activities. Traditionally, any gains or losses resulting from changes in fair value of derivatives and hedging activities were either ignored or disclosed in footnotes to financial statements. Under SFAS No. 133, all derivatives are recorded at their fair value on the balance sheet as assets or liabilities, and changes in their fair value are reported on the income statement or balance sheet depending on their intended use and their designation as either a fair value hedge, cash flow hedge, or foreign currency exposure hedge.

The balance sheet effect of adopting SFAS No. 133 is an increase in the size of the balance sheet because of the fair value recognition of derivatives as assets or liabilities. The income statement effects of changes in fair value of derivatives depend on the intended use of derivatives and whether they are qualified and designated as hedging instruments. If the derivative does not qualify as a hedging instrument or is not designated as such, any changes in its fair value and the resulting gain or loss should be recognized currently in earnings. If the derivative qualifies for special hedge accounting, the resulting gain or loss should be either recognized in income or deferred in other comprehensive income (e.g., equity). To qualify for special hedge accounting, the derivative must be designated as either a fair value hedge, cash flow hedge, or foreign currency hedge.

Adoption of SFAS No. 133 can affect risk-management strategies in several ways. Traditionally, management has used "synthetic-instrument accounting" techniques to convert variable-rate debt into fixed-rate debt by using an interest-rate swap. Prior to SFAS No. 133, "synthetic-instrument accounting" techniques had affected the income statement as if the entity had actually issued fixed-value debt. Under SFAS No.133, these techniques should qualify as cash flow hedge with essentially the same income statement effect as before; however, the balance sheet effect of these techniques should reflect the swaps' fair value and their changes in fair value that are deferred in other comprehensive income.

17.5.2 How Does This SFAS No. 133 Work?

SFAS No. 133 is very complicated, its implementation is complex, and it requires substantial changes in accounting information systems of financial institutions which use derivatives. However, SFAS No. 133 provides an excellent opportunity for financial institutions to further examine their risk management practices and policies on derivatives. SFAS No. 133 requires that all derivatives be measured at their fair value and be recognized as assets or liabilities in the statement of financial position. The accounting for changes in the fair value of a derivative (gains or losses) depends on the intended use of the derivative, the reason for hedging the instruments, and the resulting designation as a hedge of a fair value exposure, a cash flow exposure, or a net investment in a foreign currency.

The fact that derivative activities are to be made publicly available increases the responsibility of management to ensure that measurement, recognition, reporting, and disclosures are reliable, relevant, and adequately supported. The magnitude of derivatives being used by entities, coupled with their associated risk and the first-mandated source of public information about their fair value, necessitates that the affected entities organize an implementation team to effectively and efficiently adopt SFAS No. 133. The implementation team should include auditors and individuals knowledgeable in global financial markets, risk management, accounting, law, tax, information systems, operations, treasury, and asset and liability management. The implementation team should analyze and understand the nature, terms, and extent of derivatives and consult with the entity's independent auditors, advising them of key decisions. SFAS No. 133 does not delineate a specific methodology for assessing whether a hedge is expected to be highly effective or for measuring hedge ineffectiveness. The implementation team should clearly define the intended use of derivatives, because the only requirement under SFAS No. 133 is that there be a "reasonable basis" for assessing hedge effectiveness.

Extensive information system modification may be necessary to ensure compliance with substantial fair value requirements of SFAS No. 133. The implementation team should: (1) identify all derivatives that meet the definition of derivatives as stated in SFAS No. 133; (2) determine whether existing hedging strategies qualify for hedging accounting under SFAS No. 133; (3) consider the changes in the existing accounting system and disclosure policies that should be made to satisfy the fair value accounting requirements of SFAS No. 133; (4) assess and document the entity's risk-management strategies including objectives and policies consistent with the requirements of SFAS No. 133; and (5) communicate the financial and managerial impacts of adopting SFAS No. 133 to all internal (e.g., executive management, audit committee) and external (auditors, shareholders) parties.

17.5.3 Financial Requirements

Financial institutions should establish accounting policies and procedures pertaining to the classification and reasons for holding derivatives. The proper classification of derivatives is important because SFAS No. 133 requires that accounting for and reporting of gains and losses resulting from changes in fair value depend on the purpose and reason for holding derivatives. For financial reporting purposes, derivatives should be specifically designated as: (1) a fair value hedge of an existing asset, liability, or firm commitment; (2) a cash flow hedge of a forecasted transaction; (3) a hedge of a foreign operation; or (4) not intended as a hedge. The hedge accounting should consider: (1) the type of hedge relationship (e.g., fair value, cash flow, or foreign currency); (2) how effectively hedged items are measured; and (3) potential alternatives to existing hedging strategies.

Financial institutions' accounting systems should: (1) measure, recognize, and report fair value of derivatives and hedging activities including related gains and losses in financial statements; and (2) provide adequate disclosure while not revealing critical data about characteristics of related assets to competitors. The complexity and extensive use of derivatives requires that the financial institution's accounting information system: (1) accurately assess valuation considerations in light of the related derivatives' risk; (2) provide income adjustments for fluctuations in fair value of derivatives and hedging activities; (3) keep track of other comprehensive income fair value adjustments and their subsequent recognition in earnings; and (4) consider the procedures for bifurcating and subsequent measurement of the component of hybrid instruments. Financial institutions, according to provisions of SFAS No. 133, should also provide documentation of: (1) the reason for issuing or holding derivatives; (2) derivatives' intended use and resulting designation; (3) the nature of cash hedge strategy; (4) the nature and assessment of the risk that is being hedged; (5) how the hedging instrument's effectiveness is being assessed; and (6) the designation of derivatives and hedged items in hedging relationships.

The FASB, in June 2000, issued an amendment to SFAS No. 133 entitled "Accounting for Certain Derivative Instruments and Certain Hedging Activities" to address major implementation problems of adopting SFAS No. 133. The amendment postpones the effective date of the adoption of SFAS No. 133 to January 1, 2001, for many companies. The amendment was intended to resolve major implementation problems of SFAS No. 133 including restrictions on cross-currency hedges, specific risks that can be hedged, expansion of the normal purchase and normal sales expectations, hedges of interest rate risk, and hedges of foreign-currency-denominated assets and liabilities. The amendment: (1) permits the use of a benchmark interest rate that excludes the sector spread; (2) relaxes restrictions on hedging recognized foreign-currency-denominated assets and liabilities; and (3) reduces earnings volatility resulting when the changes in those foreign-currency items are measured at fair value.

17.5.4 Disclosure Requirements

Financial institutions should disclose the objectives for issuing or holding derivatives, the context needed to understand the objectives, and strategies for achieving those objectives. SFAS No. 133 requires disclosure of the classification of derivatives into: (1) those designated as fair value hedging instruments; (2) those designated as cash flow hedging instruments; (3) those designated as hedging instruments for hedges of the foreign currency exposure of a net investment in a foreign operation; and (4) all other derivatives. Financial institutions should indicate the risk management policy for each of these types of hedge, including a description of the items or transactions for which risks are hedged. Furthermore, the SEC requires disclosures based on the type of market risk that is being hedged (e.g., interest rate, foreign currency, commodity). If appropriate and feasible, qualitative disclosures about objectives and strategies for using derivative instruments should be provided.

The extensive disclosure requirements of SFAS No. 133 are classified into qualitative information and quantitative information. Qualitative disclosures are: (1) the entity's objectives and strategies for holding and issuing derivatives; and (2) a description of the transactions or other events that will result in the recognition of gains and losses in earnings resulting from changes in fair value of cash flow hedges, deferred in accumulated other comprehensive income. Quantitative disclosures are: (1) the net gain or loss recognized in earnings for the period representing aggregate ineffectiveness for all hedges and the component of the derivatives' gain or loss excluded from the assessment of hedge effectiveness; (2) an estimate of the amount of gains and losses related to cash flow hedges, included in other comprehensive income that will be recognized in earnings within the next 12 months; (3) the amount of gains and losses reclassified into earnings as a result of the discontinuance of cash flow hedges because it is probable that the original forecasted transaction will not occur; (4) the maximum period of time over which the entity is hedging cash flows related to forecasted transactions; and (5) the net amount of the foreign currency transaction gain or loss on the hedging instrument included in the cumulative translation adjustment during the period.

17.6 TAX CONSIDERATIONS OF DERIVATIVES

Financial institutions should identify and examine the applicable tax rules on derivatives to determine: (1) how derivatives should be classified for tax purposes (debt or equity); (2) how their related trading revenues (gains or losses) should be measured and classified (capital or ordinary); and (3) what is the timing of derivative gains or losses for tax purposes. Determination of the tax treatment of derivative transactions depends on: (1) the type of derivatives; (2) the status of the taxpayer holding derivatives (e.g., corporations, individuals, dealers, and investors); (3) the purpose of holding derivatives (e.g., capital asset, inventory, and holding instrument); and (4) the manner of acquisition, holding, or disposition of derivatives.

The tax effects of the transition adjustments should also be considered. Transition adjustment is the difference between a derivative's previous carrying amount and its fair value at the time of the adoption of SFAS No. 133. This transition adjustment should be reported in net income or other comprehensive income, as appropriate, as the effect of a change in accounting principles and presented in a manner similar to the cumulative effect of a change in accounting principles as described in APB Opinion No. 20. Many of the transition adjustments, required under SFAS No. 133, create temporary differences. Depending on the nature of the hedge relationship (e.g., fair value or cash flow hedge), the deferred tax impacts of the temporary differences should be netted in the cumulative effect of adoption on net income or on other comprehensive income as set forth in the statement. Consult with tax experts (e.g., public accounting firms) and seek advice from the Internal Revenue Service (IRS) to provide reasonable assurance of compliance with tax laws regarding classification, measurement, and recognition of derivative transactions for tax purposes.

17.7   AUDIT OF DERIVATIVE TRANSACTIONS

Financial institutions should communicate the financial and managerial impacts of issuing and/or holding derivatives to all interested parties including executive management, the audit committee, shareholders, creditors, regulators, and independent auditors. Risk management strategies will be more visible under SFAS No. 133 primarily because of the required extensive justification and documentation regarding how derivatives and hedging activities are initially designed, measured, recognized, and subsequently tracked and disclosed. SFAS No. 133 eliminates managerial practices of "synthetic or accrual accounting" with the intention of keeping derivatives off the balance sheet with net periodic settlements being recorded through earnings.

Adoption of SFAS No. 133 may increase volatility in earnings and equity through comprehensive income. The degree of volatility, resulting from the requirement for recognition of any changes in fair value (gains or losses) in either earnings or components of other comprehensive income, depends on the reason for holding derivatives or hedging activities. The balance sheet effect of adopting SFAS No. 133 is an increase in the size of the balance sheet because of the fair value recognition of derivatives as assets or liabilities. The income statement effects of changes in fair value of derivatives depend on the intended use of derivatives and whether they are qualified and designated as hedging instruments. If the hedged item fails to meet general criteria applicable in all circumstances as well as criteria specific to the type of hedge (fair value, cash flow, or net investment in a foreign operation), it cannot be treated as a hedge and would be marked to market with no offset. If the derivative does not qualify as a hedging instrument or is not designated as such, any changes in its fair value and the resulting gain or loss should be recognized currently in earnings. If the derivative qualifies for special hedge accounting, the resulting gain or loss should be either recognized in income or deferred in other comprehensive income (equity). Auditors' involvement in assessing and classifying derivatives is important in preparing financial statements in conformity with accounting standards (SFAS No. 133) as well as in complying with applicable laws and regulations on derivatives. External auditors should be provided with appropriate answers to the set of questions suggested by the American Institute of Certified Public Accountants (AICPA)[12] and other authoritative bodies (e.g., FASB). The questions are as follows:

- Has the board established a clear and internally consistent risk management policy, including risk limits (as appropriate)?
- Are management's strategies and implementation policies consistent with the board's authorization?
- Do key controls exist to ensure that only authorized transactions take place and that unauthorized transactions are quickly detected and appropriate action is taken?
- Are the magnitude, complexity, and risks of the entity's derivatives commensurate with the entity's objectives?
- Are personnel authorized to engage in and monitor derivative transactions well qualified and appropriately trained?
- Do the right people have the right information to make decisions?
- How are the fair value of derivatives and hedged assets and liabilities determined?

- Do derivatives previously designated as hedges continue to qualify under the requirements of SFAS No. 133?
- How is management responding to the possible volatility in earnings and equity resulting from the changes in fair value of derivatives and hedging items?
- Are there any derivatives that qualify as hedges under SFAS No. 133 which previously were not considered as hedged items (e.g., foreign currency futures in certain hedging relationships)?

The AICPA suggests that "objectives of audit procedures for derivative transactions might include those designed to test that:[13]

- Derivatives contracts have been executed and processed according to management's authorizations.
- Income on derivatives, including premiums and discounts, are properly measured and recorded.
- Derivatives accounted for as hedges meet the applicable criteria for hedge accounting.
- Changes in the market value of derivatives have been appropriately accounted for in the circumstances (whether or not hedge accounting is used).
- Information about derivatives in the financial statements is accurate and complete and has been properly classified, described, and disclosed."

17.8 SOURCES OF INFORMATION ON DERIVATIVES

Many of the derivative failures have been caused by allowing individual employees to trade or invest in derivatives without proper knowledge as well as lack of supervision and authorization of top-level management. Senior management should establish proper policies and procedures for issuing and/or holding derivatives and monitor effective implementation of these policies and procedures.

Financial institutions should provide in-house training and education for employees directly involved with derivative transactions and SFAS No. 133 on a continuous basis. Financial institutions should obtain and study existing publications on derivatives and provide education for employees dealing with derivative transactions and hedging activities. Employees should be provided with the most recent publications, regulations, and accounting standards on derivatives. Some of the current initiatives on derivatives are: (1) Derivatives: Practices and Principles, Group of Thirty, 1993; (2) Financial Derivatives: Actions Needed to Protect the Financial Systems, U.S. General Accounting Office (GAO), May 1994; (3) Banking Off the Balance Sheet: Using Derivatives for Risk Management and Performance Improvement at Commercial Banks, Bank Administration Institute (BAI) and McKinsey and Company, 1994; (4) Risk Management Guidelines on Derivatives, Basel Committee on Banking Supervision, July 1994; (5) Risk Management of Financial Derivatives: Questions and Answers, Office of the Comptroller of the Currency (OCC), Bulletin 94-31, May 10, 1994; (6) Examination Guidance for Financial Derivatives, Federal Deposit Insurance Corporation (FDIC), May 18, 1994; (7) Statement of Financial Accounting Standards (SFAS) No. 119, Disclosure about Derivative Financial Instruments and Fair Value of

Financial Instruments, Financial Accounting Standards Board, October, 1994; (8) Financial Accounting Series, Special Report, "Illustrations of Financial Instruments Disclosures," Financial Accounting Standards Board, December 1994; (9) new government initiatives and Congressional legislation on derivatives; (10) SFAS No. 113, "Accounting for Derivative Instruments and Hedging Activities," Financial Accounting Standards Board, 1998; (11) U.S. Securities and Exchange Commission (SEC), "Disclosure of Accounting Policies for Derivative Financial Instruments and Derivatives Commodity Instruments and Disclosure of Quantitative and Qualitative Information about Market Risk Inherent in Derivative Financial Instruments, other Financial Instruments, and Derivative Commodity Instruments," Release No. 33-7386, 1997, Washington DC; (12) the FASB Implementation Task Force on Derivatives; (13) the Supervisory Policy Statement on Investment Securities and End-User Derivatives Activities which was issued on April 23, 1998 by the Federal Financial Institutions Examination Council (FFIEC); (14) Risk Management of Financial Derivatives, Comptroller of the Currency Banking Issuance Circular 277, October 27, 1993; (15) Six Common-Sense Questions About the Use and Risks of Derivatives, American Institute of Certified Public Accountants, 1994; (16) Internal Control Issues in Derivatives Usage: An Information Tool for Considering the COSO Internal Control—Integrated Framework in Derivatives Applications was issued by the Committee of Sponsoring Organizations of the Treadway Commission in 1996; (17) Derivatives—Current Accounting and Auditing Literature issued by the American Institute of Certified Public Accountants, 1994; and (18) Banking Off the Balance Sheet, Bank Administration Institute and McKinsey and Company, Inc., 1994.

SFAS No. 133 has been issued with many unanswered implementation questions and, accordingly, implementation guidelines will evolve as the Statement is adopted by affected entities. To facilitate the proper adoption of SFAS No. 133 and to provide adequate answers to implementation questions, the FASB has appointed the Derivatives Implementation Group, which is a task force to assist the FASB in identifying implementation issues and in answering the related questions. The task force is in the process of compiling an implementation guide to highlight and resolve significant implementation problems in advance of the adoption of the statement. The status of the guidance will remain tentative until it is formally cleared by the FASB and will finally be incorporated in a FASB staff implementation guide.

17.9 DERIVATIVES VALUATION MODELS

The increasing use of derivative contracts available over the counter, on exchanges, and through private placements has raised serious concerns regarding their proper valuations. A number of valuation models for different types of derivatives (e.g., option, call, swap) have been developed based on the premise that if the suggested model accurately determines the value of a derivative, its market price should equal its theoretical fair value. Many of these models go far beyond the intended level of this book. The models range from the relatively simple models (e.g., binomial option pricing model) to more complex and sophisticated models (e.g., Black-Schobes model, digital contracts).

17.9.1 Binomial Model

To simplify, the binomial model presented here is the one-period binomial option pricing formula.[14] This model determines the option price as a weighted average of the two possible option prices at expiration, discounted at the risk-free rate. Mathematically the option price is calculated as follows:

$$C = \frac{PCu + (1 - P)Cd}{1 + r}$$

where

    C = the theoretical fair value of call option

    Cu = the price of call when it goes up = Max $[0,S(1+u)-E]$ where S is stock price, E is the exercise price of call, and u is the percentage increase in value of stock

    Cd = Price of call when it goes down = Max $[0,S(1+d)-E]$ where d is the percentage decrease in value of stock

    P $= \dfrac{r - d}{u - d}$ where r is the risk-free rate

17.9.2   Binomial Model—An Illustrative Example

Assume that a stock is currently priced at $150 and can go up to $177, an increase of 18 percent, or down to $120, a decrease of 20 percent, in just one period. Furthermore, the exercise price of a call option is $125, and the risk-free rate is 12 percent. The theoretical fair value of the call is calculated as follows:

$$C_u = \text{Max } [0,S(1+U)-E] = \text{Max } [0,150(1 + .18)-125] = \$52$$
$$C_d = \text{Max } [0,S(1+d)-E] = \text{Max } [0,150(1 - 20)-125] = \$\phi$$
$$P = \frac{r - d}{u - d} = \frac{.12 - (-.20)}{18 - (-.20)} = \frac{.32}{.38} = .842$$
$$1\text{-}P = 1\text{-}.842 = .158$$
$$C = \frac{PCu + (1 - P)Cd}{1 + r} = \frac{(.842)(52) + (.158)0}{1 + .12} = \frac{43.78}{1.12} = \$39$$

17.9.3   The Black-Scholes Call Option Valuation Model

In the world of no taxes and no transaction costs, one could adjust hedge positions almost constantly within the short time period. Black and Scholes (1973) developed a call option pricing formula known as the Black and Scholes option pricing model, which has been modified and used by valuation professionals to determine the theoretical fair value of call options.[15] The Black and Scholes call option valuation formula as described below determines the call value based on the stock price, exercise price, risk-free rate, time to expiration, and variance of the stock return. The formula is

$$Pc = P_s N(d_1) - \frac{E}{e^{rt}} N(d_2)$$

$$d_1 = \frac{In\left(\dfrac{P_s}{E}\right) + \left(r + \dfrac{1}{2}\delta^2\right)t}{\delta\sqrt{t}}$$

$$d_2 = \frac{In\left(\dfrac{P_s}{E}\right) + \left(r - \dfrac{1}{2}\delta^2\right)t}{\delta\sqrt{t}}$$

where:

P_c = the current price of the call option
P_s = the current value of the stock
E = the exercise price of the call option
e = 2.71828
t = the time remaining before expiration (in years)
r = the continuously compounded risk-free rate of return
δ = the standard deviation of the continuously compounded annual rate of return on the stock
$In\left(\dfrac{P_s}{E}\right)$ = the natural logarithm of $\dfrac{P_s}{E}$

$N(d_1), N(d_2)$ = cumulative normal probabilities which is the probability that a derivative less than d will occur in a normal distribution with a mean of zero and a standard derivation of one.

The Black-Scholes option valuation formula can be applied to a variety of financial derivatives in light of the following assumptions:

1. There are no taxes or transaction costs.
2. The stock pays no dividends prior to expiration.
3. The risk-free rate is constant throughout the life of the option.
4. The standard deviation of the return on the stock is constant throughout the life of the option.
5. The rate of return on the stock follows a lognormal distribution of a normal curve.
6. The calls are European-style with a single payoff received on a maturity date known at the contract's inception.

17.9.4 An Illustrative Example of the Black-Scholes Valuation Formula

Consider a stock is currently priced at $75. Assume a call option with an exercise price of $86. The risk-free rate is ten percent, and the standard deviation of the continuously compounded annual return is 50 percent. The time remaining before the expiration is three months.

$$d_1 = \frac{In\left(\dfrac{75}{86}\right) + \left[.10 + \dfrac{1}{2}(.5)^2\right].25}{.50\sqrt{.25}} \approx -.319$$

$$d_2 = \frac{In\left(\dfrac{75}{86}\right) + \left[.10 - \dfrac{1}{2}(.5)^2\right].25}{.50\sqrt{.25}} \approx -.545$$

$$N(d_1) = N(-.319) = .3725 \text{ (from a normal curve distribution)}$$
$$N(d_2) = N(-.545) = .2912 \text{ (from a normal curve distribution)}$$
$$P_s = P_s N(d_1) - \frac{E}{e^{rt}} N(d_2) = (75 \times .3725) - \left[\frac{86}{e^{.10 \times .25}} \times .2912 \right] \approx \$10.29$$

17.9.5   Digital Contracts for Valuation of Derivatives

Digital contracts are simple building blocks that provide a unified approach for determining formulas for a wide variety of financial instruments. Unlike these specialized formulas (e.g., Black-Scholes) that can only be applied to the specific asset for which they were derived, digital contracts are applicable to a wide variety of financial assets. Digital contracts are simple because their payoffs are either "on" or "off, " indicating that a digital option pays at maturity either one dollar (on) or nothing (off), depending on its payoff event.

Ingersoll (2000) suggested a three-step valuation process with digital contracts. The first step is the determination of the (risk-neutral) probability of a particular payoff event. The second step involves development of the formulas for the digital contracts. The third step is to use these instruments (formulas) to value financial derivative contracts.[16] To simplify mathematically, a pure European-style call option can be valued as follows:

$$P_c - \sum_i a_i k(S_i t_i T_i M_i) + \sum_j b_j L(S_j t_j T_j M_j)$$

where $k(S_i t_i T_i M_i)$ is the value at time t of receiving \$1 at time T, the maturity date, if and only if the event M occurs, and $L(S_j t_j T_j M_j)$ is the value at time t of receiving one share of stock at time T (no dividends), if and only if the event M occurs.

The probability of event M happening depends on the current stock price (S), so the values of k and L are determined based on stock price (S). Thus, the value of the call option is determined based on the value of stock.[17]

Financial institutions should establish managerial policies and procedures regarding issuing and/or holding derivatives. Management should initially brainstorm various methods that can be used in issuing and holding derivatives in order to maximize the expected return and minimize the potential risk. Derivatives should be used in a manner consistent with the entity's overall financial and investment activities as well as risk management. The managerial policies on derivatives should be clearly defined, including the purposes for which derivatives are being issued or held, because the classification and the accounting for changes in the fair value of derivatives, under SFAS No. 133, depend on their intended use. These policies should be reviewed and revised as business and market circumstances change to properly determine the value of derivatives. The institution's risk management philosophy should be properly documented and assessed in achieving the overall risk management objectives.

17.10   CONCLUSION

Derivatives have grown significantly in volume and complexity from the traditional interest-rate and currency-swap to more sophisticated computer-driven risk management derivatives.

The magnitude, complexity, risks, and incomplete as well as inconsistent accounting and reporting practices for derivatives have raised some concerns. Improved oversight requirements, regulatory initiatives, and new accounting standards have been suggested as a means of addressing these concerns. SFAS No. 133 standardizes the accounting for derivatives by requiring that derivative instruments be measured at fair value and recognized in financial statements. Financial institutions should obtain a thorough knowledge and understanding of the provisions of regulatory requirements and accounting standards about derivatives.

The widespread use of derivative transactions presents new challenges and opportunities for financial regulators, the accounting profession, and the business community. Derivatives provide a means to: (1) access low-cost funds; (2) earn higher investment returns;(3) adjust investment portfolios to take advantage of miss-pricing between stock baskets and stock index futures; and (4) combine derivatives with other financial instruments to create new and more-powerful financial products. The FASB accelerated its financial instruments project and first issued SFAS No. 119, which requires disclosures about amounts, nature, and terms of derivatives in October 1994, two years later issued the Exposure Draft, and finally in June 1998 issued SFAS No. 133, which requires all derivatives to be measured at fair value and reported as assets or liabilities in the statement of financial position.

The adoption of SFAS No. 133 would cause financial institutions to report a fuller picture of their financial exposures by requiring measurement, recognition, and reporting of fair value of derivatives in their financial statements. The balance sheet effect of adopting SFAS No. 133 is an increase in the size of the balance sheet because of the fair value recognition of derivatives as assets or liabilities. The income statement effects of changes in fair value of derivatives depend on the intended use of derivatives, whether they are qualified and designated as hedging instruments. Adoption of SFAS No. 133 may increase volatility in earnings and equity through comprehensive income. Implementation of provisions of SFAS No. 133 is very complex and requires substantial changes in affected entities' financial information system, internal control structure, and risk-management strategies. Currently, many financial institutions use derivatives for a variety of purposes, including accessing low-cost funds, earning higher investment returns, and creating more powerful financial products. Financial institutions must continually assess their risk management practices to ensure that their derivatives are properly valued and in compliance with the board-authorized policies and procedures approved to facilitate the implementation of leveraged trading strategies.

ENDNOTES

1. The Federal Reserve Board, 1999. Remarks by Chairman Alan Greenspan on Financial Derivatives before the Futures Industry Association, Boca Raton, Florida (March 19).
2. Group of Thirty, 1993. "Derivatives: Practices and Principles."
3. U.S. General Accounting Office (GAO), 1994. "Financial Derivatives: Actions Needed to Protect the Financial Systems."
4. Federal Financial Institutions Examination Council (FFIEC), 1998. Supervisory Policy Statement on Investment Securities and End-User Derivatives Activities (April 23).
5. The Federal Reserve Board, 2000. Remarks by Governor Laurence H. Mayer before the Derivatives Risk Management Symposium Institute on Law and Financial Services. Fordham University of Law, New York, New York, February 25.

6. loct. Group of Thirty, 1993.

7. Deloitte and Touche LLP, 1996. The Committee of Sponsoring Organizations of the Treadway Commission. Internal Control Issues in Derivatives Usage: An Information Tool for Considering the COSO Internal Control-Integrated Framework in Derivatives Applications.

8. Financial Accounting Standards Board (FASB), 1998. "Accounting for Derivative Instruments and Hedging Activities," Statement of Financial Accounting Standards No. 133 (FASB, June, Norwalk, CT).

9. The Wall Street Journal, 1994. "Beleaguered Giant: As Derivative Losses Rise, Industry Fights to Avert Regulations" (Thursday, August 25) reported that "notional value" of outstanding global derivatives contracts at $35 trillion which exceeds the estimated total value of the world's bond and stocks of $32 trillion. While this notional value of outstanding derivatives contracts may not exactly present the size of the financial derivatives market, it provides some indications of potential payments and growth associated with derivatives. Indeed, the recent report of the United States General Accounting Office, "Financial Derivatives: Actions Needed to Protect the Financial System," GAO/GGD-94-133, May 1994, indicates that the notional amount of derivatives outstanding grew from $7 trillion in 1989 to $17.6 trillion by year-end 1992.

10. The six Wall Street firms that established the new standards for derivatives are CS First Boston, Inc.; Goldman, Sachs & Co.; Salomon Brothers, Inc.; Merrill Lynch & Co.; Lehman Brothers Holdings, Inc.; and Morgan, Stanley & Co.

11. U.S. Securities and Exchange Commission (SEC), 1997. Disclosure of Accounting Policies for Derivative Financial Instruments and Derivative Commodity Instruments and Disclosure of Quantitative and Qualitative Information About Market Risk Inherent in Derivative Financial Instruments, Other Financial Instruments, and Derivative Commodity Instruments, Release No. 33-7386. Washington, DC: SEC.

12. American Institute of Certified Public Accountants, 1994. "Derivatives—Current Accounting and Auditing Literature." (Accounting Standards Executive Committee. Financial Instruments Task Force.)

13. Ibid.

14. Chance, Don M., 1995. *Option Pricing Models: An Introduction to Derivatives* (The Dryden Press, Third Edition).

15. Black, Fischer, and Myron Scholes, 1973. "The Pricing of Options and Corporate Liabilities." *Journal of Political Economy* (Vol. 81, No. 3, May/June): 637–654.

16. Ingersoll, Jr., Jonathan E., 2000. "Digital Contracts: Simple Tools for Pricing Complex Derivatives." *Journal of Business* (Vol. 73, No. 1): 67–89.

17. See Ingersoll (2000) for a more sophisticated mathematical illustration and examples of using digital contracts in determining the value of derivatives.

CHAPTER 18

Real World Bank Valuation Complications

Not all bank valuations will involve normal conditions and clean banks that have healthy prospects for reasonable returns in the future. There are numerous instances where special circumstances require adjustments to the standard valuation approaches. This chapter describes the application of the various valuation approaches under eight real world complicating circumstances:

1. A bank that has experienced losses in recent years because of low spreads, high overhead expenses, or excessive loan losses
2. A bank with inadequate capital levels
3. A bank that faces very uncertain loan loss exposure on a significant portion of its portfolio
4. A bank whose equity base consists of both preferred and common stock, but only the value of the common stock is needed
5. A bank that is highly leveraged
6. A branch of a bank that is to be purchased
7. Bank assurance
8. Initial Public Offering (IPO)

Each of these situations requires slight modifications to the valuation approaches used in Chapter 14.

18.1 BANKS EXPERIENCING RECENT LOSSES

Banks and banking organizations in the United States have reported eight consecutive years of record earnings, showing financial health and strength in rebounding from the financial difficulties of the late 1980s and early 1990s. In 1991, the Federal Deposit Insurance Corporation Improvement Act (FDICIA) introduced mandatory procedures called prompt corrective action (PCA), which requires regulators to promptly close depository institutions when their capital falls below predetermined quantitative standards.

The banking industry during the past eight years has been profitable and financially healthy with the average annual return on assets (ROA) of above one percent and the average annual return on equity (ROE) of above 15 percent. However, the chairman of FDIC in her February 8, 2000 testimony before the U.S. House of Representatives raised some concern regarding several recent failures of insured institutions.[1] Exhibit 18.1 shows the frequency of banks' and thrifts' failures from 1980–1999.

Exhibit 18.1 also reveals that in light of the existing health of the economy in general, and the banking industry in particular, the frequency and trend of bank failures has been low during the past five years. In addition, recent loss rates, stated as the loss to the deposit insurance fund as a percentage of the total assets of the failed banks, have not been significant and are considered to be within the acceptable 12 percent range of the FDIC.[2] The primary reasons for recent bank failures are (1) extensive activity in subprime lending without prudential standards with regard to borrowers with blemished or limited credit histories and inadequate safeguards (e.g., capital) to meet anticipated losses; (2) valuation and liquidity risk resulting from "retained interests" generated from the securitization of high-risk assets for institutions with excessive concentrations of these assets in relation to capital; and

Exhibit 18.1   Bank and Thrift Failures 1980–1990

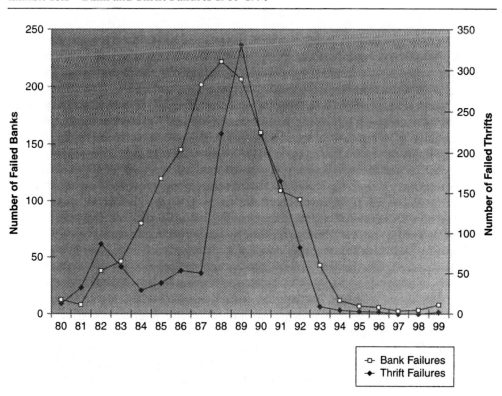

Source: Author's calculations based on data from the Federal Deposit Insurance Corporation.

(3) fraudulent financial activities by failed bank managers and directors (e.g., BestBank, Keystone, Golden City Commercial Bank, Hartford-Carlisle Savings Bank).[3]

The minimal recent bank failure rates, coupled with profitable financial services, more diversification of risks, and maintenance of a greater amount of capital encourage some banks to relax their lending standards. This has increased the number of "3," "4," or "5" rated state member banks to 43, the highest since 1995.[4] Banks can minimize the risk of failure by engaging in the following activities:

1. the use of a more sophisticated risk management system;

2. the use of a risk-focused approach of emphasizing the adequacy and effectiveness of the internal control system;

3. continuous testing of the loan portfolio and other transactions to ensure that prudent risk-taking is occurring;

4. continuous assessment of an institution's risk management system and overall risk profile;

5. ongoing monitoring of control activities to ensure that the designed control activities are functioning effectively as intended;

6. in-depth review of the loan portfolio;

7. identification of problems at an early stage; and

8. fraud prevention policy of reducing incidents of fraud.

An increasingly common situation in bank mergers and acquisitions is when the selling bank has experienced losses in recent years. Use of the market approach may not accurately reflect true value, and the income approach may be distorted by the recent losses. There are two options in such a situation. If the losses are expected to continue for at least the next few years—that is, if a turnaround is unlikely for whatever reason—it may be appropriate to estimate the bank's net asset value—the market value of the bank's assets less the market value of its liabilities. In extreme situations, the liquidation value of the bank may be the most appropriate value measure. Liquidation value is the lowest price a business commands—a business is worth no less than what remains after assets are liquidated and liabilities satisfied.

The more likely situation is a bank that has experienced recent losses being evaluated by a buyer who will be able to improve its performance. In this case, it is first necessary to construct a detailed balance sheet as it would exist on the date of acquisition. This balance sheet should reflect adjustments to clean up the bank so that its performance can be forecast as a healthy entity. This clean balance sheet would be the starting point for the new income statement. It is essential that the new income statement immediately reflect the expenses associated with cleaning up existing problems, recognizing loan losses, undertaking needed deferred maintenance, and so on. The income approach as described in Chapter 14 could then be used. The difference is that cleanup costs are reflected as immediate outflows of cash when calculating available cash flow.

Exhibit 18.2 provides a simple example. In this case, the available cash flows have been forecast based on an acquired balance sheet free of problem assets. Without cleanup costs the value of the bank is $94 million, but because of problems requiring $25 million, the value of the bank is only about $69 million. This simple example illustrates how estimated cleanup costs would be reflected in value calculations.

Exhibit 18.2 Illustration of the Impact on Value as a Result of Balance Sheet "Cleanup" Costs ($000,000)

	Year 1	Year 2	Year 3	Year 4	Year 5	Year 6	Year 7	Year 8	Year 9	Year 10
Available cash flow*	$10.0	$10.5	$11.0	$11.5	$12.2	$13.0	$13.8	$14.8	$16.0	$17.2
Discount rate	14%	14%	14%	14%	14%	14%	14%	14%	14%	14%
Capitalization rate on year 10 cash flow	—	—	—	—	—	—	—	—	—	11%
Sum of present values of cash flow	$57.8									
Present value of capitalized value of year 10 cash flow	$42.2									
"Clean" value**	$94.0									
"Cleanup" costs	($25.0)									
Value considering cost to "cleanup"	$69.0									

*Based on a clean balance sheet that reflects the results of cleanup, such as realizing losses on an investment portfolio, taking loan losses, and so on.

**The value had the buyer acquired the clean balance sheet.

18.2   BANKS WITH LOW EQUITY CAPITAL

A situation closely related to low earnings is a bank with low equity, often below regulatory minimums. In such a situation, it is difficult to apply the market approach unless banks with similarly low equity levels have been sold recently and can be used as comparables. A better approach is similar to the one described above. Project value by the income approach after a capital injection, then adjust the value to reflect that capital injection.

The difference between the low equity situation and the recent losses situation has to do with where the money goes. The cost of cleaning up the bank described above presumably went to outside parties. In a low equity situation, a capital injection stays with the bank and helps with earnings but essentially is unavailable to the owners until the bank is sold or is sufficiently profitable that internal capital creation is adequate. For example, if a buyer is required to inject one dollar of new capital upon acquisition, the assets will increase by one dollar, as will equity. All or virtually all of the additional dollar can be invested in earning assets, thus improving the income of the bank. And when the bank is sold, the one dollar is still part of the equity base. Contrast this scenario with one in which one dollar is a direct loss (say from the sale of investments). The dollar is removed from the bank, with no current or future benefit.

Despite the differences in effect, the valuation of a bank with low equity can be undertaken essentially in the same manner as for a bank with recent losses. The key is to establish a starting balance sheet reflecting the capital injection. Exhibit 18.3 illustrates how a buyer would adjust a balance sheet of a $160 million bank to reflect a $6 million addition to equity. An income statement would then be projected based on this starting balance sheet. Available cash flow would be adjusted downward to reflect the required equity injection, with value estimated based on the income approach.

Exhibit 18.3   Reflecting Capital Injections in Starting Balance Sheet ($000,000)

	Acquired Balance Sheet	Capital Injection	Starting Balance Sheet
Assets			
Cash and Due Froms	$ 10		$ 10
Securities & Fed Funds	20	+5	25
Total Loans	130		130
(Loan Loss Reserves)	(10)		(10)
Net Loans	120		120
Premises & Fixed Assets	5	+1	6
Other Real Estate Owned	3		3
Other Assets	2		2
Total Assets	$160	+6	$166
Liabilities & Equity			
Noninterest-bearing Deposits	$ 25		$ 25
Interest-bearing Deposits	115		115
Total Deposits	140		140
Other Liabilities	17		17
Equity	3	+6	9
Total Liabilities & Equity	$160	+6	$166

Another possibility is that the balance sheet is so weak that it cannot be cleaned up within realistic financial or time limits. In such an extreme case, the liquidation value, as described earlier, may be the most appropriate measure of value.

In some instances the net asset value may be negative; that is, the value of the bank's assets may be less than its liabilities. This is the typical situation with an FDIC-assisted sale. In this case, the buyer requires the FDIC to inject sufficient capital (and hold back certain nonperforming assets) to ensure that the acquired balance sheet is reasonably clean.

18.3   BANKS WITH UNCERTAIN FUTURE LOAN LOSS EXPOSURE

A third complicating situation is when the bank being valued faces uncertain future loan loss exposure. In other words, the loss facing the bank in its loan portfolio is difficult if not impossible to assess with any reasonable degree of accuracy, and existing reserves may or may not be adequate. This can be a particular problem in smaller banks where a few large problem loans have a disproportionate impact on the bank's financial condition and subsequent value to a buyer.

One way to reflect such uncertain exposure is to identify separately those problem loans on the projected income statement of the bank. Instead of one line item called Loan Loss Provision, there would be two: Loan Loss Provision for Identified Problem Loans and Loan Loss Provision for All Other Loans. The total of these two would be the loan loss provision for the bank. The normal income approach could then be used to value the bank.

The advantage of this separation technique is that a normal annual loan loss provision could be applied to all other loans, while the specific impact of the problem loans on the value estimate can be assessed. Different assumptions of degree and timing of collectability can be simulated to determine how franchise value might be affected.

Loans and loan losses are somewhat unique aspects of banks (and other financial institutions) for several reasons:

- Loans (which are, in effect, accounts receivable) constitute a large part of the asset base
- Losses on loans can be difficult to predict

It is this second aspect that is of most concern in the valuation process.

In the valuation of Example Bank in Chapter 14, the loan loss provision was based on a target loan loss reserve of 1 percent of total loans with a charge-off rate of 0.3 percent of total loans. Had these projections been different, the resulting value would also be different. Exhibit 18.4 illustrates how the value impact can be affected by relatively minor changes in assumptions. For every 0.05 percent increase in net charge-offs to average assets, the value of Example Bank declines by about $1.0 to $1.1 million.

It should be noted that increasing or decreasing any expense item (salaries, occupancy, and so on) would have the same impact on value. The difference is that most operating expenses of a bank are either fairly predictable or controllable, or both. Loan losses are unique because they can be unpredictable. Banks in a given peer group tend to have much more consistent operating expense ratios than loan loss ratios. Loan losses are related to many factors outside the bank's control. Consequently, when a bank is being valued, it is critically important that the loan loss assumptions be as accurate as possible and based on a full knowledge of pertinent facts.

Exhibit 18.4   Impact on Estimated Value of Example Bank with Varying Assumptions of Loan Losses* ($ Millions)

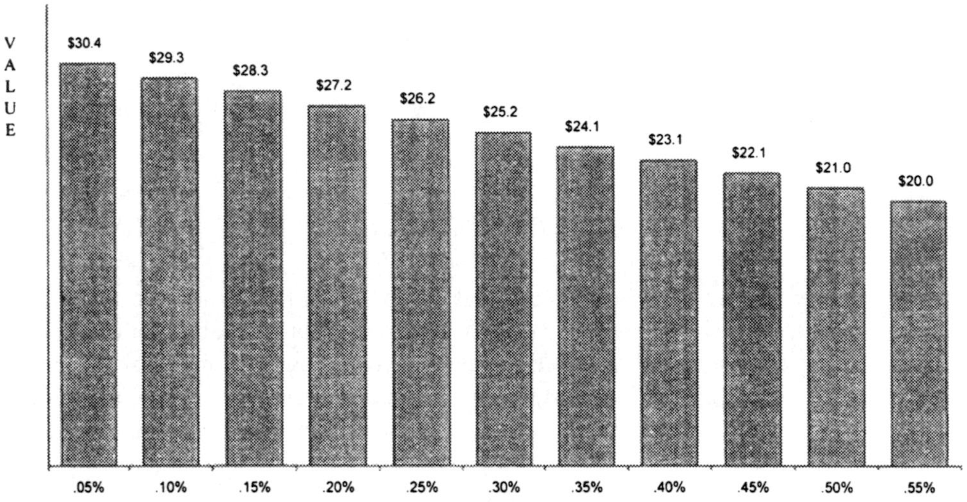

Net Charge-offs Each Year, As a Percent of Total Loans (with constant 1% reserve for loan losses)
*From data in Chapter 14.

18.4   PREFERRED AND COMMON STOCK

In cases where a bank has both common and preferred stock, there are instances where a buyer is interested in the value of only one or the other. The technique is relatively straightforward. Preferred stock can be valued by either the market approach (comparing one issue with similar issues of preferred stock) or the income approach (the net present value of interest and return of principal).

To value just the common stock of a bank that has both preferred stock and common stock requires that the bank first be valued as a total economic entity. The market and income approaches used to value Example Bank in Chapter 14 provide this total economic entity value. The preferred stock value is then subtracted from the total economic entity value, with the result being the aggregate value of the common stock. This is the value on a 100 percent common stock ownership basis. Any minority position valuation would require that an appropriate minority and/or marketability discount be applied.

18.5   HIGHLY LEVERAGED BANKS

Banks, or more likely bank holding companies, that have high debt-to-equity ratios may have historical earnings that belie the underlying earning potential of the institution. If a bank has a large debt burden, its fixed interest charges can have a significant impact on net income and available cash flow. Leverage ratios can vary widely among different size holding companies.

Valuing a highly leveraged bank is best accomplished by examining it on a debt-free basis, both historical and projected. Historical income statements can be adjusted to reflect what income would have been without the debt, or with a normal level of debt. Projected income is then estimated on a debt-free basis. Normal market and income approaches to value can then be used. The amount of debt is subtracted from the debt-free value to arrive at a with-debt value. This is essentially the approach described in the discussion of total enterprise value versus value of equity in Chapter 6.

18.6   BRANCH ACQUISITIONS

As consolidation continues in the banking industry, more and more banks are finding that redundant branch coverage is causing excessive costs. Moreover, with a greater focus on optimal asset utilization, some banks are withdrawing entirely from selected markets. The net result is that branch acquisitions have become commonplace. Buyers of branches confront an unusual set of circumstances, including the problem of defining exactly what is being acquired. Some branches are almost self-contained banks with their own loyal customer base, while others are simply service centers for routine deposit and loan services.

In most instances, the value of a branch is more than the physical premises, furniture, fixtures, and equipment. If only these parts of a branch are being acquired, typical real estate and equipment valuation methods are sufficient. The more likely, and more complex, situation is when a bank is selling a branch as a business unit, including earning and non-earning assets and the customer relationships.

The most straightforward technique to valuation of a bank branch as a business unit is to compute its net asset value. Exhibit 18.5 illustrates this approach. The first column shows the book value of the assets and liabilities to be computed as part of the branch sale. (As is the case with many branch acquisitions, there are more assigned liabilities than assigned assets.) The second column shows the adjustments of assets and liabilities to market values. The third column shows the balance sheet the buyer would have. It reflects a $5.2 million injection by the seller and includes core deposit intangible value.

In essence, when a branch is acquired with equal assets and liabilities, the price paid reflects the value of the core deposit intangible—the customer base. Consequently, the buyer must be confident that a significant number of depositors will not move their accounts when the branch is sold. If this were to occur, the deposit base upon which to value the intangible would be smaller, thus lowering the premium.

Another approach is to forecast the income and cash flows from the assets acquired and liabilities assumed. The normal income approach could then be used to value the branch. When using this approach, the required additions to capital must be factored into the available cash flow calculation. For example, if a branch with $20 million in assets and $20 million in liabilities is being acquired, the incremental equity capital needed for the buyer to inject, assuming a 5 percent equity-to-assets ratio, would be $1 million. Such a requirement should be considered in the valuation.

In some cases the purchaser of a branch is taking over only the deposits and fixed assets of the branch. No assets except for the physical structures are being acquired. This is the

Exhibit 18.5   Example of Net Asset Valuation of Branch to be Acquired ($000,000)

	Book Value of Assets and Liabilities	Market Value of Assets and Liabilities	Buyer's Opening Balance Sheet
Assets			
Vault cash	$ 10	$ 10	$ 10
Investments	20	18	$ 70*
Total loans	105	100	100
(Loss reserve)	(5)	(5)	(5)
Net loans	100	95	95
Fixed assets	15	20	20
Miscellaneous	5	5	5
Core deposit value	—	—	10
Total assets	$150	$148	$210
Liabilities			
Deposits	$200	$200	$200
Total liabilities	$200	$200	$200
Net asset value	($ 50)	($ 52)	$ 10

*Reflects $5.2 million injection by seller to balance market value of assets and liabilities.

typical scenario for an FDIC branch sale. In determining the value of this type of branch acquisition, the purchaser will pay a premium for the customer base. This premium represents the value of the core deposit intangible.

The premiums paid for a deposit purchase vary considerably, but most fall into the 2.5 to 5 percent range. This means that for every $100 of deposit the bank takes over, it will pay the seller $2.50 to $5.00 in addition to taking over the liability. The premium will depend on the types of deposits being acquired and the contractual interest rates the purchaser will have to pay depositors. Lower cost stable deposits (such as checking and passbook savings) tend to command higher premiums.

18.7   EUROPEAN BANKING MODEL

Consolidation, convergence, and global competition in recent years have encouraged banks to engage in insurance and investment activities. Especially, the passage of the Gramm-Leach-Bliley Financial Modernization Act (GLB) of 1999 allows banks to establish financial holding companies (FHC) which could engage in a wide variety of financial services activities including insurance and investment activities. The banking model under the GLB Act in which banks can fully integrate insurance and investment businesses into their core product and service offerings would resemble the European banking model of "bancassurance." The bancassurance model has been successfully used by European banks and would be possible for U.S. banks under the GLB Act.

Traditionally, the investment marketplace was driven primarily by institutional investors and wealthy individuals. Recently, especially during the 1990s, individuals across all income and demographic segments have become active investors by investing in the reward-

Exhibit 18.6   Trends in the Growth of Mutual Funds Assets and Bank Deposits

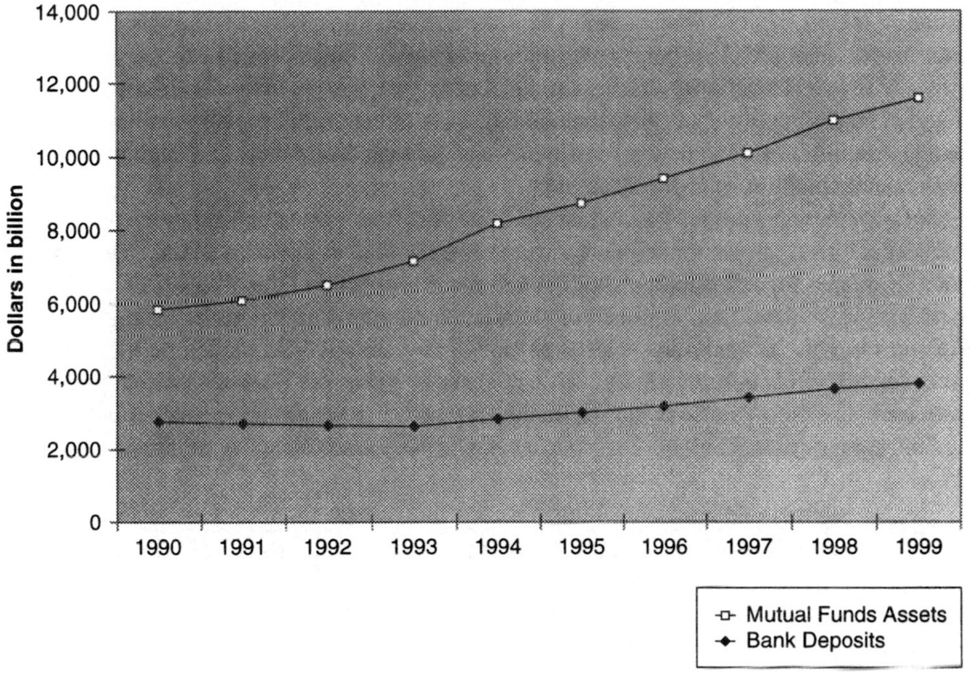

Source: Author's calculation based on bank deposit data from the Financial Deposit Insurance Corporation and mutual fund assets data from the Investment Company Institute

ing stock market, 401(k) plans, and mutual funds. Exhibit 18.6 shows that during the 1990s the amount of assets in mutual funds exceeded bank deposits and grew at a rapid pace. The passage of the GLB Act enabled U.S. banks to adopt and apply the European banking model of "bancassurance" to increase their market share and profitability in nontraditional markets such as mutual funds. Banks will be able to meet all of their customers' basic financial needs by integrating insurance and investment products with their core banking operations.

This wave of convergence will create a number of challenges for banks in shifting away from offering traditional banking services (e.g., deposits, loans, transaction activities) and moving toward engaging in nontraditional markets including insurance and mutual funds. By enacting the GLB Act, the United States was almost the last developed economy to eliminate convergence restrictions in the financial services industry and to allow the financial systems to respond to changes in the global marketplace. With this convergence now being possible in the financial services industry, several issues arise about the future structure and directions of financial service providers. These issues are: (1) the possible impacts of the passage of the GLB Act on future mergers and acquisitions in the financial services industry; (2) whether the convergence, specifically between banks and insurance companies, will limit consumer choice; and (3) whether banks and securities companies combine without imposing excess and unjustifiable levels of risk on the consumer and the economy in general. These and other related issues should be addressed in complying with the provisions of the GLB Act and in adopting the European bank assurance model in the United States. The effective and successful convergence requires banks to combine with insurance companies and mutual funds according to the provisions of the GLB Act. To achieve a successful level of convergence, banks should modify their financial reporting as well as their internal risk assessment policies and procedures. These changes require compliance with insurance and mutual funds laws and regulations and make bank valuations more complicated.

During the past decade, the mutual fund industry has grown substantially to the unprecedented level of over $6 trillion and surpassed the total deposits at banks.[5] The Investment Company Act of 1940 requires calculation and reporting of the net asset value (NAV) per share for a mutual fund. Mutual funds are not taxpaying entities; their earnings pass directly through to shareholders who report individual earnings information on their tax returns. Mutual funds calculate daily NAV per share by using the market value of funds' investments. The daily reporting of NAV in the financial press permits investors to determine the fair market value (FMV) of their investments. NAV is calculated as follows:

$$\text{NAV} = \frac{\text{market value of shareholders' equity}}{\text{outstanding shares of mutual funds}} = \frac{\text{assets (at FMV)} - \text{liabilities}}{\text{outstanding shares of mutual funds}}$$

Exhibit 18.7 shows the calculation of the daily net asset value for the hypothetical ABC mutual fund.

Exhibit 18.7   Calculating the Daily Net Asset Value (NAV) for the ABC Mutual Fund

Assets	
Cash	$ 1500
Interest receivable	325,000
Dividend receivable	416,000
Investment at cost	395,000,000
Net appreciation of investments*	15,000,000
Total assets at FMV	$410,742,500
Liabilities	
Investment purchases payable	$ 2,100,000
Accrued expenses	216,000
Total Liabilities	$ 2,316,000
Shareholders' equity	
Capital stock	$391,000,000
Net appreciation of investments	15,000,000
Retained Earnings**	2,426,500
Total shareholders' equity (at FMV)	$408,426,500
Shares outstanding	$ 18,000,000

Net asset value (NAV) = 408,426,500 ÷ 18,000,000 = $22.69.

*The "net appreciation" and "net depreciation" of investments represent unrealized holding gains and unrealized holding losses.

**Retained earnings consist of capital gains, income, expenses, and distributions.

18.8 INITIAL PUBLIC OFFERING (IPO)

Initial public offering is another business area that requires determination of fair value of the company going public in order to assess the IPO pricing and fair value of the minority interests prior to the IPO. In the IPO process the privately held company in the transition process provides the public with the opportunity to buy shares in the public stock markets. The financial institution in the transition process of "going public" may be considered attractive to the public stock markets for the following reasons: (1) generating new capital from the IPO; (2) increasing earnings capacity resulting from the new capital invested; (3) increasing growth prospects resulting from new capital and increased earnings capacity; and (4) accessibility to a public market for offering stock in an active market to a great number of potential shareholders.

In most of the aforementioned valuation services, the considerations in dispute are not bought and sold every day by able and willing involved parties. In other words, there is not a readily available fair market value for them, and accordingly the proper valuation method should be employed to assess their value. Valuation experts utilize a number of valuation methods commonly derived from theories of finance (e.g., discounted cash earnings, capital asset pricing model) to calculate a business's value.

The eight situations described in this chapter are not uncommon and are likely to be confronted in the course of most bank valuations. A summary of the approaches that should be considered is shown in Exhibit 18.8.

Exhibit 18.8 Summary of Valuation Approaches in More Complex Situations

Situation	Valuation Approach
Bank has experienced losses in recent years.	If losses are expected to continue, use the market value of equity approach, which essentially measures liquidation value. If losses are not expected to continue, develop a projected income statement based on detailed analysis of current balance sheet and yields, costs, etc. Factor in any costs necessary to divest of assets or liabilities that are draining earnings. Then use income approach.
Bank has very low equity.	If the current balance sheet is clean, a projected income statement can be prepared based on the yields, costs, etc. Then use the income approach, taking into account any needed immediate capital injection. If current balance sheet is not clean and level of required equity is very high relative to likely asset quality, the liquidation value approach may be warranted.
Bank faces uncertain loss exposure on a selected portion of its portfolio.	A detailed analysis of the problem loans should be undertaken to reduce the uncertainty as much as possible. Then, two line items for loan losses should be included in the projected income statement; one for the problem loans, another for all others. This way, the problem loans can be evaluated separately from the rest. The normal income approach can then be used.

(Continued)

Exhibit 18.8   Summary of Valuation Approaches in More Complex Situations—*continued*

Situation	Valuation Approach
Bank has preferred and common stock, and only the value of the common stock is desired.	The total value of the bank is equal to the value of common stock plus the value of preferred stock, or conversely the value of the common stock is equal to the total value of the bank less the value of the preferred stock. Therefore, the first step is to value the bank in total, then value the preferred stock using techniques described in Chapter 6. The difference is the common stock value.
Bank is highly leveraged.	Value bank on debt-free basis using income approach, then subtract debt to be assumed to arrive at value with debt.
Branch purchase.	Compute net asset value taking into account the value of the core deposit intangible asset or construct an opening day balance sheet of the branch, then project the income statement based on the yields, costs, etc. Value by the income approach taking into account any capital injections needed to support the acquired assets.

ENDNOTES

1. Tanove, Donna. 2000. "Testimony on Recent Bank Failures and Regulatory Initiatives before the Committee on Banking and Financial Services." U.S. House of Representatives (February 8, FDIC).
2. Ibid.
3. Ibid.
4. Governor Lawrence H. Meyer. 2000. Testimony, 1999 Banking Failure before the Committee on Banking and Financial Services, U.S. House of Representatives (February).
5. Gorman, Joseph F. and Joseph M. Hargadon. 2000. Mutual Fund Accounting. *Strategic Finance* (April): 49–53.

Index

Accounting Principles Board (APB):
  goodwill and, 7.4, 13.1
  pooling accounting requirements,
    7.3.2
Accounting procedures:
  generally, 3.3, 7.3—7.4
  pooling accounting requirements,
    7.3.2—7.33
  pooling versus purchase accounting,
    7.3, 7.4
  typical valuation examples, 7.4
Accounting-based valuation approach,
  14.10.2
Aggregation method, future income
  level projections, 6.4.6
Allocated transfer risk, financial analysis, expenses composition, 9.11.3
Allocated transfer risk reserve, loans,
  financial analysis, 9.3.4
Alternatives principle, described, 5.5.1
American Institute of Certified Public
  Accountants (AICPA), 2.1
American Society of Appraisers,
  (ASA), 2.1
Amortization:
  amortizable versus nonamortizable
    assets, 8.2
  core deposits valuation, 16.1. See
    also Core deposit base valuation
  going concern value, 5.2
  intangible asset valuation, 6.5, 8.5.
    See also Intangible asset valua-
    tion
  useful life measurement, 8.3
AmSouth case, 16.3.3
Annual budget, financial analysis, 9.1.5
Antitrust, merger and acquisition
  process, 12.3.2
Antitrust Department, 3.4
Appraisal, cost approach, 6.2
Appraisal Foundation (AF), 2.3
Appraisal plan, 2.93
Appraisers, 2.1
Appraiser's traits, 2.10
Arbitrage pricing theory, 17.2

Assembled work force. See Work force
Asset composition. See also Financial
  analysis; Financial assets valuation process; Fixed assets; Intangible assets; Physical assets; Tangible asset valuation
  balance sheet analysis example, 9.12
  financial analysis, 9.3
  property factor, internal characteris-
    tics assessment, 10.2.8
Asset composition peer group
  comparison, financial analysis,
  balance sheet analysis example,
    9.12.3
Asset growth rates, financial analysis,
  balance sheet analysis example,
  9.12
Asset/liability (A/L) management
  report, financial analysis, 9.1
Asset size, business enterprise valuation process, comparability basis,
  14.5.2
Asset transfer transaction (Type D reorganization), nontaxable transactions, valuation process, 7.1.1
Asset valuation, business enterprise
  valuation process contrasted, 12.1
Associated company, asset composition, 9.3.8
Assumption changes, business enterprise valuation process and, 14.7,
  14.8
Audit Committees, 4.12.4
Available cash flow, income type
  selection, 6.4.4

Balance sheet:
  financial analysis, 9.2
  projection of, business
    enterprise valuation process,
    14.6.2-14.6.3
Balance sheet analysis example, 9.12
  asset composition, 9.12.2
  asset composition peer group com-
    parison, 9.12.3

asset growth rates, 9.12.1
capital levels and trends, 9.12.7
liability composition, 9.12.5
liability composition peer group
  comparison, 9.12.6
liability growth rates, 9.12.4
Balanced scorecard (BSC), 10.3.3
Banc One case, 16.3.2
Bankers acceptance, customers' liabili-
  ties, financial analysis, 9.3.9
Bank examination report, financial
  analysis, 9.1.5
Bank and thrift failures, 18.1
Bank holding company:
  BHC, 1.2.2, 4.2.2, 4.11
  capital components, 9.7.2
  special considerations, 9.17
Bank Holding Company Performance
  Report (BHCPR), 9.1.2
Bank supervision, 4.4
Banking franchise concept, business
  enterprise valuation process, 14.2
Basel Capital Accord, 1.4.4, 3.5
Basel Committee, 1.4.4
Below-market rate lease, intangible as-
  set valuation, 8.4.3
Binomial Model, 17.9.1
Block-Scholes Option Pricing Model,
  17.2, 17.9.3
Book value:
  adjusted, to compute market value of
    equity, business valuation, 6.6.4
  defined, 5.2
Borrowed money, financial analysis, li-
  abilities, 5.4.4
Branch acquisitions, valuation process
  complications, 18.6
Budget, annual, financial analysis,
  9.1.5
Business enterprise valuation process,
  Chapter 9. See also Business valuation
  asset valuation contrasted, 14.1
  assumption changes and, 14.7
  banking franchise concept, 14.2

cost approach limitations, 14.5
income approach, 14.6
    balance sheet projection, 14.6.2
    cash flow measurement, 14.6.1
    example, 14.6.4, 14.7
    generally, 14.6
    income, expenses, and cash flow
        projections, 14.6.3
    model overview, 14.6.1
market approach, 14.5
    advantages and disadvantages of,
        14.5.5
    comparability basis, 14.5.2
    comparable transactions identifi-
        cation, 14.5.1
    example of, 14.5.4
    generally, 14.5
    publicly traded companies as com-
        parables, 14.5.3
    stockholders and, 14.11
    strategic versus tactical valuations,
        14.3
    value creation opportunities, 14.8
Business to Business (B2B), 1.4
Business Valuation Standards, 2.1
Business valuation, 6.6. See also Busi-
    ness enterprise valuation process
    book value, adjusted, to compute
        market value of equity, 6.6.4
    generally, 6.6
    liquidation value, 6.6.5
    preferred stock, 6.6.3
    total enterprise value versus value of
        equity, 6.6.2

Call reports, financial analysis, 4.11,
    9.1.3
CAMEL factor, 4.4.4, 12.3.2
Candidate identification, merger and
    acquisition process, strategy
    phase, 12.1.5
Capital: 9.6
    Components, 9.7.1
    Reserves, 9.6.4
    Risk-based, 9.8
Capital, risk-based, financial analysis,
    9.8
Capital Asset Pricing Model, (CAPM),
    6.4., 6.4.7, 14.10.1, 17.2
    discount rate, and, 6.4.7
Capital composition, financial analysis,
    9.6
Capital standards, 1.4.4
Capitalization rate:
    business valuation, preferred stock,
        6.6.2 income approach to valua-
        tion, 6.4
    internal characteristics assessment,
        potential factor, 10.2.10
    selection of, income approach to val-
        uation, 6.4.7
Capitalized leases, financial analysis,
    liabilities, 9.4.5
Capital levels and trends, financial
    analysis, balance sheet analysis
    example, 9.12.7

Capital reserves, financial analysis,
    9.6.4
Cash and due froms, financial analysis,
    asset composition, 9.3.1
Cash flow, available, income type
    selection, 6.4.4
Cash flow measurement, business en-
    terprise valuation process, income
    approach, 14.6.1
Certificate of Deposit (CD):
    core deposits valuation, 16.5.2
    interest expense, financial analysis,
        9.10.1
Chambers of commerce, external
    environment assessment, 11.2
Citizens & Southern Bancorporation
    case, 8.5, 16.3.4
Closely held corporations (CHC), 6.8
Closely held stock, 2.8
    generally, 2.8
    IRS Revenue Ruling, 6.8.1, 7.1.1
    marketability, lack of, discount for,
        6.8.3
    minority position/premium for con-
        trol, discounts for, 6.8.2
Collateralized Mortgage Obligation
    (CMO), 15.2.1
Commercial loans, tangible asset valua-
    tion process, 15.2.3
Committee of Sponsoring Organiza-
    tions (COSO), 4.12, 17.3
Common stock. See also Preferred
    stock
    business valuation, 6.6.3
    par value of, financial analysis, 9.6.1
    valuation process complications,
        18.4
Community impact, regulator approval,
    merger, and acquisition process,
    12.3.2
Community Reinvestment Act (CRA),
    1.2.2
Comparability:
    business enterprise valuation
        process, 14.5.1, 19.5.2
    lack of, adjusting for, 6.3.2
Comparables:
    identification of
        business enterprise valuation
            process, 14.5.1 valuation
            process, 6.3.1
        publicly traded companies as, busi-
            ness enterprise valuation
            process, 14.5.3
Competitive analysis, external environ-
    ment assessment, 11.6
Complications, Chapter 18. See also
    Valuation process complications
Consolidation, Convergence, and Com-
    petition, (3 C's), 1.2, 1.4, 2.2, 4.2
Consumer loans, tangible asset
    valuation process, 15.2.4
Continuous quality improvement, 1.4.6
Core capital, 1.4
    regulatory capital components,
        financial analysis, 9.7

Core deposit base, intangible asset val-
    uation, 6.1.2
Core deposit base valuation, Chapter 16
    cost
    savings approach
        described, 16.2
        example of, 16.7
    deposits included in, 16.4
    future income approach
        described, 16.5.3
        example of, 16.8
    historical development cost
        approach, 16.5.1
    intangible asset concept and, 16.1
    IRS position on, 16.2
    life estimation, 16.6
        historical retention, 16.6.1
        projected lifing, 16.6.2
    tax court cases on, 16.3
        AmSouth case, 16.3.3
        Banc One case, 16.3.2
        Citizens & Southern case, 16.3.4
        generally, 16.3
        Midlantic case, 16.3.1
        Newark Morning Ledger case,
            16.3.5
Corporate culture, internal characteris-
    tics assessment, 16.2.3
Cost, value contrasted, 5.2
Cost approach:
    intangible asset valuation, 8.4.1
    limitations of, business enterprise
        valuation process, 14.4
    replacement principle, 5.5.2
    valuation process, 6.2
Cost recovery method, intangible asset
    valuation, amortization, 8.5
Cost savings approach:
    core deposits valuation
        described, 16.5.2
        example of, 16.7
    intangible asset valuation, 6.53, 8.43
Customers' liabilities, financial
    analysis, asset composition, 9.3.9

Daily statement of condition, financial
    analysis, 9.1.5
Data sources. See also Financial analy-
    sis availability, comparables iden-
    tification, 6.3.1 external environ-
    ment assessment, 11.2, 11.5
Debentures, financial analysis,
    liabilities, 9.4.7
Delinquent and classified loan analysis,
    financial analysis, loan risk analy-
    sis illustration, 9.14.2
Delinquent (past due) loan report,
    financial analysis, 9.1.5
Demand notes, financial analysis,
    liabilities, 9.4.3
Demographic analysis, external envi-
    ronment assessment, 11.2, 11.4
Department of Justice (DOJ), 3.4
Deposits, financial analysis, liabilities,
    9.4.1
Depreciation, book value and, 5.2

Derivatives, 17
  authoritative guidelines, 17.1
  market, 17.2
  risk management, 17.3
  accounting, 17.5
  tax considerations, 17.6
  audit, 17.7
  sources of information, 17.8
  valuation model, 17.9
Direct approach, business valuation, 8.6.2
Discounted cash flow (DCF), 14.7
Discounted future income method, described, 6.4.2
Discount for lack of marketability, closely held stock, valuation process, 6.8.3
Discount rate, selection of, income approach to valuation, 6.4.7
Dividend capitalization model, income approach to valuation, 6.4.8
Due diligence review: 3.10.5, 12.2.4
  internal characteristics assessment, 10.1
  merger and acquisition process, 12.2.4

Earnings per share, business enterprise valuation process and, 14.4
Economic Growth, 3.7
Economic obsolescence, cost approach, 6.2
  Economic value, defined, 5.1. See also Value 80 percent rule, taxation, typical valuation examples, 7.2
Economic value added (EVA), 10.3.2
Electronic Data Interchange (EDI), 3.8
Employees. See Work force
Employee stock ownership plans (ESOPs), 10.2.2
Enhancements, value creation opportunities, business enterprise valuation process, 14.8
Equity capital:
  financial analysis, 9.6
  low, valuation process complications, 18.2
Equity valuation, book value and, 5.2
Equity value:
  book value adjusted to compute, business valuation, 6.6.4
  total enterprise value versus, business valuation, 6.6.2
Excess Earnings Method, 6.5.4
Erratic trend pattern, stabilized level of income estimation, 6.4.5
Examination report, financial analysis, 9.15
Excess earnings method, intangible asset valuation, 6.54
Expenses composition, 9.11
  generally, 9.11
  income taxes, 9.11.4
  interest expense, 9.11.1
  loan and lease losses and allocated transfer risk, 9.11.3

noninterest expense, 9.11.2
Expenses projection, business enterprise valuation process, income approach, 14.6.3
External environment assessment, Chapter 11. See also Internal characteristics assessment
  competitive analysis, 4.6
  data sources, 11.2, 11.5
  demographic analysis, 11.4
  economic analysis, 11.5
  market-wide versus small area analysis, 11.3
  value and, 11.1
Extraordinary gains or losses, financial analysis, income composition, 9.10.3

Fair market value: 2.1, 2.2, 2.3
  book value and, 5.2
  business valuation, 6.6
  defined, 5.2
  goodwill value and, 5.2
  investment value and, 5.2
Fair value accounting (FVA), 4.6, 4.10
Fair value standards, 2.2, 3.7
Federal Deposit Insurance Corporation (FDIC):
  FDIC Act, 1.2.1
    external environment assessment, 11.2, 11.6
    liquidation value. 5.2
    low equity capital complication, 18.2
Federal Financial Institutions Examination Council (FFIEC), 9.1.1
Federal financial safety net, 1.2.1
Federal Home Loan Bank Board (FHLBB), 4.6
Federal Home Loan Bank System, 1.2.1
Federal Reserve Bank, 14.5.1
Fed funds sold:
  asset composition, 9.3.3
  liabilities, 9.4.2
Federal Reserve Board, 1.4.5, 3.4.1
Final agreement, merger and acquisition process, 12.3.1
Finalization and integration phase, merger and acquisition process, 12.3. See also Merger and acquisition process
Financial Accounting Standards. Board (FASB), 9.3.6
Financial analysis, Chapter 9
  asset composition, 9.3
    cash and due froms, 9.3.1
    customers' liabilities, 9.3.9
    fed funds sold and reverse repos, 9.3.3
    intangible assets, 9.3.10
    investment securities, 9.3.2
    loans and lease financing receivables, 9.3.4
    other assets, 9.3.11
    other real estate owned, 9.3.7

premises and fixed assets, 9.3.6
  trading account assets, 9.3.5
  unconsolidated subsidiaries and associated company investments, 9.3.8
balance sheet analysis example, 9.12
  asset composition, 9.12.2
  asset composition peer group comparison, 9.12.3
  asset growth rates, 9.12.1
  capital levels and trends, 9.12.7
  liability composition, 9.12.5
  liability composition peer group comparison, 9.12.6
  liability growth rates, 16.12.4
  summary, Exhibit 9-4
bank holding company considerations, 9.17
capital composition, 9.6
data types and sources, 9.1
  Bank Holding Company Performance Report (BHCPR), 9.1.2
  call reports, 9.1.3
  generally, 9.1
  internal data sources, 9.1.5
  private sources, 9.1.4
  Uniform Bank Performance Report (UBPR), 9.1.1
expenses composition, 9.11
  generally, 9.11
  income taxes, 9.11.4
  interest expense, 9.11.1
  loan and lease losses and allocated transfer risk, 9.11.3
  noninterest expense, 9.11.2
external environment assessment
  demographic analysis, 11.4
  economic analysis, 11.5
financial statements, 9.2
  balance sheet, 9.2.2
  generally, 9.2
  income statement, 9.2.1
income composition, 9.10
  extraordinary gains or losses, 9.10.3
  interest income, 9.10.1
  noninterest income, 9.10.2
income statement and profitability analysis illustration, 9.13
  overall income and expenses, 9.13.1
  profitability sources, 9.13.2
  summary, Exhibit 9-6
internal characteristics assessment
  portfolio factor, 10.2.5
  potential factor, 10.2.10
  liabilities, 9.4
  liquidity and investment portfolio analysis illustration, 9.15
  loan risk analysis illustration, 9.14
  off-balance sheet items, 9.5
  regulatory capital components, 9.7
  risk-based capital, 9.8
Financial assets valuation process, 15.2
  commercial loans, 15.2.3

consumer loans, 15.2.4
  generally, 15.2
  investment securities, 15.2.1
  lease financing. 15.2.6
  loan portfolio, 15.2.6
  mortgage loans, 15.2.5
  nonperforming loans, 15.2.7
Financial Electronic Data Interchange
  (FEDI), 3.8
Financial Holding Company, 1.1, 1.2.2
Financial Institutions Reform, Recovery, and Enforcement Act (FIR-
  REA), 2.3
Financial statements, 9.2
  balance sheet, 9.2.2
  generally, 9.2
  income statement, 9.2.1
Financial Structure, 3.10.8
First Pennsylvania case, 8.3.2
Five-year asset growth, business enterprise valuation process, comparability basis, 14.5.2
Five-year return on assets, business enterprise valuation process, comparability basis, 14.5.2
Fixed assets:
  financial analysis, 9.3.6
  property factor, internal characteris-
    tics assessment, 10.2.8
Forced liquidation value:
  defined, 5.2
  value relationships and, 5.4
Forecasting:
  balance sheet projection, business
    enterprise valuation process,
    income approach, 14.6.2
  future income level projections,
    income approach to valuation,
    6.4.5
  income statement projection, business
    enterprise valuation process, in-
    come approach, 14.6.3
  projected lifing, core deposits valua-
    tion, 16.6.2
Franchise concept, business enterprise
  valuation process, 14.2
Functional obsolescence, cost
  approach, 6.2
Future benefits principle, described,
  5.5.4
Future income approach:
  core deposits valuation
    described, 16.5.3
    example of, 16.8
  income approach to valuation, 6.4
Future income level projections, income approach to valuation, 6.45

General Accounting Office (GAO),
  4.12.3
General Utilities, Section 338 election,
  taxable transactions, 7.1.2
Generally Accepted Accounting Princi-
  ples (GAAP), 2.9, 4.6, 4.11
Generally Accepted Auditing Standards
  (GAAS), 4.12.1

Glass-Steagall Act of 1933, 1.2.1,
  3.4, 13.1
Global marketplace, 1.4.3
Going concern value, defined, 5.2
Goodwill value:
  Accounting Principles Board
    (APB), 7.4
  defined, 5.2
  financial analysis, 9.3.10
  intangible asset valuation, 8.2
  value relationships and, 5.4
Government Agency Securities,
  tangible asset valuation process,
  10.2.1
Gramm-Leach-Bliley (GLB) Act, 1.1,
  1.2.2, 3.3, 4.5
Growing erratic trend pattern, stabilized level of income estimation,
  6.4.5

Herfindahl-Hirschman Index
  (HHS), 3.4
Highly leveraged banks, valuation
  process complications, 18.5
Historical development cost approach,
  core deposits valuation, 16.5.1
Historical loan risk analysis, financial
  analysis, loan risk analysis illustration, 9.14.3
Historical retention, core deposits valuation, 16.6.1

Immateriality, intangible asset identification criteria, 8.1.1
Improvements, cost approach, 6.2
Income, intangible asset valuation, 6.5.2
Income approach, 6.4
  business enterprise valuation
    process, 14.6
  balance sheet projection, 14.6.2
  cash flow measurement, 14.6.1
  example, Exhibit 14-6
  generally, 14.6
  income, expenses, and cash flow
    projections, 14.6..3
  model overview, 14.6.1
  capitalization and discount rates
    selection, 6.4.7
  discounted future income method,
    6.4.2
  dividend capitalization model, 6.4.3
  future benefits principle, 5.6
  future income level projections, 6.4.5
  income type selection, 6.4.3
  inflation and, 6.4.9
  intangible asset valuation, 8.4.3
  overview of, 6.4
  stabilized income method, 6.4.1
  stabilized level of income estimation,
    6.4.5
Income composition, 9.10
  extraordinary gains or losses, 9.10.3
  interest income, 9.10.1
  noninterest income, 9.10.2
Income forecast method, intangible asset valuation, amortization, 8.5

Income statement:
  business enterprise valuation
    process, income approach,
    14.6.3
  financial analysis, 9.2.1
Income statement and profitability
  analysis, 9.13
  overall income and expenses, 9.13.1
  profitability sources, 9.13.2
  summary, Exhibit 19-6
Income taxes, financial analysis, expenses composition, 9.11.4. See
  also Internal Revenue Service
  (IRS); Taxation
Indirect approach:
  business valuation, 6.6.1
  future income level projections, 6.4.6
Individual component analysis, intangible asset valuation, 8.3.2
Inflation, income approach to valuation, 6.4.8
Inseparability, intangible asset identification criteria, 8.1.1
Information technology, 1.4.2
Initial public offering (IPO), 18.7
Institute of Business Appraisers, 2.1
Insurable value, defined, 5.2
Intangible assets:
  financial analysis, 9.3.10
  going concern value, 5.2
  goodwill value, defined, 5.2
  valuation and, 5.3
  value relationships and, 5.4
Intangible asset valuation, 6.5, Chapter
  8. See also Tangible asset valuation
  amortizable versus nonamortizable
    assets, 8.2
  amortization, 8.5
  core deposit base, 8.1.2
  core deposits valuation, Chapter 16.
    See also Core deposit base valu-
    ation
  cost savings and, 6.5.3
  excess earnings method, 6.5.4
  generally, 6.5
  good will, 8.1.9
  identification of asset criteria, 8.1.1
  income and, 6.5.2
  leasehold interests, 8.1.7
  loan servicing contracts, 8.1.3
  proprietary computer software, 8.1.5
  replacement cost, 6.5.1
  safe deposit box contracts, 8.1.4
  support for, 8.6
  trust accounts, 8.1.6
  useful life measurement, 8.3
    generally, 8.3
    individual component analysis,
      8.3.2
    unique experience, 8.3.1
  value establishment, 8.4
  work force, 8.1.8
Integration, 3.10.10, 12.3.5
  problems, internal characteristics as-
    sessment and, 10.1

Interest expense, financial analysis, expenses composition, 9.11.1
Interest income:
  financial analysis, income composition, 9.10.1
  net business enterprise valuation process, income approach, 14.6.4
    core deposits valuation, 16.5.3
  profit factor, internal characteristics assessment, 10.2.1
Internal characteristics assessment, Chapter 10.
  See also External environment assessment framework of, 10.2
  people factor, 10.2.2
  personality factor, 10.2.3
  physical distribution factor, 10.2.4
  planning factor, 10.2.9
  portfolio factor, 10.2.5
  potential factor, 10.2.10
  processes factor, 10.2.7
  product factor, 10.2.6
  profit factor, 10.2.1
  property factor, 10.2.8
  objectives and benefits of, 10.1
Internal control structure, 14.12.2
Internal Revenue Service (IRS): **2.3**
  core deposits valuation, 16.2.
    See also Core deposit base valuation
  excess earnings method, 6.5.4
  going concern value, 5.2
  intangible asset valuation, 8.2.2, 8.6
  338 election, taxable transactions, 7.1.2, 7.2
  useful life measurement, 8.3, 8.3.2
  value-in-use/value-in-exchange, 5.2
Internal Revenue Service (IRS) Revenue Ruling 7.1.1, closely held stock, valuation process, 6.8.1
International Accounting Standards Committee (IASC), 13.1
Intrinsic value, 5.2.4
Investment securities:
  financial analysis, asset composition, 9.3.2
  tangible asset valuation process, 15.2
Investment value: **5.2.2, 14.5**
  business enterprise valuation process, 14.6
  defined, 5.2

Keefe, Bruyette & Woods, 9.1.4

Lack of comparability, adjusting for, market approach, 6.3.1
Lease financing, tangible asset valuation process, 15.2.6
Lease financing receivables, financial analysis, asset composition, 9.3.4
Leasehold interests, intangible asset valuation, 8.1.7
Lease losses, financial analysis, expenses composition, 9.11.3

Leases:
  below-market rate lease, intangible asset valuation, 8.4.3, Exhibit 8-2
  capitalized, financial analysis, liabilities, 9.4.5
  premises and fixed assets, financial analysis, 9.3.6
Letter of intent, merger and acquisition process, 12.2.3
Leveraged banks, valuation process complications, 18.5
Liabilities:
  balance sheet analysis example, 9.12.4—9.12.6
  financial analysis, 9.4
Liability composition peer group comparison, financial analysis, balance sheet analysis example, 9.12.6
Liability growth rates, financial analysis, balance sheet analysis example, 9.12.4
Life estimation, core deposits valuation, 16.6
Liquidation value:
  business valuation, 6.6.4
  defined, 5.2.7
  value relationships and, 5.4
Liquidity and investment portfolio analysis, 9.15
Loan losses:
  financial analysis, expenses composition, 9.11.3
  uncertain future exposure, valuation process complications, 18.3, Exhibit 18-3
Loan loss provision, financial analysis, 9.13.2
Loan portfolio, tangible asset valuation process, 15.2.2
Loan risk analysis, 9.14, 9.14.1
Loans:
  financial analysis, asset composition, 9.3.4
  nonperforming
    business enterprise valuation process, 14.1
    tangible asset valuation process, 15.2.2, 15.2.7
  performing, tangible asset valuation process, 15.3
Loan servicing contracts, intangible asset valuation, 8.1.3
Local government securities, financial analysis, 9.3.2
Losses. *See also* Loan losses
  recent, valuation process complications, 18.1, Exhibit 18-1
  uncertain future loan loss exposure, valuation process complications, 18.3, Exhibit 18-3
Low equity capital, valuation process complications, 18.2

Malcolm Baldrige National Quality Award (MBNQA), 1.4.6

Management:
  merger and acquisition process, integration, 12.3.5
  people factor, internal characteristics assessment, 10.2.2
Marketability, lack of, discount for, closely held stock, valuation process, 6.8
Market approach:
  business enterprise valuation process, 14.5
    advantages and disadvantages of, 14.5.5
    comparability basis, 14.5.2, 14.5.3
    comparable transactions identification, 14.5.1, Exhibit 14-1
    example of, 14.5.4
    publicly traded companies as comparables, 14.5.3
  intangible asset valuation, 8.4
  substitution principle, 5.5.3
  valuation process
    comparables identification, 6.3.1
    generally, 6.3
    lack of comparability, adjusting for, 6.3.2
Market comparison method, discount rate selection, 6.4.7
Market discipline, 4.4.1
Market position, planning factor, internal characteristics assessment, 10.2.9
Markets:
  external environment assessment, economic analysis, 11.5
  merger and acquisition process, strategy phase, 12.1.1
Market type, business enterprise valuation process, comparability basis, 14.5.2
Market-wide analysis, small area analysis versus, external environment assessment, 11.3
Mass asset rule, intangible asset valuation, 8.3.2
Merger and acquisition process, Chapter 12
  finalization and integration phase, 12.3
    final agreement, 12.3.1
    final review, 12.3.3
    integration, 12.3.5
    regulator and shareholder approval, 12.3.2
    transaction finalization, 12.3.4
  negotiation and investigation phase, 12.2
    candidate contact and preliminary negotiation, 12.2.2
    due diligence review, 12.2.4
    generally, 12.2
    letter of intent, 12.2.3
    strategy for, 12.2.1
  overview of, 12.1, Exhibit 12-1
  strategy phase, 12.1, 12.1.1—12.1.7
    candidate analysis, 12.1.6

candidate criteria, 12.1.4
candidate identification, 12.1.5
generally, 12.1
overall plan, 12.1.1
plan for, 12.1.3
preliminary valuation and financial feasibility study, 12.1.7
team for, 12.1.2
tangible asset valuation process and,
15.3
Mergers and acquisitions (M & A):
1.2.1, 3.3, 3.7, 3.10, 13.3, 14.9
accounting procedures, 7.3, 7.3.1—
7.3.3, 7.4, Exhibit 7-5
generally, 7.3
pooling accounting requirements,
7.3.2
pooling versus purchase accounting, 7.3, 7.3.1—7.3.3, 7.4
typical valuation examples, 7.4
book value, 5.2.6
branch acquisitions, valuation
process complications, 18.6
goodwill value, 5.2.4
income approach to valuation, 6.4
taxation
generally, 7.1
nontaxable transactions, 7.1.1
taxable transactions, 7.1.2
typical valuation examples, 7.2,
7.3, Exhibit 7-1
taxation and, 7.1, 7.1.1, 7.1.2, 7.2
value creation opportunities, business enterprise valuation
process, 14.9
Midlantic case, 16.3.1
Minimum capital regulation, 4.4.3
Minority position/premium for control,
discounts for, closely held stock,
valuation process, 6.8.2
Mortgage loans:
financial analysis, liabilities, 9.4.6
tangible asset valuation process,
15.2.5

National Association of Certified Valuation Analysts (NACVA), 2.1
National Association of Regional
Councils, 11.2
Negotiation, 3.10
Negotiation and investigation phase,
merger and acquisition process,
12.2, 12.2.1—12.2.4. *See also*
Merger and acquisition process
Net amount, liquidation value, 5.2.7
Net interest income:
business enterprise valuation
process, income approach,
14.6.3
core deposits valuation, 16.5.3
Net asset value (NAV), 18.7
Net interest margin, financial analysis,
income statement and profitability
analysis illustration, 9.13.2
Net lease financing receivables, financial analysis, 9.3.4

Net loans, financial analysis, 9.3.4
Newark Morning Ledger case, 16.3.5
Nonamortizable assets, amortizable assets versus, intangible asset valuation, 8.2.1, 8.2.2
Noninterest expense, financial analysis,
expenses composition, 9.11.2
Noninterest income:
business enterprise valuation
process, income approach,
14.6.3
financial analysis, income composition, 9.10.2
Noninterest income to total income, financial analysis, 9.13.2
Nonperforming loans. *See also* Loans
business enterprise valuation
process, 14.1
tangible asset valuation process,
15.2.2, 15.3
Nontaxable transactions, mergers
and acquisitions, 7.1.1
North American Industry Classification
System (NAICS), 1.1

Obsolescence, 6.2
Off-balance sheet items:
financial analysis, 9.5
risk-based capital, financial analysis,
9.8
Office of the Comptroller of the Currency (OCC), 1.4.2, 4.3, 16.7
Office of Thrift Supervision (OTS),
11.2, 11.6
Operating expenses, per dollar of total
income, financial analysis, 18.2
Orderly liquidation value, defined,
5.2.7
Organizational structure, internal characteristics assessment, 10.2.2
Other assets, financial analysis, asset
composition, 9.3.11
Other liabilities, financial analysis, liabilities, 9.4.8
Other comprehensive basis of accounting (OCBOA), 2.9.2
Other real estate (ORE) owned:
business enterprise valuation
process, 14.1
financial analysis, asset composition,
9.3.6

Par value of stock, financial analysis,
9.6.1
Past due loan report, financial analysis,
9.1.5
Patents, intangible asset valuation,
6.5.2, Exhibit 6-7
Payment form, business enterprise valuation process, comparability basis, 14.5.3
People factor, internal characteristics
assessment, 10.22
Performing loans, tangible asset valuation process, 15.2.2. *See also*
Loans.

Permanent differences, financial analysis, expenses composition, 9.11.4
Personality factor, internal characteristics assessment, 10.2.3
Personnel. *See* Work force
Physical assets, tangible asset valuation
process, 15.1
Physical distribution factor, internal
characteristics assessment, 10.2.4
Physical obsolescence, cost approach,
6.2
Planning. See Merger and acquisition
process
Planning agencies, external environment assessment, 11.2
Planning factor, internal characteristics
assessment, 10.2.9
Pooling accounting:
purchase accounting versus, 7.3,
7.3.1—7.3.3, 7.4
requirements for, 7.3.2
Portfolio factor, internal characteristics
assessment, 10.2.5. *See also* Liquidity and investment portfolio
analysis; Loan portfolio
Preferred stock. *See also* Common
stock
business valuation, 6.6.2—6.6.4
par value of, financial analysis, 9.6
valuation process complications,
18.4, Exhibit 18-3
Premises, financial analysis, 9.3.6
Premium for control/minority position,
discounts for, closely held stock,
valuation process, 6.8.2
Price, value contrasted, 5.2.1, 14.11
Price/earnings *(PIE)* ratio, 6.4.7:
business enterprise valuation process
and, 14.11
discount rate selection, 6.4.6
Pricing value, reporting value versus,
valuation, 5.6
Process factor, internal characteristics
assessment, 10.2.7
Product factor, internal characteristics
assessment, 10.2.6
Profitability sources, financial analysis,
income statement and profitability
analysis illustration, 9.13
Profit factor, internal characteristics assessment, 10.2.1
Profits:
business enterprise valuation process,
comparability basis, 14.5.3
improvement in, internal characteristics assessment, 10.1
undivided, capital, financial analysis,
9.6.3
Projected lifing, core deposits
valuation, 16.6.2
Projections. *See* Forecasting
Property, valuation and, 5.3
Property factor, internal characteristics
assessment, 10.2.8
Proprietary computer software, intangible asset valuation, 8.1.5

Publicly traded companies, as comparables, business enterprise valuation process, 14.5.3
Purchase accounting, pooling accounting versus, Mergers and acquisitions, 7.3, 7.3.1-7.3.3

Rate of return:
  income approach to valuation, 6.4
  risk-free, discount rate and, 6.4.5
Real estate:
  cost approach, Exhibit 6-1
  other real estate (ORE) owned
    business enterprise valuation process, 14.2
    financial analysis, asset composition, 8.3.7
    property factor, internal characteristics assessment, 10.2.8
  valuation and, 5.3
Recapitalization transaction (Type E reorganization), nontaxable transactions, valuation process, 7.1.2
Recent losses, valuation process complications, 18.1, Exhibit 18-1
Regression analysis, future income level projections, 6.4.5, Exhibits 6-9, 6-10
Regulations, 1.4.1
Regulator approval, merger and acquisition process, 12.3.2
Regulatory Accounting Principles (RAP), 3.7, 4.11
Regulatory capital, 9.6, 9.7, 9.7.1
Replacement cost, intangible asset valuation, 6.5.1
Replacement principle, described, 5.5.2
  Replacement value, defined, 5.2.9
Reporting value, pricing value versus, valuation, 5.6
Repos, financial analysis, liabilities, 9.4.2. See also Reverse repos
Reproduction value, defined, 5.2.9
Residual value, discounted future income method, Exhibit 6-6
Revenue Pulling, 59-60, 2.2
Revenue Reconciliation Act (RRA) of 1989, 10.2.2
Reverse repos, financial analysis, asset composition, 9.3.3. See also Repos
Riegle-Neal Interstate Banking and Branching Efficiency Act of 1994, 1.2.1, 3.4
Risk:
  allocated transfer risk, financial analysis, expenses composition, 9.11.3
  financial analysis, loan risk analysis illustration, 9.14, 9.14.1, 9.14.2, 9.14.3 Exhibits 9-8, 9-9, 9-10, 9-11
Risk assessment, 3.10.6
Risk-based capital, 4.4.3
  financial analysis, 9.9
  off-balance sheet items, financial analysis, 9.5

Risk-free rate of return, discount rate and, 6.4.6
Risk premium, discount rate, and, 6.46

Safe deposit box contracts, intangible asset valuation, 8.1.4, Exhibit 8-1
Safety and soundness, regulator approval, merger and acquisition process, 1.4.1, 12.32
Sales dates, business enterprise valuation process, comparability basis, 14.5.2
Salvage value, defined, 5.2.10
Scrap value:
  defined, 5.2.10
  value relationships and, 5.4
Seaboard case, 8.3.2
Section 338 election, taxable transactions, 7.1.2
Securities and Exchange Commission (SEC), 4.3, 4.11.1, 9.1.3
Shareholder approval, merger and acquisition process, 12.3.2. See also Stockholders
Sheshunoff Information Services, financial analysis, 9.1.4
Small area analysis, market-wide analysis versus, external environment assessment, 11.3
Stabilized income method, described, 6.4.1
Stabilized level of income estimation, income approach to valuation, 6.4.4
Staffing, internal characteristics assessment, 10.2.2
Standard Industrial Classification (SIC), 1.1
State Banking Departments, 14.5.1
State government securities, financial analysis, 9.3.2
Statement of Financial Accounting Concepts (SFAC) No. 7
Statement of Financial Accounting Standards (SFAS), No. 115, 4.7
Statement of Financial Accounting Standards (SFAS), No. 133, 17.5
  investment securities, financial analysis, 9.3.2
Statement on Auditing Standards (SAS) No. 81, 4.8
Statutory merger, nontaxable transactions, valuation process, 8.1.1
Steady trend pattern, stabilized level of income estimation, 6.4.4
Stock, par value of, financial analysis, 9.6.1. See also Common stock; Preferred stock
Stock-for-assets transaction (Type C reorganization), nontaxable transactions, valuation process, 7.1.2, 7.2
Stock-for-stock transactions (Type B reorganization), nontaxable transactions, valuation process, 7.1.1
Stockholders, business enterprise valuation process and, 14.11. See also Shareholder approval

Strategic valuation, tactical valuation versus, business enterprise valuation process, 14.3
Strategy phase, merger and acquisition process, 12.1,12.1.1—812.1.7. See also Merger and acquisition process
Subordinated notes, financial analysis, liabilities, 9.4.7
Substitution principle, described, 5.5.3
Summation method, discount rate selection, 6.4.6
Superadequacy, cost approach, 6.2
Supervision, 4.4.2
Supervisory activities, 1.4.5
Surplus capital, financial analysis, 9.6.2
Synergy, physical distribution factor, internal characteristics assessment, 10.2.4

Tactical valuation, strategic valuation versus, business enterprise valuation process, 14.3
Tangible asset valuation, 5.3, Chapter 15. See also Intangible asset valuation
  financial assets, 15.2, 15.2.1—15.2.7
    commercial loans, 15.2.3
    consumer loans, 15.2.4
    generally, 15.2
    investment securities, 15.2.1
    lease financing, 15.2.6
    loan portfolio, 15.2.2
    mortgage loans, 15.2.5
    nonperforming loans, 15.2.7
  mergers and acquisitions process and, 15.3
  physical assets, 15.1
Taxation. See also Internal Revenue Service (IRS)
  business enterprise valuation process, 14.4
  income taxes, financial analysis, expenses composition, 9.11.4
  intangible asset valuation, 6.5, 8.5
  mass asset rule, 8.3.2
  mergers and acquisitions
    generally, 7.1
    nontaxable transactions, 7.1.1
    taxable transactions, 7.1.2
    typical valuation examples, 7.2, 7.3.1
  valuation process, 7.1, 7.3.1. 7.3.2, 7.2
Tax consideration of fair value, 4.9
Tax court cases, core deposits valuation, 16.3, 16.3.1—16.3.5
Tax Reform Act of 1986, 7.1.2
Technological innovations, 4.2.1
Technology:
  physical distribution factor, 10.2.4
  property factor, 10.2.8
  10-K report, financial analysis, 9.1.3
  338 election, taxable transactions, 7.1.2, 7.2
Time method, intangible asset valuation, amortization, 8.5

Timing differences, financial analysis, expenses composition, 9.11.3

Total capital, regulatory capital components, financial analysis, 9.7.1

Total enterprise value, value of equity versus, business valuation, 6.6.1

Total income, business enterprise valuation process, income approach, 14.6.3

Trading account assets, financial analysis, 9.3.5

Trust accounts, intangible asset valuation, 8.1.6

Type A reorganization, nontaxable transactions, valuation process, 7.1.1, 7.2

Uncertain future loan loss exposure, valuation process complications, 18.3, Exhibit 18-3

Unconsolidated subsidiaries, investment in, financial analysis, 9.3.8

Undivided profits, capital, financial analysis, 9.6.3

Uniform Bank Performance Report (UBPR), 9.1.1:
  external environment assessment, 11.2, 11.6
  financial analysis, 9.1.1, 9.4.1

Uniform Standards of Professional Appraisal Practice (USPAP), 2.3

Unique experience, intangible asset valuation, 8.3.1

U.S. Department of Commerce, 11.2

U.S. Government securities:
  discount rate selection, 6.4.6
  financial analysis, 9.3.2
  tangible asset valuation process, 15.2.1

U.S. Treasury demand notes:
  interest expenses, 9.11.1
  liabilities, 9.4.3

Unity of use concept, intangible assets, valuation and, 5.8

Useful life measurement, 8.3, 8.3.1, 8.3.2
  generally, 8.3
  individual component analysis, 8.3.2
  unique experience, 8.3.1

Valuation, Chapter 1
  limitations of process, 5.7
  pricing value versus reporting value, 5.6
  principles of, 5.5
    alternatives principle, 5.5.1
    future benefits principle, 5.5.4
    replacement principle, 5.5.2
    substitution principle, 5.5.3
  property types, 5.3

value, defined, 5.1
value concepts, 5.2. See also Value
value relationships, 5.4, 7.4, Exhibit 7-5
Valuation process, Chapter 2
  accounting procedures and, 7.3, 7.3.1—7.3.3, 7.4. See also Accounting procedures
  business enterprise valuation process, Chapter 14. See also Business enterprise valuation process
  business valuation, 6.6, 6.6.1—6.6.5
    book value, adjusted, to compute market value of equity, 6.6.4
    generally, 6.6
    liquidation value, 6.6.4
    preferred stock, 6.6.2, Exhibit 6-19
    total enterprise value versus value of equity, 6.6.1
  closely held stock, 6.8, 6.8.1—6.8.3
    generally, 6.8
    IRS Revenue Ruling, 6.8.1, 7.1.1
    marketability, lack of, discount for, 6.8.3
    minority position/premium for control, discounts for, 6.8.2
  complications in, Chapter 18. See also Valuation process complications
  core deposits valuation, Chapter 16. See also Core deposit base valuation
  cost approach, 6.2
  income approach, 6.4, 6.4.1—6.4.8. See also Income approach
  intangible asset valuation, 6.5, 6.5.1—6.5.4. See also intangible asset valuation
    cost savings and, 6.5.3, Exhibit 6-17
    excess earnings method, 6.5.4
    generally, 6.5
    income and, 6.5.2
    replacement cost, 6.5.1
  internal characteristics assessment and, 10.1
  market approach, 6.3, 6.3.1—6.3.2
    comparables identification, 6.3.1
    generally, 6.3
    lack of comparability, adjusting for, 6.3.2
  overview of steps in, 6.1
  preliminary, merger and acquisition process, 12.1.7
  tangible assets, Chapter 10. See also Tangible asset valuation
  taxation and, 7.1, 7.1.1—7.1.2, 7.2. See also Internal Revenue Service (IRS); Taxation
  widely traded companies, 6.9

Valuation process complications, Chapter 18
  branch acquisitions, 18.6
  highly leveraged banks, 18.5
  low equity capital, 18.2
  preferred versus common stock valuation, 18.4
  recent losses, 18.1, Exhibit 18-1
  summary table, Exhibit 18-5
  uncertain future loan loss exposure, 18.3, Exhibit 18-3
Value:
  defined, 5.1
  external environment and, 11.1
  relationships between, 5.4, 7.4, Exhibit 7-5
  types of, 5.2, 5.2.1—5.2.1
    book value, 5.2.8
    fair market value, 5.2.1
    fair value, 5.2.3
    going concern value, 5.2.7
    goodwill value, 5.2.6
    insurable value, 5.2.10
    intrinsic value, 5.2.4
    investment value, 5.2.2
    liquidation value, 5.2.9
    replacement value, 5.2.11
    salvage value, 5.2.12
    value-in-use/value-in-exchange, 5.2.5
Value assumption changes, business enterprise valuation process and, 14.8, Exhibit 14-8
Value-at-risk (VAR), 4.4.3,
Value-at-risk models, 9.9
Value creation opportunities, business enterprise valuation process, 14.8
Value-in-use/value-in-exchange:
  defined, 5.2.5
  value relationships and, 5.4
Value of equity. See Equity value
Value of tangible assets, 8.4
  cost approach, 8.4.1, 14.9.1
  market approach, 8.4.2, 14.9.3
  income approach, 8.4.3, 14.5.5

Weighted average, stabilized income method, 6.4.1
Weighted cost of capital method, discount rate selection, Exhibit 6-13
Western Mortgage case, 8.3.2
Widely traded companies, valuation process, 6.8
Work force:
  intangible asset valuation, 8.1.8
  people factor, internal characteristics assessment, 10.2.2

Printed in the United States
97546LV00001B/2/A